P9-DDQ-646

Physical Disability—
A Psychosocial Approach

SECOND EDITION

Beatrice A. Wright
UNIVERSITY OF KANSAS

Maria Regina College Library
1024 Court Street
Syracuse, New York 13208

SIDNEY B. COULTER LIBRARY
Onondaga Community College
Syracuse, New York 13215

HARPER & ROW, PUBLISHERS, New York
Cambridge, Philadelphia, San Francisco,
London, Mexico City, São Paulo, Sydney

1817

To the Life of M. Erik Wright,
My C.R.E.W.
and the
Enhanced Family

Sponsoring Editor: Kathy Robinson
Project Editor: Eleanor Castellano
Production Manager: Delia Tedoff
Compositor: Haddon Com Com
Printer and Binder: R R Donnelley

The first edition of this book was published under the title *Physical Disability—A Psychological Approach.*
Physical Disability—A Psychosocial Approach, Second Edition

Copyright © 1983 by Beatrice A. Wright

All rights reserved. Printed in the United States of America. No part of
this book may be used or reproduced in any manner whatsoever without written
permission, except in the case of brief quotations embodied in critical articles
and reviews. For information address Harper & Row, Publishers, Inc., 10 East
53d Street, New York, NY 10022.

Library of Congress Cataloging in Publication Data

Wright, Beatrice Ann Posner
  Physical disability, a psychosocial approach.

  Bibliography: p. 481
  Includes index.
  1. Physically handicapped—Psychology. I. Title.
[DNLM: 1. Handicapped—Psychology. 2. Rehabilitation.
HD 7255 W947p]
BF727.P57W7 1983   362.4'01'9   83–10713
ISBN 0–06–047241–3

36a.4
W

87-159

Contents

Preface to the Second Edition
Value-Laden Beliefs and Principles

In the years since the first edition of this book, important developments have taken place in the rehabilitation field. Major advances have occurred on medical and technological fronts, and landmark legislation has embodied some of the best ideas of modern rehabilitation. The past three decades witnessed a new affirmation of human and civil rights and a determination on the part of disadvantaged groups, including people with disabilities, to speak out and act on their own behalf.

But how much can we count on continued progress? Some years ago my reply was "Not very much. . . . To assert otherwise would be to invite apathy" (Wright, 1973, p. 357). The elimination of attitudinal and other barriers that deny access to opportunities in the general life of the community is a mandate of basic human rights, but human rights are fragile insofar as they are subject to the vicissitudes of broad, sweeping social, economic, and political circumstances.

The title of the original edition, *Physical disability—A Psychological approach,* has been slightly altered in the present revision.

The phrase "a psychosocial approach" is preferred because the book examines problems in terms of the individual in relation to the social environment. Concepts discussed in the earlier edition are developed further, additional research is presented, and new problems and issues are addressed.

The volume strives to contribute knowledge and understanding that will lead to constructive views of life with a disability. Technical language has been kept to a minimum in the hope that readers of varying backgrounds, including students and professionals, individuals who have a disability, and the concerned general public will find the book as a whole, or sections therein, of value.

The following discussion makes explicit those "value-laden beliefs and principles" that have guided my work in rehabilitation as a field of study and service (Wright, 1972).[1] They are offered as possible guidelines with the intent that they be examined and improved, then kept in the forefront to remind and to prompt, to check and to challenge, lest they remain inactivated and submerged by the weight of social, political, and personal pressures of all sorts.

1. *Every individual needs respect and encouragement; the presence of a disability, no matter how severe, does not alter these fundamental rights.*

A person is entitled to the enrichment of life and the development of his or her abilities, whether these be great or small and whether the person has a long or short time to live. The person must not be led to devaluate the self or to give up hope. The person is not to remain neglected and deprived. Under no circumstance is the person to be treated as an "object" or "vegetable."

Biases that declare some groups to be more worthy or deserving of services than others lead to gross inequities and must be avoided. Life, increased mobility, and better communication skills are as important to a 72-year-old as to a 12-year-old, to a mentally retarded person as to an average person, to a black person as to a white person, to a poor person as to a rich person.

The affirmation of human worth and dignity must not only be kept explicitly in the forefront when allocating limited resources but should also be reflected in adequate case-finding efforts so that no person who has a disability remains neglected.

2. *The severity of a handicap can be increased or diminished by environmental conditions.*

Although grammatical usage speaks of a "person's handicap," how handicapping a disability is depends to a great extent upon the characteristics of the person's environment. Thus, physical handi-

[1]Revised from the original 1972 version.

caps can be reduced by eliminating architectural barriers, interpersonal handicaps by overcoming devaluating social attitudes, educational handicaps by providing educational and training facilities, economic handicaps by extending work opportunities, and emotional handicaps by enhancing family and group support.

It should be stressed that the rehabilitation process itself carries an important environmental impact. Professionals and others must continuously question whether present methods or systems of operation are always or maximally helpful. They should seek ways to improve the rehabilitation process, as well as support environmental changes in the home and community that reduce the severity of handicapping conditions.

3. *Issues of coping and adjusting to a disability cannot be validly considered without examining reality problems in the social and physical environment.*

It is to be stressed that the personal-affective life of the individual generally can be most effectively strengthened within the context of dealing with reality problems that exist in the social and physical environment, rather than by treating feelings in an environmental vacuum. Supportive attitudes of family, friends, and professionals, as well as opportunities for satisfactory living offered by the community, facilitate the person's efforts to come to terms with the disability.

4. *The assets of the person must receive considerable attention in the rehabilitation effort.*

A person's healthy physical and mental attributes can become a basis for alleviating difficulties as well as providing a source of gratification and enrichment of life. Special care must be taken to avoid overemphasis on the pathologic that leaves one inadequately sensitized to stabilizing and maturity-inducing factors. Those attributes of the person that are healthy and promising must be supported and developed.

5. *The significance of a disability is affected by the person's feelings about the self and his or her situation.*

Feelings that often have to be worked through by a person who has incurred a disability are those of resentment, inferiority, guilt, loneliness, and being a burden; doubts about whether he or she will still be loved and accepted; worries about the future and how one will manage; and concern that one will be left behind. Such social-emotional concerns take time to resolve. When the person accepts the disability as personally nondevaluating and engages life positively, important rehabilitation goals have been reached.

6. *The active participation of the client in the planning and execution of the rehabilitation program is to be sought as fully as possible.*

Genuine respect for the client leads to the affirmation of the right, within very broad limits, to become actively engaged in the rehabilitation process and to make decisions that affect one's life. The client obviously also has information and ideas essential to rehabilitation progress that are not available to others.

Among the foremost consequences of active involvement on one's own behalf are the enhancing of the person's self-respect, initiative, and responsibility for carrying out decisions.

This principle requires that effort be made to determine the views of every client. Special effort will be necessary in those instances where a major problem of communication exists; for example, deafness, aphasia, cerebral palsy, mental retardation, foreign speech, ghetto speech, and stuttering.

7.   *The client is seen not as an isolated individual but as part of a larger group that includes other people, often the family.*

The problems of the client are intimately connected with those of the larger group of people whose welfare is shared. Therefore, early and active participation of such significant others as spouses, parents, siblings, and children is viewed as an important principle in the total rehabilitation process. Where the client is in fact alone, or is resistant toward including other people, this principle may remain inactivated.

8.   *Because each person has unique characteristics and each situation its own properties, variability is required in rehabilitation plans.*

Grouping persons according to a specific disability must not lead to stereotyped inferences about them. Differences in the needs, abilities, and circumstances of persons with the same or a similar disability require diverse approaches rather than the inflexible application of procedures.

Differences in problems that stem from particular characteristics of particular groups further serve to underscore the need for variability in the process of rehabilitation.

9.   *Predictor variables, based on group outcomes in rehabilitation, should be applied with caution to the individual case.*

At the present stage of knowledge the individual, if given a chance, often becomes the exception which, instead of proving the rule, challenges it. Assessment data, therefore, generally can be used more appropriately as an indication of present status and as a *guide to remediation* than as a prognosticator of future performance.

The direct application of group-based predictor variables is not questioned in regard to the behavior of groups *qua* groups, as in voting or consumer behavior, but is questioned in regard to long-range decisions about a particular individual. Moreover, prediction based on the response of the individual to the rehabilitation process, rather than on "group variables," encourages treatment corrections in accordance with continuing evaluation. The job in rehabilitation is to strive to establish the conditions under which the individual can "beat the odds."

10. *All phases of rehabilitation have psychological aspects.*

All human beings react cognitively and emotionally to events that involve them. These reactions in turn affect the further course of those events. One is compelled, therefore, to recognize that psychological factors are ever-present and often crucial in all aspects of rehabilitation—medical, surgical, educational, social, vocational, as well as primarily psychological.

The psychologist (as well as other psychosocially versed professionals) can offer help to other professions. For example, psychologists are able to describe principles and procedures that help to motivate a client, review body-mind relationships that are important in rehabilitation, assess client attributes, evaluate psychological and behavioral consequences of particular environmental situations, demonstrate ways to resolve intragroup and intergroup conflicts, and sensitize personnel to social-emotional aspects of professional-client relations.

11. *Interdisciplinary and interagency collaboration and coordination of services are essential.*

The needs of individual clients are so diverse, encompassing all problems that one might expect to encounter in human affairs, that a variety of services is necessary. Comprehensive rehabilitation, therefore, requires the effort of many professions and close working relations among the various kinds of rehabilitation agencies.

There is the persistent danger that the pressure to meet agency and professional needs most efficiently and conveniently will become the principal basis for coordinating services. To guard against this danger a clear and explicit focus on most effectively meeting client needs is required.

Because of the complexities in the system of services, the client needs a specified person to serve as "coordinator" or "advocate" in providing information and otherwise acting on his or her behalf. Such a person may come from a self-help group or any of the helping disciplines as appropriate, rather than routinely from a single profession.

12. *Self-help organizations are important allies in the rehabilitation effort.*

Self-help groups provide important programs and mutual support to their members. They also can aid rehabilitation personnel in the understanding of significant problems and the development of new directions in the rehabilitation field. More extensive collaboration between professionals and self-help groups can be expected to further shared objectives.

13. *In addition to the special problems of particular groups, rehabilitation clients commonly share certain problems by virtue of their disadvantaged and devalued position.*

Devaluation and disadvantagement are general life problems experienced by diverse groups: persons who have a physical, mental, or emotional disability; racial and religious minority groups; the poor; and so on. These common problems give rise to important rehabilitation goals that are shared among socially and economically deprived groups.

Special problems stemming from the particular characteristics of particular groups are locomotion difficulties of persons with orthopedic disabilities, communication problems of those who have impaired hearing, addiction in the case of the drug user, malnutrition of the poor, intellectual deficits of the mentally retarded, and so on.

14. *It is essential that society as a whole continuously and persistently strives to provide the basic means toward the fulfillment of the lives of all its inhabitants, including those with disabilities.*

Among the obligations of society are the establishment of needed housing, schools, work opportunities, transportation, hospitals, recreation facilities, and other services. Professionals and others bear a responsibility in helping to meet these obligations by initiating and supporting appropriate legislation and programs.

Where national and community resources are limited, ways to make more effective use of them or to expand them must be sought. Inertia and resistance to change lead to ignoring pressing problems and must be replaced by a determined effort to work toward better solutions.

Extending the goals of rehabilitation to their ultimate implications requires that effort be directed toward the prevention of handicapping conditions. Improvement of health care, reduction of accidents, control of pollution, overcoming of prejudice, diminution of poverty, are all major societal responsibilities. Professionals and the general public cannot remain indifferent to them.

15. *Involvement of the client with the general life of the community is a fundamental principle guiding decisions concerning living arrangements and the use of resources.*

Under special circumstances, where vital considerations indicate the advisability of some form of institutional living, every effort should be made to help the resident participate in community activities and services. Involvement with the community can also be served by sharing institutional resources and activities with the public. Periodic visits on the part of the resident with family, friends, or in foster homes, should become established procedure. The location of institutions within, rather than outside, communities facilitates such integration.

The development of halfway houses and other interim steps that encourage community involvement is imperative. Housing designed to meet special needs should be available in the community to persons with disabilities.

The client who chooses specialized living arrangements should continue to have the option and opportunity to move elsewhere as circumstances permit. In the interest of life enrichment, the space of free movement of a person should be enlarged rather than restricted.

16. *People with disabilities, like all citizens, are entitled to participate in and contribute to the general life of the community.*

Persons who have a disability should not only fulfill the role of consumers. They also have abilities and talents that offer a significant resource that should be utilized for the betterment of the community. The removal of attitudinal and environmental barriers that prevent full participation in community life must be pursued on many fronts, including research, public education, legislation, and other forms of action.

17. *Provision must be made for the effective dissemination of information concerning legislation and community offerings of potential benefit to persons with disabilities.*

Large numbers of persons with disabilities remain unaware of available services from which they could benefit. Professionals are also often unaware of them and thus do not serve adequately as sources for information and referral. Solution of the problem requires a variety of approaches by which both professionals and clients can be kept abreast of opportunities that might be of benefit.

18. *Basic research can profitably be guided by the question of usefulness in ameliorating problems, a vital consideration in rehabilitation fields, including psychology.*

Basic research can be useful research in the sense of being oriented toward the alleviation and overcoming of problems faced in rehabilitation. The converse is also true: useful research can be basic research in the sense of advancing knowledge through the discovery of general principles that apply beyond the borders of the immediate situation. It is misleading and stultifying to identify basic research with "pure" research, the unwitting assumption being that any guide to research other than that given by "knowledge for its own sake" renders it impure and somehow less basic.

It is, therefore, urged that the question of usefulness be regarded with favor as a guide to research. Basic research can profitably become real-life oriented in its conception and from its inception by considering usefulness as a value in the selection of problems, analysis of data, communication of results, and application of findings. In bridging the gap between theory and research, psychological concepts need to be examined and new ones introduced in the light of their usefulness in dealing with everyday life problems of persons who have a disability.

19. *Persons with disabilities should be called upon to serve as coplanners, coevaluators, and consultants to others, including professional persons.*

It is important that the rehabilitation field take advantage of the special knowledge and viewpoints of people who have a disability. Such persons have had first-hand experience with the rehabilitation process and are directly involved with problems that personally affect them. Their ideas should be especially sought concerning ways in which rehabilitation services can be improved and the lives of people with disabilities enriched.

Organizations on behalf of persons who have a disability should make it a point to include representatives of client groups on their advisory boards. Examples of such organizations are rehabilitation centers, private and governmental health agencies, foundations, schools, and hospitals. Rehabilitation agencies should make certain that persons with disabilities serve in professional and nonprofessional capacities.

With respect to research on problems of rehabilitation, the special sensitivities and understandings of persons who have a disability can be utilized by having them serve as consultants and coinvestigators.

20. *Continuing review of the contributions of psychologists and others in rehabilitation within a framework of guiding principles that are themselves subject to review is an essential part of the self-correcting effort of science and the professions.*

The values and beliefs expressed in the foregoing set of principles need to be periodically reviewed for two main reasons. First, change in emphasis and content may be indicated by new knowledge and changing times. Second, specification as to how the principles can best be implemented requires constant examination and study if their effectiveness as guides in rehabilitation is to be increased.

In many cases, the sheer process of seriously examining a principle will reveal instances in which it is not reflected in actual practice as well as ways to improve the situation. Serious examination is directly available to everyone and when carried out in brainstorming group sessions can be especially productive.

Beatrice A. Wright, Ph.D.

May 1981

Preface to the First Edition

Throughout recorded history, and probably before, man has been intrigued by the possibility that the outward characteristics of physique might in some way be a guide to the inner nature of man, to his temperament, his character, his personality. It is not difficult to understand how such a deep-seated belief might become established.

In daily contacts there are many cues from physique, posture, clothing, and other aspects of outward appearance that serve to give information about a person's calling and habits. This identifying information readily breeds the impression that one "knows" more about the individual's personality than is actually the case. The philosophical tenet that holds man to be an essential unity, that the mind and the body are different aspects of the same individual, lends intellectual support to the belief in the intimate interdependence of physique and personality. Scientific investigations of psychosomatic medicine provide many indications of the effects of sustained emotional states upon the physical condition of man. Inversely, there are instances in which obvious physical stigmata, such as in cretinism, imply defects in mental functioning. Finally, it is only with sophisticated restraint that one guards against the jump from the incontrovertible fact that physique is an important determiner of behavior to the tempting conclusion that personality is manifested in physique.

There has been a sobering balance to the readiness to accept body-mind connections uncritically, however. Most of the inferences about personality based on physical signs have found no factual support in systematic investigation. Where relationships are revealed, the correlations are typically low. Ideologically speaking, the belief in free will has led some to look askance at physical constants that impose limitations on man's nature. If features of the face, or deformities of the body, or meanderings of body chemistry bespeak and determine personality, then man to some extent becomes a pawn of impersonal forces. The democratic viewpoint has also tended to find it more congenial to focus on environmental conditions, especially those controllable by man, rather than on immutable hereditary and physical factors under which man must bow. Particularly in American democracy, which upholds the value of man's rugged individualism and prefers the notion that man's future is determined by his own dogged will and ingenuity and not by coercive limitations on any front, did the emphasis tend to become the one of choice. Deeper analysis, of course, shows that there is no basic contradiction between these ideological viewpoints and the search for body-mind interrelationships, for the fact that man to some extent is influenced by impersonal factors does not keep him from influencing the course of events as well. He is as much a determining organism as one that is determined.

The present volume is concerned with one segment of the relation between man and his physique, namely, the somatopsychological problem as seen in disablement. The emphasis is on the kinds of social-psychological situations that confront a person with an atypical physique, and how he copes with them. Factors within the person and factors attributable to the environment are considered in terms of how they aid psychological adjustment or, on the negative side, how they create difficulties.

Many topics of importance to the problem of adjustment to disability do not appear within the pages of this volume, the reasons for exclusion being varied. First of all there is the matter of author limitations. The theoretical background and range of experience and competency naturally tend to prescribe certain questions and exclude others. Foreign references, unfortunately, are notable by their absence. Then there is the direction indicated by available research and the considered thinking of others. Moreover, the scope of a single book must perforce be limited, and the outlines become dictated in part by the substance initially worked through.

There is no doubt that to some extent the contents of this volume have been shaped by preconceived notions, but it should also be noted that they have been reshaped as the evidence of scientific investigation and considered opinion added to the perspective of the person as an active agent in meeting the impositions of a disability. Since fiction far more than fact characterizes many ideas about psychological aspects of disability, it is well to embark upon the reading of this book with an eye critical of those personal views that have long been cherished as well as of those that may here be proposed in their place. Certainly not all the assertions made have scientific validity. But it is hoped that many of them are supported by sound psychological thinking and by research evidence where possible. In any case all of them are advanced "until further notice."

I should like to say a few words about the personal documents as used herein. Because most of them are taken from literary productions written by the person himself, they sample predominantly the introspections of persons who are highly verbal, thoughtful, and who have a solid complement of psychological resources as well. But the purpose of these documents is not to prove the theoretical position advanced—rather the purpose is to illuminate it. Through the documents a vividness is achieved, a concreteness and exemplification of what might otherwise appear as too abstract and theoretical for the reality of psychological man. It is for this reason that the book was designed as a combination text and case book. Those readers who have a good deal of familiarity with problems of disability will easily be able to skim over the case material, but for others it illustrates the living situations in which the problems under discussion occur. It is also believed that many of the psychological events portrayed in the personal accounts are not unlike, in principle, those which touch the lives of the more drab, plodding, and unimaginative. Insofar as psychological principles are being expounded, the specification of causes and effects allows exemplification through the pertinent life history. At the same time, longitudinal records of the lives of persons among the less articulate and less successful with different disabling conditions would be valuable as a source of new insights as well as a check of old ones.

This volume was written for the practitioner in the field of rehabilitation, especially for the professional in training, though I would like to believe that the research worker will also find some leads for productive exploration. Because "the practitioner" covers a wide range of professions—medicine and nursing; occupational, physical, and speech therapy; social work, psychology, and psychiatry, to mention a few—and because in some instances the patient as well as his family may be interested in the material, an attempt was made to avoid technical language communicable only to "the trade." That some readers will find particular sections "too simple" or "too difficult" is foreseen, which situation can be used to advantage if the individual reader will select for more careful study those chapters that hold promise for him.

The recognition that one's own work is also in many ways the product of those from whom one has learned leads me to think about my psychological lineage. If I had to single out a handful of my teachers and colleagues who had the greatest impact on my thinking as a psychologist, the following would be high on the list: Solomon Asch, Roger Barker, Tamara Dembo, Fritz Heider, Kurt Lewin, Carl Rogers, and Erik Wright. Their mark is indelibly impressed in many of the ideas elaborated in this book and would be detectable even if no mention had been made of them.

I wish to express my thankfulness to those who have read all or parts of the manuscript: Roger Barker, Louise Barker, David Klein, June Kounin, Gardner Murphy, Stephen Richardson, Phil Schoggen, Anthony Smith, and Erik Wright. Their suggestions have led to wise clarification in the treatment of several of the problems discussed. The editorial acumen of David Klein was especially valuable in tightening the manuscript and detecting obscurities. It is also a pleasure to mention with gratitude the Association for the Aid of Crippled Children, who provided a grant and editorial assistance in support of this undertaking and patiently awaited its completion in spite of the vicissitudes that marked its course.

To the publishers who gave permission to use the material quoted, special thanks. The reference sources are generally indicated by author and date, referring to items in the bibliography.

I feel a special bond of friendship and indebtedness to those whose personal documents were used freely in the discussion. I only hope that reference to the details of their lives and innermost feelings, most of them from published sources, will be taken not as an intrusion into their privacy but as a contribution to the understanding of social-psychological factors important in adjustment to disability.

These remarks are strangely incomplete without the expression of my deepest feelings to my family—my husband, children, and parents—who did so much to make possible the completion of this book.

Beatrice A. Wright

November 1959

Foreword to the First Edition

Human physique has a central place in naive, commonsense psychology. It is generally believed that a person's body influences his behavior by way of the many phenomenal properties it has for him and his associates, and by way of its greater or lesser efficiency as the instrument with which he attempts to carry out intended actions. Variations in physical size, beauty, and normality, for example, are widely presumed by businessmen, artists, and athletes, by politicians, suitors, and doctors to be important causal variables within the total context of factors that determine behavior and personality. One common theory is expressed by Shakespeare in *Richard III*, where the crippled Richard, Duke of Gloucester, says:

> But I, that am not shaped for sportive tricks,
> Nor made to court an amorous looking-glass;
> I, that am rudely stamp'd and want love's majesty
> To strut before a wanton ambling nymph;
> I, that am curtail'd of this fair proportion,

Cheated of feature by dissembling nature,
Deform'd, unfinish'd, sent before my time
Into this breathing world, scarce half made up,
And that so lamely and unfashionable
That dogs bark at me as I halt by them;
. . . since I cannot prove a lover,
To entertain these fair well-spoken days,
I am determined to prove a villain
And hate the idle pleasures of these days.
Plots have I laid, ...

An opposed view is given by Robert Burton in his *Anatomy of Melancholy:*

> Deformities and imperfections of our bodies, as lameness, crooked-
> ness, deafness, blindness, be they innate or accidental, torture many
> men: yet this may comfort them that those imperfections of the body
> do not a whit blemish the soul, or hinder the operations of it, but rather
> help and much increase it.

Scientific psychology has not in the past been much concerned with these kinds of relations between physique and behavior; it has emphasized other body-mind interdependencies; for example, those between the brain and behavior, emotions and ulcers, the cochlea and hearing, genes and intelligence, and hormones and personality characteristics. When the phenomenal and instrumental interconnections between the psyche and the soma have been considered by psychologists, they have usually been discussed in terms of rather unsystematic, recondite processes such as body image, organ inferiority, and cathexis to disabled parts; or they have been seen as mere technological problems for psychological practitioners who deal with the education, employment, or counseling of disabled persons.

Dr. Wright's book provides welcome evidence that a change is taking place in psychology with respect to these matters, and that the phenomenal and instrumental significance of physique is receiving a new and deserved emphasis. *Physical Disability—A Psychological Approach* is much more than a symptom of this change, however; it makes important contributions to the new development by carefully collating available data and relevant theories, by contributing new concepts and interpretations, and by integrating the whole problem within the context of persisting psychological issues. Altogether, Dr. Wright makes an impressive case for considering somatopsychology, as it has been called, a valid subdivision of the science of psychology, with a unique syndrome of facts, theories, and investigatory and therapeutic techniques. Every psychological theoretician would do well to confront his system with the facts of life and of psychological science to which Dr. Wright draws our attention.

As is proper in the early days of a new scientific development, Dr. Wright has a place in her book for diverse viewpoints and facts. She is not limited by a narrow theoretical partisanship. On the other hand, *Physical Disability—A Psychological Approach* is not merely eclectic; an organized conception of the somatopsychology of physique emerges.

Physical Disability—A Psychological Approach marks a milestone for the professions that deal in practical ways with the behavior and adjustment of physically deviant persons. It places the psychological side of disablement within a framework of sound concepts, and in doing so contributes in an important way to making rehabilitation psychology an applied science rather than, as heretofore, a welfare specialty based largely on experience and art. Her own extensive, practical experience with these matters saves Dr. Wright from leaving reality behind and soaring too soon into scientific outer space. The wealth of concrete examples she presents and her ability to deal with complicated issues without using an unduly technical language will make the *Physical Disability—A Psychological Approach* of interest and value to a wide range of professional people.

ROGER G. BARKER
Professor of Psychology
University of Kansas

Chapter 1
Circumscribing the Problem

The following scenes sample dramatic episodes taken from the lives of three people with disabilities—an adult, a teenager, and a child.

Louise, a young woman who suffered the loss of one leg in childhood and is now on crutches, encounters prejudice in looking for a job:

> [I had] a letter in my purse which introduced me, with some flattering phrases, to the field secretary of a large national girls' organization. . . . I had operated for four summers on the Pacific Coast as a counselor in the camps of this organization. According to the Los Angeles executive, my work was highly satisfactory. She had used me in various capacities—camp craft, handcraft, swimming, hiking, etc. The children liked me and I had no discipline problems. . . .
>
> In fact, the Los Angeles executive was sufficiently impressed to express the opinion that I had something of a talent for leading the young. She encouraged me to consider seriously the possibility of a career in her organization. With this in mind, she equipped me with the introduction and suggested that I . . . discuss the matter with the national executive. . . .

I was completely unprepared for the blasting brushoff I got. . . .

She [the field secretary] told me that with my horrible handicap I should never for a moment consider an active job that involved leadership of young people or contact with the public. Her implication was not only that I was halt, but that the very sight of me would warp a sensitive young mind.

In frantic haste to justify my mad entertainment of such ridiculous heresy, I tried to tell her how fast I could swim, how far I could hike, and all about my four summers in camp and the serenely happy and uncomplicated reactions of all the children I had shepherded.

I didn't talk very well because there was a sob suffocating its lonely self in my tight throat. I finally left and walked twenty-two blocks to my hotel rather than get in a taxi and let the driver see me cry. [Baker, 1946, pp. 128–131][1]

Russell Criddle, an adolescent with sufficiently poor vision to be classified as blind, rejects pity and suffers the anguish of not being wanted as a dating partner:

I was further disturbed when I sensed that others were pitying me for my loneliness. I learned to pretend that I was not lonely, just as I pretended that I could see, but this pretense was far more difficult. A subtle advance, and a subtle rejection, one girl telling another, and it soon became general knowledge that I was an unwanted person. Had a girl felt attracted toward me it would have been humiliating indeed for her to have accepted me after ninety per cent of her associates had turned me down. I sensed all this, even then, and was ever alert for new girls, new faces, new circles of friends.

One night Bud arranged a party date for me with a cousin who was visiting his family. Bud neglected to tell her about my eyes, and she did not discover my handicap until the evening was well advanced. She had seemed to like me, and I had sensed her acceptance of me. But when she found me out she was so distraught that she left alone, without even waiting for the cake and ice cream. [Criddle, 1953, pp. 54–55][2]

Wally, a 4-year-old boy seriously crippled from poliomyelitis, is angered and frustrated as he struggles to get his coaster wagon up a low incline between the road and sidewalk, a situation easily mastered by a nondisabled child:

9:44 a.m. Using the wagon as a prop and holding onto it with both hands, he pulled himself up off the ground from a sitting position. He

---

[1]Reprinted by permission from *Out on a limb* by Louise Baker, published by McGraw-Hill. Copyright 1946 by Louise Baker.
[2]Reprinted from *Love is not blind* by Russell Criddle by permission of Norton. Copyright 1953 by Russell Criddle.

put one knee in the wagon, and with the other knee began propelling himself up the short hill to the sidewalk. About halfway up, the weight seemed to be too much for him. He struggled hard. Then he rolled out of the wagon, sat down on the ground with a helpless air and held the wagon in place with both hands on the back end of the wagon. He sat behind the wagon with an expression of futility. He rolled over on his side till he was at the side of the wagon and held on. The wagon rolled back slightly.

9:45. With one hand he picked up a clod of dirt. He seemed to be angered at the difficulty he was now having with the wagon. He threw the clod into the ditch and shouted angrily, "Damned old mud!" He sat for a moment and glared at the muddy ditch. [Barker & H. Wright, 1948–51]

That there are triumphs in the lives of persons with disabilities, triumphs that arise in disability-connected situations, is *just as important* as the fact that there are suffering and failure.

In Wally's case, as he sat throwing the clod and casting imprecations at the mud, new ways to solve the problem began to dominate his attention, with the attempt ending in victory:

9:45. Wally rolled over and, using the wagon as a prop, lifted himself up. With what seemed renewed determination, he put one knee in the wagon and with the other foot started to push the wagon up the hill. Since it was difficult for him to go directly up the hill, he tried to lessen the grade by taking a diagonal path up the hill. He turned the wagon to the left and pushed hard. He got caught in some weeds off the path along the side.

9:46. It was quite a struggle but he kept pushing strenuously. He rolled out of the wagon and tried to push the wagon with his hands. He pushed it up and tried to crawl up behind it but this was difficult because the wagon would not stay up; while he crawled, the wagon rolled back down. He had to block it with his body to prevent it from rolling all the way down the hill. Wally looked up at me [the observer]. He was getting quite annoyed at the whole procedure. He asked hopefully, "Will you pull me up?" I asked him kindly, "Well, what would you do if I weren't here?"

9:47. He smiled quizzically and coaxed, "Pull me up." I said, "Well, would you pull up yourself if I weren't here?" Again he smiled. He turned around with what seemed a little more determination. He put one knee in the wagon and, with a great effort, strenuously pushed the wagon up. The wagon moved up the hill. He looked at me and said determinedly, "I'm getting up," as though he were showing me that he could do it himself if I weren't there. After a good deal of struggling he finally pushed the wagon up onto the cement sidewalk. When he got it up onto the cement sidewalk, he gave one final hard push.

9:48. The wagon suddenly moved forward on the sidewalk and he fell flat on his stomach. He accepted this matter-of-factly. He crawled up to the wagon and got in it. Then he turned around, looked at me and said with pride in his voice, "I made it." [Barker & H. Wright, 1948–51][3]

So it was with the others. Russell Criddle, once rejected as a dating partner, eventually met the girl he was to marry. Louise, once denied a job because of her disability, persisted until she found work to her liking.

I do not wish to imply that all ends well in the lives of persons with disabilities, but it should be emphasized that satisfactions and triumphs, not only sorrows and difficulties, are well represented. This is important because of the all too frequent tendency to view the lives of people with disabilities in primarily tragic terms. People with disabilities resist, if not resent, such a pervasive negative view, not only because it belies the facts, but also because of their efforts to cope with the problems they face.

It should also be emphasized that the experiences recounted above are shared in *principle,* not only by people with a great variety of disabilities, but also by those who are regarded as nondisabled. That is to say, rejection, pity, frustration, and discrimination in some form are general human experiences. Understanding their origins, learning ways to cope with them, and discovering the means to reduce them are important to the lives of all people. I am sure that there are far fewer psychological experiences peculiar to persons with physical disabilities than an offhand guess might indicate. Even if one broadens the examples to include sensory loss, as in blindness or deafness, the psychological significance of the deprivation involves experiences with which most human beings are conversant, such as unjustified barriers to opportunities, the threat of social isolation, the need for acceptance of personal limitations, the struggle for independence, and the importance of dependency and interdependency relationships. This is one reason why the problems discussed in this book bear upon the lives of all people, those with disabilities and those without. The reader is urged to compare the examples presented to illustrate various points in the text with incidents from his or her own life. In this way, the problems of people with disabilities will become more fully appreciated as everyone's problems. Some of the comparable incidents may involve race, sex, mental retardation, or age. Actually, any personal characteristic that is devalued can serve as a source of prejudice and discrimination.

[3]From *One of a series of records made in connection with the natural living conditions of children* by R. G. Barker & H. F. Wright. Reprinted by permission of R. G. Barker.

THE GENERALITY OF PROBLEMS

That the fact of disability is not only someone else's problem is also made clear by its prevalence. About half the population of the United States is reported to have a chronic condition of some sort. Of these individuals, two-thirds are limited in some form of activity, and as many as 10 percent of the U.S. population is significantly limited in a major activity of daily living (Riley & Nagi, 1970, Table I). That almost everyone is directly affected by problems of disability is further seen if one examines families in general. At the University of Kansas more than 90 percent of a sample of 2000 college students reported that a family member toward whom they felt close (e.g., parent, grandparent, sibling, first cousin, aunt, uncle) had a *major* chronic illness or disability. Since an upward selection with respect to physical and mental health can be expected in a sample of college students, the 90-percent figure becomes even more striking. It is especially important for the "able-bodied" reader to realize that the topics to be discussed in this volume are not of special concern for a "different" group but, rather, are of special concern for the totality of humankind, for each of us must at some time face the challenge of living with a disability. This is another way of saying that physical disability is a "normal" and inevitable part of life, that all of us experience illness, that time brings impairment. The problems under discussion are our problems, not "theirs" alone.

THE SCOPE OF QUESTIONS CONSIDERED[4]

Our broad concern is with social-psychological factors that affect the lives of people with disabilities. We shall examine those personal and interpersonal forces that impede and that facilitate adjustment and participation in life satisfactions. The text deals with status problems, with the way people perceive themselves and others, with interpersonal relations that are satisfying and disturbing, with value changes that aid adjustment, with coping and succumbing as reactions to

[4]A survey of the literature is not the purpose of this volume. The reader may refer to such reviews as Barker et al. (1953), Meyerson (1957), Neff (1971), and Garrett & Levine (1973). The following are fine bibliographic sources for somatopsychological literature: *Rehabilitation Literature* (National Easter Seal Society, Chicago, Ill.) includes a section on abstracts of current literature from diverse fields; *Psychological Abstracts* (American Psychological Association, Washington, D.C.) provides a comprehensive coverage of publications that are psychological in nature. The *Annual Review of Rehabilitation* (Springer Publishing Co.) selects current topics of importance to rehabilitation theory and practice for systematic review. There also are federal and private agencies that provide computer searches on specified topics.

problems of living, with modifying attitudes and changing behavior, with fund-raising and health care messages, with professional-client relations, and with myths about disability. Again, notice that these topics have relevance to human functioning in general, although for our purpose their application will be to problems associated with disability.

These problems fall within the domain of what has been called the *somatopsychological relation,* a relation dealing with "those variations in physique that affect the psychological situation of a person by influencing the effectiveness of his body as a tool for actions or by serving as a stimulus to himself or others" (Barker et al., 1953, p. 1). This is to be distinguished from the psychosomatic relation, namely, the relationship between the psychological characteristics of a person and the predisposition toward certain types of organic dysfunction. The psychosomatic problem is conceptually distinct from the somatopsychological problem and will not be discussed here. For a systematic statement differentiating several types of connections between the person and the disability see Barker et al. (1953, pp. 1–8).

The somatopsychological relationship involves social-psychological factors, that is, factors that underlie the way disability as a value loss is perceived and reacted to by other people, as well as the self. Actually, much of the psychology of the individual requires social-psychological understanding, since the way in which one feels and behaves about many things depends in greater or lesser measure upon one's relationship to other persons. Problems that on first appraisal may seem purely personal often reveal a social basis. Consider the person whose disability permits the basic routines of living, such as dressing or eating, to be accomplished only with great effort. One might feel that the difficulty resulting from the wide gap between the person's abilities and the task requirements has nothing to do with the social environment. Yet, when we recognize that some—and often an important part—of the difficulty stems from expectations that the person must eat in a certain way or wear certain clothes, *ways of behaving prescribed by society,* we realize the impact of social-psychological forces. Or consider the person in a wheelchair who cannot enter a building because of insurmountable stairs. Does the difficulty arise because the person has a physical disability or because the person is architecturally handicapped? The latter view ascribes the source of the difficulty to the environment and not to the person, a shift that raises the social-psychological issue of *exclusion by people* from human habitats. One writer feels so strongly that the problem of disability lies exclusively in society that he defines *disability* as "the special form of discrimination, or social oppression,

that is faced by people who are in some way physically impaired"
(Finkelstein, 1980, pp. 1–2).

One can press further and examine social problems from an economic and political point of view. Sometimes this approach involves
what is referred to as a structural analysis of social problems. While
recognizing the enormous impact of the broader socioeconomic philosophy of different countries on problems involving disability, our
concern is primarily with a social-psychological perspective regarding more immediate interpersonal relationships. The analysis will
lead to an examination of beliefs and actions that can be understood
in terms of principles of human perception, values, emotions, and
motivation. Our concern will also lead us to offer suggestions to counteract those social-emotional forces that add to problems encountered by people with disabilities.

The principles discussed generally apply to children and adults
and to a wide range of disabilities. Sometimes it seemed more expedient to center the discussion on one or another age group, either because the problem appeared more directly relevant to the particular
population segment or because the research and illustrative material
dealt with people of certain ages. Nonetheless, the implications of
the point made are usually apparent across age groups. The same
holds true for specific disabilities. A cited example may refer to a person with an amputation, paralysis, epilepsy, or a sensory impairment,
but it is used only to clarify a concept or point that has wider generality. The psychological problems associated with mental retardation
are not specifically dealt with, although it should be noted that much
of the discussion has application to mental, as well as physical, impairments.

Throughout the text an effort is made to point out the generality
of the concepts used, as well as to apply generally used concepts to
the disability-connected problem under discussion. In some instances the knowledge gained from study of the psychological aspects of disability also has important implications for problems that
do not involve disablement. Just as probing into mental illness produces insights into psychological phenomena that are relevant to the
mentally normal, so the examination of problems associated with
physical illness and disability forces attention to important areas of
general human behavior that otherwise tend to be neglected. The
concept of accepting the loss of something valuable (Chapter 8) is
one such area. The phenomenon designated as the requirement of
mourning (Chapter 5) is another. Problems arising from ordinary relationships, such as helping, sympathizing, pitying, staring, questioning, and ridiculing (Chapter 13) constitute a third. The idolizing of
normal standards of behavior (Chapter 7) and the different perspec-

tives of the coping and succumbing frameworks (Chapter 9) are still others. Even the sophisticated psychologist, we believe, will find several new signposts pointing toward the understanding of unexplored and vital areas of human nature.

TERMINOLOGICAL ISSUES

It has long been recognized that language is not merely an instrument for voicing ideas but also plays a role in *shaping* ideas by guiding how we perceive and experience the world (see Sapir, 1931; Johnson, 1946; Whorf, 1947; Lee, 1947; Korzybski, 1951). It behooves us, therefore, to consider the implications of word usage as an important aspect of the psychology of disability.

Dangers of Shortcuts and Dehumanization

Is a "disabled person" one who is unable to do anything? "Of course not," is the retort—the phrase is assuredly meant to be applicable to varying degrees of disability and not just to the extreme where a person is helpless or virtually moribund. More accurately, then, a "disabled person" is also an *able* person. There are things that the person *can* do as well as things that the person *cannot* do. In fact, the person is typically more able than disabled. Then why call the person "disabled"? We may conclude that the designations "disabled person" or "the disabled" are shortcuts to psychologically more valid formulations such as "the person (or individual) with a disability, or "people who have a disability." A tolerant concurrence, combined with the feeling that this is much ado about nothing much, may greet this proposal; however, as we shall see in subsequent chapters, it is precisely the perception of a person with a physical disability as a *disabled person* that reduces the person to the disabling aspects of his or her functioning.

To be sure, the structure of our language makes it difficult to consistently use the more cumbersome but accurate form that subordinates a disability to the personhood of the individual. It is easier to refer to "the disabled" or to "the handicapped" than to "the person with a disability" or to "people who are handicapped." Persons who are blind will still be referred to as "the blind." People who have an amputation, diabetes, a heart condition, or cerebral palsy will still be referred to as amputees, diabetics, cardiacs, and C.P.'s.

Yet there is evidence that the more involved form is generally preferred. In one of our studies, subjects ($N = 50$) from a wide adult age range and diverse backgrounds were asked to indicate their preference between two designations. In one case, the physical condition was used to label the people referred to (e.g., "amputees"), whereas in the alternative, the person referent was made explicit (e.g., "persons who have an amputation"). The task involved seven such pairs presented as parts of a sentence fragment ending in "are employed as . . ." For example, "The cerebral palsied are employed as, . . ." versus "Persons who have cerebral palsy are employed as . . ."; "Arthritics are employed as . . ." versus "Persons who have arthritis are employed as . . ." Clearly a large majority of the subjects favored the person term and rejected the physical condition term.

The importance of preserving the personhood of the individual with a disability also leads us to reject any metaphors or descriptions of behavior suggestive of less than human status. One author, in describing the athetoid condition of cerebral palsy, referred to the "slow, *worm-like* movements in the limbs and body" (italics added). Instead of "worm-like," would not the words "undulating," "sinuous," or "wavy" provide an apt description in keeping with the principle of preserving personhood? One counselor, after mentioning children who were active and children who just sat around, added, "Then you've got *the wheelchairs* that can't run around at all" (italics added). Is it appropriate to refer to children as "wheelchairs"? A nurse referred to a patient as "the appendix in room four." To justify semantic usage that designates people by their disability as a matter of convenience ought to give us pause.

The situation may be somewhat different when people with a disability themselves use the disability designation to refer to their own group, such as "quads," "laryngectomees," and so forth. The situation is different so long as they recognize their human potential and use the shorthand as a familiar and nondevaluating convenience. Even so, since many people with disabilities devaluate their own group, it is well for everyone to get in the habit of using the longer verbal form as a semantic signal of human dignity.

The National Easter Seal Society (1980) has lent support to these ideas in their numerous suggestions for "Portraying persons with disabilities in print." So has the American Psychiatric Association (1980) with respect to mental disorders. The third edition of the *Diagnostic and statistical manual of mental disorders (DSM–III)* states: "A common misconception is that a classification of mental disorders classifies individuals, when actually what are being classified are disorders that individuals have. For this reason, the text of *DSM–III* avoids the use of such phrases as 'a schizophrenic' or 'an alcoholic,' and instead uses the more accurate, but admittedly more wordy 'an individual with Schizophrenia' or 'an individual with Alcohol Dependence'" (p. 6).

Terms that indicate lack of a valued personal characteristic have shown a history of being supplanted by new terms as connotations become objectionable. So it is that the word "feeble-minded" has metamorphosed into "mentally retarded." Instead of "moron, idiot, and imbecile" to indicate levels of retardation, the current terms are "moderate, severe, and profound retardation." The field of emotional disorders has seen similar changes. The etymologically sound word "insane," derived from the Latin meaning "not healthy," has given way to such expressions as "mentally ill," "emotionally disturbed," and "behavior problem." Burning people at the stake as witches had condemned the word "insane," inextricably interwoven as it was with such mistreatment. Should terms in use today accumulate negative surplus meanings provided by associated contexts, they, too, will be replaced.

A related and difficult problem concerns pejorative implications of disability terms when used as metaphors in commonly accepted language. A telling case in point is the word "blind" to connote being ignorant or unaware ("the experimenter was blind to the conditions"), something unsupported by evidence or plausibility ("blind faith"), not having the faculty of discernment ("blind to one's own defects"), being unreasonable or uncontrollable ("blind rage"), or something that offers no opportunity for advancement ("blind alley"). It is hoped that dictionaries will someday declare these usages archaic. After all, there are alternatives: "the experimenter was unaware of the conditions," "unquestioning faith," "denying one's own defects," "furious, undirected rage," and "closed alley." It is hard to believe that repeated exposure to language which extends the meaning of blindness for the worse does not also reinforce negative attitudes about blindness and people who are blind. This concern should not imply a corresponding rejection of the positive use of terms referring to sight. It is acceptable to "shed light on the matter" or to ask, "Do you see what I mean?" As we shall see later (Chapter 8), sight can be an "asset value," that is, a good thing to have if you have it, but not devaluating if you don't.

Sensitivity to word usage would not be so important were it not for the tendency for inferiority with respect to a single significant valued characteristic to spread so that the person as a whole becomes devaluated. To remind us of the need for individuality and dignity, we shall attempt to use humanizing terms even at the cost of awkwardness.

Disability Versus Handicap

The terms *disability* and *handicap* have been variously defined and additional terms introduced, such as *impairment* and *limitation,* in an attempt to arrive at a common terminology for health surveys and other purposes (Hamilton, 1950; Barry, 1971; Haber, 1973; World Health Organization, 1980). Whatever terms are used, it is important to distinguish two main concepts. One concept refers to limitation of function that results directly from an impairment at the level of a specific organ or body system. For this, we shall use the term *disability*. A word is also needed for the actual obstacles the person encounters in the pursuit of goals in real life, no matter what their source. For these we shall use the term *handicap*. This distinction is basically in line with the terms adopted by the World Health Organization (1980).

A fundamental point is that the *source* of obstacles and difficulties, that is, what actually handicaps a person, cannot be determined by describing the disability alone. Thus, although the disability itself may also contribute to difficulty in goal achievement, architectural, attitudinal, legal, and other social barriers are handicapping, as are negative attitudes on the part of the person with a disability. With some impairments, as in facial disfigurement, the handicapping factors reside entirely in negative social and personal attitudes insofar as the disfigurement itself does not involve a functional loss. Moreover, as we shall see, a person with a disability may or may not be handicapped, and a person who is handicapped may or may not have a disability.

Consider the example of certain strata of Chinese women in times past who were not considered handicapped even though they could only hobble on their bound feet. Symbolizing nobility, this condition did not interfere with the functions required of such women and therefore, presumably, was not an obstacle to their goals. Although diminutive feet may be considered an impairment, they were looked upon neither as a disability nor as a handicap. An important conclusion, therefore, is that what is regarded as a disability or a handicap depends upon the requirements and expectations in the situation, often culturally determined.

Moreover, when environmental changes are made to accommodate the needs of a person with a disability, and when that person has also undergone necessary adaptations, then even someone with a severe disability may be only minimally handicapped. A person who is blind may not be handicapped in work that does not require visual orientation. A person in a wheelchair may be no more frustrated in a barrier-free job situation than the person who takes it for granted that one has to ride the bus to work every morning.

That disability, as the term is used here, cannot automatically be equated with handicap is further demonstrated in a study of the attitudes of forty women who had poliomyelitis (Fielding, 1950). Although their disabilities were moderate to severe, 98 percent reported that they only occasionally experienced the physical defect as a disadvantage, some 20 percent affirmed that the disability annoyed them very little in physical activities, and 70 percent revealed the defect to be a help in some phases of life. These results cannot be discredited as mere products of wishful thinking, for it is now well corroborated by research and theoretical considerations that the degree of handicap associated with a disability can only be poorly predicted, if at all, from knowledge of the disability alone.

It is also important to recognize that someone may be physically handicapped even though the physical limitations are not disabilities from the physiological or medical point of view. A person with only an average voice is handicapped if he or she aspires to become a great singer. Consider also that deep dissatisfaction with some aspect of one's body is common in our society. One study found that almost all the children interviewed felt sensitive or inferior about various aspects of their bodies (Levy, 1932). The self-evaluation of the children was handicapping even though they did not have a disability.

Some might propose that the concept of physical disability implies deviation from normality, deviation from a state that is natural or average, and might offer as support the fact that humans are not judged to have a physical disability because they are not as fleet as the deer, as strong as the lion, or able to soar into the air like the bird. Nor are children considered to have a disability because as compared to adults they are less able. However, there are difficulties with this proposition. It could be asserted, for example, that the arthritic changes concomitant with aging represent a "natural" or usual course of events; yet hardly a person would be ready to concede that functional limitations resulting therefrom do not connote a disability. Evidently a more idealized standard that defines what is right and proper is invoked, rather than simply a standard of what is natural or usual. Arthritic changes, however common, are not regarded as right and proper.

In any case, it is important to draw a distinction between the disability (i.e., the functional limitations resulting from an impairment) and the handicap (i.e., the barriers, frequently social in nature, that prevent access to desired goals and opportunities).

Physical Definitions and Psychological Understanding

One might suppose that definition of the various disabilities would not involve such semantic complications. Are not deafness and blindness, for example, clear-cut disabilities? Actually, the problem of nomenclature regarding these disabilities continues to arouse controversy. Deafness is a case in point. One might suppose that all that is required is a reliable test of auditory acuity—for example, diminishing the intensity or amplitude of a sound until the subject no longer responds to it. Several issues, however, act against the uncritical application of this simple system. First, at what point of diminishing sound intensity shall it be said that a person is deaf as opposed to hard of hearing? Shall the designation of deafness be reserved for those whose auditory acuity is functionally useless? A Conference of Executives of Schools for the Deaf (1938) did in fact adopt definitions in functional auditory terms:

> *The deaf:* those in whom the sense of hearing is nonfunctional for the ordinary purposes of life. . . .
> *The hard of hearing:* those in whom the sense of hearing, although defective, is functional with or without a hearing aid.

But then, of course, one has to set up criteria both for the evaluation of functional and nonfunctional hearing and for what constitutes "the ordinary purposes of life." To complicate the problem yet further, it has been shown that two individuals with the same degree and patterning of auditory acuity as measured by pure tone threshold may differ markedly in auditory functioning as measured by speech-hearing tests (Barker et al., 1953, p. 191; Meyerson, 1956). Likewise, two individuals with similar auditory functioning may display grossly divergent sensitivity to sound. These interesting results occur because *functional* hearing depends upon many factors other than sheer auditory capacity—factors such as motivation and age at loss of hearing with respect to language acquisition.

A similar situation exists in the case of blindness. The definition of blindness varies from country to country, from state to state, and certainly from investigator to investigator. In Norway, for example, a person is legally blind who, with corrective lenses, cannot see to count his or her fingers in good illumination against a dark background at a distance of one meter (Holst, 1952). Within the United States legal blindness is based on such diverse criteria as inability to perceive motion at a distance of one foot and Snellen Chart performance of 20/200, which is roughly equivalent to the ability to read 14-point type. Whatever the criteria, however, great caution must be used in inferring what the person can and cannot do simply because there is not a one-to-one relation between visual acuity and visual behavior. Thus, in one study, 8 percent of the children in special classes for the partially seeing had central visual acuity less than 20/200 Snellen, meaning that they could be classed as legally blind—yet these children could learn by visual methods (Kerby, 1952).

The proposition that physique as defined medically in physical or physiological terms is not unequivocally related to behavior is an important one. Definitions of physical conditions are not psychological definitions. Like age or sex, they are of value in somatopsychological research chiefly as reference points that delimit gross characteristics of the individuals to be studied. They are the starting points for such crucial inquiries as: How does the person evaluate his or her disability? What are the physical limits it imposes? What are the restrictions imposed by society? How does the person perceive others' view of himself or herself? How do society and those more immediately close to the person regard the disability? These are somatopsychological questions that point to the underlying variables connecting atypical physique on the one hand with attitudes and behavior on the other.

Chapter 2
Status Position

Both positive and negative attitudes toward people with disabilities exist, although the latter may be more covert. Because negative attitudes are so troubling, there is a strong tendency for those concerned about disability problems to concentrate on them. However, dwelling on the negative, without also revealing and examining the positive, can reinforce the negative in strange ways. We shall avoid this pitfall by striving to understand, in different parts of this book, the factors involved in both positive and negative attitudes.

It is useful to compare the position of persons with disabilities to that of minority groups in general, for, as we shall see, disadvantaged groups have much at stake that is common.[1] First, commonalities will be discussed, then points of difference. The chapter will end with the proposition that the status of individuals with a disability

[1]The classical volumes of Lewin (1948) and Allport (1954) are highly recommended for their penetrating insights about prejudice. Barker's paper (1948) formulated important aspects of the underprivileged minority-group status of persons with disabilities.

is not only that of a devaluated minority group; being valued, appreciated, and respected are positive attitudes of the public that need to be recognized, explored, and extended.

UNDERPRIVILEGED STATUS

Examples of underprivileged status are far-reaching. Employment opportunities, particularly at the higher levels, are often sharply limited, *even though* the person has the requisite ability. Physical standards for all employees may exist as a matter of policy, irrespective of whether a particular job can be handled effectively by a person with a disability. The admonition of Henry Ford (1926) that "we are too ready to assume without investigation that the full possession of faculties is a condition requisite to the best performance of all jobs" (p. 107) needs to be well heeded today. Various directives and guidelines stemming from the Rehabilitation Act of 1973 and from statements of human rights now require that job qualifications match actual abilities needed to carry out the job. This position is encouraging.

The exclusion of people with a disability from educational, recreational, and other social activities also occurs. Even if they are accepted as participating members in many life areas, their disability, in the abstract, is often seen as precluding marriage. In one study of almost 100 adults, it was found that as a social relationship increased in intimacy, the acceptability of persons with various disabilities decreased (Shears & Jensema, 1969). Table 2.1 indicates the sharp decline in acceptance as a marriage partner compared to a work partner.

To guard against overgeneralization, all of us need to be reminded that the percentages in this table reflect stereotypical reac-

Table 2.1 PERCENTAGE OF SUBJECTS WHO WOULD ACCEPT CERTAIN ANOMALOUS PERSONS IN TWO TYPES OF RELATIONSHIPS

PERSON[a]	WORK PARTNER	MARRIAGE PARTNER
Physically handicapped (wheelchair)	93%	7%
Amputee (arm or leg)	91	18
Blind person	89	16
Person with a hairlip	80	8
Severe stutterer	74	7
Deaf-mute	67	10
Cerebral palsy (spastic)	51	1
Mentally ill person	37	2
Mentally retarded person	30	0

[a]The phrasing that was used to identify the person to the subjects has been preserved in this table.

tions to persons who are defined only by a labeled disability. This situation is far different from that in which social encounters take place with individuals who are known as *individuals*—that is, as individuals with a unique complement of interests, abilities, personality traits, and life circumstances. The difference is so important that it is discussed more fully later (pp. 73–78). Also, it is well to remember that the percentage of people with the indicated disabilities who are actually married exceeds the above percentages by a considerable margin despite the hurdles that are raised, and sometimes raised high, by conflicts within the couple themselves and disapproving others.

Underprivileged status may be insisted upon by those who want minority-group members not only to know their place but also to *keep* their place—that is, to feel and act less fortunate than others. Certain driving forces behind this insistence have been understood in terms of the concept "requirement of mourning," elaborated in Chapter 5. Here let it suffice to point out that the requirement of mourning stems from a need to maintain unchallenged those cherished values which may have accorded the person superior status. This dynamic is captured in the astute observations shared with Chevigny (1946), recently blinded, by a friend who said, "You're a blind man now, you'll be expected to act like one" (p. 71). "People will be firmly convinced that you consider yourself a tragedy. They'll be disconcerted and even shocked to discover that you don't" (p. 74). Aren't some people disconcerted and even shocked when ethnic and religious minority-group members advocate equality or show in other ways that they deserve as much respect and opportunity for development as anyone else?

If people with a disability are unable to participate in some activities that are highly valued, their space of free movement is restricted. Part of the restriction may be due to the physical limitation itself. A person who is deaf may not enjoy nuances of music. A person with limb or heart impairments may avoid walking more than modest distances. However, part of the restriction has its source in socially derogatory attitudes—attitudes that say, in effect, "You are less good, less worthy because of the disability. It is something to be ashamed of, to be hidden, and made up for."

Devaluation is expressed sometimes subtly, sometimes bluntly, and sometimes viciously. It is seen in the patronizing attitude of the person who gives money to "help those poor little crippled children." It is seen in disparaging allusions to the physical particulars of an adversary. Jokes about people with a disability more often deprecate and ridicule than do jokes about socially accepted classes—like farmers, salespeople, and judges (Barker et al., 1953, p. 75). The feeling "I am glad I am not like you," which may spring into consciousness upon seeing a person with a disability, betrays devaluating attitudes. We do not entertain this feeling toward persons whom we accept on an equal or superior footing, even though we might not choose to exchange places. Devaluation is seen in the alarm of a student visiting Alcoholics Anonymous for a class project who, upon being asked how long she had been coming to the meetings, thought, "They surely couldn't think *I* am alcoholic!" It is seen in the reluctance of a volunteer to accompany a mentally retarded adult to the grocery store, fearing that "someone might infer a family relationship." In an extreme form, devaluation is seen in aversion toward a person with a physical disability. The following is one incident among many variations on the same theme: Disability can lead to devaluation. Karen, a 3-year-old child with cerebral palsy, journeyed far with her parents for medical consultation. They were seeking lodging for the night:

> . . . The house was lovely—white clapboard, old and with lamplight at the windows, it looked warm and friendly. I rang the bell and the door was opened almost immediately. I stepped in out of the rain and turned to a sweet-looking middle-aged woman.
>
> "We should like a room for the night," I said, "if you can put a cot in our room for Karen."
>
> "I think I can accommodate you."
>
> She led the way into a tastefully furnished living room and invited me to sit down. I relaxed comfortably, propping Karen on my arm. . . .
>
> "Why don't you put the child down, she must be heavy," she inquired.
>
> "That's all right," I said, "I'll hold her."
>
> "Well, sit her in the chair next to you," she suggested, "I don't mind if she gets down and runs around. Traveling is hard on youngsters; she'd probably love to get down."
>
> "Karen can't get down and run around," I explained. "As a matter of fact, she can't sit up alone. Even when I'm holding her you'll notice she has difficulty holding her head erect for any length of time. That's why we're here. We've come to see Dr. C. We hope he may be able to help her."
>
> I suddenly realized that the woman was sitting in an attitude of frozen attention. Her face grew livid and she jumped to her feet. "Get out of my house!" she shouted. "Only bad, dirty people would have a child like that." [Killilea, 1952, pp. 64–65].[2]

Self-devaluation, as felt by the person with a disability, is also manifested variously. Illustrations of its many ramifications appear in this and other chapters.

---

[2]From *Karen* by Marie Killilea, published by Prentice-Hall, 1952. Reprinted by permission of Prentice-Hall and Marie Killilea.

A consistent finding in the research literature is that attitudes toward people with disabilities are correlated with attitudes toward other minority groups (English, 1971a). In one study, negative attitudes toward blind people were significantly associated with negative attitudes toward Negroes and other minority groups (Cowen et al., 1958). Similar results have been found in the case of deafness (Cowen et al., 1966), old people (Kogen, 1961), and people with unspecified disabilities (Chesler, 1965). These findings can be understood as deriving from a more basic ethnocentric attitude toward out-group members in general—an attitude that one's race, culture, or nation is superior to all others. One study (English, 1971b) used the Ethnocentrism Scale that had been developed in the classical study of the authoritarian personality (Adorno et al., 1950). It was found that negative attitudes toward blind people were related to high ethnocentric scores.

Physical limitations per se may produce suffering and frustration, but discriminatory practices against persons with a devalued physique spread far wider. They cut off a vast range of opportunities for personal development. They create difficulties in social affairs and in self-acceptance. It should also be underscored that, so long as a physically able person links disability with shame, he or she will be ill prepared for the challenge of living with a disability that may come with time. It behooves us, then, to give careful consideration to sources of prejudice and ways of overcoming them. Different aspects of this problem are examined in this and subsequent chapters.

OVERLAPPING SITUATIONS

Persons with a disability, like members of other minority groups, may be represented as subject to two different and often conflicting situations at the same time. On the one hand, considered disabled, they are subject to the expectations of how a person with a disability should act (disabled determinants of behavior); on the other hand, the wish to be "just like anyone else" predisposes them toward "normal" patterns of behavior.[3]

Illustrative of the problem is the situation of persons who are blind. As Chevigny (1946) has stressed, the world has an unusually fixed notion that a person who is blind is a tragic figure, utterly helpless and dependent. This is one situation in which individuals who are blind find themselves. The other situation is more clearly that of a "normal person," with its attendant values and expectations of

---

[3]A systematic discussion of the nature of overlapping situations and resulting behavior is given in Barker et al. (1953, pp. 27–46). Although the referents are to physical growth in adolescence, the points made have wide generality.

independence and self-acceptance. Persons who are blind may not only prefer to be in the latter psychological situation but may feel that they *are*, to a large extent or fully. They may, for example, consider their situation not tragic at all. They may have achieved adequate physical independence and a share of life's satisfactions. Helplessness and self-pity do not characterize their lives. Yet they are subject to the behavior determinants of both the "disabled" and the "normal" situation. When seeking a job, they may be directed to the sheltered workshop even though they may be able, or willing to try, to compete in the world of the sighted (see Criddle, 1953: Chapters 21, 22). In ordinary relationships, people may insist that they act like blind people are supposed to act and may be "disconcerted and even shocked" when they don't.

The expectations and directives of others are not the only source of conflict in overlapping situations. Persons with a disability may themselves be torn between acting in accord with their disability and acting like "normal" people. They may, for example, find it necessary to ascend stairs slowly, while at the same time they may wish to hide the disability and keep up with others. Conflict imposed both by society and by the individual himself or herself often coexist. A young man, quadraplegic from an automobile accident, recalls his adjustment period: "I tried so hard to look and act normal. In some ways I still do [12 years after the accident]; I don't deny it. Society demands that people act and be 'normal,' not deviate. At the same time, I was constantly reminded that I was not 'normal,' through interpersonal relationships, architectural barriers, and vocational goals" (Caywood, 1974, p. 25). Whether the conflicting situations are felt as primarily imposed by the outside or as stemming from internal conflicts will affect where the individual's resentments will be focused. In any case, a person with a disability—and, in fact, all members of minority groups—may frequently be placed, both by society's edict and by personal conflicts, in overlapping situations in which the determinants of behavior are to some extent incompatible.

GROUP STEREOTYPES

The stereotype of a person with a disability is often that of an individual who has suffered a great misfortune and whose life is consequently disturbed and damaged. Unlike bereaved persons, in whom the deep-felt pain of loss formally ceases after a year and who are expected gradually to engage in the fullness of life once again, people with a disability are frequently expected to be permanently enmeshed in the tragedy of their fate. Several factors contribute to this stereotype. In addition to the phenomenon of "spread" (Chapter 3), the "requirement of mourning" (Chapter 5), and other sources of at-

titudes examined in Chapter 19, popular misconceptions are perpetuated by reality distortions appearing in the media:

> Guilty of confirming pity stereotypes, popular culture finds ample use
> for them. Typical was the film *Moulin Rouge*, which depicted Tou-
> louse-Lautrec as a piteous, embittered dwarf, morbidly obsessed by his
> deformity and tragic in his love relationships. How far this is from the
> truth can be seen in Gerstle Mack's biography, where the artist emerges
> as a witty, engaging personality who loved Paris night life and the sport-
> ing scene. The testimony of Lautrec's friends indicates that, with the
> exception of his last mentally aberrant years, he was amusing and well
> liked, highly regarded by the artistic and literary figures of his time. By
> falling into easy stereotype, the film distorted the facts of Lautrec's life
> to play up sentimental fancies and, unwittingly, to confirm popular no-
> tions of how the handicapped are handicapped. [Maisel, 1953, p. 32][4]

Popular misconceptions are also perpetuated, unfortunately, by
scientific investigators who, expecting certain results, inadvertently
help to produce them by the very procedures that are undertaken.
An especially relevant example is the development of a self-
acceptance scale in which the investigator used both people who
stutter and nonstutterers for validating purposes, reasoning that "on
both an *a priori* and an empirical basis" those who stuttered should
score lower than those who did not stutter (Berger, 1952). When they
did not, the investigator matched the two groups on the basis of age
and sex. The resulting self-acceptance scores came out in the "right"
direction—and the investigator stopped controlling! If the results
had persisted in being stubborn, socioeconomic status, race, or religion would probably have been controlled until the desired result
had been obtained.

Where the social stereotypes of a group are stigmatizing, individuals often wish to be judged in their own right and not "known"
by membership in the group. The reason for this is not hard to find
since the stereotyped expectations and judgments often reflect underlying devaluating attitudes. Consider some common negative
misinterpretations: Persons with a disability are often considered to
be compensating when simply pursuing their strengths and interests;
they may be judged to feel inferior when they are merely holding
back because of realistic appreciation of limitations; they may be regarded as being suspicious when they are merely wondering—all because they are seen as part of a larger group with certain presumed
personality characteristics.

The dependence of a part on the whole does not always result

---

[4]From *Meet a body*, a ms. by E. Maisel. Reprinted by permission of International Center for the Disabled, New York.

in the part's taking over or assimilating the properties of the whole. Sometimes the influence is seen through the *phenomenon of contrast*. Suppose, for example, that a person who is deaf earns a living and is happily married. Such a person may be judged by others as outstanding and unusually well adjusted simply because these accomplishments contrast with the stereotype about people who are deaf. People who are deaf may not appreciate this type of compliment when the praise implies that they are exceptions proving the rule. To illustrate the generality of the perceptual phenomenon of *assimilation* versus *contrast,* the following examples are given: "In the same way do we judge the personality traits and motivations of individual Jews, Republicans, Negroes, Catholics, Russians, etc. . . . Thus, many Americans, through the operation of the assimilation phenomenon, tend to overestimate the shrewdness of a particular Jew, or the inscrutability of a somewhat reticent Russian—because they believe Jews to be shrewd and Russians to be inscrutable. Because of contrast, they tend to overestimate the intelligence of a Negro who is normally intelligent and to underestimate the religious conservatism of a Catholic who is liberal in some of his religious views" (Krech & Crutchfield, 1948, p. 97).

Assimilation appears when the difference between parts of a whole is perceived as small, contrast when it is perceived as great (Heider, 1944). It can be expected, therefore, that a person with a disability will have to cope with the problem of being stereotyped by the disability more frequently when interacting with a stranger than with a friend. This is so because a friend knows the person as an *individual,* that is, as someone whose characteristics distinguish him or her from others in special ways.

Yet the plea, "Do not stereotype me" cannot be fully realized because the individual *must* be apprehended in terms of the presumed characteristics of the group in which he or she is placed. This is not merely up to the whim of the perceiver, for there is ample evidence to show that the perceived properties of a substructure are largely determined by the nature of the whole structure. Something that looks like a rod when perceived in isolation may turn out to be a rung of a ladder or a leg of a chair when seen as part of the larger structure. A single word gets its meaning from the context of the sentence: "Light" may refer to weight in one context, to daytime in another. In like manner, a person is viewed in terms of the group with which he or she is identified. However, although we may never be able to avoid categorizing individuals into groups, "there is no reason demanding that only certain defined personality traits should be perceived as 'belonging' to any specific grouping based on such differentia" (Krech & Crutchfield, 1948, p. 98). Yet, as we shall see, the pull toward making unwarranted, damaging inferences about a person identified by a single attribute felt to be undesirable is strong. In Chapter 4 we shall consider how to counteract such negative inferences.

COMMON FATE

We have seen that attitudes toward a wide range of minority groups, including people with disabilities, are related to each other. It can be expected, therefore, that changes in the situation of one minority group will affect other minority groups. As the civil rights of one group become more fully realized, so will the needs of other groups become more loudly voiced.

A spirited notion of the force of such interdependence is given by a woman who uses a wheelchair:

> [Since the Watts riots in 1965] Blacks all over the country, other racial minorities, women, people with disabilities and multitudes of other groups who had accepted powerlessness and half-filled cups all of their lives began to scream. They all began to realize that society . . . is not going to "fix" it for you. The guy with the problem has to come up with the solution. . . . Everybody had known all along that Blacks were regularly deprived of their constitutional rights, but whoever thought people with disabilities were? The "expectation explosion" began, and "consciousness raising" attempted to ensure that everyone's expectations were as high as they should be. [Vash, 1975, p. 148][5]

Many instances could be cited illustrating parallel changes in the situation of groups disadvantaged by race, religion, sex, ethnicity, incarceration, or disability (Wright, 1973). Attitudes toward people with disabilities are not isolated phenomena unrelated to attitudes toward other minority groups or the general sweep of social change.

DIFFERENCES IN MINORITY-GROUP POSITION

Although it is important to realize that persons with a disability often share problems in common with members of other minority groups, there are important differences. One of the most significant is the usual lack of group endorsement of behavior indicative of the particular disability. Rather, the usual advice to persons with a disability is to appear as much like a nondisabled person as possible, and adjustment is often judged in terms of how skillfully the normal state is

[5]Reprinted from The psychology of disability, by C. L. Vash, in *Rehab. Psych.*, 1975, 22. By permission of *Rehab. Psych.*

emulated. Even where there is a high degree of acceptance of the disability, there is resistance to behavior that unnecessarily spotlights the disability. This is clearly seen in the following account by the mother of a child who is blind. On the basis of interviews, this mother was rated as showing good acceptance of the child and her handicap:

> We helped Mildred to overcome some of her mannerisms which are sometimes associated with blindness such as hanging her head. We explained to her that this habit was characteristic of the blind, and she earnestly tried to overcome it. We also discussed with her the frequently expressionless and vacant look on the faces of the blind, particularly when listening to speeches, etc. We tried to tell her that she must make an effort to show joy or sadness, surprise or disappointment. She seemed to appreciate and understand this when we explained that it would increase her personal attractiveness. [Sommers, 1944, p. 52][6]

In contrast, a Jew or a black person, for example, can take pride in many of the characteristics held to be uniquely Jewish or black, and such pride is looked upon as a sign of self-acceptance.

Pride, however, can be experienced by persons with a disability in the sense of meeting the challenge of a disability, surviving and moving on to valued activities, accepting oneself and one's group, and helping others surmount similar hurdles. Millie Clapp recounts her sense of pride as she doggedly pursued learning physical and mental skills made difficult by severe cerebral palsy that prevented her from speaking, walking, dressing, feeding, or bathing herself:

> If you could see me doing these things [cutting with a scissors, drinking liquids, writing] you might be saying, "She must have a strong determination to be able to cope with her handicap." Yes, I have it and I'm very proud of it because if I didn't have the determination, I couldn't have done anything as well as I do now. Besides, I have shown some people who think they have the worst luck in the world that if they would take a good look at me and see what I am trying to do with my life, in spite of the difficulty I have in controlling my muscles to do the things I do, they might feel a little ashamed of themselves. [Clapp, circa 1976, p. 4]

The position of people with a disability also differs from other minority groups insofar as their deviation is not likely to be shared by other family members. Racial characteristics are genetically inherited and religious characteristics are often socially inherited; however, individuals with a disability are often the only ones in their family so affected. As children, they may even be unaware that there

---

[6]Reprinted from *The influence of parental attitudes and social environment on the personality development of the adolescent blind* by V. S. Sommers. New York: American Foundation for the Blind. By permission of the foundation.

are others who have a similar disability and thus may feel no affiliation with any minority group. Moreover, clubs and groups organized by and for people with disabilities are rare in small communities. In the case of other minority groups, the psychological situation is often very different.

Self-help groups, where they exist, can provide the support that comes from sharing mutual problems and taking steps to overcome them; they can foster the pride that comes with appreciation of one's own dignity and worth (Borman & Lieberman, 1976; Katz, 1976). Publications by and for individuals with disabilities can also help to reduce isolation from people who are concerned with similar problems.

POSITIVE ATTITUDES

The fact that the general situation of persons with disabilities can be represented in terms of a disadvantaged minority group must not obsure the fact that favorable attitudes toward persons with atypical physiques are frequent. In one study (Mussen & Barker, 1944), students were asked to rate cripples in general on twenty-four personality traits. The median ratings fell nearest the following descriptive phrases:

Conscientiousness: Tries harder than most
Self-reliance: Tendency to have more than average degree
Kindness: More than average
Emotional restraint: Tendency to be reserved; seldom lets the world know his feelings
Persistence: Quite persistent; gives up only after definite proof of impossibility
Mental alertness: Intelligent; more alert than average
Originality: Tendency to be more creative than average
Religiousness: Tendency to be more religious than most people
Impulsiveness: Inclined to ponder possible results of behavior
Unselfishness: Marked tendency to be unselfish; generous, altruistic
Friendliness: Average
Trustworthiness: Average
Disposition: Average, for the most part moderately cheerful
Tolerance: Average
Courage: Average
Self-pity: Average
Social poise and tact: Average ability and interest in getting along with others
Vitality: Average amount of vitality, energy, pep

Self-confidence: Average
Submissiveness: Average amount of ascendance and submission
Realism: Given to reverie occasionally
Aggressiveness: Tendency to be mild; gentle in approach to others
Social adaptability: Finds it somewhat difficult to adjust to new situations
Sensitiveness: More sensitive than average

Other data (Comer & Piliavin, 1975; Ray, 1946) support the preceding study by reporting that publicly expressed attitudes toward persons with physical disabilities are frequently favorable. Of course, covert attitudes may in some, if not many, of the responses remain negative.

Table 2.2 represents responses of 2340 professionals and businesspeople between the ages of 20 and 60 who were asked whether they liked, disliked, or were indifferent to persons with a variety of physical characteristics (Strong, 1931):

Table 2.2   RESPONSES TO PHYSICAL CHARACTERISTICS OF PEOPLE

	LIKING	DISLIKING	INDIFFERENT
Sick people	22%	28%	50%
Very old people	45	11	44
Cripples	29	19	52
Side-show freaks	4	77	19
People with gold teeth	4	46	50
People with protruding jaws	6	42	52
People with hooked noses	4	38	58
Blind people	25	16	59
Deaf-mutes	16	25	59

Notice that the most common response was "indifferent." Cripples and blind persons were more frequently checked as being liked than disliked, whereas the reverse was true for deaf-mutes.

The percentages in Table 2.2 may be compared with those in Table 2.3:

Table 2.3   RESPONSES TO GENERAL CHARACTERISTICS OF PEOPLE

	LIKING	DISLIKING	INDIFFERENT
People who borrow things	3%	77%	20%
Negroes	13	32	55
Socialists	8	41	51
Athletic men	74	1	25
Conservatives	50	12	38

The evidence seems clear that publicly expressed attitudes toward persons with physical disabilities are, for the most part, not unfavorable, frequently positive, and may even indicate admiration.

Love and appreciation by family, friends, and people who care are also common. Such positive attitudes generally are apt to go unnoticed and unnamed because they do not disturb our sense of well-being, of what "ought" to be. Sometimes they are discounted as a mere cover-up for unacceptable "real" feelings. What needs to be recognized is that both the positive and the negative exist, and that negative feelings can suppress or hide genuinely positive feelings as readily as the reverse. Special attention is given in Chapter 9 to the importance of coping versus succumbing frameworks in the emergence of positive attitudes. The significance of values is stressed in Chapter 8. We shall find that once we trouble ourselves with the untroubling positive attitudes associated with disability, their still waters run as deep as the undercurrents of inferior status.

SALUTARY STATUS AND OUTSTANDING SUCCESS

When special achievement becomes sufficiently prominent, it may serve as the organizing characteristic for status evaluation around which other characteristics of the person will be seen. Outstanding success may therefore counteract devaluation by leading to the realization that the individual is not a disabled person but a person with a disability. Physique then becomes subordinated to other characteristics that give status to the person. Success may also highlight the variety of ways of coping and adapting to a disability.

If one were to point out those among the famous who were blind, deaf, paralyzed, had lost limbs, or had other disabilities, the list would be long indeed. Such a list, taken from an earlier German compilation, has been reproduced in Boorstein (1935, pp. 106–110). It includes the names, and in some cases short biographies, of almost 500 people with disabilities. Such individuals are associated *first of all* with their achievements; their disabilities, when disclosed, thereby assume a position of secondary importance.

However, outstanding success is not a reliable path to salutary or even equal status. One usually cannot wear one's laurels for all to see, not even in the manner of a titular appellation as M.D. or Ph.D. Henry Viscardi (1952), born with dwarfed, misshapen legs, was a champion marbles player among his friends but an "ape man" to others. Franklin Roosevelt may be admired by countless persons—but one must note that being President of the United States is sufficiently distinctive to make the fact of disability interesting but not central. Moreover, admiration based on surpassed but basically low expectations may connote underlying devaluation of persons with a disability. Finally, presumed outstanding characteristics of a group may actually serve to confine its members to typecast roles rather than encourage a broad range of opportunities. Good intentions notwithstanding, the statement has been made that "Blind workers, with their sense of touch often extremely highly developed to compensate for the lack of sight, have made superior assemblers, inspectors, sorters and counters" (reported by Morganstein, 1975). This is the kind of accolade that people with disabilities can do without.

Equal or salutary status is primarily accorded only to those individuals who, having achieved in spite of their disability, are considered to be unusual. The majority of persons with a disability do not enjoy such positive status. The individual who surpasses expectations may—sometimes.

DILEMMA OF CONTRADICTORY STATUS

Finally, it should be mentioned that feelings and beliefs which bring about inferior status exist side by side with those which bring about salutary status. This juxtaposition may lead to a complex admixture of both devaluating pity and respect in the same social relationship, as exemplified in an incident recalled by Karsten Ohnstad (1942) while he was a pupil at the school for the blind:

> The woodworking room was one of the favorite stops of visitors to the school. They swelled our heads with admiration for our work, then deflated us with pity. One of them looked sadly at my basswood box.
> "Is he blind?" she asked the instructor.
> "Yes," said the instructor, as sadly as she. "He's blind."
> I could feel the woman looking at me incredulously. There was a long pause.
> "And he has such fair skin," she mourned, finally. [p. 129][7]

Contradiction in the status of the person with a disability may lead to disturbing conflicts. A person who is deaf, for example, may be held in great esteem because of accomplishments as a writer but may be regarded by some as an unsuitable marriage partner. A similar dilemma with respect to other minority groups has been described by Hughes (1945) who points out that being a Negro "tends to overpower, in most crucial situations, any other characteristic which might run counter to it. But professional standing is also a pow-

---

[7]Reprinted from *The world at my fingertips* by K. Ohnstad, published by Bobbs-Merrill.

erful characteristic. . . . In the person of the professionally qualified Negro these two powerful characteristics clash. The dilemma for those who meet such a person is that of having to choose whether to treat him as a Negro or as a member of his profession" (p. 357). Such dilemmas clearly demonstrate that status is not an abstract quality that a person "has"; rather it is always related to social standing of a person within prescribed roles. Inconsistency of social attitudes brings about situations of psychological uncertainty for the person with a disability regarding how he or she will be received (see Chapter 6).

It has rightfully been said that insofar as a disability is made more handicapping by the neglect, prejudicial attitudes, and discriminatory practices of society, it is society that needs treatment and rehabilitation, not only persons with disabilities. Underprivileged minority position creates difficulties of two kinds: the hardships and suffering resulting from restrictions imposed by a dominant majority as well as devaluative feelings about oneself and one's own disability.

To ward off possible false conclusions, it is important to stress that feelings of inferiority are *not* more common among people with disabilities *as a group* than among their able-bodied counterparts (see Chapter 7). Moreover, people with disabilities and the able-bodied are hardly distinguishable as groups in overall adjustment or in life satisfaction (Cameron, Titus, Kostin, & Kostin, 1973). These facts may partly be accounted for by the existence of positive attitudes that are also part of the social surroundings of persons with disabilities, as well as by powerful personal adjustive efforts and other factors. Equivalence in adjustment and life satisfaction, however, should not be interpreted as meaning that *life conditions* are satisfactory. Value judgments about life conditions, whether they are good or bad, depend upon beliefs about the nature of barriers to the fulfillment of human potential and how they may be eliminated, as well as upon ideas of justice.

That there are basic factors in the broader socioeconomic-political conditions of both industrial and nonindustrial societies affecting the status of persons with disabilities was recognized at a meeting of the United Nations (United Nations, 1977). That meeting also recognized the importance of attitudes in creating social barriers. The point was made that "Discriminatory behavior may take place either because a person is prejudiced or because prejudices have been built into the laws, regulations, and customary norms and requirements of different social structures and institutions" (p. 11).

Psychological factors that influence attitudes will be our concern in several chapters throughout this book. Chapter 3 introduces a number of general concepts basic to the understanding of how we perceive and evaluate people, followed by a chapter that examines more specific factors in the appraisal of persons.

Chapter 3
Perceiving the Causes and Effects of Disability: Some Basic Concepts

How one reacts to a negative event, like the imposition of disability, whether in oneself or others, is significantly influenced by its presumed causes and effects. What makes the perception of causes and effects so problematic and fraught with consequences is that it generally involves cognitive-affective processes that are irrational as well as rational; that is, the perceived connections between events are not dictated by logical reasoning alone. And yet it is the perceived causes and effects of something that significantly defines its very nature and undergirds attitudes that become widely generalized. Beliefs reflect such perceptions and are tenaciously held because they seem so necessarily true.

In general, cognition refers to processes by which the world is grasped and understood. It includes perceiving, judging, and reasoning, although the conclusions reached are not necessarily rational or accurate. The hyphenated term cognitive-affective indicates the interdependence between cognition and feelings, each affecting the other. The statement that a disability is generally perceived as negative introduces feelings from the start.

SPREAD

The term *spread*, introduced by Dembo et al. (1956; reprinted, 1975), refers to the power of single characteristics to evoke inferences about a person. This power is strikingly demonstrated in the experiment mentioned earlier (pp. 25–26), in which subjects were asked to rate "cripples" in general on twenty-four personality traits (Mussen & Barker, 1944). If one pauses to consider that nothing more was said about the group to be rated, it is significant that the task could be executed at all. In a second experiment, high-school students were shown six photographs of college men to be ranked according to a number of behavior and personality characteristics (Ray, 1946). A photograph of a man sitting in a wheelchair was presented to half the subjects; to the other half, the same picture was presented with the wheelchair blocked out. When depicted as being in a wheelchair as compared to able-bodied, the stimulus person was judged to be more conscientious, feel more inferior, be a better friend, get better grades, be more even-tempered, be a better class president, be more religious, like parties less, and be more unhappy.

The phenomenon of spread also occurs in regard to other characteristics of groups—such as nationality, ethnicity, race, religion, and sex. In a classical experiment, Katz & Braly (1933) studied racial and ethnic stereotypes by asking subjects to select from a list of traits those most typical of ten groups. An important, but understressed, finding was that the subjects felt able to rate groups with which they had had no contact (for example, Turks).

Frequently, although not always, the inferences are positive or negative according to the valence of the precipitating characteristic (see "Spread and Similarity of Traits," pp. 61–63). That is, a negative attribute, like a disability, may lead to negative associations, and a positive attribute to positive associations, *especially* where there is little additional information to check the spread. Thus, a person who has a disability may be thought of as less mature emotionally and less able intellectually, although as we have already seen, positive inferences may also occur.

The interesting question is, how can subjects generalize from a single characteristic, such as crippling, to a vast array of expectations concerning personality and behavior? Fruitful empirical data on this question could be directly obtained by asking the subjects themselves to elaborate and explain their judgments. What, for example, would a particular subject say who rated "cripples" as having a marked tendency to be unselfish? One subject might say, "They have suffered so much that they have become more sensitive to people's wants." Another might say, "This is one way they try to be accepted by others."

Such responses suggest that the subjects' impressions need not necessarily simply be arbitrary but may be supported by their view of disability. They are able to generalize from the physical characteristic because to them this represents a crucial deviation that affects a person in ways they presume to understand. That is to say, judgments are partly based on hypotheses as to the effects of crippling as a value loss. For example, the suffering stemming from disability may be seen as helping the person become more sensitive to others' needs. Also, if crippling is regarded as a state to which one can adjust, judgments can be expected to differ markedly from the view of crippling as an overwhelming calamity.

Even subjects who rate persons with a disability sometimes favorably and sometimes unfavorably are likely to hold not only arbitrary and discrete impressions but also impressions that are coherent to some extent. One can see that if a person describes people with orthopedic disabilities as trying harder and being more sensitive than the average, the views are not necessarily inconsistent.

Sometimes the process of spread functions in the reverse. That is, instead of the fact of disability leading to inferences about personality traits, a trait that is *known* about the person is freely *explained* by the disability, even in the absence of supporting evidence. Thus, a child's studiousness may be gratuitously ascribed to the fact that the child can't run like other children. Given the studiousness and the crippling, an automatic linkage is established. The term *physique as prime mover* has been applied when traits are automatically attributed to physical characteristics of the person (Wright, 1960). That spread to inferred characteristics and spread involving physique as prime mover designate different, although not independent, processes can be seen when we consider the likelihood that a person who ascribes studiousness to a child's crippling does not generally infer studiousness from knowledge that a child is crippled (see Figure 3.1).

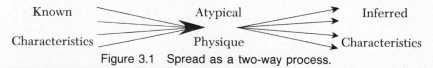

Figure 3.1   Spread as a two-way process.

Because of spread, the degree of disability is often perceived as more severe than it actually is. This is exemplified in the exaggerated estimates of the proportion of mentally retarded persons who have IQs below 50. In one of our studies, the average guess of some 500 college students was around 30 percent, whereas the true proportion is close to 5 percent.

If a person who is below standard in one characteristic is viewed as less adequate *only* in that regard and not more generally, the judgment would be a realistic one. Unfortunately, so sane an appraisal

Maria Regina College Library

1024 Court Street

Syracuse, New York 13208

of personal liabilities is not the rule. Physique (as well as other salient, personal-social characteristics) evokes a wide variety of impressions and feelings about people. Not only are specific characteristics of the person inferred from physique, but the person as a whole is sometimes evaluated accordingly. The problem becomes especially harmful when global devaluation takes place so that the person *as a person* is felt to be less worthy, less valuable, less desirable.

Experiments on the "fortune phenomenon," first explored by Dembo et al. (1956; reprinted 1975), clearly demonstrate the readiness with which a group is viewed as unfortunate on the basis of a label that signals devaluation. In one set of experiments, women from a variety of groups rated themselves, their own groups, and the other groups in the study on 11-point scales ranging from very fortunate to very unfortunate (Wright & Howe, 1969). Women from the socially devalued groups were mental hospital patients and welfare clients; the groups of higher status were middle-class housewives and college students. An important finding was that *all four* groups rated mental hospital patients in general and welfare clients in general significantly below average in how fortunate they were, in spite of the fact that virtually all subjects from these two groups rated themselves *as individuals, at least average* in this respect. Persons with physical disabilities at a rehabilitation center also rated themselves at least average (Wright & Muth, 1965).

It is well established that the observer need not be aware of the physical characteristics of another in order to be influenced by them. Winkler (1931), for example, presented action pictures of children with and without disabilities to 200 physically normal subjects who were to judge them according to personality traits. Some of the children with disabilities were not consciously recognized by the subjects as having a disability. Unfavorable judgments regarding the nondisabled children constituted 46 percent of all judgments about them, whereas 60 percent of the judgments made about the children *who were not recognized as having a disability,* were unfavorable. Possibly the postures of these children although not sufficiently peculiar to be consciously recognized as different, served as a stimulus for an unconscious negative reaction. Other evidence supports the validity of these findings (Barker et al., 1953, p. 77).

Examples from Everyday Life

Physical disability may be perceived as spreading to other physical, mental, social, and emotional characteristics of the person—even to his or her life situation as a whole. Spread to physical areas is commonly seen when a sighted person, without thinking, speaks unusually loudly to someone who is blind, as if lack of vision signals impaired hearing, as well.

In the following example, spread appears to also encompass mental abilities. Even in the face of ongoing evidence to the contrary, the person in question persisted in behavior that disregarded the actual capabilities of Karsten Ohnstad, a man who is blind. The setting is a library frequented by Karsten and his companion. One librarian always addressed the companion as if Karsten weren't present at all. Karsten recounts:

> "What book does he want?" she would ask, looking straight at Oscar who was standing beside me.
> Oscar would turn to me. "What book did you say you wanted?"
> *"Les Miserables* by Hugo."
> Oscar would turn back to the librarian. "He wants *Les Miserables* by Hugo."
> The librarian got the book. "Does he want to take it with him?"
> "Do you want to take it with you?"
> "Yes, I want to take it with me."
> Oscar would turn wearily back to the librarian. "Yes, he wants to take it with him."
> The librarian put the book on the table. "Does he want it signed in his own name?"
> "Do you want it signed in your name?" Patient Oscar.
> "Does he . . ." began the librarian.
> "No, he doesn't," I said, "He's changed his mind. He doesn't want a book." I hurried out of the building.
> "Now whatever do you suppose got into him?" I heard the librarian asking Oscar. [Ohnstad, 1942, pp. 62–63][1]

Spread can exert such a powerful force that even friends and relatives, not only strangers, are coerced by it. In the following account, a camp counselor narrates his excitement at discovering that 11-year-old Chris, a child with cerebral palsy, could read, and then his dismay at realizing that he had assumed that Chris could not:

> Chris had very poor motor control, could not speak well enough to be understood unless you knew beforehand what he was going to say, and had to be fed. He was easy to please. If he liked you, he was sure to let you know it. He was very patient with others and took their mistakes all in stride.
> Chris communicated with an electronic message board. He had a magnet attached to his wrist by which he could activate the machine to spell words, build sentences, and do math.
> One day I asked him if there were any books he liked to look at. I assumed he liked to look at the pictures. The familiar name, Dr. Suess, was put on the

---

[1]Reprinted from *The world at my fingertips* by K. Ohnstad, published by Bobbs-Merrill.

digital reader. When I gave the book to Chris, he started reading it out loud. I could follow with him and understand his words. Chris could read a book! I started to rush out of the room to tell everyone the good news.

Half way down the hall I stopped dead in my tracks. Of course he can read! How else could he use the message board? He could read, spell, construct proper sentences (his grammar and spelling were much better than my own!) and even swear and cuss on his "mini computer." In spite of all this I had assumed he could not read. (Personal communication)

Overprotection on the part of those close to the person with a physical limitation may in some measure be a consequence of spread. If a child's remaining abilities are underrated because of spread effects, it is readily seen how the child's ability to learn to cope with the physical and social environment will also be underrated.

An extreme manifestation of spread is the all too ready judgment, on the basis of a disability, that a person's life is a tragedy from which there is no reprieve. Some people have expressed the thought, "I would rather be dead than stone deaf or blind or . . ." On the other hand, the recognition that participating in life's satisfaction is not necessarily precluded by a physical disability requires putting physical characteristics in a position of sharing consequences with other factors.

The unrestrained spread of physique is again seen in the attitude that persons who have a disability stand apart from, rather than are a part of, the community of others. It has been said, for example, that "a handicapped child can *never* have the satisfaction of being just like other children" (italics added). Does this mean that physical difference is always so central that it looms as the major feature of every situation? Surely there are times when most people with a disability feel essentially like other people, even though they may become especially aware of their difference in certain situations. Besides, there is strong evidence that people don't want to be just like everyone else, that there is an urge for uniqueness and a pursuit of human difference (Snyder & Fromkin, 1980). In any case, for a person who has a disability to be viewed first and foremost as a person and only secondarily as a person with a disability is a significant sign of maturity. Such titles as *Understanding the disabled* help to foster the invidious tendency to perceive disability as creating psychologically different kinds of people. All too readily it is assumed that people with disabilities take a great deal of knowing before they can be understood or accepted on the usual level.

People who have a disability are themselves subject to the spread process. We shall see that Frances regarded perfect hearing as the open sesame to all worthwhile things in life, from marriage to career, and impaired hearing as the impenetrable barrier (see pp.

118–121). People with a hearing loss do get married and do have careers, but for Frances her physical limitation meant widespread blocking in many social areas as well.

Examples of *physique as prime mover* abound in everyday life. Once a person has a physical deviation that stands out, there is a strong tendency to attribute wide-ranging personal characteristics and events of life to that deviation. Even theorists reflect the power of physique as prime mover in their views, an especially pointed example of which is the theory of compensation as indemnity (see pp. 147–149). The following excerpt is representative of this kind of thinking: "A well-known psychologist brought together some very interesting and enlightening factual information concerning some famous personalities who achieved greatness and distinction through relentless effort to compensate for organic inferiority and physical limitation" (Wilson, 1950, p. 192). The author then goes on to mention several accomplished athletes who achieved, it is supposed, *because* of their physical deficiencies—for example, Annette Kellerman, who "compensated for her frail body by rigorous swimming and became one of the great women swimmers of all time" (p. 192).

To us, it is still a moot question whether Annette Kellerman's performance should be seen primarily as compensatory. The issue is even more clearly drawn in the following remarks, made specifically to illustrate the principle of compensation:

> The record in the field of intellectual accomplishment is even more amazing. Robert Louis Stevenson was racked with tuberculosis and kept moving from one health resort to another. Charles Darwin was so sickly that he was limited in his work to only a few hours each day. Lord Byron's whole life was altered by his club foot. Edgar Allan Poe was the victim of a lung condition. The philosopher Kant carried on his writings in a state of continual pain caused by gout and his sunken chest. The philosopher Nietzsche, conscious of his frail body, conceived a philosophy of the superman. Aristotle and Demosthenes were physical defectives. The poet Goethe always complained that his life was all pain and burden, and once stated that in his whole life of seventy-five years he had not even four weeks of general well-being. Beethoven was pockmarked and snubnosed. He was continually harassed by asthma and digestive disorders, and at the age of twenty-eight, became deaf. . . . [Wilson, 1950, p. 193]

This passage clearly exemplifies how the power of physique as prime mover can distort the meaning of crucial aspects of a person's life. The disability is seen not only as entering everywhere but as the critical element in the events of life. Surely, the fact that "Charles Darwin was so sickly that he was limited in his work to only a few hours each day" is not sufficient to account for his absorbing interest in evolutionary processes. A review of his intellectual and emotional life would probably reveal that physique played a role, but most assuredly not *the* role, not the one factor primarily responsible for the directions his life assumed.

It is important to appreciate that physique as prime mover steers a person away from recognizing the possibility that people with a disability might pursue an area of work because they find it satisfying. Instead, positive motives, such as interest, enjoyment, and accomplishment, are seen as compensatory.

The next two examples show that persons with a disability are themselves coerced by the power of physique as prime mover to interpret events in terms of their disability. In the first example, Henry Viscardi, dwarfed through congenitally malformed legs, is 7 years old. By this time he had several harsh experiences which taught him that, except to those who knew him, he was an object of pity to be ostracized and ridiculed. He jumped to the conclusion that he could not enter the church because he was crippled—and it was a wrong conclusion:

> But as we stopped by the holy-water font a man at the church door looked at me sharply and whispered something to papa. The other people stared at us too.
>
> What is wrong? I wondered. *Do you suppose crippled children* are not allowed to come to church any more? [Italics ours]
>
> Papa took my hand and led me outside. "Let us go for a walk in the park," he said, smiling brightly.
>
> My eyes were smarting. "What's the matter, papa?" I finally said. "Why didn't we stay for Mass? Is it because I'm crippled?" I could hardly get the words out.
>
> Then Papa threw back his head and laughed. And he laughed again. "Oh, this is very funny," he said.
>
> I did not think it was funny, and I wished I had never come to church with him. I had a salty taste in my mouth.
>
> Then he put both his hands on my shoulders and looked right into my eyes. "Oh, this is very funny—no children allowed at eleven o'clock Mass. What a way to run a church!" I laughed too, just to be polite. [Viscardi, 1952, pp. 24–25][2]

In the second example, Karsten Ohnstad was sure that the girl stopped writing to him because he was blind. Was he right?

> A letter arrived from an unexpected source—from the pretty blonde girl back home. I listened with a glow of pleasure and embarrassment as I sat on my bed while my favorite nurse read the letter aloud. I had not expected to hear from the girl. . . . A nurse wrote the reply I dictat-

[2]From *A man's stature* by H. Viscardi, Jr. Reprinted by permission of Paul S. Eriksson, Pubs.

ed. The blonde girl had said in her letter that she would write again. I waited—one week, a month. I made a decision. She had written purely out of sympathy. I took her letter and tore it to bits. This, I decided, was part of my new education. [Ohnstad, 1942, pp. 29–30][3]

There simply is not enough evidence for a reliable verdict as to the circumstances surrounding the girl's silence, and such ambiguity repeats itself in the lives of people with a disability. The important point is that both the person with the disability and the nondisabled person are prone to draw conclusions despite lack of evidence, and physical disability is readily singled out as the inferential base.

The spread phenomenon is not unique to atypical physique. Anything salient that is regarded as a personal characteristic can serve this function. In the following example a student cites the unconscious raising of one's voice when speaking to a foreigner:

> While living in the Philippines, my family employed a maid who didn't speak English well. In daily living with her and other Filipinos we would raise our voices in trying to make ourselves understood. Until our maid brought it to my Mother's attention that she was not hard of hearing, and that if my mother would simply slow her speech rate she would understand much better, no one in the family realized that this had been taking place. Upon attempting to correct our mistake, we found that we exhibited this behavior with anyone who gave any indication of not understanding. (Personal communication)

Since any salient fact about a person can serve as a stimulus for the spread phenomenon, all of us are affected, both as the recipients and as the actualizers of spread. In this and subsequent chapters we shall examine a number of factors influencing the spread process, with particular reference to persons with disabilities.

PERSON VERSUS ENVIRONMENTAL ATTRIBUTION

In its most general meaning, attribution refers to "what is attributed to what and why." Heider's original work on this question (1958) caught the imagination of many investigators who followed up its profound implications in a large number of studies (Harvey et al., 1981; Jones et al., 1971). Attribution theory deals with the conditions under which we assign attributes (causes, characteristics, properties) to various entities in our world, such as people, things, events, and situations. Of special interest is the problem of causal attribution, especially with respect to whether the cause of something is attributed to the person or to the environment. By the environment we mean other people, physical events, the situation—that is, anything that is not the person whose behavior is being explained.

[3]Reprinted from *The world at my fingertips* by K. Ohnstad, published by Bobbs-Merrill.

Consider the following two names that had been suggested for a committee organized to reduce architectural barriers at a large university: "Committee for the Physically Handicapped" and "Committee for the Architecturally Handicapped." The latter designation was chosen because it rightfully assigns the source of difficulty not to the person but to the environment. The author of the book *Designing for the disabled* considered using the more pointed title *Architectural design criteria for people with physical disability who are handicapped by buildings* (Goldsmith, 1967, p. 7).

This section examines some of the factors that lead to overlooking the environment as a source of difficulties (Wright, 1980). Although attribution analysis will be illustrated primarily with problems involving disability, it applies to other problems as well. Several studies on poverty, for example, have led to the essential conclusion that the public view of people who are poor (that they are lazy and lack ambition) has little relation to fact and is largely immaterial in view of environmental factors over which they have no control (Feagin, 1972; Goodwin, 1973; S. R. Wright, 1972).

Conditions Underlying Attribution to Person Versus Environment

We all know that people vary in their characteristics. One person is recognized as being more outgoing than another, quicker, more domineering, more honest. These personal attributes are drawn upon to account, in part, for differences in behavior. We also know that the behavior of a person varies according to the situation. A person is more outgoing in some situations than in others, or quicker, more domineering, more honest. It is the nature of the situation, then, that also has to be examined when accounting for a person's behavior. Yet, the impact of the situation can easily be overlooked, with the consequence that remedial efforts become centered on the person and scant attention paid to the environment.

That the perceived source of difficulties critically affects treatment decisions was demonstrated in an important experiment in which subjects served as counselors in a simulated referral agency (Batson, 1975). After hearing a client describe his problems, the counselor first indicated whether the problem lay "with the individual" or "with his social environment" and then recommended one of a range of service agencies to help the client. When the problem was seen to lie primarily with the person, referrals were more likely to be directed to institutions oriented toward changing the person and protecting society (e.g., the mental hospital or residential treatment center), whereas when the client's social situation was held account-

able, referrals were more likely to institutions oriented toward protecting the individual and changing the social situation [e.g., social
services or an employment agency (Batson, 1975, p. 460)].

A general law of behavior states that behavior is a function of
both the person and the environment (or situation). This is sometimes expressed by Lewin's (1935) formula, $B = f(P,E)$, although it
should also be recognized that all three terms in the equation recip-
rocally influence each other; thus, as indicated by Bandura (1978),

$$B \longleftrightarrow E \quad P$$

Why the situation is so frequently ignored is the problem before us.
How behavior, in turn, affects the person and the situation is not the
concern here.

· *Proximity Between Person and Behavior.* One important reason why
the person becomes the focus in accounting for behavior is that the
person's behavior is perceived as "belonging to" the person. In general, a person appears where his or her behavior occurs. The person
and the behavior are in close proximity to each other. Walking, talking, or working doesn't occur unless the person is there to walk, talk,
or work.

As made clear by the Gestalt psychologists, proximity in space
or time is a strong factor in unit formation, that is, in the perception
of what belongs together. Consider the difference in the following
two arrangements:

x x o o x x o o x x o o   xo ox xo ox xo ox

The first series is readily perceived as consisting of pairs of x's alternating with pairs of o's. In the second series, this pairing is not present; the factor of proximity makes it easier to perceive an x and an
o as a unit. In like manner, proximity leads to the perception of person and behavior as a unit, that is, as belonging together. Being part
of the unit, the person is readily seen as causing the behavior. The
environment, not being part of this unit, is more apt to be omitted
from the attribution process. The unit relation between person and
behavior is so strong that grammatically we attach the behavior to
the person by using the possessive case when we speak of a person's behavior.

· *Saliency of Person as Figure, Environment as Background.* Another reason for overlooking the role played by the environment in behavior
has to do with saliency. The environment often assumes a background character against which the behaving person stands out as

a figure, prominent and concrete. The person is an active entity, changing position in space and commanding attention. The environment is vaguer, less active, less visible, and therefore less apprehensible as an important factor. The environment is the medium that allows the person to act, just as sound waves are the medium that allow the person to hear (Heider, 1926). In both cases, the sound heard and the person acting are more easily apprehended than the mediating conditions.

The two factors of proximity and saliency apply to the general tendency to underrate the role of the environment in behavior. The next factor, covariation of behavior, applies more particularly to atypical behavior and therefore has special significance in the case of persons with a disability.

· *Covariation of Behavior with Person or Situation.* In his classical work, Heider (1958) points out that "If we know that only one person succeeded or only one person failed out of a large number in a certain endeavor, then we shall ascribe success or failure to this person—to his great ability or to his lack of ability. On the other hand, if we know that practically everyone who tries succeeds, we shall attribute the success to the task" (p. 89). That is to say, where behavior is atypical, causal attribution to the person is compelling.

Let us attempt to understand why there is such a strong propensity to attribute the source of atypical needs and behavior to the person with relatively less emphasis on the environment. One explanation concerns the type of comparison being made; that is, whether inferences are drawn on the basis of comparing people or comparing situations (Kelley, 1967, 1973).

To begin with, the determination of whether behavior is typical or deviant requires knowledge of the behavior of numbers of people; that is, the behaviors of people have to be compared. If explanation of the behavior in question, whether it be typical or atypical, can be found in the presumed charcteristics of the people observed, person attribution takes place. There is then no need to seek further explanation in the environment. Stopping the explanatory process at this point occurs readily in the case of atypical behavior. It is relatively easy, for example, to account for a child's inattentiveness in terms of presumed hyperactivity, mental retardation, or some other characteristic when most children are able to complete the assigned task. So long as such attributes of the child appear adequate to the explanatory task, there is no need to pursue the matter further by inquiring about possible contributing factors in the situation: whether the child receives an adequate breakfast, whether the school tasks are too hard or too easy, whether there are sufficient adults in the classroom to give the child the needed attention. There is even no felt need to ask whether the child is inattentive in other situations, such as on the playground. In short, the atypical behavior is seen to vary with the person, not with the situation, and therefore it is attributed to characteristics inherent in the person.

In the case of typical behavior, however, the course of events often takes a different turn. As has already been noted, comparing behavior of people necessarily occurs initially, for it is this comparison that leads to the perception that the behavior in question is typical. If the perceiver then discovers a common trait to account for the typical behavior, the explanation often rests with person attribution and no situational considerations are entertained. But this is not always easily accomplished.

Consider the case where almost all members of a classroom are inattentive. It is not ordinarily concluded that the class is hyperactive, mentally retarded, or delinquent because these traits are not ordinarily perceived as being sufficiently widespread to account for the general behavior. An observer would tend to reserve such judgment for special classes of labeled children. Instead, the teacher's skill in keeping order might be questioned or the overcrowded classroom noted. Such probing enlarges the casual network to include the situation. Thus, *when the search for personal traits is not adequate to the task of accounting for common behavior, the perceiver moves to the next possible explanatory source—the situation.* Apparently, also, once attention is directed to the situation, other situations are implicitly invoked for comparative purposes. If an observer holds overcrowding accountable for the inattentiveness, it is because the inattentiveness is felt to contrast with behavior in less crowded circumstances. Similarly, behavior typical at a tennis match is ascribed to the nature of the situation only because the behavior is seen to change with the situation. People do not ordinarily go about their daily activities turning their heads from side to side!

In short, where behavior is perceived to vary with the person, explanation is sought in terms of person attributes. Where behavior is seen to vary with the situation, characteristics of the situation are held accountable. Person attribution is more frequently invoked in the case of atypical behavior than typical behavior. The reverse is true in the case of environmental (situational) attribution; that is, environmental attribution more frequently becomes the explanatory source for typical rather than atypical behavior.

This analysis suggests that the role of the situation in the behavior of a person with a disability will be revealed more readily if *different* situations are specifically examined. For example, a person with impaired hearing may find it difficult to communicate in a noisy room but not in a quiet room, an observation that immediately highlights environmental aspects of the problem. A general question to help reveal possible situational contributions to a problem is: Does the person behave this way or have this problem in all situations? A "no" answer means that the behavior depends at least partly on the situation. Technically speaking, covariation between behavior and situation begins to emerge.

A second approach to increasing awareness of the environment is to show that what are usually regarded as atypical needs are not atypical. Unmet needs are more readily related to environmental conditions when they are regarded as common needs rather than as atypical needs. In the case of atypical needs, the focus often remains on the person to the exclusion of possibilities for change in the environment. It is for this reason that there is an advantage in stressing, for example, that *most people* are handicapped by inadequate architectural structures, not just those with physical disabilities. By including children, pregnant women, the elderly, people with cardiac conditions, workers carrying heavy loads, and others, the generality of the problem can be recognized and the burden more readily placed on environmental change. In support of this approach, it should be noted that improving the architectural environment for particular groups often works to the advantage of others in diverse and sometimes unanticipated ways. Curb cuts are preferred by many, not just by people in wheelchairs; ramps are used more frequently than steps when both are side by side. By stressing how common the problem is, the environment becomes more easily recognized as a main source of difficulty and more properly an essential focus for change.

This does not mean that the person side of the issue should be ignored. Helping the person with a physical disability negotiate environmental barriers through skill training and improved prostheses is obviously important. Helping the person assume responsibility for his or her behavior is also obviously important. The environmental side is stressed here because it is so often overlooked in causal attribution, especially in the case of atypical needs.

Ecological psychologists have developed the concept of *behavior settings* to indicate the dependence of behavior on the place in which it occurs (Barker & Associates, 1978). The point has been made that the implications of the principles and supporting data of behavioral ecology "will affect human behavioral science in profound ways. One area that will be affected strongly is the area of human assessment. It will no longer be so tenable or defensible to assess *a person's* performance. Rather we will have to assess performance by settings, simply because variations in settings produce variations in performance" (Willems & Halstead, 1978, p. 186).

· *Position of the Person as Insider or Outsider.* Differences in the way difficulties and problems are perceived by the person experiencing them (the insider) and by someone else (the outsider or observer) are discussed at length toward the end of this chapter (pp. 47–51). Here we will merely point out that the insider is more likely than the outsider to take the nature of the situation into account. This is not to say that the insider is not prey to the forces toward person attribution, for these are pressing indeed. The statement rather is a *relative* one: The sensitivity of the insider to factors in the environment tends to be greater than that of the outsider.

The special sensitivity of insiders to situational factors may arise, in part, from the need to adapt one's own behavior to the demands of the situation. What commands the insiders' attention are the ongoing events to which they are reacting. Their own behavior, therefore, is more apt to be self-perceived as varying with the situation than when someone else's behavior is being observed. Outsider-observers, on the other hand, focus their attention on the person being observed. They perceive the behavior of the person as belonging to that person, as being "attached to" the person and covarying with him or her.

Overlooking the Environment Illustrated

Examples in which the environment is neglected when accounting for behavior, needs, or problems are legion. The poor are blamed for their poverty. The unemployment of people with disabilities is attributed to their disability. Consider the following example: The reviewers of a study in which only two of thirty-three persons with cerebral palsy who had attended college were using their education for earning a livelihood concluded that "these results would seem to indicate that decisions regarding their education were essentially unrelated to knowledge concerning their weaknesses" (McLarty & Chaney, 1974, p. 45). Notice that only person attributes were held accountable for the failure. Nowhere were environmental barriers, such as employer attitudes, transportation and architectural lacks, community unemployment levels, or family obstacles even considered as possible contributing factors. Because this side of the problem was totally disregarded, the recommendation that "Adequate evaluation of the individual's strengths and weaknesses may help to prevent occurrences such as these" (p. 45) could pertain only to person attributes.

Contrast the preceding view of the problem with the following example (Nayer, 1971): Cynthia, a nurse in training, is paralyzed from the waist down following an automobile accident. She gets herself from her apartment to the hospital in a car with hand controls.

She makes beds, turns patients, lifts and bathes them, and actively participates in nursing school as well as in private life. This was made possible because the physical facilities of her nursing school had been modified so that students in wheelchairs and on crutches could maneuver with little or no assistance. What if these environmental barriers had not been eliminated? Would not her exclusion from nursing training have been ascribed to her disability, to the fact that she used a wheelchair?

Environmental barriers can also be reduced or eliminated with the aid of mechanical devices, as seen in the following illustration (Garris, 1974). A client using crutches wished to be trained as a television repairman. He was faced with the problem that TV chassis were too heavy for him to lift to the workbench. Ordinarily he would have been disqualified because of his physical limitations. In this case, however, an elevator platform was constructed that enabled the worker to move the TV set from the floor to the platform, which then could be raised to any convenient height. Safety features were built in. Incidentally, the device could also be used by able-bodied workers.

The point to be stressed is that people are often excluded from jobs because the job requirements are perceived as fixed. Yet, if the tasks and the physical and social environment are regarded as potentially and justifiably modifiable, solutions can emerge that make employment possible. With the spread of this idea, the concept of "reasonable accommodations," as mandated in the Rehabilitation Act of 1973, can be expected to encompass an expanding range of possibilities.

Bringing the Environment into Focus

For people who have a disability, the consequences of underrating the significance of environmental factors in causal attribution are severe, for it hinders the realization that circumstances can enormously increase or reduce the extent of a handicap. Common experience, as well as research, has shown that if the cause of difficulties is ascribed to the person, the locus of change becomes the person; if the cause is seen as environmentally created, then attention is directed toward altering conditions in the environment (Batson, 1975).

Five suggestions are offered in an effort to counteract common attribution errors:

1. Always remember that behavior is a function of properties of *both* the person *and* the environment. When a problem is attributed to traits of the person, insist that a review of possible contributing environmental circumstances be made.

2. Compare the behavior of the person in different situations, not only the behavior of different people. Behavior seen as varying with the situation will reveal the influence of situational properties; behavior perceived as varying with the person will be understood in terms of person properties. Because it is so compelling to attribute the source of atypical behavior and problems to the traits of the person, it is imperative to search out situations in which the atypical behavior or problem varies with the situation. A good general question to ask is: Does this behavior or problem occur in all situations?
3. Place atypical needs and their solution within a broader context of common needs. The environmental focus is more readily maintained when it is shown that an environmental change needed for a particular group is also helpful to people in general. The elimination of architectural and attitudinal barriers, of employment and educational barriers, of legal and leisure barriers, can be shown to benefit society as a whole.
4. Keep in mind that when change or help is indicated, environmental accommodation is as important as personal adaptation. Adopting a dual focus on the person *and* the surrounding situation (physical and social environment, role and task requirements) can help to spot cases of misplaced causal attribution.
5. Obtain the views of the person whose atypical needs and behavior are being reviewed. That person tends to be more sensitive to environmental sources of difficulty than the person whose needs and behavior are not impeded by the environment.

POSITION OF THE PERSON AS INSIDER VERSUS OUTSIDER

Tamara Dembo, the distinguished pioneer in rehabilitation psychology, has repeatedly stressed that the difference in viewpoints by the insider and outsider must be taken into account in the discovery and utilization of psychological knowledge (Dembo, 1964, 1970). The insider (also referred to as actor) is the person himself or herself, the person experiencing or evaluating his or her own behavior, feelings, or problems. The outsider is the person observing or evaluating someone else's behavior, feelings, or problems. Increasing research supports the view that there are important differences in the way the insider as experiencer and the outsider as observer perceive the situation in question, with important consequences for the rehabilitation situation itself.

The disparate perspectives of insider and outsider can be strikingly demonstrated in what we have called the "mine-thine problem" (Wright, 1975). In the following experiment, the position of the person is both that of insider and outsider; that is, insider with respect to his or her own problem and outsider with respect to someone else's problem. A simple way to approach the mine-thine problem is: Participants are reminded that everyone is handicapped in some way, physically, mentally, or emotionally. They are then asked to write what they regard as their own worst handicap on a slip of paper, together with a code number. The collected slips are randomly paired, the pairs of handicaps as expressed in the *original words,* together with their code numbers, are displayed in some form before the group (e.g., on a blackboard). On a second sheet of paper, the participants are instructed to record the first pair in which their own handicap appears, to underline their own handicap, and to star the one they would choose if they had a choice between the two. The results are then tabulated and discussed with the group. This experiment has been carried out with many different groups of subjects: college students, children, hospital aides, rehabilitation and medical professionals, parents, and headstart teachers. The results are consistent and dramatic. From 62 to 95 percent of the subjects reclaimed their own worst handicap. The inclination to reclaim one's own problems still holds true when the handicaps are confined just to physical disabilities.

It is in the group's attempt to explain the results that the difference in the *span of realities* of the insider and outsider become appreciated in a personally direct way. As explanations, participants refer to the following ideas: They are used to their own handicap (*familiarity* factor), they know what it entails (*coping* factor), it is part of the self and the person's history (*self-identity* factor), there are certain advantages in one's handicap *(positive aspects,* sometimes *secondary gains),* they would not know how to manage with the other person's handicap *(coping* factor, *fear of the unknown),* the other person's handicap would replace something valuable that they would have to give up (*reactance* factor, Brehm, 1966), it would take a lot of change in one's life to deal with a different handicap (factor of *energy conservation*), and the other person's handicap is much worse (often this reflects a *spread* factor).

The following six subjects, paired in terms of the same two handicaps considered, illustrate how these explanations make sense to the person in accounting for the preference for one's own handicap. The underlined handicap is that of the subject; the asterisk indicates that it was chosen over the alternative:

*Grand mal epilepsy
No willpower

"Grand mal epilepsy isn't so bad with all the drugs that can be used. But if you didn't have any willpower, you would just sit and not do anything. Maybe you would only do things you liked to do. But other things have to be done too."

Grand mal epilepsy
*No willpower

"I don't have much willpower, but that's my problem and I'm working on it. If I try hard enough, I can beat it. But epilepsy can't be conquered by willpower. I would hate to think I could fall down anytime."

*Poor eyesight—legally
blind without glasses
Overweight

"My eyesight is easily correctable with glasses or contacts and though it's a hassle, I'd prefer that to fighting a weight problem, because being overweight would make me feel very negative about myself."

Poor eyesight—legally
blind without glasses
*Overweight

"I would rather be a little overweight because it is less permanent, and I really could do something about it."

*Muscular atrophy of
feet and hands
Inability to withstand
anger emotionally

"I know what to expect, having lived with it so long. I am not sure what inability to withstand anger emotionally really means. Perhaps a rage so great that a murder could be committed. Perhaps my problem helps to identify me, is what helps me be what I really am."

Muscular atrophy of
hands and feet
*Inability to withstand
anger emotionally

"I believe that I can and have to a large extent begun to overcome the one I preferred [my own]. Muscular atrophy cannot be overcome, and I could not stand not having the use of my hands and feet."

The insights gained through discussion help the participants to appreciate the adjustive forces that enable people to cope and live with their own difficulties. Further, the insights reveal forces that sometimes lead people to resist change, even for the better as seen by the outsider, and sometimes by the insider as well.

The position of the person also influences causal attribution. Several lines of investigation have shown that the insider is more apt than the outsider to attribute his or her own behavior to properties of the environment, whereas the outsider-observer relatively more frequently sees the person's traits as being the source of the behavior (Goldberg, 1978; Jones & Nisbett, 1971). This was pointedly shown in an experiment in which subjects were asked to describe five people, including themselves, by selecting from each of twenty pairs of trait opposites the trait that most nearly applied to the person (e.g., energetic versus relaxed), or by checking the alternative option "depends on the situation" (Nisbett et al., 1973). The subjects made more frequent use of the "depends on the situation" category when describing themselves than when describing someone else (e.g., best friend, peer acquaintance).

In another experiment, the insider's visual attention was shifted to approximate that of outsiders' by having the subjects view a videotape of themselves conversing with someone else (Storms, 1973). Subjects made ratings, in the original live situation and later in viewing the video tape of themselves, of the degree to which they felt their own behavior (how friendly, talkative, nervous, and domineering they were) was affected by (1) their personality and (2) the nature of the situation. In the videotape ratings, as *quasi-outsiders,* the subjects attributed their behavior significantly less frequently to characteristics of the situation than in the live situation.

The fact that the insider is relatively less inclined toward personal attribution than the outsider suggests that the phenomena of spread and prime mover may also be less pronounced among the insider group. As applied to atypical physique, this would mean that one's own disability is less apt to spread to other personal characteristics or to serve as prime mover in the case of the person with the disability himself or herself. This is not to say that spread and prime mover are alien to the insider. It is important to keep in mind that the difference in attribution is a relative one. The correct formulation is that, *relative* to the outsider, the insider is more inclined toward environmental attribution and less toward personal attribution.

It is also important to keep in mind that persons with a disability are insiders with respect to their own problems and situation, but are outsiders with respect to other people's, even those whose disabilities are similar to their own. In the latter case, the position may be closer to that of the insider, but not equivalent to it, for each person's span of realities has its own uniqueness. The term *quasi-insiders* may be used to define the position of persons with similar disabilities or of persons who care and are intimately connected with the life of the insider, as in the case of family members and friends. Typical of the *outside* position is that of strangers or persons who feel little connection with the fate of the person with the disability.

The following amusing incident (Zola, 1972) provides a pointed example of how innocently the outsider's perspective can lead astray and how necessary it is for the insider to provide corrective feedback:

> I entered the workshop of a prosthetist who had been in the business for over 50 years. Noting that I had polio and used a cane to walk, he motioned me to come near.
>
> HE: "I wonder if you'd try this cane."
> Z: "I did."
> HE: "Well what do you think?"
> Z: "It seems solid enough."
> HE: "Now watch this." He then proceeded to take the cane from me and pushed a little button about three inches from the handle and out popped a twelve-inch blade.
>
> Before I could say another word, he went on: "This one is even handier; Look!" Taking another cane, he also pressed a button and now brandished what might be called a ten-inch iron blackjack. "You know," he went on, "In times like these, crime in the streets and all, things like this self-defense cane should be pretty handy."
>
> Z: "Yes," I replied in my best tongue in cheek fashion, "particularly if the thief lets me lean on him for support while I dismantle my cane." [p. 182][4]

The different perspectives of insider and outsider help us appreciate why people with disabilities have been such a vital force in the elimination of environmental barriers. Ordinary *and* repeated experience reminds them that they are handicapped by attitudinal and other environmental barriers as much or more so than by their own limitations. Further, the different perspectives support the idea that people with a disability must become actively involved in their own rehabilitation. It is the insiders' views that are so essential in helping to define and solve the problems that have to be confronted.

---

[4]Reprinted from The problem and prospects of mutual aid groups, by I.K. Zola. In *Rehab. Psychol.*, 1972, 19. By permission of *Rehab. Psychol.*

Chapter 4
Impressions of People with Disabilities

In this chapter, factors that influence the way we perceive people in general are applied to impressions of people with disabilities. As the discussion proceeds, it will become clearer that the *context* in which a disability appears exerts a major influence on how the individual is perceived. It makes a difference whether the disability is a disembodied abstraction or is embedded within a complex of personal traits, whether these traits have a positive saliency or a negative saliency, whether the disability is relevant to the situation or not, whether the disability pertains to a stranger or a known person, and so forth. The context refers to the conditions presented to the perceiver who, in turn, interprets and forms an impression about the person(s) under scrutiny based on those conditions.

Because it is the perceiver who processes and interprets information provided by the context, it should be borne in mind that forces within the perceiver always play a vital role in the impressions that are formed. These internal forces stem from the values, needs, motivation, and habitual modes of reaction of the perceiver. After all, it is these internal factors that, despite the same context, produce heterogeneity, not unanimity, in opinions and impressions. Although much of what follows pertains to the kind of information with which the perceiver is presented and upon which the perceiver makes a judgment, internal forces contributing to the impression are also considered.

CENTRAL AND PERIPHERAL CHARACTERISTICS

In his series of classical experiments, Asch (1946) initiated wide interest among researchers in the systematic exploration of how we form impressions of personality. His approach became paradigmatic for subsequent researchers, and his insights have been recognized among the outstanding contributions to the field. He distinguished between qualities that furnish the key to a person and those that are subsidiary—that is, between central and peripheral characteristics. In one experiment, two groups of subjects were read a list of identical personality traits, with the exception that one group heard the person described as "warm" and the other group as "cold," thus:

Group 1. Intelligent, skillful, industrious, *warm*, determined, practical, cautious;

Group 2. Intelligent, skillful, industrious, *cold*, determined, practical, cautious.

If the character traits "warm" and "cold" are central aspects of a person, they should affect the total impression of personality. That this is the case is shown in the results obtained when the subjects were asked to select from a checklist of pairs of traits, mostly opposites, the quality that best fitted the impression they had already formed. The positive terms of each pair appear in Table 4.1. The "warm" person was described as being generous, wise, happy, good-natured, humorous, sociable, popular, humane, altruistic, and imaginative much more frequently than the "cold" person. There were also qualities that were not affected by the warm-cold variable, for example, physical attractiveness, reliability, strength, and seriousness. Thus, though the central characteristic affects the impression of the total personality, it does not function as an undiscriminating "halo effect." Moreover, when the warm-cold traits were omitted from the original list describing the person, the selection of fitting characteristics was significantly altered.

That trait opposites do not always drastically influence personality impressions was demonstrated in a second experiment in which the terms "polite" and "blunt" were substituted for "warm" and "cold." Under these circumstances, the difference between the impression of the polite person and the blunt person *within the same*

Table 4.1 CHOICE OF FITTING QUALITIES (PERCENTAGES)

	WARM N = 90	COLD N = 76	POLITE N = 20	BLUNT N = 26
Generous	91	8	56	58
Wise	65	25	30	50
Happy	90	34	75	65
Good-natured	94	17	87	56
Humorous	77	13	71	48
Sociable	91	38	83	68
Popular	84	28	94	56
Reliable	94	99	95	100
Important	88	99	94	96
Humane	86	31	59	77
Good-looking	77	69	93	79
Persistent	100	97	100	100
Serious	100	99	100	100
Restrained	77	89	82	77
Altruistic	69	18	29	46
Imaginative	51	19	33	31
Strong	98	95	100	100
Honest	98	94	87	100

context of traits was far less than in the case of the warm-cold variation (Table 4.1). Clearly, the trait contrast warm versus cold was markedly more effective in differentiating personality impressions than was polite versus blunt.

THE IMPORTANCE OF CONTEXT

Centrality as a Function of Context

Asch's theoretical position helped him to appreciate that not only does a central trait significantly influence other impressions about a person, but that the position of centrality itself depends on the context in which the trait is viewed. He studied this question by including the term "warm" in the following series: obedient, weak, shallow, *warm*, unambitious, vain (Asch, 1946). In the new context, in contrast to the earlier trait series (see p. 53), warm was not a central characteristic. Its relative ranking of importance dropped to peripheral status. Warm was now seen as dominated by other far more decisive traits, as exemplified in the written protocol of one subject: "I think the warmth within this person is a warmth emanating from a follower to a leader" (p. 267). This and other experiments led Asch to conclude that as soon as two or more traits are understood to belong to one person, they cease to exist as isolated traits. Instead they come into immediate dynamic interaction, and the process instigated possesses, in a striking sense, certain qualities of a system. In the course of this process some characteristics assume special importance. But it is the whole system of relations that determines which will become central. Central characteristics, while imposing their direction on the total impression, are themselves affected by the surrounding characteristics. In other words, the meaning and functional role of a trait changes with the context.

Context need not only refer to a network of personality traits. In fact, whether a disability assumes the role of a central characteristic is influenced by the broader situation in which the person is viewed. A study of the social usefulness of the cosmetic glove is revealing in this connection (Cattell, Dembo et al., 1949). The cosmetic glove is designed to approximate the appearance of the natural hand. Data were derived from several field settings. In one setting a person with a cosmetic hand prosthesis entered a store. While engaging the salesclerk in conversation, he tried to draw the salesclerk's attention to the cosmetic hand by putting it on the counter, by gesturing, scratching his face, and smoking. The contact lasted between 5 and 20 minutes after which the customer left, and the experimenter approached the salesclerk for an interview designed to elicit his reactions to the cosmetic hand.

Though on closer inspection the cosmetic hand is noticeably different from the natural hand, 80 percent of the sales personnel did not recognize the cosmetic hand as such and were completely unaware of any difference. The investigators account for this by distinguishing between the *region of visual presence* and the *region of visual concern.* The region of presence encompasses those objects that are perceived but not inspected, the region of concern those which command the focus of attention. The cosmetic hand, when in the region of presence, sufficiently matches the normal hand so as not to be noticeable, whereas when it becomes a part of the region of concern, obvious differences emerge. In casual contacts we do not usually concern ourselves with the hands of other persons. In this experiment, it was the situation that predisposed toward casual contact and relegated the prosthesis to peripheral status.

In another experiment (Schachter, 1951), one person in the group assumed the position of a deviate by strongly opposing the group's views on how juvenile delinquents should be treated. When the issue was directly relevant to the group's purposes, as in the case of an editorial club, the deviate was more strongly rejected on sociometric data than in groups where it was irrelevant, such as a radio club. Again, the situation influenced how central the deviate's views were regarded.

Atypical Physique in Positive and Negative Contexts

Contexts vary in their valence; that is, in their positive or negative character, whether they attract or repel. An especially enlightening, yet simple demonstration of how reaction to disability depends on the valence of its context is a study of attitudes toward "blindness" and "physical handicap" as compared to "blind people" and "physically handicapped people," respectively (Whiteman & Lukoff, 1965). In each instance, people with the handicapping condition were perceived more favorably than the condition itself. The difference can be understood by the far-reaching proposition that the *positive context of a person* constrained the negative spread.

Other research has extended the human context by elaborating the type of person depicted. In one study, reactions to people identified solely by what is generally regarded as a negative label (mentally retarded, amputee, former mental patient) were compared to reactions when these labels were included in a sketch of an adequately functioning person (Jaffee, 1965, 1967). The sketch described the person's appearance, adjustment, marital status, and job:

> Frank Jones, a 24-year-old man, is of average height and weight. He works as a stock clerk for a department store. He has been married for two years and expects his first child soon. He presents a neat appearance. Although he has his share of problems, he feels that things are going all right for him. Jones is usually a pleasant fellow who gets along with others and his friends. And [for amputee] he had a leg amputated several years ago and walks with an artificial leg. [For retarded: He attended special classes for mentally retarded children in public school. For former mental patient: He was a patient in a mental hospital several years ago.] [Jaffe, 1965, p. 21]

The persons referred to by the labels (mentally retarded, etc.) and by the sketches were rated on 7-point scales to indicate the degree to which each of a number of adjectives fitted the particular person. The results were clear. Less-favorable reactions were aroused to each of the three labels than to the corresponding sketch person. Notice that the context in which the disability was mentioned in the case of the sketch person was essentially positive; the person was depicted as functioning adequately, although not unusually so.

The problem of the differential effects of negative versus positive contexts was the focus of a study in which different groups of subjects were presented with a set of four personality traits of a person whose physical status was listed first (Leek, 1966). The physical status was indicated as physically disabled, crippled, able-bodied, or robust, depending on the subject group. The personality traits were either all positive or all negative and were opposites of each other. Sample sets are:

Set 1 (+ context)	*Set 2 (− context)*
Physically disabled	Physically disabled
Industrious	Lazy
Courageous	Cowardly
Generous	Selfish
Pleasant	Unpleasant

Subjects expressed their impressions of the target person by rating adjectives on 7-point scales and by writing sketches of the person. A main and significant finding was that *only* in the context of negative personality traits was the person with the physical disability (or crippled status) evaluated more unfavorably than the able-bodied (or robust) person. Moreover, in the context of positive traits, there was a tendency for the person listed as having a physical disability to be evaluated even higher than his able-bodied counterpart. Thus, a significantly greater number of extremely positive statements (for example, "He never makes excuses for himself") appeared in the sketches written about him.

Such intensified reactions in both favorable and unfavorable directions, depending upon the context, relate to Erik Erikson's astute observation that a member of a minority group has to be very, very good in order to keep from being very, very bad. The phenomenon has also been demonstrated with respect to race and mental illness. In one study, black and white persons were described as holding certain beliefs and values (Dienstbier, 1970). The black person received greater acceptance than the white person when these beliefs and values were socially desirable and vice versa when undesirable beliefs and values were ascribed. In another study, subjects displayed heightened positive or negative reactions to persons presumed to be mental patients, depending on whether their behavior had favorable or unfavorable consequences for the subject (Gergen & Jones, 1963).

Explanations of heightened reactions are of interest. One explanation draws upon the factor of expectation discrepancy (see Chapter 5). The idea is that individuals may be considered to be especially outstanding when their performance is perceived as sufficiently better than expected. The contrast with the expectation enhances the achievement.

Ambivalence is another explanatory concept. Ambivalent attitudes are considered by some psychoanalytic writers to account for exaggerated positive or negative reactions to the person (Freud, 1961). Resolving the conflicting love-hate forces involves withdrawing energy from one impulse and adding it to the other. The concept of guilt has been added to that of ambivalence by Katz and his associates (Katz et al., 1973; Katz et al., 1977). They have theorized that ambivalence leads to amplified reactions because it potentiates guilt. It is the excessive arousal of guilt that mediates not only exaggerated negative reactions but also positive behavior such as helping, in the attempt to relieve the guilt. In one set of experiments, subjects who felt the greatest ambivalence toward "the physically handicapped," as measured on a pretest, showed a greater negative change toward a person in a wheelchair whom they thought they had harmed than those with low ambivalence scores (Katz et al., 1977). The explanation is that if the initial attitude had been simply hostile, the other person would be perceived from the start as deserving harm, and there would be no strong need to justify the harm-doing through further derogation. Or, if the attitude had been simply friendly, the subject would perhaps feel some guilt, but less guilt than if an ambivalent attitude would have given some reason to suspect that a hostile impulse were being gratified at the other's expense.

The problem of context raises the question of the relative potency of positive and negative attributes. There is strong and accumulating evidence that under some conditions people tend to weigh negative aspects more heavily than positive aspects (Kanouse & Hanson, 1971). The following experiment is illustrative (Feldman, 1966). Subjects rated each of twenty-five statements containing a different adjective to describe the person, given the context "He is a [e.g., wise] man." A 9-point rating scale was used ranging from good to bad. Each subject also rated the statement when it included one positive and one negative adjective (e.g., wise and corrupt). The potency of each adjective was determined by comparing the ratings of the statement when the adjective was used alone and when it appeared as a pair. The results were clear. The most powerful adjectives were negative. That is, ratings of people described by positive and negative adjectives were more negative than would be predicted by simply averaging the scale values assigned to the adjectives when used singly. That negative information may carry more weight than positive information has also been demonstrated in other areas, such as risk-taking (Kogan & Wallach, 1967).

Several explanations of the negativity bias have been proposed. First, negative information may become more salient than positive information because it arouses vigilance. Also, negative experiences do not let go of the person; the person ruminates about them, and in so doing their potency is increased. Moreover, the norms of society are positive: Anything that deviates sufficiently from these norms stands out and is perceived as being even more negative because of the perceptual factor of contrast (see p. 22). Another explanation for the disproportionate weight given to negative attributes is that they are more likely to reduce or cancel the value of positive attributes than vice versa. Finally, it has been suggested (Kogan & Wallach, 1967) that the negativity bias may have a physiological basis insofar as evidence exists for the relative independence of reward and punishment systems in the brain (Stein, 1964). These separate systems may have evolved in the Darwinian sense, producing approach and avoidance tendencies of unequal strength.

In the case of a negative attribute, as when a physical disability is judged to be undesirable, the negativity bias poses an added problem. The context in which a disability appears assumes special significance because of it. At the very least, the context must be that of a human being whose abilities are appreciated in terms of what the person can do, not diminished because of what the person cannot do.

Order Effects: Primacy and Recency

Again it was Asch's classical experiments (1946) that stirred continuing interest in the importance of the order of appearance of personal attributes on impression formation. His characteristically simple experiment involved two series of identical personality traits differing only in their order of presentation:

> Series A. Intelligent, industrious, impulsive, critical, stubborn, envious;
> Series B. Envious, stubborn, critical, impulsive, industrious, intelligent.

Each series was read to a different group of subjects.

Observe that the order of traits is merely reversed, Series A opening with positive qualities, Series B with questionable qualities. In general, the subjects' impression of A was that of an "able person who possesses certain shortcomings, which are not serious enough to overshadow his merits" whereas B impressed the majority as "a 'problem' whose abilities are hampered by his serious difficulties." Asch stressed that first impressions are especially potent in that they set up a *direction* that exerts a continuous effect on later impressions: "The view formed quickly acquires a certain stability; later characteristics are fitted to the prevailing direction when the conditions permit" (Asch, 1952, pp. 212–213).

The order-effects problem involves the issue of the power of primacy (early information) versus recency (later information) in influencing perception and memory. Asch's results favored the importance of primacy effects inasmuch as it was the assimilation of later information to the initial perception that brought coherent meaning to the impression of the person as a whole. If, however, the traits are listed in random order without regard to their positive and negative value, then it is difficult to establish the kind of initial orienting impression that guides the processing of later information. Under these circumstances, the connotations of the trait adjectives do not influence each other in an orderly way. Instead, the overall evaluative impression of the person (as determined by ratings on a scale ranging from highly favorable to highly unfavorable) can be closely approximated by averaging the ratings of favorability assigned to each adjective regarded individually.

In pursuing this problem further, other factors have emerged, some contributing to primacy effects and some to recency. Besides *assimilation* as a factor accounting for primacy effects, later (i.e., recent) information may be given little weight because of *waning attention* due to distraction, fatigue, or boredom. *Discounting* recent information may also occur and for the following reasons: the information doesn't fit with the initial impression, it doesn't fit with what the person wants to hear, the person believes that the items of information are not equally valid, the characteristics observed initially appear unusually stable, or the person makes a commitment based on early information.

On the other hand, there are factors that support recency effects, namely, clarity of memory for recent events and displacement of early events by later information. Thus, in real life, where naturally occurring events emerge over far longer periods of time than in the laboratory situation, one would expect recent information to be remembered more vividly than that more remote in time. As for displacement of information, recent developments may supplant prior information whenever change is expected, as in the case of maturation or learning. Despite different factors pulling toward primacy effects and recency effects, however, the impact of initial information appears generally to be especially potent. The reader is referred to Jones & Goethals (1971) for a full review of factors important in order effects.

In light of the significance of order effects on impressions of persons, a visible disability can be expected to play an unduly precipitous role on at least two counts. First of all, a person's physique is an immediately apprehensible characteristic in face-to-face contact and thereby readily conditions subsequent impressions. Second, physique is a relatively stable characteristic, so stable, in fact, that a person's identification largely rests on his physical appearance.

In a penetrating analysis, Ichheiser (1949) stresses visibility as a main determinant of social reality. He points out that coercion is more objectionable when it is evident in outright violence than when it is subtle (i.e., invisible). Likewise, bodily appearance assumes a major role because the *visible* appearance of an individual, not the invisible personality, constitutes the main basis of identification. The following dramatic sketch is offered as an example:

> Suppose Jane Doe would change all her inner personality characteristics such as her attitudes, opinions, tendencies, character, temperament, and whatever else. At the same time, suppose she would retain unchanged her bodily appearance. Then, obviously, she would continue to be considered and identified as "the same person." Other people would probably say that Jane Doe has radically changed, but it would be still Jane who has changed. If, on the other hand, Jane would maintain all her inner personality characteristics but would by some miracle altogether change her bodily appearance so that she would look like Susan Smith, then she would cease, in terms of social reality, to be "the same person." People would then, obviously, consider and identify Jane as being Susan, and they would probably wonder why Susan talks and behaves like Jane. [Ichheiser, 1949, p. 17]

SPREAD AND SIMILARITY OF TRAITS

Dating from the time of the early Gestalt psychologists, notably Wertheimer (1923), the similarity between objects or entities has been recognized as a main factor in perceiving them as belonging together; that is, as a unit. A simple demonstration is the following series, which is perceived as consisting of pairs of stars alternating with pairs of dashes with something left over at the ends:

- ** -- ** -- ** -- ** -- ** -- *

In fact, one has to strain to defy the force of similarity in an attempt to group the dissimilar figures. "Birds of a feather flock together" aphoristically reflects the potency of similarity as a unit-forming factor.

Since the spread phenomenon involves the bringing together of different personal characteristics, we can expect that the factor of similarity also plays a role in how individuals are perceived. In the following example, Bob's expectations of Randy, a young man with cerebral palsy, were initially controlled by the factor of similarity in the *form* of anticipated traits: "First of all, my thoughts were, he is so racked with spasms, he is jerking so. *I expected his thoughts to be jerky also.* He could type with his big toe, which he did to communicate. His thoughts turned out to be completely adequate" (personal communication from Bob, a student).

An especially salient type of similarity between traits is their affective quality; that is, their negative or positive valence (value). Things that are positive are alike in implying a force *toward* them, negative things *away from* them. To combine a positive and a negative quality would subject the person to forces opposite in direction. In his "balance theory," Fritz Heider made a major contribution to psychological understanding by including sentiments among the unit-forming factors (1958, Chapter 7). He concluded that "a state of harmony or balance exists if entities which belong together are all positive, or if they are all negative" (p. 258). The term "halo phenomenon" has been applied to the tendency to view a person as all positive or all negative.

Asch, in his studies of impression formation, noted that when subjects were asked to describe a person by selecting traits from a list of adjectives, the checklist choices "tended to be consistently positive or negative in their evaluation" (1946, p. 265). It is important, however, to appreciate that not all choices sorted themselves in this way. That is to say, the halo effect did not engulf all attributes of similar valence. Subjects generally perceived the person they were describing as having some characteristics that were of opposite sign to that of the preponderant evaluative selection.

It is proposed that, although it is cognitively easier to combine attributes of similar valence, forces also exist toward recognizing traits of opposing valence (Wright, 1964). For example, we do not feel comfortable with a person who is either all good or all bad. Thus, the person who aspires to the purity of a god is soon damned. At the other extreme, even the most disreputable person is raised a notch by the awakening of compassion. It is as if some counterpoint is required in which a more complex, but more interesting picture of the person emerges whose features are both positive and negative. Of course, when we know someone, we become aware of differentiated aspects of that person's functioning, some of which are positive and some negative. It is likely that the all-good–all-bad evaluation tends to be reserved for more primitive states, such as can occur with heightened emotionality, when one hates or loves intensely or is overwhelmed by fear or anxiety. We would also expect children, because of their relative immaturity, to demonstrate like-valence spread more frequently than adults. Additionally, a need to be fair, to balance the score, may be at work in bringing traits of unlike valence together. Even a free-association process in which a stimulus word elicits its opposite may occur and interrupt the proliferation of like-valence associations. Love evokes hate, hot evokes cold, and so on.

As applied to atypical physique, the idea of disability may be balanced by ability-connected thoughts, as when a person is seen as able in special ways, perhaps made cogent by a theory of compensation or coping. For example, the person who is blind or crippled may be thought to have a sixth sense, a depth of understanding, or a will to conquer adversity. Not to be discounted is the possibility that traits of unlike valence may be similar in form in the Gestalt (structural) sense; for example, a flash of anger and a burst of generosity may share qualities of being impulsive or histrionic. These factors, as well as others, account for the fact that attitudes toward a group, even when identified by a single attribute assumed to be negative ("the disabled," "the blind," "people with cerebral palsy"), can best be characterized as ambivalent.

PERCEIVED SIMILARITY BETWEEN DISABILITY AND ITS CAUSE: SIN AND PUNISHMENT

We have just seen how spread may lead to inferred personality traits similar to that of disability in valence or form (figural properties) or both. Similarity of valence and form may also be expected to influence the perceived cause of disability. In the words of Heider, "in general one may say that factors making for figural unit formation also make for causal integration" (1944, p. 362).

Let us consider an example from the neighboring field of emotional disability. In the past, and in some circles today, the cause of derangement was viewed in terms of the occult. Although such an association appears foolish from the perspective of modern science, its basis is the phenomenal similarity between the strange and inexplicable behavior of persons with serious emotional problems and the strange and inexplicable behavior of the occult. In short, there is a similarity in the form or quality of something and its perceived cause, just as the imprint in the sand fits the shape of the foot that formed it (Scheerer, 1954, p. 103–104).

Perceiving the cause of insanity in terms of witches and demons prompts what appear to be appropriate reactions. The beating and burning of emotionally disturbed persons, or the offering of sacrifices to mollify devils, are seen as neither unjust nor irrational, for these are reactions that are in keeping with the perceived cause. As science advanced the theory of mental *illness*, however, such treatment became abhorrent because it clashed with the new understanding concerning the cause of the disorder. This example serves to remind us that at least certain attitudes, beliefs, and behavior toward persons with atypical conditions are not willy-nilly affairs that arise and change as fashion dictates, but are grounded in perceived cause-effect relationships.

To return to the matter of atypical physique, the phenomenal cause of illness and disability can be expected to be sought in negatively evaluated events insofar as disability is perceived as negative. More than that, the negative evaluation is often invested with moral indictment. Thus, illness and disability are sometimes seen as a punishment for transgression.

It has been stated that the nondisabled unconsciously believe that the cripple has committed some evil act and is therefore dangerous; or, if he has not done so, that he will do something wrong in order to warrant his punishment (Meng, 1938; reported in Barker et al., 1953, p. 87). That evil acts are associated with marked physical deviation has been shown in an experiment in which nondisfigured persons reacted to photographs of persons with facial anomalies (Magregor et al., 1953). One photograph showed a 30-year-old man who had a low, narrow forehead, a prominent, convex nose, a receding, pointed chin, narrow, deep-set eyes, large buck teeth, and lop ears. The fact that he had superior intelligence and earned a good salary as a junior executive in a chemical corporation was not mentioned. The following conclusions were drawn: "He is mean and small—not bright. He might be a follower in a gang. He's a dope addict. Man seems to look like a maniac. Has desire to kill" (p. 77). The investigators concluded that "facial features which served as false clues led respondents not only to impute to these patients personality traits considered socially unacceptable, but to assign them roles and statuses on an inferior social level" (p. 79). In the same study, a patient with a disfigured face resulting from war injuries recounted, "When I parked my car in front of a jewelry store, two cops came up and asked me for my identification card. They thought I was a gangster" (pp. 70–71).

In an experiment with children, it was concluded that beauty and high moral qualities are rarely disentangled in young children (Spiegel, 1950). To the question "Whom would you rather play with—a beautiful boy (girl) or an ugly boy (girl)?" a 9-year-old boy replied "A beautiful boy—an ugly boy won't want to do anything. Start to hit you. . . . A beautiful boy won't get into trouble." An 11-year-old girl chose "A nice looking girl [because] ugly girls are fresh, play fresh." The few children who did not associate appearance with conduct, were both older and brighter on the average than the others.

That disability sometimes stirs thoughts of wrongdoing is also true of persons with disabilities themselves, as well as their loved ones. The wrongdoing may be ascribed either to someone else or to themselves, but the need to blame is compelling and a likely target is sought. In the following example, Doug, crippled from polio years ago as a youth, blames someone else:

INTERVIEWER: You sound as if you felt that DDT was the cause of your getting polio.

DOUG: That's right. You never hear anything about it, but does that mean it couldn't have been so? DDT was doing a fine job for everybody at the time. I'm just saying maybe some bobnoble [sic] chemist didn't take the time to find out what the long range effects would be. (Personal communication)

In other cases, self-blame is evident. In a study on reaction to physical disability, as many as 50 percent of the children with various disabilities expressed self-blame or some idea of their illness as punishment (Dow, 1965). In asking the seemingly naive question that often besets a person who has suffered a disability or a deep loss: "Why did this have to happen *to me?*" is not one looking for a personal meaning or offense that might justify the hurt? A slight change in the question to "Why did this happen?" represents a major change in the meaning of the disability, a change in which objective nonpersonal attribution is uppermost and guilt is less apparent. In other instances the source of the affliction may be attributed to the negligence of a second person, in which case it is often felt as willful negligence even though objective consideration may deny premeditation. Imputing an intention augments the sin to a level appropriate to the disastrous consequence.

Thus, hardly a parent of a child who has a disability can escape the conviction that in some way avoidable mismanagement was a contributing cause if not *the* cause of the disability. The mother may blame herself or her doctor for the sedation that might have caused the birth injury of her child. Someone has to be blamed, for disability is all too easily perceived as having its source in wrongdoing. This is brought out in a study of the attitudes of parents of children who are blind (Sommers, 1944). On the basis of interviews with the mothers, the investigator distinguished four attitudes toward blindness:

> Blindness as a symbol of punishment: "What have we done that God should wish this on us?"
>
> Fear of being suspected of having a social disease: "I am sure the neighbors say this about me because they have mentioned it in reference to other handicapped children in the vicinity."
>
> Feelings of guilt due to transgression of the moral or social code or to negligence: "I blame myself for not having had a doctor."
>
> Blindness as a personal disgrace to the parents: "Our family felt it was a disgrace and were ashamed."[1]

[1]Reprinted from *The influence of parental attitudes and social environment on the personality development of the adolescent blind* by V. S. Sommers. By permission of The American Foundation for the Blind, New York.

There is other evidence that disability and illness are linked to causes of a negative, evil signification. To the ancient Hebrews, illness and physical defect marked the person as a sinner. Twelve blemishes are enumerated in the Bible that disqualified a priest from officiating. Among those mentioned are "a blind man, or a lame, or he that hath a flat nose, or anything superfluous, or a man that is brokenfooted, or brokenhanded, or crookbackt, or a dwarf, or that hath a blemish in his eye, or be scurvy, or scabbed, or hath his bones broken . . ." (Hentig, 1948a, p. 16). Gradually other bodily imperfections were added, of which the later Talmudists mention no less than 142. A Roman priest also had to be free from physical infirmities, and the same rules apply to the Catholic priest to this day (Hentig, 1948a). It was a strict commandment of the Old Testament that "The blind and the lame shall not come into the house." Illness was considered both a punishment and a means of atonement.

The Hindu theological concept of *Dharma* explains an existing personal condition as the inevitable result of past behavior in previous incarnations (Hanks & Hanks, 1948). It is consequently reasonable that sympathy for persons with defects is lacking because they have brought their affliction upon themselves. That the attribution of responsibility is an important factor in attitudes toward persons who have a disability has been consistently demonstrated in research (Shurka et al., 1982). In Western society, the person tends to be held more accountable for alcoholism, mental illness, and obesity than for sensory and orthopedic impairments, and therefore is especially stigmatized on this account.

In some societies, as among the Trobriand Islanders, an affliction is blamed on an enemy thought to have caused it through sorcery (Hanks & Hanks, 1948). It has been noted that the term "ugly" in its aesthetic sense was preceded by a moral significance. It is derived from a root meaning "dreadful, fearful." In connection with weather, it means "threatening" (Hentig, 1948a, p. 64). We also note the equivocal meaning of such allusions as "his *bad* leg," "my *bum* arm," what is "wrong" with the person, the child who is not "quite right." Hentig goes so far as to say that all peoples have had the idea that physical defect and punishment for some sort of wrong, committed perhaps by an ancestor, were somehow connected (1948a, p. 17).

Several factors may be operating in support of moral imputation. The first concerns early socialization practices in which children are threatened with illness as the price for infringement of health rules. They are warned of catching cold if they go out without coat or rubbers. If they eat too much candy, their teeth will decay. They also accumulate sufficient evidence to back up the connection between illness and punishment. The day quantities of the forbidden candy were eaten, an unforgettable digestive upset was the reprisal. Continuing knowledge teaches that rule infractions increase the probability of illness and injury. Disabilities are incurred when driving at high speeds. Illness is more likely when neglecting diet and exercise. It need not take much evidence to support what may be sensed as the natural and proper order of things.

It seems that human beings feel that suffering or punishments, like joys or rewards, should be deserved (Asch, 1952; Heider, 1958), a belief that has been aptly referred to as the "just world phenomenon." That belief in a just world can be maintained by blaming the victim has been shown in a series of laboratory experiments (summarized in Lerner, 1970). A "just world scale" has been developed to measure individual differences concerning this belief. It has been found that believers are more likely to admire fortunate people and derogate victims than nonbelievers, thus maintaining the notion that people in fact get what they deserve (Rubin & Peplau, 1975).

The gratuitous connection between illness or disability and sin may represent an *emotional syllogism*, a term first introduced by Franz Alexander (1938) to describe elementary emotional sequences. That suffering is caused by wrongdoing appears to be grasped without additional elaboration. We inveigh against events that bring suffering to the innocent. Suffering perceived as stemming from virtue is not self-evident. For this to become comprehensible and acceptable other connecting links must be introduced. For example, one may conceive of suffering as a test for lofty future roles, as a means of attaining deep understanding (see pp. 186–192), or as a consequence of self-sacrifice in the interests of higher purposes. Thus, there are cripples among the gods; in the Nordic mythology, Wieland, god of smithery, was lame (Hentig, 1948a, p. 74). The Christian doctrine introduced the view that disease may be a means of purification and a way of grace. Where suffering stems from good, good must be its product. The suffering cannot be for naught. "That they shall not have died in vain" carries with it tremendous force just because the comfortable emotional sequence is threatened. On the other hand, when suffering stems from evil, it is sufficient unto itself. The matter can simply rest there. The *a priori* connections are complete. Evidently, the quality and nature of suffering and evil are more compatible than those of suffering and virtue. Crosscultural reference should, therefore, find frequent evidence of the former association, and of the latter only when elaboration leads to the necessary congruence.

Not only is the source of illness and disability sometimes felt to lie in sin, but the *consequences* may also be felt to be sinful. "A twisted mind in a twisted body" captures this devaluation of the total person. Thus, with illness and disability both the perceived cause and the perceived effects sometimes, if not often, match the negative qualities of illness and disability. Moreover, the cause-effect relationships sometimes, if not often, have a moral reference. This may be one reason why the theory of compensation as indemnity (see pp. 147–149) has so firm a hold on the minds of experts and laymen alike; the wrong is righted through compensation.

Lest there be a too hasty overgeneralization, it bears repeating that a substantial number of people connect suffering or even tragedy with such positive effects as deeper understanding and higher values (see pp. 264–268). In these instances the association is linked through a more complex network of cause-effect relationships.

THE DIFFERENT AND STRANGE

"To be different" is to be "set apart," which, in the language of interpersonal relations, may signify rejection. During adolescence, conformity to the ways of the peer group is so commanding because "belonging" is highly valued. Many writers have also attributed rejection of a person with a disability to the fact that he or she is *different*.

In his balance theory of sentiments, Heider (1958) provides a basis for negative reactions to the different and strange. Stated briefly, this theory posits an interdependence between a person's liking for someone (sentiment relation) and the feeling of belongingness (unit relation) with that person. There are many factors that give rise to the feeling that two persons form a unit—that is, that they belong together in some way. These are called unit-forming factors. For example, two persons may be associated together through kinship; through similarity of beliefs, nationality, and religion; through familiarity and interaction. The idea is that when person p identifies with another person o because of any one of the unit-forming factors, a tendency for p to like o will be induced. The inverse relation also holds: if p likes o, a tendency to perceive similarities between them will arise. Parenthetically it may be noted that the concept of unit-forming factors had been systematically investigated by Gestalt psychologists who demonstrated their importance in perception. Heider incorporated the concept within a theory of sentiments. He also added such peculiarly human unit-forming factors as similarity of beliefs, the strong connection between people and their deeds, and between people and their property (ownership).

In Heider's work, many examples of a relationship between liking and similarity between individuals are given from research and everyday life. The point of many proverbs is that similar individuals tend to associate and to like each other. In an experiment on social relationships, it was shown that the subjects perceived persons they liked best as more similar to themselves than those they liked least (Fiedler, Warrington, & Blaisdell, 1952). In another experiment, subjects rated either a blind or able-bodied student whose attitudes were fictitiously conveyed as being either similar or dissimilar to the subject's. Attitudinal similarity increased the attraction toward both the blind and able-bodied student (Asher, 1973).

Familiarity has also been shown to induce liking. One experiment that studied this factor in a particularly ingenious way made use of reversed facial images (Mita et al., 1977). It was hypothesized that because of greater familiarity with one's own mirror image as opposed to one's true image, people should prefer their mirror image, whereas the reverse should hold in the case of preference of the person's image by others. A single frontal facial photograph of the person was printed in such a way that one print corresponded to the person's true image and another to the mirror image. In two studies, the person was found to prefer the mirror image over the true image, whereas the reverse tendency characterized the choices of the person's friend or lover. For a review of research dealing with familiarity and liking see Harrison (1977).

The opposite cases of these factors—namely, the effects of dissimilarity and unfamiliarity—have direct bearing upon feelings toward persons with a disability. Heider's theory postulates that there will be a tendency for the dissimilar and strange to evoke a negative affection in p for o. An example is that of xenophobia, where the hesitancy in befriending a foreigner is accounted for by the dislike induced by the dissimilarity and perhaps also unfamiliarity of the alien member.

Heider attributes the negative effects of unfamiliarity to at least two factors. The first concerns uncertainty engendered by new situations. An unfamiliar situation is cognitively unstructured. It is full of possibilities that may be sufficiently threatening to an insecure person to lead to withdrawal. Conflict and unstable behavior result. The second factor is a more purely intellectual and aesthetic component of resistance to the unfamiliar. "The strange is experienced as not fitting the structure of the matrix of the life space, as not filling one's expectations. The adaptation or change in expectations which is required by meeting the unfamiliar demands energy. It is more comfortable to wear old clothes and to talk with old friends" (Heider, 1958, p. 194).

The theoretical formulations of other investigators can also be drawn upon in the search for understanding of negative reaction to the different and strange. In terms of the concept of body image as developed by Schilder (1935), the other person's physical difference creates uneasiness because it does not fit with a well-ordered body image. Moreover, a person's unconscious body image of the self may be threatened by the appearance of a person with a missing part or deformity, inasmuch as he or she identifies to some extent with that person.

A neurophysiological theory to account for the fear response to the strange has been proposed by Hebb (1946), based upon observations that both humans and chimpanzees show spontaneous fear of mutilated and unresponsive bodies (dead or anesthetized bodies). The statement of the theory that applies most particularly to reaction to disability is that "fear occurs when an object is seen which is like familiar objects in enough respects to arouse habitual processes of perception, but in other respects arouses incompatible processes" (p. 268).

Actually, the evidence that similarity and familiarity induce liking is much more consistent than that dissimilarity and unfamiliarity induce disliking. Heider, on the basis of work stemming from his theory (Cartwright & Harary, 1956), raises the possibility that whereas similarity and familiarity may lead to a real feeling of unity between p and o, dissimilarity and unfamiliarity may not necessarily lead to disunity, but rather to a mere absence of the unit relation in some cases. Evidence for an actual disjunctive force would be resistance against moving toward the unfamiliar. Heider is careful to point out that there are many instances where the unfamiliar and the different have their own allure. One possibility is that we may be interested in something different because of a need for variety and challenge, providing that the context is sufficiently familiar so as not to be too threatening. The idea has been advanced that infants *seek out* the novel within a familiar context and thereby develop intellectually (Hunt, 1946). People often strive to be different in some ways, to sense their own uniqueness, to stand out as individuals (Snyder & Fromkin, 1980).

We need to know more about the nature of differences and unfamiliarities, as well as the surrounding conditions that evoke indifference on the one hand and withdrawal or fear on the other. In any case, as applied to disability, the distinction between absence of a unit relation and its disjunction means that a person with a disability need not necessarily be seen as separated from the able-bodied by an unbridgeable chasm.

The preceding discussion suggests certain measures in the interest of enhancing constructive attitudes toward disability on the part of the community at large. It argues that children with disabilities should attend regular schools wherever feasible, rather than segregating them in special schools, so that familiarity with atypical physique may take place in everyday life. The recommendation assumes, of course, that the integrated context is predominantly a positive one (see also Chapter 8). The preceding discussion also calls attention to the proposition that it is not so much physical deviation as such that creates a feeling of being different as psychological characteristics imputed to the person through the phenomenon of spread. This means that education, to the effect that physical anomaly does not betray personality, is of the first importance. All one knows about a person with a disability is that the person has the disability. Until one knows more, one can hardly say more. Once negative spread has been held in check, physical dissimilarity may become a relatively minor feature among the many other characteristics that unite people. After all, the person with a disability is first of all *a person who shares essential similarities* with other people.

LABELING, SPREAD, AND CORRECTIVE MEASURES

A striking testimony to the power of spread is the feeling that the bit of information provided by a label tells a good deal about a person or group. The problem moves from the scientific arena to that of social and personal concern when a label serves to interfere with actualizing the human potential of a particular group. Where spread leads to underrating the abilities of a group, environmental opportunities will correspondingly be limited by those who control the dispensation of resources. Labeling a person as mentally retarded, for example, has come under indictment for just this reason. Being so labeled, a person may be placed in an institutional or educational environment ill-designed for adequate development. The resulting poor learning has been challenged as a self-fulfilling prophecy by the public media, as well as scientific investigation (Rosenthal & Jacobson, 1968). In setting off one group from another by their labels, the propensity to perceive the nature of problems in terms of person attributes is heightened; the role played by situational factors becomes still further obscured. (See "Person Versus Environmental Attribution," Chapter 3.)

Another major problem with labels is that they homogenize people instead of revealing the great heterogeneity that exists within any labeled group. How different Jane and Bill appear when their uniqueness is conveyed by individualized descriptions (Hobbs, 1975):

> Jane shows up on summary school records and state reports as "mentally retarded, educable." What is not recorded is that Jane cannot read, that she is attractive and pleasant, that she needs dental care, and that she is very good with children and has held a child-care job with a family for five years. [pp. 106–107]
>
> Bill shows up on summary school records and state reports as visually handicapped. . . . What is not recorded is that Bill is a diabetic,

that he has an IQ of at least 160, and that he is a superb musician.
[p. 107]

In his excellent book, Hobbs (1975) discusses in depth the social, psychological, and legal complexities of the problem of labeling.

However, a negatively charged label does not always adversely affect the person identified with that label. In one study, the effect of labels on the attitudes of teachers toward children with special problems varied depending on the diagnostic category (Combs & Harper, 1967). When the label "mentally deficient" was added to a description of the behavior of a child who was mentally retarded, the child was perceived *less* negatively than when the label was omitted. On the other hand, when the labels psychopathic, schizophrenic, and cerebral palsied were applied to behavioral descriptions of children with these disorders, the children were evaluated more negatively than when unlabeled. Perhaps teachers, being familiar with mental retardation, found the behavior of children so identified to be less threatening and less strange than if the child had been assumed to be normal. Teachers may generally be less familiar with the other disorders; therefore, instead of making the child's behavior seemingly more understandable, the labels may have only heightened the teachers' uneasiness. The varying results of this study support the recommendation that potentially stigmatizing labels should be applied with *great caution* and only after serious consideration is given to *who benefits* and *who is harmed* by the label. (For a review of the mentally retarded label, see MacMillan, Jones, & Aloia, 1974.)

To be sure, not all labels that adversely affect people can be avoided. Certain facts about a person, visible in a public sense, serve to separate people into groups whether or not they are formally labeled. Among these are many physical and ethnic characteristics, modes of behavior and dress, and even ideological viewpoints that are shared with others. Although such facts can be excluded from official records in many cases, in face-to-face contact they are generally apprehensible. The problem of reducing unwarranted negative-spread effects, therefore, calls for measures over and above cautious labeling.

The key idea of some approaches to counteract negative impressions engendered by labels is to expose the public to information, semantic formulations, and experiences that will provide a broader set of positive expectations. Public media are therefore encouraged to present all sorts of people with different types of disabilities fulfilling all sorts of *nonstereotyped* roles as a way of reducing exaggerated notions of limitation. Contact with persons who have a disability and who are of equal status also serves this purpose. Publicizing the contributions of individuals with disabilities who have achieved eminence is a further approach to countering the arbitrary spread of disabling effects. Certain language constructions have also been introduced to block negative spread, as in the word "handicapables," the phrase "person with a disability," or the thought "It is ability not disability that counts." Individualized descriptions of people rather than labels is another general recommendation to counter stereotypy.

Still another approach concentrates on the moral, political, and economic values that both support and are supported by the separation of people into particular groups of hierarchical status. The effort, then, is directed toward altering those values and those political and economic structures that are found wanting. Legislation may be implemented to protect the civil and human rights of persons who are disadvantaged. Sometimes, even the very basic economic structure of society is challenged, as when unemployment and inflation rates are high. In these instances, negative-spread effects are attacked indirectly by emphasis on human dignity, injustice, and societal change.

Despite continuing efforts to enhance human potential, the probability remains that negative spread will continue to exist as a social-psychological obstacle, although hopefully less pervasively so. This follows because not all conditions underlying the phenomena of spread can be eliminated by changing belief systems, value systems, or socioeconomic systems. Where a negative characteristic is viewed as a central personal characteristic and where the context in which it appears is sparse, negative-spread effects can be expected.

A few precautions may help to check some of the abuses of labeling and negative spread:

1. Ask who benefits and who is harmed by the label.
2. Be sure to assume abilities, thereby encouraging the search for those abilities that would otherwise remain hidden beneath a stigmatizing label.
3. Be alert to the fact that labels underscore person attributes while ignoring environmental factors that contribute to the problem.
4. Remember that the individuals within any labeled group vary *enormously* with respect to important personal and situational characteristics.

THE STRANGER'S VIEW: A PAUCITY OF CONTEXT

The situation where little is known about the person with a disability appears especially conducive to negative-spread effects. The fact that the context is so sparse provides few constraints against perceiving the person as generally less endowed and less fortunate in an overall sense than the able-bodied. Such is the case between strangers. In the stranger relationship, the obviousness of a disability becomes the outstanding characteristic. Other facts that may be apprehended in passing, such as age and sex, are usually so general that they hardly compete in being given preponderant weight.

That a visible disability is more apt to dominate the relationship between strangers than between people who know each other is supported by research. Thus, one of our studies has shown that people are apt to view strangers with a disability as more unfortunate than they view a friend with the same disability. Moreover, people with disabilities feel that strangers regard them as being more unfortunate than do their family or friends.

Sometimes, and probably frequently, a member of the family is not thought of as having a disability in spite of a major physical impairment. This is seen in the following reflections of two able-bodied young adults who participated in a discussion organized by students concerned with disabilities:

> What was striking to me is that I have always been telling myself and others that I had never had any interaction with people with disabilities. David, a disabled person himself, helped me to explore myself and it dawned on me that my grandparents became disabled when my grandfather lost the use of his right hand and my grandmother her left leg. I had never regarded these as disabilities. It still baffles me why, up until this moment, I had closed myself to realize that. It could be that I had come to accept them as they were and never stereotyped them. [Personal communication].

> Dave, who uses a wheelchair because of polio, asked if any of us had any experiences with disabled people. I said no, everyone in my family was healthy. Then I started laughing. My own father walks with a severe limp. He has been that way since he was 5, so he rarely mentions it. To me, that is just part of my father. I know it is there, but it isn't a conscious fact. When I walk with my father, I am not aware of his limp, and when he needs help, I automatically hold out my arm for him to hold on to. When walking on gravel, or grass, or snow, or going upstairs, he needs help in maintaining his balance. (Personal communication)

For these two people, the disability was incidental and peripheral because the individuality of the person with the disability and the totality of family relationships made it so. With a stranger there is little to overshadow the disability, and the disability becomes central.

Admonitions not to stare or to ask questions are particularly pointed toward strangers, just because of the contextless nature of the relationship. For this reason, also, the aforementioned study on the cosmetic glove (p. 55) recommended that "during a first meeting with someone, which may be the initial stage of a lasting relationship, the cosmetic hand is seen as useful, because it allows the non-wearer to get to know the wearer as a person before the fact of a prosthesis and feelings about the injury and amputation come into play" (Cattell et al., 1949, p. 28).

Should the relationship between strangers become more than a passing one, the influx of new information and the feeling of familiarity that comes with repeated contact serve to alter initial impressions. The relationship changes by virtue of the fact that the disability becomes less dominating; other personal characteristics have a chance to assume ascendancy. This transformation is seen in the following account by a college student who worked as a teacher's aid with four children who were severely mentally retarded. During her contact of two hours per week for three months, she realized profound changes in her own feelings:

> I chose to work with these severely handicapped children because I have had little exposure to this type of child and needed to know for the future if they were the type of children I would like to work with. I must say that my initial impression had to have been the epitomy of the worst. All I could think of was "Oh, those poor children, they can't do anything." They couldn't talk, couldn't take commands well, couldn't sit in their seats for long. Not only were their behaviors low but their motor coordination was poor and two of the children drooled. I was dismayed and (yes) disgusted with their behaviors and appearance. However, after I began to work with them and got to know them a little better that attitude began to change. I could see little things—often very little things—that they were improving on. They all are becoming more responsive and all but one can vocalize "bye-bye" with a prompt from me when I leave. I have learned to pick out things that one can do that perhaps another one can't and realize that they are children that have problems—but they have feelings and emotions like anyone else. I think that at first I was detached and uninvolved; I considered them objects for observation. After I began to get involved with them, I began to appreciate and see them as people. (Personal communication)

In an important study that compared children with disabilities and their able-bodied counterparts, the results were attributed to the fact that in the settings in which the observations took place, the people knew each other well (Schoggen, 1978). The study was concerned with the kinds of action directed toward the children in home and school. Of the many comparisons made, the overall finding was that the intrapair differences between the children with and without disabilities were neither consistently larger or in one direction. The investigator concluded that the data "provide no support for the proposition that the social environment of children with physical disabilities tends in general to be either oversolicitous or rejecting and indifferent" (p. 133). The explanation that was given is far-reaching and fits well with the theme of the present chapter:

The behavior of others toward these children appeared to be determined by the total complex of personal attributes, of which physical disability was only one small part. The child friends and adults who interacted with one of these children appeared to be responding to the whole child as a person, and the fact of physical disability seemed to be virtually disregarded or at most to play a very minor role. This one characteristic of disability seemed to the associates of these children to be embedded in the larger context of all the child's personal qualities. They were not responding to a "crippled child" but rather to Nick and Patrick or Libby, as persons who, almost incidentally, had a physical disability.

If this interpretation seems hard to accept, let us remind you that we were observing children with disabilities in ordinary, everyday situations at home and school where they were intimately or at least well known to nearly all other persons with whom they came into contact. Moreover, in every case the disability was a stable characteristic of some duration—everyone who knew the child was familiar with his limitations. There was nothing novel about Robert's prosthesis, Libby's wheelchair, or Danny's sling and crutches. . . . Under these circumstances, the focus of an associate's attention shifts from the superficial characteristics of physical appearance to deeper, more important traits of personality and behavior. It is possible that observational studies have a nearly unique advantage in being able to tap really natural behavior of others toward persons with disabilities. Perhaps interviews, questionnaires, and attitude tests can hardly avoid giving an inaccurate picture, because they almost necessarily isolate disability . . . as the characteristic of special interest or importance. [pp. 144–145]

The difference between the stranger relationship and other relationships is so important that great caution should be taken lest conclusions drawn from studies of relationships between strangers are inappropriately generalized. A case in point is a study in which the subject had the task of teaching paper-folding skills to two confederates over a period of two training sessions (Kleck, 1969). One of the confederates simulated the role of a person with a left leg amputation through the use of a specially constructed wheelchair. Only during the *first* training session did the subjects maintain a significantly greater physical distance from the person in the wheelchair than from the "normal" person. That is to say, at the time of the second training session, the situation was no longer novel and some acquaintance with the partner had taken place. This helped to reduce the impact of disability as such. In citing this study, more than one author has overlooked the change that had taken place in even the brief time span of two sessions.

The stranger situation is unique just because its sparse context more readily anchors the relationship to the disability. A good deal of disability research involves disability as an abstraction or disability in the context of interactions between a subject and someone who is unknown to the subject. Unfortunately, the temptation is great to generalize these findings to relationships between people who know each other. The thrust of this chapter, stressing as it does the importance of context, clearly makes such an extrapolation unwarranted. In short, the psychology of disability must not be made equivalent to the psychology of disability in stranger relationships or to the psychology of disability as a disembodied abstract concept.

The ideas presented thus far will appear again, along with others, as we examine a variety of problems. Context issues, value questions, perspective differences, and so forth keep cropping up in our attempt to bring about psychological clarification of some of the problems confronting people with disabilities—and in a broader sense, all of us—so that opportunities may be widened and constructive views of life with a disability enhanced.

Chapter 5
Requirement of Mourning and Expectation Discrepancy

Thus far we have examined how impressions of people with disabilities depend upon factors important in the spread or inferential process. These impressions lead to expectations of how people with disabilities feel and act. This chapter will first consider the problem of the requirement of mourning as it relates to the expectation of suffering and will end with an analysis of the general case of expectations that are discrepant with reality. The problems presented have considerable impact on interpersonal relations.

REQUIREMENT OF MOURNING

To begin with, it should be made clear that "the requirement of mourning" is not the same as "the period of mourning"; the latter is part of the process of adjustment to loss and is discussed in Chapter 8. The original requirement-of-mourning hypothesis (Dembo et al., 1956, p. 21) stated: When people have a need to safeguard their values, they will either insist that the person they consider unfortunate is suffering (even when that person seems not to be suffering) or devaluate the unfortunate person because he or she ought to suffer and does not. Because the need to safeguard one's own values comes from quite different sources, it is useful to distinguish three types of requirement of mourning; namely, (1) empathic requirement of mourning, (2) self-aggrandizing requirement of mourning, and (3) ought requirement of mourning.

The *empathic requirement of mourning* arises from the many perceptual factors already discussed that lead to the expectation of suffering in the case of a disability judged to be negative and unwanted, imposed and not chosen. In imagining how the self would feel with the advent of disability, one imagines distress. It is this self-perception that becomes projected onto the other person in the form of expectations. In expecting suffering, one tends to perceive it (see "Believing Is Seeing," p. 273), and it is in this sense that one requires the person to suffer. Should the expected suffering not become evident, the perceiver continues to struggle with the unexpected state of affairs, wondering "how come?" The person with a disability may then be seen as courageous and may be admired for keeping "a stiff upper lip." Genuine concern for the person may be felt. Notice that in these instances, because of an inability to see the world from the insider's perspective, the onlooker retains the idea that the person really is suffering at some level. However, where ongoing evidence helps to answer the question "How come the person is content and not suffering or unhappy?" the empathic requirement of mourning gives way to understanding and one's expectations become revised accordingly.

An example of revising one's expectations as an outcome of the empathic requirement of mourning is given in a student's reaction upon realizing that an attractive young woman in his class had one arm:

> As I entered the class, I glanced around the room giving it the once-over when my eyes fell upon a girl who seemed to pulsate with a beauty I had not seen before. It was not so much a physical beauty, however. Her physical attributes were most becoming, but it was more of a radiant or inner beauty that captivated me. As I made my way toward the seat next to hers, I tried to figure out just what it was that was so attractive about this young lady. As I got close to her, it dawned on me just what was so attractive. In a room of fifty faces, hers seemed to lack the anxiety, the anticipation, or the worry that was on the faces of others. She seemed so peaceful.
>
> As I took my seat, I started a conversation with her. As we talked, I took an instant liking to this young lady because she was very easy to talk to.
>
> After the class had ended, we rose to leave and for the first time I noticed that she had an artificial arm. My first reaction was one of shock as I thought to myself how could something like that happen to someone as nice as her? For the rest of the day my mind kept returning to thoughts of this girl and the question, *how can she be so happy with such a terrible handicap?* [Italics

added.] I just could not believe a person could lose a part of her body and yet be so content.

    As the semester grew on, we became closer friends and I found to my surprise that she could accomplish with her hook just about anything anyone else without this disability could. She drove a car as well as anyone and to my surprise could even type. So, as time passed, I again saw in her the same person I had seen when I first walked into the class, only I saw a person with a disability instead of a disabled person. (Personal communication)

One should understand that perceiving the person with a disability as being able to accomplish "just about anything anyone else could," as in the above example, is not a prerequisite to the successful resolution of the empathic requirement of mourning. Rather, the point is that the expectation of suffering became modified in accordance with the feelings and abilities that were revealed by the young woman with the artificial arm.

Not always, however, does wondering "how come" lead to an understanding of why the person is content. The perceiver's evaluation of what it takes to be content may be too strong to be revamped by the wondering. The perceiver may then feel sorry and genuine concern for the person, evidence that the empathic requirement of mourning is persisting. This outcome is seen in the following report of a respiratory therapist: "David was 20 years old and in the final stages of cystic fibrosis. He was always cheerful and helpful to those of us who were trying to sustain him against the devastating effects of the disease. At the time I used to wonder how anyone could be happy at a time such as this. I couldn't help feeling sorry for him." Notice that in this case the therapist, who viewed dying as an inconsolable value loss, felt sorry but there was no hint of pleasure or righteousness.

In sharp contrast is the *self-aggrandizing requirement of mourning* in which the dominant motive is the need to preserve and elevate one's own status. The person wants the one considered unfortunate to suffer as a sign that one's own status is recognized as superior. "Consider a woman to whom 'position is everything in life.' She must consider as unfortunate those who are omitted from the social register. If she does not it would mean that her position is not so valuable after all. If they do not accept the fact that they are unfortunate, she must consider them either too stupid to know better, or insensitive, or shamming; otherwise her own position is threatened" (Dembo, Leviton, & Wright, 1956, p. 21).

In the following account, the self-aggrandizing requirement of mourning is laid bare as the narrator became aware of her own status needs and "crippled thoughts." Notice how she denigrated the evident good fortune of the deaf saleswoman by insisting that her lot was lamentable:

It was an early Saturday morning in January when I paused in front of a shop and read the sign—Judy Jansen Upholstering. I entered the store and a slight woman approached me smiling.

I don't know whether she made a sound or whether I inquired about the headboards and spreads in response to her most engaging smile. However, I immediately realized that she had a hearing problem and that she had not attempted to converse with me. I felt a tinge of disappointment because she was unable to give me the desired information. She gave me a business card, implying by pointing to the number, that I could call for further information.

When I returned to the shop a week later, I was greeted by a very handsome looking, energetic, middle-aged man. He gave me the information I wanted and I placed an order with him. When I mentioned that I had been in before and had "talked" to a lady, he immediately said that I must have found it a little difficult to do so because she is deaf. He further stated that the lady, Judy by name, is his wife. Judy—the card. I readily recalled both. *I was surprised that this man was her husband. Really shocked.*

In further conversation with Mr. Jansen he gave the impression that he was very proud of her. In talking about the business his conversation was dotted with "we this" and "we that" and Judy was a part of the we.

How could a nondescript person with a handicap as serious as hearing have such a handsome husband who was, obviously, very proud of her accomplishments. Is my husband so proud? I bet she does all the work and he loafs around. I am sure that is it, now that I think of it.

I thanked Mr. Jansen, and he assured me that my order would be ready at the specified time. I left with this assurance, but I also took along with me my "crippled" thoughts. (Personal communication, italics added)

A somewhat different version of the self-aggrandizing requirement of mourning arises when the perceiver becomes threatened by the apparent adjustment of a person with a disability because one's own ego is found wanting by contrast. The following personal account is illustrative:

I have had students report to me that my lack of distress made them feel uneasy. They said they perceived me as a happy, successful person who copes with a wheelchair without apparent frustration. They felt that if they landed in a wheelchair, they would be so upset that they would probably "go blow their brains out." They concluded that if I, and others, can take conditions in stride that they thought they would find unbearable, there must be something wrong with them. Hence, they felt uneasy because I made them feel inferior. (Nancy Kerr, personal communication)

To avoid being confronted with the contrast of one's own weaker ego, the perceiver would prefer that the person with a disability not show such capability and equanimity in living with a disability.

The *ought requirement of mourning,* the third type, stems from the need to preserve codes of proper behavior, that is, how one ought to feel and act. Maintaining the ought standards of proper conduct connotes moral obligation. A case in point is bereavement during which it is generally expected that one should show proper mourning for the deceased. One student reported:

> The mother of my best friend, a 40-year-old woman, was widowed when her husband died suddenly of cancer of the liver. When her friends realized that she was dating within three months of her husband's death, the general reaction of her friends was one of disapproval and misunderstanding. Upon announcing her intention to remarry after only seven months as a widow, the general reaction shifted to one of shock and angry disapproval, verbalized by statements such as "How can she be so disrespectful of Tom." (Personal communication)

A parent of a terminally ill child recounted being told by a friend, "How could you have a birthday party at this time" (Friedman et al., 1963), implying the inappropriateness of celebration when one is expected to be grief stricken. The ought requirement of mourning can also reflect the belief that disability is a punishment for sin and therefore the person ought to suffer (see Chapter 4, pp. 63–68).

It should be clear that the requirement of mourning occurs not only in regard to illness and disability but in any situation where there is a need to safeguard one's values. The events that followed a football game is a particularly frank example of the self-aggrandizing requirement of mourning:

> On a sunny Saturday afternoon after a surprise upset of the nationally ranked "N" football team by our poorly esteemed "K" squad, I found myself caught in a traffic jam for about 10–15 minutes. One factor discriminated me from other homeward bound, rejoicing K's—I had N license plates on my car. Expressions aimed in my direction ranged from Bronx cheers by chortling urchins to superior smirks from condescending adults. Falsely identified, I was consigned to the ranks of grieving N's. "Go ahead and cry, admit you are heartbroken." This seemed to be the feeling of virtually every supercilious K that inched by. (Personal communication)

Research on the requirement-of-mourning hypothesis can be found in a study of hospitalized surgical patients and their caregivers (Mason & Muhlenkamp, 1976). Examples of the patients' surgery are: amputation, colostomy, and mastectomy. The caregivers were nurses, assistants, physicians, and so forth. The patients were asked to select those adjectives from a long list which best described how they felt at that specific time. Caregivers most directly acquainted with the particular patient were asked to also select those adjectives they believed the patient would select. High scores on derived measures of depression, anxiety, and, to a lesser extent, hostility were interpreted as reflecting the state of mourning. On the basis of the requirement-of-mourning hypothesis, the researchers predicted that since health and body-whole are valued highly, caregivers would judge the patients as being more disturbed than the patients' own responses would indicate. The results bore out the prediction. Other results led the authors to discount patient denial as a possible explanation of the difference. Experiments on the fortune phenomenon are also relevant to the requirement of mourning (Wright & Howe, 1969). Self-ratings by mental hospital patients and welfare clients regarding how fortunate they were in comparison to the general population were significantly higher than the ratings given by others to these groups. In another study, airline stewardesses, who were expected to value physical perfection more highly than typists, were consequently expected to have less positive attitudes toward persons with physical disabilities (English & Oberle, 1971). This reasoning accords with the requirement-of-mourning hypothesis and was borne out by the results.

Although lending support to the basic requirement-of-mourning hypothesis, these studies do not deal with differences among the three types of the requirement of mourning. What is common among the three types is that the observer, in order to protect highly held values, exaggerates suffering on the part of the person (recipient) considered unfortunate. However, in the event that the recipient does not appear to be suffering or as unhappy as expected, the outcome differs in the three cases. In the case of the empathic requirement of mourning, the observer puzzles about the unrealized expectations and either modifies them, feels concern and sorrow, or admires the presumed sufferer for being able to cope so well with the difficulties. Where the empathic requirement of mourning is operating alone, devaluation has little place. In sharp contrast is the case of the self-aggrandizing requirement of mourning. Not only is there insistence that the recipient is suffering, but there is personal pleasure or satisfaction at the recipient's plight and disdain at what is declared to be pretense should the suffering not become apparent. The ought requirement of mourning also involves devaluation should the recipient not reveal proper distress, but when suffering is evident, there is approval rather than personal pleasure. The essential distinctions among the three forms of the requirement of mourning are charted in Figure 5.1.

Clearly, few recipients of the self-aggrandizing and ought types of requirement of mourning would welcome being pitied or the source of another person's aggrandizement or righteousness. The situation is less clear with empathic requirement of mourning. Where the observer quickly adjusts his or her expectations to fit those of the recipient, the initial affective discrepancy may be fleeting and taken in stride. Where, however, the observer continues to presume inordinate difficulties that require inordinate courage to be undefeated by them, the situation quickly becomes problematic. Admiring a person for having special courage is easily experienced as pity, especially in the case of strangers where there is no ongoing relationship to be

Empathic ROM (Projection of Own Perspective)
1. Expectation that the person is suffering
2. Wonder why the person does not appear to be suffering
3. Outcome:
   a. Expectation revision ⎱ Understanding; empathic ROM is reduced or eliminated.

   b. Concern and sorrow ⎱ Empathic ROM persists.
   c. Admiration of the person ⎰

Self-Aggrandizing ROM (Feeds Personal Status Needs)
1. Desire or insistence that the person is suffering
2. Outcome:
   a. Satisfaction over the person's suffering ⎫
   b. Devaluation of the person who is suffering ⎪ Self-aggrandizing
   c. Devaluation of the person who is not ⎬ ROM persists.
   suffering, or ⎪
   d. Distress when the person is not suffering ⎭

Ought ROM (Preserves What Is Right and Proper)
1. Insistence that the person ought to suffer
2. Outcome:
   a. Approval of person's suffering ⎱ Ought ROM persists.
   b. Devaluation of the person who is not suffering ⎰

Figure 5.1 Requirement of mourning (ROM). (Stems from need to perserve one's own values.)

assuring of good will. A woman with cerebral palsy roundly expressed her resentment when "strangers see me talking and laughing and then tell me I am so brave." There is a difference between respecting a person for coping with whatever difficulties may be presumed and emphasizing those difficulties by intrusively bestowing accolades irrespective of the recipient's situation and mood.

The person with a disability is faced with a strange paradox. On the one hand, lacking physical normality, the person is expected to suffer. That is the requirement of mourning. On the other hand, society frowns upon displaying one's hurt and frustration in public. One should keep a "stiff upper lip" and "keep on smiling"—a "requirement of cheerfulness" as it were. The paradox is expressed in the following note:

Overt mourning in the early stages of disability is almost uniformly condemned by rehabilitation personnel. Patients who cry instead of entering enthusiasticaly into hospital routines are often criticized, badgered and berated—either to their faces or behind their backs. Later, even though the requirement of mourning persists long after the person with a disability is through mourning, there is still a strong requirement that the person be friendly, outgoing, cheerful and well motivated. Continually, I learn from students, special education teachers and rehabilitation workers that there is quick and uncompromising condemnation of anyone with a disability who has a "bad attitude," gripes about some injustice, shows hostility, or is not interested in doing whatever the "outsider" thinks should be done. Of course, disability aside, it is usually more pleasant to be around happy rather than sad people. But when the person has a disability, there seems to be less allowance made for the fact that many people have "good days" and "bad days." The phenomenon is especially interesting when the demand for cheerfulness is made simultaneously with the requirement of mourning (Nancy Kerr, personal communication).

EXPECTATION DISCREPANCY

Expecting suffering when the person doesn't appear to be suffering was the problem presented in the requirement of mourning. There are other kinds of expectations having to do with ability and adjustment that are also frequently discrepant with the presenting evidence. In this section, the general case of expectation discrepancy will be discussed.

Expectations can be worse than the apparent reality or better. The person who has these discrepant expectations will react with some feeling appropriate to the gap between the expected and apparent state of affairs and the direction of that gap. Where the expectations are worse than what is observed, the person may experience the following emotions:

> Surprise: "Despite their severe disabilities, the mental health of the veteran paraplegics as a group is surprisingly good."
> Incredulousness: "It's unbelievable, but he can even shave with those hooks!"

Where the expectations are higher than the presenting facts, the emotions may be:

> Anguish: "I felt sick. The last hope that I might again see perfectly was gone."
> Disappointment: "I had hoped this final operation would be successful, but she still can't bend her knee."

Assuredly, there is a wide gamut of emotional reactions to expectation discrepancy. Such feelings as amazement, wonder, curiosity, dismay, horror, frustration, and futility could be added. It seems reasonable that if the direction of the expectation discrepancy is in accord with the person's wishes, a positive affect emerges, such as pleasant surprise or hopefulness. If, however, the expectation discrepancy runs counter to wishes, a negative feeling is experienced, such as disappointment and anger.

Though it might appear that a positive reaction would be typical in cases where the state of affairs turns out to be better than anticipated, we must not forget that the person might wish a worsening or a maintaining of the unfortunate situation. We have already seen that where the self-aggrandizing or ought requirement of mourning is operating, the observer may actually be dismayed should the person with the disability be perceived as better off than expected and be quite content to find the reverse. Sometimes persons with a disability may themselves wish to exaggerate their unfortunate status when secondary gains are in the offing (Cordaro & Shontz, 1969).

Where the person experiences a discrepancy between his or her own expectations and the evidence, there is frequently a need to explain the discrepancy, to reconcile the two halves of the equation; that is, expectations on the one hand and the apparent reality on the other. How this reconciliation takes place has important consequences for the evaluation of a person with a disability, but first we need to inquire as to the conditions that give rise to expectation discrepancy.

Conditions Underlying Expectation Discrepancy

Several conditions bring about a discrepancy between the presenting reality and what one had expected:

1. *Spread:* The perceiver views the person (or the self) as a "disabled person." That is, the person is seen as disabled not only with respect to physique but with respect to other characteristics as well—for example, personality and adjustment (see pp. 32–39). Because of spread, the observer tends to overgeneralize the disability and therefore *expects* the lot of the person with a disability to be *worse* in many ways than the apparent reality (even though particular difficulties actually experienced by the person may not be recognized). Such spread paradoxically becomes a condition for the subsequent wonder and admiration at the accomplishments of the person with a disability.

2. *Position of the person:* When the perceiver is not the person who has the disability, the problems involving the disability will be viewed from the perspective of the outsider (see pp. 47–51). Not having had experience with the disability, not having to learn and discover new ways of meeting the problems, the outsider may regard the problems as frightfully frustrating and even insurmountable, thereby leading to exaggerated negative expectations. Were the person closely aligned with the disability situation, either as insider (i.e., the person with the disability) or as someone close to that person,

the necessity of meeting problems of living would reveal ways of managing and meeting the challenges. When perceived coping is enhanced, negative expectations tend to be reduced.

3. *Self-aggrandizing requirement of mourning:* When the status of the observer depends upon physique as a high status value, he or she will insist that the lot of a person with a disability is an unfortunate one (see pp. 80–81). Exaggerated negative expectations are part and parcel of this self-aggrandizing need and point to an important source of expectation discrepancy.

4. *Wish for improvement:* Sometimes the wish that all will be well is so strong as to lead to unrealistic expectations of marked improvement or eventual recovery. Even though current difficulties may be played down because of this same wish, the fact that the hopeful expectations cannot materialize means a discrepancy with reality that is at best disappointing and at worst heartbreaking. We should also expect that a person with such a strong wish would show other differentiating emotions; for example, he or she is less likely to be amazed or surprised at the positive adjustment and accomplishments of a person with a disability and more likely to be pleased than would the outsider who does not actively entertain the wish for improvement.

Reconciling Expectation Discrepancy

It is part of human nature to search for explanations and connections in order to make experience comprehensible. So it is in the case of expectation discrepancy. It is frequently disturbing to the person when expectations do not match the presenting facts although sometimes one doesn't bother with the discrepancy. Where there is a felt need to clarify the discrepancy, cognitive changes are attempted. These will be discussed in terms of expectation revision, altering the apparent reality, and anormalizing the person.

Let us consider the frequently occurring expectation discrepancy where the performance of a person with a disability outstrips the expectations of an outsider. In attempting to explain the discrepancy, the outsider may shift from ruminating about succumbing to the difficulties (i.e., emphasizing all the things the disability denies) to involvement with the coping aspects (i.e., the ways in which the person has managed). In doing so, the outsider begins to learn about and appreciate the adjustment possibilities of living with paraplegia, blindness, epilepsy, and so forth, and is then able to agree in principle with Miers (1953) who pointed out that his athetosis ". . . is not half the nuisance you think. Straws for drinking, a typewriter for putting my thoughts on paper, an electric razor, in the main cut down this disability to life size" (p. 7). Not only will the coping aspect of difficulties have shifted into the focus of attention, but the outsider will also have shifted position toward that of the insider.

These two shifts give a new direction to the original amazement over the adjustment of the person with a disability. *Expectation revision* has occurred. The expectations of the observer have been revised upward, thereby leaving little room for incredulity. This does not mean that the residual affect is neutral. The observer may now feel respect for the persistence shown by the person with the disability in meeting difficulties, or may appreciate the courage it took or the ambition or earthy common sense regarding the realities of life. That these positive feelings emerge when coping with, as against succumbing to, difficulties is in the field of concern.

Although this cognitive-affective change for resolving the discrepancy is to be desired, the social-psychological position of the outsider is not always conducive to such a shift. Not only may there be little opportunity for the outsider to learn just how the person with a disability does manage, but often the outsider has little felt need to create such opportunities. Instead, other means at reconciliation may be sought.

The outsider may, for example, *alter the apparent reality* by disregarding or doubting evidence concerning the adequacy of the emotional adjustment and abilities of persons with a disability. Thus, the outsider may feel that these persons are shamming, simply acting as though they were adjusted and managing well, that they are defensively denying their unfortunate state. The outsider may suppress evidence regarding the coping aspect of difficulties; for example, when he or she does not "see" how well the child with braces gets around but instead emphasizes the child's halting gait. The outsider may attribute many problems and distresses of life to the person's disability that are not at all so related, and in spite of indications to the contrary, may insist that the person's lot is insufferable. Chevigny (1946), who became blind as an adult, sometimes could not help feeling that the world "doesn't want to be convinced that I am not altogether helpless, despite the plain evidence to the contrary" (p. 76). Unfortunately, this means of fitting together the expected state of affairs with the apparent state is probably not infrequent. Where the "requirement of mourning" (see pp. 78–85) insures the security of the outsider, altering the apparent reality in this way becomes the method of choice.

Finally, the discrepancy between expectations and the apparent reality may be reconciled through *anormalization;* that is, the outsider attributes to the person with the disability certain unusual characteristics, even supernatural ones, so that the ordinary expectations do not apply. It is very much like the kind of anormalization one might experience in the event of winning the sweepstakes; the incredibility soon becomes imbued with a strange feeling that one has been blessed or fated to win in the face of extraordinary odds. Similarly, when the outsider expects a person who is blind to fumble and stumble and instead finds well-oriented locomotion, it is easy for the outsider to "explain" this discrepancy by concluding that a sixth sense is operating.

Anormalization of persons who are deaf is seen in the following fictional sources:

> In Gian-Carlo Menotti's contemporary opera, *The Medium*, the title character and fraud, Madame Flora, intones about the deaf-mute boy she has taken into her home: "Just because he cannot speak we take him for a halfwit, but he knows a great deal. He knows more than we think. There is something uncanny about him. He sees things we don't see." Her vague apprehensions are ambiguously justified in the course of the opera. Assuming that the deaf-mute is the real medium for inexplicable phenomena, she is frightened into killing him, and thus brings about her own downfall.

> Madame Flora's recitative is taken up in full chorus by a whole group of inhabitants of a small town in Georgia, in Carson McCullers' novel, *The Heart Is a Lonely Hunter.* The spiritually desperate characters come to regard Mr. Singer, a deaf-mute who lives in their community, as a kind of God substitute, and attribute to him many of the characteristics traditionally ascribed to deity. The author simultaneously points up the irony of the equally anguished concerns of Mr. Singer's own life, so remote from the supernatural vision of him conjured up by the needs of the other townspeople that his eventual suicide becomes a poignant mystery and defeat to them.

> The same idea again finds expression in a popular movie, *Flesh and Fury*, where the boxing skill of a champion prize fighter seems mysteriously to hinge upon his status as a deaf-mute. When his hearing is restored, and he has learned to articulate, he finds himself at a total loss in a championship match, as inept in the face of his opponent as the shorn Samson before the Philistines. Fortunately, a blow in the course of the fight deprives the hero of his hearing long enough for him to win the bout. [Maisel, 1953, pp. 216–217][1]

Persons with a disability may themselves feel a kind of supernatural intervention in the face of what appears to be insuperable difficulties. Karsten Ohnstad (1942) describes the problem that confronted him when, in crossing a busy thoroughfare, his usual sound

[1]From *Meet a body*, a ms. by E. Maisel. Reprinted by permission of International Center for the Disabled, New York.

SIDNEY B. COULTER LIBRARY
Onondaga Community College
Syracuse, New York 13215

cues were disrupted by wind and the rumbling noises of trucks. Upon arriving safely at the curb, he felt that in some way he had been magically protected (p. 68).

When Karsten gained thorough *control* over traffic hazards by using a white cane, the anormalization became even more a part of his very person:

> ... The cane was a nuisance, clattering against everything and catching in my trouser cuffs as I twirled it idly about like a baton; but at street corners it proved its worth. Car drivers saw it and stopped. I held it out before me and walked across the pavement with an assurance that I had never felt before. I was a worker of miracles. I was the Moses of the metropolis. I held out my staff over that roaring, honking sea, and lo! the traffic parted, and I stepped up on the opposite curb sound as a dollar. [Ohnstad, 1942, p. 69][2]

The factor of personal control is probably conducive to the feeling of deification in contrast to the kind of anormalization in which the person is felt to be a pawn of fate or subject to control by other supernatural events. Such personal deification was experienced by Raymond Goldman (1947) when, unable to walk because of polio, he mastered the "unattainable" through the strength of his own will:

> ... Other children learn naturally and without conscious effort to move about and crawl and stand up. Not I. I had to achieve those things so deliberately, at the cost of so much pain and sweat and tears, that the attainment of each was a separate triumph. I stood almost in awe of my own power to accomplish. I was like a god [p. 38].[3]

Anormalizing the person with a disability means that the laws of ordinary mortals are transcended so that expectations relevant to normal persons do not apply. There is one important difference between the quality of deified eminence and that of the esteem generated when, through concern over coping with difficulties, expectation revision takes place in which higher though entirely normal expectations are maintained. In the former case, the person with a disability is viewed as a different kind of person; one who is set apart from normal persons and whose accomplishments are seen as resulting from some kind of mystical intervention. Expectations concerning that person's group still remain generally low. Only in the specific instance of defied expectations is the person held up as

[2]Reprinted from *The world at my fingertips* by K. Ohnstad, published by Bobbs-Merrill.
[3]Reprinted with permission of Macmillan Publishing Co., Inc., from *Even the night* by R. L. Goldman. Copyright 1947, and renewed 1975, by Raymond Leslie Goldman.

something special. Small wonder that many persons with a disability reject such anormalization. The situation is different in the case of expectation revision where the accomplishments of the person with a disability are perceived in terms of normal human functioning.

Conditions for anormalizing the person appear to be favorable when the perceptions of the two sides of the equation are difficult to change. Again let us turn to blindness as an illustration: (1) An outsider with respect to blindness, a sighted person expects that the locomotion difficulties attendant upon blindness are insuperable. Moreover, this perception is difficult to change. (2) When a person who is blind unperturbably moves about, there is a discrepancy with what had been expected. This perception is also difficult to change. Seeing is believing, and the outsider cannot deny that the blind person has safely crossed the street, traveled alone, or located his or her books.

In these circumstances, it is perhaps comprehensible why the person who is blind should be looked upon with reverence and felt to be equipped with unusual powers. In fiction, the most frequent stereotype of blind persons is that of the idealized and abnormally good person (Barker et al., 1953, p. 274). In religious practices, blind persons have been accorded privileged positions (Barker et al., 1953, p. 273). Modern Turkey regards persons without sight as indispensable assets to religious ceremonies and funerals (Maisel, 1953, p. 23). In Greek legend many clairvoyants were blind (Hentig, 1948b, p. 23). Among the Koreans it is believed that blind persons have acquired an inner vision and are therefore held in high esteem (Maisel, 1953).

For a review of the factors important in resolving expectation discrepancy, the case of deafness serves well. Commonly, with respect to a person who is deaf, the outsider holds higher expectations than are borne out by what ensues because the deaf person, looking just like anyone else, is expected to act like anyone else. The outsider, expecting the person who is deaf to be able to communicate easily, encounters difficulties in this regard. Reconciliation of this expectation discrepancy is then initiated. The expectation of the outsider may be revised downward. The outsider may seek to understand "what is wrong" and may discover that his or her expectations were unrealistic in the light of the newly uncovered facts. If in the process of expectation revision the difficulties of deafness are seen in the light of coping rather than succumbing, positive evaluation of the person will occur.

However, there will undoubtedly be strong resistance against lowering the expectation level where there is a strong wish for the person to hear better, this not infrequently being true of someone close to the person. In this case, the outsider may alter the apparent reality by regarding the discrepancy as a temporary one that will be erased through the efforts of continued language training and medical advance; the apparent reality is looked upon as eventually rising upward to close the gap. In the meantime, insofar as the gap persists, the apparent reality will be perceived as progressively better. Thus, the person with a hearing impairment who undergoes surgery, and those close to him or her, will tend to feel that there is improvement in hearing even when this is not the case. Eventually, it is possible for the forces of objective reality to become so great as to make such misperception difficult and the person may then turn to a reevaluation of the expectation level.

There are instances of expectation discrepancy in which both the expectations and the apparent reality resist change. This is true of some outsiders where there is neither a need or opportunity to comprehend the difficulties of deafness nor a need to shift the apparent reality upward. The discrepancy is resolved by anormalizing the person who is then dubbed strange or even bewitched. Anormalization that reconciles a discrepancy in which the expectations are lower than the apparent reality leads to sanctification, but where the expectations surpass the apparent reality, anormalization leads to vilification.

It should not be supposed that one attempt at resolving expectation discrepancy is sufficient. The following newspaper account reveals the shifting interplay of the different forms of resolution as the reporter describes the feats of a clarinetist who is blind (*Kansas City Times,* November 9, 1964; italics added):

Newspaper Account	Comment
Headline: Blind Clarinetist Never Misses Step or Note	By its grossly exaggerated statement, this headline reveals anormalization. After all no human being *never* misses a step or note.
Everytime Louis Fioritto, 17 years old, marches with the 120-piece Euclid High School band, fellow bandsmen *shake their heads in wonderment.*	Shaking one's head suggests an attempt at altering the manifest reality. One shakes one's head from side to side, a movement indicating disbelief, as if saying, "It can't be!" Contrast this with nodding one's head in agreement. The added phrase, "in wonderment," perhaps suggests an ongoing explanatory search that may lead to other forms of discrepancy resolution.

The youth who wears dark glasses *never misses a beat regardless of how* fancy or highstepping the routine.

Evidently the attempt at altering the apparent reality was unsuccessful, for the youth continues to be seen as marching right along with the others. The reporter, then, again resorts to anormalization, this time buttressing the attempt by affirming and underscoring the great difficulty of the routines.

Yet they keep wondering how someone who was born blind can do it. . . .

Once again the attempt at anormalization gives way. The reporter appears to be searching for some realistic explanation leading to expectation revision.

A member of the band as a clarinetist since junior high, Louis asked Dale Harper, band director, for a chance to march at the football games. *He was a success at the first practice.*

Expectation revision is still not in evidence. Rather a bit of anormalization persists. Is anyone a success at the first practice?

All Louis needs during the drills is a nudge in the right direction supplied by his close friend, Rip Baldini. Louis and Rip say they "sometimes mess things up in practice just to keep the rest of the band on its toes."

With the discovery of the cues used by Louis in performing the routines, *expectation revision* finally begins to reduce the initial discrepancy between expectation and reality. Performance errors are no longer denied, but their interpretation still preserves the original anormalization method of discrepancy resolution.

A number of factors significant in the emergence and resolution of expectation discrepancy have been discussed, namely, spread, the position of the perceiver as insider or outsider, the wishes of the perceiver, the opportunity for reevaluation, and the ease with with which expectations and the apparent reality can be changed.

The reader is invited to examine a variety of personally experienced incidents in which the requirement of mourning, and/or the expectation discrepancy can be seen to play a significant role. It would be well to include nondisability- as well as disability-connected events. It is then that the wide-ranging application of these concepts will become more fully appreciated. Also, such a review will help to underscore the point that the social psychology of disability is truly a general social psychology whose principles have bearing upon diverse situations and fields not restricted to problems of disablement.

Chapter 6
Frustration and Uncertainty

In light of the discussion thus far, it is not surprising to learn that a physical disability is commonly *viewed* as bringing about excessive frustration. Thus, few persons would see anything contestable about such a statement as: "The handicap of seriously defective vision or no vision is so obviously shackling, so frustrating, so dispossessing, that when borne by a child small wonder those who love him feel he is intolerably afflicted" (Stern & Castendyck, 1950, p. 73). A second assumption is that irritability and other negative effects of frustration are more common among the ranks of those with physical disabilities. Yet none of these assumptions is borne out by research and systematic observation.

The word "systematic" should be emphasized, for certainly a casual and haphazard glance at everyday experience seems to verify the *a priori* connections between disability and frustration. Examining relevant research and attempting to account for the myths will lead to a clearer understanding of the significance and management of frustration as applied to problems of disability.

EVALUATING THE FIRST COMMONSENSE NOTION: AMOUNT OF FRUSTRATION

The first assumption that must be considered is that persons with disabilities are more frequently frustrated than the nondisabled. The few available studies, however, actually belie the *generality* of this assumption.

Shere (1954) studied the parent-child relationships of thirty pairs of twins, one of whom in each pair was a child with cerebral palsy. The pairs included ten pairs of identical twins, nine pairs of like-sex fraternal twins, and eleven pairs of boy-girl twins, ranging in age from $1\frac{1}{2}$ to 16 years. The disability of twelve twins was judged to be mild to moderate, nine considerable, and nine extreme. This study is one of the few systematic twin studies found in disability research.

The following statistically significant findings, based on several rating procedures, are relevant to the present discussion. The behavior of the parents toward the twin with cerebral palsy as compared to the able-bodied twin differed only in certain areas:

Parents tended to more understanding of the potentialities of the twin with cerebral palsy and to get along with him or her with less friction. They also tended to expect the twin who did not have cerebral palsy to assume more responsibilities and to act in a more mature manner than his or her age or capabilities warranted. Moreover, the parents appeared to be aware of the problems of the child with cerebral palsy but oblivious to those of the twin. The author concluded that the lack of conformity exhibited by the able-bodied twin and the consequent disciplinary friction with the parents was part of the behavior pattern of the rejected child.

In other areas the behavior of the parents was actually more desirable toward the able-bodied child than it was toward his or her twin. The able-bodied child was accepted in an objective matter-of-fact way, accorded a place in all family activities, given help when necessary, protected from real dangers, encouraged to participate in new activities, and allowed to govern his or her own activities as much as possible. In contrast, the parents tended to overprotect the twin with cerebral palsy, to give the child little or no active part in forming family policies, and to direct the child's activities in a loving but arbitrary manner.

The behavior of the twins differed. The able-bodied child was more curious and more ready to explore than was the twin with cerebral palsy. However, the child with cerebral palsy was more cheerful than the able-bodied twin. The child with cerebral palsy was less easily excited and less prone to violent emotional outbursts, was less stubborn and resistant to authority, was more willing to wait one's turn without becoming impatient, and was not as sensitive to either flattery or disparagement as was the able-bodied twin.

These findings lead to the important conclusion that, for this sample, those children with cerebral palsy experienced fewer frustrations in their relationships with their parents than did their nondisabled twins.

The ecological study by Barker & H. Wright (1955) is even more startling in its findings for it covers naturally occurring situations both inside and outside the home. The three findings most pertinent to the topic of frustration are based on behavioral observations throughout an entire day in the lives of twelve nondisabled children and four children with appreciable disabilities (inability to walk following polio, cerebral palsy, spinal bifida, congenital heart dysfunction). The children were between 2 and 11 years of age. The number of children is small, but the consistency of the findings and their theoretical implications give them an importance of the first order:

1. For each of the children, there was a relatively low frequency of episodes ending in success, frustration, and failure. Summing the percentages for these three experiences yields a median of 2 percent for the group. Thus, "life for these children appears to have been less a matter of high ups and low downs than one might be led to expect from the amount of attention often given to these outcomes of action in research and writings on children's behavior" (p. 298).
2. For every child the percentage of good endings—attainment, gratification, and success—is higher than the percentage of bad endings—nonattainment, frustration, failure. (The rating "success" was reserved for episodes in which there was clear evidence of pride in having accomplished something difficult. Satisfaction in goal accomplishment without especially crediting the self was rated as "attainment," or as "gratification" where credit was bestowed upon another.)
3. There is no suggestion of difference between the nondisabled children and the children with disabilities; a contention that motor disability necessarily implies more frequent occurrence of bad episode endings is simply not supported.

The far-reaching implications of these findings are conveyed in the following major conclusion: "The outcome of behavior episodes in so far as it is related to release of tension, success, failure, frustration, etc., is in children virtually unrelated to motor and intellectual abilities. The fact that the 2-year-olds and the 10-year-olds, the physically disabled and the normal children were perceived to experience the same episode outcomes would seem to indicate that some governing apparatus is functioning to protect the weak and disabled from too great [negative] psychological consequences of their limitations" (p. 465).

Both the twin study and the ecological study are studies of children. To my knowledge, no comparable observational studies of adults exist to indicate whether or not the amount of frustration tends to be greater among those with disabilities as compared to their able-bodied counterparts. There is, however, a relevant questionnaire study that dealt with the life satisfaction of adults (Cameron et al., 1973). In this study the responses of almost 200 persons with various physical disabilities were compared with those of a "normal" control group. No differences were found between the two groups in their response to the following items: Do you find life frustrating? (never, infrequently, sometimes, frequently, constantly). These days my life is (just great, more than satisfactory, satisfactory, less than satisfactory, just miserable).

A matter must be cleared up: Because physical status may not be related to the *amount* of frustration does *not* mean that the issue of frustration in the lives of people with disabilities can be ignored. Some frustrating situations may be inevitable or even desirable from the learning point of view, but others represent injustices and discriminatory practices. The amount of frustration as such may not be as important as the significance of particular frustrating conditions.

In any case, it is the commonsense notion that disability generally produces extraordinary or intolerable levels of frustration that is being challenged here. This assumption would not be so disturbing to persons with a disability were it not for the fact that an attitude of devaluating pity often accompanies it.

EVALUATING THE SECOND COMMONSENSE NOTION: FRUSTRATED PERSONALITIES

Sometimes it is assumed that persons with a disability react more immaturely to frustrating situations, that they are more irritable and easily frustrated, for example. Studies with adequate controls challenge the validity of the assumption.

The following study of the effect of disability on behavior in frustrating situations is important because it exercised a degree of scientific care rarely found in disability research (Kahn, 1951). Three groups were compared, each consisting of fifteen children between the ages of 9 and 11: A group with normal hearing, a moderately hard-of-hearing group with loss of 15 to 35 decibels, and a severely hard-of-hearing group with still greater losses. The first two groups attended public schools; the severely hard-of-hearing children attended a special day school. The subjects were equated on age, sex, school grade, socioeconomic status, and intelligence level.

Two measures of reaction to frustration were used. One was based on the responses of the subjects to a projective test consisting of twenty-four pictures involving frustration (Rosenzweig et al., 1948). The children were directed to write down what they thought the child in each picture would reply to the person talking to him. The second measure was based on reaction to frustration in a realistic situation. The children were directed to arrange sixteen blocks according to a specific pattern. The test was discontinued when the child had been thwarted by ten of the designs.

The reactions of the children in the two situations were rated on a dozen categories: Behavior was rated as extrapunitive when aggression was directed toward the external world, as intrapunitive when aggression was directed against the self, and as impunitive when the child tried to avoid blame and aggression entirely by passing over the frustrating situations lightly. The behavior was also rated according to the degree to which it showed "obstacle-dominance" (concentration on the barrier itself), "ego-defense" (defense of the self), and "need-persistence" (emphasis on solution). Finally, the behavior was evaluated in terms of six variants of ego-defensive scores.

The main overall findings may be summarized as follows: ". . . few differences exist between the groups in terms of response to frustration. What differences do appear . . . seem to indicate a consistent tendency [though slight] for the hard-of-hearing children to meet frustration more constructively than the non-handicapped children" (p. 58). The evidence strongly suggests that these children do not have lower thresholds for frustration than normally hearing children.

A second study compared thirty adolescents who had moderate to severe orthopedic disabilities with a comparable group of nondisabled young people (Fitzgerald, 1950). Initially, the line of reasoning guiding the research was as follows: (1) Limitation of normal mobility and activity implies the presence of a frustrating situation; (2) increased frustration, according to the frustration-aggression hypothesis, results in an increased tension state (see Dollard et al., 1939); and (3) therefore, the reactions of the subjects with orthopedic disabilities might be expected to deviate from normal because of increased tension.

Contrary to expectations, reaction to frustration as manifested by behavior with difficult form boards was not differentiable on grounds of physical status. Instead, interview data led the investigator to conclude that the ability to perform a task under stress is more closely related to personal feelings and attitudes about home than to status as a physically handicapped or physically normal adolescent. Thus, the adolescents who felt dissatisfied with their home life did more poorly than those reporting fewer deviant home conditions.

Our task now is to account for the persistence of the myths that equate disability with frustration.

THE SIGNIFICANCE AND MANAGEMENT OF FRUSTRATION

Accounting for the Myths

The reasons disability and frustration are so readily linked are varied. We shall number them in order to highlight their different slants on the problem:

1. Fundamental is the proclivity of the human being to view the situation of another from one's own perspective (see position of the person as insider versus outsider, pp. 47–51). Even in empathy we typically react the way we imagine we would feel in a like sitution without realizing that new learnings and adjustive forces within our own psychic economy would so alter the meaning of the situation that our emotional reaction would correspondingly be different.

Thus, in the following scene, as Lila is viewed laboriously building a tower, most persons would probably feel an "anticipatory" frustration that in fact was not there at all. Lila is 8½ years old. Cerebral palsy has affected her hand and arm movements so that only with a great deal of patience and persistence does she manage to accomplish tasks requiring fine movements. Of course, the judgment that it took a great deal of patience and persistence is itself based on the norms imposed by the outsider; Lila may not have perceived her effort that way at all. It took Lila more than two minutes to place the six blocks one upon the other, a task that could ordinarily be completed by a child her age in a fraction of the time:

> Lila picked up the red block carefully and set it down directly in front of her.
> Then she slowly picked up the orange block. She laboriously placed it on top of the red one.
> Lila carefully picked up the yellow block. As she picked it up, it fell out of her hand. She picked it up again. The yellow block was carefully put on top of the orange one.
> Then she picked up the green block. It took her almost twice as long to put the green block on top of the yellow one. Finally she got the green one fitted on top of the yellow one.
> She picked up the blue block. She laboriously tried to put the blue one on top of the green one but the tongue and groove didn't match. She looked at it for a moment.

Then she slowly took the blue one off. She put it down on the desk. She turned it around in her hand. Then again she carefully tried to put it back up. This time she put it on so that it fit securely in place.

She took the smallest block, the purple one, and carefully put it on top. After a few moments she got it in place.

As soon as she got the block in place, she banged her hand and squealed in delight. [Barker & H. Wright, 1948–1951][1]

Lila would have been frustrated only if her goal had been to complete her task in short order, for then she would have been blocked by her physical limitations. Instead, the goal itself was molded in terms of the reality of her situation.

2. In addition to being unaware of adjustive changes within the *outlook* of the person, the outsider also tends to be unfamiliar with specific ways and aids in circumventing difficulties. Instead, the disability is perceived as an insurmountable barrier to the achievement of many goals. For example, many persons would be certain that the following activities are closed to those who are blind: playing ball, mowing the lawn, traveling, roller skating, and so on—until the list becomes frighteningly long. It is with surprise and admiration that sighted people learn that none of these activities is foreclosed, that the manner of carrying them out can be appropriately modified.

3. Because disability is perceived as a negative state, any frustration that may in fact be connected with the disability will tend to be perceived by the outsider as especially frustrating.

4. Another aspect of this spread phenomenon is what we have called physique as prime mover (see pp. 33–34, 37–39), the phenomenon that gives disability such a central position that it is held accountable for unrelated events in the life of the person. Accordingly, whatever failures and frustrations the person with a disability may experience tend to be seen as disability-connected.

5. The presumption that disability brings about frustration leads the observer to expect frustration, an expectation that highlights evidence supporting the expectation and suppresses or distorts facts that conflict with it. Perception selectively serves one's biases and expectations in many situations (see Chapter 5).

These reasons explain why the outsider tends to make an exaggerated claim for the connection between disability and frustration. But obviously it should not be implied that frustration is never tied to the fact of disability. The following incident, one of many that could have been selected, shows that (1) the person is unable to reach his goal because of limitations imposed by his disability and (2) the

[1]From *One of a series of records made in connection with the natural living conditions of children* by R. G. Barker & H. F. Wright. Printed by permission of R. G. Barker.

totality of circumstances makes it difficult to alleviate the frustration by a shift in goals or in means. It is the same 4-year-old Wally whom we met trying to push his wagon up the bank. He is unable to walk because of a polio attack a few years before. The scene is a backyard shed where he and his cousins, Ben and Jim, ages 6 and 8, are playing:

Both Jim and Ben were on an old auto seat in the southwest corner of the shed. Between that and the doorway where Wally was, lay quite a bit of debris, including some heavy electric wire.

Ben said invitingly and commandingly, "Come and get on this, Wally," meaning on the auto seat. Wally paid no attention to them but crawled away toward the door from the shed into the Wolfson's garage.

Ben came to Wally and said shortly, "I'll carry you." He picked Wally up under the arms and proceeded to drag him across the debris and wire to the auto seat.

As he squirmed, Wally protested loudly, "I don't want over there." Wally's reluctance seemed just to make Ben more insistent. He dragged him over and dumped him on the end of the auto seats.

Wally, with impotent anger, said, crying as he said it, "Take me back, I don't want over here. Take me back."

Jim said in a lofty and quite nasty way, "You can take yourself over. You can take your *own* self over."

This enraged Wally. He shouted, "You big shit-ass, you. Goddamn it, you take me over."

Ben and Jim joined forces and taunted, "Take yourself over."

Wally, whipped into a frenzy, yelled, "Goddamn it," again. "You *will* take me over."

The two boys together teased, "No. Take yourself over."

Wally slipped off the end of the auto seat. Crying and shouting, he tried to make his way back to the shed door, crawling over the debris. He got entangled in the heavy electric wire that was in the way.

Jim and Ben took hold of the wire and pulled on it to pull him back. One of them said playfully, "We've got a big fish on this wire."

Wally took hold of the wire but his strength was not sufficient to counterbalance that of the other two boys. He was in a frenzy. "Goddamn you," he yelled, angry and crying.

He fumbled around, evidently for something to throw at the boys. Wally picked up a corn cob and threw it at them as hard as he could. One of them immediately threw it back at Wally. Wally threw another corn cob. They threw one back at him. Jim and Ben were teasing Wally; they were not angry.

Wally was really angry and obviously wanted to throw something at them to hurt them. He got hold of the handle of the big ax. He said fiercely, "I'll throw *this* at you," as he tried to lift it. It was too heavy for him to really lift adequately.

Ben immediately, recognizing Wally's real anger, came and took hold of the ax and pulled it away from him.

Wally picked up a piece of a bushel basket that was broken and threw that at the boys but didn't hit them. Then he found a short heavy board and pulled it up and started to throw it at them.

Ben came and easily took that away from him.

Wally pulled himself loose from the wire. He crawled over to the doorway and got out of the door, crying and whimpering as he crawled toward the kitchen door.

His mother appeared at the kitchen door. I [observer] heard him call to his mother from the ground, "They've been teasing me," complaining bitterly. [Barker & H. Wright, 1948–1951].[2]

It is clear that Wally was frustrated to the point of tears and could do little about it. It is also clear that if he were sound of limb he could have escaped and avoided much of the unbearable frustration.

Although frustration heaped upon frustration as a vague and overgeneralized negative-spread effect is erroneously perceived as characterizing the lives of people with disabilities, *awareness of the nature and specific sources of frustration* is nonetheless typically lacking on the part of the outsider. Addressing himself to the experience of living with multiple sclerosis, Ernest Hirsch writes:

> As with so many other conditions, a person who is not suffering from multiple sclerosis cannot truly appreciate how someone else feels when he's afflicted with this illness. While the well-meaning person may assure me that he knows what I'm going through, this simply can't be so. Another person can't know what it feels like to be tired and weak through and through, what it feels like to be concerned with how to go about getting into a friend's home, or how it feels when one is not able to use his eating utensils as well as he would have liked or cannot speak as well as he had wanted, how it feels to be concerned about what both the immediate and the distant future will bring, or how to open a book or fold a newspaper successfully. [Hirsch, 1977, p. 157][3]

The Value of Frustration: Coping and Learning

A matter of considerable importance for disability-connected frustration concerns the possible growth-promoting value of frustration. Since frustration itself is such a negatively experienced emotional state, it is not surprising that its negative consequences tend to be emphasized with little attention being given to possible positive

[2]From *One of a series of records made in connection with the natural living conditions of children* by R. G. Barker & H. F. Wright. Printed by permission of R. G. Barker.

[3]From *Starting over: The autobiographical account of a psychologist's experience with multiple sclerosis* by E. A. Hirsch. Reprinted by permission of Christopher Publishing House.

by-products. And yet it is virtually a truism that some frustration is a precursor to much that is important in learning. Imagine what it would be like if gratification were simultaneous with desire. One would neither experience gratification nor desire! More than that, psychologists are of the opinion that the baby could not learn to distinguish the self as an entity different from the surrounding environment if life were frustration-free.

Besides, when some activities are blocked, energy may be released for other purposes. This is one basis for advocating sublimation as an important psychological adaptation in accepting necessary restrictions of the social and physical environment. Psychoanalysts hold that sublimating sexual impulses renders the psychic energies serviceable for other purposes, such as art, science, and creative enterprise in general, or in the negative case, for asocial ends. The main problem, then, is to channel energy constructively. Undoubtedly there are more or less permanent renunciations demanded of all members of society as the price for the benefits of social living, but these "socialization privations" may be turned to constructive outlets.

Furthermore, the fact that catastrophe and other unplanned, trying events do inevitably occur requires that individuals develop a tolerance for frustration if one is to remain undefeated by them. This tolerance doubtless cannot arise in the absence of prior experience with frustration. Rosenzweig (1938, p. 153) believes that frustration tolerance can be fostered by allowing children to experience small amounts of frustration, amounts they can handle. Extreme deviation from this optimal dose will produce difficulty. If children are overindulged, they will develop insufficient tolerance. If, on the other hand, they are frustrated beyond their ability to cope with distress, low frustration tolerance or complexes may be created and the ground prepared for behavior disorders.

In a significant study on improving children's reactions to failure (Keister, 1937), the training program was designed to introduce the children progressively to more and more difficult tasks, thus enabling them to build up mature and desirable responses to later difficult situations. During the training, the children were encouraged to persist with tasks that were difficult for them, depend less on an adult for help, offer fewer rationalizations in the face of failure, and attack a problem with a certain amount of composure. The children who experienced the training showed marked gains, whereas a comparable group of untrained children showed little change in their habitual response to frustrating situations.

Analyzing the effects of frustration from another point of view, Barker (1938) considered two different kinds of problems: (1) the effect of frustration upon ability to overcome the difficulty from which the frustration arises and (2) the effect of frustration upon ability when an individual gives up and turns to other activities; in other words, what is the effect of a frustrated need upon the level of behavior not directly related to the satisfaction of that need? In both cases, the reaction may lead either to a lowering of intellectual (cognitive) functioning, as when regression occurs, or to creative behavior of a high order.

In the following experiment, though the typical reaction was one of regression and primitivization, some of the children showed an increase in their level of constructiveness (Barker, Dembo, & Lewin, 1941). Thirty nursery school children were observed individually on two occasions: first, in a standardized playroom where the child's play was rated by observers on a constructiveness scale; secondly, when the room had been enlarged and the old toys incorporated with more attractive play materials. After the child became thoroughly interested in the new toys, the situation was changed to a frustrating one by making the toys unobtainable, even though they could still be seen through a wire barrier. The old toys were available, and the amount of constructive play with them was compared with the previous play in the standard situation.

Barker makes clear that the constructive level of behavior is depressed when the person is torn between *preoccupation* with the frustrated goal and the current goal. On the other hand, constructiveness may be enhanced when the stepped-up tension stemming from frustration is deflected toward other goals that are able basically to satisfy the same needs or raises the energy level of a person who would otherwise be more passive in the situation (Barker, 1938, p. 149).

Frustration may also stimulate the person to new solutions of current difficulties. One's efforts, however, cannot be so intensely concentrated on the goal or its barrier that one becomes shortsighted for lack of adequate perspective. Along with persistence, the person must achieve sufficient flexibility to survey alternatives.

Frustration can even unite people as they seek the support of shared interests. Witness the thousands of self-help groups in this connection. In one experiment (M. E. Wright, 1943), friendship between children increased when they experienced a frustrating situation together. The conclusion is inevitable that the frustration of goal achievement and the failure of tension reduction may lead to a variety of adaptive *or* maladaptive behaviors.

With respect to the problem of adjusting to disability, the previously mentioned governing apparatus that protects "the weak and disabled from too great psychological consequences of their limitations" (see p. 98) may be placed within two foci—namely, *adjustive changes within the person* on the one hand and *environmental accommodations* on the other. *The value of reducing excessive frustration is not to eliminate frustration from the lives of people, but to enable the person to deal with and learn to tolerate new frustrations that inevitably accompany new challenges.*

With respect to the person side of the frustration problem, we have already pointed out that considerable learning often takes place in coping with frustration. The person learns about frustration tolerance as well as the source of the frustration, what can and cannot be done, and the nature of the physical environment and its human inhabitants, all of which are important differentiations of reality. A general consequence of such learning is that one adjusts one's goals, referred to as the level of aspiration, according to the experience of success and failure. With success, aspirations usually rise; with failure they decline. This balancing mechanism of the level of aspiration can be thrown out of kilter, but it is certainly not typical for a person to continue to concentrate on unattainable goals.

Sometimes the adjustment involves not the lowering of goals but finding a way to circumvent the difficulty. This restructuring of paths to goals is seen when Wally, unable to push his wagon straight up the incline, turned it at an angle and, with the help of other adaptive maneuvers, achieved his goal. (For details of this incident see pp. 3–4.) Sometimes specific features of a goal are modified to accord with one's abilities. Examples are wheelchair sports and beep baseball for those who are blind. Reducing frustration sometimes involves substituting a goal of an entirely different character, yet one that meets important needs.

Changes in values held by the person accompany these shifts in goal orientation. We shall have a good deal more to say about value changes important in acceptance of loss in Chapter 8, but suffice it here to point out that new and different satisfactions emerge as the person copes with frustration, disappointment, and the limitations of disability. Ernest Hirsch (1977) addressed this point as he gradually came to terms with great physical incapacitation resulting from 21 years of multiple sclerosis. He required considerable help in toileting, bathing, and dressing; he had difficulty lifting even light objects; he could barely sign his name; and yet he writes:

> I've become increasingly grateful for being able to successfully perform very little things in life. For example, I'm grateful to sit well in my chair so that I don't have uncomfortable pressure from my pillow. [p. 111]

I'm very pleased when I can stand with help. And I'm thankful when bowel and urinary functions proceed without difficulty. And I'm glad when I can read in the evening without becoming too tired. My values certainly have changed, and I find myself deeply appreciating things that most people take very much as a matter of course. [p. 112]

Often I experience a feeling that "it's not really that important." I no longer have the same striving for status or for fame. I feel much more satisfied with what I am, with what I've achieved, with what I probably will be able to achieve. . . . [p. 159][4]

It must be remembered that not only adjustive changes within the person, but also environmental accommodations, are important in reducing frustration. Examples of the latter are: considerations in the home that take into account the special needs of each person, school curricula geared to individual and group differences, architecture that accommodates the varying physical attributes of people, legislation on behalf of persons with disabilities. These are frustration-reducing accommodations. On the other hand, the social environment, through mistaken notions, lack of interest, or thoughtlessness can contribute greatly to unnecessary frustration in the lives of people with disabilities.

Unfortunately, the person-environment governing apparatus is not foolproof, either for persons with physical limitations or for those without. The world has all too many persons who are excessively frustrated, distraught, bothered, unfulfilled. On the person side, one of the most common and powerful factors militating against constructive substitution of means and goals in coping with frustration is "idolizing normal standards" (see pp. 121–123). If the person feels valued in relation to the degree to which his or her goals and behavior are the same as they would have been without the disability, then deeply felt persistent frustration is bound to occur. The following protocol is of a counseling session with a 16-year-old young man with cerebral palsy. It shows the depths of despair that can result from rigid adherence to standards of the nondisabled state:

YOUNG MAN: "I just don't know why the doctors let me live when I was born. I'm no use to anyone the way I am."
COUNSELOR: "You feel that you are of no value to society and that discourages you."
YOUNG MAN: "Yes, I know what I want to do and I can talk O.K., but

[4]From *Starting over: The autobiographical account of a psychologist's experience with multiple sclerosis* by E. A. Hirsch. Reprinted by permission of Christopher Publishing House.

every time I try to do anything I'm stymied. I can't walk or even eat without some help."

COUNSELOR: "You feel, because of your physical condition, that you can't do many of the things you want to do and you feel frustrated when this happens."

YOUNG MAN: "It's worse than that. When I can't succeed in something and when I know I could succeed if I weren't a C.P. [cerebral palsy], I get more than discouraged because I'm so helpless. You're stuck and you hate yourself for being stuck." [Cruickshank, 1948, pp. 81–82]

Some will hold that with such a severe disability, overwhelming frustration is inevitable, and yet we must remind ourselves that it was this young man's vision of accomplishments unfettered by disability ("I know I could succeed if I weren't a C.P.") that was crucial in fixing his aspirations so rigidly that appropriate modifications could not bring satisfaction. Contrast this case with that of Hirsch, described earlier (p. 103), who, despite equal incapacitation, could say, "But I find my life quite satisfying and enjoyable . . ." (1977, p. 141). It must be emphasized that value changes and aspiration changes represent the person side of meeting the challenge of frustration. There is of course an environmental side.

The environmental side needs special attention to counteract the tendency to concentrate on the person in accounting for frustration and failure (see "Person versus Environmental Attribution," pp. 39–47). This tendency is especially strong where the person is perceived to be atypical. In the frustrating incident involving Wally earlier (pp. 102–103), was the frustration due primarily to Wally's limitations or to the teasing of the older boys? To what extent were insufficient environmental accommodations responsible for the despair of the 16-year-old young man with cerebral palsy?

The main theme of this discussion is that though a disability may act as a barrier to the achievement of certain goals, in adjusting to this reality, the person tends to alter his or her aspirations, values, and way of life in such a way that oppressively frustrating situations are avoided. Add to this the environmental accommodations that take special needs into account and we can begin to understand why lives filled with frustration are not generally more common among persons with a disability than among the able-bodied.

In any case, it should be understood that the level of frustration cannot determine issues of justice and human rights. Injustice may be great when frustration is high or low. Many institutional environments are not especially frustrating but neither are they conducive to human development. Resigning oneself to difficult circumstances may reduce frustration, but may also mean resigning oneself to injustice. Raising consciousness and expectations often increases frustration in people who previously had "known their place." When to strive to overcome limitations either of the self or of the environment and when to accept them is as much a question of values as of reality.

UNCERTAINTY AND NEW PSYCHOLOGICAL SITUATIONS

Puzzling over a problem, applying for a job, being in an unfamiliar town, entering a social situation well under way, all have in common the fact that in certain respects the situation is psychologically a new one. This means that the directions toward a desired goal are unknown and that the behavior one embarks upon is simultaneously positive and negative; that is, each act may place one closer to the goal (positive) or move one further from it (negative). Such a situation provokes cautious behavior. To the extent that the situation is a dangerous or crucial one, it provokes anxiety and insecurity as well.[5]

Examples of Insecurity

Situations that are psychologically new in the sense that they are perceptually unclear, unstructured, or ambiguous arise in regard to a person's disability when (1) The person is unsure as to whether the situation can be managed physically. For example, architectural barriers may pose a problem. (2) The person is unsure of the reception by others. For example, the person may not know whether he or she will be accepted or rejected, shown sympathy or devaluating pity, reacted to with fear or treated naturally or ignored. (3) The person is unsure of his or her own self-concept. For example, there may be difficulty in reconciling a physically imperfect body with personality characteristics that are acceptable and even complimentary. See p. 233 for the anguish and conflict suffered by a young woman every time her mirror image shattered her self-illusions.

Whether or not a physical disability in general tends to increase the frequency with which new psychological situations are encoun-

---

[5]For a more detailed and systematic account of the properties of new psychological situations, see Barker et al. (1953, pp. 30–37); the thinking therein stems from the work of Lewin (1936, 1938). The concept of new psychological situations and their derived behavior—namely, behavior characterized by conflict, emotionality, alertness, and instability—has been applied to a variety of cases, such as adolescents (Lewin, 1939; Barker et al., 1953), autocratic groups (Lippitt, 1940), and persons with disabilities (Barker et al., 1953; Meyerson, 1955b).

tered requires ecological investigation. Some psychologists have taken a firm position that it does (see Meyerson, 1955b, p. 48). But relative frequency is always difficult to establish and depends on many inconstant conditions. If one argues, for example, that the able-bodied person is not troubled by unknown architectural features (such as whether a building has steps or an elevator), one can counter that the able-bodied person might more frequently engage in activities that would involve other kinds of uncertain physical-geographic situations. Whether in greater or lesser degree, nonetheless, the problem of uncertainty resulting from new psychological situations seems especially salient in the case of particular physical disabilities: for example, deafness, blindness, epilepsy, and progressive disorders.

The following account shows the extreme consequences of uncertainty created by seizures that overtake the person without warning:

> When I have an attack, I sort of go into my shell. I stay at home, am absent from school and just sit around thinking. I am afraid that I might get another attack any minute. When a few days have passed since my attack, I may go out of the house, perhaps for a walk. But I am still very anxious about my physical condition and make sure that I get home quickly. It takes about a week before I feel like returning to school and seeing outside people. Even when I'm back at school I can't help thinking about getting an attack there, or in the street or in the subway. It seems as if I'm always ready to jump within my shell, as I like to put it, at the slightest disturbance. [Arluck, 1941, pp. 64–65]

In this case, the persistently "new" psychological character of the person's situation was not due to his never having experienced seizures before but to his inability to structure the situation in a stable way because at any moment events could shift dangerously beyond control. The tension, caution, conflict, frustration, alertness to every cue—behaviors derivable from the forces characterizing new psychological situations—are apparent. The fact that most people with epilepsy are able to control seizures with proper medication means that they are spared the fearfulness of unexpected physical assault. Even in such cases, anxiety-arousing new psychological situations may occur because of uncertainty of social reception or because of vacillation between identifying with the healthy and the sick (G. Lewin, 1957).

The insecurity of changes that threaten a person with a progressive disorder is described by Hirsch after years of living with multiple sclerosis:

With a progressive illness such as multiple sclerosis, . . . it's necessary that year after year, month after month, sometimes even week after week, new adaptations have to be made, adaptations which can last only as long as the condition remains the same. Since, even with a plateau, the condition usually does not remain the same for very long, new adaptations constantly have to be instituted. Perhaps worst of all is not knowing where things will eventually end. Will I be totally helpless? Will I be bedridden? Will I be able to move at all? By constant adaptation I mean that as one problem is vanquished and as peace is made with regard to it, this problem gives way to a new one, and this problem in turn gives way to another one, only for another to take *its* place. Thus, walking normally gives way to walking with a cane, the cane gives way to a walker, the walker gives way to pushing oneself in a wheelchair, and pushing oneself finally gives way to being pushed by another person. Similarly, writing gives way to typing, which gives way to printing, which gives way to only scrawling one's signature. [Hirsch, 1977, pp. 151–152][6]

That the uncertainty of new psychosocial situations is frequently independent of the fact of disability must also be recognized. Because the following incident clearly illustrates this and because it also demonstrates a type of behavior commonly occurring in new psychological situations, it is recounted in full. Karsten tells about the time he and a girl, both blind high-school students, were out together for the first time. Especially prominent is cautious, exploratory, trial-and-error behavior. Underlying tension and resulting frustration may be presumed. Notice that in this case the uncertainty is independent of the blindness:

. . . I found a small brick alcove jutting out from the wall with a high concrete step at its base. I brushed the snow from a small area, and we sat down on either side of it about three feet apart. The girl was a bit timid, I thought. For a long time we sat in silence. Snow settled on my hat. The cold air pried into my overcoat and through my shirt. I rummaged about in my brain trying to find something to talk about.

"It's kind of cold out tonight," I said finally.

The girl drew her coat more closely about her.

"Yes," she said, her head still turned straight ahead.

I shivered. I turned up my collar and wished that I had put on my winter underwear.

"I think it will be warmer tomorrow though, if it doesn't turn colder,"

[6]From *Starting over: The autobiographical account of a psychologist's experience with multiple sclerosis* by E. A. Hirsch. Reprinted by permission of Christopher Publishing House.

I went on. Words came out of me like a dull razor sawing through dry whiskers. The girl took a handkerchief from her purse and blew her nose cautiously.

"Yes," she said.

I had a vague feeling that things were not progressing. I put my hands in my pockets and curled my toes, trying to find a warm spot by the heel. There must be other interesting subjects that we could talk about!

"You live quite far from here, don't you?" I asked.

She deliberated.

"Yes," she said.

I was uncomfortable. I managed to keep some warmth in my hands and feet, but the concrete I was sitting on did not seem to warm up at all. We sat staring into the snow. The girl moved uneasily, but I said nothing. It was her turn to ask questions. I did not want to hog all the conversation. Snowflakes clattered loudly on the crown of my hat. I wondered what Ben and his girl were talking about on the other side of the building. My companion blew her nose again and turned slightly.

"Do you like that new song we are learning in chorus?" she asked.

I fumbled about for a brilliant answer. Our conversational infant needed a verbal whack that would put life into him.

"Yes," I replied.

She deliberated again.

"I think the sopranos sing a little flat, don't you?"

"Yes," I said.

We lapsed into another long and profound silence. My thoughts moved sluggishly, like broken ice on a prairie river. It was getting late. In a short time the girls would have to leave. Impulsively I put my hand on the concrete behind her back and leaned forward.

"My lips are kind of puckery tonight," I said nonchalantly.

"Are they?" she brightened. Her voice was like chocolate and raspberry jam. She leaned toward me. Her face was not over two feet away. "What do you suppose makes it?" she asked.

I took my hand from behind her back and turned the other way again.

"I don't know," I said, rubbing my lips reflectively. "Been practicing too much on my cornet, I guess. . . ."

We were half buried in snow when Ben and his girl came around the corner again. When the girls were two blocks or more away, Ben and I started trudging slowly along. Ben was silent. I wondered what he was thinking of—most likely of all the things he and his friend had talked about.

"What sort of a girl was she, Ben?" I asked.

Ben plodded along.

"Yes," he said hollowly.

I waited. He seemed unaware of my presence.

"I said: 'What sort of girl was she?' "

"Yes," Ben repeated mechanically.

I shook my head sadly and blew a cloud of steam inside my collar to thaw my cheeks. Together we trudged along over the drifts toward home. [Ohnstad, 1942, pp. 146–148][7]

Reducing Uncertainty and Anxiety

It is the coping spirit of the human being that pushes toward extracting whatever positives can be found in threatening situations with which one must live. We have been witness to Hirsch's anxiety in connection with multiple sclerosis (see pp. 110–111). Yet he sees certain advantages in progressive disorders as compared to sudden injury:

> This slow and constant adaptation, however, also has its advantages. In the severe spinal cord accident, for example, the patient is suddenly faced with a dreadful loss, a major need to change his entire style of life. In multiple sclerosis, on the other hand, although adaptations keep having to be made, they take place gradually, over a period of time, and they can therefore be prepared for. Constant adaptation, in other words, is easier in a way because it is slow, gradual and rarely a source of sudden, unexpected surprise. [Hirsch, 1977, p. 152][8]

Another approach to counteracting anxiety in new, threatening situations, one that is of the greatest importance, is to determine whether the anxiety arises because the person has not accepted the disability. Much uncertainty and tension stem from the fact that, in hiding one's disability, the person prevents clarification of behavior possibilities (see p. 147). The overwhelming anxiety that can be self-imposed in this way is seen in the account by Raymond Goldman, who, hard of hearing, could not tell when the teacher called upon him or what point in the text the recitation had reached (see pp. 129–130 for incident). If only Raymond had allowed himself to inform the teacher of his hearing difficulties, he could have been spared much of the uncertainty of a perceptually confused situation. He could have been placed in a strategic position to speech-read more adequately; someone could have followed along in the text with him, and so on.

Situations that are psychologically new differ from one another in an important respect: some are crucial and even dangerous to the

[7]Reprinted from *The world at my fingertips* by K. Ohnstad, published by Bobbs-Merrill.
[8]From *Starting over: The autobiographical account of a psychologist's experience with multiple sclerosis* by E. A. Hirsch. Reprinted by permission of Christopher Publishing House.

person and some are not. Being on thin ice, either literally or figuratively, is an example of a new and dangerous psychological situation. Working through a problem in automobile mechanics or in room decorating are examples of new but relatively safe psychological situations. It is safe even though the directions to the goal are not fully known and even though one is bound to make false steps in spite of caution. The safety accrues either from the fact that the inevitable false steps are reversible or because the worst eventuality, failure, is not crucial to the security of the person. As applied to disability, this means that a psychologically new situation may, with personal adjustment and environmental accommodations, shift from one that spells danger to one that is less threatening or not threatening at all.

First, as to the matter of reversibility. The person can develop facility in structuring otherwise unknown situations. In case of a hearing impairment, for example, the person can ask people to face him or her, to speak louder, to repeat. The person who is blind can begin to use a white cane or ask someone to accompany him or her when the need arises. Obviously, these actions are not independent of the person's acceptance of disability, which, as we shall see in Chapter 8, is contingent upon important changes within the value system of the person.

As for the matter of how crucial the situation is, this too, in many instances, is subject to reevaluation. If the self-esteem of the person hinges on whether one can converse like any normally hearing person, on whether one can find one's way around town unaided, on whether one can walk as far as the next person, then situations requiring these abilities are crucial and any perceptual unclarity will give rise not only to cautious behavior but to anxious behavior as well. But if, as a result of adjustive changes, individuals are able to accept their limitations, then failing to keep up with others is simply not decisive. They may remain alert as to how best to manage, but the emotionality of conflict and self-evaluation need not be prominent accompaniments.

The preceding coping devices pertain to the person side of the problem of reducing uncertainty. The social or environmental side of the problem is no less important. Architectural accessibility, social security programs, provision for interpreters for the deaf, all help to reduce unnecessary anxiety stemming from uncertainty.

We would like to stress that it is not the newness as such of psychological situations that should be avoided (though a superabundance of such situations, with the problem solving required, may become burdensome). If all situations were well structured—that is, if the directions to goals were always known—we would neither be alerted nor challenged to make new discoveries. Probably the notion of an optimum balance between the known and unknown is applicable here.

In this chapter, frustration and uncertainty were examined in terms of their sources, the positive and negative aspects of their consequences, and the conditions that mitigate their deleterious effects. The commonsense notion that oppressive frustration is a probable, if not inevitable, accompaniment of disability has been challenged by a review of pertinent research findings and theoretical considerations. However, reducing frustration is a valid goal that enables the person to become involved in new, challenging situations. It is also valid when issues of justice and injustice call into question certain frustrating conditions. Environmental accommodation and changes within the person must become the two foci in understanding how frustraton and the uncertainty of new psychological situations can be met satisfactorily. One of the main impediments to finding adequate solutions is the high value placed on "normal" standards of behavior.

Chapter 7
Disability and Self-Esteem

That positive attitudes are part of the social surroundings of persons with a disability may well contribute to the significant fact that feelings of inferiority are *not* more characteristic of people with disabilities as a group than of their able-bodied counterparts (see pp. 149–151). Nonetheless, many persons with a disability have such feelings (as do many nondisabled persons), and probably all have at some time during the course of their adjustment. We shall now turn our attention to feelings of shame and inferiority associated with having a disability.

Shame, self-pity, and inferiority are difficult psychological states, and the person will muster varied and persistent efforts to overcome them. The effort to raise one's self-esteem may be directed toward one's own self-acceptance, or toward hiding or weakening one's identification with the devalued group. The latter strategy is the focus of the present chapter; the struggle for self-acceptance is examined in the chapter that follows. The discussion draws heavily from the work of Dembo and her associates on the problem of adjustment to misfortune (1956; reprinted 1975).

"AS IF" BEHAVIOR

In the initial stage of adjustment the person commonly tries, tenuously or more resolutely, to conceal his or her disability—and for understandable reasons. The person, like others of the general culture, typically views disability as something that detracts from one's acceptability. The obvious way to eliminate the negative consequences is to eliminate the fact of disability. Where this can be accomplished through surgical and other therapeutic procedures, the person will feel relieved and may objectively effect a change from the handicapped to the nonhandicapped position. Where this cannot be accomplished, however, the person is likely to attempt to hide, forget, or even deny what is viewed as a deficiency. The need to cover up in order to be acceptable as a person may be so strong that, even when the deviation is minor and temporary, the individual may fumble through patent devices: thus 17-year-old Chip "went about grinning with his tongue turned over to cover the almost unnoticeable gap" left by a recently extracted eye tooth (Linduska, 1947, p. 128). The person may even succeed in denying painful facts to oneself. The psychoanalytic literature on repression leaves no doubt that escape forces may be so strong as to alter one's memory and perception of the unacceptable.

I do not wish to imply that all efforts to cover up stem from personal depreciation. A particular fact about oneself may be accepted and yet concealed because of the belief that awareness on the part of others would contribute to disturbed social relations. This is one basis on which the cosmetic hand instead of the hook or no prosthesis is recommended in casual relationships (Dembo & Tane-Baskin, 1955).

Sometimes the concern is that others will make more of the disability than it warrants. A person who is color-blind writes:

> I must admit to a reticence to reveal my color deficiency because . . . this disclosure leads to questions which imply that defective color vision *must be a problem.* Another attitude which I sometimes meet is best described as solicitous: The individual who wants to help me by naming the colors of objects. The danger in this kind of treatment is that the color-blind person can come to believe that . . . he really does have a problem. [Snyder, 1973, p. 54][1]

Sometimes the concern is that knowledge of a disability may create barriers to acceptance in employment or other situations, thus

[1]Synder, C. R. The psychological implications of being color blind. *The Journal of Special Education,* 1973, 7, 51–54. Reprinted with permission.

leading the person to withhold such information. The pros and cons of whether to disclose a hidden handicap to a prospective employer was discussed at length in interviews with professionals and clients in a study of important rehabilitation concerns (Leviton, 1973).

In many cases, however, the person rejects his or her minority-group identification. Concealment then stems from the belief that having a disability inherently makes the person less desirable, less good. Consider the following autobiographical reminiscences of Frances who was hard of hearing. As a small child she heard her aunts speak about a neighbor as "so stone-deaf he might as well be dead." In the value-atmosphere of the home, she began to see physical perfection as the road to success in all areas of life, including one of the most important, that of love and acceptance by others:

> "Stop slipping your braces off," Aunt May said. "If you have crooked teeth you'll be sorry."
> "Stop reading all the time and ruining your eyes," Aunt Harriet scolded. "If you have to wear glasses, you'll be sorry."
> "Stop eating so much fudge; your complexion's bumpy, you're much too plump. Don't you want to be slender and beautiful and marry into a fine family like your oldest sister?"
> "Stand up straight. Don't you want to be athletic like your second sister who is so popular and is invited everywhere?"
> "Brush your hair a hundred strokes every night. Don't you want to have thick shiny braids like your sister Ann's?" [Warfield, 1948, p. 22].

Frances, then, had no alternative but to conceal, however precariously, the fact that she couldn't hear well:

> I mustn't let on I couldn't hear perfectly. People didn't like it. It made them scornful like Ann or exasperated like Aunt May and Aunt Harriet when they called and I didn't answer right away. . . .
> I must listen hard. Sometimes, when I didn't hear at first, it would flash over me, a second later, what had been said. I must never look blank. No matter how much I wanted to, I must never say "What?" "What?" was perilous. "What?" would give away my secret and I'd be exposed to deadly danger. [pp. 4–5]

For Frances the deadly danger was being rejected because of her deafness, perhaps even sent away. And this rejection was expected by Frances and even supported by her because *she agreed that deafness made a person unworthy,* that a hearing loss was something to be ashamed of. Since a shameful fact cannot be accepted as long as it remains shameful, Frances tried to hide, deny, or at best compensate for her hearing loss. It was only later, after Frances discovered the futility of her pretense, that she began to reevaluate the meaning of disability.

The effort to forget one's disability is supported by the presumption that relief from the intolerable state can be achieved by blotting it out or by acting as though it did not exist. If in some magical way one could only forget, one could then act like a normal person—and be, in fact, a normal person.

This kind of magical thinking is displayed more clearly in devised rituals which, if followed exactly, will reward the performer. Frances, for example, "knew" that she would get her hearing back after her adenoidectomy at seven, but just to make sure she secretly pursued the rites of magic:

> . . . Crouched in my hideaway behind the lilac bushes in the yard, I closed my eyes and put my fingers in my ears and repeated, "wrinkels-tiltskin" seven times every day. I even devised fancier magic, such as avoiding cracks in the pavement and touching every other railing of every fence I ever passed. [Warfield, 1948, p. 12]

The fact that unrealistic and even fantastic attempts to overcome disability are clung to tenaciously may be due to a deep emotional need for their promised effects, but the choice of a particular mechanism emerges from a conscious or unconscious belief in the reasonableness of its action. All of us have at one time or another achieved solace in forgetting; all of us have sought relief in sleep, an escape from the immediate troubles that beset us, an interlude during which we consciously forget. All of us have attempted to conceal or deny some personal fact: the child refuses to admit taking the candy; the young mother closes the door on the unmade beds. In so doing we may sometimes have successfully shielded the shameful fact from becoming a social reality. It is the social reality of an undesirable personal characteristic, awareness of it on the part of others, that threatens one's group status. To attempt to hide, to deny, to forget is common sense, although it does not make adjustive sense. It does not make adjustive sense because acceptance of a disability requires that the person absorb it within one's psychological outlook in such a way that it is no longer a painful fact that must be concealed.

Even the more clearly magical ruse undoubtedly originates in some experience that makes it "logical." When Frances at the age of 7 realized that her operation did not produce clear hearing, she decided that when she started school she would have perfect hearing *because lightning would strike her kite and restore her hearing!* On the face of it, this seems truly magical. But to Frances, it was completely comprehensible because "Aunt Harriet had read a newspaper story aloud to Aunt May about a woman who had been sitting beside an open window during an electrical storm with a pair of scissors in her hand. Lightning had struck her scissors. According to the newspaper story, the woman had been somewhat deaf, but when her scissors were struck by lightning her hearing was restored" (Warfield, 1948, p. 15). Even Frances' choice of a kite was not accidental, for she had admired a life-size statue of Benjamin Franklin and dreamed of herself discovering electricity and being so acclaimed. It is the commonsense feel of these techniques as paths to the goal of full membership in the favored group that leads the person to persist in using them in the face of objective facts which negate them.

The attempt to conceal the disability, to act "as if," demands ingenuity and alertness, for the situations that require covering up are endless. Again let us share Frances' life (Warfield, 1948):

> . . . I had never even felt faint, really—just a sickish little ball of panic in the pit of my stomach sometimes when I wasn't hearing and was afraid someone was going to say, "What's the matter—cotton in your ears?" The dressmaker who made my wedding dress had kept mimbling and mumbling, down on the floor with her mouth full of pins. Several times during the fittings I'd pretended to feel faint to explain my not answering her. Feeling faint was a good alibi. [p. 19]

> I heard better when I could see people's faces; . . . In firelit rooms or on summer evenings on the porch, I would fall into reverie or pretend to go to sleep. I knew dozens of ways to get people to repeat what they had said without actually asking. For example:
> Aunt May: "Will you remember to bring me some wrinkelawreedles on your way home?"
> I (dreamily): "From the post office?"
> Aunt May (tartly): "Since when does one buy darning needles at the post office?" [p. 21]

> I tried hard to be as funny as possible all the time. I invented a side-splitting story to explain why I took Aunt Harriet's crochet pattern to Mrs. Schlee instead of to Mrs. McGee. I was a daydreamer and a wool-gatherer; I faked absent-mindedness, boredom, indifference. [p. 21]

> I had learned by experience to do all the talking when I walked along the street with a boy. Indoors I could keep voices raised by playing the victrola; outdoors I was in danger of missing what was said. I always walked fast, rattling on at random, trusting to luck that when a boy wanted to ask me to a dance he'd call me on the telephone. [p. 24]

> I didn't mind being teased about snoring, because I snored purposely. Stella [my roommate] was a great whisperer after lights were out and sleep was my alibi for not answering. [pp. 29–30]

Musical shows were all right; there was plenty to see and the plot didn't matter. Plays dragged; I'd get bored imagining, and itch to know what the play was about. Naturally I never asked. During intermissions I might inquire offhand what Stella thought would happen next; with luck I'd get an inkling of what had already happened. That is, if I heard what Stella said. [p. 34][2]

The price of trying above all to hide and forget is high. It is high because the effort is futile. A person cannot forget when reality requires time and again that the disability be taken into account. The vigilance required for covering up leads to strain, not only physically but also in interpersonal relations, for one must maintain a certain distance in order to fend off the frightening topic of the disability.

There is ample evidence in autobiographical materials to support this thesis; yet objective evidence is largely lacking. What little there is remains unclear. Landis & Bolles (1942) hold, on the basis of interviews with 100 women with disabilities, that those using the "obliterative method" of adjustment (refusal to admit that they were incapacitated in any way, equivalent to our "as if" behavior) showed the best adjustment to handicap and general life adjustment. But the likelihood that these same subjects would also deny any other difficulties, thus leading interviewers to form a spuriously high impression of their adjustment, as well as other considerations, prevent our relying upon these observations.

On the basis of our thesis, the following paradox becomes clear: Trying to forget is the best way to remember. In trying, one must be ever aware of one's disability, for otherwise the disability might not be adequately concealed. On the other hand, to be able to disregard the disability in situations in which it is not relevant, the person must first accept the disability as a fact, and ultimately as a fact that does not diminish one's self-worth.

IDOLIZING NORMAL STANDARDS VERSUS NORMALIZATION

The fervent desire to forget or cover up one's disability in the hope of being "normal" also has important consequences for the standards and values that guide the person's behavior. The normal ideal becomes *idolized*. Normality is then viewed as the only passage to all that is prized, and standards of behavior that define normality become the only hallmark of what is appropriate.

Idolizing normal standards should be distinguished from the

---

[2]Reprinted with permission from *Cotton in my ears* by F. Warfield. New York: Viking Press, 1948.

principle of normalization, a concept originated by the Swedish proponent Nirje (1969). This principle affirms that the *conditions of everyday life* for people with disabilities, including the mentally retarded, should approximate the norms and patterns of the mainstream of society as closely as possible (Wolfensberger, 1972). Normalization calls for integration of people with special problems into the community wherever possible as opposed to segregated residential, educational, employment, and social settings. It means utilizing existing community resources and developing new ones to meet underserved needs. Where special residences or workshops are called for, it means designing them in the manner of other homes and businesses in the community. Normalization generates the notion that special workshops could well be located in regular factories or other places of business, thereby reducing separation from ordinary life still further. It gives rise to the idea that these clients should be called workers and that places of work should be separated from places of living (Brickey, 1974). The normalization principle draws upon a normal way of life as a guide for including diverse segments of society within community life. The danger occurs when it becomes confused with *idolizing* normal standards. Then, instead of allowing flexibility in what is regarded as appropriate behavior and situations, standards become fixed according to the normal ideal.

Idolizing normal standards, on the other hand, means that the normal standards of behavior are rigidly defined and held forth as the *single* criterion for the desirable or even allowable. Those who fall below those standards are devaluated. Their needs are underserved, their well-being neglected. Persons with a disability who themselves idolize the normal will continue to battle feelings of inferiority even when they approach criterion.

Idolizing the normal is particularly apparent during early attempts at adjustment to a disability, although it may persist with reduced intensity later on. Recently injured persons cannot easily decide, for example, that it is all right to limp when the normal gait had been regarded as the only really proper way to walk. If, with bodily injury, our values automatically underwent appropriate accommodations, we would be able to see beauty in the laboring locomotion of a person who is meeting the residuals of polio and to view the hand prosthesis as "working hands" rather than "claws." Although such perceptions reflect good adjustment to disability, they require major alterations within the value system of the person, alterations that are only gradually realized in the struggle for acceptance (see Chapter 8). An individual does not lightly toss over the basis for strivings and evaluations taken for granted during the foregoing lifetime, just as an immigrant does not leave native customs behind when coming to a new land.

The person with a disability clings to the standards of the normal majority for another, very different reason. We have seen that in the primitive effort to forget and conceal the disability, the person tries to act "as if" the disability did not exist. This means that the person should act as much like someone without the disability as possible and that others should ignore the disability and treat the person like anyone else. The standards of behavior relevant to the nondisabled state become enshrined as the ideal, as the preeminent guide for the person's own behavior and relationships with others.

Arbitrarily holding up "normal" performance as the model of behavior unnecessarily commits many persons with a disability to repeated feelings of failure and inferiority. Careful experimental work has demonstrated that the experience of success and failure is largely independent of the person's performance per se but is determined by the person's goals, expectations, and aspirations (Lewin et al., 1944). Usually people set their aspirations near the top of their abilities. After success, goals are usually raised; after failure they are usually lowered. In other words, the level of aspiration operates as a protective mechanism so that most persons, whatever their abilities, experience success. Where normal performance is unattainable, the person who idolizes this as the standard must suffer the ignominy of repeated failure. Performance that may represent genuine progress over past achievement may merit only dissatisfaction because it is still far from the elusive but imperious normal ideal. Moreover, even should the person with a disability achieve or surpass the standards of normal performance, this by no means guarantees a success experience, for as long as the disability is viewed as a stigma, the feeling that at best one is an imperfect facsimile of a "nondisabled person" must retain its sting.

The Case of Raymond

Let us share part of Raymond Goldman's (1947) life for exemplification. At the age of 4 he was stricken with polio. Laboriously he learned to sit up, to crawl. At the age of 8 he was fitted with long leg braces. By the time he was 12, he could walk straighter and faster and tripped less frequently. At about the age of 14 he was fitted with half-leg braces and could walk better than ever. Finally, he attempted the impossible and succeeded. Contrary to the prediction of his doctor, at the age of 17 he learned to walk without braces.

And yet, though he triumphed over severe difficulties, though his gait represented remarkable improvement over the years, his feeling of achievement in situations where the normal standards remained exemplary, as in contact with girls, was abruptly replaced by shame and dismay. At the beach he swam early in the morning to avoid people who would see his legs. "The very sight of my own uncovered legs stabbed me to the heart" (p. 86). In the afternoons he sat on the beach, in trousers and shoes. "I even made friends with a group of fellows and girls of my own age who came down every afternoon, my self-consciousness subsiding as I got to know them better; subsiding, that is, *to a certain point* beyond which it could not go. *When the girls were present I didn't walk*" (p. 89, italics added). What had been true accomplishment in terms of progress was now seen as defeat and failure because in this situation the normal standards of walking were glorified into how one *should* walk.

Furthermore, idolizing normal standards serves to support not only inferiority feelings but also guilt feelings. (The emotional syllogism by which the *cause* of disability becomes associated with evil is discussed on pp. 63–68.) To the extent that the wrongdoing is attributed to oneself, the person will feel the uneasiness of guilt, though in a vague and uncomprehending way because its source is unclear.

It has also been pointed out that guilt feelings and inferiority feelings tend to reinforce each other (Alexander, 1938). Although the following statement refers to a person who has committed a crime, the principle is a general one: ". . . in order to escape inferiority feelings the criminal is driven to commit acts which give him the appearance of toughness, bravado, and aggressiveness. But this behavior which seeks to avoid the Scylla of inferiority feelings drives him into the Charybdis of guilt feelings" (p. 47). So it is in the case of an individual with a disability who tries to escape inferiority feelings by denial, "as if" behavior, and excessive competition. Because these maneuvers are conflicted, they add to the person's guilt.

In some way the normal standards of behavior themselves may become endowed with a quality very close to a moral imputation that it is right and proper for one to walk or talk in a certain way. At least under certain conditions, the shame of inferiority at being below standard is tainted with the shame of guilt at violating an ethical code. Raymond, the boy crippled through polio, in thinking of his youth poignantly compares his emotional reaction to that of a culprit: "It is hard to believe that I am describing the emotions of a youth who is guiltless of crime against society. His frantic fear of human eyes could not be more terrible if he had robbed a bank, committed murder, or escaped from a penitentiary. He is lame, that is all; and his soul is fevered with a burning shame" (Goldman, 1947, p. 66).

Idolizing normal standards relegates the person to an inferior position, not only objectively, in terms of a particular characteristic, but may also do so morally, as a total person. In turn, the feeling of shame and inferiority prompts "as if" behavior, which itself heightens the potency of normal standards, for in the frenzy of emotional logic, the success of forgetting, denying, and concealing requires that the person emulate the styles and standards of the nondisabled. Thus, the means of extricating oneself from more shame becomes the very means of submerging oneself further. (In Chapter 8 we shall consider value changes important to the acceptance of a disability that hold greater promise for the ultimate realization of the self as a worthy and whole human being.)

The possible positive consequences of maintaining the standards of the "normal" majority must also be examined. It might be argued that the ideal of normal performance provides the necessary motivation for persistent self-improvement, that without it the person would be satisfied with a more awkward gait or a less pleasant-sounding voice or a narrower range of activities than could be achieved. Almost any autobiography documents the fact that the feeling of inferiority, fed by the normal ideal, can serve to prod the person to greater effort. Some theorists even assert that all accomplishment primarily reflects compensation for inferiority.

It is revealing to examine several incidents in the life of Raymond Goldman (1947), the man who was both lame and hard of hearing, with the following questions in mind: Could Raymond's accomplishments have been brought about by driving forces other than the striving to be like a "normal" person? At what price were his accomplishments made? What were the positive implications for adjustment and what were the negative consequences?

When Raymond was fitted with full-length leg braces at the age of 8, the trying problem arose of motivating him to use them. Until then he had had little feeling of inferiority. He did not miss the companionship of other children his age, for they belonged to a world he knew nothing of. He was the center of his own world, where everyone loved him and took care of him. He not only had high self-esteem but did not think of himself as having misshapen legs (see p. 223 for a vivid example of his lack of awareness of his deformity). When the braces were fitted, he hated them. They hurt, and only because of the prodding and solicitousness of his parents did he cooperate at all:

> During that summer I wore my braces at least thirty minutes every day. I dreaded and hated them and made little effort to learn to walk. For a few weeks I would not attempt to walk at all, but sat down after they were put on and waited miserably for them to be removed. . . .
>
> Quite naturally I preferred riding in the gocart to pedaling the velocipede, crawling to walking. But mother rose to the occasion. She tolerated my attitude for a while, then became annoyed with me.
>
> "Get up and walk!" she commanded me, handing me my canes. "You'll never learn how to walk sitting in a chair."

I got up and practiced walking. Mother watched me, suffering, I am sure, even more than I. Propping myself up with the canes, I swung one weighted leg after the other, taking a step, resting, taking another step. The braces were half as heavy as I was. After getting across the room and back I was spent; I felt nauseated and dizzy with pain and weariness. Then Mother took off the braces, laid me on the bed, removed my stockings and rubbed me well with alcohol, gently patting the red bruises on my ankles and knees.

As the summer passed, the skin of my ankles became tougher and tougher, calluses began to appear. I wore my braces longer than half an hour a day; I wore them several hours. I got around the house—though I could not take the stairs—and I walked a little outside after I was carried down the front steps to the sidewalk. . . .

My happiness at entering school was all the greater when I learned that I was not to wear my braces there. Six hours in them was more than I was expected to endure. That torture would be reserved for late afternoons, after I returned from school. If I got along well at school, I thought, perhaps Mother would see the uselessness of wearing them and would throw them away. Mother was just being stubborn about it. Anyone could see that I got along much better without them. Without them I could crawl all over the house in the time it took me to walk across a room with them on. [pp. 30–32]

Then occurred a momentous experience that was to usher in a totally new attitude toward himself and the world around him. At the age of $8\frac{1}{2}$ Raymond entered school for the first time. The ridicule and torment to which he was subjected was overwhelming (see pp. 224–225 for the description of this nightmare). The hammer of comparison beat into him the barbs of shame. The standards of the "norm" began to have for him the character of a compelling ethic:

. . . I knew now that legs *should* be stout and shapely and that mine were skinny and deformed. I knew that I *should* walk and could not. I learned indeed that I was a cripple, a pariah among the strong and straight, an object of pity to grown-ups and of scorn to children. [p. 39, italics added]

Now that Raymond had suffered shame, his braces took on a new meaning. Before, they meant pain to him, and a way of locomotion that was less efficient than his tried and true method of crawling. Now they meant a way of becoming *like other children,* of meeting the standards of the normal majority, of escaping the pity due a disgusting, crippled boy. Small wonder that after school he asked for his braces:

. . . Thereafter, day after day, week after week, month after month I struggled to walk. I put on my braces as soon as I got home from school and I kept them on until I went to bed. About forty pounds of boy, I dragged twenty pounds of steel across the room and back, across the room and back, holding myself upright with my canes. I must walk, I told myself, I must walk. I must get out of that shameful gocart, out of the arms of people who carried me. Of course I could do it! Hadn't I learned to crawl, even down the steps? [pp. 39–40]

An important question is whether Raymond would have learned to walk had he not been prodded by shame. Hadn't his parents tried to motivate him with reason, kindness, and command, but with limited success? And yet, we reply in the affirmative, relying on the emergence of new needs that emerge in new situations and that may remain free of shame. Hadn't Raymond learned to crawl down the stairs when he was 6 in spite of great fear because he wanted to get there without being dependent on others? And shame did not crawl along with him!

. . . I learned to climb up the stairs, but going down stumped me for a long time. In the upper hall I would venture to the head of the long carpeted stairway and look down. It was as forbidding as a bottomless pit and I would turn away only to return again and look down while I lashed my courage. If I wanted badly enough to go downstairs, I called someone to carry me; but there was no real satisfaction in that. . . . I was at the top of a long flight of steps, looking down, waiting to go down, held back by fear. Then, without conquering my fear but in spite of it, I started down, head first, and kept on going until I reached the bottom. [pp. 12–13]

Likewise, it is highly probable that Raymond would have found it unsatisfactory to have to wait until someone could carry him or wheel him in school from room to room and sooner or later would have turned to his braces, in spite of the pain, as a way of achieving greater mastery over his environment. Walking might have been delayed, but, without the catalyst of shame, accomplishment represents the rewards of triumph over adversity unsullied by the sinking feeling that one is not yet up to par.

But, to press further, under such circumstances would Raymond have continued toward maximum improvement? Would he, nine years later, have defied the expert opinion of his doctor that he would never walk without braces and endured the sweat and tears it took to accomplish the impossible? His doctor had said, "You ought to be satisfied" (p. 29). Would a Raymond free of shame have persisted, "But couldn't I try it? It couldn't do me any harm to try, could it?" We do not know. Perhaps the inconvenience of repeated broken braces, of heavy gear, would have led him to attempt discarding them. Perhaps not.

But even so, a challenging query is "So what?" Reducing the dis-

ability in no way assures a better adjustment. There is already sufficient research to establish as a fact that there is but little relationship
between adjustment and degree of disability (see pp. 149–151).
Was the gain of walking without braces worth the price of self-
debasement? The feeling of inferiority is painful enough, but when
the normal ideal not only spurs the person onward but also sparks
deception and defeat, one wonders what it all adds up to. The con-
suming desire to be like other boys led Raymond, like a rat in a maze,
to explore frantically first one closed alley, then another.

Sometimes the gateway was labeled "Lie, and you will be like
other boys." For example, when Raymond was in the fifth grade, an
idea came to him as he was watching a telephone repair man climb
to the top of the pole by using the irons strapped to his legs. The next
time Raymond was asked what he was wearing on his legs, he answered, "Tree-climbers."

Sometimes the gateway was labeled "Treat me like anybody
else, no matter what!" This meant that he wanted not only to have
the good things in life enjoyed by other boys but also the punishment
that other boys received. One day he set out upon a deliberate cam-
paign to change his teacher's attitude toward him from one of gentle-
ness to that of the strict disciplinarian she was to all the other boys:

> . . . In the silence of study period I clanked my steel braces against
> the iron stanchions of the desk.
>
> "Raymond, will you please try not to make that noise?"
>
> Not angrily, as she would have spoken to another boy. Not leaping
> up from her desk and striding down the aisle like a wrathful demon.
> What was the matter with her? I thought bitterly. Didn't she know I
> was doing it on purpose?
>
> I came to school with a pocketful of marbles. I dropped one with a
> solid click and let it roll down the floor. I dropped another and another.
> Miss McIntyre left her desk and came to my seat.
>
> "Let me have those marbles," she said, holding out her hands for
> them. "Give me every one of them."
>
> I took them out of my pocket and poured them into her cupped
> palms.
>
> "I want to talk to you after class," she said, so quietly I was afraid that
> the other children had not heard her.
>
> I was triumphant. I had made her leave her desk and come after me.
> I was being kept in after school like the worst boys in the room. She
> had taken a knife away from one boy and several tops from another,
> and they had never gotten them back. She wouldn't give me back my
> marbles, either. Maybe, I thought, she'd whip me, though I had never
> heard of any boy actually getting a whipping.
>
> I sat at my desk after the others marched out and Miss McIntyre
> squeezed sideways into the seat in front of me. She took one of my
> hands in hers and held it tenderly while she spoke to me. I was such

a smart boy, she said, and she knew I was a very good boy. I just didn't understand that good, smart boys didn't do things to disturb the class. . . . While she spoke, tears came into my eyes. She thought, no doubt, that they were tears of repentance, but they weren't. They were tears of bitter disappointment and resentment. To make matters worse, she gave me back my marbles.

That was the time I boasted to the boys next day about Miss McIntyre's anger and the severity of her punishment. [pp. 48–49]

Sometimes the very performance prompted by the normal ideal itself suffered. In high school, Raymond tried very hard to walk *as others did.* But the more he tried, the more awkward he became:

When I walked through the corridors from one class to another, my braces clanked loudly on the floor. *If I tried to walk less heavily, I became more noticeably lame.* I am sure that none of those girls I passed in the corridor paid any attention to me, that only a few of them gave me even a passing glance. But I imagined that every one of them looked at me—not at me but at my legs—with a shudder of revulsion or, even more terrible to contemplate, a wave of pity. [p. 67, italics added]

Raymond tried to communicate *as others did.* But the more he tried, the more he felt like a dunce and a fool:

I am in a classroom. The class is at Latin recitation. We hold our books open at a certain page and one by one, as the teacher calls our names, we rise and translate the text, the bidden student taking up where his predecessor left off. I studied conscientiously the night before; I am thoroughly prepared. Yet, agony fills me. I am cold with terror, wretched with desperation, stricken by a sense of impending disaster.

I do what I can to avoid the horror of catastrophe. I try to save myself with my eyes. But I ask too much of my perceptive wits. My eyes must be on the teacher's lips whenever she happens to call my name. Even so, shall I know whether she says Goldman, or Goldsmith, or Gorham, or Bowman? I must be careful not to rise if it is one of the others whose name has been called.

And how shall I know where to begin, granting that I rise at the correct time? I know with what page we began; I made certain of it by looking over the shoulder of the student in front of me. I turn a page whenever the others turn theirs. But where, on two pages, are they? I watch the reciting student. If he is behind me, I turn and see his face, but I cannot read Latin from his lips. If he is in front of me, I watch the back of his head. I can tell whether we are on the left-hand or right-hand page. The head is turned slightly to the left; the chin slowly sinks; then suddenly the chin goes up and the head turns a little to the right. The right-hand page! But what paragraph? What sentence? My classmate sits down. Look at the teacher! Oh, God, why does she hold down her head that way, looking at the recitation cards! What did she say? Gorham, Goldman, Bowman . . . ?

In spite of my desperate efforts I wasn't always successful. There were times when I didn't rise when the teacher called my name, and sometimes I rose when she called on someone else. On one occasion I thought she spoke my name and I got up and began to recite. The class broke into laughter. Behind me, the boy whose name had been called, had risen and begun to recite before I got to my feet. When I got up and joined in, like a second alto coming into a musical round, the teacher had every right to look startled. [pp. 67–68]

After his first year in high school, Raymond quit. He stayed out of school for a year during which time he worked in his father's furniture store. The normal ideal, instead of encouraging him toward greater achievements, mocked him into despair. In grade school, he had achieved considerable success and much satisfaction in writing, but now his aspirations were destroyed, at least temporarily, because no matter how much he taxed his motor and auditory capabilities, he did not fit the pattern of his normal ideal.

Raymond had to learn the hard way that a "crippled boy is essentially the same as any other boy; that man did not walk and run his way out of beastliness, but thought his way out; that man is not ashamed because his legs are relatively crippled as compared with the legs of a deer, and his arms relatively muscleless as compared with the strength of a gorilla" (p. 51). According to our interpretation, the normal ideal of being physically like other boys was *not* the source of the reawakening of his ambition. The source was, rather, his gradual recognition that life is more than physique and that other values are important and satisfying.

The experiences that contributed to this realization are enlightening:

1. Raymond's initial job assignment—addressing envelopes—was completely unsatisfying to him. It was boring and yielded little pay. He was also ashamed, but not of his lameness or of his impaired hearing, for when he was seated behind a desk where no one spoke to him these limitations were of little importance. He was ashamed at the thought of sitting there among women addressing envelopes. What had occurred here was the emergence of a *new* standard, a standard that did not define the necessary physical characteristics of a person but concerned the value "manliness" as determined by the kind of work he did.

2. Raymond's second job assignment was writing furniture descriptions for newspaper advertising. When he saw his work in print, something stirred within him. He dreamed again of authorship and after a while began to write. His revived ambition was stimulated at home by conversations about the suc-

cess of other writers. Stories by a distant relative were beginning to appear in magazines, and his neighbor, Fannie Hurst,
recently had had several stories published in the *Saturday
Evening Post.* What had happened here? Again, Raymond became absorbed with new values. Physique, instead of being
the determiner of all of life, began to recede into the background as he again became attracted to literary pursuits, an
interest that dated from years before.

3. These value changes paved the way for the tremendous discovery that shame and strain are fed by concealment. Once
   he realized that physique was not *that* important, that other
   things were far more crucial, he could confess his deafness
   for the first time. This he did, to Fannie Hurst, and experienced a calmness and understanding which taught him that
   though he could never get away from deafness he could get
   along with it.

In this brief review, we have seen in process several of the value
changes to be analyzed in more detail in Chapter 8. These are: enlarging the scope of values (i.e., the disability is not the only thing
that matters); subordinating physique relative to other values (i.e.,
other values are more important than physique); and containing disability effects (i.e., the disability does not affect all situations).

Raymond was now able to return to school, a private high school
for boys. During these years the ideal of normal physique remained
relatively dormant. Because other values and ideas occupied him he
found life, unsapped by shame, exciting and rewarding.

Yet the transformation of physique from a comparative value to
an asset value (see pp. 178–183), the value change par excellence that
would strip normal physique of its character as a status standard for
him, had not as yet taken place. Raymond was therefore still vulnerable to shame. Normal physique as an idol still could rear its terrifying
head. At graduation from high school, the old shame returned to Raymond as he saw *the girls* in the crowded auditorium and faced the
prospect of standing there on the stage, reciting his poem, with all
eyes upon him. Once again he had to come to grips with a world in
which normal physique was an important criterion for personal evaluation.

And in coming to grips again and yet again, Raymond learned
several important lessons: The thought that he could be accepted as
he was, even by girls, began to come to him. During the summer following his graduation, young and beautiful Edna was willing to sit
and talk with him at the beach even though, because he hadn't dared
to walk in her presence, she thought he couldn't walk at all! With

this revelation, the battle raged furiously within him. Could he, would he, allow others to see him as he was? The answer fought its way through:

> Next afternoon I went down to the beach as usual. I took off my trousers and shoes and waited for the others to arrive. I let them see me as I was, I let them see my legs, the entire skinny, deformed length of them. Edna, too. I walked with her down to the sea, naked with a nakedness known only to a cripple. [p. 91]

Raymond also began to realize that his disability could be of real advantage in some situations. In the college gym course he discovered that he could chin far more times than anyone else. His upper trunk had been well developed during the years of exercise in his own gym, and his legs had little weight to be lifted. The instructor was impressed with his achievement and called the other members of the class to watch (p. 94).

In thinking over this experience, Raymond achieved even greater insights. He realized that coping with a disability in itself merits recognition and that what he had sometimes taken as pity was in fact respect for his striving (see p. 276 for an account of this insight). He also learned that respect for accomplishment depends upon what is expected of you and what you expect of yourself, not merely upon doing something better than someone else.

By the time Raymond was 30, these, as well as other experiences and insights, led him to formulate his mature view of the problem of normal standards:

> [1.] I did not measure success by what others had accomplished, but by what it was possible for me to accomplish. Along with shame, I had put envy and self-pity out of my life forever [p. 101]. I walked anywhere without fear of being noticed, proud that I could walk at all. I was unconcerned about the skinniness of my legs. I said, "Pardon me, what did you say? I don't hear very well," as easily as I might have said, "Pardon me, will you tell me what time it is? I have no watch with me." [p. 102]
>
> [2.] I can live a normal life *although* I am *not* the same as other men [p. 115]. . . . while I was not quite the same as other men, I was, nevertheless, not so very much different. [p. 138]

In short, a normal physique ceased to be the standard by which Raymond measured and evaluated himself. This is not to say that he preferred his imperfect physique to a more adequate one. Rather, he could appreciate all the good things his body could do for him because he no longer compared himself with the normal ideal. The things he *could* do became proficiencies. He could walk without braces, and that was good. A hearing aid improved his hearing, and that was good. He notes:

. . . I derived happiness from the queerest sources, things that meant nothing to other people, mere trivialities such as walking—just walking—down the street, climbing or descending steps; for who else save a few, could remember . . . ? [p. 126][3]

In effect, normal physique had become an asset value for him—for example, a good thing to have when present, but not a disturbance when absent (see Chapter 8).

This value shift, the dethroning of the idol of normal physique, did not, as some might suppose, remove the source of motivation toward improvement. Raymond continued his four-days-a-week workout at the gym—not because the normal standard egged him on but because he treasured his own health and strength. He was able to get married—not because of a challenge to overcome his inferiority but because he wanted to share his life with the woman he loved. He applied himself diligently to writing, in which he achieved considerable success—not because the image of a deformed physique stalked behind him but because the satisfaction of writing enticed him onward.

And the value shift prepared him for the years of anguish that awaited him. Within a short time of each other, the two persons closest to him, his father and his wife, died and the emptiness that followed was soon to be capped by a new disability, severe diabetes. But during those years of deep despair the philosophy of life that was to carry him through the void remained dormant and not dead. He had learned life's lessons well. Could he not meet the onslaught of diabetes when he had already learned to get along with the best he had? Could he not meet the pain of bereavement when he had learned to look upon hardship and suffering as part of life, as meaningful and challenging and not as worthless and humiliating? The ideal of physical normality had nothing to do with the reawakening of his will to live, with his savoring again the glory of thinking and feeling and caring and writing. On the contrary, had it played a role, his despair might well have lasted even longer.

Misapplied Standards: Further Examples and Considerations

The role of misapplied standards has been explored in other contexts. To give a brief notion of its generality, the matter of neurosis and sexual deviation may be mentioned. Personality theorists have stressed self-rejection as etiologically significant in the neuroses. Many persons become emotionally disturbed because they are un-

[3]Reprinted with permission of Macmillan Publishing Co., Inc., from *Even the night* by R. L. Goldman. Copyright 1947, and renewed 1975, by Raymond Leslie Goldman.

able to "accept their own nature . . . and to shape their aims according to their assets" (Meyer, 1948, p. 539). Newcomb (1950) has discussed sexual deviation, such as homosexuality, as a function of the degree of rigidity in the prescribed standards for male and female behavior. Margaret Mead (1949) has considered in similar terms other facts relating to sex roles. She points out that women who enter an occupation defined as masculine may do so in order to act as males or to prove they are as good as males. This drive, being compensatory and derivative rather than primary, "will blur their vision and make clumsy fingers that should be deft as they try to act out the behavior of the other sex deemed so desirable." Even should they enter such an occupation because of intrinsic interest, "they will find themselves handicapped at every turn by the style that has been set by the other sex" (p. 377). The parallel case holds true for men. During the seventies some countries leaped forward in the breaking through of rigidly defined sex roles. Flexibility of behavior styles, with proper regard for societal needs, allows people to carry out tasks and roles most satisfactorily in the way that is right for them.

The same applies to persons with a disability who attempt to abide immutably by the standards and styles of "normal" performance. Too often their own performance will suffer, not only because of the psychological strain of striving to be what they are not, but also because modifications appropriate to their individual needs and characteristics are forestalled.

Even should the person achieve and surpass "normal" standards, this *in itself,* we hold, is no criterion for successful adjustment. Yet individuals with disabilities who have become outstanding sports figures are held up as models to be emulated, as examples of persons who have overcome their handicaps. Thus the statement about a young man who lost a leg in a railroad accident while still a child: "That he has found the loss no handicap is evidenced by the fact that he was a collegiate boxing and fencing champion, captured the men's badminton singles title in his home town . . ." (Shortley, 1948, p. *iv*). We believe, on the contrary, that such a criterion for adjustment, especially when regarded as primary, is psychologically unsound. Competing on the basis of regular boxing rules may mean precisely that the person has *not* accepted his disability but has instead been motivated to achieve in this particular area just to prove that his amputation does not matter. Actually it *does* matter, and often matters a great deal.

What we are trying to point out is that *"acting like a normal person"* is not the same as *"feeling like a normal person"*—that is, a worthy human being—and that emphasis on the former may militate against the latter. This is not to say, however, that persons with disabilities should never participate in sports designed for the able-bodied, but it is to say that the way of participation should fit the circumstances of the participants. It does not make sense to cling to the established rules of the game *just because* the physically able play that way. Such rigid adherence reminds us of the immaturity of the young child who in no circumstances can modify the rules of a game because "rules are rules," whereas older children are able to do so in agreement with the other participating members (Piaget, 1932). All too often, one pays a price for the apparent success when the motivation is to prove that one is "as good as anybody else."

Though the overriding potency of "normal behavior" as such is to be decried, there are important considerations that support abiding by such standards under certain conditions. First of all, striving toward the normal ideal may lead to the value change called "containing disability effects," in which the effects of disability are seen as restricted rather than pervasive (see Chapter 8). By engaging in "normal" activities, the person may become aware that these activities are really not precluded after all: "It was great . . . doing the things you thought you would never do again" (Ohnstad, 1942, p. 157). Persons with a disability, particularly in the case of a recent injury, are subject to the same spread phenomena as are the nondisabled majority (see pp. 32–39). They too will perceive their disability as extending far beyond the necessary limits, spreading into what could be unaffected physical and nonphysical areas. In this case, the push to act like anyone else serves the positive function of making certain activities accessible.

Secondly, it may be necessary to cling to the normal ideal before one can give it up, to try to be like everyone else before one can find the comfort and the reward in being oneself. This may be particularly true in a society that ill prepares its members for the eventuality of disability and, on the contrary, fosters the ideal of superman in many phases of its life, as in industry and sports, for example. We have not found any autobiographies in which the person was able to sidetrack this phase of the adjustment process. But it is equally important to notice that we have not found in any autobiography that achieving the normal standards in activities impeded by disability was the primary basis for adjustment or acceptance of the disability.

Thirdly, to adhere to certain modes of behavior, though they might not be as natural where a particular disability is involved, may be recommended when (1) they involve *little actual stress* and (2) the natural alternative will be met with social disapproval. An enlightening case in point is teaching table manners to the blind child. This child should be cautioned against the tendency to put one's nose close to the food or to use the tongue in an attempt to find out what food is on the plate; it is easy enough to tell the child what is being served. On the other hand, blind children should not be discouraged from developing their own special and sometimes strange means of "space testing" when there is no adequate "normal" substitution for informing oneself about the environment. "Blind children have been observed . . . clapping their hands, snapping their fingers, smacking their lips, and clicking or popping their tongues. All these slightly explosive sharp sounds produce high frequencies and help the child to know more about his environment, how big and spacious it is, how far away the walls are, whether it is empty or filled with objects, etc." (Lowenfeld, 1971, p. 63)[4]

Finally, adhering to the normal ideal may in some instances be worth the price of strain and pain, especially if the person does not feel that such achievement is all-important. To be able to do things in the manner of others or to look like others may smooth the way in social relations. A person may be justified in undergoing expensive and painful plastic surgery for purely cosmetic reasons just because certain aspects of life will thereby be eased.

The critical decisions concerning standards and goals must involve a careful weighing of the possible gains and possible losses. Because the issues are not clear-cut, because some of them pull in opposite directions, the matter is not a simple one for mechanical solution. It takes wisdom based upon accumulated research and upon the art of sifting the important from the superficially attractive. In the foregoing discussion, the dangers of uncritically maintaining normal performance standards have been stressed more than certain positive effects of these standards, primarily because in the total process of adjustment more weight must be given to the former. Furthermore, in the common sense of adjustment to disability, the need for reevaluation of standards is generally neglected.

It is certain that, when the implications of maintaining the normal ideal as a standard are better understood and accepted, rehabilitation practice will be modified, for the implications are crucial to the central problem of what to work toward and how to get there. Cruickshank has made the point that education for people with cerebral palsy "has permitted feelings of inadequacy as a result of overstress on normalcy" (1955, p. 334). Meyerson has challenged on the same grounds the educational philosophy of teaching deaf children. His statement of some of the issues is so incisive that it bears verbatim recounting:

[4]From B. Lowenfeld, *Our blind children,* 1971. Courtesy of Charles C. Thomas, Publisher, Springfield, Ill.

Everyone will agree that speech and lip-reading are useful tools for the deaf child. In their finest development they enlarge the life space of the child tremendously, permit increasingly finer differentiations or growth, and reduce the communication barriers between the child, his family, and the world. For reasons that are presently unknown, however, not every deaf child learns to speak and lip-read. For reasons we can only conjecture, many who do learn, after 12 to 15 years of continuous drill, later do not use their hard-won skills. Perhaps they discover the deceit of the implicit promises held out to them that "if only you learn these skills and behave like other people, society will accept you." Perhaps many discover that their speech and lipreading are good only in a limited circle of family and friends. Outside of it they may experience great difficulty in understanding or being understood. They may discover that others are amused or annoyed at their voices.

Is a child necessarily a less valuable child if he uses other modalities and communicates by finger-spelling or pad and pencil? Is nothing else so important as speech and lipreading? It is true that in some schools there is a tendency to establish a status hierarchy of "good" oral pupils and "poorer" manual pupils, but there is no psychological justification for this. Perhaps parents should evaluate a school by determining whether its students have anything worthwhile to communicate beyond being able to say "a top, a ball, a fish." Perhaps they should ask if the children have learned to solve problems by themselves, whether they have learned to take turns and respect the rights of others, and whether they have "good" adult power figures with whom they can easily identify. [Meyerson, 1955a, pp. 163–164][5]

Lillian Smith (1954) has even insisted that sameness and normality (in the sense of typicality) have no place in human beings.

In certain quarters the philosophy of rehabilitation is absorbing the view that instead of normal behavior being the golden guide for "what to do and how to do it," the abilities and disabilities of the particular person more wisely fulfill that function. The counsel given decades ago in a small illustrated booklet to patients at the Institute for Physical Medicine and Rehabilitation on the question of standards of performance still needs to be more widely applied:

There are hundreds of ways of doing all these things [that make us independent]. Maybe with your disability you won't be able to do them the same way you used to do, but that certainly doesn't mean you can't learn to do them some other way. And that's why our people are here—to teach you to do these things the best possible way with your disability. [Rusk & Taylor, 1946, p. 85]

[5]Reprinted by permission from Lee Meyerson. A psychology of impaired hearing. In M. Cruickshank (Ed.), *Psychology of exceptional children and youth.* Copyright, 1955, Prentice-Hall, Inc., Englewood Cliffs, N.J.

The account is told of Alice, severely crippled with polio, who learned to ascend stairs:

> . . . [Alice] learned to do at least one thing that seems practically impossible for a person with her limitations: Alice is able to walk upstairs on crutches without using a handrail. Her technique is to go up the steps backwards balancing herself on her two crutches as she pulls up her lifeless legs. She balances herself on her two crutches, pushes down on their handles, thus lifting the entire weight of her body. As her feet reach the step level, she swings them backward and catches her heels on the step. [Rusk & Taylor, 1946, p. 92][6]

Had the "normal" way of ascending stairs been Alice's model, her own techniques would probably never have been discovered.

The goals of rehabilitation and education need, therefore, to be evaluated and reevaluated. We need to ask, Are the goals set reachable and if so, at what price? Bear in mind that this emphasis on reevaluation fits the principle of normalization so long as idolizing normal standards is rejected. Instead of uncritically imposing normal standards as the guide for behavior and action, the concern is that along with appropriate personal adaptation, *necessary accommodations* within community settings must be brought about so that persons with a wide range of physical and mental abilities can participate in community life.

GROUP IDENTIFICATION

As we have seen, "as if" behavior is in many instances a direct expression of the fervent wish to change one's group identification from the handicapped group to that of the favored group. Paradoxically, the very attempt to hide the disability often prevents the person from feeling part of the advantaged group. Concealing the disability does not eradicate it; it still remains in the eyes of the person as the barrier to acceptance by the sought-for group. The stigma of disability that prompts efforts to cover up at the same time negates those efforts. Not accepting the truth, one has to pay the consequence of being in the ambiguous position of a marginal person who belongs fully to no group (see pp. 19–20). Like the man without a country, the person will wander in search of acceptance that cannot be achieved without acceptance of self.

Persons threatened by identification with a particular group will

[6]From *New hope for the handicapped* by Howard A. Rusk & Eugene J. Taylor. Copyright 1946, 1947, 1948, 1949 by Howard A. Rusk. By permission of Hrper & Row, Publishers, Inc.

also avoid contact with that group. Thus, those who want to forget their economically meager past will not wish to associate with people "on the other side of the tracks." Such contact recalls intolerable conflicts resulting from deceit; it reminds them of their implicit "belongingness" to that group from which they have tried to separate but whose hurt they well understand. Such contact may also threaten discovery, for by the mere fact of contiguity they fear that likeness will be exposed. They may also fear that someone like themselves will see through their mask. A similar psychological situation has been explored among Jews (Lewin, 1948, Part III) and among Nisei (Yatsushiro, 1953) for whom "the Americanization process was so thorough that in many cases there developed . . . a feeling of hostility toward 'things Japanese,' including frequently their unacculturated immigrant parents" (p. 205).

So it is with persons with a disability whose overpowering wish is to be considered nondisabled. They will be inclined to "look the other way" at a social gathering to avoid meeting the eyes of a person with a visible disability. They are likely to resist the employment of a person with a disability in their own place of work; they will tend to become hypersensitive to behavior and mannerisms that earmark a person with a handicap.

The *principle of vigilance* operates. This principle refers to the tendency of the person to respond to threatening situations with increased alertness (Bruner & Postman, 1948). It accounts for certain experimental findings on prejudice: in these studies, persons high in prejudice not only saw more faces as being Jewish than those low in prejudice but also were more accurate in their detection (Allport & Kramer, 1946; replicated by Lindzey & Rogolsky, 1950). Though these studies dealt with how majority-group members perceive minority groups, the explanation of the findings applies to minority-group members who are alerted to identifying characteristics of their own group. "The question of racial [or in our context, disability] identity is of small importance to the person free from prejudice. Yet it is of considerable importance to the bigot [or to the person threatened by group identification], and for this reason the bigot apparently learns to observe and interpret both facial features and expressive behavior so that he can more swiftly spot his 'enemy' " (Allport & Kramer, 1946, p. 17).

By the same dynamics, people who wish to conceal their disability will notice disability-revealing mannerisms in another person. Moreover, they are likely to resent those mannerisms that advertise the fact of disability, for in wishing to conceal their own disability they wish others to conceal theirs. Thus it is that the person who is hard of hearing and who strives to hide this fact will be annoyed at the old woman who cups her hand behind her ear. Flaunting the disability is a threat because it stirs up the guilt of having denied one's own group, as well as the possibility of being exposed. Surreptitiously realizing the other person's secret and maintaining a silent agreement that both should play their "as if" roles may be preferred to having the other person challenge one's pretense by confiding his or her own. Individuals who have not accepted their own disability may even develop an active dislike for people who have a disability and may especially resent being classed with those who have a disability more severe than their own. One reason why people hard of hearing were moved to establish separate organizations from the deaf was just this desire to avoid identification with a more stigmatized group (Barker et al., 1953, p. 189).

Some of these reactions to group identification are seen in Frances Warfield's (1948) personal document. It will be recalled that Frances was terrified lest others should discover her imperfect hearing. She feared exposure by members of her own group:

> . . . I was terribly afraid of deaf people—they didn't like me; I couldn't talk loud enough; I was too shy. Moreover, I thought they might be on to my secret. I thought that, being deaf themselves, *perhaps they could tell by looking at me I didn't always hear.* [p. 9, italics added]

She felt uncomfortable in the presence of other deaf persons:

> Marge Martin gave me the willies. She was very pale, with blond hair and staring pale-blue eyes. She reminded me a little of Alice Hart, the girl who had been electrocuted years ago, back home. Marge talked in a flat voice that was sometimes so faint no one could hear it and sometimes so shrill that people turned to look at her. That was because she couldn't hear herself accurately, people said, and therefore couldn't regulate her voice. . . .
>
> Whenever I met . . . [her] on campus I smiled and sang out, "Hello, how are you?" heartily and hurried past. I didn't want to stop and talk to her if I could help it. *It was embarrassing.* You didn't know whether to shout or mouth words silently, and it gave you a funny feeling to have her watching your lips. [p. 43, italics added]

She felt her secret would be revealed if she associated with other deaf persons:

> Besides, I didn't want to associate even casually with Marge. *Somebody . . . might get the idea we were alike,* that our voices sounded alike, or something. [p. 43, italics added]

She preferred mutual pretense on the part of others who were hard of hearing:

I went through a series of glubglub part-time maids before I found Poppy, a large, plush-upholstered Negro with a rich, plushy voice. Then I had to fire Poppy; I heard her telling the back elevator man he'd ought to speak up, her young lady didn't hear too good. Poppy was followed by a middle-aged Irish woman named Vera, and at last I was safe in my own home, thank goodness. Vera was hard of hearing herself. We played our game together. When Vera suggested peas for dinner and I ordered cheese instead, she never let on it wasn't cheese she'd wanted all along. When Ellen Pringle telephoned and Vera's note on the pad read "Miss Trinket called" I said Mrs. Pringle sounded exactly like Miss Trinket and, anyhow, people should learn to speak up in this world. [p. 119].[7]

Not only do those who view their disability as a stigma tend to feel uncomfortable in the presence of other persons with disabilities but they may also resist association with persons who excel in precisely those traits in which they are lacking. For example, a man disturbed by his own short stature will furtively be interested in the height of a prospective associate, and should the latter be notably tall, will silently mark this against him or her. Persons wishing their deficiency to remain obscured do not welcome a contrast that accentuates it. Thus they are hounded on both sides; they resist associating with others like themselves and with others unlike themselves.

It is always meaningful in science to demonstrate the same basic phenomena manifested in different overt behavior and in a wide range of situations. The generality adds validity to the underlying concepts. For this reason it is relevant to note the behavior of members of a government housing project who resented having to live with "low-class" people and who for various reasons could not move (Festinger, 1953). It was observed that severe limitations were placed on the kinds of contacts they could have with the surrounding community because they imagined that outsiders would also look down on people from the project. Thus the project residents, because of their shame over having to live in the project, remained clearly in a state of relative social isolation both from members of the project (own group) and from people in the town (respected group).

The Case of Noreen

We should now like to offer a clinical demonstration of the fact that acceptance of one's disability is a prerequisite not only for group identification with other persons who have disabilities but also with

[7]Reprinted with permission from *Cotton in my ears* by F. Warfield. New York: Viking Press, 1948.

other persons who are regarded as nondisabled. Noreen had contracted polio at the age of 24. The following sequence captures some of the phases that she passed through in her gradual acceptance of kinship toward others with disabilities (Linduska, 1947).

At first, even though dangerously ill, she refused to consider the possibility of polio and insisted that her ailment was "just the flu" (p. 22). Later in the hospital Noreen vacillated between recognizing and denying her illness. On the one hand she inquired about the Sister Kenny treatment and combed all the newspapers for every account of polio that was printed. On the other hand she continued to attribute her paralysis to various other diagnoses, such as diphtheria, streptococcic sore throat, malnutrition, and even mental alienation.

Noreen's gradual willingness to recognize herself as a polio patient is seen when, many months later, as a convalescent who had learned to sit but not yet to walk, she began writing magazine articles about her experiences with polio. However, she still resisted her new group identification and avoided answering the letters from her readers who had a disability, rationalizing that people should not segregate themselves for the sake of sympathetic company (when actually desiring sympathetic company is a healthy and honorable motive and need not imply segregation). When she was asked to become a regular contributor to a monthly magazine for the disabled, she became troubled: "I then realized that I had slipped into a different group of society and I didn't like it" (p. 129).

The true beginning of a feeling of identification with persons who had a disability is seen when, during convalescence, Noreen attended a Sister Kenny rally and felt a sudden kinship with the crippled children on the platform:

> I couldn't ascend the platform, so the nurse helped me to a chair in the front row. It wasn't bad. I munched the peanuts, and out of the corner of my eye, I watched the rest of the hall fill. Then the children who were to sit on the platform began to arrive, and a strange kindred feeling arose midway when our glances met. I saw a little boy with a chromium-plated brace on his back and his arm stuck out on a shelf extending perpendicularly from the body. They put him in the front row. [p. 162][8]

But this feeling of group belongingness was unstable and gave way to strong resistance when the unreality of her present situation loomed forward in the wake of her reaching out for her past, normal existence:

[8]Reprinted by permission of Farrar, Straus & Giroux, Inc. From *My polio past* by Noreen Linduska. Copyright © 1947, 1974 by Noreen Linduska.

. . . Suddenly the peanuts stuck in my mouth, and my whole body surged with an emotion I could not identify. I began to breathe faster, and I simply could not decide whether to laugh or cry.

What kind of a crazy, upside-down cockeyed dream was this! CRIP-PLED CHILDREN! Remember Father's Elks' parties? Remember the Girl Scouts! Remember the Woman's Clubs! Hey! Just a moment! I don't belong with crippled children! I'm on the wrong side of this fence! [p. 162]

Soon after, in describing a splash party in the hospital swimming pool, Noreen was able to feel a real identification with polio patients:

In our own bathing suits, we polios were rolled off the hospital carts which conveyed us to the pool. . . . [p. 167]

It is no accident that Noreen's glimmering feelings of kinship with the minority group were concurrent with her awareness that crippling was an adjustable state, one that still provided tremendous scope for meaningful activity. During the rally, Noreen was lost in thought:

Who said that cripples are unfortunate? Do they, or do you? . . . Polio is not sad—it is just darned inconvenient. . . . [pp. 164–165]

The morning before the rally, Noreen had visited the children's polio ward and realized that the world had room for differences:

. . . Here I was in a roomful of the tiniest "victims" as the newspapers called them. . . .

In this room were the little shoes that would be lifted into the Orthopedic School Bus that used to pass our house every morning as I was running down the front stairs to catch the 7:45 "L." These little shoes wouldn't fit into roller skates or skis or be exchanged for soldiers' boots. These would know a different world than that of being center-fielder on the local dry goods baseball team. It wasn't sad—it was simply different, and I knew undramatically that there is a place all picked out in this world for every one of those baby faces. [p. 157]

It is equally significant that as Noreen began to appreciate the adjustable side of crippling, there were major shifts within her system of values: moral imperfection became far more important and deplorable than physical disability:

Why and when had physical perfection become so important, when mental imperfection, more easily remedied, went along so unnoticed. Little crippled boys were given sympathy because they could not walk, but how about the little boys who had never been taught to read or write. How about the minds of the children who lived in the same room where the adults in the family slept. Would their minds be crippled?

Would somebody pity them if they could run very fast but didn't believe in the future of honesty? Would they be pitied if they lacked whatever it takes to love the dark-skinned children whom they had gone on strike to ban from their high schools? Would they be pitied if they grew up to think that sex was the only thing in life worth working for, and that to be a pin-up girl in a movie studio was the greatest honor a woman could achieve? [pp. 158–159]

This is in sharp contrast to her prepolio outlook where physique and good health had been key criteria for status judgments:

> . . . I had belonged to a generation of laughers. My "crowd" was gay and alert. We liked everything new, and if it wasn't new enough, we would invent something that was! I liked to move about all the time. I was thrilled with tennis and volley ball and swimming—and I adored dancing. I had made a hobby of the Russian Ballet ever since I had written an eighth grade term-paper about it. I had secretly been vain about my grace and I loved to remember the man who tried to persuade me to become a part of his adagio team. I had always wanted to be a dancer, but not that kind. The fact that my parents did not approve of dancing as a career did not keep it from being a secret ambition.
>
> Good health was the most important thing in the world, and we even unconsciously scoffed at people with too-frequent sniffles. [pp. 176–177]

Noreen was further along the path of adjustment than was Jay, a young man also convalescing from polio. He was greatly troubled by the anticipated pitying attitudes of people outside the hospital. Noreen was better able to take this prospect objectively and to concern herself with its coping aspects. Her adjustment was strengthened by a reevaluation of the meaning of life that involved a reconsideration of the relative importance of significant values.

Jay vividly described the deep struggle against being pushed into an alien group, that of the handicapped. His resistance against being dislocated from his former position was so great that he could not begin to see what his new circumstances had to offer. As long as he felt that he did not belong to the group with a disability, he would continue to feel that he did not belong to the "other half" either. The price for refusal to acknowledge membership in one's own group is great:

> . . . When you are healthy all your life, and suddenly in the best years of it, you slip into the other kind—you are naturally unhappy. You are out of your element, a fish out of water. You find yourself where you do not belong. You remember how the other half lives, but you can't live with it. You won't concede your former position—you won't even turn your head to see how comfortable the new category might be. You liked the old places, and there you want to stay—there you don't belong any more, but there you want to stay—so you do—miserably! [p. 194]

Physique, which was a central value for Jay, provided the foundation for his powerful resistance against belonging to the "disabled" group. For Noreen, physique was becoming a relatively superficial characteristic, other values being of far greater importance. Consequently, she was now able to more comfortably accept her disability with the result that she was also able to more comfortably feel a part of the nonhandicapped group as well. In answering Jay, she said:

> ... "When you once belong to a group, you always belong. You belong to it because of a lot of reasons you have nothing to do with—race, religion, position, education, inherited traits and talents. Those things are not physical, but they make you belong someplace. Sometimes these uncontrollable factors combine and people of unlike religions or talents make up a group—but somewhere there is a common, compatible factor. Just because you can't hop off a chair or go running down some stairs doesn't mean that you belong to a different group—the common factors are never that shallow." [p. 194]

To sum up, the preceding analysis revolved around the following points:

1. During the initial phase of her illness, Noreen refused with all the psychological maneuvers she could muster to accept the fact of her disability.
2. Her prepolio values provided a strong foundation for this resistance. Health had been all-important, with physical skills and grace in close second position.
3. But the facts of her illness were unrelenting.
4. And something was being done about her condition. She was massaged, hot-packed, and so on.
5. Gradually she became less preoccupied with the threatening, succumbing aspects of disability and more involved with ideas of coping with it.
6. Concurrently, changes occurred within her value system. Moral and personality values became more important than physique, which shifted to being but a shallow characteristic.
7. These changes helped Noreen find her place within the group with disabilities and consequently also within the ranks of other groups.

But the pendulum must not swing the other way. To accept one's disability and oneself as a person with a disability by no means implies an all-absorbing interest in disability-connected problems. Too much preoccupation may be as much a sign of maladjustment as ostensibly too little. Generalizing to all group memberships, Lewin correctly points out: "If an individual's membership in any one group, e.g., the Jews, is of dominant interest to those around him in all situations, or a dominant value for him in all situations then he is living in an unhealthy totalitarian social setting from the point of view of group dynamics, no matter whether this dominating membership is his family, his race, his religion, or his nation" (or, we add, his disability) (Lippitt, 1945, p. 26).

But accepting one's disability and oneself as a person with a disability does imply a certain feeling of kinship with others who have the disability, a feeling of knowing such a person a little even though a stranger, in the same way that meeting an American abroad makes for an immediate tie, albeit a temporary one. This hypothesis may be integrated within Heider's (1958) theory which relates sentiments to unit formation (see pp. 68–69). Accepting one's disability allows the factor of similarity to bring about unhampered the formation of a group, which in turn arouses a positive feeling toward the other person. This phenomenon is seen in the personal experience of Louise Baker (1946), a woman whose leg had been amputated as a child:

> I have met a great many crippled people since then and some of them have developed into real friends. Even the most casual contacts, however, have been rewarding. One-leggedness is a common ground on which individuals of vast difference in background can meet and communicate. I have had fascinating conversations with handicapped persons whose lives were so divergent from my own that in the normal course of a two-legged life, I never even would have crossed their pathways.
>
> A jolly drunk who sold newspapers on a city corner and who happened to wear a peg leg, gave me a full, though perhaps slightly alcohol-flavored, account of himself one day while I waited for a bus. Similarly, I've learned all about the private lives of a taxi driver, an ex-policeman, a sculptor, a factory worker out on parole from a woman's reformatory, a little one-armed Negro orphan, a Japanese fruit peddler, an architect, etc., etc. We speak to each other. We flaunt our fraternity badges. Whatever our limping walks in life we are all people of parts—missing. We stand on common ground. We may remain transients; we usually do. We meet; we pass on; but we enrich each other in the passing. [p. 156][9]

Accepting one's disability and oneself as a person with a disability does mean that belonging only to the majority is not all-important, for in belonging to the minority as well one belongs to humanity, a group that knows no majority-minority boundaries.

[9]Reprinted by permission from *Out on a limb* by Louise Baker, published by McGraw-Hill. Copyright 1946 by Louise Baker.

THE ECLIPSE OF BEHAVIOR POSSIBILITIES

The insecurity of the person who tries to forget and conceal his or her disability is yet further increased because concealment interferes with clarifying what the person can and cannot do. We have seen (pp. 118–121) how Frances, whose hearing was impaired, bluffed her way through all kinds of social occasions instead of asking for more light in order to lip-read or for someone to speak louder or repeat what was said (Warfield, 1948). Frances figured out elaborate strategies to cope with "dinner lulls," intermissions at concerts, football games, dances, and so on, in order to protect her secret. But they served only to make her more uncertain, and in turn more cautious, and in turn more uncertain. Thus, Frances had it down pat that at a dinner party she should (1) sit next to someone with a strong voice; (2) choke, cough, or get hiccups if someone asked her a direct question; and (3) take hold of the conversation, ask someone to tell a story she had already heard, ask questions the answers to which she already knew (Warfield, 1948, p. 36). But what if she were placed next to a mumbler? What if, after her coughing, the person persisted in asking questions? What if? The uncertainty and panic snowball. Behavior resulting from new and uncertain situations follows (see Chapter 6).

The person does not allow clarification of behavior possibilities because, in order to do so, one must first be able to acknowledge, "this is my disability. . . ." Only then can a wider range of possibilities for more adequate functioning be examined.

COMPENSATION AS INDEMNITY

Overcoming inferiority is also sought by way of compensation. At the outset, two significantly different meanings of the term *compensation* should be made clear. One refers to the *adaptive ways* of meeting life demands by taking deficiencies into account and circumventing them. This type of compensation is to be endorsed. It indicates a coping approach toward problem solution and is illustrated in the following account of how a man who is color-blind compensated for this deficiency:

> The person with defective color vision must operate in the world of color normals. He therefore must learn to compensate for his deficiency. . . . In my case I tried to learn the normal colors or labels which people apply to objects. . . . I initially learned: fire engine = red; snow = white; water = blue; automobile tires = black; oranges = orange; sun = yellow. . . . Further, a rough rule of thumb . . . is to appraise the shade of the object. Generally, I have found that moving from dark to light,

colors run as follows: black, purple, red, brown, blue, grey, orange, yellow, and white. . . .

A personal experience exemplifies how a person can compensate for color-defective vision. Several years ago I worked as a salesman in a men's clothing store. Surely one would assume that this requires keen color sense. Not so: If the customer asked to see a blue suit, I found that I only had to take him to the suit section and he would then search for the shade of blue he wanted. [Snyder, 1973, pp. 52–53][10]

The second meaning of the term *compensation* has destructive implications and is our main concern here. This meaning is given in the definition of compensation as "the individual's attempt to make up for an undesirable trait and the consequent discomfort by emphasizing or exaggerating a desirable trait" (Maslow & Mittlemann, 1951, p. 575). Instead of adaptation to life demands being its main purpose, compensation in this case is an indemnity, that is, a way to "make up for" a shortcoming in order to *redeem oneself.* Essentially it reflects shame and guilt.

The concept of compensation in the sense of indemnity was given a prominent place in adjustment theory through the writings of Alfred Adler (1917a, 1917b) who felt that organic or constitutional inferiority was basic to the striving for adaptation to the world. In compensating for this inferiority, the person may either be led to constructive achievement or to a neurotic power drive.

That this type of compensation occurs cannot be denied, but it is not the spring of all, or even most, motivation. Also questionable is the view that compensation as a prodder of achievement is a way toward mental health. These issues are especially germane to the psychology of disability because of the readiness with which all behavior is linked with the disability. Thus, accomplishment tends to be seen as compensatory, particularly when the achiever has an obvious disability.

Cutsforth (1948), a clinical psychologist, himself blind, deplores the approval that educators and social agencies for the blind place upon compensation: "The attempt to compensate for the feelings of inadequacy drives the individual oftimes to the achievement of successes, but never to personality adjustment" (p. 67). Persons with a physical disability have, in fact, nothing "to make up for"—that is, unless they feel inferior because of the disability. The following admonition captures the essential devaluating supposition underlying such an adjustment theory of compensation: In order not to be especially bad, the person with a disability (or any minority-group member) must be especially good.

[10]Snyder, C. R. The psychological implications of being color blind. *The Journal of Special Education*, 1973, 7, 51–54. Reprinted with permission.

The fact that a disability imposes limitations in certain situations does not mean, perforce, that the person has to sing better, or write better, or do something else better. It means only that he or she, like everyone else, has to pursue those activities that are possible and rewarding. When unsuitable for one undertaking, the individual may seek another and pursue it because the experience is satisfying rather than compensating. The person who cannot become a doctor because of limited financial means may choose instead to become a biologist, not necessarily because he or she is compensating, but because limited financial resources is but one among other important considerations. All major decisions take into account an array of factors in order to lead to the best choice. The final decision is not compensatory *just because* it has included consideration of limitations.

Actually, if the prime motivation for striving continued to be compensatory, the person's full satisfaction of achievement would be spoiled by persistent inferiority feelings. Achievements, no matter how great, do not alter the fact of disability, and as long as the person deals with this fact through compensation as indemnity, so long will inferiority be its passport. Byron, the great British poet, Talleyrand, the great French statesman—each was born with a club foot. Byron evidently showed as much ambition to excel in violent exercises as the most robust youth of the school. Though both rose to the heights of world fame, it is reported that neither could ever forget for a moment that he was lame and both suffered the ignominy of attempts at dissimulation and feigning (Hentig, 1948a, pp. 75–76).

In only one sense would we propose that compensation as indemnity has anything to recommend it. The driving force that pushes a person to new pursuits may produce major alterations in the individual's system of values. The new areas may reveal satisfactions and values which become more important than the old ones that led the person to compensate. A person who paints *because* of a limp may discover that art is a significant value too, that a person's worth need not arbitrarily be connected with physique.

PERSONALITY EFFECTS: OPINION AND RESEARCH FINDINGS

One might suppose that a stigmatized underprivileged social position would predispose individuals toward feeling more inferior than their able-bodied counterparts. Although this is a commonsense view, it is *not* supported by the vast amount of research that has accumulated to date. And yet, experts and laypeople alike frequently mention inferiority feelings as being one of the important characteristics of groups identified by a disability. In a study of the expert opinion of professional workers with the handicapped, feelings of inferiority (with a frequency of about 25 percent) headed the list of behavior characteristics mentioned by twenty-six authors in general articles about the handicapped (Barker et al., 1946, p. 71). A study of the opinion of high-school students revealed that, when the stimulus person was presented as crippled, he was rated as feeling more inferior and unhappy than when presented as able-bodied (Ray, 1946; detailed on p. 32).

However, when we turn to the research literature on the *actual* feelings of persons with disabilities, a far less clear-cut picture emerges. In some studies, the group with a disability earned scores indicative of *greater self-respect* than their "normal" controls: In one study (Seidenfeld, 1948), subjects who had poliomyelitis showed a greater sense of personal worth on a personality test than the group on which the test was standardized. In another study (Coleman, 1973), children with disabilities who were matched with able-bodied children on age, race, sex, IQ, socioeconomic status and family constellation scored significantly higher than their matches on a standardized personality test measuring sense of personal worth and tended to show greater self-reliance and better self-concepts as a whole. In still another study (Arluck, 1941), children with epilepsy and children with a cardiac condition more often *felt superior* to most children in respect to attitudes, feelings, and interests than did their able-bodied controls, as measured by a self-rating scale. Further, the self-concept and self-acceptance of blind adolescents in a study were found to be significantly more positive than those of a matched group of sighted adolescents (Williams, 1972).

In other studies no relationship was found between specific physical characteristics and inferiority feelings. The blind adolescents in one study (Sommers, 1944) scored about the same on sense of personal worth as did the standardization population. And negligible correlations were found between inferiority feelings and height and weight of men and women in another study (Faterson, as reported in Paterson, 1930).

On the other hand, studies do exist that show a relationship, albeit a low one, between feelings of inferiority and physical defect. Children with epilepsy in the study mentioned above (Arluck, 1941), but not children with a cardiac condition, tended to feel that they were inferior in respect to their *behavior*, though not in respect to their *feelings*, more often than did their "normal" counterparts. In another study (Shelsky, 1957), hospitalized patients with tuberculosis but not those with amputations tended to be more self-rejecting than the control patients who were hospitalized for minor illnesses. In still another study (Faterson, 1931), a rating scale for measuring inferiority was administered to a group of entering university students and the resulting scores were correlated with degree of physical defect as determined from each student's medical report. A physical-defect score was obtained by giving one point for each physical defect reported on the medical blank, such defects being included as fallen arches, menstrual disorders, heart murmurs, poor posture, nasal obstruction, orthopedic defects, diseased tonsils, insomnia, and tiredness. The correlations between inferiority feelings and physical defect for men and women were low (under .25) but positive. (Note that the physical-defect score included deviations such as insomnia and tiredness, which might easily have a large psychosomatic component.)

The main point is that no matter how the studies are grouped, the data cannot be ordered so that scores of inferiority are in any systematic way related to type of disability or to such aspects of disability as duration or degree. This point can be broadened to state that, on balance, research shows that people with a disability fare as well (or as poorly) on general measures of personality adjustment as do their able-bodied counterparts, provided that socioeconomic status and other confounding factors are eliminated.

OVERSIMPLIFIED CONNECTION BETWEEN DISABILITY AND INFERIORITY FEELINGS

To attempt clarification of the preceding problem, several ideas need to be considered. First of all, disability is not the only characteristic that places a person in an inferior status position. Underprivileged minority status touches those of particular races and religion, of low socioeconomic level, and of slow mental development. Even children, women, and in some respects men are placed in the psychological position of inferior status. The reader will be able to think of many other circumstances that provide an occasion for devaluation. In short, *all of us* have within us the experience of being looked down upon as individuals or as part of a larger group.

But, the protest might be made that persons with a disability have the stigma of disability superimposed on whatever other devalued characteristics they might have; they have a greater load of inferior status to bear and a more persistent one. Ought not this fact lead to more pronounced feelings of inferiority? Evidently not. And the reason is an important one. *Psychological processes do not add up in a simple way.*

For clarification, let us consider the relationship between *degree of disability and adjustment.* One might assume that the greater the disability, the more difficult it is for the person to accept it or to achieve good adjustment. However, the facts provoke serious question of this assumption. Though some studies (Brunschwig, 1936; Kammerer, 1940; Landis & Bolles, 1942; Weiss et al., 1971) have shown a relationship between degree of disability and poor adjustment, other studies (Springer, 1938; Donofrio, 1948; Tracht, 1946; Shontz, 1971) have shown no relationship, and still others (Macgregor et al., 1953; Miller, 1958) have shown the reverse relationship.

To explain these inconsistencies, it may be postulated that persons with a mild disability may, because they are *almost* normal, have a greater need to hide and deny the disability, thereby thwarting adjustment, whereas those whose disability is so severe as to be undeniable have little recourse but to grapple with the problem of accepting themselves as a person with a disability. Support for this hypothesis may be drawn from the point made by Heider (1958) that a near approach to what we desire seems to make its attainment more possible, and from Dembo's observation in experiments on anger that the subjects were more disturbed when they *almost* succeeded in the task (throwing rings on a peg) than when the failure was more clear-cut (1931; translated 1976).

The observation has also been made that the child with cerebral palsy who has a mild handicap appears to have more severe adjustment problems arising from disturbed parent-child relationships than does the child with severe cerebral palsy (Miller, 1958). One study directly tested the hypothesis of stress and marginality by comparing partially with totally blind children and partially with totally deaf children (Cowen & Bobrove, 1966). The marginally involved children showed greater personality disturbances in twenty of the twenty-eight data comparisons. As we have noted above, however, research has not shown a consistent correlation of adjustment with degree of disability. This is because all the favorable factors do not appear on one side of the disability continuum. Thus, it may also be postulated that a mild disability, by imposing fewer frustrations due to the barrier of physical limitations, makes adjustment easier. Doubtless there are other factors associated with degree of disability, some favoring and some hindering good adjustment, the resultant effect being quite removed from the objective fact of severity. Notice that we have moved from the *physical* fact of degree of disability to *psychological* concepts, such as need to hide the disability, perception of probability of goal attainment, and frustration, in order to account for the associated personality and psychological behavior. Such psychological concepts are known as *intervening variables* and are necessary for the understanding of somatopsychological problems.

By like reasoning, we cannot say that frequency or intensity of social devaluation is related in a direct or one-to-one way to personal feelings of inferiority. With increase in social devaluation may come an increased need for a new look into one's values, which may do much to counteract the destructive power of inferior social status (see Chapter 8).

In addition to change in one's values, there are other ways human beings attempt to preserve their own sense of personal worth. Research has shown that we are more likely to care greatly about what others who have a favorable opinion think of us than when they hold us in low regard (Rosenberg, 1973). Also, we selectively tend to associate with those who have favorable or at least accepting attitudes, thereby minimizing our exposure to the barbs of others.

Furthermore, inferior status is not the only psychological situation in which people with a disability are placed. At times they may be looked up to and may even enjoy an exalted position. Henry Viscardi (1952), dwarfed by misshapen legs as a child, remembers how much becoming an expert marbles player did for his standing in the gang:

> In the years that followed, under the tutelage of Marble Bags I gradually became the immies champ of our block, and my self-esteem grew along with my big bag of marbles. In later years I was often to think with pride of that little achievement, as I watched amputees and paraplegics regain a feeling of personal dignity through mastering the art of doing something well with their hands. [pp. 27–28][11]

The majority group may sometimes bestow genuine commendation, as when the person is acknowledged who achieves in spite of a disability. Certainly respect, encouragement, and acceptance from family members and friends are not infrequent. That salutary status and acceptance by others are not foreign to members of minority groups are undoubtedly important in checking self-rejection.

In an important study on well-adjusted children (Langdon & Stout, 1951), it was discovered that despite tremendous differences in the background and physical characteristics of these children, many of which could be considered as social or physical handicaps, there was one outstanding similarity: the children were loved by their parents in an atmosphere of warm though not necessarily demonstrative acceptance. Of the 261 well-adjusted children, some wore glasses, one used a hearing aid, a few were described as over-

---

[11]From *A man's stature* by H. Viscardi, Jr. Reprinted by permission of Paul S. Eriksson, Pubs.

weight, some underweight, several were left-handed. One was said to have a spastic condition, another a heart lesion, another diabetes. The children were oldest, youngest, in the middle. Some were from poor homes and some from middle-class homes and higher. Several children came from one-parent families through divorce, separation, or death. There were children with parents of mixed religious beliefs. There was such a diversity of discipline procedures as one can hardly imagine, ranging all the way from "They do what I say or else" to "We want them to want to do what is right." Yet all these children were well adjusted! And all the parents, without a single exception, expressed in some way the following thoughts as being most important of all: Loving them and letting them know it, thinking of them as people and treating them so, appreciating what they do and trusting them and telling them so, and above all letting them know they are wanted. This study is important in showing that conditions commonly accepted as being deleterious to personality development do not necessarily bend the twig into a deformed tree; the tree may flower and prosper because of deeper psychological soil made rich by growth-promoting interpersonal relationships.

The thesis presented here does differ from Alfred Adler's (1917b) theory, which holds that ". . . the possession of definitely inferior organs is reflected upon the psyche—and in such a way as to lower the self-esteem, to raise the child's psychological uncertainty. But it is just out of this lowered self-esteem that there arises the struggle for self-assertion . . . the predisposed child in his sense of inferiority selects out of his psychic resources expedients for the raising of his own value . . . among which may be noted as occupying the most prominent places those of a neurotic and psychotic character" (p. 3). The Adlerian doctrine would lead one to expect a high incidence of neurotic and psychotic tendencies in individuals with a physical disability and specifically of marked feelings of inferiority. The available evidence, however, supports none of these expectations and forces one to the conclusion that there has been a gross oversimplification of the connection between physical impairment and maladjustment.

Moreover, even when inferiority feelings in an individual are strongly tied to impaired physique, we must, in order to understand and evaluate those feelings" . . . deal with the individual in relation to and as part of the family, and with the family in relation to and as part of the individual's cultural environment" (Sommers, 1944, p. 98). As has been pointed out, "When the relationship between the child and its parents and its effect on the development of the former's personality is studied, it becomes evident that this feeling of inferiority has causes other than the physical defect, although these causes are associated with and conditioned by it" (Allen & Pearson, 1928, p. 234).

Our position must be further clarified. It does not assert that physical disability plays no role in the development of inferiority feelings or other problems. On the contrary, it is *likely,* although not inevitable, that stigmatized and undesired self-attributes will stir some feeling of shame and inferiority *initially* as one struggles toward self-acceptance. This has been amply indicated in the earlier section on "as if" behavior. Our position does imply, however, that *the objective fact of disability is an extraordinarily poor criterion for judging which individual is unduly beset by self-depreciation and which individual is not.* Moreover, we are forced to conclude that people with disabilities as a group are not distinguishable from the nondisabled with respect to inferiority feelings and that the presumed association between inferiority feelings and atypical physique is unwarranted by the facts.

It is important to realize that the reasoning presented here regarding the self-esteem of people with disabilities also applies to other minority groups. Thus, in a valuable review of a dozen studies on race and self-esteem, Rosenberg & Simmons (1971) conclude that ". . . despite the immense disprivileges to which blacks are subject in our society today, they do not have lower self-esteem" than whites, despite expectations to the contrary (p. 145).

A second point that has to be underscored is that many of the problems with which the individual with a disability is faced stem directly from discriminatory practices and neglect on the part of the wider society. Obviously, if people with disabilities had access more generally to suitable housing, transportation, work and other important settings, basic conditions of life would more satisfactorily be met. Also obviously, if devaluation in interpersonal relations were reduced, personal suffering on that account would also be reduced.

Thus far we have been concerned with initial efforts of the individual to escape the stigmatizing effects of disability, efforts that often persist but are not sound, for they disguise negative feelings but do not overcome them. The discussion dealt with forgetting, concealing, avoiding group identification, eclipsing behavior possibilities, compensation as indemnity, and idolizing normal standards. It was seen that these phenomena are prompted by a basic rejection of the disability when it symbolizes that "I am less worthy, less good, less desirable than others."

Despite the stigma attached to disability, however, the considerable body of research forces the conclusion that people with a physical disability are not generally distinguishable from their able-bodied counterparts in terms of inferiority feelings. Reasons for this include: (1) All people have the experience of being devaluated or stigmatized for something, whether as individuals or as part of a larger group. (2) The frequency or intensity of social devaluation is not related in a direct way to personal feelings of inferiority, partly because the individual does not passively become more and more scarred with each successive blow. (3) Adjustive forces within the person, such as those leading to important value changes, serve the person's self-esteem. (4) The person also gives greater weight in the long run to the opinions of those who are accepting rather than rejecting and selectively associates with the former. (5) Respect, encouragement, and acceptance from family and friends are not foreign to members of minority groups and are crucial in checking self-rejection.

Yet, people with a disability, as almost everyone, do experience gnawing feelings of inferiority more or less intensely at some time in their lives. These feelings may be tied to having a disability. The discomfort that results from rejecting the disability and therefore the self helps the person to recognize that pretense produces repeated feelings of failure, shame, guilt, and estrangement from oneself and others. The wish to accept oneself as a person with a disability and to have others accept oneself as such strengthens the person's adjustive efforts. The value changes that are part of these adjustive efforts are discussed at length in the following chapter.

Chapter 8
Value Changes in Acceptance of Disability

We have seen how people who feel ashamed and inferior because of a disability avoid identification as a person with a disability. By keeping the disability to oneself, the person tries to prevent it from becoming a social fact, hoping that rebuff from society can thereby be eluded. There is a rational basis for this course of action inasmuch as having a disability will provoke rejection by some persons and discrimination in some situations of importance, as in employment. By hiding a disability it seems possible to avoid negative experiences. If concealment is not possible, then as long as the person feels inferior because of it, he or she will try to act as though the disability makes no difference, outdo himself or herself in maintaining normal standards, and in general appear as much like a nonhandicapped person as possible (see preceding chapter). But even should the disability be concealed, the person cannot feel the security of being a complete and worthy individual, for admission that a difference exists is a prerequisite to the further step of accepting the difference as personally nondevaluating.

If, as was already shown, the cultural attitudes toward atypical physique are conflicting (on the one hand being a sign of inferiority, and on the other being neutral or even an indication of virtue and goodness meriting special reverence), why is it that the person with a disability struggles so much with the personally more devastating side of the conflict? It is primarily because the first view (sign of inferiority) is so threatening that it demands attention. And when the individual in some way associates disability with punishment or idolizes the normal ideal, the feeling that disability is and ought to be a sign of inferiority is confirmed. Moreover, under certain conditions an inferior position on one characteristic tends to spread to other characteristics and to the total person. These and other factors contribute to the importance that disability-as-personal-inferiority assumes *at first* and that determines the more primitive efforts of escaping the intolerable rejection of the self.

The maladjustive reactions to disability, however, are important first efforts in the process of accepting one's disability and oneself. Gradually and intermittently, the individual may become aware of the strain that nonacceptance of the disability imposes and that one can live on satisfactory terms with the disability. Frances Warfield (1948), who admitted her hearing loss only to her medical and quack therapists, devised elaborate schemes to hide her impairment and at the same time perceived the foolishness of such behavior *when the actors were other people.* She spoke of them as "silly ostriches . . . who didn't fool anybody but themselves" (p. 26). It may take a longer time and many upsetting personal experiences before one can admit the foolishness in oneself. Admission carries the obligation of altering one's behavior, of giving up the methods one wants so desperately to succeed, of examining anew the values one cherishes, values that seem so compelling and driving and by which one lives.

ACCEPTANCE AS NONDEVALUATION

The importance of accepting oneself has become a cardinal principle among psychotherapists ever since the far-reaching role of such psychological processes as repression and guilt have become more clearly understood. However, we need to go further and ask what kind of self-acceptance we have in mind, for as a general term it cloaks a diversity of values and concepts. When a person in psychotherapy becomes aware of his or her hostile feelings and defiantly begins to insult associates and cater almost exclusively to personal needs, is that accepting oneself? At the moment the person may be accepting these hostile feelings, but also the premises that they need no controls and that the goal of self-acceptance means accepting oneself as one is with no requirement for change. This is not the meaning of self-acceptance as we shall use it.

Nor by self-acceptance will we mean a preference for one's own characteristics or group, although self-acceptance is sometimes used in this way. There certainly are many among underprivileged racial and religious minority groups who are glad that they are blacks, Indians, or Jews, who wish their children to be proud of their heritage, who accept and prefer their group membership. The book *It's good to be black* culminates in the young girl's conviction that she could be proud that she was black (Goodwin, 1953). Moreover, she felt "genuinely sorry for everybody in the world lighter than the brown pair of . . . shoes laced on my dancing feet" (p. 256).

Acceptance in the sense of preference is certainly not unknown among people who have a disability. There are those who would not relinquish the disability even if they could. There are those who are glad that they are deaf and even wish their children to be. Before the judgment "Aha, secondary gain, rationalization" is made, we must again remind ourselves of how seriously mistaken outsiders can be when led astray and deluded by the compelling nature of their own values and perspective. (See "Requirement of Mourning," Chapter 5; "Position of the Person," Chapter 3.) A disability can become an inextricable part of one's identity and one's life. To cast it aside can signal too basic a restructuring and a relinquishing of aspects and values that are too important.

In any case, the problem of acceptance as dealt with here is not concerned with the conditions that will bring about preference of one's own state over others. Nor does it deal with the other end of the scale, that of acceptance in the sense of resigning oneself to the inevitable. Resignation connotes a bowing to misfortune, patiently uncomplaining, rather than meeting its challenge in a positive sense. We are more concerned with the conditions facilitating *acceptance of one's disability as nondevaluating.* The disability may still be seen as inconvenient and limiting. The person may still strive to "improve the improvable" where improvement will facilitate certain aspects of life. With acceptance, unencumbered by resignation and self-devaluation, the person may exercise daily to graduate from crutch-walking to cane-walking but will not abandon the crutches prematurely in order to be as much like a "normal" person as possible. The person will not feel personally debased and suffer the strain and shame of hiding and pretense.

We shall begin our discussion of value changes with a description of the period of crisis as experienced by a person who endured a major neurological assault.

THE PERIOD OF CRISIS

The following account summarizes a surgeon's reactions during the first two weeks of a progressive neurological disease (Guillain-Barre type of polyneuritis) that left him with permanent paralysis of his hands and lower legs (Sharman, 1972). It was selected because it highlights the crisis period during which complex sets of intermingling thoughts, feelings, and events flare up, subside, and smoulder, only to be aroused again in response to the inordinate stresses of the situation. The breakdown by days is to keep the reader apprised of the temporal course of events and to mark off some notable transitions. The account takes the reader through the acute stage of the disease to the point where the patient began to take stock of his changed circumstances in an effort to redefine a place for himself.

> *Days 1–3:* Became aware of the spreading paralysis. Filled with stunned disbelief. Such a thing could not happen to *me*—a medical doctor was "immune" to serious disease. Kept checking out reality by trying to move my limbs. Angry at "Fate," at the disease itself, at the profession who could not stop the disease's progression. Deeply resented unimpaired persons. They were "whole." I was not. Thought of my illness as inconvenience, not as a threat to my way of life.
>
> *Days 4–7:* Paralysis advanced to above elbows and knees. Hands useless. Could no longer stand. Could only watch as a major portion of my body was destroyed. Anger flared. Have taken more than enough of this. Became convinced that an uncontrollable disease was overtaking me. Diffuse feelings of anxiety displaced anger. My personal world gradually shrank and became focused on my body. Concern for my professional responsibilities never entered my mind. Still felt hope that the paralysis would spend itself and progress no further. Anxiety subsided, I believe through processes of denial and isolation of affect. People's reactions affected me a great deal. Everyone, except my wife, felt uncomfortable in my presence. Was especially sensitive to the anxiety of the doctors and felt that they tried to avoid me. Silently angry at the doctors' emotional detachment. Felt that they were consciously lying. Angry at myself for being afraid to ask that I be informed. I remained quiet, aloof. Became increasingly anxious and angry and hurt within. Deep inner sense of hurt came over me when it seemed that other people preferred to remain uninvolved with my undesirable and unworthy self. My wife only person who wanted genuinely to stay close by. Talked mainly about daily activities of our two children. Dared not ask her any crucial questions.
>
> *Days 8–9:* Respirator placed in readiness. No one had discussed the respirator with me. Became afraid, not that I would die, but that I would be alone, isolated from people. My hope was at stake. Flowers from friends began to signal last respects to a dying man. Angry and resentful over the idea that I no longer merited the hope of others. Anxiety and

fear mounted. Physical helplessness almost total. My arms and legs totally paralyzed. Retained full control of only my head, neck and trunk,
including respiratory and sphincter function. Frightened that if these
latter functions were lost I would be reduced to a "living brain."
Thoughts were blurred by intense anxiety and fear. Felt abandoned,
helpless and without hope. Panicked at the thought of being alone with
a machine. Was close to an emotional break. Feared that if I sobbed or
screamed out in despair I would lose control of everything.
Day 9: Turning point because of simple compassion of doctor who assured me that he would stay with me if respirator became necessary.
Almost burst out crying because of a sudden feeling of relief and exaltation. Somehow I had been put back on the track, after a temporary de-
railment, by a friend and doctor who cared, who would see to it that
I lived. From that point on, everything from within and without seemed
to begin to stabilize. No longer felt alone. Fear and panic dropped away
although I continued to feel uneasy.
Days 10–14: Acute phase over. Feeling of great relief that paralysis
progressed no further. Reassessment of myself and the world about me
begun.

The crisis period of this patient could be described by the following reactions: disbelief and denial; anger and resentment; fear, anxiety, and panic; self-devaluation and guilt; rationalization; reality testing; narrowing of personal world; aloofness; helplessness and despair;
hope and encouragement; feelings of being comforted; feelings of
abandonment; worry and uneasiness; blurring of thoughts; emotional
decompensation; relief and exaltation; emotional stabilization; and
reevaluation.

Such a list, however, is inadequate for a number of reasons. To
begin with, the reactions did not occur in sequential order, but rather
fluctuated in time. Such fluctuations are typical and led Shontz (1965)
to describe the crisis period as consisting of rapidly recurring cycles
during the early stages that become less pronounced as the person
begins to acknowledge the reality of the situation.

What is equally limiting is that such a list separates emotions
from cognitions. Cognitions give emotions their content. They include the person's thoughts and perception of events associated with
the emotion in some way, often as causes of them. To state that the
patient felt angry at "Fate" is quite different from saying that he felt
angry at the medical profession for not halting the disease, or angry
at the emotional distancing of doctors and friends. Even if these reactions are collapsed into the one classification, anger, they assuredly
represent three qualitatively different psychological events, a differentiation that may be important in considering which of the disturbances could have been avoided. For example, knowledge that the
emotional detachment of professionals provoked anger points the

way for amelioration, whereas "Fate" as the perceived provocative agent does not.

Other examples of the cognitive anchoring of the emotional processes experienced by this patient are:

Denial—disbelief at the spreading paralysis.
Rationalization—a medical doctor is immune to serious disease.
Anxiety—over the spreading paralysis.
Narrowing of personal world—focus on body.
Hope—paralysis would be halted.
Guilt—at being afraid to ask for information.
Isolation of affect—remaining aloof.
Self-devaluation—others wished to avoid his undesirable self.
Feeling of being comforted—by wife who genuinely wanted to remain close.
Fear—of being abandoned.
Resentment—at people who were whole.
Anger—that paralysis was progressing.
Panic—at the thought of being alone in a respirator.
Testing of reality—by trying to move limbs.
Relief—when paralysis ceased progressing.
Emotional stabilization—attributed to compassion of doctor who cared.

Only sometimes are emotions "free floating," without content. Usually, the person latches on to something that will give a sense of reasonableness to the feeling. It is a feeling in search of a cause, as it were.

Various writers have conceptualized the crisis period in different ways. What they have in common is the recognition that the emotional buffeting and defensive reactions that follow the trauma eventually give way sufficiently to allow the person to begin to take hold in the light of the new circumstances. The process is one of struggle and growth, as a result of which the person sometimes, in the words of Karl Menninger, becomes "weller than well." The significance of restitutive forces has been studied in different cases of physical trauma: the dying patient (Kübler-Ross, 1969), persons who are chronically physically ill or have a physical disability (Dembo et al., 1956; Shontz, 1965; Fink, 1967), persons with progressive illness (Matson & Brooks, 1977), and families of children with polio (Davis, 1963).

Now we ask, what helps the person begin to "take hold" and continue to strive to regain his or her bearing and sense of personal worth? We shall examine this question in terms of the evolving and shifting changes that take place within the person's value system.

VALUE CHANGES

Dembo and coworkers (1956; reprinted 1975) conceived the problem of acceptance as centering upon the concept of "acceptance of loss." By loss is meant the absence of something valuable, experienced as a personal misfortune. By acceptance is meant viewing the value loss as *nondevaluating*. It does not imply resignation or ignoring aspects of the self or of the environment that can be improved.

The following discussion is an extension of the Dembo analysis of changes within the value system of the person that are important in overcoming the feeling of shame and inferiority resulting from disability as a value loss. These value changes are designated as: (1) enlarging the scope of values, (2) subordinating physique relative to other values, (3) containing disability effects, and (4) transforming comparative-status values into asset values. Bear in mind that the value changes apply to both the insider and the outsider, the latter when the task is to accept the disability of another as nondevaluating. The presentation, however, will focus on the insider.

Enlarging the Scope of Values

We have seen that during the crisis period, one's resources are mustered to fight the physical and psychological assault to one's integrity. As part of the shock reaction, there occurs a narrowing of the person's world and a preoccupation with the loss itself.

Preoccupation with loss, referred to as the period of mourning, has been compared to mourning in bereavement. It may cover a longer or shorter time span during which the person comes to terms with the loss. The *period of mourning* should be distinguished from the *requirement of mourning* which was discussed at length in Chapter 5.

Where preoccupation with loss is intense, the first value change posited to occur is "enlarging the scope of values." This value change means emotionally appreciating the existence of values in addition to the one(s) lost. It represents an awakening interest in satisfactions that are accessible and facilitates coming to terms with what has been lost. An understanding of the awakening process will be furthered by a discussion of the significance of the period of mourning.

· *The Significance of Mourning.* Some writers have stressed that although mourning may be a common reaction to a major loss, it is neither universal nor a necessary precondition to adjustment (Cook, 1976). The position one takes on this question depends upon whether the concept of mourning refers only to all-inclusive preoccupation with loss involving a depressed general mood and outlook or whether it also encompasses more moderate states in which the person is able to give weight and attend to ongoing values and goals. There is no doubt that many people can confine their sense of loss more narrowly to the loss itself and "deal with what has to be dealt with and go on from there." They are not pervasively depressed, although they may experience intermittent sadness and other dysphoric feelings connected with the loss, such as worry, regret, and anger. As we shall use it, the concept of mourning refers to a continuum, one extreme being all-inclusive suffering.

Caretakers can be expected to overestimate the degree of depression admitted by patients. This proposition is derived theoretically from the difference between the position of the person as insider versus outsider (see pp. 47–51). It is also supported by research (Hamera & Shontz, 1978; Mason & Muhlenkamp, 1976; see also research on the fortune phenomenon, p. 34 and on the mine-thine problem, pp. 48–49). Since "one's life depends on it," the need to cope is strong in the person faced with a challenge. It is this need that directs the person to discover and hold on to hopeful signs and positives in the situation. This, of course, does not preclude the fact that many people struggle with all-inclusive suffering while mourning a major loss.

A person with a disability experiences the loss in terms of personal and social satisfactions that are now felt to be denied. Mourning for personal loss is expressed in the following ruminations as Harold Russell (1949) realizes for the first time that he has no hands:

> I looked up and saw my arms. For the first time. Their ends were wrapped in bandages. They were pulled up over my head and fastened to a wooden frame above the bed. I couldn't move them. I could hardly move my body at all. It made me think of the days before I went to the Army, when I worked in the market. My arms reminded me of two sides of beef hanging on hooks. . . .
>
> Then it hit me.
>
> It was my *hands* that were gone. Those things at the end of my arms. Those things with five fingers on them. They hadn't been much to look at. Quite ugly, in fact, and dirty most of the time.
>
> Suddenly I knew how useful those hands had been to me. I had always taken them for granted. Like my eyes, legs, ears, tongue. They had always been there when I needed them, ready to work. If I wanted to cut and weigh a piece of meat, if I wanted to drive a golf ball, if I wanted to write a letter to Rita or pull the ripcord of a parachute, they were always there to serve me. I never had to ask, Will you do this for me? They were always there, by my side, prepared, willing, unhesitating, obedient, loyal. A pair of stout, strong friends, not beautiful, but dependable. . . .

I tried not to think about them. . . .

But I kept coming back to my hands. I couldn't get them out of my mind. What wonderful, efficient machines they were. Hands. So simple. Just some bones, muscles, nerves, blood vessels and skin. Nothing to them, really. And yet, how valuable, how perfect, how cunningly contrived to do so many marvelous things. Like pitching a ball or painting a picture or caressing someone you loved. [pp. 4–5][1]

The social loss content of mourning may be conveyed in the following: "People might stand my presence but not accept me as they used to." "I never had to depend on others. Now I will be a burden." "People will pity me." "Others will go ahead while I will be left behind."

With intense mourning, the loss aspects dominate the emotional stage. In extreme bereavement, "the loss seems to pervade all areas of the person's life. Whatever he thinks about, whatever he does, he is troubled, pained, and distressed. There is no differentiation between areas of the person which are and are not injury-connected. All that matters are the values affected by the injury and they are lost. No other values in life are important or even existent" (Dembo et al., 1956, p. 36). In the grip of such an emotional onslaught, the person may become apathetic, numb to all conscious feeling. Goldman (1947) captures the essence of this state in his recollection of the period following the death of his wife:

. . . I tried not to look back; I couldn't look forward, for ahead was a wall of blankness. It is difficult to put into this chronicle the record of my emotions. I seemed to have none; I was empty as a wormed shell. I no longer felt even the twisting pain of grief. . . .

. . . I wanted to die . . . to be rid of the galling burden of futile struggle. The thought of taking my own life never once entered my mind. . . . Just passively I wanted to die. [p. 168][2]

Pearl Buck (1950), upon learning that her retarded child could never be normal, was overcome with a despair so profound that it threatened to destroy her thought and feeling:

. . . there was no more joy left in anything. All human relationships became meaningless. Everything became meaningless. I took no more pleasures in the things I had enjoyed before; landscapes, flowers, music were empty. Indeed, I could not bear to hear music at all. It was years before I could listen to music. Even after the learning process had gone

[1]Reprinted by permission of Farrar, Straus & Giroux, Inc. From *Victory in my hands* by Harold Russell & Victor Rosen. Copyright 1949 by Harold Russell & Victor Rosen. Copyright renewed © 1976 by Harold Russell.
[2]Reprinted with permission of Macmillan Publishing Co., Inc., from *Even the night* by R. L. Goldman. Copyright 1947, and renewed 1975, by Raymond Leslie Goldman.

very far, and my spirit had become nearly reconciled through understanding, I could not hear music. I did my work during this time: I saw
that my house was neat and clean, I cut flowers for the vases, I planned
the gardens and tended my roses, and arranged for meals to be properly
served. We had guests and I did my duty in the community. But none
of it meant anything. My hands performed their routine. The hours
when I really lived were when I was alone with my child. When I was
safely alone I could let sorrow have its way, and in utter rebellion
against fate my spirit spent its energy. [pp. 29–30][3]

Deep despair may also occur in the recently injured person
when the experience of loss and change from one's former state is
so overpowering that the suffering seems boundless, not only in extent but also in time. The idea of suicide may then present itself or,
more moderately, the gnawing feeling that one will now be useless.

There are a number of forces that keep the person within the
mourning state. One of the most persistent is the *need to hold on
to the preferred state* that was. By mourning the loss, the person
brings the past into the present and does not give up the past.

The person also *needs time* to begin to absorb the new changes
into one's self-concept. As has been pointed out, the shock reaction
to loss ". . . seems to be an emergency defense against the threat of
dissolution of the ego by eruption of overwhelmingly painful affects.
The affects are thereafter allowed to emerge bit by bit so that they
can be handled by the ego piecemeal . . ." (Blank, 1957, p. 11).

In addition, the *perceptual factor of contrast* contributes to the
persistence as well as the existence of mourning. In the sheer act of
comparing the present with the past, one is prone to concentrate on
the changes and to ignore the commonalities. Perceptually, the
things that are different stand out and the remainder, in its sameness,
becomes obliterated. In the case of disability, *the difference is the disability* and thus the loss may be seen as the main feature of the new
state.

Mourning may also express the *need to make a public pageant
of grief.* This may be associated with a bid for sympathy, indulging
in self-pity, or fulfilling the formal requirements of propriety.

That the mourning reaction to loss, though common, is not the
only reaction is seen in a study of World War II injured men (Randall,
Ewalt, & Blair, 1945). In the case of noncombat casualties, severe depression (mourning) was the preponderant reaction immediately following the injury. However, in the case of battle casualties the modal
reaction was the feeling of being lucky, with depression, though com-

---

[3]From *The child who never grew* by P. S. Buck, published by John Day. Reprinted
by permission of American Institute for Mental Studies.

mon, taking second place. These results can be accounted for by the perceptual factor of contrast, that is, by the likelihood that the battle casualties felt that they easily could have been worse off; instead of comparing their present injured state with their previous able-bodied state, the comparison was with their anticipated annihilation. The outstanding difference in these circumstances is not the loss aspect of the new state but rather its gain. The percentage of cases (76 battle injuries, 24 noncombat injuries) reacting variously, as determined by social histories from Red Cross files, analysis of unidentified Rorschach records, and psychiatric examinations, is shown in Table 8.1.

Table 8.1 PERCENTAGE OF REACTIONS TO INJURY

	IMMEDIATELY FOLLOWING INJURY		IN BASE HOSPITAL	
	BATTLE	NONCOMBAT	BATTLE	NONCOMBAT
Shame	0	0	11	33
Self-pity	1	0	9	0
Lucky	42	0	7	0
Worry about family	16	13	0	0
Depression	30	61	13	21
Psychiatric	4	13	3	8
No emotional response	7	13	57	38

The reaction of the battle cases is more favorable in both time phases. In the second phase the feeling of both "lucky" and depression decreases, and the feeling of shame and self-pity increases. Finally, it is apparent that depression was not the only prominent reaction. How many of the "no emotional response" reactions can be considered symptomatic of what we have called mourning is not known.

During pervasive mourning, the need for the lost values, the perception of difference with the compared state, and even the propriety of mourning concentrate the energies of the person on the *loss* aspects. It now becomes clear why the first step in overcoming such preoccupation entails enlarging the scope of values to encompass those values that are still available to the person. Only then can the person look to the satisfactions existing in the present and begin to see life, as well as the self, as having something to offer.

In the following section, the focus is on all-inclusive suffering, although the discussion and suggestions will also be useful to the person whose suffering is less pervasive.

· *Overcoming Mourning.* A variety of experiences prod the person out of the worst moments of despair by forcing the realization that there is meaning to life, that all is not lost by the disability. Dembo and her coworkers (1956) suggest that the essential value, *life,* may be regained the moment the person decides to give it up. Here again the contrast phenomenon plays an important role in perceiving what constitutes change. In a contemplation of suicide, the characteristic that differentiates the two states, before and after, is *life.* Instead of pervasive suffering, life, for the moment at least, may occupy the person's energies. This may provide the first hold, the feeling of strength and hope called the "stamina experience" and lead to new positive awareness in life. Doug, a 46-year-old man who had had polio in his twenties recalled:

> Before I got polio, I'd always been able to unload 100 pound sacks of feed. I remember saying and agreeing with my buddy that both of us would rather be dead than be crippled up to where we couldn't use our bodies like we had just done, but I'll tell you for sure that when the Doctor told me I had polio, I started praying to come through it alive. I don't remember once praying to come out of it without being crippled. I'd say probably everybody at one time or another has said they'd rather be dead than in a wheelchair, but if people were really faced with the choice I'd bet nearly all of them would do just like I did and not once think back to rather being dead. (Personal communication)

Perhaps the shock of almost having lost his life helped Doug to appreciate life itself.

The *perceptual factor of contrast* is also in evidence when a person, in seeing others with different disabilities, first realizes his or her own assets. Speaking of his many employees with disabilities, the head of a company, who himself had an amputation, observed: "It is valuable psychologically to have different types of disabled workers together in the same company. . . . The blind man considers himself much better off than his deaf-mute co-worker. The deaf-mute would not trade places with the infantile paralysis victim who cannot walk. The infantile paralysis victim feels sorry for the one-armed person. Each one, when he sees someone else and realizes the limitations forced upon the other fellow by handicaps he himself does not have, feels he is not so badly off" (Rusk & Taylor, 1946, p. 188).[4] This contrast phenomenon is of therapeutic value when, through it, people become aware of their own assets or abilities, and that they can participate in their own way, as others can in their own way, in this multivaried world.

Even when the person may believe that nothing matters any longer, many dormant values remain that may be aroused. Dembo et al. (1956) give an example in which the depression of a wounded

[4]From *New hope for the handicapped* by Howard A. Rusk & Eugene J. Taylor. Copyright 1946, 1947, 1948, 1949 by Howard A. Rusk. By permission of Harper & Row, Publishers, Inc.

soldier was eased when a close friend ridiculed and scolded his self-pity. This resulted in awakened pride as a remaining value.

In less depressed states, the sheer necessities of living may contribute to the turning away from the past and dealing with the here and now. The person with paraplegia, for example, has to attend to bodily needs. Needs prod the person to try to move, turn over, and sit up; and in coping with these problems the person may find a challenge in dealing with the problems at hand. We can now see the important place, in the process of enlarging the scope of values, of mastering *activities of daily living* (ADL) that modern rehabilitation introduces early to the patient (although mastering ADL is surely not sufficient for engaging a new lease on life).

Films that show a person with a disability managing the ordinary affairs of living can provide tremendous support for a person who has only recently become faced with the challenge. The psychological impact of such a film is seen in Harold Russell's (1949) experience two months after he lost his hands:

> . . . *Meet McGonegal* was the story of a man who had lost his hands in World War I. McGonegal . . . had been faced by the same problem I was up against and he had licked it. . . . There was no plot to the movie, at least not in the ordinary sense. But for me it had a tremendous impact. It told me that any handicapped person could get along fine and take a normal place in society if he really wanted to. The picture showed a typical day in Charley McGonegal's life: It showed him dressing himself, shaving, brushing his teeth, combing his hair, eating breakfast, smoking, drinking, reading, shooting a game of pool and writing a letter—with a fountain pen, like a grownup, instead of with a pencil, like a child.
>
> It was the most exciting movie I had ever seen. When it was over and the lights went up again I said to myself, if he could do it, I can do it, too. [pp. 105–106][5]

It is also likely that a *satiation factor* will affect behavior, helping the person to overcome absorption with loss. One can maintain an emotional state only so long. One can be ecstatically happy, but the peak wanes with time even when the circumstances remain the same. Similarly, a person may be deeply depressed over a loss, but in time there is an ebbing of depression. This may be accompanied by a numbness. The person feels wrung dry. It is as though that person were satiated with emotion and preoccupation with loss. One has mourned and mourned and mourned. One becomes tired of mourn-

[5]Reprinted by permission of Farrar, Straus & Giroux, Inc. From *Victory in my hands* by Harold Russell & Victor Rosen. Copyright 1949 by Harold Russell & Victor Rosen. Copyright renewed © 1976 by Harold Russell.

ing. Suddenly the person is ready for something new, something different. The dominance of loss now is abated and, in searching for diversion, the person rediscovers the wider reality. Satiation may be one important factor permitting a person "to snap out" of a feeling of hopelessness and grief by himself or herself.

Though it is necessary to leave the state of mourning behind as one adjusts to life with a disability, it would be a mistake to conclude that this should be done with dispatch. There is good reason to believe that the period of mourning, whether it is experienced deeply or less intensely, can be a healing period during which the wound is first anesthetized and then gradually closed, leaving the least scarring. Lack of recognition of the psychological value of mourning was the basis for an indictment against one of the military rehabilitation centers for blind veterans where, "because of an enthusiastic and efficient attempt . . . made there to help the blinded soldier master problems of external reality," it was believed that the inner work of mourning could not be accomplished (Blank, 1957, p. 12). This, then is an issue clearly affecting the nature of rehabilitation programs treating the newly injured.

We have seen earlier that the mourning reaction to loss need not always be an intense and protracted experience. However, the period of mourning should be recognized as a period that can help the person prepare himself or herself before taking the leap to meet the challenges that lie ahead. To facilitate the transition, the early introduction of activities of daily living and the opportunity to meet other people with disabilities (similar to as well as different from one's own) who are satisfactorily managing can be recommended. To discredit the value of mourning is not seen as helpful.

Certain societies seem better able to prepare their members for bereavement (Volkart & Michael, 1957). One example of variable cultural mores affecting the ease of meeting bereavement is the matter of "replacing" the one lost. Some societies have instituted obligatory remarriage or adoption, this serving to reestablish the role vacated by death. Our society, on the other hand, tends to emphasize the loss aspects of death. One even should not speak ill of the dead. However, the period of mourning during which homage is paid to the dead and healing takes place is formally halted at one year, a convention that encourages the person to resume fully the affairs of the living. Whether "the year" is generally and optimally satisfactory and whether it has equal relevance with respect to mourning a physical loss touches upon important psychological issues.

Mourning, clearly, is not a state through which one passes and then leaves behind. It is experienced intermittently after the deepest pangs are mitigated. Moreover, "one should not draw any strong inference about psychiatric diagnosis and ego strength from the severity of the symptoms in the shock stage" (Blank, 1957, p. 12). As the outlook of the person is further altered by the value changes to be discussed in the following pages, mourning becomes less persistent until finally the person is able to look upon the loss with unconcern or a feeling of tenderness rather than hurt, "with that tenderness which old people not infrequently feel toward the reminiscences of their youth," now gone, but still a part of them (Dembo, Leviton, & Wright, 1956, p. 39). During the later phases of adjustment to disability, after the person has found a first hold and can carry on in meaningful activity, further enlargement of the scope of values is necessary.

The following important processes in overcoming mourning have been considered: comparison of one's state with other states, arousal of dormant values, satiation, and involvement in necessities of living. There are others, but these are sufficient to demonstrate the important practical and theoretical problems involved in overcoming mourning.

Subordinating Physique Relative to Other Values

As mourning subsides, the scope of values that hold meaning widens to include values still available to the person from which satisfaction can be gained. However, enlargement of the scope of values as such is not sufficient, for even when there is no doubt that life is worth living, the person may still feel gravely troubled either because of the excessive value placed on physical normalcy, or because other values are given insufficient weight. The person may recognize, for example, that life means friendship, work, and so on, but still feel uninspired or apathetic, unworthy or otherwise beset because these satisfactions are insufficiently valued to override the potency of physique.

Dembo et al. (1956) describe two examples of value change in which nonphysique values increase in value and become the important determinants in the evaluation of the person. In the first example, physical appearance matters less than personality; in the second, physical ability matters less than doing one's best:

1. *The problem of appearance versus personality.* It is proposed that devaluation resulting from damaged appearance will be diminished to the extent that surface appearance is felt to be less important for the evaluation of the person than personality. This shift is facilitated when the person is convinced of the fundamental importance of nonphysique values such as kindness, wisdom, effort, and cooperativeness. Earl Schenck Miers (1949), a man with cerebral palsy, has

expressed this relative subordination of physique values to personality or character values: "The intolerance of ignorance, the ruthlessness of avarice, the insanities of lust for power and domination, the unfeeling heart that must nurture the shameless, all-consuming pride—such handicaps as these are most to be regretted and most to be avoided, for from them come much of the world's eternal suffering."

Actually, the perception of the physical appearance may itself change when seen in the light of such personality variables. Thus, whatever the objective conditions of the surface appearance may be, when one reacts positively to the person, the appearance may be felt to be attractive.

In certain circumstances, as among strangers, the influence of personality remains in the background and that of surface appearance becomes a focus of attention. On the other hand, many people naturally judge a person's attractiveness in terms of personality. This is especially true in close relationships, where the personality of the other is felt. It is also true that some people show little concern with physical appearance because other more highly valued aspects of life command a good deal more of the available time and energy. We are not advocating, of course, neglect of personal grooming, but we are asserting that placing personality above physical appearance will reduce devaluation of persons with visible disabilities.

2. *The problem of ability and achievement versus effort.* Dembo, Leviton, & Wright introduce the problem as follows:

> To call someone disabled implies that performance determines the evaluation of the person. In our society, people are frequently compared with each other on the basis of their achievements. Schools, for example, are predominantly influenced by the achievement or product ideology. High grades are not given to the one who worked hardest but to the one who performed best. Under certain circumstances, of two persons who reached the same performance level, the one who did so with greater ease is considered the better. He is seen as potentially a better producer than the one who had to work harder. Thus, effort is not only considered a positive value, but paradoxically, sometimes as a liability.
>
> If one would follow the maxim which also exists in our society to the effect that, "All that is expected of you is that you do your best," it would mean that the person would not be compared with others in regard to ability; it would mean that only his own state matters and thus that it does not matter whether he lost or lacks ability. Actually, one wishes to say, a person does not lack ability; he can only *have* it. In everyday life we do evaluate as equally good citizens those who pay taxes according to their financial state. The injured who applies himself with effort contributes the most that he can as a *person*. Though the unsatisfactory

physical tools of his body may have limited his production [along specific lines] his personal contributions are at the maximum. As a *person*
he is not different from the noninjured. [Dembo, Leviton, & Wright,
1956, p. 40][6]

In the preceding discussion, we stressed the weight given to personality qualities over which the person has more control. One may
wonder what would happen to the person who cannot claim credit
for effort or some other particular personality trait. If we had been
discussing acceptance of one's personality shortcomings, the question could be raised as to whether acceptance of such traits is justified. Should acceptance of the presumed shortcoming be in order,
as for example one's shyness, then diminishing the importance of ex-
troversion as a value or increasing the importance of other traits
which the person possesses would be indicated. Sometimes evaluating the behavior in question more positively is in order. An example
is behavior that has been labeled "laziness" but then reinterpreted
to signify unconcern for material possessions. With respect to physical disability, devaluation will be diminished insofar as personality
traits become more important or physical normalcy becomes less important. In the words of Shakespeare:

> In nature there's no blemish but the mind;
> None can be called deformed but the unkind:
> Virtue is beauty, but the beauteous evil
> Are empty trunks, o'erflourished by the devil.
> (*Twelfth Night*, Act III, Scene 4)

Whether the importance of physique is decreased or the importance of other values is increased, in both cases the *relative* weight
of physique is reduced. Both shifts in emphasis appear helpful. In the
latter case, however, it is possible that the absolute value of physique
is retained. This was shown in one study that examined the relationship between subordination of physique and acceptance of disability
(Balunas, 1972). Subjects with a visible physical disability were asked
to engage in a conversation with another person for 15 minutes. In
half the cases, the other person was seated in a wheelchair, and in
half the cases in a regular chair. After the conversation, the subjects
were asked to list ten qualities that described the other person and
rate the importance of each on a 20-point rating scale. The ten traits
were later classified into three categories: physical appearance, ability and achievement, and personality. The subject's score on a stan-

---

[6]Adjustment to misfortune: A problem of social-psychological rehabilitation, by T.
Dembo, G. L. Leviton, & B. A. Wright. Reproduced from *Artificial limbs*, National
Academy Press, Washington, D. C., 1956.

dardized measure of Attitudes Toward Disabled Persons (ATDP) was regarded as an indication of acceptance of one's own disability (Yuker et al., 1966). Two results of this study are pertinent to the present discussion: (1) There was a significant correlation between the ATDP scores and the ratings of importance assigned to personality qualities. That is, the subjects with a disability who showed greater acceptance of persons with a disability (and presumably therefore of themselves) tended to give *more weight* to personality when evaluating the other person (whether or not he was in a wheelchair). (2) However, the ratings of importance assigned to ability or appearance did not vary with the ATDP scores. In this study enhancing other values was related to acceptance of disability as a value loss, whereas diminishing the absolute importance of physique was not.

That assigning low absolute importance to a trait on which one fares poorly can be related to self-acceptance was shown in another study (Rosenberg, 1965). Adolescents rated themselves on seventeen traits and rated how important each of the traits was to them. A measure of self-esteem was also obtained. The findings most germane to our discussion are: (1) Subjects who rated themselves low on particular traits *and* who cared little about those traits (low importance) had higher self-esteem than those who rated themselves equally low but cared a great deal. (2) The relationship between subjects' self-evaluation on a specific trait and their global self-evaluation was much stronger if they regarded the trait as important than as unimportant. In other words, a poor showing on a trait does not appear to have major consequences for one's ego if the person gives little weight to that trait.

Another study investigated the hypothesis that the emphasis placed on physique by nondisabled persons would be inversely related to positive attitudes toward people with disabilities (English & Oberle, 1971). Airline stewardesses were selected as a group that could be expected to place a relatively high emphasis on physique and female typists as a group with relatively lower emphasis. The hypothesis was verified: airline stewardesses scored lower on the test of attitudes toward persons with disabilities than the typists.

To avoid one misconception, we should like to stress that it is possible to consider physique an *asset value* of high importance without affecting judgments of personal worth. (See "Transforming Comparative-Status Values to Asset Values," pp. 178–183).

Culturally, body-whole, body-healthy, and body-beautiful are given enormous weight. Ellis presents a lively account of the beautification of beauty (1954, Chapter 1). It behooves us to recognize that certain physical attributes are overvalued. Physical fitness is a case in point. It has been noted that there is "no real evidence in humans that unusual physical fitness imparts immunity or resistance to disease" (Rusk & Taylor, 1946, p. 199). Moreover, though it is commonly acknowledged that there is a relationship between physical fitness and ability to work, we know that motivation, training, and the absence of attitudinal and other barriers are far more significant.

A question arises as to whether subordinating physique relative to other values is to be recommended in all cases. Should not one stress the importance of physical health? We would answer affirmatively, but if individuals who are chronically ill are not to be devaluated by this very emphasis, the remaining two value changes (i.e., containing disability effects and transforming comparative-status values into asset values) will have to occur. Of particular importance is the latter in which good health can be seen as an asset value rather than a comparative-status value.

Containing Disability Effects

The phenomenon of spread has already been discussed and illustrated (Chapters 3 and 4). Spread results in unwarranted implications of disability in many facets of life. Containing disability effects, therefore, represents an important value change, because not all areas of life are disability connected, and those that may be are affected in ways not commonly presumed.

A number of conditions conducive to containing disability effects have been examined. In Chapter 4, evidence was presented to show that the power of a personal characteristic to evoke inferences about a person depends on the centrality or saliency of that characteristic. It was further shown that centrality in turn depends upon the context in which that characteristic is imbedded. In the preceding section of the present chapter, the matter of the relative importance of values was discussed. The obvious implication is that containing disability effects can be facilitated by decreasing the relative importance of a value that signals personal shortcomings. Now we shall turn to the interesting problem of what makes something identifiable as a personal characteristic in the first place.

This problem was first raised in the monograph of Dembo and her coworkers (1956). It was pointed out that the same thing may be perceived as a *possession* or as a *personal characteristic*, a distinction that has important implications in the case of overcoming devaluation:

> If a value is seen only as a possession of a person and not as a personal characteristic, devaluation of the person cannot take place. Thus beautiful pictures may be evaluated highly, yet those whose homes do not

boast of even one old master are not devaluated. Though this seems clear, the terms "personal characteristic" and "possession" are in themselves problematic. . . . Whether something is seen as a part or characteristic of a person or as a possession seems to depend upon the judge. The person who has lost someone dear to him may feel that he has lost part of himself. Clothes may be thought of as a material possession and "being well dressed" as a personal characteristic. Where some judges would perceive a "man who owns a house," others would perceive a "home-owner," a substantial and responsible member of the community" (Dembo, Leviton, & Wright, 1956, p. 23).[7]

To understand the forces that lead to the perception of a disability as a personal characteristic, we remind the reader of several factors that have already been discussed. The first concerns proximity between the person and the disability (see Chapter 3, p. 41). Proximity is such a strong unit-forming factor that two entities can be seen to belong together because of it. Visibility and permanence of the disability are further factors that favor regarding the disability as a characteristic of the person. Also, there is the "just world phenomenon"—the belief that people get what they deserve, implying that disability is a personal characteristic (Chapter 4, p. 67). Finally, and of great importance, is the general tendency, particularly pronounced in the case of atypical behavior, to neglect the role of the environment, a neglect that keeps attention focused on the person (see Chapter 3, pp. 40–45).

Counteracting forces, fortunately, enable a greater separation between the person as a whole and the disability: The person, insider or outsider, may not have a strong belief in the inevitability of a just world. In the case of outsiders, knowing the person with a disability as a friend leads to seeing the disability as more peripheral. This contrasts with relationships with strangers where the disability assumes a prominent position because the person remains largely undifferentiated as an individual (see Chapter 4, pp. 73–77). Moreover, the coping framework, elaborated in the following chapter, is conducive to viewing disability as an impaired tool.

Perceiving disability as an impaired tool helps to contain disability effects. Appreciating that physical abilities are tools for action implies that when a tool becomes impaired it is possible to substitute other means for carrying on. In that way, important aspects of one's life that otherwise would be foreclosed may not in fact be denied the

[7]Adjustment to misfortune: A problem of social-psychological rehabilitation, by T. Dembo, G. L. Leviton, & B. A. Wright. Reproduced from *Artificial limbs*, National Academy Press, Washington, D. C., 1956.

person. The essential function of walking as a tool can be seen to be served by a prosthesis, crutches, or wheelchair, for example. The preservation of important values by such functional substitution is seen in the spontaneous remark of a child in a school for children with disabilities who said: "Let's go for a walk," whereupon all the children wheeled themselves around the courtyard.

To take another example, consider sexuality as a value. People with spinal cord injuries, chronic back pain, arthritis, and heart disease may need to enlarge their conception of normal sexual expression. They may need to learn new techniques and appreciate new ways of relating to their partners. The Sexual Attitude Restructuring (SAR) process was developed by the National Sex Forum (1975) for that purpose. Participants are exposed to a wide variety of films and slides on emotional and genital aspects of sexuality in order to desensitize them to fettering taboos. The sharing of feelings and ideas that follow are part of the process leading to an appreciation of new ways to achieve sexual satisfaction.

"Do it another way," the essence of means substitution, applies to a vast array of human activities. It also applies to all people, not only because all of us are limited in some way, but also because a flexible approach to problems that remain unresolved by habitual modes of thinking and acting creates the opportunity for solutions. Do it another way allows the "it" to become possible by altering the means to its attainment.

The following recollections of Harold Russell (1949), who lost both hands during World War II, illustrate the deeply felt wish on the part of a person with a disability to contain negative effects of disability but being powerless to do so in the early stages of acceptance of the disability. He longed desperately to maintain his relationship with the woman he loved, but his disability, he felt, ruled this out:

> My reason told me I should and must give her up, but all my instincts told me I should cling to her, that she could be my ultimate salvation. If only I could be sure she loved me—*really* loved me—not out of pity, not out of loyalty, not out of a sense of duty! To know that I was still desired, to know that a woman could still love me as a man, that was the all-important thing. That knowledge, I felt, could lift me over the highest hurdles. It could give me new hope and courage. It could make me into a human being again, instead of a helpless freak.
>
> But I knew that could never be. I knew that no matter what she said—no matter how fervently she proclaimed her love—no matter how many times she told me she still wanted to marry me—I knew that

I would have to give her up. There was no other way. [Russell, 1949, p. 45][8]

What has happened here? Because at this time Russell's negative view of disability was *the* thing of importance, occupying his entire thinking, the horror and aversion spread to himself as a total person—he became a useless freak, a travesty on the human being he had been. Only with the passage of time was he able to engage in the kind of value reorientation that enabled him to contain negative spread effects.

Sometimes, rather than containing disability effects, becoming more aware of its negative aftermath may be in order. An example is a person who continues to deny and defy the limitations imposed by a disability, notwithstanding repeated evidence to the contrary. In that case, overcontainment on the behavioral level may be said to have occurred, although the behavior may be ascribed to an underlying and profound fear of the implications of disability.

All persons, those with a disability and those without, must come to appreciate that though a physical disability is a physical fact which may affect other areas of the person's life, the effects can be contained within those more narrow areas that actually involve the disability. Not all of life is influenced, let alone determined, by disability. Moreover, not all effects are negative. The view emphasizing containment of disability argues that disability is but one among an array of factors that determine the nature and direction of life. As a value loss, a disability can be seen as lack of a tool for which adequate substitutions can often be found; it can be seen as a peripheral characteristic that does not identify the essential core of the person although it may be part of the person's identity. Moreover, it is important to appreciate that the restrictions in functioning faced by a person with a disability stem from societal barriers as well as personal limitations. Essential features of containing disability effects as a concept are captured in the following two statements: *A disability involves certain limitations in certain situations. The source of limitation is due to barriers imposed by society and not only to personal incapacity.*

Transforming Comparative-Status Values into Asset Values

The attributes of a person—for example, the person's looks, capacities, and background—may carry status implications for the person

---

[8]Reprinted by permission of Farrar, Straus & Giroux, Inc. From *Victory in my hands* by Harold Russell & Victor Rosen. Copyright 1949 by Harold Russell & Victor Rosen. Copyright renewed © 1976 by Harold Russell.

evaluating them. In this case, the attributes in question may be said to have status value for the evaluator, and the evaluator may be said to invoke status values. Because they always involve comparison with a standard along a scale of better and worse, *status values* have also been referred to as *comparative values* (Dembo, Leviton, & Wright, 1956). For other evaluators, those same attributes may not be judged along a status dimension at all. They are then evaluated in other terms, for example in terms of usefulness or intrinsic value. The focus is the value of the attribute, not the person's position relative to that of others. Because this mode of evaluation allows something to be seen as an asset which would, in the case of status judgments, be viewed as below standard, it is called *asset evaluation* and the values involved are called *asset values.* Thus, the ability to use crutches can be viewed as an asset and not devaluated as signifying inferiority.

When status judgments are made, the standard for comparison may represent the presumed average, as when a person is judged to be bright or slow; it may represent formal requirements, as when a person is evaluated for membership in a social club; it may represent "ought" injunctions, as when it is felt that one ought to be a certain kind of parent in order to be a good parent. In all these cases, the outcome is a judgment of status, of worthiness as a person.

Although status evaluation is common in our culture, it is likely that asset evaluation occurs more frequently than we realize. We may enjoy an artistic performance without comparing it to anyone else's work. Friends often relate to each other without the distorting lens of status comparisons. In fact, should they be competitively inclined toward each other, the friendship is threatened.

Some persons appear to be very status oriented, frequently sizing up others in comparison with the self or with some symbol of status such as wealth, power, or education. They become consumed by status questions even when such questions are irrelevant to the situation. Other persons predominantly hold asset values in cases where relative standing of persons is not the issue. Their use of status values is reserved only for competitive situations, as in judging athletic events or in hiring the best applicant for a position. The problem before us is to eliminate the use of status comparisons when they are unnecessary and harmful.

Clarification is needed on several points. Not all comparisons are status comparisons in the sense of determining relative standing in a hierachy of prestige. For example, a person may keep a chart of how long or far he or she is able to walk in order to determine progress toward a goal. The person may feel pleased or disappointed in the progress made; the person may change the regime according to the evidence, but one's worthiness as a person is not thereby altered.

We might say that the comparisons permitted by such charting is a means of assessing whether there is anything to be gained from the approach to walking—that is, whether it has asset value.

A second point is that one can appreciate the asset value of something without purposely invoking a comparative standard, as when one enjoys a balmy evening or a musical performance because of the pleasure one gets from their inherent qualities, not because they are better or worse than something to which they are compared. In the same way one can value the functional usefulness of a prosthesis or wheelchair without putting them down as less functional than the intact body. Very young children, in fact, hardly make use of scales, comparisons, or standards in their valuing process. They do not have the concept of better or worse or of sequential ordering that is a precondition to establishing a scale. Their pleasure with a toy springs from the toy itself, not because it is better than another.

Still another point is that the inherent qualities of something may be negative as well as positive. The pain of a headache is negative, not because it is better or worse than some other kind of pain, but because it is intrinsically so. In this case the pain or the headache would more appropriately be designated a dysvalue than an asset value.

Finally, asset values can refer to values that are highly important without provoking judgments of relative personal merit. Thus, high asset value can be placed on walking, music, and so forth because these are good things to do or to have, but not devaluating if you lack them.

Let us look in on 5-year-old Raymond crawling for the first time since polio struck him almost a year and a half earlier. He is sitting on the floor with his toys surrounding him:

> On one momentous occasion I gave the engine a great shove, failed to hold on to it, and it rolled away beyond my reach. I hesitated to call Celia [the nurse], for she fussed, but I wanted my engine, and I decided to try to go after it myself. I placed my hands, palms down, on the floor in front of me. I moved my legs from the hips, moved them more than I had ever moved them before, until they were behind me and under me and I was on my knees. I put my right hand forward and pulled my right leg forward. I put my left hand forward and pulled my left leg forward. I repeated the actions and soon I was across the room where my fire engine waited for me.
>
> . . . I remembered the act and the emotion, the ineffable joy that flooded me, the sense of power, of achievement, of a miracle wrought. . . . Later I was to feel the crushing weight of shame, but the memory of what happened to me that day helped me to bear up and struggle on. I crawled six feet across the carpeted floor and the course of my life was charted.

When I reached my fire engine, the enormity of what I had achieved flashed upon me. I twisted my body around and sat down. My eyes filled with tears of happiness. I had been over there and now I was over here, and I had done it all myself! [Goldman, 1947, pp. 10–11][9]

Raymond was exalted by the wonder of his accomplishment because of its asset or intrinsic value. He did not compare his performance with that of someone else but marveled at the idea that for the first time he was able to retrieve his own toy. This was valuable, a good thing to be able to do. It was an asset value that did not require a comparative standard to be appreciated. The shame he was later to feel occurred when this priceless asset value was undercut by locomotion as a status value in which criteria for the right and proper way to walk became the comparative standard.

The person with a disability has much to gain psychologically if physique can be looked upon in terms of its intrinsic or essential characteristics—what it permits and restricts the person to do—without basing the evaluation on comparisons with other individuals or with one's own previous nondisabled state. The perception of what physique permits and restricts is influenced, of course, by knowledge of what other persons can do. A person would not think of his or her hearing impairment as a restriction if everyone else were similarly affected, just as we don't mind being unable to hear the high frequencies that a dog can hear. Nevertheless, when physique has the function of an asset value, the person is able to appreciate those inherent satisfactions that are but disappointments the moment physique is taken as a comparative value with status implications. "It's all a bit of a folly . . . spending all this time comparing":

I spend a lot of time comparing myself with others. Frankly, it doesn't seem to do me much good. But I still keep doing it. Sometimes I feel good when I seem to be like others; sometimes I feel good when I feel different from others. It's all a bit of a folly, though, I mean, spending all this time comparing. Maybe if I stop, I can be me. [Snyder, 1974, p. 1]

Dembo (1953) has linked the idea of spread and comparative (status) evaluation by hypothesizing that when the evaluator is in a comparative frame of mind and views disability as below the standard of normalcy, other characteristics of the person that are not the primary focus of the evaluator's attention will also be regarded as below normal. The process is conceived as follows: In comparing a person with a standard, one is interested only in a particular characteristic (e.g., physique, intelligence). Because this characteristic dom-

[9]Reprinted with permission of Macmillan Publishing Co., Inc., from *Even the night* by R. L. Goldman. Copyright 1947, and renewed 1975, by Raymond Leslie Goldman.

inates the field of concern, it acquires considerable potency. Other characteristics, being vague, shift into "below" or "above" the standard position by virtue of the cognitive-affective set established by the initial comparative evaluation. In a diffuse way, the one being judged may even be regarded as inferior as a person.

Since some people are more strongly comparative minded than others, having a generalized need to establish the relative standing of persons along dimensions important to them, a correlation between such comparative mindedness and inclination to spread can be expected. This hypothesis was supported in a study in which scores on a test of spread correlated significantly with scores on a test of comparative evaluation (Butts & Shontz, 1962). The test for spread required subjects to indicate how certain they were that each of twelve persons described by two different traits would also have other named personality traits. The greater the degree of confidence was, the higher was the spread score. The measure of comparative evaluation required subjects to select from several alternatives that varied according to comparative mindedness, those that applied best in a variety of different situations. The more frequent the choice of comparative-minded items was, the higher was the score.

It has been noted that "even social workers accustomed to dealing with all types often find it difficult to think of a normal, pretty girl as being guilty of a crime. Most people, for some inexplicable reason, think of crime in terms of abnormality in appearance, and I must say that beautiful women are not often convicted" (Monahan, 1941, p. 103). At this juncture we are able to suggest two explanations for this "inexplicable reason." One has to do with the unit-forming factor of similarity that guides the inferential process; in this case beauty, as a positive characteristic, is not easily associated with something negative (see spread and similarity of traits, Chapter 4, pp. 61–63). A second explanation argues that the social worker finds difficulty in thinking of a pretty girl as guilty of a crime when he or she holds beauty as a comparative-status value. In that case, when the girl's beauty is in the field of concern, its property of being above standard spreads to other characteristics of the person so that the social worker would also see a moral girl. The spread effects are incompatible with a below-standard characteristic such as criminality.

The following reminiscence of Noreen about her prepolio days when she was highly comparative minded, reveals the phenomenon of comparative values and diffuse spread:

> . . . I am simply inconsolable at horse-races or relays of any kind, for worrying about the unhappiness of the contestant who comes in last. At gala night-club scenes in the movies, I always search out the background for extras who sit at the gay tables with unconscious envy

painted on their pretty faces as they watch the star perform. At weddings I watch the least of the bridesmaids, and at graduation exercises, the little girl whose dress has the widest hand-made hem. [Linduska, 1947, p. 15][10]

Why does Noreen's heart go out to the person who is last, an extra, a lesser bridesmaid, or a girl with the widest handmade hem? These may be facts, but they have no necessary connection with being unfortunate. The wide hem may belong to the girl who is brimming over with the anticipation of marrying her beloved after graduation. The contestant who comes in last may be pleased to have been part of the race at all. Not everything that can be rank-ordered involves a contest. But for Noreen, relative position on this or that characteristic meant so much that it spread to the evaluation of the total person. Being below par on one characteristic signaled being an unhappy person.

Physique as an asset value provides a sound basis for the commonly heard dictum, "It is not what you have lost, but what you have left that counts." It is significant that when Harold Russell first began to realize the truth of this dictum he also began to take himself to task regarding his loss of hands: "I would have to stop regarding myself as a freak. I would have to stop sneaking into dark corners and hiding my hooks. . . . I would have to realize that I had nothing to be ashamed of" (1949, p. 142). These admonitions express the dim recognition that physique can become an asset value, a view that would free him of inferiority. Only then would shamming and shaming no longer pursue him. With asset evaluation, a healthy and intact body can remain an asset; that is, a good thing to have if you have it, but not devaluating if you don't.

ACCEPTANCE AND ADJUSTMENT

The question remains as to whether accepting a disability implies general personality adjustment. We have argued that the four value changes lead to accepting a disability as nondevaluating and free people to act in ways befitting their own characteristics rather than those of an idolized normal standard. We could expect that acceptance in these terms represents the outlook of a mature person.

Yet there is quite a jump between accepting one's disability in particular and accepting oneself in general. The self-accepting person has been defined (Berger, 1952, as modified from Sheerer, 1949) as one who:

[10]Reprinted by permission of Farrar, Straus & Giroux, Inc. From *My polio past* by Noreen Linduska. Copyright © 1947, 1974 by Noreen Linduska.

1. Relies primarily upon internalized values and standards rather than on external pressure as a guide for behavior.
2. Has faith in one's capacity to cope with life.
3. Assumes responsibility for and accepts the consequences of one's own behavior.
4. Accepts praise or criticism from others objectively.
5. Does not attempt to deny or destroy any feelings, motives, limitations, abilities, or favorable qualities which one sees in oneself, but rather accepts all without self-condemnation.
6. Considers oneself a person of worth on an equal plane with other persons.
7. Does not expect rejection from others.
8. Does not regard oneself as totally different from others or generally abnormal.
9. Is not shy or self-conscious.

There is also a jump between accepting oneself in general and being a mentally healthy person. The emotionally mature person has been characterized (Saul, 1947, Chapter 1) as one who:

1. Is independent and responsible.
2. Has little need to regress.
3. Is giving and productive, although still able to receive.
4. Is cooperative rather than egotistical and competitive.
5. Is in relative harmony with one's conscience.
6. Is reasonably free of inferiority feelings, with anxiety at a minimum.
7. Has attitudes toward sexuality that show a balance between freedom and responsibility.
8. Has minimal hostility toward others and toward the self, yet the hostility is freely available for defense and constructive use.
9. Has a grasp of reality that is clear and unimpaired by the emotional astigmatisms of childhood.
10. Is discriminating and highly adaptable.
11. Has not only the *capacity* for such attitudes and functioning but also the ability to *enjoy* them fully.

It is not difficult to reason that a person whose scope of values has been enlarged, who has shifted the relative importance of values, who has contained disability effects, and, particularly, who has come to regard physique as an asset value will rate well on these self-accepting and mental health criteria. Yet, research and systematic observation remain as the ultimate court of validation.

The most directly relevant research employed a measure of acceptance of disability (AD scale) based on the four value changes herein described (Linkowski, 1971). In one study (Linkowski & Dunn, 1974), this AD Scale was filled out by college students who had a disability. The scores were then correlated with two measures that the students had taken two years earlier, one being a measure of self-esteem and the other of satisfaction with social relationships. Despite the protracted time interval, significant correlations were found between acceptance of disability and self-esteem and between acceptance of disability and satisfaction with social relationships. In a second study (Sieka, 1974), scores on the AD Scale of adults with facial disfigurements were correlated with a measure of sex-role esteem based on an evaluation of one's role as a man or woman, husband or wife, dating partner, and so on. Again, a significantly high correlation was found between the two measures. Parenthetically, it may be pointed out that self-esteem is an asset value when "feeling good about the self" is not based on being better than someone else.

Further evidence that adjustment is related to value changes in acceptance of disability is found in a study of the reaction of men with visible disabilities to negative statements about disabled persons (Grand, 1972). Subjects were divided into relatively high and low acceptors on the basis of certain attitudinal and behavioral correlates of acceptance of disability. When exposed to a film in which a nondisabled person expressed negative views about disabled persons, the high acceptors of their disability were less anxious than the low acceptors.

Another study (Butts, 1962; Butts & Shontz, 1962) restricted itself to comparative evaluation in examining conditions underlying coping effectiveness. Four groups of men judged to represent groups of increasing coping effectiveness served as subjects: an institutionalized group of people with schizophrenia, an institutionalized group with physical disabilities, an institutionalized socially disabled group, and a group of noninstitutionalized "normals." The relative use of comparative-status evaluation in everyday life situations, measured by a test specifically designed for that purpose, was found to decrease significantly as coping effectiveness increased, a finding in support of the importance of asset evaluation in general adjustment. (See the preceding sections for additional research supporting the separate value changes.)

To be sure, the problem of unwarranted social and environmental restrictions is crucial to issues concerning adjustment and the quality of life. However, viewing one's disability as nondevaluating is also crucial. The one should not diminish the other, even though the person side or environment side of the issue may take precedence at particular times and places. The following personal reflections of a psychologist who uses a wheelchair underscores the necessity of accepting one's disability, not as a second-class citizen, but as nondevaluating. This realization came to her after her own divorce. Until then she had agreed with those who emphasized modifying unfair practices rather than the person:

> I decided to invest . . . in ten psychotherapy sessions to see if I could get my head together. One of the first things the man said to me was, "The trouble with you is you haven't accepted your disability." "Oh brother," I thought, "I should never have come to a psychologist who hasn't had experience with disabled people. He doesn't know how inappropriate that remark is, even if it were true. I obviously have accepted my disability. I am working in a responsible position, making enough money to pay for my own attendant, am openly and unabashedly on the dating market and doing reasonably well. I have lots of friends, social and recreational activities. I paint, write poetry, and work 80 hours a week. How can he say I haven't accepted my disability? . . . . True, I wasn't exactly happy and couldn't figure out why. It took a few months to realize that one reason was, I hadn't accepted my disability. [Vash, 1975, p. 152][11]

The observations of a 30-year-old man, injured five years earlier in a motorcycle accident, expresses the deeply felt impact of value changes that so altered his outlook on life that he wouldn't go back to his preinjury days: "Life's a lot more pleasant now than it was. . . . I've slowed down and can see life now. . . . I've come to realize that there's more to life than I ever thought. Being able to walk is a very minor thing. I wouldn't trade it [my present life] for what I had. . . . Now if I've done something good, I feel I've really accomplished something" (Young, 1956).

SUFFERING AND UNDERSTANDING

> Regardless of the various viewpoints expressed by the psychiatrists and psychologists, those who have worked closely with the physically disabled know that having once made the emotional adjustment to their disabilities, they possess a depth of understanding, patience, and tolerance which is rarely found among those who have not endured some soul-torturing experience. They have been forced to discard the superficial and to find the fundamentals. They have discovered what Robert Burton wrote over three hundred years ago: "Deformities and imperfections of our bodies, as lameness, crookedness, deafness, blindness, be they innate or accidental, torture many men; yet this may comfort them that those imperfections of the body do not a whit blemish the soul, or

[11]Reprinted from The psychology of disability, by C. L. Vash, in *Rehab. Psych.*, 1975, 22. By permission of *Rehab. Psych.*

hinder the operations of it, but rather help and much increase it!" [Rusk & Taylor, 1946, p. 224][12]

The view that deep understanding emerges from suffering has been advanced through the ages by philosophers, poets, writers, and scientists. It is one of the important factors that evokes respectful regard for persons disabled in some way. In its more general application it is represented by the belief that life should not be made too easy for children in school and society, because only through hard work, frustration, and tribulation can the fullness of creativity and wisdom be realized.

Not only professional personnel, but many laypeople and persons with disabilities themselves connect suffering and even great misfortune with fundamental improvement in the person. In one study on values, for example, subjects were asked whether they would wish tragedy for their child (Dembo, 1953a). About half the subjects answered affirmatively on the ground that in this way depth of understanding is reached. In another study, virtually none of the subjects (40 men in the professions) expressed disagreement with the statement: "I believe we are made better by the trials and hardships of life." Even when other subjects (an experimental group of 50) were confronted with a presumed group consensus toward disagreement, only one-third went along, whereas two-thirds took a position supporting the statement (Crutchfield, 1955).

Persons with disabilities have, in looking over their lives, also expressed the belief that, through the manifold experiences of living with a disability, they have gained a profound awareness of truly human values. Harold Russell (1949), who lost his hands as an adult, puts it this way: ". . . this seeming disaster has brought me a priceless wealth of the spirit that I am sure I could never have possessed otherwise. I have enjoyed a life that has been full and rich and rewarding, a life that has had a meaning and depth it never had before" (Russell, 1949, p. 278).[13] Raymond Goldman (1947), who faced infantile paralysis as a child, deafness as an adolescent, diabetes as an adult, expresses it this way: "Now, I thought, I could understand the true meaning of life, could see a *reason* for the physical and mental anguish I had had to endure, could see the *reward* for the struggle I had made. How else could one gain victory except through defeat?

[12]From *New hope for the handicapped* by Howard A. Rusk & Eugene J. Taylor. Copyright 1946, 1947, 1948, 1949 by Howard A. Rusk. By permission of Harper & Row, Publishers, Inc.
[13]Reprinted by permission of Farrar, Straus & Giroux, Inc. From *Victory in my hands* by Harold Russell & Victor Rosen. Copyright 1949 by Harold Russell & Victor Rosen. Copyright renewed © 1976 by Harold Russell.

... How else could one know happiness except through suffering and despair?" (p. 159).[14]

Research has shown that a substantial number of people who have a disability recognize some good related to it. One study (Weinberg & Williams, 1978) asked the question, "Do you think your disability has any advantage?" Of the seven response categories delineated, the first six indicate gains in understanding and experience, namely: The disability (1) provided a challenge, goal, or purpose for which to work; (2) made one more sensitive to and more tolerant of other people; (3) increased the range of experience; (4) gave one a greater appreciation of life; (5) helped one to be better prepared and realistic about life; (6) provided the opportunity to help educate and give hope to other people; and (7) entitled one to special treatment services.

In the following account we are brought into a life experience that arose because of a disability. It took place within three years of a man's blindness and because it did so very much to challenge his understandings and shape new ones that carried him far in his own adjustment, it is reproduced here at some length. The world could well learn the lessons of that one incident and the reevaluation of fundamentals that followed in its wake. It is told by Chevigny (1946), who became blind at the age of 40:

> ... one noon I was walking up 53d street on my way to the restaurant I usually frequent for lunch. I heard a genial hail; it turned out to be someone I knew only as Billy, the office boy at a publishing house where I am acquainted. I said hello in return, we fell into step—he was going to lunch too—and I suggested he join me. Billy hesitated, then asked, "Are you sure they'll serve me?" "Of course," I answered, "why shouldn't they?" The next few minutes were among the most profoundly embarrassing I ever passed. Billy had to tell me a fact about himself of which I was completely unaware; he is a Negro.
>
> My embarrassment arose in my instant realization of the predicament in which I had placed him. ... Then what seemed a brilliant solution occurred to me. I said, "You were on your way to lunch—why don't you take me to the place where you're going?"
>
> "That's a thought," Billy said, and we changed the direction of our walk. Then I remembered my own problem. Would Bill's restaurant admit Wiz [the Seeing Eye dog]? I put the question up to him and it was his turn to be embarrassed—for me. He didn't know about the policy of his restaurant regarding dogs. He was shocked at the thought that any restaurant would exclude a man with a Seeing Eye dog. I had my

[14]Reprinted with permission of Macmillan Publishing Co., Inc., from *Even the night* by R. L. Goldman. Copyright 1947, and renewed 1975, by Raymond Leslie Goldman.

hand on his arm as we walked and I felt his muscle stiffen as he said, "They'd better let you in. If they don't, they'll have a little trouble putting the roof back on when I get through raising it." It was a remark that filled me with profound shame. I hadn't offered to raise any roofs for him. Yet the reasons for his exclusions from restaurants had infinitely less justification than the reasons for mine.

This story might seem more dramatic had we had the argument we expected on reaching the restaurant, but we didn't. We were courteously shown to a table, I put Wiz under it, and we ordered lunch. But it was eaten in silence, both of us being much too preoccupied with the consideration of the separate accidents of fate that made our relations with the world difficult.

Walking back to my office, alone with Wiz, my mind was busy with the implications of this scene. There was the thought of Billy's kindness; it was no different from that given me by any other man. And had I not been told, in so many words, that he was a man marked out from the majority I would have attached no undue importance to it, I would not even have sought to detect any difference in him. But there was another thought, one almost terrible in its significance.

Were the whole world blind, there would be no race prejudice. There couldn't be. The only sense which could have told me that Billy is what is called a Negro was my sight. No other sense detected any difference. I had nothing but Billy's own word for it. It was a concept shaking to the intellect. The whole structure of the majority-minority relationship was perceived in a clear light; its foundation is that which can be seen, and nothing else. The color of hair, the shade of skin, the shape of nose—what can perceive them but the eye? It takes hearing to perceive what is in the heart and mind, and civilized man is too busy using his eye to listen. [pp. 254–256]

My inmost dislike has always been for seeming different from the rest of my fellow men. Every act of my life has been in the direction of making myself as close to the norm as possible. I therefore could not now accept the notion that I had suddenly [when blindness occurred] become inherently peculiar, and that is the feeling which drove me forward to reattaining as much of my old position as I could.

It was a nice comfortable position, my old one, very normal and ordinary. The tabulated card that represents me in the files of the Census Bureau has always, in passing through the electric tabulating machines, dropped into the pockets containing the biggest and fattest bunches of cards. My height and weight were average, I belonged to the white race, there was nothing exotic or unusual about the church I attended, my politics were ordinary enough, and I was neither rich nor poor. The only time my card ever fell in with the smaller package of cards was in tabulating professions; but even as a writer I was distinguished by being neither very good nor very bad. I was safe in the bosom of the majority. . . .

Now suddenly an important difference had developed between the majority and me. . . .

That I resented it shows that my thinking was of the very stuff of which intolerance is made. I was of the majority and I thought like it. That means I was conscious of such things as differences between people and classes and groups.

It took a long time, and not until after the meeting with Billy did I fully realize that I was carrying with me the very body of fixed notions against which my resentment was now directed. Those fixed notions were based on sight, that sight I no longer had; . . . Now, if I wanted to do it, I could get to the heart and the mind of a man right away without first reading into him a whole set of attributes because I could see the color of his skin or the shape of his nose.

I think a good deal of the inward part of my adjustment formed about that time. . . . What happened was that there didn't seem any longer to be too much need to belong to the majority, to be a regular. The important body to which to belong was mankind itself, every member of which laughs when tickled and bleeds when pricked. That there is such a body—well, that too I had merely been told; now I could know it emotionally.

The rich experiences with friendships of the past previous months fell into place with these new concepts. The friends who so magnificently came to my assistance were Christians, Jews, and men of no faith at all. Their political beliefs were as varied. Yet when they came to my bedside as I lay in the hospital and offered the means to erase worry from my mind about both the present and the future, their thought was only that I was a fellow man who needed help. They defended me from the tragedy of my position; I can do no less, when the need arises, than to defend them from the tragedy of theirs.

These are among the understandings of living I have gained under blindness. As a writer they are of great importance to me and have added much to my desire to express what I know and feel. They are of even greater importance to me as a human being; I still can hate, but only ideas—not people. [pp. 258–261][15]

A hundred new thoughts occurred to Chevigny that day. And in the end not only did he attain higher social values but he also made possible an inward adjustment that was fundamental and satisfying. He realized in the depths of his emotional core that one does not have to belong to the majority group in order to be fully human. He realized that sight, the queen of the senses, may also become the servant of malice that divides person against person on the basis of the most superficial criteria. And in so realizing, he and others through him gained that which is priceless.

Chevigny is a man of high intellect. Could the ordinary person

[15]H. Chevigny, *My eyes have a cold nose*, Yale University Press, 1946. By permission.

with a disability reach such fundamental understandings? Harold Russell (1949), on the basis of wide observation, thinks so. He is convinced, for example, that racial intolerance wanes in the sick and disabled in general:

> During my tour . . . I visited dozens of Army and veterans' hospitals. I talked, not only with hundreds of amputees like myself, but with paraplegics, spastics, and the badly mutilated. I also visited several Canadian Army hospitals. I carried away one more conclusion from these hospitals: Neither differences of nationality, race, nor religion counted for much among the sick or disabled. All were united by the common bond of illness and suffering. It was only among the so-called healthy that I found the seeds of disunion and hatred. [p. 237][16]

As far as we know, there are no objective studies on this point. Clearly much is needed in the way of research that will sharpen our understanding of the connection between certain kinds of life experiences and the attainment of deep understanding of what really matters. We would support the hypothesis that "soul-*searching*" experiences are essential for the attainment of depth of understanding of the truly important, but we at least question the role of "soul-*torturing*" experiences. Although there is good evidence that one *may* rise to great heights of emotional understanding from the depths of despair, this may not be the only or best course. The course may be too thorny, too tortuous, and consequently too few may reach the light through the darkness. It is the *process* of adjusting to suffering that leads to sifting out the trivial from the important and culminates in a deeper understanding of the basic underpinnings of human values.

This chapter conceptualized the problem of acceptance of disability in terms of four kinds of change within the value system of the person. Supporting evidence was also provided. It should be clear that there may be other value changes and that those that have been delineated are interdependent. Thus, enlarging the scope of values appears to be favorable to diminishing the relative importance of physique, for in the perspective of other values, physique may become less dominant. Diminishing the relative importance of physique is also apt to lead to containing disability effects. Transforming comparative-status values into asset values is likely to support other value changes. Evidence for such interdependence is found in a sta-

[16]Reprinted by permission of Farrar, Straus & Giroux, Inc. From *Victory in my hands* by Harold Russell & Victor Rosen. Copyright 1949 by Harold Russell & Victor Rosen. Copyright renewed © 1976 by Harold Russell.

tistical analysis of a test of acceptance of disability whose items were based on these value changes (Linkowski, 1971). A second measure of acceptance of loss, conceptualized in terms of these value changes has also been developed (Osuji, 1975).

Value changes accompany the person through an arduous and complex journey. "Values seem to be a basic and fundamental part of who we are, what we believe, and how we behave. . . . In mourning, there is a sadness not only over the lost body part or functioning, but over the whole nexus of values connected with that physical loss, with the nexus of behaviors connected with the values, and with the part of one's personal identity connected with those values that are now lost . . . how deep a process this loss of value can be" (Mangione, 1979). And correspondingly, how deep are the value changes that aid in the process of acceptance of loss.

The various value changes may be recommended in the following circumstances:

1. Enlargement of the scope of values is indicated in the case of all-inclusive suffering where the problem is to see as valuable those aspects of life not closed to the person.
2. Shifting the relative importance of values is indicated where the importance of the particular value has been overrated and others underrated.
3. Containment of the effects of disability is indicated where diffuse spread has occurred and where the disability need not have disabling effects.
4. When a value retains substantial importance, as in the case of physique, what is required for full acceptance is transformation from a comparative to an asset value in situations that do not require comparisons involving merit.

It is our judgment that the change to asset values is essential for the full and lasting feeling of the dignity of the individual. We agree with those who decry the automatic invoking of social comparisons as a way of relating to people. The kernel of feeling epitomizing the state of comparative-status values on the one hand and of asset values on the other can be described as, first, "I am nothing but an incomplete, injured person who has always to mourn my loss," and in the second case, "I am as I am, and though I don't have all the possible assets that can be imagined, I am fully a whole person."

Chapter 9
Coping, Succumbing, and Hoping

A woman, in musing about injured war veterans, remarked, "When I thought of the courage it took to ignore those handicaps, I felt humble. I felt that anyone who overcomes a handicap like that wins an added amount of respect from everyone" (Dembo, Leviton, & Wright, 1956, p. 24). In contrast, in thinking of severe disabilities others feel that, "It wouldn't be worthwhile to live." "I'd go into hiding and not show my face for the rest of my life" (Dembo, Leviton, & Wright, 1956, p. 24).

What are some of the immediately underlying differences between these two points of view? Although the person in the first instance appreciated the seriousness of the disability, she focused on the adjustable or coping aspects. She saw the difficulties associated with a disability as something that could be faced or overcome in some way. Those who voiced the second kind of comment saw the difficulties as a quagmire through which there was no path. Perhaps one so consumed with the imagined suffering of the disabled state doesn't even seek a path. The difficulties are in command and one succumbs to them. The two viewpoints just expressed are conceptualized in terms of two vastly different perspectives designated as the coping versus succumbing frameworks. It should be understood at the outset that these frameworks apply to both the insider and the outsider. People with a disability, as well as the able-bodied, may be coerced by the succumbing framework or reassured by the coping framework in experiencing the significance of disability.

THE COPING-VERSUS-SUCCUMBING FRAMEWORKS

Conceptualizing the Difference

The characteristics of the coping and succumbing frameworks are delineated in Figure 9.1. They are presented as pure cases, although in real life vacillation between the coping and succumbing frameworks, or mixed forms of them, are frequent. Briefly, the succumbing framework highlights the negative impact of disablement, giving scant attention to the challenge for change and meaningful adaptation. Prevention and cure are seen as the only valid answers. Satisfactions and assets are minimized or ignored. The emphasis is on the heartache, the loss, on what the person cannot do. Such a state is viewed as pitiful and tragic. The person as an individual with a highly differentiated and unique personality is lost.

The coping framework, on the other hand, orients the perceiver to appreciate the abilities of the person in terms of their intrinsic or asset value. People with disabilities are regarded as having an active role in their own lives and in the community, not as being passively devastated by difficulties. The problem of managing difficulties has a double focus. One is geared toward environmental change; that is, changing those alterable conditions that add to the person's handicap such as architectural barriers, discriminatory practices, lack of employment opportunities, family problems, and inadequate education, housing, and transportation. The second focus concentrates on change in the person through medical procedures that reduce the disability, education and training that lead to new skills, and value restructuring that allows the person to accept the physical condition as nondevaluating. As for the suffering associated with disability, the coping framework is oriented toward seeking solutions and discovering satisfactions in living. Moreover, it recognizes the disability as only one aspect of a multifaceted life that includes gratifications as well as grievances, abilities as well as disabilities.

It should be understood that concentrating on the coping possibilities does not imply glossing over the difficulties themselves. Disregarding difficulties could not lead to coping with them. Coping means dealing with difficulties, not pretending that they do not exist.

COPING	SUCCUMBING
1. The emphasis is on what the person *can do.*	1. The emphasis is on what the person *cannot do.*
2. Areas of life in which the person can participate are seen as worthwhile.	2. Little weight is given to the areas of life in which the person can participate.
3. The person is perceived as playing an *active role* in molding his or her life constructively.	3. The person is seen as *passive,* as a *victim* of misfortune.
4. The accomplishments of the person are appreciated in terms of their benefits to the person and others (asset evaluation), and not devaluated because they fall short of some irrelevant standard.[a]	4. The person's accomplishments are minimized by highlighting their shortcomings (comparative-status evaluation, usually measured in terms of "normal" standards).[a]
5. The negative aspects of the person's life, such as the pain that is suffered or difficulties that exist, are felt to be manageable. They are limited because satisfactory aspects of the person's life are recognized.	5. The negative aspects of the person's life, such as the pain that is suffered or difficulties that exist, are kept in the forefront of attention. They are emphasized and exaggerated and even seen to usurp all of life (spread).
6. Managing difficulties means reducing limitations through changes in the social and physical environment as well as in the person. Examples are: a. eliminating barriers b. environmental accommodations c. medical procedures d. prostheses and other assistive devices e. learning new skills	6. Prevention and cure are the only valid solutions to the problem of disability.
7. Managing difficulties *also* means *living on satisfactory terms* with one's limitations (although the disability may be regarded as a nuisance and sometimes a burden). This involves important *value changes.*	7. The only way to live with the disability is to resign oneself or to act as if the disability does not exist.
8. The fact that individuals with disabilities can live meaningful lives is indicated by their participation in valued activities and by their sharing in the satisfactions of living.	8. The person with a disability is pitied and his or her life essentially devaluated.

[a]The coping framework does not preclude instances where the nature of the situation requires that people be ranked on a given dimension (as in competitive activities such as sports and merit examinations), but it does preclude instances where comparative-status evaluation is actually irrelevant to the situation.

Figure 9.1   Characteristics of the Coping-Succumbing Frameworks

Adjustment, Attraction, and Aversion as Expressions of Coping-Succumbing

It is proposed that perceiving a person with a disability as coping with the problems at hand or as succumbing to them has contrasting effects on how well adjusted that person appears. When people with a disability are *perceived* as attempting to utilize their assets and improve their lives, they are regarded as determined or courageous. They may be respected, even admired. In contrast, when the perceiver is preoccupied with the undermining or succumbing aspects of the situation, the person with the disability tends to be diminished. He or she may be looked upon with aversion and be pitied or even condemned. Such negative reactions will occur so long as the evaluator, whether insider or outsider, maintains the succumbing perspective. In a test of this hypothesis, the coping and succumbing frameworks were experimentally coerced by having subjects view a videotaped interview of a person in a wheelchair who was depicted as either coping or succumbing (Shurka, Siller, & Dvonch, 1982). In the former case, the person in the wheelchair was rated significantly more favorably than when perceived as succumbing.

The emphasis on the succumbing as against the coping possibilities is one important factor, we believe, in the surprise, if not doubt, of many persons when informed that people with disabilities are for the most part indistinguishable from their able-bodied counterparts with respect to health of personality.

In the case of what has been called all-inclusive suffering, coping on the part of the person with the disability, even when halfhearted, may provide the spark for the adjustive change designated "enlarging the scope of values" (see pp. 163–171). Coping may also provide the opportunity for "containing disability effects" (see pp. 175–178), for it leads to new learning and solutions that overcome difficulties. People who become blind, for example, must learn to go from the bedroom to the kitchen, and *in trying* discover that visual cues are not the only stimuli that can guide them. "Then you perceive suddenly that there is order and reason and communication within the vast darkness which had seemed only chaos" (Ohnstad, 1942, p. 42). The way Karsten Ohnstad relearned to write soon after he became blind illustrates well how coping is the true mother of invention. He became impatient with having to depend on the nurses for doing his writing, and after trying unsuccessfully to produce a legible product on his own, he discovered that he needed something to hold his paper steady and to keep the lines straight across the page:

> . . . I found a medical-chart holder—a flat piece of metal with rubber-tipped clamps at the top. The rubber clamps held the paper firmly

in place. As a guide for making a straight line, I laid an envelope across the sheet and folded the left end under the chart, so that it could slide up and down along the edge without becoming crooked. A rubber band slipped around the entire chart held the envelope in place at whatever point I pushed it. It worked! When I made a *g* or an *f* or any letter that dropped below the line, I lifted the edge of the envelope until I had made the loop and then dropped it again. The lines were no longer run together. Completing a line at the right-hand side of the sheet, I pulled the envelope downward the approximate distance of the line, and there it remained, held fast by the rubber band. I handed the letter to a nurse and glowed with the pride of accomplishment as she read it word for word rapidly and without hesitation. [Ohnstad, 1942, pp. 48–49][1]

Psychologists have become increasingly concerned with positive strivings in people, with the factors that lead them to face and cope constructively with problems. The emphasis was explicitly recorded in the First Conference on Psychology and Rehabilitation (Wright, 1959). Among the twelve principles and assumptions defining rehabilitation listed therein are included (1) the importance of stressing the "assets of the person" and (2) the necessity of dealing with "reality factors," those difficulties within the actual social and physical environment with which the person with a disability has to cope. Since that conference, the importance of endorsing the assets of the person and eliminating attitudinal and architectural barriers that limit opportunities has continued to be stressed (Wright, 1972).

The coping versus succumbing frameworks not only affect the way disability-connected matters are grasped intellectually but the way they are reacted to emotionally. Reactions to the sight of blood, to an exposed stump, to braces and crutches are sometimes matter-of-fact and even positive, sometimes strongly aversive. One might turn away from the sight of blood when it signifies a crushing accident, suffering, and pain but be quite calm when it connotes the lifesaving material for the blood bank. One might be bothered by the sight of a stump and consider its exposure indecent or see it as well healed and ready for a prosthesis.

The same holds true for aesthetic reactions to prosthetic devices. During Harold Russell's (1949) initial reaction to his handlessness, he thought of hooks in terms of their devastating implications—as "claws" and "flippers," "hollow in sound." On the other hand, a man whose hands had been amputated for many years thought of his hooks as loyal friends who had served him well; to him they were "nice shiny little hooks." Harold notes: ". . . The prospect of going

[1]Reprinted from *The world at my fingertips* by K. Ohnstad, published by Bobbs-Merrill.

through life with steel claws terrified me. That would mean I'd be openly advertising the fact that I was a cripple and a freak. Besides, they were gruesome and repulsive to look at" (1949, p. 42). He therefore looked toward the cosmetic artificial hand in the hope that it would cover up his handlessness. Desperately he asked an old-time hand amputee, "Were they [the cosmetics] any good? How well did they work? Did they really look like the genuine article?" (p. 43). The old-timer replied:

> "Ah reckons they ain't so hot, son, else more folks'd be usin' 'em." He chuckled and clacked his hooks together like a seal clapping his flippers; they gave off a dismal, hollow sound. "No, suh! Gimme mah nice, shiny little hooks anytime! Yuh c'n do anythin' with 'em, positively anythin', suh!" [p. 43]

Harold continued to be sorely troubled at the thought of going through life with hooks until he discovered for himself that the hooks worked, whereas the cosmetic hands did not. Significantly, from then on he thought of the hooks as hooks or working hands (never as "claws") and of the cosmetic prosthesis as "phony hands."

> It didn't take me long to discover my mistake. The "cosmetics" looked all right, though the gray gloves gave me a clammy feeling and reminded me of pall-bearers hauling a coffin. What was more important, however, was that they didn't work. To begin with, only the thumb and index finger could be moved at all; the other three fingers were stationary. Then the normal position of the two functional ones were open. That meant that when I wanted to grasp something and hold onto it I had to exert constant pressure in order to keep the fingers closed. That was both tiring and disturbing. If I relaxed for just an instant, I'd drop whatever I was holding. I was under steady physical and mental strain everytime I picked up something.
>
> The following morning I went back to the workshop. I traded the phony hands for a pair of hooks. Maybe they didn't look so good, but they worked. I found that out right away. I pulled out a cigaret and lit it. It took a little struggling, but I was able to do it, which was more than I could say for the hands. I left the shop feeling that maybe things weren't going to be so bad, after all. [pp. 99–100][2]

Though at this point Harold still had a long way to go before he could approach full acceptance of his hooks, the groundwork was well laid. The hooks had become secured within the framework of coping rather than of succumbing.

[2]Reprinted by permission of Farrar, Straus & Giroux, Inc. From *Victory in my hands* by Harold Russell & Victor Rosen. Copyright 1949 by Harold Russell & Victo Rosen. Copyright renewed © 1976 by Harold Russell.

By the same dynamics, Noreen Linduska (1947) was able to see her braces as aesthetically pleasing, whereas they were aversive to a particular outsider. When Noreen described them as beautifully chromium plated, a woman felt that she was being "gruesome" (p. 189).

Another incisive example is the reaction of Karen and her mother when they saw Karen's crutches for the first time. Karen, now 7, had never walked. For years she had been slowly conquering the limitations of cerebral palsy by diligent application toward self-help in feeding, washing, and dressing and by development of sitting balance, active reciprocal motion, and so forth. After what seemed like interminable waiting, the crutches finally arrived. They were glorious because they meant not incapacity but tools with which to walk:

> . . . I [Karen's mother] threw the package on the couch and scampered off for a pair of scissors. It took a few minutes but finally I was down to the box. I took the box and placed it on the floor in front of Karen. Reverently I raised the lid. I looked at Karen. She was staring down, spellbound.
>
> There in all their gleaming beauty were our crutches. "Isn't the wood beautiful," she said in a hushed voice.
>
> Lifting her out of the bars, I sat her on the ottoman. My hands trembled as I lifted the crutches from their box. Wood or wings? [Killilea, 1952:215][3]

Of course, the perception of succumbing aspects and the resultant aversions may be invested with quite widely differing emotional contents. An example of deeply morbid preoccupation is the reaction of Miss M., observed in an experiment on the emotional reactions of nondisabled persons to the cosmetic hand (Cattell et al., 1949). The subject was in a small group that included a young man wearing a cosmetic hand prosthesis. Unable to bear the sight of the hand, she left; when interviewed later she spontaneously said:

> "It nauseated me. That's why I ran out. The sandwich [which she had been eating] began to smell . . . I smelled it again. The look of the hand where it came to the ridge . . . discolored, yellow-greenish" (grimaces and shows disgust and shrinks from the discussion and has to be encouraged to go on). [p. 62]

After continued discussion Miss M. pointed out that "It looked like nothing. It looked like death" (p. 63).

What is important to realize is that Miss M.'s marked aversion

---

[3]From *Karen* by Marie Killilea, published by Prentice-Hall, 1952. Reprinted by permission of Prentice-Hall and Marie Killilea.

to the yellow-greenish color is comprehensible when seen as linked to emotional contents that destroy the person, in this case the association with death. What may be gruesome to one may be gratifying to another, for in the one case it signifies troubles and heartaches and in the second case solutions and satisfactions.

Conditions Underlying the Coping-Succumbing Frameworks

The pressing question, then, concerns the conditions that shift the focus to the coping possibilities or the succumbing possibilities in situations involving serious difficulties. A number of factors need to be considered: perceptual contrast, insider-outsider position, insecurity in new situations, secondary gains of disability, requirement of mourning, and cultural prescriptions.

· *Perceptual Contrast.* The principle of perceptual contrast has already been encountered. It states that when two sufficiently different situations are compared, those features that indicate difference will be highlighted. In the case of disability, it is the disability that differentiates the nondisabled and disabled conditions. Examined in this light, it is the disability that stands out and assumes great power in spreading its negative sign on wide areas of the life space, even those that are not necessarily disability-connected. The areas in life that remain in fact untouched by the disability, that are similar to the nondisabled situation, or that are not adversely affected by the disability remain in the background, unrecognized and unreported. This is one important reason why, with the advent of a disability, the person may suffer the pain of self-pity and sometimes despair; in comparing oneself to the previous state of well-being, the disability stands out as the difference. The outside viewer who makes this comparison also falls easily into the succumbing framework.

Yet, perceptual contrast can also serve to orient the person toward coping. When a person with a disability sees another person with a different disability, the comparison may be a reminder of one's own assets. Or, when it is realized how much progress has been made since the injury, the person may be motivated to seek out further coping possibilities.

· *Insider-Outsider Position.* Another factor of importance to the coping-succumbing focus is whether the position of the person is that of the person who has the problem (the insider) or someone else (the outsider). The significance of this distinction has already been discussed but here its connection with the coping-succumbing problem will be more specifically addressed.

In the case of the insider, the person not only wishes for improvement but is actually faced with the necessity of coping with the difficulties; both *wish* and *necessity* keep prodding various coping possibilities. In contrast, the need to cope with disability problems may not be felt by the stranger or casual acquaintance. Nor is it *directly experienced* by professionals or other caretakers. We would expect, then, that insiders would be more inclined than outsiders to identify with, and look with favor on, assistive devices that enable them to function better. This was shown in a study in which rehabilitation patients on acute and chronic wards evaluated the idea of a wheelchair more positively than did nurses and aides (Antler et al., 1969). The evaluations tapped affective connotations of the meaning of a wheelchair by using Semantic Differential measures of "Evaluation," "Potency," and "Activity." For example, with regard to the Evaluation dimension, the subject rated the concept of "wheelchair" in terms of good-bad, beautiful-ugly, clean-dirty, and so forth. The patients were forced by circumstance to realize and experience directly the personal benefits of a wheelchair. The coping framework is therefore more salient in giving positive meaning to "wheelchair" than in the case of outsiders who are more removed from its emotional impact as a personal *resource*.

That the coping framework guides the feelings and views of the insider more spontaneously than of the outsider was demonstrated in the "mine-thine" problem previously presented (see pp. 48–49). In these experiments, one's own worst handicap is randomly paired with someone else's, and both persons are given an imaginary choice between them. By far, the majority of subjects reclaim their own handicap because, in comparing difficulties, the coping aspects of one's own situation come to the fore.

The "fortune phenomenon" described earlier in the discussion of spread (p. 34) also attests to the positive thrust of the insider position. It was seen that people generally rate *themselves* at least average, and typically above average, in how fortunate they are, even when the group with which they are identified is judged to be unfortunate by society. Thus, clients at a rehabilitation center rated themselves above average in how fortunate they were in contrast to the below average ratings given to rehabilitation clients by outsiders. Similar results were found for a group of mental hospital patients and a group of mothers on welfare.

"Quasi-insiders"—for example, friends—also view the situation of a person with a disability as more fortunate than when they are in the position of full outsiders. In one study (Wright, 1977) 60 percent of the subjects rated a friend with a particular disability as more fortunate than a stranger with the same disability, and none considered the imagined stranger to be more fortunate (40 percent of the subjects rated both targets equally). The socioeconomic status of the subjects did not affect their ratings.

The greater impact of the coping orientation of the insider as compared to the outsider is suggested in still another experiment in which college students described in detail a situation in which they themselves had been very worried and upset (Wright, 1976). The following two accounts are examples:

One student wrote: Probably one of the most disturbing situations that I've encountered in the last couple of years concerns a very personal matter. Last year, I met a girl in a lab section of one of my classes. Immediately we became friends, and I've always considered her as a very nice girl. Eventually I asked her out and she accepted. Over a period of 6 months, I saw her and dated her with some frequency. I had in mind getting to know her so that we could really know each other; but unfortunately, my part of the relationship became more involved.

She was a very serious student and studied a great deal. I really felt I was getting to know her, and I was enjoying it immensely. I thought that she felt somewhat the same. Anyway, just out of the blue, she said that our situation was a complication that she'd rather not deal with, and that we should forget it. Of course, I was surprised but what could I do?

I regret now never really understanding why she changed her mind. I wish I knew, just to answer some of my own questions about myself. I've often thought that someday I'll ask her out again but then I think that I was possibly too big of a fool already.

This little paper was a great idea, because I've never yet had a chance to really discuss my feelings on this subject even with my best friends. Still I feel as though there is still this cloud hanging over my head. It was very depressing; I couldn't concentrate on my studies and I was rather listless. It's a slow recovery from an event like this, for me anyway. But I realize that you have to go on.

Another student wrote: The experience I am talking about is one of total failure on my part to show love and concern.

My elderly grandmother had lived with us for several years. She had poor leg circulation and had one leg amputated—thereafter she stayed in a rest home. But while she lived with us I enjoyed caring for her, and when she moved, I liked to go visit her. By this time I was in high school and felt that my mother really appreciated my help.

After my freshman year in college I came to Nebraska to visit my brother and his wife—and also a young man with whom I was corresponding. After I had been with my brother a few days we got a call from my parents saying that my grandmother had died. During the call, I expressed my sympathy and sadness. I cried a long time that night. I had also asked my mother if she wanted me to come home, but she didn't, as my three week visit had just begun—and there wasn't much I could do anyway.

The next morning my sister-in-law said I could call home, but I felt that if I did I'd only cry and make my mother feel worse. So—as time went on I neglected to write, call, send flowers, or anything. I seemed to be completely oblivious to the sorrow, pain and hurt my mother was going through.

Finally I called just before I was going to leave for home. My mother said, "Oh, so you finally decided to call." It didn't sound like her, and then I began to realize what I had done. I almost hated to go home I felt so ashamed, but home I went and was welcomed.

My mother related everything that had happened to my grandmother. She expressed that she thought she had failed my grandmother too in not being with her when she died. She also expressed her hurt at my lack of concern. She said she could somewhat understand my brother not responding, but she could hardly believe my not responding since I was usually so compassionate. I apologized sincerely. She forgave me lovingly, but I can still hardly forgive myself.

The accounts were randomly grouped in sets of seven according to sex. In a second session, each subject received the set in which his or her account appeared and was asked to rank the troubling experiences according to how much the authors learned from the experience and matured as a person. In this way, each account was ranked seven times, once by the person who wrote it and six times by the other subjects whose experiences appeared in that set. The results were clear and significant: Most subjects perceived their own troubling experience as having greater adjustment value than their average ranking of other people's troubling experiences.

· *Insecurity in New Situations.* The insecurity of the unknown coerces the person, both insider and outsider, to focus on any possible threatening aspect. When moderate, the threat may lead to constructive coping, but when sufficiently alarming, it can lead to a dedifferentiation of the person's outlook so that the disability assumes unusual potency in spreading its presumed negative effects in an overly generalized way (Wright, 1964). As the person learns about new situations with which he or she is confronted, the sheer familiarity mutes its negative aspects. The succumbing framework begins to shift to that of the coping framework. Thus, reducing unfamiliarity by presenting problems of disability within a coping framework would help both people with disabilities and the able-bodied to overcome succumbing attitudes.

· *Secondary Gains of Disability.* When people feel relieved of responsibility because of their condition, or enjoy the dependency it imposes or unconsciously atone for guilt by the thought of being punished by disablement, motivational forces to maintain a succumbing orientation are strong. These are usually referred to as the secondary gains of disability.

On the other hand, there are many kinds of physical, social, and emotional gains from the disability experience that do not involve the exploitation of other people or the perpetuation of neurotic conflicts. People with disabilities do undergo change in values that allow them to recognize newly appreciated positives in their lives. They can achieve a sense of pride in being survivors and meeting adversity with will and effort. They can capitalize on opportunities that become available because of their disability and derive satisfaction from the gratification they afford. They can become part of self-help groups concerned with improving the quality of life. They can sense a deeper understanding of the difference between the trivial and the important. These are healthy, secondary gains of disability that serve to support the coping framework.

· *Requirement of Mourning.* The nondisabled person, too, may net personal gain by keeping someone else in effect subjugated by disability. The requirement of mourning, already elaborated at length in Chapter 5, is of special interest here. Particularly in the case of the self-aggrandizing requirement of mourning, people protect their own values and sense of well-being by devaluating another. They then insist that the other person is suffering or should suffer even when that person is seemingly content. In this way the requirement of mourning accomplishes for the favored person what unhealthy secondary gains of disability accomplishes for the insider. In both phenomena the person's own needs are fed by stressing the disabling, succumbing aspects of disability.

The requirement of mourning has such wide generality that it intrudes into all sorts of hierarchical relationships involving status and power. Agencies serving the handicapped, doctors serving patients, professors serving students, and parents serving children not infrequently affirm their own importance by behavior that betrays a need to keep those served in positions of inferiority, weakness, and incompetence. Because the requirement of mourning tends to be deflected from consciousness, it is essential that all of us attempt to raise our own awareness by periodically examining how we relate to other people.

· *Cultural Prescriptions.* Contributing to the relative potency of the coping and succumbing frameworks are cultural attitudes that dictate the way in which a person is taught to view disability. These in turn are affected by the basic undercurrents that drive the society. Thus, highly competitive societies with the elitist emphasis on status and power would appear to be susceptible to viewing "the less fortunate" as "less worthy." On the other hand, where a society can muster its philosophic and economic resources to support a constructive view of life with a disability, it will recognize the imperatives of eliminating attitudinal and environmental barriers and viewing disablement as nondevaluating. Above all, the inviolable faith in the value, worth, and dignity of each human being, when supported by the wider culture in outlook and deed, becomes the strongest base upon which the coping framework rests in organizing the way in which problems of disability are thought about and acted upon.

Implications for Rehabilitation and Education

Originally, agencies on behalf of persons with disabilities were organized to give comfort to the afflicted, to make the lot of "the disabled" somewhat easier. Increasingly, the efforts of organizations are being directed away from charity and toward constructive effort. Fraternal and social organizations of all kinds are making tangible contributions toward rehabilitating persons with disabilities rather than merely solacing them. The focus on succumbing to disability leads to charity, the focus on coping to rehabilitation.

· *Activities of Daily Living.* The best rehabilitation procedures contribute enormously toward bringing the possibilities of coping with difficulties into focus. The emphasis on "activities of daily living" directs the person to deal with the concrete here-and-now demands of getting along. When a patient who is paralyzed learns to move from the bed to the wheelchair, something more important than a new physical skill is being acquired; he or she is learning that one's situation can be improved and that in coping with the many "little things" the gain is self-respect. It has been said that working with daily-activity skills is the basis for all subsequent rehabilitation processes (Rusk & Taylor, 1953). This is as true for the restoration of self-respect as it is for the restoration of physical independence. The emphasis on coping is illustrated in the two rules stressed by the Institute of Rehabilitation Medicine at Bellevue Hospital, New York: "You can't disable ambition" and "you still have a lot more ability than you have disability."

· *Success Stories.* Success stories can also aid a person with a recent disability by highlighting the reality of coping successfully with the attendant difficulties. The story is told of a Marine flying officer whose left heel and entire right foot were amputated by the propeller of an enemy plane while he was parachuting from his own destroyed plane. Upon landing in the water, he inflated his life raft, applied a tourniquet, and waited to be picked up by a crash boat. When he was later asked what his thoughts were while administering first aid he answered, "I thought of an article I had read about Alexander de Seversky and how, although he lost a leg in the First World War, he was able to continue flying, and became one of the great men of the world in aviation. I thought, if he could do it, I could, too!" (Rusk & Taylor, 1946, p. 12). What this Marine officer realized was that the world still could reserve a useful place for him, that all the important things of life were not lost with his foot.

Without a doubt, some success stories serve to augment the feeling of self-pity. Inspirational stories about a person with a disability may exude self-aggrandizing feelings on the part of the writer that kindle the flames of devaluation in the reader. It is enlightening to sensitize oneself to the emotional undertones of the following news story about Pete Gray, the baseball player, who lost his right arm when he fell from a truck at the age of six: "Gray is an inspiration to practically every wounded veteran. The mere fact that a one-armed ball player has crashed the big leagues opens up new and electrifying vistas for each of them. If he can overcome his handicap in such fashion, there is hope for them all" (Rusk & Taylor, 1946:140). The last phrase, "there is hope for them all," particularly carries the sting of "You poor fellow, don't worry, there is still hope for you."

In contrast, consider the following account of Bill Talbert, the United States Davis Cup tennis star, who must daily remember the fact that he has diabetes. "In the fourteen years Talbert has played tournament tennis, he has competed in some five hundred events, has traveled more than three hundred thousand miles, and taken more than ten thousand insulin injections. Diabetes has not interfered with either Talbert's tennis playing or his personal life, for he has learned to live with his disability" (Rusk & Taylor, 1946, p. 131).[4] There is no pity in this description. But there is an awareness that the disability plays a role in Talbert's life, a role defined by his efforts to cope with its impositions.

· *Seeing Others Manage.* Even more than success stories, knowledge of how others with like problems manage successfully may provide

---

[4]From *New hope for the handicapped* by Howard A. Rusk & Eugene J. Taylor. Copyright 1946, 1947, 1948, 1949 by Howard A. Rusk. By permission of Harper & Row, Publishers, Inc.

the realization that it is possible to do so. As a parent of a retarded child, Pearl Buck received such support when she needed it most:

> I learned at last, merely by watching faces and by listening to voices, to know when I had found someone who knew what it was to live with sorrow that could not be ended. It was surprising and sad to discover how many such persons there were and to find how often the quality I discerned came from just such a sorrow as my own. It did not comfort me, for I could not rejoice in the knowledge that others had the same burden that I had, but it made me realize that others had learned how to live with it, and so could I. I suppose that was the beginning of the turn. For the despair into which I had sunk when I realized that nothing could be done for the child and that she would live on and on had become a morass into which I could easily have sunk into uselessness. [Buck, 1950, p. 31][5]

The positive psychological effect of seeing others *like oneself* manage is an important reason for employing rehabilitation personnel who have disabilities similar to those of their patients or clients. An occupational therapist with a hook prosthesis can teach people with arm amputations a good deal more than the mechanical use of prosthetic devices. He or she can teach them that it is possible not only to become physically independent but also to feel satisfaction in achievement that comes from viewing a disability as nondevaluating:

> . . . Sure, it was easy for her [an able-bodied occupational therapist] to show me how to turn on a water faucet or drop a coin in a box. All you did was thus and so, and then they'd demonstrate for me. That didn't mean much to me. Of course they could do it themselves. They had hands. But if someone with hooks had demonstrated how to open a window or turn a faucet not with hands, but with hooks, he would have made a deep and lasting impression on me. Then I wouldn't have left Occupational Therapy every day saying to myself, That's all very fine and wonderful, *but*—[Russell, 1949, pp. 104–5]

Parenthetically, an occupational therapist who has the particular disability is likely to have worked out tricks and shortcuts that may not be a part of the nondisabled therapist's repertoire:

> . . . they taught me in Occupational Therapy to pick up a cup of coffee by slipping my hook through the handle. That was all wrong. I had no control over it that way. The weight of the liquid would pull it down. To keep it from spilling I'd have to steady it with my other hook. After awhile I learned by myself that it was better to grip the handle between

[5]From *The child who never grew* by P. S. Buck, published by John Day. Reprinted by permission of American Institute for Mental Studies.

the prongs of one hook, thus leaving the other free. [Russell, 1949, p. 103][6]

· *Disability Symbols.* The guiding idea here is that prosthetic aids should be imbedded within a coping context of acceptance. This means that words that connote positive functioning should be selected in favor of more aversive terms. On these grounds, the designation of *working* or *functional hands* is far better than *claws* in designating an arm prosthesis.

Acceptance within the coping framework also means that advertisements should avoid basing their appeal on how inconspicuous the prosthesis is. By stressing the invisibility of the hearing aid, for example, that "no one will know," the message reminds its readers that impaired hearing is something to be ashamed of, a message that fits the succumbing framework all too readily. The retort that such an approach will more easily sell hearing aids than will a positive approach is simply not borne out by the evidence. Manufacturers sell eyeglasses by glamorizing them and in so doing encourage people to purchase them and wear them with the comfort of self-acceptance. Hearing aids, too, could be adorned to meet various tastes.

Even when a commercial appeal has nothing to do with disability, it is suggested that having a person with a disability advertise a product could do much to nonintrusively convey the idea that having a disability is common, that it does not engulf all of life, that it can be accepted and lived with. People with disabilities ought to appear far more frequently in the communication media, on television and stage, in newspaper and magazine, not as "disabled people," but as people engaged in the wide-ranging panorama of living experiences.

· *Widening Opportunities: The Possible-Impossible.* Another set of implications of the coping-succumbing differentiation concerns the perception of the possible and impossible, a matter of grave consequence in regard to employment, and more generally in regard to what a person is allowed to do. It is sobering to think how powerful this basic difference is, for it opens up employment opportunities or shuts them off; it screens people in or keeps them out.

An enlightening case is the experience of Robert Acosta, a man who is blind. As a student, it took much convincing before he was permitted to pursue a teaching career. It took convincing because

[6]Reprinted by permission of Farrar, Straus & Giroux, Inc. From *Victory in my hands* by Harold Russell & Victor Rosen. Copyright 1949 by Harold Russell & Victor Rosen. Copyright renewed © 1976 by Harold Russell.

everyone believed that blindness made it impossible to carry out the duties of a teacher, particularly of sighted children. The prejudice precluded thoughts of possibilities. At first he was only allowed to serve as a substitute teacher. It was only after he was proclaimed one of the ten outstanding young Americans of 1968 that he was allowed to become a regular classroom teacher. When he began to teach successfully, people asked, "How does he grade examinations? How does he teach geography without maps? What about discipline? Use of the blackboard?" These are coping questions that gear the effort to discovering how problems can be worked out rather than prematurely written off as too difficult or impossible to solve. In many, many cases the impossible becomes possible when myths that exaggerate limitations are overcome, personal assets are developed, barriers to opportunities are eliminated, and reasonable accommodations are instituted. The list of foregone conclusions that deny opportunities to all sorts of persons with all sorts of disabilities because of the succumbing attitude is long indeed.

· *Brainstorming.* An excellent way to expand coping possibilities is through the creative problem-solving approach known as brainstorming. The following brief description of what took place with a group of parents whose children had cerebral palsy demonstrates its value (Schiller, 1961).

After the parents indicated the problems they would like to work on, they were invited to offer as many ideas as they could to stimulate possible solutions without regard to whether the ideas were wild or practical. The 30-minute brainstorming session devoted to a problem yielded about 100 suggestions in each case. The following is a small sample of the range of ideas that emerged to help a 7-year-old boy increase his desire for accomplishment. The boy had trouble gripping things, swallowing anything but liquids, and reaching his mouth with food. He was learning to use crutches. He took a long time to dress and feed himself, was content to dawdle in the morning, and had a problem getting to the school bus on time. He was fond of TV and sports. The suggestions included:

> Allow more time for him to dress; get him up earlier. This means he'll have to go to bed earlier and miss some of his TV programs. As he speeds up eating and dressing, he can stay up later.
> Interest him in firefighters and make believe he is one. Refer to the alarm clock as a fire alarm. Stress that "firefighters don't dawdle."
> Let him sleep in some of his clothes to speed up dressing.

Button the lower part of his shirts when they are folded; then he can slip them over his head and have only the top buttons to do.

Get him clothes that go on easily, such as loafers instead of shoes with laces.

Build up handles of fork and spoon so he can get a better grip on them.

Make a game out of spearing the food on his plate. You might use paper plates with a "bull's-eye" painted on them. Place the food in the bull's-eye, and keep score.

Draw lines on the basement floor and have him follow them on his crutches. Set a goal each day, five steps, seven steps.

Utilize his interest in sports to spur his desire to conquer his crutches. Show him how to support himself with one crutch and make use of his free hand to engage in sports activities like bowling.

Provide him with peg games that will compel him to use his fingers in handling the pegs.

Build up his self-respect by giving him decisions to make: what shirt to wear, what to eat at mealtime, what to do in his playtime.

Make positive statements about his achievements, no matter how small, by telling others when he is able to overhear.

It was reported that the parents of this boy were able to make use of a number of the suggestions and that significant progress was shown by the boy as a result. Several parents found helpful suggestions on other parents' lists.

The difference between the way the coping-versus-succumbing frameworks define the very nature of disability has important implications for many issues. In later chapters its bearing on professional-client relations (Chapter 17), on fund-raising and health care messages (Chapter 18), and on modifying attitudes (Chapter 19) will be elaborated. The reader doubtlessly will find its application to other problems as well.

Conditions Suspending the Coping Framework

There are circumstances in which the coping orientation needs to be held in abeyance. The need to mourn a deep loss, be it of a close person or body function, often experienced after the numbing impact of the loss has worn off, is one of these (Dembo et al., 1956; Wright, 1968). During this period, the person may want and even need to remain with the sorrow, to grieve, and even sometimes to suffer self-recrimination. The "work of mourning" during this period enables the person to gain a positive hold on the task of living and coping with loss, but it is work that can be forestalled if efforts to snap the person out of despair deny the person the right to grieve. What is often needed is to stand by the person for the time being, to let the person know that there are people who care, that their support and services are available when the person is ready to receive them. This does not mean that the person should be encouraged to keep on mourning the loss. Nor does it mean that participation in activities of living should be set aside. It means that the coping framework, with its stronger emphasis on positive functioning, can bide its time.

Another set of circumstances that may preclude the coping framework concerns the freedom of the writer or artist to depict a person with a disability in any way that fits one's purposes. So long as one is *not* concerned with promoting rehabilitation efforts or constructive views of life with a disability, having a disability can be portrayed as a tragedy pervasive in extent and time, with the power to defeat, to crush with pain and despair, to strip one of hope and satisfaction and anything else. Besides the fact that such states of devastation are not unknown, all existential views of the human condition should have a hearing.

But, when one is concerned about helping people meet the problems of living with a disability, it is the coping and not the succumbing framework which should provide the thrust of the effort. In the case of public media, the communication must be of sufficient dimension to allow those positive forces to be appreciated that make it possible for people to live satisfactory lives with their disability. It is probable that brief communications such as those used in advertisements, fund-raising campaigns, and newspaper releases are insufficient to the task of dealing with despair within a coping framework. It is also probable that longer accounts and personal documents, providing the possibility of describing the complexity of emotions and behavior as a fluctuating process involving change and growth, can handle the emotional drama within a time perspective that makes room for the working through of severe problems.

HOPING

"Physicians in their observations of patients, survivors of concentration and prisoner-of-war camps, mountain climbers in acute physical distress, all report that they can 'see,' that they 'know,' when an individual gives up hope and subsequently will die. Conversely, hope, suddenly entering the doomed and resigned, gives instant strength and activity to a wasted mind and body. . . . Hope appears to be energizing, hopelessness de-energizing" (Korner, 1970, 135–136). In this statement, hoping is seen as a sustaining force, giving vitality to the will to live and cope. Yet, there are often misgivings about the value of hoping, as expressed in the aphorism: "He who lives by hope will die of hunger." The concern seems to involve an opposition between acting realistically on the one hand and hoping on the other.

One study confronted clients and professionals with this opposition by asking the following question: "Would you support a hopeful outlook or a very realistic approach to the future" (Leviton, 1973). When the issue is posed in this way, most hospital patients placed emphasis on the importance of a hopeful outlook, whereas most hospital professional personnel leaned toward the realistic approach. On the other hand, members of self-help groups, as well as vocational counselors, were more evenly divided on this issue. An important conclusion of the study was that "dichotomizing hope versus reality appears to be less profitable than specification" of the following aspects of hopes:

1. Content of hope: Some hopes can be supported more readily than others.
2. Time dimension: For the immediate future, realistic tasks must be emphasized; for the long run, uncertain new discoveries that may be promising may be considered.
3. Probabilities and possibilities: The situation may be discussed both in terms of probabilities, which is important for planning and professional credibility, as well as in terms of possibilities, which gives recognition to more farfetched hopes and acknowledges the lack of omniscience of the expert.
4. Hoper characteristics: Hope may be supported in cases where the person is coping in contrast to passively "waiting for miracles."

Where hoping is not juxtaposed against reality, the strong need of adults to seek a reality base for their hopes emerges. In a study on the process and tasks of hoping (Wright & Shontz, 1968), parents, teachers, and therapists of children at a school for crippled children, as well as the children themselves, were asked about their hopes for the particular child when that child became an adult. In contrast to child hopes, an important characteristic of adult hopes was the need to ground hopes in reality: more than 90 percent of the adults spontaneously offered supporting evidence for their hopes, whereas none of the children did so. Moreover, 70 percent of the adults felt some uncertainty about the realizability of their hopes, whereas very few of the children did so.

To account for these differences, two factors may be suggested.

One pertains to the developmentally greater conceptual ability of adults that allows them to differentiate hopes from wishes, reality from unreality, and a more uncertain future from the present. The second concerns different role expectations regarding the responsibility of children and adults: "To the child, the future is not part of his responsible sphere of action, and as such he can express hopes without needing to become concerned about outcome probabilities. The future is far off and will be taken care of by omnipotent adults. Even the adolescents in the study tended to be indifferent to reality issues, perhaps because all their lives important decisions were not theirs to make" (Wright & Shontz, 1968, p. 324).

The need of the adult to undergird hopes is seen in the variety of ways in which phenomenal reality grouding takes place. In the study, over a dozen ways were distinguished. One common way is to point out favorable environmental circumstances, as did the father of 14-year-old Jed who had a suprapubic cystotomy at one week of age and poliomyelitis at age 5. When asked about hopes for Jed as an adult, the father said:

> "Well, I think, if we can get him through high school, I can send him to Horkins school. They have business courses out there, which I think would be the best thing for him. I graduated twice out there, from high school and from the vocational program, and they do have a two-year business course—typing, shorthand, bookkeeping, but generally I think that, once I get him through high school, why they'll be able to more or less teach him a trade, so he can earn a living, which is not impossible." [Wright & Shontz, 1968, p. 327]

Another common way to support hope is to stress the assets of the child, as did Jed's teacher:

> "Actually, I hope that Jed can go on through school to receive the type of certificate or diploma that would mean that he would be able to get some type of training, because his *upper extremities are good, his hands are good, and he should be able* to go into some trade or vocation that would, you know, give him a nice livelihood." [p. 327]

A further analysis of the interviews led to a differentiation of the process of adult hoping according to the way in which the survey of reality is paced and the uncertainty of the future is handled.

Even when an unpromising or bleak future is acknowledged, the adult tries to achieve a hopeful attitude by intentionally keeping the future poorly defined and taking "each day as it comes." The positives are then preserved by concentrating on realistic values in the present. The case of Donald, a 14-year-old with a progressively debilitating disease, aptly illustrates this means of maintaining hope:

MOTHER: Well, I mean as far as hoping, we've just never [pause]
FATHER: We've never given up hoping [pause]
M: You never give up, I mean, to a certain extent he might be handi-capped in one way [note the understatement here] but you hope that eventually he will gain more in another part, that someday [pause]

The lack of adequate reality support shortly shifted the conver-sation to the need for living in the present:

M: There was a time when he [Donald] worried terribly about what he was going to do when he was going to get old, whether, you know, about making his own living and of course it shocked me. . . . I said, "You don't want to think that far ahead, you just live today, and then tomorrow morning when you get up you live for that day." I said, "Don't live so many years in advance." Well, now, ever since that he's kinda, you know, lived for the present, not for the future so much.

The father then continued the conversation, still focusing on the present and thereby renewing his own morale:

F: As far as his interests go, he's still as, just as much a normal kid, I mean. He's crazy about baseball, and he likes football, basketball, and he's always had a great thrill for racing, building model racers, and stuff like that like most boys his age. As far as his morale, it's always pretty good, I mean, he's never let himself down in the dumps to think that, "Well, it's just here and that's it." So he's got high hopes. [pp. 327–328]

The parents' desire to make the most of the present by focusing on here-and-now rewarding activities allows them to hope. When the future is kept only vaguely defined, it can reflect the positive glow of the present.

The reflections of the parents, teachers, and therapists led the investigators to distinguish four cognitive-affective tasks of hoping:

1. Reality surveillance: A cognitive function directed toward co-ordinating hopes with reality in order to insure the fulfillment of hopes. It also serves as a base for substitute hopes should one's original hopes have to be given up.
2. Encouragement: The affective side of coordination of hopes with reality as the person sees reality. It motivates, sustains, and comforts the person who is hoping.
3. Worry: The affective counterpart of cognitive uncertainty. It forces the person to reexamine reality.
4. Mourning: The affective consequence of having to relinquish a hope. Mourning prepares the person for the task of reap-praising values and accepting hope substitutions.

A general principle is that weight should be given to each of the four tasks of hoping: "This leads to the conclusion that encouragement should not be so all-important as to bypass the productive outcomes of worrying and mourning. Conversely, it also leads to the conclusion that objective reality considerations should not be pursued in a highly differentiated way if so doing would destroy encouragement. Sometimes wishful expectations may have to be countenanced and realistic expectations muted in order to keep encouragement alive" (p. 330).[7]

Two additional guiding principles may be offered: First, the realistic state of affairs as it relates to *current planning* must be discussed with the person, but even then hope for improvement in the situation need not be discredited. For example, it may be important to convince the person that his or her hearing cannot be restored so that the necessary speech training program can be initiated as soon as possible. The person may have to be convinced many times over that current medical knowledge is of no avail, but this does not mean that hope for medical advance and eventual hearing need summarily be dismissed. Second, the emphasis given to the reality of the future can be guided by whether the person gives an indication of readiness to know it. The question is whether the difficult reality needs to be unfolded all at once or more gradually paced. Despite wishful thinking, most people do gradually absorb the reality that has to be faced. The four tasks of hoping psychologically prepare the person, making it unnecessary that the person be shocked into reality by the blunt if not callous words of the professional.

Some will disagree with this advice. It may be held that a wound, however deep, is better when it is clean-cut. The point of view presented here, on the other hand, maintains that for the wound to be clean-cut, the area must first be prepared by the proper care. The four tasks of hoping admirably fulfill that care. If one is grateful for the "bitter truth," it is because one has been prepared; one already "knows" and needs the verdict of the authority to give certainty to that knowledge, a certainty that provides relief only after floundering amid the unknown and being exhausted by it. Even then hope is not precluded.

A study of parental hopes for their child with a disability (D) and a nondisabled sibling (ND) supports the tasks of hoping by showing that dormant values emerge as hopes according to the concerns and priorities for the child (Brown, 1968). For example, the percentage of hopes for D concerning physical abilities was twice that for ND; whereas, the percentage of hopes for D concerning interpersonal re-

[7]From Process and tasks in hoping, by B. A. Wright & F. C. Shontz. In *Rehab. Lit.*, 1968, 29, 322–331. Reprinted by permission of *Rehab. Lit.*

lations was half that for ND. Moreover, a greater number of hopes was submitted for D than for ND even though the parents rated the hopes for D lower in realizability than for ND.

Dembo made an important contribution to the psychology of hoping in her distinction between probable and possible outcomes (1955). Probable outcomes are based on the belief that the future can be predicted from the present. The notion of realistic expectations is based on such probabilities. Possible outcomes on the other hand yield more to wishful thinking. All that is required is that there is a possibility for a hoped-for eventuality. The person is encouraged by that possibility. Not only is suffering thereby alleviated, but in warding off despair, the person is better able to deal with present realities. The task of reality surveillance in hoping will then assure that there will be grounds for substituting a hope when the time comes.

There is one more important point that must be considered. Not infrequently misconception and prejudice masquerade in the name of reality. When Karen's doctor told her mother, "I don't believe that cerebral palsy children have any mentality" (Killilea, 1952, p. 29), he thought he was being realistic and that she ought to know the dire facts. When another doctor advised the parents to take Karen to an institution and leave her and forget they ever had her (p. 34), he also thought he was being realistic. The judgment of reality depends partly on whose eyes are perceiving. By and large the eyes of the insider become very good perceivers when time and opportunity to see and to feel as well as to hope and to substitute hopes are given. It is then that reality holds promise for the future. Hundreds of cases could be cited in which the dream of today became the reality of tomorrow (Wright, 1968).

Coating reality with hope does not mean living in a world of unreality. Accepting a disability does not mean banishing hope. Even when one has reached the most wholesome adjustment to disability—namely, that of viewing physical intactness as an asset value—hope is not ruled out. As a general principle, shocking a person into reality has doubtful value. As the person struggles to adjust to the loss, reality takes shape. But the person needs time and experience with the disability to face it. Although one cannot or ought not live by hope alone, when allowed to fulfill its tasks hoping can be a leavening agent that lightens one's burdens.

Chapter 10
Development of the Self-Concept

The kind of person you think you are becomes endowed with remarkable powers. It influences, and often decisively, the way one perceives the intentions of others, the choice of associates, the goals set for oneself, and much more. The self-concept, then, is an important part of one's world or life space and has been so recognized by our eminent psychological forebears who have given serious attention to its development. Contemporary thinkers are continuing the investigation of this important area. In broad outline, we shall attempt here to describe how the concept of the self is formed and the forces that direct its fate, with particular reference to problems of disability. That aspect of the self-concept which pertains to attitudes, experiences, and functions involving the body is referred to as the *body-image.*[1]

---

[1]Extensive coverage of theory and research on topics involving the self-concept appears in Wylie, 1979. A broad survey of thought and research concerning body-image phenomena may be found in Fisher & Cleveland (1968, Chapter 1), and in Shontz (1969; 1975, Chapter 5).

The composition of the self-picture is an intricate one, consisting of a variety of particular characteristics that define for the person his or her *identity,* as well as a global self-evaluation of personal worth. We develop a notion about our own body, what satisfactions it offers and denies us; we discover that we have certain interests and abilities, likes and dislikes; we begin to think of ourselves as shy, outgoing, or in-between, as irritable, calm, or anxious; we learn something of the way we affect others, that we are liked or resented, for example. We learn about our heritage. Not only does the individual evaluate these separate personal characteristics, but an overarching feeling regarding self-esteem also emerges. All these perceptions and evaluations make up that separate entity in the individual's world variously designated as the "I," the "me," the "self," and the "ego."

For our purposes, no distinctions between these terms will be made, though some psychologists have made them. Freud (1933) for example, distinguishes the superego or "conscience" of the person from the ego, whereas Sherif & Cantril (1947) see no need for this separation. Ausubel (1952) makes a distinction between the body, the self, the ego, and the personality.

It is well to keep in mind that the boundary between what is the self and what is not a part of the self, even in the mature person, is not as sharp as it might seem. One's children, for example, are felt to be a part of oneself, though at the same time there is recognition of their independence. Even an object may become so intimately bound up with the emotions of a person that, should it become necessary for the two to become separated (e.g., the person moves from a home of many years) a feeling of having left behind a part of the self is common.

DIFFERENTIATING THE WORLD AND INTEGRATING THE SELF

Psychologists generally agree that young infants do not make any distinction between what is the self and what is not. If they should happen to pull their hair or scratch their face, they will cry out, but they do not realize that *they* are pulling *their* hair or scratching *their* face. With maturation of the nervous system and increased interaction with the environment, however, *differentiation* takes place in which there gradually emerges a very special part of the universe which is felt as the self or "I." For example, the baby's interest in his or her hands initially appears to be no different from interest in other objects, such as a rattle or crib post. Soon, however, new experiences emerge. Not only can the baby control the fingers' wiggle but, more than that, the baby feels the wiggle in a way different from the wiggle of the rattle. In time the baby will realize that the hand is a part of the self whereas the rattle is not. Psychoanalytic theory places special importance on the physical self both in the differentiation of the person from other realities and in the continuing development of the ego. Fenichel (1945), an exponent of the Freudian viewpoint, presents this emphasis in these words:

> In the development of reality the conception of one's own body plays a very special role. At first there is only the perception of tension, that is, of an "inside something." Later, with the awareness that an object exists to quiet this tension, we have an "outside something." One's own body is both at the same time. Due to the simultaneous occurrence of both outer tactile and inner sensory data, one's own body becomes something apart from the rest of the world and thus the discerning of self from nonself is made possible. The sum of the mental representations of the body and its organs, the so-called body image, constitutes the idea of I and is of basic importance for the further formation of the ego (Fenichel, 1945; pp. 35–36).

This process of self-identification is hastened by the fact that the baby meets resistance in the external world. Needs are not and cannot be satisfied the moment they arise. The unsatisfied needs not only sharpen self-awareness but prompt the baby to search for ways to gratify them and as a consequence, the baby's world becomes yet further differentiated. It may very well be that frustration is a necessary experience in personality development, for if all needs could receive immediate gratification, there would be no differentiation between the self and external reality.

Learning about the self occurs through various modalities. There is, first of all, the direct sensory experiences of the baby, as when the baby discovers the different sensations of the hand in contrast to the rattle. Since vision is presumed to serve more efficiently than the other senses to differentiate external objects from one another, as well as the self from other objects, it has been hypothesized that among children who are congenitally blind there should be some delay (but not necessarily a permanent defect) in the development of ego functions (Blank, 1957, p. 7).

Secondly, the child learns about the self through the leads provided by others. The child learns that one is a boy or girl, has a certain name, and is not allowed to do certain things, for example. The child also develops certain attitudes about these facts, and therefore about oneself, through contact with the viewpoints of associates.

Self-knowledge gained directly through the senses is not always consistent with that socially induced. According to Rogers, when the person denies the former in favor of the latter, the conditions become favorable for neurotic ego development (Rogers, 1951, Chapter 11). Part of the adjustment process then becomes one of attribution; that is, notions about the self must become more correctly ascribed to evidence directly experienced and personally evaluated on the one hand and to evidence socially mediated on the other.

Since knowledge about the self is built up through sensory experience and through the viewpoints of others, as well as through inferences based on these sources, it is possible for the body to become invested with significance beyond its concretely apprised functions. Body parts begin to assume such connotations as good and bad, clean and unclean, adequate and inadequate. The hands, for example, may not only be regarded as tools for grasping and manipulating but also contaminated by shame and evil should the child have been traumatized when caught masturbating or in fecal play.

Psychoanalytic theory gives special prominence to the symbolic meaning of body parts and considers these meanings to be crucial in adjustment to disability. The problem of adjusting to amputations, for example, is felt to be largely a problem of dealing with castration anxiety. (See p. 449–450 for a more detailed discussion of this.) Such was the interpretation given to the following remark of a patient: "Even though the eye is useless and I will look better with a glass eye I don't want any part of me cut out" (Blank, 1957, p. 17). When the patient was analyzed within this theoretical framework it was reported that she mastered the problems of surgery and the use of the prosthetic eye. Without debating the specific symbolic associations attributed to the eyes and other body parts by different interpreters, it is undoubtedly true that the meaning of the body has significance that extends far beyond the concrete apprehension of function and appearance.

The ever-enlarging array of facts and attitudes about the self, however, is not built into the self-picture in a haphazard way. There is good reason to believe that at least in many if not all instances, new self-attributes are *integrated* within old ones either by modifying the meaning of the former or the latter or both. This holds true for attributes pertaining to the body as well as those pertaining to other aspects of the self. Integration need not require a reasonableness that adheres to adult logic, but rather is a "fitting-in process" in which new facts or attitudes or values are assimilated by being attached to existing beliefs so that the old and the new cohere as a Gestalt. In this way a certain stability and consistency of the self-picture is achieved.

The principle of integration through modification of the old and the new applies, as psychology has clearly established, not only to the self-concept but to all sorts of perceptions, beliefs, and even behavior. A clear demonstration of the principle appears in a study in which college students were asked to form an impression of a factory worker on the basis of a list of traits presented to them (Haire & Grunes, 1950). The inclusion of "intelligent" as an attribute was disturbing to these subjects, who, having had a well-organized picture of a working man that was generally somewhat patronizing and snobbish, found that an intellectual trait did not easily fit with their existing system of beliefs and values. They either had to ignore this trait, tamper with its meaning, or revamp their total concept of a factory worker. There are many other studies directly dealing with perceptual and cognitive phenomena that show the interacting process between part and whole in the service of integration.

Returning to the self, we get a glimpse of the process of differentiation and integration with specific reference to body-image in the following account. Billy was born without arms. Attached to his right shoulder was a small part of a palm and three tiny fingers, and to his left shoulder were two webbed appendages. When Billy was about two years old, he was led to believe, through what he had heard from time to time about his body as well as information gained through his own senses, that his right hand, with which he could feed himself and hold things, was his good hand, whereas his left hand, which was practically useless, was his broken hand. The development of this perception is seen in the following incident told by his mother:

> . . . in the playground, one of the children noticed Billy's lack of arms for the first time and kept asking over and over if his arm had broken off. He was too little to understand a real explanation so I finally said, yes, it had broken off, and walked away. I thought no more about it, because similar incidents had happened so often, until that night when I was giving Billy his bath. He felt his little two fingers that protrude from his left shoulder anxiously, as if to reassure himself that he, too, has something there. Then he held up his right arm and said, "This good hand, other broken hand." [Bruckner, 1954, p. 140]

Sometime later Billy denied not having an elbow because (and we interpret) this fact was simply inconsistent with his existing belief that his right hand was his good hand:

> One day as she [Karen, Billy's sister] was doing something, and Billy was trying to copy her, she noticed that he could not do it. She looked truly surprised as she said, "Mother, I just noticed that Billy doesn't have an elbow and he can't lift his hand up high like I can."
> I hadn't thought that Billy had heard her because he was so absorbed in what he was trying to do. But he immediately answered her.

"I do so have an elbow and look at me lift my hand up high. See, Karen." [Bruckner, 1954, pp. 146–147][2]

It is certain that once Billy learns more precisely what an elbow is, he will recognize its absence in his own anatomy, with the consequence that other changes in his self-picture will take place in order to effect the necessary integration. He may realize, for example, that his right hand is not, in fact, a "good hand"; though it is better than his left, it still has major shortcomings. How this will affect other attributes of his self-concept, his self-esteem in particular, will depend upon the further direction the integrating forces take. We shall have more to say about this shortly.

At this point it is important to note that the principle of integration need not imply a self-picture that is integrated in all its aspects. The findings of one study, for example, suggest that the ideal self is a complex rather than a unitary entity, making it possible for inconsistencies to persist without tension (McKenna, Hofstaetter, & O'Connor, 1956). It is more than likely that not only the ideal self but also the self in its existing structure consists of subparts, each of which may be fairly well integrated but not necessarily related to every other part in an integrated way. For example, Mr. A. may consider himself a handsome man but a scoundrel: his appearance self and moral-behavior self are relatively independent, by which we mean that a change in either of these subparts of the self has little effect on the other. Subparts, however, may show a high degree of interdependence and therefore integration, as when Mr. A feels himself a scoundrel *because* he is repulsed by his appearance. We believe that personality descriptions in terms of the relatedness of subparts of the self would provide pertinent data about the individual.

Schilder (1953) asserts "that single sensations [about the body] do not stand helter-skelter side by side in memory, but are ordered into a total image of the body—or, to use Head's expression, into a schema. Every new stimulus is met by previously fixed structures, by a body-image . . ." (p. 93). Though basically in agreement with this point of view, we prefer to take the more moderate position that integration of a new stimulus or sensation need not require ordering into a total image of the body, but rather a subpart may be sufficient.

INTEGRATION AND SELF-EVALUATION: A TWO-WAY PROCESS

One of the most interesting and direful facts about the integration process is that congruency is frequently established between what

[2]Reprinted from *Triumph of Love* by Leona Bruckner, Copyright by Leona Bruckner.

we might call a single attribute of the self on the one hand and
self-esteem on the other. This fact has been encountered earlier in
the discussion of the phenomenon of spread (see pp. 32–39).
Self-esteem refers to the more or less general evaluation of the self
as a worthy or unworthy *person*. The perception of a single attribute
may be molded by self-evaluation, or the evaluation of the self may
be affected by a single attribute in such a way as to bring about the
necessary integration.

Both processes may occur, and both are seen very clearly in Raymond Goldman's (1947) life history. It may be recalled that Raymond
was the boy whose legs became disabled from infantile paralysis at
the age of 4, and who in his teen years struggled against increasing
deafness. The first example shows that even what objectively may
be a startlingly clear and unambiguous fact concerning the self,
namely the glaring condition of his legs, may be distorted by the
power of the general evaluation of the self. The scene is the doctor's
office where 8-year-old Raymond is waiting to have long leg braces
fitted. His self-esteem at this time glistened with the high and mighty
omnipotence of a childish ego. All along he had been king-pin in a
world in which he had been loved, lauded, and protected:

> Most of the seats were occupied by waiting patients and their moth-
> ers. It was the first time I had ever been close to a large group of chil-
> dren—there were about ten or twelve in the room—and I regarded
> them with curiosity. They were all crippled and deformed, and I saw
> what braces were like. There were different kinds. The little girl who
> sat across from me wore one on her head. It protruded from the neck
> of her dress in the back and ended in padded circular fingers that
> gripped either side of her head just above the ears. When she wanted
> to look to one side or the other she had to turn her whole body from
> the waist. The boy who sat beside her wore braces on his legs as did
> nearly all the children. But each brace differed from the others and I
> wondered what my braces would be. Did they hurt? I wanted to ask
> the boy who sat next to me, but so deep a hush lay over the room that
> I did not dare. . . .
> I preferred looking at the folding doors to looking at the children.
> I couldn't bear the sight of them; they were ugly and sickening. I almost
> hated them. Their legs were thin and misshapen. Their faces, somehow,
> were too old and wise. I felt that way, *not realizing that I was there
> as one of them.* [Italics added.] If someone had reminded me that *my*
> legs were thin and deformed, dangling there helplessly from the edge
> of the chair, and that *my* face, perhaps, revealed a kind of wisdom that
> only long, deep suffering can impart, I would have been shocked. [Gold-
> man, 1947:24][3]

[3]Reprinted with permission of Macmillan Publishing Co., Inc., from *Even the night*
by R. L. Goldman. Copyright 1947, and renewed 1975, by Raymond Leslie Goldman.

Even though Raymond could not walk and pain was still a frequent intruder, even though he had watched other children run and play, a deformed body image was simply out of keeping with his self-evaluation as a lovable and powerful individual. Integration between these two attributes of the self was achieved by not recognizing on the conscious level that his body was deformed! There is some evidence, however, that subconsciously Raymond was aware of his own deformity, and in fact hated it. For example, the deep aversion he felt toward the other children who were in the doctor's office seems explicable on the basis of such awareness.

The next example shows how a single attribute is molded by self-evaluation and, conversely, how the perceived attribute, through its evaluatory connotations, can largely determine the person's self-esteem. The following incident took place a short time after Raymond's visit to the doctor (previous incident). It is Raymond's first day at school:

I finished my lunch and dropped the remains into the can that I was able to reach. Other boys came to drop their refuse in the can. One of them stopped to look me over.

"What's the matter with you?" he asked me.

"Nothing," I said.

"Can't you walk?"

"I can walk a little," I said. "I can crawl real fast, though."

"Jiminy Christmas!" he exclaimed.

I took this to be an expression of admiration. I looked up into his face, eager to be friendly. No one else had spoken to me, though many had looked at me intently, and I was grateful for this attention.

We attracted the attention of other boys and soon a crowd was gathered in a semicircle around us.

"Lemme see, will you?"

"Quit shoving or I'll—"

"This kid can't walk. He says he can crawl real fast though."

I was pleased and honored. It was like one of my dreams.

"I can even crawl up and down steps," I told them. "They won't let me crawl here because I'd get dirty."

The boys began to laugh. I wondered what was funny about that statement. Through my mind flashed the weeks and weeks of efforts before that feat had been accomplished. Now my boast—and I had really said it boastingly—was greeted with laughter.

"That's pretty good, fellas! He can crawl up and down steps!"

I felt easier when I heard that. So they did think it was pretty good! Their laughter, then, had been prompted by admiration.

One of the boys leaned down and touched my leg. He circled it with thumb and forefinger.

"Look how skinny!" he shouted triumphantly. "I can wrap it with two fingers!"

"Let's see!"

"Sure 'nough!"

"Gee, what skinny old legs!"

A feeling of inferiority began to batter against the bulwark of my illusions. I sensed the ridicule before I comprehended it. I had never been fully conscious of the fact that my legs were emaciated. Now I looked down at them and then at the legs of the other boys. The damnable hammer of comparison beat the truth into my consciousness.

"Let go my leg!" I said, letting anger rise to cover rising horror.

"Why? Does it hurt?"

"No. But let it go."

"Who says so?" the boy demanded, but he released my leg and stood up. "Let's see you crawl."

"No."

"Jiminy!" he said. "Those ain't legs. You got broomsticks!"

That prompted another sally of laughter. The room echoed a jeering repetition of "Broomsticks!" I looked at my tormentors with burning eyes. I saw them through a film of tears. I wanted to kill every one of them, to hit them and claw them and bite them. In my hand was an imaginary dagger, sharp and glistening. I saw myself leaping from the bench and slashing right and left with the murderous blade. My victims screamed and fell, bleeding, dead at my feet.

The boy—perhaps it was the same one—reached down and grasped my leg again. I flung myself forward off the bench, grabbing him as I fell. The boy went over backward and we went down with me on top. I heard his head hit the concrete and I was glad. I sat astride him, pounding my fists into his face, screaming with tears streaming down my face.

Then I felt myself being lifted up while my fists were still flailing.

"Stop it! Stop it! Behave yourself, Raymond!"

I suddenly realized that it was Mr. Stevens' [the principal's] voice and that I was on his arm. I buried my face in his shoulder and sobbed. [Goldman, 1947, pp. 35–37]

Following this incident Raymond Goldman was a changed person. "A few ill-mannered boys had implanted in me the seed of shame from which I was to conceive a monster" (p. 38). Thereafter, until more maturing forces took hold, Raymond suffered the hurt and shame of inferiority. The perception of a single attribute, that his legs were deformed, had the power to annihilate fairly thoroughly the general esteem he had heretofore felt.

If we examine the foregoing incident in order to reveal more explicitly what was happening in the process of alignment between attribute and self-evaluation, three phases may conveniently be distinguished:

1. Self-evaluation dominates perception: When Raymond went into the lunchroom, he felt proud of himself and his accomplishments. Ambiguous social events were integrated within

this schema and interpreted accordingly. Thus, when Raymond became the center of attention through staring and queries, he basked in illusory glory, for was not all this admiration over the wonder that he was?

2. There is temporary incongruence between self-evaluation and outside events: Then the boys began to laugh. To Raymond the laughter was puzzling, for it seemed inappropriate for a hero who, by dint of *sheer perseverance*, had accomplished so great a feat as crawling. But his self-esteem remained unshaken and his uneasiness allayed when that segment of the comments made by the boys that could be seen as consistent with his high self-regard was partialed out; he latched onto the statement, "That's pretty good, fellas! He can crawl up and down steps!" Raymond was then again able to interpret the laughter as being prompted by admiration, the laughter being sufficiently ambiguous to be fitted into the pattern of his highly valued self.

3. Single attribute dominates self-evaluation: Then came the turning point when the events outside Raymond's skin were not so malleable. The children pointed out how skinny his legs were, that two fingers could wrap around them, that they were broomsticks. What is more, they were unrelenting in their jeers until Raymond was all but bludgeoned into perceiving the stigma of his physique. We would like to speculate as to what might have gone on in Raymond's mind as these invectives were being hurled at him:

They call my legs skinny, and broomsticks. They are not skinny! I can prove that they are as stout and shapely as anybody's. See—look at mine and look at yours. Oh no! They are skinny! They are broomsticks! I have broomsticks for legs. You shouldn't have broomsticks for legs. They asked me if I can walk. I can't walk but I can crawl. That's just as good as walking. No it isn't. I *should* be able to walk. I'm ashamed. It's awful. It's horrible!

Notice that, before Raymond's new perception of his legs could affect his self-esteem, the perception had to take on an evaluative quality of good and bad, what should be and what should not be. Although Raymond sensed the ridicule before he could comprehend it, the ridicule had the power to bewilder *but not to shame* until the ridicule became *attached to* his own perceptions of what should be and what should not be.

Integration then took place along many paths: fact with fact —Raymond perceived his legs as broomsticks. Fact with value—he perceived that his legs should be stout and shapely and not like broomsticks. Evaluated fact with self-esteem—he perceived his self as inferior in keeping with an inadequate physique.

The integrative process is one reason why the self-concept is difficult to change. The very thing that is to be changed has considerable power in molding the experiences impinging on the person to fit its own image so that they are interpreted as not conflicting with that self-concept. It takes much convincing before a drastic remodeling of the self-concept can take place in either a negative or positive direction (Rogers, 1951). Just as Raymond had to be "bludgeoned" into perceiving the abnormalities of his physique, so it took years of internal struggle before he became convinced that he was still a man for all that.

The resistance against positive change in the self-concept is especially interesting since it runs counter to what would seem to be the wishes of the person. Would not everyone rather feel better about himself or herself? The resistance, however, is simply one of the consequences of the integrating process. Once self-abnegation involving a central core of the person has taken place, old and new events tend to be interpreted to fit a negative self-concept. Raymond, for example, could no longer really think of his performance as accomplishments because such an evaluation, which previously had fitted in well with his high self-regard, now had nothing to which it could be anchored.

When a disability is sustained after the self-concept has been formed, the integrative process requires some change in the self-concept, but by no means a major overhaul. In a study dealing explicitly with the effect of disability on the self-concept (Shelsky, 1957), subjects were asked to describe themselves as they were before the disability and as they perceived themselves at the time of the survey. The particular disabilities involved were tuberculosis and amputation. All the subjects were adults, still hospitalized, and were examined at least 2 months posttrauma, the average length of time since determination of the disability being about 6 months. The investigator found that both groups of patients did recognize some difference between their present and past selves but far less than one might have expected. Those with an amputation described themselves as having been more active, adventurous, and energetic, and less awkward than they were at present—all realistic perceptions of the effects of loss of a limb. This realism is also observable in the perceptions of the patients with tuberculosis as having previously been more healthy and active. They also saw themselves as having been more foolish, impulsive, and hurried than at present.

It seems that these subjects did not, at least on the conscious level, experience any violent upheaval of the way they perceived themselves as persons. Of 300 possible traits, including such commonly assumed disability-related characteristics as *anxious, complaining, confused, dissatisfied, high-strung, irritable, moody,* and *nervous*—or, to take a sample of positive attributes, *adaptable, contented, courageous, enterprising,* and *inventive*—the subjects evidently felt that only a very few differentiated their former from their present selves. For the most part, the acknowledged changes related to realistic and clearly disability-linked attributes. Moreover, the results did not show these changes to have major consequences for traits not directly related to the disability or for one's general self-evaluation as expressed by such feelings as contented, capable, and self-confident—at least not on the conscious level.

As for the ability to adjust to or cope with a disability, the integrative process implies that the predisability personality plays a significant role. Therefore, instead of treating all individuals with the same disability as a homogeneous group, some studies have examined the influence of specific personality traits on adjustment. Examples are studies on "internal versus external locus of control" (Rotter, 1966). Individuals high in internal locus of control believe that they have a good deal of personal control over what happens to them, whereas those with an external locus believe that their lives are largely determined by chance, fate, luck, or powerful others. Results indicate that internal locus of control as a personality trait favors adjustment to disability (Trieschmann, 1980). Trieschmann's thorough review of personality aspects that bear upon adjustment in the case of spinal cord injury led to the following conclusions: "Some independence and aggressiveness, creativity, many goals for the future all favor good adjustment or productivity after spinal injury. Education and theoretical interests favor vocational success. Basically, it seems that those who were successful at coping with life prior to injury have a greater probability of coping with spinal injury" (1980, p. 80). These relationships apply as well to a wide range of disabilities.

THE CONCEPT OF SELF AND THE SOCIAL LOOKING GLASS

That the self-concept is a social looking glass expresses the belief that ideas and feelings about the self emerge largely as a result of interaction with others. Yet the self-concept does not simply mirror the views of others or of society at large. We have seen, for example, that people with disabilities do not, in general, feel more inferior than their able-bodied counterparts in spite of common beliefs to the contrary (see Chapter 7). Research has also shown that the self-concepts of people with disabilities concerning a great variety of traits do not fit widely held projections. One study (Weinberg-Asher, 1976) found that college students with a disability saw themselves in much the same way that a group of able-bodied college students saw themselves, despite the fact that they were expected to be less intelligent, less cheerful, less popular, less aggressive, less happy, lacking in social interactions, more courageous, and so forth. These expectations were based on the views of college students that had been solicited in an earlier study (Weinberg, 1976).

In short, self-concepts do not directly correspond with others' expectations and views. There are several reasons for this. To begin with, the self-concept cannot reflect all views encountered, only some. The two-way integration process guarantees and assures that the individual plays an important part in fashioning his or her own self-concept. Most persons do not take belittling views of others without struggling to protect their egos and affirm their own worth. They give differential weight to the opinion of others in order to support a more adequate self-concept. They modify their own values. They learn to sort out the views of others from their own, and are selective in their associates. Undoubtedly there are other reasons, but these are sufficient to underscore the realization that the self-concept is actively worked over by the person himself or herself and is not a direct reflection of the verdict of others. Some people, of course, are more successful than others in developing and preserving a basically positive sense of self, whether or not they have a disability.

TWO GRADIENTS IN THE SPREAD FROM SINGLE ATTRIBUTE TO SELF-EVALUATION

Once again we encounter the phenomenon of spread, and once again we raise the question of how a single fact about a person can become so potent as to print its negative (or positive) stamp on the person as a whole. Previously, this phenomenon was related to such factors as similarity of valence and context (Chapter 4) and comparative values (Chapter 8). We should now like to approach the problem from the point of view of the structure of the self-concept by isolating two general factors—namely, the self-connection gradient and the status-value gradient.

The *self-connection gradient* refers to how central or close to the "essence of the self" or the "essential me" is an attribute of the self. One's blood type, for example, typically is quite alien to this central core, whereas one's ability and appearance are typically very close. A close connection between the attribute in question and the self-core is often expressed by the verb "to be" as in the following: I *am* smart, you *are* good-looking, and he *is* dishonest. A weaker connection is often expressed by the verb "to have," as in the following: I *have* false teeth, you *have* a clear complexion, and she *has* fine motor coordination.

What creates closer or weaker connections with the self-core is a challenging problem requiring further investigation. A few leads are immediately apparent, several of them directly related to what has been called ego-involvement. From the perceptual point of view, it appears that events involving the face and torso are more closely connected with self-essence than events associated with the appendages. Thus it is to be expected that adjustment to a facial disfigurement would, in general, involve a greater problem from the point of view of the self-connection gradient than adjustment to a leg disfigurement, for example. This is also at least one reason why we speak of a girl as being pretty if her face is pretty but not generally if her hands are pretty. The face seems to be a more intimate part of the person than the hands or legs. The close identification between face and self is seen in the case of a little boy who feared that if he wore glasses nobody would know him. In a study of facial deformities, it was noted that "disfigurement which occurred during adulthood always seemed to have a disorganizing effect on the integration of the person" (Macgregor et al., 1953, p. 195).

Evidently, too, there is less connection with the self-core when a body attribute may be looked upon as a tool than as a personal characteristic (Dembo, Leviton, & Wright, 1956, p. 22). For example, false teeth may be thought of as a tool for eating or indicative of one's decline—that is, as a personal characteristic.

Also, certain personal characteristics about the self appear to be more crucial to one's identity than others. People identify themselves as men or women, for example, and not as broad-headed or long-headed. Since gender identification is often a central personal characteristic that serves to define the person to oneself and others, it can be expected that any circumstance that endangers this identification will have marked effects on the self-concept. The same little boy who faced the prospect of wearing glasses expressed the fear that he could not be a rough-and-tumble boy any more, an *a priori* connection which, threatening the child's gender identification, made him envision himself as a strangely different person. To take another example, leg amputation is sometimes viewed as a symbol of castration. Feeling "half a man" points to one of the main areas of adjustment often having wider implications for personal well-being than the sheer ability to get around.

Another personal characteristic high on the self-connection gradient is often symbolized by the kind of work one does. One's very essence may be felt to be that of a scholar, a miner, a musician, or a homemaker. The self-concept, then, might be expected to suffer stress when circumstances—retirement or injury, for example—force one to give up the work. Preparing for retirement in advance means reshaping the self-concept to fit a new role. If adjustment is to take place, other personal, positive attributes must assume a high position on the self-connection gradient. Unfortunately, the science and practice of mental health have not as yet seen the equal necessity of preparing for disablement.

Personal characteristics, of course, carry with them status implications. But independent of their status value, personal characteristics vary in their closeness to the self-core. This point is clarified in the following section which deals with the status-value gradient.

An examination of cases in which the body becomes so detached from the self that it is looked upon or felt to be an object is revealing. For instance, Bettelheim (1943, p. 431) reports that as a Nazi prisoner he was able to endure the torture and indignities inflicted upon him because, right from the beginning, he became convinced that these horrible and degrading experiences somehow did not happen to him as a person but only to him as an object. There is also a psychotic separation between the body and the self in which the person *disowns* his or her body or experiences it as belonging to another person. A more familiar example of body-person separation is the case where professionals treat their clients or patients as they would any other object coming under serious scrutiny. For them, physique has been removed from any connection with feelings, attitudes, or essence of the other person's self.

In this last example, the separation is effected in a second individual, the professional, rather than in the person being examined. Undoubtedly, body-self separation occurs less readily in oneself than in the outsider who, intentionally or not, more easily remains cut off from the personal qualities of the other person. Thus without qualms a stranger can stare at a person with a disability just because this person is the *object* of his or her attention. Should their eyes meet, the body-person separation is destroyed, for "eyes are the mirror of the soul," and the stranger looks away.

It is also noteworthy that people resist such separation all the more when it denotes a loss of integrity of the "essential self." We resent being stared at when we feel "like a monkey in a zoo." On the other hand, there are circumstances, as in the case of the aforementioned concentration camp prisoner, where dissociating the body from the self-core helps to maintain personal integrity.

In regard to adjustment to disability, clinical records indicate that disowning the defective part impedes self-acceptance. The person who feels psychologically that the withered limb is not a part of the self will not be able to make most effective use of it. A study of patients with facial disfigurements bears on this point (Macgregor et al., 1953). Patients who had been reared not to mention and even to hide their deformity had not integrated it well into the body-image, whereas those who were reared to regard the deformity realistically were able to give a fairly accurate description of themselves. Moreover "a poorly integrated deformity seemed to favor dissatisfaction with the operative result, whereas a clear concept of the body image seemed rather to predispose to postoperative satisfaction" (p. 199). Similarly, a study of persons with an amputation has shown that an individual's adjustment to a prosthesis is dependent to a considerable degree upon the self-concept (Fishman, 1949).

The disability must become an integrated part of the self, not severed from it, though research will have to show whether its optimum position on the self-connection gradient is at a distance from or closer to the self-core. Viewing a body attribute as a tool does not mean disowning it. Clearly, the development of theory and research is also needed to identify further the conditions determining position on this gradient.

The *status-value gradient* refers to the relevancy of an aspect of the self for the evaluation of personal worth or self-esteem. In the American culture, for example, success and achievement commonly have a higher level of status value than diligence or cooperation. One of the determinants of status value may very well turn out to be the degree of connection with the self-core (and vice versa), but undoubtedly there are other determinants as well, for the relative status value of two attributes may sometimes be the reverse of their position on the self-connection gradient. Thus, some people may enjoy high status because of their political influence rather than ostracism because of their reprehensible character, even though this second attribute may be more tied in with the core of the self than the first.

In Chapter 8, several value changes were discussed that have the potential of reducing the status value of physique: enlarging the scope of values, containing disability effects, shifting the relative importance of values, and transforming comparative-status values into asset values. Also, we saw in Chapter 9 that the coping and succumbing frameworks have significantly different effects on the status value of physique.

Where the essential "I" of a person who has incurred a disability is centrally associated with an intact body and where the status value of body-whole, body-well, and body-beautiful is high, traumatic consequences for the self-concept appear inevitable. In fact, the consequences may be so traumatic that the person may be unable to integrate the new body-image into the self-concept at all. This anguished difficulty is effectively described by Katherine Butler Hathaway (1943) who suffered from a tubercular infection of the spine and was bedridden throughout her middle childhood:

> When I got up at last . . . and had learned to walk again, one day I took a hand glass and went to a long mirror to look at myself, and I went alone. I didn't want anyone . . . to know how I felt when I saw myself for the first time. But there was no noise, no outcry; I didn't scream with rage when I saw myself. I just felt numb. That person in the mirror *couldn't* be me. I felt inside like a healthy, ordinary, lucky person—oh, not like the one in the mirror! Yet when I turned my face to the mirror there were my own eyes looking back, hot with shame . . . when I did not cry or make any sound, it became impossible that I should speak of it to anyone, and the confusion and the panic of my discovery were locked inside me then and there, to be faced alone, for a very long time to come [p. 41].
>
> Over and over I forgot what I had seen in the mirror. It could not penetrate into the interior of my mind and become an integral part of me. I felt as if it had nothing to do with me; it was only a disguise. But it was not the kind of disguise which is put on voluntarily by the person who wears it, and which is intended to confuse other people as to one's identity. My disguise had been put on me without my consent or knowledge like the ones in fairy tales, and it was I myself who was confused by it, as to my own identity. I looked in the mirror, and was horror-struck because I did not recognize myself. In the place where I was standing, with that persistent romantic elation in me, as if I were a favored fortunate person to whom everything was possible, I saw a stranger, a little, pitiable, hideous figure, and a face that became, as I stared at it, painful and blushing with shame. It was only a disguise, but it was on me, for life. It was there, it was there, it was real. Every one of those encounters was like a blow on the head. They left me dazed and dumb and senseless every time, until slowly and stubbornly my robust persistent illusion of well-being and of personal beauty spread all through me again, and I forgot the irrelevant reality and was all unprepared and vulnerable again. [pp. 46–47][4]

And yet the person cannot comfortably remain one kind of person when "looking in the mirror" and another kind of person when suppressing the disturbing facts of the physical self. The integration that will allow the person to continue to think well of himself or herself, however, requires important value changes.

When the effects of disability are felt to be widespread, it would seem that the disability has greater possibilities of assuming a high position on both gradients. At the same time one has to be most cau-

---

[4]Reprinted from *The little locksmith* by K. B. Hathaway, 1943. By permission of Coward, McCann & Geoghegan.

tious in concluding that a severe disability will automatically have a more drastic consequence on the perception of self than a mild one. An excellent example of more than a minor disability having a relatively insignificant effect on the perception of the person (though it deals with interpersonal perception rather than self-perception) occurred when a father, confronted with the news that his son lost a leg, rebutted:

> "Lost a leg, has he? What's so bad about that? Rest of him's in good shape, hain't it?" [Viscardi, 1952, p. 143][5]

On the other hand, as we have seen in the example of eyeglasses presented in the preceding section, even a mild disability may affect areas in the person's life that are closely tied to the self-core and to status.

In answer to the original question concerning how an evaluation of a single attribute becomes imposed on the evaluation of the total person, we may now stipulate two functions. The power of a single attribute to influence self-esteem will be greater (1) the closer the connection between it and the self-core and (2) the higher the status value it possesses.

Two conclusions follow. First, since a disability is generally negatively evaluated, since physique almost always has some connection with the self-core (though in specific cases its position on the self-connection gradient may be low), and since physique in most cases has some status-value relevancy (though in some cases a low value), self-esteem will be threatened by disability for most people. The threat may be little or great. A caveat is in order. Because of the danger of false generalizations, we must note that this conclusion does *not* state that persons with disabilities tend to feel more inferior than the able-bodied (see pp. 149–156).

Second, though shame stemming from the negatively evaluated aspects of disability may be experienced, such shame can be reduced or eliminated when the coping framework brings the view of life with a disability into proper focus. When the coping aspects are attended to, new *positively evaluated attributes* will appear which establish high positions on the self-connection and status-value gradients, thereby building up self-esteem. For example, the person may feel good because of striving and having succeeded in improving one's situation in spite of severe handicaps. Such personal attributes as perseverance, independence, intelligence, moral stamina, and so forth, may give genuine support to an ego that may be flailed by negative social implications of disability.

[5]Reprinted from *A man's stature* by H. Viscardi, Jr., 1952. By permission of Paul S. Eriksson, Pubs.

AGE OF OCCURRENCE OF DISABILITY

During the life of an individual, the body, of course, undergoes change. It grows, matures, and ages. The change may occur gradually, as during childhood and adulthood, or more suddenly, as during adolescence or as a result of disability. Typically, even a gradual change is consciously first recognized all at once, as a sudden and startling fact. This occurs when the meaning of the changing physical trait is of such nature as to effect significant modifications in the self-concept. Thus the wrinkles and the greying hair that had been accumulating over a period of time may not even be noticed until the person suddenly realizes, "I am becoming middle-aged!" To take another example, many an adult remains happily unaware of what to others is an unmistakable increase in weight, interpreting blunt remarks as inconsequential and meaningless jests until the person is shocked into the realization, "I *am* fat. Is that I? I once was so slender and youthful. It couldn't be."

Often, however, what are looked upon as major changes or "turning points" in a lifetime are brought about by special events that significantly alter the self-concept. Marriage, parenthood, graduation, or victory or defeat in important contests are examples. Raymond Goldman's first day at school was a turning point for the same reason (see pp. 224–225). Subjectively, the person may feel a strangeness about himself or herself. In the extreme one may feel like a different person altogether. Ordinarily, however, one still recognizes the self as the same person in spite of remarkable changes. The process of integration, which requires that new feelings and notions about the self be absorbed within old ones, makes possible the feeling of continuity between the past and the present in a life history. It is this property which cautions us against the generalization that a physical trauma, even a major one, must create a violent upheaval in the self-concept.

Because of the great need to simplify in order to understand, generalizations continue to be made to the effect that it is easier to adjust to a disability when one is "born that way," or when it is acquired in childhood or in adulthood. There are several good arguments for each of these alternatives. In the case of congenital disability, one does not have to cope with alteration in the self-concept and therefore, on this score, adjustment is facilitated. On the other hand, in the case of adventitious disability one is not faced with the possible stigma of hereditary defect. One could also argue that the adult is better able to adjust to a disability because of greater maturity, in contrast to the child who is more vulnerable; or the reverse could be stated—the child, being more plastic than the adult, can more easily accommodate changes in self-perception. One could add that the child is not burdened with earning a living and the heavy demands for independence that confront the adult. In addition one could point out special psychological stages in the life cycle that affect adjustment to disability incurred at that time. Thus, on the basis of certain phases of psychosexual development, the conclusion has been stated that "all other factors being equal, we expect blindness occurring at age nine or ten to be less traumatic to the ego than at age five or age thirteen" (Blank, 1957, p. 17).

Probably all the aforementioned factors, as well as others, bear upon adjustment to disability. But evidently their weight varies with the groups studied, for research has simply not shown with any consistency that adjustment to disability is easier or more difficult at certain ages of incurrence than at others. The status of the findings in regard to deafness may be taken as representative of research with other disabilities. Barker et al. (1953) summarize thirteen studies analyzing adjustment in terms of age at loss of hearing with the statement that the findings of these studies are inconsistent. "A few tend to show greater problems of adjustment when loss of hearing occurs at young ages; others tend to show the reverse. Most of the relationships are statistically unreliable" (p. 233). Of course, with respect to particular challenges, age is important. Thus, age at which a hearing loss is acquired is a significant factor in ease of oral communication. Taking age of onset into account is important for understanding the particular life circumstances, tasks, and problems with which the individual with a disability must cope; however, age of onset as such does not appear to be a decisive factor governing the psychological *outcome* of the adjustment process.

CONCLUSIONS FOR CHILD-REARING PRACTICES

We have attempted to give some indication of the processes of differentiation and integration in the development of the self-concept and how self-evaluation and the evaluation of a single attribute become reconciled. Now we shall consider the problem of self-evaluation and integration from the point of view of the prevention of psychological trauma:

Using Raymond Goldman's (1947) childhood as an example, we might agree that the following were undesirable:

1. Raymond's denial of his own deformities during the period in which he regarded himself as a paragon.
2. Raymond's denial of his own worth at the time when he was forced to recognize the disabling and pitiful aspects of his disability.

Each of these perceptions defied the evidence of reality. That the first occurred was a good guarantee that the second would also occur, because it indicated that the disability as a *negatively evaluated fact* could not be assimilated into the self-concept without threatening it. To avoid this, gross distortion became necessary. The inevitable occurred, however, when Raymond's schoolmates denied him the bliss of his pretense and insisted that he acknowledge the inferiority of his legs. What had heretofore been a stable and high self-esteem gave way to an undeniable reality; his self-esteem plummeted and shattered to the depths of despair and shame. Raymond's "wakening to shame and the consciousness of reality was inevitable. If it had not happened that day under those circumstances, then it would have happened another day under other circumstances" (p. 38).

We should like to ask in what circumstances would Raymond have been better prepared to face his deviations without having had to pay the price of his sense of personal worth. The main principle offered is that negative or devaluating aspects of disability must be brought to the young person's awareness, along with the coping aspects, by those who know and love him or her. This principle may be referred to as *realization amid interpersonal acceptance.* Accordingly, it was important for Raymond to have talked and thought about the fact that his legs were in fact more poorly developed than those of most children so that he could have assimilated this fact into his self-concept with knowledge that he was loved and accepted *in spite* of his crippling. In terms of the previously described self-connection gradient, this would mean that the devaluating aspects of physique would not be closely attached to the self-core: "I and my crippling are not the same because I am loved though my legs leave something to be desired." A comparable shift on the status-value gradient, especially if accompanied by the value changes described in Chapter 8, permits a healthful integration of the disability into the self-concept.

The principle of realization amid interpersonal acceptance is best put into practice when the person close to the child discusses disability-connected matters in the framework of their coping aspects and in situations where this topic comes up naturally. Lowenfeld (1971) advises parents of blind children as follows:

> . . . When he [your child] has recognized that he cannot see, he may ask you why this is so. If you tell him that he is blind because his eyes do not work, but that he has his hands with which he can feel, his ears with which he can hear, his nose with which he can smell, and his tongue with which he can taste, his attention will be focused on what

he can do rather than on what he cannot do. Telling him alone would of course not be enough, but by the time he asks this question, he should have experienced so many things with his senses that your reply will be accepted by him as satisfactory. [Lowenfeld, 1971, p. 94][6]

Following is a concrete account of how one mother made a start on bringing her son to the realization that he was blind. Davey, now 4, had been blind since birth:

> We came out of the house, and spring was in the air. Things smelled sweet and new, and the sky was bright with stars.
> "Smell, Davey," Al [his father] said, drawing his breath in deep. "Doesn't it smell sweet?"
> "Um," said Davey, inhaling with gusto.
> "Um," Mary Sue [sister] echoed, sniffling up her small nose with short brief sniffs.
> I hugged her against me, and then I glanced up at the sky.
> "Look, honey," I said. "Look, Mary Sue, up at the sky. See the stars."
> Davey put up his hand. "I want to see the stars, too," he said.
> I looked over at Al, and his face was blurred in the dark or maybe it was my sudden tears that made it seem blurred. For a minute, my throat closed over, and I knew a pain so sharp I thought I could not bear it. But then I knew that this was my opportunity, the time I had been seeking for. So I put Mary Sue in Al's arms, and I sat down on the steps beside Davey.
> "Listen, honey," I said, and I turned his face toward me. Then I stopped, and for a second, there were no words to say. But then the words came, and I said them. "Davey, some people in this world can't see things with their eyes. Those people are called blind people. They have to look at things with their fingers, the way you do. Annabel [a blind social worker whom Davey knew and loved] is like that, and you are, too."
> "But couldn't I touch the stars?" said Davey, and there was, of course, no loss or sorrow in his voice. He had found that very beautiful things could be seen with his fingers. He was only four years old, and so he did not miss color or light when he had shape and substance.
> "No, honey," I said, and I did not want to cry, not any more. "No, some things in this world are too far away to touch, ever, and the stars are like that. Those things you'll have to learn about by hearing of them. Understand?"
> He nodded his head against my shoulder.
> "Sure," he said. But, of course, he didn't. He probably never would, not completely. But I had told him. [Henderson, 1954, pp. 112–113]

In this brief scene, several important ideas were introduced: the meaning of blindness, Davey is blind, other people are blind too,

---

[6]From B. Lowenfeld, *Our blind children: Growing and learning with them* (3d ed.), 1971. Courtesy of Charles C Thomas, Publisher, Springfield, Illinois.

blindness entails certain restrictions (disabling aspects), and thus certain aspects of life must be met in a different way (coping aspects). But these marks of difference from others were brought out with a deep but simple feeling of love and acceptance. One such scene may not be enough, for ideas sometimes "sink in" slowly and may require repeated exposures for the self-picture to be positively imprinted with full values that are able to withstand assault.

In Raymond's case, however, a comparable scene apparently never took place (Goldman, 1947). That he was different in some ways from other children and would continue to be different was never mentioned. He was praised for cooperating with the exercises and striving to crawl and do other things, but no special reference was evidently made to the shortcomings of his legs. "They [his parents] entered into a fine conspiracy of cheerfulness, hope, and courage, and throughout my childhood I was treated the same as my brother and sisters" (p. 6). Raymond came to identify being loved with being perfect as epitomized in the frequent scenes in which his parents, nurse, and older sister "kissed me [being loved] and said lovely things about me [being perfect] to each other while I listened from my seat in childhood's heaven" (p. 11). Whatever subconscious awareness he had of his own physical inadequacies was counterbalanced by an active fantasy life in which he envisioned "a personal vigor and physical strength that were Gargantuan. I dashed about the city streets, uprooting tall trees with my bare hands. Or, more constructively, I ran like the wind on my own fleet legs to spread the alarm of fire to every inhabitant" (p. 3).[7]

Through the techniques to be described in Chapter 14 Raymond could have been prepared for the prejudices he would inevitably encounter. Storytelling, role playing, and discussion would have all been in order. Not only would such activities have equipped him with certain social skills but, in exposing him to the negative aspects of his disability, the necessary reorganization of the self-concept would have been evolving in a protective atmosphere. The companionship of other children with disabilities, in an accepting atmosphere of the home or nursery school, would have provided the opportunity for "the mental and emotional experience of recognizing another human being as possessing simultaneously a recognizable disability and a lovable self" (Garrett, 1955, p. 447). This, as in group counseling, favors the assimilation of the negative aspects of disability within a self-concept that could remain positive.

Being brought face to face *for the first time* with one's shortcom-

---

[7]Reprinted with permission of Macmillan Publishing Co., Inc., from *Even the night,* by R. L. Goldman. Copyright 1947, and renewed 1975, by Raymond Leslie Goldman.

ings in a hostile and rejecting environment can be such a devastating experience that precautions must be taken to avoid this, particularly in childhood. It makes all the difference in the world if painful facts about the self are first realized in a friendly and caring atmosphere. In the case of the child who was blind there was an assimilation between the self-core and the negative fact, whereas in Raymond's case there was a complete break. Therefore, if by the age of 8 Raymond already had come to some grips with the displeasing aspects of his physique in his own home where he was loved and accepted, his self-concept would have had a far greater inner strength to withstand the barbs being thrust at him by the boys who were so unfriendly on that first day at school. He still would have fought and cried, but the strong core of his self-esteem would not have been shattered.

When discussing a child's disability with the child, one can avoid common errors by observing the value concepts important in accepting one's disability as nondevaluating (Chapter 8). In the following scene, a parent makes the mistake of invoking comparative-status values rather than asset values:

> DEBBIE: Do you think I'll ever be able to walk like everybody else?
> MOTHER: Probably not. But even if you can't walk as well as some people there are other things that you do better than some people.

To demonstrate the difference when asset values guide the interaction, the scene is changed as follows:

> DEBBIE: Do you think I'll ever be able to walk like everybody else?
> MOTHER: Probably not, but you are learning to walk better and that is good. And do you know that there are lots of other things you can do? Let's name some of them.

On most occasions status comparisons between people are unnecessary and should be avoided. Asset values provide a far better guide for strengthening a sense of self-worth in human development.

GENERAL RESULTS ON ADJUSTMENT AND PERSONALITY

It should not come as a great surprise, in the light of previous discussions (see pp. 149–156; 228–229; 235–236), to learn that there is no substantial evidence to indicate that persons with an impaired physique differ as a group in overall adjustment from their able-bodied counterparts. (This statement does not apply to impairments of clearly psychosomatic origin, although even in such instances that evidence is far less consistent than might be expected.) Some studies show a somewhat greater number of persons with physical disabilities who have lower adjustment scores than their controls; however, in most of these cases the differences may well be experimental artifacts. At this time, it can be said with considerable assurance that *the great overlap in the level of adjustment of physically impaired and able-bodied groups is at least as significant as the relatively small margin of difference found in some of the studies.*

This is not to say, of course, that most persons with physical disabilities are well adjusted, any more than it is to say that most physically "normal" persons are well adjusted. Good adjustment can be conceptually defined independently of how it is distributed in the population at large. But the findings do strongly point to the conclusion that most persons with physical limitations make about as good a personality adjustment as do the nonhandicapped.

There is also no clear evidence of an association between type of physical disability and particular personality characteristics, a conclusion that has been reached in serious reviews of this question (Barker & B. Wright, 1954; Shontz, 1971). Folklore such as the euphoria and hypersexuality of persons who have tuberculosis or the paranoia of persons who are deaf are not supported by the data. Even when neural lesions are involved, as in the case of cerebral palsy, the individuals do not exhibit common characteristics of personality (Barker et al., 1953, p. 64; Cruickshank & Bice, 1955).

The following statement by Johnson (1950) with reference to stutterers may be generalized with impunity at the present stage of our knowledge to other physical disability groups. The statement is based on over 100 scientific studies of stuttering in older children and adults, and six investigations involving more than 200 young children, stutterers and nonstutterers: "I believe any expert can safely be challenged to go into a room in which there are 100 adult men and women and pick out the ten stutterers whom we shall include in the group. He may use any tests whatever, except that he may not hear anyone speak, nor may he obtain any information about each individual's personality and mental ability so long as this information in any way relates to the question of how the person speaks or used to speak. I should be surprised if the expert could make significantly better selections with his test than he could by means of the eenie-meenie-minie-moe" (p. 7). The specific kinds of direct cues to be avoided, of course, will have to be specified for the particular disability in question.

The same point has been made in a study of whether emotional disturbance, when it occurs, assumes pathognomic patterns among children with cerebral palsy (Miller, 1958). Children with cerebral palsy and physically normal children had been referred to a child guidance clinic because of severe learning and behavior problems.

The conclusion reached was that if only test data on these groups were available, with no identifying data as to the physical handicap, one would be unable to select out the handicapped except as problems in perception and coordination existed. The test data gathered in the study included tests of intelligence and projective tests of personality.

Shontz (1970) lists three kinds of evidence that would be needed to show that personality and disability are directly linked in a systematic way: (1) Persons with disabilities who have little in common except the disability in question must be shown to differ on some measure indicative of personality from persons without disabilities; *and* (2) Persons with one type of disability must be shown to differ from persons with other types of disability; *and* (3) The degree of manifestation of personality characteristics must be shown to be correlated appropriately with severity, duration, or some other medical feature of the disability. The point is that all three types of evidence would have to appear with sufficient consistency in well-designed research to warrant confidence in the direct connection between disability and personality. The basis for such confidence is currently lacking.

The following summary of fifteen studies utilizing personality inventories with blind subjects illustrates the inconsistency of findings typical of the literature on the problem relating disability to personality and adjustment (Barker et al., 1953, p. 282):

1. In six studies, both the subscale test scores and the total test scores are in the direction of greater maladjustment for the blind as compared with seeing groups.
2. In the other nine studies, the visually handicapped did not consistently fall significantly below seeing controls on subscale and total test scores.
3. Studies using the same tests produce different results. Of two studies using the California Test of Personality, one showed that the blind scored lower than seeing controls on social adjustment, and the second showed the two groups equal in this respect. Of two studies using the introversion scale of the Bernreuter Personality Inventory, one found that the majority of blind subjects scored as introverts, whereas the other showed the blind to be no different from the controls. Moreover, the investigators of both studies note that test results and observational data were not in agreement.

Even the more sophisticated type of laboratory experiment, which avoids certain methodological weaknesses common to the use of personality inventories, shows diversity of results to be the rule. This is well illustrated by the review of studies on the goal-setting behavior or level of aspiration of persons with disabilities. Some of the studies indicate that the goal-setting behavior of the subjects who had a disability differed in some way from their normal controls (Rotter, 1943; McAndrew, 1948; Wenar, 1953; Rutledge, 1954). Others, however, found no differences (Arluck, 1941; Heisler, 1951; Johnson, 1954).

Such inconsistency and diversity among findings force serious attention to the dangers of overgeneralization. With respect to subject overgeneralization, the matter can be put simply by the obvious, although often ignored, maxim that because some subjects with the same disability show certain reactions, it does not follow that all or most subjects with the disability behave similarly.

There is also overgeneralization of a different sort, *behavior* overgeneralization. Not infrequently, on the basis of one behavioral manifestation, conclusions are made as to the generality of that behavior; yet it is entirely possible that different situations would yield different results. An interesting example is found in an experiment on rigidity in the personality of deaf children (Johnson, 1954). The investigator used not one but several different tests of rigidity. It was found that the relative rigidity of deaf children as compared with their hearing controls depended on the particular testing situation. The experimenter, therefore, was led to the conclusion that "deaf children are *not necessarily* more rigid than hearing children. . . . Deaf children may sometimes, in some situations, behave less rigidly than hearing children" (p. 71).

This conclusion is far-reaching because it directs thinking to additional situational and personal variables important for rigidity, which can then be pursued in continued investigation. For example, the experimenter, on the basis of the nature of the situations that produced "inconsistent" results in relative rigidity between deaf and hearing children, hypothesized that deaf children will be flexible in many situations that involve acute visual perception (p. 75). The necessity of including an adequate sampling of situations in research, as well as an adequate sampling of subjects, has been urged upon psychological science by Brunswik (1947) and is referred to as the problem of representative design.

Inconsistency and diversity among findings, in addition to cautioning against overgeneralization, also provide a basis for challenging myths and formulating new ways to look at the significance of disability. One basic idea is that a somatic abnormality as a physical fact is not linked in a direct or simple way to psychological consequences. Instead, factors that pertain to intrapsychic events in the person and to external forces in the situation must be considered in accounting for variable effects of disability.

Perhaps it is necessary to add that although consistent group trends linking disability to personality and adjustment have not been found, it is clear that physical disability can have a profound effect on the person's life, as our ample use of personal documents demonstrates. Instead of pursuing elusive if not illusory personality correlates of disability, it would seem far wiser to be concerned with uncovering psychosocial factors that create difficulties on the one hand and resolve difficulties on the other.

The special case of the adolescent with a disability is discussed in the following chapter. It will be seen that the extraordinary weight given to physique in regard to gender role relationships as a man or woman poses a challenge to self-esteem and the process of adjustment. It is not easy to maintain a strong or comfortable self-concept at every turn throughout the life span. We can, however, strive to impart to the developing person those values and coping approaches that enable one to take stock and affirm oneself anew when confronting social indignities and personal challenges during the course of a remarkable life journey.

Chapter 11
The Adolescent with a Physical Disability

There are several reasons why the period of adolescence deserves special consideration. First, it is a period during which the self-concept undergoes important changes. Secondly, physique plays an especially prominent part in the new look at the self; it assumes a high position on the status-value gradient and a close connection with the self (see Chapter 10, pp. 229–234). Thirdly, the psychological situation of the adolescent can be represented as overlapping both childhood and adulthood determinants of behavior. In an earlier discussion (pp 19–20) overlapping situations were also seen to represent important aspects of the psychological situation of people who have a disability and of minority groups in general.

HEIGHTENED IMPORTANCE OF PHYSIQUE DURING ADOLESCENCE

During adolescence there are many reasons which intimately bind physique to re-formation of the self-concept.

1. The striking physical changes of adolescence bring about a change in what others permit and expect of the young person. This may be illustrated by the expectations of parents and teachers for two pairs of girls, each pair consisting of girls who differ greatly in physical maturity (Barker et al., 1953, pp. 30–33). Though of the same chronological age (13–14 years), one girl of each pair appeared to be a fully developed teenager, dressing accordingly, whereas the other looked like a child of 10 or so. The parents and teachers of each girl were asked to judge which of a list of activities (e.g., buys dress by self) they considered proper for the girl. The physically more mature girl of each pair was judged to be mature enough for adultlike activities more frequently than the physically less mature girl, even though each pair of girls was in the same grade, of the same mental age, and came from the same socioeconomic background.

2. The young person looks at his or her physique in the new light of gender appropriateness. Not only do the more purely biological urges contribute to this awareness, but the values of society also bring tremendous pressure on the young person to examine the self in terms of the criteria of his or her gender role. Particularly during adolescence, these criteria follow rigid standards as to what the feminine and masculine models should be. Marriage and children are deeply ingrained values of society and, in fact, are often necessary passports to full adult status. Small wonder, then, that as adolescents grow into adulthood there is considerable anxiety as to whether they can make the grade. The final score requires not one but many looks at the self as each experience with members of the other sex is assessed. The status value of physique assumes tremendous potency because of its identification with rigid and idealized notions of what is admissible to each sex. In one study, two-thirds of the adolescent boys who were dissatisfied with their physiques were troubled with aspects that the authors describe as "sexually inappropriate," for example, development around the nipple area, size of genitals, scanty pubic hair, fat hips, and facial blemishes (Stolz & Stolz, 1944).

In the following personal account, the impact of gender appropriateness on the adolescent's evaluation of a physical trait and of the self as a person is dramatically clear. What had been a disturbing fact became a source of pride at the very moment that its significance changed from inappropriate to ideally suited to the gender role aspirations of this young woman:

> All through my grade school years, I was the tallest in the class, and, as a matter of fact, was rather proud of it. However, the summer before I entered Junior High School at the age of thirteen, I grew to just an inch below my present five-feet-eight. I towered above every girl and

boy in our class; and it seemed to me that I was the tallest girl in the world. *None of my family's comforting words made it easier for me to walk across the room at school.* In high school, two girls taller than I entered the class. *But they weren't in our crowd,* so I continued to feel like a giraffe when I went out with the girls. I suppose the fact that several of the boys grew to six-footers helped dispel that shrinking feeling. But the crowning touch came in the spring of my junior year. The school paper published a list of characteristics of a composite "Ideal Girl." Lo and behold, my name was listed after "Ideal Height." I haven't felt too tall since. [Sherif & Cantril, 1947, p. 228]

It has been concluded that once the boy feels accepted as a man and the girl as a woman, they "become more stable and predictable. Teachers and parents say they have 'settled down' " (Sherif & Cantril, 1947, p. 237). Such acceptance is often not the smooth consequence of natural development we would like it to be. Doubts in the area of sexual adequacy are kept actively astir by the assumed and rigid standards of what constitutes appropriate physique, by the preconceived notions as to what the sexual relationship ought to be, by the necessity for postponing marriage long after sexual maturity, and by the fact that *any* real or imagined physical deviation readily becomes the scapegoat for all personal difficulties.

3. Physique affects the new self-look during adolescence in yet another way. Unlike younger children, adolescents tend to regard their physique as the final edition of themselves. They are aware of physical decline with age, but that indefinite future is unrelated to their present state. They are now grown up, in the prime of life, and their physical equipment is the best that they can hope for. On the other hand, realizing that they are growing and therefore changing, children can more readily discount a rejected body as a temporary imposition and look toward a more suitable physique that the benevolent future will bestow. The child's perceptions are, in fact, more amenable to the influence of wishes on the "level of irreality" than are the adult's (K. Lewin, 1936, p. 204). Carlson (1941), who was born with severe spasticity, recalls that as a child "I formed a passionate faith that a . . . miracle would be achieved when I grew up: that halting feet, shaking head, writhing arms and legs, and troubled speech would all be healed" (p. 19). But as an adolescent ". . . I became so self-conscious about my handicaps. . . . For the first time the realization that I was different from other people sank home" (p. 22). The immutability of physique has the important effect of placing physique close to the self on the self-connection gradient, thereby giving it a commanding role in the process of reevaluation of the self during adolescence.

It has been pointed out that, through the convenient mechanism of displacement, somatic defects can be made the scapegoat of all adjustive difficulties and the cause of all anxiety feelings regardless of their original source. Because physique becomes a prominent and important characteristic during adolescence, it may very well fulfill this scapegoat function with surprising uniformity.

Although physique carries a particularly heavy emotional loading during adolescence, it is not correct to conclude that any single physical deviation will invariably *or even probably* produce distress. "The psychological consequences of deviation will depend on 'social and individual attitudes toward non-conformity,' the strength of intrinsic attitudes of self-acceptance and the possession of compensatory assets" (Ausubel, 1952, p. 102), as well as the meaning of that particular deviation for the individual. To give a concrete example of the individuality of reaction to deviation, we again refer to the study of adolescents by Stolz & Stolz. Of the seven boys who were concerned about their shortness, four were actually among the shortest (15 percent of the 92 boys) all through the adolescent period. But there were five other boys in the same short group who gave no evidence of being disturbed about it. And two of the seven were as tall as 20 percent of the total group (Stolz & Stolz, 1944, p. 87). This is one important reason why studies that correlate variations in physique such as size, strength, and attractiveness with adjustment measures almost invariably yield but slight, if any, relationship (Barker et al., 1953, Chapter 2). ". . . the reader should remember that just what the meaning of variation in somatic conditions will be to any boy or any girl can only be determined by a study of the individual" (Stolz & Stolz, 1944, p. 80).

OVERLAPPING SITUATIONS IN ADOLESCENCE

"In American society there is a child culture and an adult culture. There are ways and goals of behaving that are accepted as appropriate for children, and quite different ways and goals of behaving that are considered appropriate for adults. Correct ways for children to eat, sleep, dress, talk, and work, for example, differ in many respects from the ways that are correct for adults" (Barker et al., 1953, p. 28). During the transitional period of adolescence the individual may be described as being in an overlapping situation, being a child on the one hand and an adult on the other.

Uneven physical maturity, conflict between giving up the comforts of dependency and attaining adult status with its widening horizons, plus ambivalent adult attitudes toward the child's ambiguous status—these factors and others contribute to the stress of the overlapping situations in which young people find themselves. Inconsistency in adolescent behavior not infrequently occurs because sometimes the determinants of adult behavior and sometimes the determinants of childish behavior win out. When the person cannot satisfy both childish and more mature needs at the same time, there is the likelihood that anxiety, frustration, and heightened emotionality will ensue. Also, the uncertainty of the adolescent's role may lead to exaggeration either of adult behavior or of the childish component. Not all overlapping situations lead to disruptive behavior, however, since it is possible for behavior appropriate to each to be compatible. This is seen, for example, in the adolescent who plays childish games (child situation) with the small child left in his or her charge (adult situation).

The concept of overlapping situations has been found useful to describe not only the psychological world of the adolescent but also, as we have seen, that of the person with a disability who is exposed to the pressures of what may be called the "disabled determinants" of behavior and "normal determinants" of behavior (see p. 19–20). Where these determinants are incompatible, then inconsistent, emotional, and exaggerated behavior can be expected to result, depending on the particular constellation of forces. For example, a person with impaired hearing may show inconsistencies in the use of a hearing aid when he or she wants on the one hand to act as though there were no impairments (normal determinants) and yet also wear the prosthesis in order to participate in conversation (disabled determinants). Emotion may be expressed in the aversion a person feels toward one's braces. And exaggerated behavior may be evidenced when a person with a mobility impairment refuses help in situations of ordinary courtesy. We have used the verb "may" here because the same overt behavior may be due to divergent factors. Thus, help may be refused in situations of ordinary courtesy, not necessarily because of conflicting overlapping situations but because the person may want to take every opportunity to learn on one's own.

For an adolescent with a disability, two of the more lasting and problematic kinds of overlapping situations will be those due to (1) the operation of "child" and "adult" determinants of behavior and (2) the operation of "normal" and "disabled" determinants. The following two incidents are taken from the autobiography of Frances Warfield (1948), who, it may be recalled, struggled against a progressive hearing loss throughout her adolescence. The first is an example of overlapping situations in which child and adult determinants of behavior operate at the same time; the "adult" situation representing freedom and independence is clearly positive, the "child" situation clearly negative. The resulting behavior is an exaggeration of behavior symbolic of adulthood. The incident took place when Frances was visiting England upon graduation from college:

> I began going alone around London, poised and journalistic, I and my one-dollar Certificate of Newspaper Credentials. Anna Mary [a college-mate] was jealous. If only she had a job ahead, she grumbled. If only she could be free and independent, as I was, to go around having adventures.
>
> I loitered at No. 10 Downing Street, and was rewarded by a glimpse of the Prime Minister. Paying tribute to the Peter Pan statue in Kensington Gardens, I saw a man who might well have been Sir James M. Barrie. I walked up to the bar in a pub in Hammersmith and ordered Guinness because I'd read it was the ruin and solace of London char-women. *It was dark, sickish stuff, but I forced it down, feeling every inch a roving journalist, smoking a Gold Flake cigarette.* That was the first time in my life I ever smoked a cigarette in public, though, like all my friends, I had been smoking surreptitiously for several years. Just imagine Aunt Mary's and Aunt Harriet's faces if they could have seen me standing in a London pub drinking Guinness and smoking a cigarette! Judas Priest. I was so tickled that on the way home I stopped in a swank shop in Bond Street and bought myself a small pipe. [pp. 72–73, italics added][1]

In the next example, the overlapping situations are directly related to Frances' disability. It is during adolescence that the conflict between the "normal versus disability" determinants of behavior often becomes acute, for it is during this period that physique tends not only to assume a heightened importance but also to become rigidly standardized as to what constitutes appropriateness. As a person in the "disabled" situation, Frances should say, "What? Speak a little louder, please." As a person in the "normal" situation, she should carry on a smooth conversation. But Frances at this time in her life was both kinds of people. Though the former was negative and the latter positive, Frances' physical status did not permit her to act in accord with the normal determinants of behavior to the exclusion of the disabled determinants. Instead, the behavior required by each of the situations was modified by the other, resulting in such "solutions" as dominating the conversation and double-talk. Notice, too, the manifestations of emotionality resulting from the conflicting situations. Frances is now 14:

> I had learned by experience to do all the talking when I walked along the street with a boy. Indoors I could keep voices raised by playing the victrola; outdoors I was in danger of missing what was said. I always

[1]Reprinted with permission from *Cotton in my ears* by F. Warfield. New York: Viking Press, 1948.

walked fast, rattling on at random, trusting to luck that when a boy wanted to ask me to a dance he'd call me on the telephone.

But this time my tongue was tied—transfixed between fear that Roger was going to ask me to the dance (he'd be sure to mumble) and fear that he had already asked Pamela.

He said, "Hello." We scuffed along in silence. My heart jolted against my red sweater and my ears set up such a roaring that I couldn't have heard a fire alarm at ten paces. When we reached my gate, Roger asked me a question. It might have been about algebra. It might have been about football, fudge, or fiddlesticks. It might have been about going to the dance.

I opened my mouth but nothing came of it. What could I say? I certainly wasn't going to say "What?" Well, hardly. And risk the Seven Deadly Words? Risk having a boy—and Roger Evans of all boys—jeer, "What's the matter—cotton in your ears?"

Mentally I ran through my standard dodges—feeling faint, being absent-minded, and so on. They wouldn't do. A big dance was at stake. And I couldn't just stand there.

I swung the gate back and forth. Suddenly I exclaimed, "Wrinkeloh-wrinkellet-downyourhair!" [Wrinkel was an imaginary childhood companion that always came to Frances' aid.]

"Say, what kind of lingo's that?" Roger demanded.

"Wrinkelingo."

"What's wrinkelingo?"

"Wrinkeli wrinkelthink wrinkelyou wrinkelare wrinkela wrinkel-prune," I improvised glibly.

"Come again?"

I repeated it, swinging the gate confidently.

"Wrinkelprune yourself, smarty," he said.

"Yah, wrinkelsap." I swung the gate to and started up the walk.

Roger telephoned that evening and wrinkelasked me to the wrinkel-dance. [pp. 24–25]

The adolescent with a disability, then, has to cope with two kinds of persisting overlapping situations: situations owing to disability and situations owing to transitional status as a child-adult. The conflicting nature of the former will be reduced (in frequency and intensity) to the extent that the person has stripped the disability of shame and inferiority.

The overlapping situations of childhood and adulthood may persist beyond the usual span of years, and in fact may recur as more than one episode in the lifetime of an individual. Whenever both the emotional patterns of childhood and those of mature adult self-responsibility vie for ascendancy, the person will be caught up by the need for reevaluation of the self typical of the adolescent.

Moreover, whenever the "rites" of adulthood are denied or postponed (as may occur where a disability exists), the adolescent marginal position tends to persist. In some societies children learn their roles in life by the time they are 6 or 7 and then must simply wait for physical maturity to assume a complete adult role (Mead, 1949, p. 361). In our society, the status of full adulthood is generally withheld until the advent of two outstanding circumstances: economic independence and marriage, or at least the establishment of a separate household. For some individuals, additional accomplishments are necessary before they and others accept their claim to full adult status: parenthood, being a property owner, admission to a fraternal order, and other symbolic attainments fall in this class. For others, no matter how many symbolic prerequisites are achieved, the dependency relationship between parent and child is never outgrown and consequently they do not *feel* adult. The establishment of a separate household, so much the American ideal, is the outward sign that the person has become economically self-sufficient and emotionally independent of parental authority.

When circumstances prolong the period of economic dependence, postpone independent living, or disallow sufficient emotional separation from the parent, the position of the individual as an adult (no matter what his or her age) is apt to be tenuous and, like that of the adolescent, marginal between adulthood and childhood. The person may well continue to experience conflicts with parental authority resulting from such marginality, to feel devaluated as an incomplete adult, and to show inconsistent, exaggerated, and emotional behavior typical of conflicting overlapping situations. It may very well be that the fact of disability in many cases tends to prolong the adolescent period.

THE ADOLESCENT PEER GROUP

The discrepancy in the perception of adults and adolescents concerning the appropriateness of adult and child determinants of behavior in different situations is one of the keys to the understanding of the tremendous importance that the peer culture assumes during adolescence. Adolescents often regard the adult as being the barrier to attaining the status of full adulthood. Until recently, in the adult-dominated world of school and home, they may have enjoyed the privileges of being older and more responsible *children,* whereas now their self-esteem may be shaken by those same adults with whom they have no standing as adults.

The simplest type of negative response to the perceived agents of frustration is direct aggression. "Hence arise hostile and defiant attitudes towards adults and adult authority, contempt for adult goals and values, and cynical philosophies of life" (Ausubel, 1952, p.

93). But the adolescent does not generally have the confidence to carry on the attack alone. Moreover, a deflated ego as a marginal adult needs propping up. The necessary support is found in the adolescent peer culture. "Through the force of numbers, precedent and organized resistance, it is able to protect the individual adolescent from excessive encroachments of adult authority" (Ausubel, 1952, p. 94). And "through its power to confer recognition and prestige, it provides a rich compensatory source of status which is partially capable of restoring damaged ego adequacy" (Ausubel, 1952, p. 93).

The demands for conformity of dress, behavior, and speech by adolescents have been commented upon by many authorities. These demands serve to delineate the group from both adults and children and to produce a group solidarity that may be helpful in the search for self-affirmation and independence. The adolescent peer culture can provide strength and comfort to the adolescent who is part of it. It also is a source of distress for the individual who would like to join but cannot, either because of rejection by the "gang" or because of insecurity. We do not know how many adolescents are outcasts. It is probable, however, that most adolescents, those with a disability and those without, experience the loneliness of not fitting solidly anywhere for *shorter or longer periods of time* during these maturing years. If rather strict conformity to adolescent codes and standards are felt to be a necessity, it is not difficult for *any* adolescent to notice some way in which he or she deviates.

A careful analysis of several autobiographies of persons with disabilities, however, strongly suggests that the conforming demands of the adolescent can make allowances for physical deviations in many kinds of group situations (Baker, 1946; Brown, 1955; Carlson, 1941; Criddle, 1953; Goldman, 1947; Ohnstad, 1942; Viscardi, 1952). In only one of the seven accounts did the adolescent lack group companionship, the case of Christy Brown (1955) who was profoundly incapacitated physically because of cerebral palsy. Each of the other personal documents reports a good deal of activity at work and at play with other young people.

Yet these accounts also reveal a deep and sometimes overwhelming loneliness. Each of the adolescents had to face and in some way cope with the physical ideal of man and woman. These young people were lonely not because of the lack of friends but because they could not share in the attachments of boy-girl relationships. The conviction that they could never enter the adult estate of courtship and marriage dawned at adolescence and did not disappear until the horizons widened to include other values besides physical conformity as criteria for suitability in romantic relationships.

SEXUALITY

We have had occasion before to refer to the significant changes brought about as people lay claim to their rights as full human beings. Among these rights is the right to be regarded as a sexual being. In response to this recognition, excellent materials on the topic of sexuality and disability have appeared in the literature and on film. An entire journal, *Sexuality and Disability,* is devoted to this area. Books and articles dealing with single types of disability (e.g., spinal cord injury, mental retardation) or covering a variety of conditions (e.g., cardiac problems, diabetes, orthopedic disabilities, etc.) are available. The book *Sex, society, and the disabled* (Robinault, 1978) includes examples from real life and research to illustrate, at each stage in development, the kinds of experience people with disabilities share with their able-bodied contemporaries, the adjustments that have to be considered, and the realistic options that exist. A listing of organizations concerned with human sexuality, bibliographies, audio-visual materials, and genetic counseling services are included in the Appendix. An article on the management of psychosexual readjustment in the cord-injured male has much to offer all sex counselors regardless of their discipline or type of disability and sex of their clients (Hohmann, 1972). The precautions listed therein should be heeded by everyone.

As described in autobiographies, personal experiences of adolescents who have a disability reveal that, although they did not lack adequate companionship, they suffered rejection most keenly in matters of courtship and marriage. Carlson, whose spasticity was severe, had three faithful friends with whom he played and studied. He did not lack companionship, but did miss social life with girls and the feeling of manliness he craved. It was not until his middle twenties that he enjoyed "a great increased sense of personal worth, thanks to having won the affection of a girl for the first time in my life" (p. 71). And the feeling of being part of the human community was his also for the first time: "He who has thought of himself as being cut off from the rest of mankind by his handicap suddenly discovers that the barrier has vanished, and he idealizes the girl who has released him from isolation" (p. 71). Even young Louise Baker (1946), a vivacious and popular girl with one leg who was president of one group or another twelve times before she was graduated from high school, suffered the frustration of believing herself "all wrong" and unwanted because she "knew" that she could never get a husband (though subsequently she did, and more than once).

In summary, autobiographical accounts indicate that, during adolescence, persons with disabilities experience trying times in heterosexual adjustments, but we must remember that this is true of adolescents in general. We are forced to conclude that there are many, many factors that enter into the creation and resolution of problems; that though physical deviation may not be the least of these factors, neither is it the greatest; and that some factors may balance out others in the resultant effect on heterosexual adjustments. Adolescents with a disability who are convinced that their difficulties in forming boy-girl attachments would vanish were it not for the disability would do well to realize that many, if not all, adolescents have problems in this area which may be no lighter than their own.

The knowledge that "someday you will meet the person meant for you," as Russell Criddle's (1953) mother often repeated, may be of small comfort to the adolescent who needs reassurance *now*, whose personal experiences spell a different conclusion, and for whom rigid standards of gender appropriateness are part of accepted values. Yet, even though knowledge may offer little conscious support, it may become part of a subconscious sustaining repertoire, drawn and leaned upon as needed, and therefore ought to be made available to the young person. The adolescent should know that physical conformity will not always remain so important a criterion for gender appropriateness. The adolescent should know that, for most persons with physical disabilities, courtship and marriage are not closed though they may be delayed.

Relevant data may speak louder than words. In one study the marital status of almost 2000 employees with various disabilities was investigated (Brighouse, 1946). The results, presented in Table 11.1, show that a majority of persons with physical disabilities were married.

In another study on the personal and social adjustment of more than 400 former patients with poliomyelitis whose present ages were 16 to 42 years, 28 percent of the men and 41 percent of the women were either married or actively contemplating marriage (Lowman, as reported in Barker et al., 1953, pp. 130–131). Table 11.2 reports the percentage of married and unmarried persons with varying degrees of disability.

The data show that marriage is within the realistic outlook for persons who have a disability. Although there is some relation between severity or apparency of disability and marriage, the relationship is not strong. It has also been shown that degree of disability is a poor predictor of satisfaction in marriage (Skipper, Fink, & Hallenbeck, 1968) and that the divorce rate among men with spinal cord injuries is no greater than among the general population (El Ghatit & Hanson, 1976).

Where the nature of the disability, however, is of such proportions that the probability of marriage is remote, the person has time

Table 11.1   MARITAL STATUS OF EMPLOYEES WITH DISABILITIES.

	PERCENTAGE MARRIED	
TYPE OF HANDICAP	MALES	FEMALES
Auditory	69	51
Cardiac	62	60
Hernias	78	
Orthopedic	52	52
Respiratory	53	57
Visual	64	54
Multiple	68	52
All physically handicapped	61	55
Physically normal control group	71	49

Table 11.2.   PERCENTAGE OF MARRIED AND UNMARRIED PERSONS WITH A DISABILITY.

	MARRIED	UNMARRIED
Very apparent	34	55
Moderately or slightly apparent	34	40
Not apparent or no deformity	32	6

to absorb this realization, and to go on from there. Christy Brown (1955), severely limited physically because of cerebral palsy, recalled his adolescence as being mostly a series of frustrations. He was terribly lonely, and his life seemed without purpose or worth. He loved one girl and then another, but could only dream of this and never partake. These experiences, however, were not pervasive. Other experiences enabled him to scale the high walls that still surrounded him. As he achieved some degree of physical independence, encouragement to write, and understanding from those who listened to him and respected him as a person, his old bitterness changed to acceptance. In his account, published when he was 22 years of age, Christy Brown notes:

> . . . I wanted so desperately to love and be loved, but—it was a bitter realization, but a true one, a necessary one. What good would it do me if I were to shut my eyes and turn my back on every unpleasant fact about myself? I was tempted to do that many times, but I was only putting off the final ordeal a little longer; it had to come sometime. It came: it made me sad, bitter for a time, but in the end it also made me stronger within myself. If I could never really be like other people, then at least I would be like myself and make the best of it. [p. 128]

We can expect that people with disabilities, including severe disabilities, will realize their human sexuality in a caring relationship more readily as they and people in general are freed from narrow conceptions of what constitutes essential physical attributes and appropriate sexual functioning. Special programs in human sexuality with this objective are available in this and other countries.

At times a specialized approach specifically geared to the needs of people with a particular type of disability is helpful. Blind young people have been allowed to explore the bodies of a live male and female model while receiving instruction in a class on sex differences, for example. This approach can be expected to become more widespread as negative attitudes toward human sexuality are reduced and the right to knowledge utilizing the most appropriate modes of communication is recognized.

An important article delineates a number of rights concerning human sexuality in general as a way of calling attention to the issues involved in according those rights to people with certain types of disability (Chigier, 1972). With editorial modification, the rights are:

1. The right to be informed about the biological and sociopsychological facts of sex behavior.
2. The right to be regarded as a sexual human being and treated as such.
3. The right to sexual expression through fantasy, self-pleasuring, sexual play with another person, and ultimately in sexual intercourse.
4. The right to marry.
5. The right to become parents.
6. The right to receive services in regard to premarital counseling, genetic counseling, marital guidance, family planning, and sexual problems.

The following elaborations are extracted from the article to show the kinds of controversies that need to be resolved in the sensitive area of human sexuality.

The Right to Sexual Expression

If other young people, male and female, masturbate, there is no reason why this should be forbidden for the disabled. Some people believe that, if the disabled has a technical problem in achieving self-pleasure, it is permissible for him to receive help, just as he would receive help in eating, walking, use of the toilet or transportation. . . . If in a particular society it is accepted that young people before marriage engage in sexual activities, there is no logical reason why this should be forbidden to the disabled living in that same society. . . . If in some societies contraceptive devices . . . available for young people who are not yet ready . . . to take on the responsibility of marriage and parenthood, there is no logical reason why the same contraceptive devices should not be available for those who are developmentally, emotionally, or physically unable to take on the responsibility of marriage and parenthood. [p. 226]

The Right to Marry

It [this right] is a controversial issue with regard to the retarded, especially the moderate[ly] to severe[ly] retarded. With greater provision of homelike facilities, better guidance programs, more social adjustment training, . . . more adequate use of and availability of contraceptive devices, it may not be too far-fetched to visualize a period where instead of two young people of the same sex living in a room together in an hostel for the retarded, that a retarded man and woman live together as a married couple under the same sheltered conditions. . . . [p. 226]

The Right to be Parents

Physically disabled have been shown to be capable of being adequate parents, as well as the blind. Even though the deaf often marry the deaf, their children, whether deaf or not, have not been shown to grow up worse than other people's children. The retarded again present a controversial question. There are less and less people today who advocate compulsory sterilization. Voluntary sterilization or adequate use of contraceptive devices may be required in these cases where the right to be a parent clashes with the right of the child to be brought up by parents with adequate social and intellectual function. As yet, there are not enough studies to indicate whether a retarded mother is automatically a worse mother than the vast numbers of non-retarded mothers. [pp. 226–227][2]

RUSSELL CRIDDLE: AN ADOLESCENT WITH A DISABILITY

Let us examine in some detail the adolescence of Russell Criddle (1953), who traces with utmost sincerity the course of his disability in the adolescent search for self-respect and independence against opposing forces. The vision of this boy, you may recall, became so seriously impaired at the age of 12 that he could not see to count his fingers at more than 2 feet in a good light, and in order to read ordinary print had to bring the book to within 2 inches of his eyes. Legally he was declared blind. During the next 17 years, when his vision was temporarily restored by a corneal graft, he fought a constant battle against being what people thought a blind person should be— namely, thoroughly incapacitated, overprotected, and ineligible as a marriage partner.

[2]Reprinted from Sexual adjustment of the handicapped, by E. Chigier. *Proceedings of the Twelfth World Congress of Rehabilitation International,* 1972. By permission of Rehabilitation International.

In the narration, the following significant points are detectable: (1) As Criddle's physique took on new meanings in adolescence, his self-concept became altered too. The processes of differentiation and integration are seen throughout these reevaluating years. (2) Criddle was by no means an isolate. He had friends with whom to play and study. (3) Yet he often knew a deep loneliness. In his preadolescence, this was felt when his disability kept him from participating in group activities. During his adolescent years, the loneliness became more firmly welded into the conviction that he could not secure the affection of a girl. (4) He had contact with girls, but except for short-lived and tenuous emotional ties, the relationships were (until his middle twenties) strictly "at a distance." (5) Like other adolescents, he rebelled against adult—particularly parental—authority and had his teenage gang with whom to rebel. (6) But in his struggle to meet the conflicting demands of the "normal" and "disabled" overlapping situations he was for the most part on his own. His mother was a source of comfort, but "solutions" evolved directly from his own experiences. (7) Two main factors combined to protract Russell Criddle's position as an adolescent. The first of these was the girl problem, which he felt denied him the status of a suitor and husband. The second was his extended economic dependence on his family, brought about by the depression years and exacerbated by his disability.

The following account is divided into age groupings that span significant changes in Criddle's life.

Age 12–13. This was the period of Criddle's initial adjustment to his disability and reinstatement, to some extent, with his gang. He did not think of himself as tragic, for he had his mother's assurance, supported by childhood's belief in the future, that his eyes would get better. But the months following his accident had been lonely months. The fellows had come around often at first, but after a while their visits dwindled until the older boys seldom came at all.

Soon he came face to face with what to him were the awful social consequences of blindness when he was openly rejected by his gang. From then on he denied that he was blind, though he was willing to admit that his eyes were bad, for blindness meant to him exclusion, dependency, and inferiority.

Criddle was correct in believing that the overlapping situations of normality and disability were not as incompatible as the stereotype of blindness would make them. But he was not correct in believing that in the long run the incompatibility could be overcome by attempts to conceal and even deny his disability. This solution, "acting as if," begun early in his career as a person with a disability, persisted for almost a decade until the wisdom of experience thrust upon him the folly of his pretense.

Criddle did become reinstated with the gang as a result of his own perseverance and the support of the gang leader, who ruled, "As long as you got guts you're still a member, even if you are blind" (p. 21).[3]

The initial, almost complete isolation gave way to a fair amount of group participation:

> . . . I can remember sliding down a steep clay bank that provided a ten-foot chute into the river [with the other fellows]. . . .
>
> I was the bat boy at ball games, though we only had one bat. I can remember hanging by my heels from the high strut of a billboard, in a game of follow-the-leader. I was the only one in the gang who could hang by his heels.
>
> We played hide-and-seek. I could hide but I couldn't seek, so I gave the last one caught before me the privilege and pleasure of giving me ten punches in the arm, in exchange for his taking "it" for me. [p. 31]

There were other occasions, and frequent ones, however, when Criddle felt alone and out of things:

> . . . there were the long, lonely hours, too, while the gang was playing some game I could not join in. I never resented their playing in the woods, or going fishing, or doing any of the hundreds of things I could not do without spoiling their play. I learned to be realistic and to play by myself while I waited out the hours and days between games I could take part in. [pp. 31–32]

With respect to his family, Criddle sensed the sympathy and understanding of his mother and in turn loved her deeply. Throughout this period and those to follow, she helped him extend his space of free movement in spite of pressures from the community to overprotect and inhibit him. Other forces worked at sharpening the incompatibility between the overlapping situations of normality and disability. His mother worked toward destroying the incompatibility:

> Mother knew what I sensed. That the difference between not being able to see and not being blind was in not being what people thought a blind person should be. She had a problem, too, in not being what mothers of blind children should be. The neighborhood felt that she was being criminally negligent in the way she allowed me to go about, playing, swimming, crossing streets, and all, and they were not reluctant to tell her so. "If that boy gets killed," I heard one irate neighbor say, "his death will be on your hands."
>
> "I know," Mother answered quietly, "and if he doesn't, his life will be on my hands. I must let him live, don't you understand? Bad eyes don't make a boy into an old man." [p. 36]

[3]Reprinted with permission from *Love is not blind*, by R. Criddle. New York: Norton, 1953.

Criddle's father provided for the family, but otherwise entered little into his son's life during this early period. The two brothers were enough younger to have their own gangs and Criddle did not often join them.

Age 13–14. As a whole, this was a lonely year for Criddle. The other boys were at school, no sight-saving classes were available, and Criddle found "life in the world of adults unbearably lonely" (p. 46). Occasionally he still boxed, skated, and went swimming with the gang. Through his mother's efforts, he was able to get a newspaper route. Criddle recalls the affectionate relationships among the family members and makes repeated reference in this and later years to his mother's wisdom in rearing a handicapped child.

Age 14–15. During this year Criddle became increasingly aware of girls as a special object of interest but had not yet fully realized the barrier of his disability in this regard. This was his first year at a sight-saving school in a nearby community which he attended until the age of 16. Evidently his days were well filled with activities at school, but he refers very little to his peer life there. He did have his first "love affair" at this school with a girl two years his junior. When she confessed her love for another boy, Criddle suffered intensely. But, because he still held the childish belief, inspired in part by his mother, that eventually he would be able to see as well as ever, he was able to assuage his ego by blaming his disability. Moreover, during this early part of his adolescence, Red, a good friend and a physically unimpaired member of the gang, was no great shakes as a Don Juan either, and at social affairs outside of school "Red and I were quite satisfied both with the cool kisses that we got from the girls whenever one of them accidentally called our numbers [at kissing games], and with the necessity of going stag" (p. 52). Criddle also could chalk off his apparent lack of sex appeal to his relative youth.

Age 15–16. It was this year that brought about some of the most drastic changes in Criddle's self-concept. His accustomed role as a child to be protected by his parents was jolted and the fear that he could never be loved by a girl descended upon him.

The rude awakening of a changed role between himself and his parents occurred when Criddle engaged in a boxing match with his father. This started as playful sparring and ended as a serious battle for superiority, with Criddle the victor. With this incident the potency of his adult position greatly increased and that of his child position weakened. The conflict over giving up personal security as the price of independence is clear:

> Bruised and horribly fatigued, I made my way to the old camp site. . . . The camp was gone, its ruins having been salvaged by another generation or another camp. It seemed to signify my lost childhood. I didn't

want to have licked my father. I didn't want to lose the protection his superior strength had given me. I didn't want to grow up. I didn't want to know that now I no longer need obey him for fear of punishment. I didn't want to lose the protection of his authority over me. Now I was a man, but I no longer had him to go to, and I felt ashamed of the tears that burned on my battered face.

I wanted to go to Mother, to have her nurse me as she always had, but when the fight was over she had run out of the front door from where she had been watching and had gone directly to Dad. She had disregarded me entirely, and I had to accept the fact that her first concern was for him rather than for me. [pp. 60–61]

With the gradual estrangement between himself and his parents that grew in the succeeding years, Criddle increasingly needed affectional ties with a girl to fill the void. But the problem of girls, with which he had been so happily unconcerned, developed during this period into the anguished conviction that the love of a girl could never be for him. His earlier rationalizations no longer worked. The adolescent's regard of his physique as being the culmination of a series of changes prevented his seeking consolation in the hope of major improvement with his eyes. Repeated experiences of a subtle advance and a subtle rejection convinced him that he was unwanted in boy-girl relationships. Not so subtle rejections and the incident recorded earlier (see p. 2) made this conviction indelible, though his hope kept alive the remote possibility that he was wrong.

In coping with this conviction, Criddle began to reason that one need not have children and a wife to be happy, that in fact one could enjoy more of the "finer things of life" without the restrictions of a family. But again the rationalization proved but a shallow covering for the relentless yearnings underneath. The fact that he could not get a dance date still foretold a life of loneliness for which he saw no alternative. The close of this period sees the cementing of the irreversible connection between loneliness and celibacy. He could not peer into the future to know that ten years later physique would cease to be the all-important criterion of gender appropriateness; that when he would have matured a little and girls would have matured a little his mother's repeated reassurances that someday he would meet the girl meant for him would be fulfilled.

Yet, during this resigned loneliness, Criddle had friends. "Anywhere from six to ten boys used to gather in either Red's cellar or my sitting room, and spend an evening in good fellowship and sparring" (p. 58). As an antidote for his loneliness his father tried to help him ". . . by making me a man among his adult friends. He took me fishing a few times that summer and though I tried to pretend to like it, he knew that I was bored. He started playing checkers with me during the evenings that he was not working, and we would have a stein of beer with the game" (p. 57). His father's efforts offered little comfort, however, for besides being a poor substitute for the real thing, Criddle felt that his father resented him because of his disability (as well as loved him in spite of it).

The ambiguous and shifting light in which parents regard their adolescent children is seen when Criddle's father on the one hand extended the symbols of manhood to him in offering the beer, and on the other hand withdrew them in demanding a curfew. The adolescent conflict with his father grew with the belief that his father required exaggerated virtue from him because of his disability. His mother, as seen by Criddle, ordered him little and understood him always.

Age 16–18. Criddle's adolescent turbulence continued unchecked. He started regular high school but, being two years older than his classmates, he had little to do with them outside school hours. At best they left him alone; at worst they rejected and ridiculed him (see pp. 331–332 for one of the more trying incidents). He bent every effort to hide his disability in order to be like anyone else, but only years later did he learn that such play carried no trumps. His gang life continued with an occasional evening of boxing and pinochle. He even made new friends and with the gang made a stab at such concrete signs of adulthood as gambling and drinking that could, at the same time, represent frontal attacks against authority. "Occasionally we would all chip in for a gallon of wine or a bottle of cheap whiskey. We seldom had enough money to do much damage" (pp. 65–66).

Criddle also saw in his escapades a bitter reaction against the loneliness of not having a girl. With indignation he challenged his mother, "So I was playing a little penny ante. What's wrong with that? The other fellows have dates all the time. What am I supposed to do, stay home and listen to the radio seven nights a week?" (p. 67). Criddle's parents continued to worry about him and keep tabs on him. Once when he had been gambling his father went to the others involved and raised a row. He told them that if it would happen again he would call the police. Criddle resented the childish position this implied even though he agreed with his parents that he was more than ordinarily derelict.

But the times that Criddle spent with his parents were also good. This point is important: though parents and adolescents may often quarrel, there are times, not necessarily infrequent, when the bond of kinship is strengthened by friendship. Criddle's father confided in him his own youthful derelictions, taught him how to play the bugle, and continued to play checkers and drink beer with him. All of this gave Criddle the feeling that, in spite of his father's resentments, he was his favorite son.

When Criddle joined the bugle corps with two of his cronies, his spare time was well occupied with practice and performance. He was even assured the company of girls at the dance after celebrations. But as emancipation from the family increased with these new exploits, Criddle's need for attachments with a girl could not remain dormant. He began to reason that if he could conceal his disability until after the girl had learned to like him—then surely she could continue to like him!

> This was a rather ambitious plan. That I could keep a girl from knowing about my eyes through the intimacies of courtship, even a rapid one, seems improbable. That I did seems a little fantastic even to me, now that I realize how little I could see at that time.
>
> This concealment became habitual. I would refrain from exposing my eye condition as unconsciously as I would refrain from touching a fire; for it was just as painful. People would notice something odd about me, but it was often a long time before they realized what it was. [p. 76]

Little did Criddle know that the adolescent, for whom physical conformity is the hallmark of gender appropriateness, could not see him as a person aside from his disability. He had to be hurt and severely hurt before his one hope in concealment, and with it his hope for happiness, was shattered:

> I remember Mary. I just happened to be standing on the corner of Fourth and West Main when Mary passed on her way to school. The day before, I had found her in music class—a new face, a new voice, a new hope, naturally to be investigated. Bud told me that she lived just around the block from my house, that she was a good-looker, and that she carried a heavy typewriter to and from school each day.
>
> And so, as I said, I just happened to be standing there when she passed. I had been happening to be standing there some twenty minutes.
>
> I pretended to be tying my shoe. Then I fell in behind her. I followed her almost to Condon's store before I mustered enough courage to advance.
>
> "May I carry your case?"
>
> "Thank you," she said with genuine gratitude. "It is heavy."
>
> She handed me the typewriter, and tossed her head to send long black curls tumbling over her shoulder. She smiled. I watched her out of the corner of my eye as we walked on. I could see a pert little nose, and she walked with a lilt, a sort of dance, but not ungraceful. Her whole personality seemed musical. I would probably have walked the rest of the way to school in silence if she hadn't spoken first.
>
> "I know you. I saw you in music class yesterday. Your name's Russell."

"How do you know?"

"One of the girls told me."

I wondered if one of the girls had told her about my eyes.

"Did she tell you anything else?"

"She said you were a sophomore. I'm only a freshman. I take music with the sophomores, though."

"I know," I said, "and your name's Mary."

She tossed her head again, and laughed, and I fell in love.

"Have you got a steady?" she asked after two more blocks of silence.

"No, I just broke up. Have you?"

"Sure. He's the hired man next to my daddy's farm. That is, he used to be. My daddy doesn't have a farm any more. I was getting tired of him anyway."

"You're pretty," I said, trying to steady my voice.

She smiled her appreciation of my compliment, and said, "You're strong."

"Aw, this ain't heavy."

I held the typewriter at arm's length, to show her how modest I was.

We stopped at the Sugar Bowl that night. Mary had a soda (15¢), so I had a dish of ice cream (10¢). I only had a quarter.

Mary sipped her soda and looked at me for a moment, then, without warning, "You're nice."

I told her I was going to be a newspaper reporter some day.

"I think newspaper reporters are romantic."

We went to the movies on Sunday night, and had a soda afterward. We walked home holding hands.

She liked horses. "My daddy had the best team of anybody," she boasted.

I laughed.

She turned abruptly and faced me. "Well, he did. My daddy said so."

"I believe you," I said.

We walked on, swinging our hands in time with her lilting steps. Then, "What are you laughing at?"

"I don't know. You, I guess."

"You're an odd person," she said pleasantly, as we reached her front porch.

"What do you mean?"

"I don't know. Sometimes I look at you and you don't seem to see me."

"Let's just say I'm deep," I said, and we laughed.

"I think you're awfully nice," she said.

I wanted to kiss her, she stood so close. But I felt guilty, it wasn't right, not telling her about my eyes.

I managed to keep Mary from knowing my eyes were bad through two dozen sodas and three movies. I used every trick I had ever learned. I paid special attention to the color of her dress each morning, and then I would keep my eyes and ears and my sixth sense alert for anyone that might be Mary. I didn't take any chances. If I wasn't sure, I would greet whoever it was with familiarity. They probably thought I was nuts, but I didn't care. I always held her hand on the way to and from the movies at night, and she led me, without knowing it, so I didn't have to feel for curbs and steps.

She said she had seen me in the library one day and that I had fallen asleep. I knew I had been studying, but I didn't tell her that.

"Why didn't you wake me up? Prof caught me."

She laughed and tossed her head, and the black curls tumbled about, and I sighed with relief and ecstasy.

"Will you go to the firemen's ball with me?"

"Sure. I was afraid you didn't go to dances," she said.

I'll never forget that date. I thought I would have to sell my bike to get funds, but Dad came through with the most beautiful five-dollar bill I have ever seen. I took a bath every night for a week. I brushed my teeth until they bled. My hair was plastered down with vaseline in the hope that it would subdue the stubborn cowlick. Mother bought me a new pair of white flannels and had my coat cleaned and pressed. I used up almost a whole box of shoe polish on my best shoes. I wore Dad's brand-new hat, and his best necktie. I was the essence of perfection as I straightened my tie and knocked at Mary's front door.

Mary's mother answered. "Come in, Russell, Mary isn't quite ready."

I almost lost faith in the worth of living as I sat in the parlor with Mary's mother, waiting for her beautiful daughter, for it started to rain. The awful stuff hit the windows like hailstones. Mary's mother probably saw my anguish, for she said:

"I think it will stop. They are big drops."

She was right. The rain had stopped when Mary came into the room. So did time. She was wearing a pink dress, all stiff and crinkled, that flared out below her slim waist and almost touched the floor. Enough perfume floated in with her to glamorize a dozen girls.

I rose and helped Mary on with her coat. She had a pink ribbon in her soft hair. Her eyes were almost black. I had thought they were.

"Come right home after the dance, and have a good time, children."

"Yes, Mother. Good night."

The rain had left the air clean and sweet, and Mary's perfume, thinned by a soft breeze, wrought havoc with my co-ordination. The shower had washed some of the greasy smoke from the town and part of it was left suspended in puddles at our feet.

With my head in the clouds, I placed my number nine shoe directly into an especially large one, splashing Mary's beautiful dress with the filthy water. Mary uttered a little scream of anguish, and the laughter left her voice as she moaned a futile, "Oh dear!" I snatched my handkerchief from where I had folded it so carefully, and dabbed at the wilting organdie, smearing it around all the worse.

Mary groaned and pulled away. "Don't. Just let it dry."

We went on toward the hall. I kept apologizing, and she kept saying it was nothing. I felt miserable as I "led" her, just a thought ahead of me, so that I wouldn't have to feel for the steps up to the dance hall.

The gaiety of the ball soon dispelled the gloom. Nobody said anything about her dress, so I guessed that it didn't look too bad. Mary danced close, and it was evident to all that she was my girl. It was pure happiness for me. I felt that Mary must somehow know about my eyes, the way she had acted about the puddle, and besides, someone must have told her by this time.

We went to the Sugar Bowl during the intermission, and we each had two sodas and a little piece of cake. After the dance, we went to the restaurant for hot roast beef sandwiches and coffee. I was happy, indeed I was. Mary didn't pity me. No one would pity me any more. I had a girl, a beautiful girl that even Bud would have liked to have, if his steady didn't already have him roped and tied. I had solved all my problems. People would no longer pity me, and even if they did, what did I care.

Mary met me the next morning with a simple "hello" that told that I was her beau. I didn't feel breathless any more; I felt contented, and happy. I looked at her and thought how wonderful she was to be able to go with a guy that nobody else would go with. It seemed to me there was no need to tell her about my eyes, that she had probably known all the time. I felt differently now. I didn't care whether anybody felt sorry for me or not. I didn't care whether they thought I was stupid or not. I had a girl.

I met Mary after school with the same inexpressible feeling of intimacy with which I had met her that morning:

"Hello. Where's your typewriter?"

"I left it in school."

We walked quietly to Main Street. Mary acted angry. She had never been that way before.

"What's the matter?"

"Nothing."

But there was, I could tell. Her manner was chilly; the music was gone from her bearing, the lilt from her step; and she was quiet. She had never been like that before.

"If I did something, I'm sorry," I said.

"It's nothing."

We walked on, almost to Condon's store.

"I wish you would tell me."

She just said, "It's nothing," but she seemed to be melting a little. It wasn't in anything she said, but her walk was a little less stilted.

Neither of us spoke again until we reached her house, and she would have left me without even saying, "I'll be seeing you." I caught her hand.

"You've got to tell me. Something is wrong."

If I could have seen her eyes, I know I would have noticed that they were shiny with tears. There was so much compassion in her voice when she finally answered that I felt sorry for her.

"I'm sorry, Russ, honest I am. I knew you were kind of odd, but I didn't know you couldn't see."

She pulled her hand from mine, and with a sob, ran into the shadow of her front porch and I heard the door close behind her. [pp. 76–83]

Criddle's misery was complete. He was now reconvinced, and this time without a shadow of a doubt, that no girl could ever love him. But more than that, he felt he was only part of a man. It was as simple as this:

> It takes six sides to make a hexagon, and a hexagon can hardly be expected to fall in love with a triangle.
>
> I'm a man in every respect but one, therefore I fall short of being a man by definition. I can't expect to be desired as a man. But I have the desires of a whole man. It's just nature. [p. 113]

Fortunately, after two years in high school, Criddle began to find a place for himself at school. To some degree this served as a substitute for his deepest pain of not being able to find a sweetheart.

Age 18–20. These two years were Criddle's first period of relative peace since the age of 14. He still missed the love of a woman sorely, but his gradual acceptance by his classmates and his life on his father's farm partially took its place. As a senior he was elected, by a popular vote of the student body, to become editor-in-chief of his high-school paper. Of one boy he says, "His acceptance of me had made my adjustment in school easier. We were close friends, and an intimate understanding existed between us" (p. 111). Nor did Criddle lack the companionship of girls:

> But though I was without a sweetheart I was not without female companionship. Girls seemed to respect and admire me. They liked me, as they told me all too often, but not in that way. They wanted me for sort of a big brother. They confided in me their conquests, their desires, and even their sins. [p. 115]

Time did not hang heavy on his hands: Aside from his improved social relations at school, his father acquired a farm during Criddle's sophomore year. Moreover, he gained the respect of the farmers and participated in the square dancing and movies of the rural community:

> My hands blistered and toughened, and I grew hard until I could spend a full day in the field and still have enough energy left for a square dance or a movie. I gained their [the farmers'] respect as a good worker, which is the ultimate as regards social status among farmers. I was respected. I was liked, too, I think, and I liked them. [p. 125]

Criddle was busy. During this period he reports no adolescent "flings" or major eruptions with his father. But though his life was far from empty, though he was productive and acclaimed, there remained an incompleteness that kept begging for closure—his wish for a sweetheart was intense. Criddle believed that he would not feel passion toward a sweetheart; that he would not desire anything from her other than companionship, understanding, and affection. He recognized that this was "a search for someone upon whom to transfer the great love I had for my mother" (p. 114). Though this incompleteness caused him great distress, it was mild compared to the compounded sufferings he had to endure following his graduation from high school.

Age 20–22. Upon graduation from high school, Criddle looked forward to achieving economic independence and with it the dignity that was his right. He achieved neither. The year was 1936, and times were hard. After battling for employment, he did manage to hold two jobs briefly but returned home sick and with the growing realization that his greatest battle would be against society's proscription that as a blind man he must live a life of asylum.

Emancipation from his family came slowly, and the inevitable parent-child conflicts piled up. Just a short while before, Criddle had enjoyed a fair amount of status as a promising reporter at high school and as a good hand on the farm. Now he had no status at all, for since he was dependent on his father, his father expected him to assume once again the subservient position of a child. He argued, in effect, "See, without my help you suffer. I will help you if you will do as I say." He beat Criddle violently whenever he stayed out after one o'clock at night or committed some comparable misdemeanor. And Criddle's reaction was to earn his board on the farm as his father directed but otherwise ". . . Dad's decree that I should do this or that was all the incentive I needed to disobey" (p. 152). And like the adolescent who sees the parent as the main source of his frustrations, Criddle recalls "I suppose I was normal enough to blame all my troubles upon my father" (p. 152). Also like the adolescent who needs some source of support for his rebellion and deflated ego, Criddle sought out companionship wherever he could find it, whether in a saloon or a pool hall, whether in a card game or at a dance. In short, Criddle, who at the age of 18 was ready to abandon the adolescent patterns of behavior for a more mature way of life, now in his twenties was plummeted back to the typical psychological situation of an adolescent with a consequent resurgence of adolescent behavior.

We tend to think of the adolescent as the one who strives for family emancipation, and yet it is the parents, too, who work toward that end in a way as uneven and ambivalent as the adolescent's striving for freedom. When, years before, his mother went to his father's assistance after the fateful battle and left Criddle without comfort, she gave him a shove toward independence. Now, when their relationships continued to go from bad to worse, it was the father who ordered Criddle from the house.

The endless trail of job hunting began again. He secured a few jobs, but as soon as his supervisors discovered the condition of his eyes, he was fired in spite of his belief that he could do a more than adequate job. Society had the fixed notion that blindness so incapacitated a man that the only possibility of functioning at all lay in the sheltered workshop. Criddle was repelled by what to him was a last resort, for it meant giving up, a helplessness and dependency that he despised. Instead he suffered cold and hunger and utter exhaustion; in humiliation he returned to his father's farm after three months rather than agree with society's verdict.

Age 22 to Maturity. By this time both Criddle and his father had changed in ways that made living together less strained. His father had learned, through the unsparing teaching of worry and remorse, that he could not impose his will on his son. Criddle had learned that he could achieve a greater freedom by admitting his disability: "I know now that the longer I kept people from knowing about my eyes, the greater became the shock when they found out" (p. 159). And having been buffeted around on the outside, he could appreciate the relief he found in farm life where he was not repeatedly subjected to social prejudice. Both parents welcomed him back and asked him to stay a while.

Criddle stayed. He worked on the farm during the harvesting season and filled in during slack periods by selling radios and cutting mine lagging. He found some semblance of peace of mind. "That half of the emotional barrier which had been within me was gone; I no longer pitied myself" (p. 196).

Then, in spite of having resisted attachments for fear of being hurt again, Criddle fell in love. What drew these two people together? Winona was fat and Criddle nearly blind. And each was ashamed of the other! In humiliation they went out together because that was better than sitting home alone. Their loneliness brought them together, and values deeper than physique drew them together. They found they had good times together. They developed a deep respect for each other, and mutual understanding flowered. They overcame the adolescent trap that defined gender appropriateness in terms of rigid standards of physical conformity. At last Criddle looked forward to marriage and as a result savored the sweet nectar of full adulthood. In spite of having become a resigned bachelor, he had felt that every self-respecting farmer *should* be married. His vision of complete status embodied the following:

> My heifers. My cows. Rather I should say our cows. That is one thing about farming, I thought: it makes a real partnership of marriage. Men have survived all sorts of handicaps on farms, except that of being without a wife.

The horses stopped for a rest and I looked toward the house and smiled. The next time I broke sod on this meadow, Winona would be there, in the house, doing whatever was to be done, perhaps cooking dinner. And when I grew thirsty she would seem to know it, and come out with a bottle of cool water, and maybe a piece of bread and jam. She would stay for a moment, admiring my work, and I would feel proud. She would probably bring some sugar for the horses, and caution me not to work them too hard. Then she would start back to the house, and I would call her back and kiss her.

I sighed at my dreams and started the team again. They would stand all day, if I let them. Winona would be a wonderful wife. I smiled again as a car went up the road. Today was Thursday and Mrs. Bryant was going to Ladies' Aid. Winona would probably belong to the Ladies' Aid too. That meant that every other Thursday I would have to get my own dinner, or eat something she would leave covered on the table for me. I guessed that would be one of the things I would have to tolerate. But the meetings always ended about four in the afternoon, and she would be home in plenty of time to get a good hot supper. [pp. 207–208]

The picture painted a blissful marriage in a setting of economic independence. Criddle's love for Winona provided all the motivation he needed to prove that he could support a family by establishing and operating a dairy farm. With the help of his father he built a stable, a barn, and a milk house. His emotional independence from his father leaped forward: "Arguments with Dad didn't seem so important any more. I could always cajole him, knowing that sometime he would go back to town and I would be boss and could run things the way I wanted" (p. 208). An interim of deep unhappiness and loneliness still lay in store for him, but the maturity he gained in this period of approaching adult status helped him to withstand the onslaught of status loss he was to suffer.

When intervening pressures led Winona to reject his love several months later, full adult status was again denied Criddle, but now, because he had achieved the important prerequisite of economic independence, he was less vulnerable to the conflicting pressures of a marginal person. Against his father's wishes and assuming full responsibility, he bought an adjoining farm that had a large farmhouse on it, for in the big house he saw a chance to have a home of his own. As a substitute for what he wanted most, he could at least "hire some widow, with a child or two, to keep house" for him (p. 220). Occasionally he went out on a binge and often drifted in search of a good time, for his need to establish himself as a man and an adult remained unfulfilled. When circumstances brought Winona to him again, his romance ended in marriage and he found a contentment "which could not be marred by pain, or fatigue or bitterness or any other thing"

(p. 226). Economic independence, marriage, a home of his own—
Criddle finally came of age.

The case of Criddle serves to show that many of the problems
experienced by adolescents who have a disability can be understood
in terms of adolescent development in general. Like their peers, adolescents with a disability undergo a change of self-concept in which
adult determinants of behavior as well as childish determinants demand a hearing. They, too, have conflicts with their parents as these
determinants vary in potency. And they, too, seek a peer group for
companionship and support as they defy parental authority in an effort to assert their own independence. For them, too, physique becomes evaluated in terms of rigid standards appropriate to each sex
and they also have an intense interest in all matters that have to do
with the establishment of one's status as a man or woman. As in the
case of other young people, the period of adolescence may be pro-
longed by protracted economic independence and by not having established a separate household, preferably with a mate. In addition,
adolescents with a disability have to cope with conflicts engendered
by the overlapping situations of "normal" and "disabled" determin-
ers of behavior.

Undoubtedly, there are large variations in adolescent peer life
among the group with disabilities as well as among the group without. Probably most adolescents, for one reason or another and for
briefer or longer duration, experience the gnawing feelings of loneliness. Assuredly, not all persons need to feel part of a sizable group
to satisfy the need for support and companionship. One friend may
be sufficient. Finally, it is likely that the adolescent with a disability
is able to find age-mate companionship more easily than establish
one's status as a man or woman. Evidently, a physical deviation need
not be a barrier to peer group supportive and status-giving functions,
even though it may be felt to threaten role suitability in romantic
attachments and marriage.

Chapter 12
Self-Concept and the Perception of Interpersonal Relations

"BELIEVING IS SEEING"—ILLUSTRATED

Harold Russell (1949), the soldier who lost his hands, reacted differently in the following two situations involving discussion of his injury:

> SCENE I. *In a bar during Russell's first pass to town from the hospital.*
> We had just ordered our first round when I noticed someone at the bar staring right at me. I tried to ignore him, but he wouldn't stay ignored. I could feel him watching me. Presently he came over. He was a blubbery hunk of fat and had three or four chins dripping down his vest. He pulled up a chair and made himself at home. Apparently he believed that everyone loves a fat man. He ordered a round of drinks for all hands.
> "Thanks, mister," I said, "I still got one."
> "So you'll have another! On me, Joe! Always good to have reserves on hand. That's how we win battles." He winked and looked around us, trying to milk a laugh. None of us made a sound. He squirmed momentarily, then shifted to the subject that he was really interested in. "Tell me, sergeant, how did—"

"—you lose your hands?" One of my buddies finished the question for him.

"Why, how did you know what I was gonna ask?"

"Maybe you'd like to tell me how you lost your teeth?" I said.

"Just tryin' to be sociable—" he said, backing away nervously, beads of sweat glistening all over his fat face, his tiny opossum's eyes darting from one to another. "No offense in-in-intended—I—I—I'm sure—no offense—"

"Scram!"

"Before I give you these!" I added, shaking my hooks at him. [pp. 122–123]

SCENE II. *Sometime later in a restaurant shortly before Russell was ready for discharge from the hospital.*

The night we were at Ruby Foo's [restaurant] I was wielding my chopsticks at a great rate—I'd learned how in Boston's Chinatown —when a man came over from another table.

"I was noticing," he said, "how well you managed those things."

"These?" I held up the chopsticks.

"No—I—er—mean those—" He swallowed hard and nodded at the hooks. "Well—*those*—"

"Oh! You mean, my hooks?"

He sighed with relief. It was obvious he had been embarrassed to call them by their right name.

"I couldn't help noticing how skilful you are with them," he said. "You can just about do everything with them, can't you, sergeant?"

"Everything," I said, grinning, "except pick up a dinner check."

That drew a laugh. I could see the man relax at once. That made me relax, too. [p. 151].[1]

What was the difference that made a difference to Russell, so that in the first incident he felt he had been insulted, whereas in the second he had actually enjoyed the situation? Was the difference in the *other* person, in the one case blustering and pitying, and in the second more reserved and respectful? Perhaps to some extent, but there is evidence that in the interim between the two scenes Russell *himself* had undergone change, a change that drastically affected his perception of the intentions of others. Russell, after many experiences in which he felt self-conscious and like a freak on exhibition, in which he froze up in regard to discussion of his hooks, began to arrive at important new understandings. He notes:

. . . Gradually, it began to seep through my skull that folks were not just being morbid and inquisitive, but that they were genuinely inter-

---

[1]Reprinted by permission of Farrar, Straus & Giroux, Inc. From *Victory in my hands* by H. Russell & V. Rosen. Copyright 1949 by Harold Russell & Victor Rosen. Copyright renewed © 1976 by Harold Russell.

ested in me. When a stranger offered to buy me a drink it wasn't cheap charity, but a kind of acknowledgment of a debt he felt he owed to all who had served. I began to notice, too, that I wasn't the only GI who was being offered free drinks. Almost every man in uniform, whether disabled or not, was getting his share of them. [p. 150]

Moreover, this changed perception paralleled significant transformations within Russell's system of values, heralding progressive acceptance of his disability. The following introspections point to the kinds of reevaluations occurring in his outlook on life.

Containing disability effects (see pp. 175–178):

Sooner or later, I had to face the problem of how I was going to earn a living. After giving it a great deal of thought, I discovered a startling fact: my hands had not been as important as I thought. *There were lots of occupations where I wouldn't be too seriously handicapped.* [Italics ours] [p. 147]

Subordinating physique relative to other values (see pp. 171–175):

. . . That was the great lesson of his [Franklin D. Roosevelt's] magnificent fight. That was the innermost secret of his triumph. He had overcome not only his physical handicap but his spiritual one, as well. He had accepted his disability. For what he had missed he had gained something immeasurably more valuable. He was the master of himself and his destiny [p. 142]

Transforming comparative-status values into asset values (see pp. 178–183):

. . . I would have to realize that I had nothing to be ashamed of. . . . I began to see that it's not what you've lost that counts, but what you have left. [pp. 142–143]

As long as Russell regarded his disability as degrading, any social interaction, real or imagined, that so much as touched upon his disability would signal personal threat. In the first scene, Russell was in the process of accepting his disability. When, however, the meaning of his disability began to change, as indicated by the reevaluations indicated above, social interactions correspondingly appeared different to him. The phrase "began to change" bespeaks the fact that the process of acceptance of loss is not accomplished once and for all, nor does it march through fixed stages to ultimate acceptance. The process rather is variable, with progress and relapses marking the struggle to accept oneself as a person of dignity and value.

That social perception is a function, among other things, of self-perception is strikingly shown in Goldman's reminiscences in which the *same* situation was first interpreted in one way and then antithetically, *only* because his self-concept had undergone fundamental change. In the first example, Raymond Goldman (1947), legs crippled from polio and now 8 years old, is meditating about the feelings of other persons toward himself. Until recently, he had known little of shame. His family had been loving, and his efforts to do things had been greeted by praise and encouragement. But now he had become fully aware of the fact that he was not like other children. During his first day at school he had been taunted and ridiculed (see pp. 224–225 for the incident): he "learned" that he was "a pariah among the strong and straight." What had before seemed like kindness and admiration was now defiled by pity and scorn:

> . . . I knew now why strange women on the street smiled at me when Christina [his sister] wheeled me along in my gocart, sometimes stopping to chuck me under the chin or pat my head. It was because they pitied me, not because they admired me. I knew now why children along the way stopped their play and stared at me. It was not because they liked me and wished they could play with me, but because they were disgusted by the sight of a boy my age riding in a gocart. [p. 39][2]

The second example, ten years later, reveals the reverse direction in which a previously negatively interpreted relationship is now viewed positively. This change, as in the case of Harold Russell, reflected basic adjustive value transformations during Goldman's struggle with acceptance of disability (see pp. 125–133 for an analysis of this struggle):

> . . . When I had played ball with the boys, wearing heavy braces, passers-by had often stopped to watch me. I had thought they were pitying me and I had hated them for it. Now I knew that I should have been grateful to them for that meed of recognition of my striving. [p. 94]

It has long been recognized that those who do not believe themselves to be lovable are unable to love others, for self-love and love of others go hand in hand (Horney, 1937; Fromm, 1939). Mounting research evidence lends support to the proposition that there is a positive relationship between self-acceptance and (1) acceptance of others, as well as (2) *felt* acceptance by others (Sheerer, 1949; Berger, 1952; Fey, 1955; Wylie, 1979). In short, if you like yourself, you will tend to like others and to perceive that others like you, whether or not that is the case.

As Santayana is reported to have said, "The empiricist . . . thinks

---

[2]Reprinted with permission of Macmillan Publishing, Inc., from *Even the night* by R. L. Goldman. Copyright 1947, and renewed 1975, by Raymond Leslie Goldman.

he believes only what he sees, but he is much better at believing than at seeing" (Korzybski, 1951, p. 176).

INTERPRETATION OF SOCIAL RELATIONSHIPS IN THE FRAMEWORK OF PERCEPTION

The problem concerning the relationship between feelings about the self and the interpretation of the behavior of other people toward oneself is part of the larger problem of variables within and without the person that influence perception (Witkin et al., 1954; Blake & Ramsey, 1951; Symposium, 1949). The role of expectations or mental set has been demonstrated in laboratory experiments.

In Kelley's (1950) experiment, students were asked to rate an unknown instructor on such traits as conscientiousness, popularity, intelligence, and humor, after he had led the class in a 20-minute discussion. Some students had been informed that the instructor was reputed to be "rather cold" and other students that he was "very warm." One of the main results was that the warm-cold variable produced large differences in the evaluation of the behavior of the instructor. Students given the "warm" prior information consistently rated the stimulus person more favorably than did those given the "cold" prior information. Thus, the information as to whether the instructor was a warm or cold person geared the subject to select and highlight those aspects of his behavior in keeping with that mental set.

Of course, expectations of the perceiver do not always primarily determine the interpretation of another's behavior to the exclusion of objective events. Clearly, the conditions "out there" affect one's perceptions. Kelley's experiment, in addition to demonstrating the potency of expectations in evaluations, also demonstrated the influence of the instructor's behavior itself. It happened that two instructors who were very different in personality and behavior served as the stimulus person in the several groups of subjects used. There were marked differences in the *degree* to which the warm-cold variable was able to produce differences for the two instructors. For example, even though the "warm" observers rated instructor B more favorably on the popularity and humor scales than did the "cold" observers, he was still rated as "unpopular" and "humorless," evaluations that agreed with his typical classroom behavior.

There is further experimental evidence to indicate, however, that what may objectively be determined as solid and irrefutable evidence may still be denied or distorted when the subject has a strong expectancy of contrary fact. An experiment by Bruner & Postman (1949) is particularly relevant. Subjects were presented with playing cards, some of which had suit and color reversed (e.g., black hearts and red spades), for brief exposure periods. Initially, almost all the subjects saw nothing unusual about the trick cards. Congruence between color and suit was effected by misperceiving either the suit or the color at exposure levels well above the threshold for such recognition. Thus, a red six of spades was reported with considerable assurance as being either the red six of hearts or the black six of spades. An equally significant fact, however, is that with increase of exposure time the percentage of correct recognition of the bizarre cards progressively increased. That is, *expectations held greatest sway under conditions of ambiguous stimulus information* and became less influential as the stimulus input became more reliable.

The complexity of the interdependence between stimulus and person variables for perception is seen in the following hypothesis offered by Krech & Crutchfield (1948, pp. 95–98): If the stimulus differs but slightly from the expectation, the perception will tend to be assimilated to the expectations; however, if the difference between the stimulus and expectation is too great, the perception will occur by contrast to the expectation and will be distorted in the opposite direction.

It is to be noted that on the environmental side the degree of ambiguity or unreliability of the stimulus information can vary: the more clear-cut and reliable the input information, the more effective it will be in structuring the percept. The degree of ambiguity has been controlled in the laboratory by the use of such experimental techniques as dimly illuminated pictures or words, tachistoscopic (briefly exposed) materials, ambiguous drawings, and so forth. As for the person, the strength of expectations can vary: the stronger the expectation for certain events, the greater its potency in structuring the percept. Expectancy strength has been controlled in the laboratory by information, past experience, and other kinds of set.

In summary, it can be stated that as the features of the environmental stimuli become more ambiguous, one's perceptions increasingly adhere to one's own expectations. The expectations become an organizing principle according to which facts are made to fit. It is especially important to understand the factors that influence expectations concerning the behavior of others toward oneself because such behavior is often perceived according to one's expectations.

THE ROLE OF SELF-CONCEPT IN EXPECTATIONS

The opening section of this chapter illustrated the significance of self-perception for social perception. The expectations of Russell and Goldman in the situations where the behavior of others was positively evaluated clearly differed from those in the situations evoking negative evaluation. In turn *these expectations depended upon how they felt about themselves, their self-concept.* When they viewed their disability with shame, they could expect only that others felt likewise; this is how they interpreted the questioning, the staring, the help of others. When they were able to accept their disability more fully, it became sensible that others could view them as self-respecting, worthwhile, and even admirable. Instead of ignoring this expectation as a possibility, they could then entertain it, and once entertaining it, they could see the corresponding positive attitudes in the behavior of others, or, in the contrary instance, misinterpret negative attitudes to fit the positive expectation. In his studies of personality and social behavior, Maslow (1939) has reported that women low in dominance "can not 'take' compliments in spite of . . . their need and hunger for them. This is because they are apt at once to discount the compliment as untrue and seek suspiciously for other motives. Often, for example, they may think the compliment is making fun of them, holding them up to ridicule, or else trying to get something out of them" (p. 21).

There are several reasons why the self-concept plays a role, often decisively, in the interpretation of social relationships. An important reason is that it is a necessary (though not sufficient) part of the total situation. When we see someone reacting to the self, we must take the self into account as an object of stimulation. The kind of "account" one takes is usually drawn from the self-concept, for in most social situations there are few other clues as potent in defining the kind of person one is. People have a full and deep experience of the self. We see ourselves in a more-or-less-incisive way, even though upon further introspection we may well become ambivalent and confused. In particular situations we feel that we are right or wrong (or at least in between), that we are competent or not (or at least in between), that we are good looking or not (or at least in between). We do not have as direct access to the other person's regard of ourselves.

It might seem that all that is necessary when one is interested in the behavior and intentions of another person is to attend to the person's *actual* behavior, inasmuch as that is the direct expression of what the person is feeling. That this is not always the case is indicated by sound research. The well-known problem and experiments on the interpretation of human emotions from photographs are particularly relevant (Woodworth & Marquis, 1947, pp. 354–360). Though the findings indicate that the emotion portrayed is not often mistaken for its opposite, they also show that a knowledge of circumstances leading up to the emotion may be an important condition of emotional recognition. To take Asch's example: "The sight of the relaxed face of a man who is watering his garden has one physiognomic quality; the same expression has a wholly different value if the man has just committed a murder" (1952, p. 194). In the case of an emotion directed toward me, *my* characteristics as an "object" of stimulation to the other person and available to me via the self-concept, are a highly relevant part of the surrounding conditions.

A second set of factors leading to the preeminent position of the self-image in the interpretation of social interactions is that the clues reflecting the attitudes of the other person are often ambiguous and difficult to pin down. There are several reasons for this. First, such attitudes as respect, warmth, annoyance, or disapproval on the part of others toward oneself are expressed in multifarious ways. The affection of one person may spill over effusively, whereas in someone else it may be restrained. The same overt behavior may be interpreted differently, particularly when only part of the circumstances is open to view. For example, the same obstreperous behavior of a child may be judged as an expression of fatigue, stubbornness, anger, or the struggle for independence. Furthermore, attitudes are complex and often conflicting. It is possible for a mother, for example, to become irritated with the demanding behavior of her child but at the same time love and cherish the child. Similarly, attitudes toward a person with a disability not infrequently reflect both positive and negative feelings, either simultaneously or at least in rapid succession. Thus, people with a disability may be admired for their accomplishments and yet pitied because they are still "cripples." Clinical experience leaves no doubt that ambivalence toward others occurs frequently, perhaps even typically, as a consequence of the multifaceted aspect of our relationships to other persons.

Sometimes, however, people may have independent information as to how someone feels about them. The information may be hearsay; it may be based on repeated and unequivocal past experience with the other person. In certain circumstances they may be able to set aside their own self-image and substitute the picture of oneself as drawn from the perspective of the other person.

Nonetheless, because of the particular relevancy of the self-concept in social interactions and of the ambiguity of the behavior of the other person, the self-concept acquires an importance that surpasses its actual effectiveness in gauging correctly the attitudes of others. The person comes to expect certain attitudes and feelings toward the self, expectations rooted in the self-concept.

EXPECTANCY STRENGTH

The *strength* of expectations largely determines the degree to which they affect perception. This holds true for expectations in general, whatever their source, and not only those arising primarily from the self-image. Because of our special concern with problems of acceptance of disability and because of the special role of the self-concept in social expectations, we shall largely restrict our examples to expectations anchored to the self-concept.

The work of Bruner (1951) provides a soundly considered and well-integrated conception of some of the important determinants of the strength of an expectation. His work forms the basis of our application to disability-connected problems.

Bruner's fundamental proposition is that perceiving begins in an organism tuned to select certain features of the environment by an expectancy or hypothesis or set. These terms are used to give the flavor of the highly generalized state of readiness to perceive in a given way. The assumption is that "we are always to some extent *prepared* for seeing, hearing, smelling, tasting some particular thing or class of things" (p. 124). Whether any organism is ever completely "untuned" need not concern us here. Our concern is more with those conditions that affect the power of the "tuning" to channel perception into meaning and evaluation.

Bruner offers three propositions concerning the concept of expectancy strength: The stronger an expectation, (1) The greater its likelihood of arousal in a given situation; (2) the less the amount of appropriate information necessary to confirm it, and (3) the more the amount of inappropriate or contradictory information necessary to refute it.

The expectations with which a person enters a situation, therefore, not only put the spotlight on what the person will see but also, as a function of their strength, delimit the degree of incompatibility with objective fact that can be tolerated. Thus, when a person has strong feelings of shame and inferiority, the more often will experiences tend to bear out the expectation that one is indeed to be pitied and cast aside. The person will see confirmation in even the most modest evidence, and disruption of the expectation would require considerable proof to the contrary. Expectancy strength can now be seen as of central importance in determining whether acceptance of a disability will proceed as a matter of course or whether it will meet difficulties along the way as the struggle is tested in life's experiences.

What, then, are some of the conditions that strengthen or

weaken an expectation? Bruner (1951) proposes five such determinants. In his exposition he has carefully attempted to tie them to experimental findings.

1. *Frequency of past confirmation.* The more frequently an expectation has been confirmed in the past, the greater will be its strength: It will be more readily arousable, require less environmental information to confirm it, and will, conversely, require more contradictory evidence to negate it than would be required for a less frequently confirmed expectation.

The significance of past confirmation for expectancy strength has been demonstrated in a variety of experiments. For example, in the playing-card experiment described above, the fact that it took a far longer exposure time to recognize the cards that had suit and color reversed than those that did not is explained by a strong expectation for normal suit and color combinations built up through many past confirmations (Bruner & Postman, 1949).

Laboratory experiments have also shown, however, that frequency of confirmation does not operate in a simple way to increase strength by uniform increments. Sometimes a single contrary experience can markedly weaken or even wipe out an expectation that previously had many confirmations. Again we draw upon the playing-card experiment. Once the subject "caught on" that suit and color might be reversed, an expectation for incongruous as well as normal cards was established that served to measurably weaken the initial sole expectation. For a clinical example, the life history of Raymond Goldman (1947) may be recalled. During the first four years of his disability, he had many, many experiences in which he was respected, lauded, encouraged, and loved. His expectation that others felt positively toward him was hardly if at all sullied by doubt until his first day at school, when in one "fell swoop" the violence done to his self-concept correspondingly affected his expectations (see pp. 224–225 for incident).

The conclusion is warranted that expectancy strength is a function of frequency of past confirmation in which the confirming or infirming power of a single experience varies enormously, depending upon its effect on the cognitive outlook of the person. This does not contradict the commonsense feeling that frequent exposure to devaluating experiences in the important areas of life, such as home, school, and job, provides fuel for the smoldering conviction that one is an object of pity. It simply forces recognition of a second commonsense feeling—namely, that frequency as such is not everything and that one experience can be more effective or destructive than another. It would be unfortunate if frequency alone mattered, for then therapy would have the impossible task of altering the attitudes and percepts of an individual that had been built up over a lifetime of experience.

2. *Monopoly.* The smaller the number of alternative expectations held by the person, the greater their strength will be.

Bruner (1951) describes relevant experimental evidence and points out that though it is rather scanty, it is unambiguous (p. 129). He mentions the study in which less exposure was required for the recognition of words having to do with food when the subjects were given the instruction to find such words than when they were told to find food words *or* color words (Postman & Bruner, 1949).

Applying this determinant of expectancy strength to disability problems, we may compare the person whose expectation that others will look down upon him or her has full reign with the person in whom this expectation is shared with such others as "My disability may not matter to them"; "they may not even notice me"; "they may admire my accomplishments." In the former case, the expectation of devaluation will be confirmed by less evidence than in the second case, and also it will be more tenaciously retained in the face of contradictory information. This suggests that exposing the person to alternative and more positive attitudes toward disability facilitates psychological rehabilitation.

3. *Supporting context.* [3] A particular expectation is embedded in a larger system of supporting hypotheses and beliefs. The larger or more integrated the number of supporting hypotheses is, the stronger will be the expectation. Bruner cites one experiment in support of this—namely, that a reversed letter is less easily detected when it is embedded in a meaningful word than in a nonsense word. In the former case, the supporting context of a meaningful word strengthens the incorrect expectation that all letters are facing correctly (p. 129).

This determinant points up a crucial step in adjustment to disability—namely, that the overcoming of shame and inferiority may be facilitated when supporting hypotheses are eliminated. Examples of hypotheses that support disability as a sign of personal inferiority are:

1. My disability is a punishment.
2. It is important to conform, not to be different.
3. Most people are physically normal.
4. Normal physique is one of the most important values.
5. Physique is important for personal evaluation.
6. A deformed body leads to a deformed mind.

[3]Bruner's term for this is *cognitive consequences.*

7. No one will marry me.
8. I will be a burden on my family.
9. My deformity is repulsive.
10. I am less valuable because I can't get around (or see, or hear) as others can.

Which of these supporting beliefs can be eliminated is a challenging issue to consider. Some of them may be discarded or at least weakened through factual and scientific knowledge: for example, "most people are physically normal"; "a deformed body leads to a deformed mind." Others require basic changes in one's value system or outlook on life: for example, "normal physique is one of the most important values"; "it is important to conform, not to be different." Even the last hypothesis, that because of a disability one is less valuable than others or than one "would have been," a hypothesis regarded as almost axiomatic by many, is challengeable. Pearl Buck (1950) learned this through suffering for her retarded child, and meeting that suffering:

> So by this most sorrowful way I was compelled to tread, I learned respect and reverence for every human mind. It was my child who taught me to understand so clearly that all people are equal in their humanity and that all have the same human rights. None is to be considered less, as a human being, than any other, and each must be given his place and his safety in the world. [pp. 51–52][4]
>
> Parents may find comfort, I say, in knowing that their [retarded] children are not useless, but that their lives, limited as they are, are of great potential value to the human race. We learn as much from sorrow as from joy, as much from illness as from health, from handicap as from advantage—and indeed perhaps more. [p. 57]

And because Pearl Buck challenged hypothesis 10 and others, she was able to sincerely advise parents of atypical children:

> Be proud of your child, accept him as he is and do not heed the words and stares of those who know no better. This child has a meaning for you and for all children. You will find a joy you cannot now suspect in fulfilling his life for and with him. Lift up your head and go your appointed way. [p. 59]

4. *Motivational consequences.* Expectations satisfy the needs of a person in varying degrees. The more relevant the confirmation of an expectation may be to the satisfaction of needs, the stronger the expectation will be: it will be more readily aroused, more easily confirmed, and less readily repudiated.

---

[4]Reprinted by permission of Harold Ober Associates, Inc. Copyright, 1950, by Pearl S. Buck.

Bruner (1951) cites various lines of evidence substantiating the role of motivational support in strengthening expectations and also calls attention to the complexities involved (p. 130).

With regard to disability problems, this proposition leads to what has been called "secondary gains of disability," a theoretical position of significance. A disability may serve many purposes. The person may wish to insure continuing financial compensation that the disability provides, or may welcome the dependency facilitated by disability; the disability may satisfy a masochistic need for punishment, or may afford social sanction for avoiding feared competition. All these are motivational supports that lead a person to cling to expectations confirming the *disabling* aspects of his or her disability. The person will then resist value changes such as containing disability effects, subordinating physique, and evaluating in terms of asset values; these bring out the abilities and positive strivings of the person instead of the disabling aspects.

By the same analysis, the counterparts of these motivational supports should strengthen those expectations in which the disability is contained. Individuals who have a strong need for independence, for example, will on this account expect fewer limitations from their disability. They will also require less evidence to confirm their expectation and their hope that disability effects can be contained.

5. *Shared verification.* An expectation may be strengthened by virtue of its agreement with the expectations of other persons to whom the perceiver may turn.

Asch's classical minority-of-one experiment (1952, Chapter 16) supports this proposition. Subjects were asked to report verbally, in small groups, the relative lengths of lines whose dimensions were clearly different. In the main experiment, all the subjects but one had been instructed to oppose the critical subject by reporting incorrect judgments at certain points, leaving the critical subject a minority of one. In these circumstances, though the input information was clear-cut, the critical subject of each group became generally insecure and yielded to the incorrect majority in one-third of his or her responses. When, however, a partner was introduced who supported the critical subject by consistently giving the obviously correct responses, the majority effect was markedly weakened. In only one-eighth of their responses did the critical subjects yield. The presence of a single confirming voice served to strengthen the subject's conviction and enabled the subject to follow more consistently and independently his or her own sensory information. Festinger (1954) developed a theory of social-comparison processes based on hypotheses that stress the importance of shared verification in supporting one's judgments. One of the corollaries states that in the absence of both a physical and social comparison, subjective evaluations of opinions and abilities are unstable (unless, we add, asset evaluation is invoked; see pp. 178–183).

Applying the factor of shared verification to disability problems, we may conclude that if a person is surrounded by the judgment that a disability is a calamity that precludes all the important satisfactions in life, then it will be more difficult to change this expectation than if the person's social verifiers support a more moderate view.

Since expectations influenced by the self-concept carry so much weight in the perception of interpersonal relations, we may wonder how one ever manages to be on the right track, perceive the intentions of others correctly, and have harmony in social relations. Ichheiser (1949) has written a perceptive analysis of sources of misunderstandings in human relations with emphasis on cognitive factors. We wish now to discuss how understandings can and do take place even though in many social situations we see things in some measure as *we* are rather than purely as *they* are.

EXPECTATIONS AND SOCIAL UNDERSTANDING

Several factors lead the person, *p*, and the other person, *o*, to see things sufficiently alike to allow for mutual understanding. First, as we have noted previously, there is the role played by reality itself. Under clear-cut environmental conditions, expectations play a less dominant role. In some social situations the behavior of another has such a firm and indisputable structure of its own that it forces its own meaning on the interaction in spite of the fact that the self-concept and consequent expectations may be at variance with it. This may be more apt to occur after several exposures to the other's behavior just because expectations have a strong influence. The following example is illustrative of this point.

Mary, a young woman who required bed rest for several days during an illness, rejected the genuine attempts of her friends to help in meal preparation, caring for the children, and providing transportation to the doctor. Each offer was resisted until finally Mary said, "Everyone's been so nice to me. It makes me feel that they like me." Mary, who for a long while had regarded herself as unworthy, at first could only interpret the help as mere formality. It was only when the offers were repeatedly made over her protestations that she could accept the help for what it was, an expression of real friendship. The property of the behavior of those close to her finally impressed its own character on her perception.

There is another factor, also mentioned earlier, that enables people to understand each other. There are times when the person defines the self as an object of stimulation to others not in terms of the self-concept but on the basis of independent clues, such as information. Thus, when a thief is sure that a friend knows nothing of his or her irregularities, the thief may take not the self-image but the pretended self as the basis for interpreting social interaction. Likewise, when a person with a disability *knows* that the employer has an exaggerated notion of the limitations of disability, failure to be promoted is likely to be interpreted accordingly rather than in terms of the self-concept.

Moreover, satisfactory interpersonal relationships need not require identity of perception between the person p, and the other person o. In many situations, p's self-picture as an object of stimulation may sufficiently match o's picture of p to permit harmonious interpretations. For example, o may agree to some extent with p's notions regarding p's capability. It is also possible for p to misinterpret o up to a certain point and still manage well together. Suppose p senses an annoyance in o that is mistakenly attributed to fatigue. Although o may truly be annoyed, the source of the annoyance may be entirely different—displeasure with something p did, for example. Yet both may be able to accept the irritation without delving further.

Finally, social interaction is a process that unfolds in the give-and-take between the participating members. This means that the reality—that is, what actually occurs—is not charted independently of the person's wishes, fears, and expectations but to some extent is actually shaped by them. In this way not only the reality *as perceived* but the reality *as is* may be made to fit the person's expectations and self-concept. When Goldman (1947) became aware of this he was overwhelmed with the implications:

> I've discovered something else: the gym teacher was embarrassed when he began to talk to me today. It was almost as if he felt the shame that he expected me to feel. But when he saw that I was not ashamed, his embarrassment disappeared. Is that a manifestation of a kind of power that human beings hold over each other? His attitude was in *my* control, it was *I*, not *he*, who determined what that attitude toward me should be. What kind of power is that? How far can one use it? What is its source? [pp. 94–95][5]

Russell (1949) also began to realize that "the only way I could expect to feel at ease with them [people] was if they felt at ease with me, and the only way for them to feel that way was for me to be at ease with myself" (p. 150). And once feeling at ease, he was able to

[5]Reprinted with permission of Macmillan Publishing, Inc., from *Even the night*, by R. L. Goldman. Copyright 1947, and renewed 1975, by Raymond Leslie Goldman.

establish social techniques that put others at ease. Let us compare the following two situations involving his hooks, the first when he was beset with embarrassment and shame, the second when he felt comfortable about his hooks and thought of them as "working hands."

The scene is Russell's first homecoming since his injury. He has just deplaned:

> When I finally got off I carried my bag in one hook and hid the other in my pocket. I hoped they [those meeting him] wouldn't notice the one with the bag right away. I tried to keep it out of sight, but the bag kept bumping against my legs.
>
> Rita [his sweetheart] spotted me first. She shouted and waved at me. Then mother and Fred [a sailor friend] began doing the same. My first impulse was to wave back at them. Then I realized how grotesque that would be. I kept the hook in my pocket. It was only a hundred yards to where they were standing, but it seemed like I was on one of those twenty-five-mile marches. And with every step I became more uncertain, more jittery, more scared. I wanted to go straight back to the hospital.
>
> Mother was the first to reach me. She folded me in her arms. "Darling! It's wonderful to have you back!"
>
> I kissed her. I started to put my arms around her. I caught myself just in time.
>
> She pushed me away from her and looked me over. "My, but you look fine!" she said. I noticed she was careful to avoid where my hands had been.
>
> Now Rita snuggled up to me. She gave me a long, tender kiss. I had a hard job not taking her in my arms. I didn't dare. It might ruin everything. Imagine having those hard, cold claws biting into your back! I could feel a shiver run through her body as she pressed against me. I knew that as soon as she was alone she'd let herself go. . . .
>
> All during the ride to Cambridge I could sense Rita and mother stealing glances at the hooks. I felt like shaking them in their faces and shouting, "Here! Take a good look at them! Fascinating, aren't they?"
>
> I was sitting next to Fred. He was driving. All the time he kept looking down at his hands guiltily as though he'd stolen something. That made me freeze up even more. I couldn't keep my eyes off the wheel and he kept taking one hand off it and sticking it in his pocket as if to hide it. [pp. 129–131][6]

The second scene is after Russell was discharged from the hospital. He is thinking about different ways to put people at ease when they meet him and his hooks for the first time:

[6]Reprinted by permission of Farrar, Straus & Giroux, Inc. From *Victory in my hands* by H. Russell & V. Rosen. Copyright 1949 by Harold Russell & Victor Rosen. Copyright renewed © 1976 by Harold Russell.

First of all, I found it was extremely important to shove my hook out at a person when I met him, just as if I were shaking hands with him. That had the psychological effect of telling him I wasn't worrying about my hooks, so why should he? Of course, I knew that most people dreaded gripping that cold hunk of steel the first time and I could hardly blame them, so I was always careful to make that first handshake as casual, informal and friendly as possible.

Then there was the cigaret gag. That was invariably good for a laugh. Whenever I'd walk into a restaurant, bar, or party I'd whip out a pack of butts, open it ostentatiously, take one, light it and sit back puffing on it contentedly. That almost always attracted attention. People would stare and I could almost hear them saying, My! Isn't it wonderful what he can do with a pair of hooks? Whenever anyone commented on this accomplishment I'd smile and say, "There's one thing I never have to worry about. That's burning my fingers." Corny, I know, but a sure ice-breaker. . . .

It wasn't long before my plan paid off. I soon found people were taking me and my hooks for granted. There would be that first shocked moment of confusion and bewilderment. Then I'd throw my hook out, we'd shake, I'd pull one of my gags and everybody would laugh. From then on everything would go smoothly. [pp. 166–167]

The difference between these two episodes has snowballing effects. In the first, Russell felt ashamed and expected others to be repelled and to show pity. He behaved accordingly, guiltily hiding his hooks, and so forth. And the events that followed bore out his expectations. Others did feel embarrassed; others did shy away from his hooks. In the second, Russell had made important headway in accepting his disability. He had already found out that he could talk and think about his disability without feeling self-conscious or ashamed. Believing this, he could expect others to begin to accept his hooks; it thus made sense for him to try to put others at ease. And again the events that followed bore out his expectations. People began to take his hooks for granted. In both episodes, the social reality fulfilled Russell's expectations *as much because Russell's behavior helped form that reality as because he was set to interpret the behavior of others in certain ways.*

We should stress once again that though expectations and self-regard have such a directive role, they do not control all social reality. Russell, no matter how good he felt about himself, perceived "that first shocked moment of confusion and bewilderment," for example.

This discussion of expectations and social reality brings us to several comments regarding adjustive relationships between a person with a disability and others. If, as there is a good reason to believe, the so-called nondisabled hold both positive and negative attitudes toward persons with disability, the positive attitudes will more readily be aroused when one accepts one's own disability and believes that others can accept it too.

It may happen that a well-adjusted person, in not looking for rejection, may not see the rejection that actually exists. But this unawareness need not be unfortunate. As Ichheiser (1949) has put it, it is highly probable that certain illusions possess a positive function and value. It remains a question whether all human relations would always operate more smoothly or with greater satisfaction if they were altogether free of illusions. In not seeing the rejection, the person may behave in ways more attuned to the positive chord in another and thus fan the "pilot light of the flame of love." Should the rejection be so strong as to eventually come through, the person's hurt would have a different quality from that which is heaped upon self-rejection. It might be a hurt of sorrow that others are unjust or do not understand, or that certain activities and relationships are foreclosed, but it would not be a hurt that, indeed, the self warrants rejection. At the end of his life story Russell (1949) states:

> People like to feel sorry for me. I suppose that's only natural, too. Once it used to bother me but it doesn't any more. It isn't important now what or how anyone feels about my being without hands. The only thing that matters is that I've learned to live without them and that I have mastered my handicap, instead of letting it master me. [pp. 278–279]

Expectations concerning the attitudes of others toward oneself are crucial in the perception of those attitudes. To go one step further, the self-concept is crucial in forming those expectations. The self-concept is psychologically of such great importance that it can hardly be overstressed, though to be sure other factors, such as *environmental conditions* and the *actual attitudes and behavior of others*, must not be understressed.

In the next chapter interpersonal relationships that are common and frequently disturbing between a person with a disability and others are examined with a view toward reducing the source of disturbance and increasing the potential for satisfaction. Recommendations are primarily focused on the other person, that is, on the outsider.

Chapter 13
Grievances and Gratifications in Everyday Relationships

People with disabilities frequently refer to ordinary incidents that arise with the nondisabled. They describe situations involving curiosity, staring, help, sympathy, devaluating pity, being treated differently, social participation, and taunting (Goffman, 1963). There is hardly an autobiography that does not bring up several of these incidents, sometimes as positive and sometimes as negative experiences. It is important to uncover psychological conditions that determine the acceptance or rejection of such relationships, for it is an impossible task to provide recommendations for each and every concrete social act that may arise.

Research has shown that in *stranger relationships* between people with and without disabilities, discomfort arises on both sides. In a series of experiments by Kleck and his associates, physically normal subjects, when interacting with a person with an apparent disability as compared to an ordinary-appearing person, generally behaved less comfortably and admitted feeling less comfortable in the situation (Kleck, 1966; Kleck, Ono, & Hastorf, 1966; Kleck, 1968a; Kleck, 1969). A parallel experiment showed greater discomfort on the part of persons with a disability when interacting with a physically normal person than with a person who had a disability (Comer & Piliavin, 1972).

Research has also shown that reducing the novelty of seeing a person with unusual physical characteristics reduces discomfort. This was nicely demonstrated in an experiment in which prior exposure to such a person through a one-way mirror where staring was permissible reduced subsequent discomfort when talking with that person (Langer et al., 1976). The positive effect of reducing novelty was also seen in one of Kleck's experiments (1969) in which the greater physical distance originally maintained by subjects between themselves and a person using a wheelchair as compared to an able-bodied person disappeared in the second session. Reducing strangeness under nonthreatening conditions can generally be expected to reduce discomfort.

The discussion that follows deals with friendship relationships as well as interactions between strangers. It draws heavily upon the research of Dembo and her associates (Dembo, Leviton, & Wright, 1956; 1975; Ladieu, Hanfmann, & Dembo, 1947; White, Wright, & Dembo 1948; Ladieu, Adler, & Dembo, 1948). The research will here be referred to as the Dembo study. The basic method of this study was an interview, usually lasting about an hour and a half, aimed at uncovering the kinds of difficulties existing in the relationships between persons with and without disabilities. The subjects were 177 adults with visible disabilities and 65 nondisabled adults. Of those with disabilities, 100 had arm or leg amputations, 40 had facial disfigurement, and the remainder were distributed among such orthopedic disabilities as poliomyelitis, transverse myelitis, osteomyelitis, and congenital deformities.

THE PROBLEM OF CURIOSITY AND DISCUSSION OF THE DISABILITY

The investigators of the problem of curiosity regarding a disability point out that a disability as a characteristic and inseparable part of the body may be felt by the person with the disability to be a private matter (White, Wright, & Dembo, 1948). Yet its visibility makes it known to anyone whom the person meets. A visible disability differs from many other personal matters in that anyone can deal with it regardless of the wish of the person; anyone can stare at the disability or ask questions about it and in this way communicate one's feelings about the disability to the person. It is its visibility that makes intrusion easier, an intrusion that the person may feel powerless to control or at best able to control only by how one reacts and handles the situation.

The subjects of the Dembo study rejected curiosity about their disability for several reasons: They viewed reminders of painful disability-connected memories as unwelcome and expressed a desire to keep their disability private. They spoke of the fear of being considered different, and outright resentment of morbid curiosity. At the same time, it became clear that the evaluation of communication about the disability was dependent on the circumstances. Eighty-four percent of the subjects neither fully accepted nor fully rejected questioning and talking about the disability with nondisabled persons. Even staring, though generally rejected, was still considered all right in certain circumstances by one-third of the subjects—for example, when it did not persist.

Conditions Underlying Evaluation

Several important factors emerged as contributing to the reaction of the person with a disability to staring, questions about one's disability, and one's willingness to discuss it.

Self-regard was discussed at length in connection with the interpretation of the behavior of another toward the self (Chapter 12). There it is pointed out that when the person with a disability has a well-balanced, accepting attitude toward the disability, the person is more likely to feel that others question and stare because they simply are wondering—how he or she gets along, how the prosthesis works. If, however, the person views the disability as devaluating, the curiosity of others will be strongly rejected as indicating aversion and pity. The person is also likely to refrain from referring to his or her disability because of the feeling that it is something to be ashamed of, a mark of inferiority, a skeleton to be hidden. Underlying the different reactions in the two cases is the fact that the self-concept defines the kind of person one is as an "object" of stimulation to others.

There is also the factor of *situational context* that contributes to the person's reaction. The subjects sometimes urged that others should not talk about the disability unless it comes up naturally, meaning that reference to the disability should be part of a broader conversation or should arise out of the demands of the situation. Such references are less likely to be felt as an intrusion into privacy. They are also less likely to be felt as emphasizing the disability as such, but rather may be seen as secondary to the purpose of the broader context. The peculiarly distasteful experience of being stared at can be partially attributed to the fact that it is not seen as emerging from a situational context; instead it is purely an expression of the needs of the onlooker. Staring often goes on in an extremely unstructured situation, so unstructured that it lacks a situational context. Under such ambiguous conditions the worst anxieties of the person may come to the surface and determine the nature of perception. Should "extended looking" be required by the situation, as when a doctor examines a wound, the activity is no longer thought of as staring.

Besides the situational context, there is also a *personal context* representing the more lasting relationship between two persons. This accounts for the marked tendency on the part of persons with disabilities to make a distinction in favor of talking about the disability with friends or family members rather than with strangers. People with a disability recognize that their friends generally see them as persons whose personal qualities are more important than bodily appearance. They have less fear that "it is not I but my disability" that is uppermost in the other person's mind. Staring on the part of strangers represents a grossly impersonal context. The very act of talking is to some degree symbolic of a human relationship, but one does not ordinarily stare at another person. One does not talk to a monkey in a zoo or to a freak in a sideshow—one only stares. As a result, the relationship is easily perceived as one of a person (the non-disabled) to an object—a curiosity.

The wish to be and to appear to be well adjusted, which may lead to strong resistance against talking about the disability, sometimes may act to diminish that resistance. The subjects often brought out their wish to be considered "normal" and especially the wish to prove that they were not defeated by their disability. Trying not to be bothered by the curiosity of others is a way to prove that one is not sensitive, that one is not ashamed, that the disability did not make one maladjusted. Thus, along with the feeling of being hurt that questioning and staring may produce, there is the struggle itself against this feeling. The person will, however, restrict the discussion to a superficial level of factual information and to casual feelings. If the conversation is carried on with an understanding person, the experience may make it possible for the person with the disability to discover that talking about the disability was not nearly as difficult as had been thought. In this way, even a superficial level of discussion may provide an opening wedge for change in the meaning of disability.

There are indications that the person *has a desire to be understood,* that the person needs and wants to talk about one's disability with those with whom one feels secure and in situations that enhance one's security. The person wants to talk because of a basic wish to be accepted as one really is, with actual needs and feelings, and not as one appears to be on the surface. The person may also feel a need for reassurance that he or she is worthy as a person or that one's attitudes and behavior toward others are justified. The person may feel a need to recognize more clearly how the disability has affected his or her life and how to manage more satisfactorily. However, it may be difficult for the person to express this need, for at the same time the wish to be nondisabled and to be treated as such may be overpowering. Moreover, those with whom the person is interacting may also feel uncomfortable and embarrassed in regard to the disability. There is thus a pretense on both sides; both try to act as though the disability did not exist.

This pretense causes an emotional strain, both in the person with the disability and in his or her associates. An estrangement between the one who has the disability and others may result, for when feelings are not shared, when much is not said but is guessed at and misinterpreted, the distance grows and the relationship suffers. Equally disturbing in the persistent "as if" behavior is the feeling that the person with a disability is only seemingly accepted—that is, that he or she is not really accepted at all. Realization of the impracticability of ignoring the disability and of the negative consequences of attempting to do so removes a large barrier to communicating about the disability.

The conditions that underlie the person's evaluation of curiosity and talking about the disability affect, of course, the manner in which the person actually meets the reality of such communication. It is the management that guides the social interaction and therefore may serve to reduce or increase interpersonal tensions.

Management by the Recipient

A person with a disability, meeting time and again the questioning and staring of others, gradually develops ways of coping with such situations. The manner of approach will depend partly on the person's general evaluation of the situation and partly on the social skills he or she has developed in the course of trying out different techniques. Some tactics appear satisfying; the person feels comfortable in their use, and they seem to be effective in their results. Other tactics leave the person disturbed, and he or she may continue to brood about the incident. The following scenes from autobiographical accounts demonstrate commonly used coping techniques. They have been grouped according to three general evaluations of the situation in which the other person is felt to be an intruder. In the first situation, attacking the offender, the person with the disability regards the intruder as a fatuous boor and wants above all to retaliate, if necessary by utilizing the disability in the attack. In the second, excluding the disability from the situation, the recipient is dominated by an imperative need to eradicate the disability as a socially real fact.

And in the third, minimizing the disability and preserving the relationship, the recipient wishes to maintain communication about the disability as well as the social relationship at a congenial level. There are other psychological situations and ways of handling them, but these will suffice to give an appreciation of ways of coping with the situation and their effectiveness in social situations that are felt to be threatening.

· *Attacking the Offender.* The other person, usually a stranger, is seen as being idly or morbidly curious and therefore really interested not in the recipient personally but only in the disability. Sometimes the recipient senses (correctly or not) that the other pries in the hope of savoring a lurid tale and thereby aggrandizing himself or herself at the expense of the recipient. In any event, the reaction to the intruder is a deeply negative one; the recipient wishes to retaliate in a cutting manner and cause the other person to appear foolish. This is accomplished with the techniques, deftly maneuvered, of biting sarcasm and dramatic prevarication.

Biting sarcasm is illustrated in the following exchange between a "snoopy old biddy" and Louise, a young college graduate who lost a leg in childhood and uses crutches to get about:

> "My poor girl, I see you've lost your leg."
> That's the opportunity for the *touche*, "How careless of me!" [Baker, 1946, p. 97]

Friends, too, can "ask for it." In the following sample, the recipient is the mother of Noreen, a young lady convalescing from polio:

> One day one of mother's friends telephoned to inquire about me.
> "How is she?" he asked.
> "Why, she is just fine," Mother said. "She is getting stronger, and we think she will be coming home soon [from the hospital]."
> "Yes," he insisted, "but how *is* she? I mean is she really all right?"
> "Why, of course," Mother said. "She will be just fine!"
> "You don't understand me," he urged. "I mean, well, has she slipped a little? Does she think clearly? Does she remember everything?"
> "Oh!" my mother said, and when she recovered, "Oh no—she has dreams! And she doesn't remember everything either, she can't remember where she put her red printed scarf that she wore last summer!" [Linduska, 1947, p. 189][1]

Dramatic prevarication as a plan of attack was also exploited by

---

[1] Reprinted by permission of Farrar, Straus & Giroux, Inc. From *My polio past* by N. Linduska. Copyright © 1947, 1974 by Noreen Linduska.

Louise, above. Eventually she became quite cavalier about satisfying the curiosity of intruders with imaginatively exciting tales:

> One of my choicest little epics was the heroic account of a swooping venture on skis. Down a precipitous mountainside I *slalomed,* a sick baby in my arms, only to collapse at the doctor's door, the infant saved, but my poor right leg frozen stiff as a poker. It was so completely refrigerated, in fact, that the doctor, without administering so much as a whiff of anesthetic, chipped it off with an ice pick.
>
> Even unrehearsed repartee came easily. The flapping-eared recipient of the latter fancy cheerfully swallowed the hook, and was all agape for the line and sinker. How did it happen that my left leg was so providentially spared, she wanted to know, not satisfied with what I already regarded as a very generous slice of my imagination.
>
> "Well, I've been educated about weather," I said. "Me, I'm a Norska from Oslo. I was smart enough to anticipate chilblains. I decided I'd preserve at least one leg. Owed it to myself, I figured. I skied on only one foot, after pinning up my spare in a blanket."
>
> "Well, I do declare!" The hypnotized listener didn't bat an eyelash. [Baker, 1946, pp. 92–93][2]

· *Excluding the Disability from the Situation.* In this case, the person with the disability wants above all to avoid reference to the disability. He or she may handle the challenge, not by attacking the intruder, but by excluding the disability from the situation. This is accomplished by what we have called the ostrich reaction and redirecting the interaction course.

The ostrich reaction is the most direct expression of the need to exclude the disability by escaping from the situation. Such literal behavior is more characteristic of children; not infrequently the child runs out of the room or buries his or her face in the mother's lap. Henry Viscardi, dwarfed through congenital deformity of his legs, offers the following example:

> . . . My mother took me home on a street car. It was open on the sides and had high steps. She had to lift me up onto the straw seat, then she got in. I sat with my boots straight out in front of me but they did not reach the edge of the seat. Across the aisle a woman in an orange coat nudged the woman next to her and pointed at me. I held my mother's hand tight. Then I saw that everybody on the street car was looking. My mother put her arm around me and I hid my face next to her coat. I wanted to run away from all those people. [Viscardi, 1952, 10][3]

[2]Reprinted from *Out on a limb,* by L. Baker. New York: McGraw-Hill, 1946. By permission of Blassingame, McCauley, & Wood.
[3]Reprinted from *A man's stature* by H. Viscardi, Jr., 1952. By permission of Paul S. Eriksson, Pubs.

The direct blocking out of the disagreeable is less readily open to an adult. It appears too childish and exposes too blatantly the personal hurt that an adult generally also wishes to keep private. The adult's efforts to escape the situation, therefore, take more subtle form. The adult recipient may return an icy stare that freezes the atmosphere. Viscardi, as a college student less than four feet tall, describes his more adult management of staring, staring that he encountered day after day after day:

> There were the thick-skinned ones, who stared like hill people come down to see a traveling show. There were the paper-peekers, the furtive kind who would withdraw blushing if you caught them at it. There were the pitying ones, whose tongue clickings could almost be heard after they had passed you. But even worse, there were the chatterers, whose every remark might as well have been "How do you do, poor boy?" They said it with their eyes and their manners and their tone of voice.
>
> I had a standard defense—a cold stare. Thus anesthetized against my fellow man, I could contend with the basic problem—getting in and out of the subway alive. [Viscardi, 1952, p. 70]

The person with a disability may lower his or her eyes and look past the intruder and hate the source of this anguish. Goldman, lame from polio, recalls an incident in his adolescence:

> I stand in the doorway to a restaurant, as yet unnoticed, my heart sinking, my body filling with a great tumor of anguish. The sensation is akin to both swelling and shrinking. I wish that I would shrivel away to nothing, like a paper curling to ashes in the grate, or that I would burst with the swelling.
>
> People! Eyes! Eyes!
>
> Something in the back of my mind moans, O God, O God, O God! I lash my courage: *Enter! Get it done and over with! What the hell? What's the difference? The hell with 'em!* I want to be bitter, get mad, put the blame on them—those people sitting there with eyes. I want to hate them so that I won't care what they think.
>
> I press my teeth together. I clench my fists. Every muscle of my body tightens and I enter with my head up. I walk down the aisle between the rows of tables, looking neither to left nor right.
>
> But you need not see eyes; you can feel them. Even when you know that you are past them and they are behind you, they reach out with something that touches you.
>
> The aisle is miles and miles in length but at last I reach my table and seat myself. I relax. There is a light dew of sweat on my face. I'll be all right in a minute. The tablecloth is long, my legs are under the table. Now to order, eat, and enjoy a hard-earned meal. I don't want to look

too far ahead. After a while I must get up and walk out again. [Goldman, 1947, pp. 65–66][4]

In *redirecting the interaction course,* one tries to escape the unpleasantly intrusive question by stopping it before it is uttered and then taking control of the conversation. Louise, with one leg amputated, was a frequent target of the curiosity of others. She developed a manner that said in effect, "I know what you're thinking, but keep it there" (Baker, 1946, p. 91)

And when an intruder has already made some headway, the recipient is sometimes able to ignore it with a matter-of-fact, otherwise empty comment that reveals nothing of the self but serves to rechannel the interaction to nondisturbing areas. This is seen in the following interchange between Frances, a college girl with impaired hearing who is frightened of deafness, and Victorine, a casual acquaintance:

"Why don't you try a chiropractor?" she [Victorine] asked me, chewing corned beef, giving no slightest indication that she was about to knock the bottom out of my world. "Dr. Fletcher told me he's curing one of his patients of deafness."

My heart skittered, in panic, against my ribs. What did she mean?

"My dad's deaf," she revealed. "I can spot a deaf person anywhere. That soft voice of yours. And that trick of letting your sentences trail off—not finishing them. Dad does that all the time."

The bottom fell out of my world. What was she saying? That she spotted me for a deaf person? That it was perfectly plain to anyone that I didn't hear well? That wasn't so. It couldn't be so. Nobody could possibly guess I didn't hear well; I had everybody bluffed. Besides, I could hear all right. Nobody could call me a deaf person. Nobody with long spindle legs and a bad complexion and fuzzy yellow hair that looked as if she never brushed it.

My head spun with fury. Did I trail my sentences? I did, often. Often I'd see, from the expression on another person's face, that I was talking on the wrong track, that I'd misheard something. . . .

"Dad's wonderful," Victorine was saying. "He can't hear thunder without an earphone and not very much even with an earphone, but he keeps trying. He's got our dining-room table and his favorite chair in the living-room all wired up for sound; you can't move without tripping over electric wires and storage batteries. Just lately one of the hearing-aid companies came out with a portable model that he can carry around in a black box. It weighs . . . [Victorine continued to ramble

[4]Reprinted with permission of Macmillan Publishing Co., Inc., from *Even the night,* by R. L. Goldman. Copyright 1947, and renewed 1975, by Raymond Leslie Goldman.

on in this fashion, oblivious of the panic she had created. Finally, Frances, with a forced indifference, interrupts.]

"Really? We'd better be getting back for the Math exam," I said freezingly. [Warfield, 1948, pp. 44–45].[5]

· *Minimizing the Disability and Preserving the Relationship.* There is also the situation in which the recipient accepts the disability as a social fact but wishes to moderate the intensity of involvement with it. Instead of a serious concern centering around the disability, the desire is to keep the discussion at a superficial level. At the same time, not feeling any ill will toward the intruder, the recipient wishes to maintain a congenial relationship. This may be accomplished through the techniques of good-natured levity and superficial discourse.

Good natured levity is the approach used by some persons who build up a repertoire of light remarks that can be used in appropriate settings. Russell (1949) found that strangers more quickly took him and his hooks for granted after some such icebreaker. He might make a crack about how the one thing he could not do with his hooks was to pick up a check at a restaurant, for example. In providing a light touch, such remarks set the social climate. They say, in effect, "I am not disturbed by my disability. So you may feel comfortable about it too, and we can go on to other things from here."

Superficial discourse is shown in the following conversation between two young teenagers, Criddle who recently lost his sight in a childhood accident, and Red, his friend:

> "What's it like to be blind?" Red asked.
> "How do I know?" I said, still irritated by the word. "I ain't blind. I just got bad eyes, that's all."
> "That's what I mean," he placated. "What's it like?"
> "It ain't like nothing. You just can't see, that's all."
> "Does it hurt?"
> "Nah, you bump your shins sometimes, and that hurts, that's all."
> "Is everything dark?"
> Knowing Red was fascinated by my blindness, I exploited the opportunity, and drew on what mother had said: "It's like looking through a frosted glass, like we have in our bathroom only not so frosted. Your ears, smell, and touch make up for your eyes."
> "You mean you can see with your ears?"
> "No, of course not. You just hear better, that's all."

[5]Reprinted with permission from *Cotton in my ears* by F. Warfield. New York: Viking Press, 1948.

"And smell better?"
"Sure." [Criddle, 1953, pp. 25–26][6]

Criddle avoided talking about the deeper and more personal meanings of blindness by brushing off any insinuation that he is seriously handicapped. He effectively guided the conversation to moderate inconveniences and at the same time maintained a comfortable relationship with his friend.

Again, a word about stranger relationships. If the person with a disability does nothing, the stranger has little to respond to except the disability, and may gawk like a spectator at a side show. However, the person with a disability can take the initiative and make a casual comment, for example about the weather, that may provide the social lubricant for an inoffensive and brief interchange. The person with a disability can also respond to a question about one's disability by briefly providing information to allay curiosity. One young woman reported that she found it helpful simply to reply: "I had cancer when I was eight years old and my leg was amputated at that time" [personal communication]. The air was cleared, and no further questions were asked.

· *Situations Not Requiring Social Tactics.* Thus far we have analyzed situations in which the questioner is felt to intrude, actually or potentially, into the privacy of the recipient. Sometimes, however, communication about the disability does not threaten privacy. The attitude toward the disability may be so matter-of-fact on both sides that the discussion can arise very naturally. This occurred during Karen's first day at kindergarten. Around the sandbox, Lucy, a schoolmate, asked Karen if her braces were broken at her knees. "Karen explained that her braces had joints where her legs had joints so she could move right, and then added very matter-of-factly, 'I have cerebral palsy, you know. I'm a spastic. Are you hungry? I am' " (Killilea, 1952, p. 114).[7]

Also, as discussed earlier, there are times when the person with the disability needs and wishes to talk about the disability. Sometimes the person may introduce the topic to someone close, to a therapist, or more rarely, to a stranger. Sometimes it is the situation that brings up the disability. When the person wishes to talk and the listener is

[6]Reprinted with permission from *Love is not blind*, by R. Criddle. New York: Norton, 1953.
[7]Reprinted with permission from *Karen* by Marie Killilea. © 1952 by Marie Lyons Killilea. Published by Prentice-Hall, Inc., Englewood Cliffs, New Jersey 07632.

understanding, discussion about the disability may continue without special maneuvering on the part of the recipient. Russell Criddle offers an example of this. He had been in a "fight to the death" at his high school with Mike, a boy who had been taunting him relentlessly about his blindness (see pp. 331–332 for incident). The next day, certain that he would be expelled, Criddle was called into the principal's office. At first he was sullen and would not participate in the conversation. Then the principal said something that struck a sympathetic chord and Criddle poured out what had long been kept within him. The principal said:

> . . . "You have a good head, Russell, and you must learn to keep it. People like Mike and me can afford to lose theirs once in a while, but a man that is blind needs to keep his. Society will not tolerate normality from you; you will either have to be nearly perfect or completely bad."
> "I know," I said. "I expected to be expelled."
> He seemed surprised at this. There was real curiosity in his voice as he asked, "You did? Why?"
> "People pity me," I answered, "and it hurts them. They want me to go away all the time. They're afraid of blindness," I went on, "and they think I feel afraid all the time, like they think they would be if they were like me. It's because they think I'm scared that they think I'm dumb. People are always dumb when they are scared, that's why people can't use their intelligence when they think about me, and want to help me. They're scared of blindness. That's why Mike kept hurting me, because he was afraid of me. People, most of them, hurt people they are afraid of." [Criddle: 1953, p. 104][8]

And the conversation that continued was good and full and central. Social tactics had no place, for in this situation Criddle had nothing to guard.

· *The Special Problem of Curiosity in Children.* Many social forms have emerged because they permit or even give rise to congenial interpersonal relationships. Children have to learn these social expressions of politeness and to regard them as logical, natural, or helpful toward comfortable relationships among people. For example, the adult ordinarily greets a visitor. A child, however, may just as naturally merely glance at the guest and turn away to immediate interests with nary a gesture of recognition or welcome. To the adult this behavior may appear so incongruous that it seems amusing, or it may be taken as downright rudeness or a sign of poor breeding. In any case, the child has to learn that greeting a visitor is the usual way

[8]Reprinted from *Love is not blind,* by R. Criddle. New York: Norton, 1953. Reprinted with permission.

of making the visitor feel welcome. Similarly, there are social forms that regulate the manner of satisfying one's curiosity. Although, as we have seen, adults often overstep accepted propriety, children, albeit unwittingly, probably do so more frequently and more openly. It is only gradually that they learn to refrain from asking people directly about their disability, to wait until a person is out of earshot before asking the mother questions, to keep from staring and pointing, and so on.

To some persons the frank curiosity of children is not markedly disturbing. They feel that it is a natural expression of interest, void of malice, and therefore should be responded to in a matter-of-fact and friendly way even though one may not have chosen to engage in the transaction. The story is told of an elderly woman whose chin trembled. When asked by a small child why her chin went up and down like that she simply replied, "Well, you know, I have something that makes my chin go like that." The child looked some more and then passed on to other things (Dembo, Leviton, & Wright, 1956, p. 50). To other persons, children remain a constant threat. If the person believes or tries to believe that his or her disability is not very noticeable, it is all the more disturbing when a child innocently calls attention to it. Not only do young children barge in, but they are so preoccupied with their own curiosity that they can remain insensitive to the other person's discomfort. Even though the recipient may appreciate that the curiosity of the child is natural, he or she may at the same time feel confused, embarrassed, and resentful.

It is well for individuals who will inevitably face the curiosity of children to think over how to meet it. In thinking it over, in talking with others about their reactions, they may become aware that their own feelings about their disability and self-regard are among the more important factors in how one reacts to the curiosity of others.

· *Indicated Research.* Clearly, further research is needed to determine which of the strategies discussed above are most appropriate to particular situations and to the needs of the recipient. A classical investigation of a related problem exemplifies one fruitful approach to problems of management of social tensions in general (Citron, Chein, & Harding, 1950 pp. 125–126). The study dealt with the handling of antiminority prejudice through appropriate counteracting retorts by a bystander. In setting up the experiment, the investigators decided that:

The study would concentrate on the behavior of the answerer rather than on the behavior of the bigot or the object of the bigot's attack.

An ideal answer should meet the following criteria: Its effect on the bigot should be to dissuade him or her from expressing his prejudice in public. It should raise the personal morale of the minority group member and of the answerer. It should minimize in the bystanders any increase in prejudice that might have resulted from the bigot's remarks, and should encourage potential answerers in the audience to become actual answerers in the future. Because of practical considerations, an answer must be made in a few words, simply expressed, suitable for a variety of incidents, and not demanding histrionic skill.

During the exploratory phases of the research, many types of answers that appeared promising with respect to the criteria above were tried out in a number of different situations. Two answers were selected for experimental study. These were the American Tradition argument, which stressed such values as fair play and the fact that this nation was built by all races and creeds, and the Individual Differences argument, which stressed that one should not generalize from one or two cases. In the main experiment, each answer was presented half the time with high emotion and half the time in a calm manner. This yielded four types of counterargument.

The incident selected for the experiment involved a public situation in which one of the characters in the scene managed unintentionally to offend one of the other characters, who in turn insulted the ethnic group to which the first person belonged. A bystander challenges this.

The incident was presented to the subjects as a dramatic skit. The script for the incident with the American Tradition counterargument follows:

The scene is an employment bureau in which several men are seated waiting to be interviewed, some filling out application forms, some smoking and chatting:

SECRETARY: "Who is next?"
    (Two men stand up and exclaim simultaneously.)
GOLDSTEIN AND JONES: "I am."
SECRETARY: "Well, I don't know for sure who is next. It's hard to tell with so many fellows coming and going. Suppose this gentleman (pointing) comes in now, and another interviewer will be ready for you in a minute. May I have your name, please?"
GOLDSTEIN: "My name is Harry Goldstein."
SECRETARY: "This way, please, Mr. Goldstein."
    (Goldstein exits with secretary. The other man turns to resume his seat and exclaims disgustedly so that the others cannot help hearing him.)
JONES: "He was not next! Goldstein, huh? Another Jew who can't wait

his turn. These Jews are all alike. Who do they think they are anyway?" (Mutters.)

American Tradition counterargument:

BYSTANDER: "Take it easy, fellow. I wouldn't say that if I were you. We
don't want that kind of talk in America."

JONES: "Ah-h . . . these Jews are always trying to get away with something. Pushing ahead. . . ."

BYSTANDER: "That's no way to talk. What kind of country would we
have if we didn't stick together? We'd be easy suckers for someone
to make trouble."

JONES: "What business is it of yours?"

BYSTANDER: "I'm telling you it's unfair to pick on the Jews, or any other
group, for that matter. Everybody in America should get the same
square deal."

JONES: "Why are you so worried about the Jews?"

BYSTANDER: "It's not just the Jews I'm worried about. It's the danger
of that kind of talk to our democracy that worries me. This country
is made up of all races and religions and it's up to us to see to it that
they all get an even break."

(Secretary returns and speaks to Jones.)

SECRETARY: "It's your turn now—may I have your name?"

JONES: "My name is Jones, Edward Jones."

SECRETARY: "All right, Mr. Jones. Please follow me."

(Exit Secretary and Jones.)

Attitudes toward Jews measured after the play were compared with
those expressed on the same questionnaire previous to the counter-
arguments.

Of the four types of answers presented in the dramatic skits two
showed a significant net reduction in prejudice. These two were the
American Tradition argument made in a calm, quiet manner, and
the Individual Differences argument made in an excited, militant
manner. Because audiences prefer a calm handling of the situation,
the investigators recommend the former.

Notice that the investigators had first to decide on the criteria
for an ideal answer before they could select possible answers for experimentation and tests for their effectiveness. Likewise, in curiosity
research one would have to make explicit what the recipient might
strive to accomplish in a given interaction and the different techniques whereby this might be realized. As we have indicated, if the
recipient is mainly geared to punish the intruder, certain behaviors
will make sense; if the desire above all is to exclude the disability,
other behavior will be more effective; if the main goal is to preserve
the relationship, another approach may be indicated; and if the wish
is to affect the attitudes of others positively, still other means may

be in order. Work in the area of assertiveness is relevant here (Galassi & Galassi, 1978). Social skills or their lack are the practical expression of the meaning of a social relationship as determined by events in the environment and events within the person. The following chapter describes some approaches to training in this important area.

Recommendations

To avoid being hurt by the other person and to make communication possible when desired, the subjects of the Dembo study gave recommendations to the nondisabled. In different ways they expressed the following rules (White, Wright, & Dembo, 1948):

1. Don't talk about it unless the person with the disability brings it up.
2. Don't talk about it unless he or she wants to.
3. Don't ask questions immediately.
4. Take into account the mood of the person.
5. Don't dwell on it.
6. Don't try to get the person away from the subject.

A principle underlying these recommendations is that the person with a disability should determine when and how the discussion should *start* and the *course* it should take. However, the clues by which the nondisabled person may be guided are rarely clear-cut and definite. They are often subtle, elusive, and may even be covered up. When the communication is an outgrowth of a definite situational or personal context, it is easier to interpret the clues correctly, since the broader context helps to structure their meaning. By refraining from communication about the injury "until it comes up naturally," therefore, the other person can be more effectively guided by the wishes of the person with a disability.

The following example is an interesting case in point. It is taken from the life of Frances Warfield, the young woman with a hearing disability to whose reminiscences we have frequently referred. It may be recalled that she tried at all costs to hide her hearing impairment. Finally, after secretly going from one doctor to another, after trying all the patent cures she came upon through newspapers and quacks, she became resigned to wearing a hearing aid. Life was, she felt, over for her. Almost every facet of her being had been identified with her hearing disability, and now with the hearing aid that publicized it. In spite of these efforts to repudiate her disability, she was able, in the following episode, *for the first time* to mention her hearing loss, however falteringly, because it came up naturally with a person close to her—Phil, her suitor discovered the aid while rumpling her hair. Notice, too, that the topic was not dwelt on and that to a large extent Frances channeled the direction it took:

> When Phil came to take me to dinner that evening I was dead.
>
> He rumpled my hair, as he always did. Then—"What have we here, Junior?"
>
> "A gimmick," I told him. This was the end. He'd send me away now. "You wear it under your hair," I said. Then you don't need to be deaf . . . You don't need to be deaf . . . You just need to be dead. . . .
>
> He nodded at me approvingly. "Good girl. I've been wondering if you wouldn't get one of those, one of these days."
>
> "You know that I'm hard of hearing?"
>
> "Everybody who knows you knows that, Junior."
>
> "Well, I'll be a sonofabitch!"
>
> "And nobody gives a damn." [Warfield, 1948, p. 151][9]

We have drawn upon this example to show that adjustive communication about the disability is more effectively cued when the context of situation and personal relationships between the parties are taken into account. The suitor, although not observing Rule 1 (i.e., Frances did not bring up the subject of her disability), recognized her covert desire to talk about it (Rule 2). Actually, one of the basic conflicts in a person with a disability—the conflict between wanting to be like a nondisabled person and wanting to accept oneself with one's disability—permits a person who is close to bring up the disability in a natural setting. Because of this conflict, the person with a disability may and may not wish to talk about the disability at the same time. Even a brief allusion to the disability may then have far-reaching positive effects, for the mere fact that it is brought up in an open, matter-of-fact way by a trusted friend may in itself help. One is silent or whispers about the terrible, but the mentionable has met the first criterion of the acceptable.

The problem of curiosity would be greatly eased if the general public became familiar with physical differences and assistive devices of various sorts that diminish difficulties. A report by Rusk & Taylor (1946) offers an example of meeting the problem of curiosity through public education:

> . . . when one of the authors was invited to speak to a group of eighth graders, . . . he took with him a number of prosthetic devices, crutches, artificial eyes, dentures, hooks, legs and hearing aids. Following a group session in which noted personalities who had severe disabilities were discussed, each of the devices was explained, and the children were in-

[9]Reprinted with permission from *Cotton in my ears* by F. Warfield. New York: Viking Press, 1948.

vited to use them. They walked around the room on the crutches, put on the hearing aids, and tried to hold the artificial eyes in their eyes as though they were monocles. Two fourteen-year-olds got one of the artificial hands, and while one held it steady, the other tried to manipulate it to pick up objects like the bucket grab bags do at Coney Island. They had not only an instructive but an enjoyable time. Their inquisitiveness was brought out in the open and satisfied, rather than being fettered to the point that it might eventually become morbid curiosity. [pp. 222–223]

Learning how prosthetic devices and environmental accommodations enable a person to function and being sensitized to the fact that a disability is just one characteristic of a person do more than abate curiosity. It fosters the kind of understanding that will not only improve relations between those with disabilities and those without but will serve the latter well for the eventuality of needing to accept a disability on their own behalf.

THE PROBLEM OF HELP

The adult able-bodied person hardly gives a thought to the problem of help because it is not a problem to him or her. Help is a good thing; it expresses concern for another, a willingness to put oneself out for that person's well-being, all of which are sanctioned in our system of values. Yet help may not simply be taken for granted by a person with a disability, for it connotes a variety of meanings and experiences, some of which are negative. In the Dembo study, the subjects with disabilities evaluated help (bodily assistance) both positively and negatively but emphasized the negative (Ladieu, Hanfmann, & Dembo, 1947). Half the subjects had more bad things than good things to say about being helped, whereas in only about one-fourth of the subjects was this relationship reversed.

Help as a Social Relationship

The act of helping may be disturbing to the recipient because it is not simply an act that may be more or less useful; it is also a social relationship that expresses a variety of attitudes on the part of the participants. As the study of the evaluation of help has stressed, the act of helping represents a hierarchical social relationship that easily leads to status judgments. The person who is always the one to be helped is likely to be considered inferior. This is one reason why it is important for the person with a disability to assume, and be expected to assume, the role of helper, as well as of being helped. More than that, as we shall see later (Chapter 16), transforming the helping relationship from a one-sided affair to a relationship of *interdependence* provides a basis for reducing inferiority, strengthening responsibility, and achieving a healthy balance between needs for dependency and independence.

Disparaging aspects of receiving help have a variety of contents. Sometimes the proffered help is interpreted by a person with a disability as meaning that he or she is considered more helpless than actually is the case, and therefore not only is the help unnecessary but it also questions one's status. Sometimes the help is felt to be motivated by hypocritical self-aggrandizement; the helper, being intent on inflating his or her own ego, is completely insensitive to the wishes of the recipient. Sometimes the act of helping is resented because it calls attention to the person's disability or is felt to set the person apart. Underlying this unwillingness to be noticed is the fear of being devaluated as a disabled person. The fear is that one's social standing is jeopardized and one's defenses against self-devaluation are shaken. Sometimes the help is seen as oozing pity, in which event it is generally rejected with bitter condemnation.

At the same time, the subjects in the help study did recognize the possible positive intentions of the helper. But what seems more striking is the fact that such approval was generally halfhearted and qualified with precautions against implications of inequality or threats to one's independence. It must, of course, be recognized that the subjects of the help study, being men, might be expected to see in help evidence of personal inferiority and threat to independence more strongly than women. Whereas helping a man might be taken as a threat to his manliness, helping a woman is not as likely to endanger her sex role.

Help as an Expediting Act

Aside from social implications, the act of helping can either advance the recipient toward desired goals or actually impede progress. Unfortunately, even when a well-intentioned helper perceives the goal of the recipient correctly, the aid is not always performed effectively. The helper may lack the knowledge and understanding of how best to help. The subjects in the help study registered an emphatic protest against what almost constitutes an unexpected attack by an awkward person who eagerly tries to help but succeeds only in getting in the way. "Help" of this kind menaces the physical security of the recipient—security which may already be shaky.

The objection to help, however, is not limited to useless or interfering acts. Many of the subjects also objected because of an indomitable need for independence. Although assistance may expedite achieving an immediate goal, the long-range goal of learning to do for oneself is blocked. These subjects protested against being babied; they spoke of the fear of becoming a burden and of being spoiled. Accepting help may lead to an anticipation of helplessness in the future, an anticipation which creates uncertainty and fear.

The *fear of being a burden* is a fear of being rejected, a fear of being inadequately cared for by others who may feel that one is imposing. It stems from the haunting conviction that one really doesn't have a right to that care and concern because of not being worth much, a fear that is especially strong in a society that equates dependency with being a burden. The only exception tends to be the dependency of children. The elderly, too, fear being a burden. Being a burden involves a *relationship* between the one who is dependent and others who resent the responsibility and care. It is surprising that little research (none as far as I know) has been done on the burden relationship inasmuch as it is so commonly experienced and feared. How the parties involved evaluate the burden relationship and attempt to cope with it are important questions for study.

Rejecting help in order to learn to do things for oneself not only increases one's independence but also enhances feelings of personal worth. Thus, with regard to expediting matters, many of the subjects restricted acceptance of help to *necessary* help; but because of the manifold meanings of help already pointed out, the concept of necessity tends to be more stringent than is commonly conceived. The degree of inconvenience tolerated by a person with a disability before considering help necessary often far exceeds the degree ordinarily tolerated by a nondisabled person. The subjects in the help study tended to use the term *necessary help* in the strict sense of absolute necessity, that is, without which a goal is excluded no matter how much effort one is willing to expend. Even then, the findings show, concern about help is due less to the question of its necessity than to the strong fear of social inferiority and dependency connoted by it.

This is not to say that help is never exploited by the person with a disability. There is ample clinical evidence to show that some individuals revel in their disability, demanding all kinds of unnecessary help as a way of ruling the roost, satisfying their need for dependency, or perversely reassuring themselves that they are loved. That these motivations for accepting help do not appear in the help study is not surprising, for they are personally unfavorable and tend to be kept private if not suppressed from consciousness.

Management by the Recipient

As in the case of curiosity, the recipient, for better or for worse, reacts in some way to situations involving help. In order to become more intimately in touch with the different meanings of being helped as well as observe how the recipient does react and cope, we shall examine several scenes from real-life experiences reported in autobiographical accounts.

Henry, a young boy with dwarfed and deformed lower limbs, went swimming with the neighborhood boys. The help he received was so natural and situation-rooted that it was just as naturally accepted:

> . . . one day some of the big boys came by and called up to ask Mamma if I could go for a walk—over by the river. Mamma finally said yes, but be careful.
>
> I walked part of the way, and when I got tired they hoisted me up on their shoulders. Then I really was tall—taller than seven feet. We came to the railroad tracks. I had never been this far from home except with Mamma or Papa, and it was exciting.
>
> "Look at that old cardboard," Marble Bags [the champion marbles player] said. It was a big piece. It must have been wrapped around a mattress or something.
>
> "Let's build a shelter."
>
> An empty freight car stood on a track and the boys put the cardboard under it and bent it like the sides of a house. Then we all crawled inside and they talked about baseball and girls. It started to rain, so we stayed. It was just like being in a clubhouse. One of the boys took out a cigarette butt and lit it.
>
> "Give me a puff," somebody said.
>
> "Look, the sun's out. Let's go swimming." Marble Bags ran across the tracks and down to the river where he peeled off his pants and shirt and dived off a big rock.
>
> The other boys picked me up, and we ran after him.
>
> I sat on the bank and watched them paddle around.
>
> "Come on in," they yelled. "We'll hold you up."
>
> Did I dare? Of course, they said. Hesitantly I took off all my clothes except my boots, and two of them let me down over the side of the rock.
>
> "It's cold," I shrieked. But as soon as I had been in the water a minute it felt wonderful. I paddled with my short legs while they held onto my hands.
>
> "I can swim! I can swim—almost," I gasped. [Viscardi, 1952, pp. 32–33][10]

[10]Reprinted from *A man's stature* by H. Viscardi, Jr., 1952. By permission of Paul S. Eriksson, Pubs.

However, the help situation is not always so comfortable. Sometimes it is hated but the recipient feels powerless to do anything but "grin and bear it." The following is an instance of boorish, self-aggrandizing help. Henry Viscardi, now a young man, is again the recipient:

> The train disgorged a mass of us at a midtown station, and I glanced again at the address of the employment agency I would "visit" today, trying to memorize the address. . . . A dried-up-looking man came by and took my arm. Despite my unresponsiveness, he drew me up a flight of stairs and all the way out of the station where he deposited me with a sanctimonious smile on the wrong side of the street.
>
> Mother of God, I thought, I bet he's the kind who goes to church and prays for those poor helpless cripples. [Viscardi, 1952, p. 71]

In the following scene, Harold Russell, whose injury caused the loss of both hands, has no alternative but to submit. Though the help was necessary, it was unrelenting torture and continued to be as he mused over it. His pride was hurt deeply, for the help stirred again the desperate doubts about his manliness. The airline hostess has just instructed the passengers to unfasten their safety belts:

> I started to pull my hooks out of my pockets, but they got stuck. I wrestled with them for a few seconds and finally I got them out after nearly ripping off my pants. Then I began fumbling with the belt. She had offered to close it before we took off, but I declined stiffly. Now she stood over me like a school-teacher, watching me struggle with it. I just couldn't seem to get a grip on that slippery metal buckle. I could almost hear her saying, "See! What did I tell you? You can't do it by yourself." That only made me more nervous. Finally she reached down, flipped it open and walked off triumphantly into the cockpit.
>
> I fell back against the seat. This was the ultimate humiliation. Only a few months before I had been the rough, tough paratrooper, boldly leaping out into the wild blue yonder. Now I had sunk so low I couldn't even open a simple safety belt without the help of a woman. I thought of what the boys in my old outfit would have said to that. I could hear them laughing. [Russell, 1949, p. 128][11]

Though help may be humiliating, recipients gradually learn how to make it more palatable in situations in which they cannot do without it. Russell Criddle, for example, while still a teenager, attempted to confine help to situations in which it was absolutely needed because of his poor vision; he then took the *initiative* as to where and

---

[11]Reprinted by permission of Farrar, Straus & Giroux, Inc. From *Victory in my hands* by H. Russell & V. Rosen. Copyright 1949 by Harold Russell & Victor Rosen. Copyright renewed © 1976 by H. Russell.

how it should take place. The boys are planning a swimming outing down the river:

> Someone grabbed my arm.
> "Go get your suit, Russ. I'll lead you, and if anybody says you're blind, I'll push his face in."
> It was Bud [leader of the gang]. He had humbled himself to such a degree just so I could go swimming. But I pictured him leading me, with the gang looking on in anguished pity, and the thought was intolerable.
> "You won't have to lead me," I said. "Just let me put my hand on your arm down by the dump and across the tracks." [Criddle, 1953, p. 28]

Criddle also developed the policy of letting the most distinguished person in the group lead him through difficult places:

> I found that it didn't seem to embarrass them so much as it did others, and it was easier for me to accept condescension from someone whom I admitted to be my superior. [p. 42]

When help is felt to be unnecessary, the recipient may regard it as a personal affront. On that first furlough home after his injury, Harold Russell recalls:

> Fred [a sailor friend] was uncomfortable, too. We didn't know how to greet each other. Somehow, it seemed gruesome to extend my hook, so we just nodded stiffly and said hello. Then he reached out to take my bag, but I yanked it away quickly. I didn't need his help. [Russell, 1949, pp. 130–131]

If no offense is presumed the person is able to reject or accept the help in a matter-of-fact or good-natured way. In the following instance the help is naturally declined. Mr. Wilke, born without arms, visited the Bruckner family whose child had a similar disability. Mrs. Bruckner relates:

> It was almost eight o'clock when he arrived. My first reaction was sheer amazement at the size of the suitcase that he had strapped to his shoulders. Hy tried to help him remove it, but he quickly said, "Thank you, I am able to manage it by myself." [Bruckner, 1954, p. 175][12]

Gracious acceptance of unnecessary help also becomes possible. Louise Baker, the young woman whose leg had been amputated, became convinced that this was by far the most agreeable reaction in most situations:

> Excess generosity is one of the problems a handicapped person faces. I have found that I am more likely to err in refusing than accepting. Seats offered me in crowded cars; special consideration in the queue

[12]Reprinted from *Triumph of Love* by Leona Bruckner. Copyright 1954 by Leona Bruckner.

at a theater; porters rushing through trains to open doors for me; shoppers giving me their turn at a busy counter in a store—and even cameos, presented by strangers. They all pose a problem.

A handicapped person doesn't win any of these on his merit, and frequently he doesn't require any such thoughtfulness. In my childhood and teens, I am sure I was very rude in my constant huffy refusals of any kind of aid. I have grown more mellow, more sensible, and, I believe, more kindly.

Frequently I accept proffered places in crowded buses or trolleys, from tired, elderly men who I know need the seats much more than I. But, according to faultless authority, "It is more blessed to give than to receive." For the most part, I am convinced it is up to the handicapped person graciously to let the giver be blessed. [Baker, 1946, pp. 117–118][13]

The person with a disability is sometimes in the position where it is necessary to ask for help. If receiving help signals devaluation, not only will one defer asking until help becomes absolutely necessary but the request will be made self-consciously or at best apologetically. When, however, the help situation connotes acceptance and good will, the request for help may come naturally and easily. Wilke, the armless visitor, sat down to eat. His hostess recalls:

> I tried to be casual as I placed his dinner plate on the table, explaining that I was serving him family style as it was quicker. I was determined not to offer to help him in any way unless he asked me to. I had thought that it might be embarrassing to him to have us all gathered around while he ate, but he very nonchalantly asked us to keep him company. He smiled at me as he said, "Oh, steak, this is a treat. But I am afraid I will need your assistance with this, Leona. This is one meat that I can't cut with a fork." I cut his steak into cubes while he continued talking. "I have a special combination knife and fork at home [which he uses with his foot], but since I try to travel light, I can't bring it along and must rely on the kindness of my hostess." [Bruckner, 1954, p. 176]

The act of helping, as we have seen, can either lead to good will and warm interpersonal relations or to ill will, personal hurt, and the disintegration of social relationships. What principles can be formulated whereby the act of helping will produce beneficial rather than negative results?

---

[13]Reprinted from *Out on a limb,* by L. Baker. New York: McGraw-Hill, 1946. By permission of Blassingame, McCauley, & Wood.

Recommendations

The investigators in the help study (Ladieu, Hanfmann, & Dembo, 1947) offer a number of practical recommendations in line with the conclusion that help is both an expression of status anxieties and a realistic means for achieving self-reliance.

1. The helper will be better prepared to meet the situation adequately if it is kept in mind that a person with a disability may want to limit help to instances of absolute necessity. This certainly does not mean that help should not be offered, but it does mean that the helper should understand that the help may not be accepted.

2. When offering help, it is mandatory in most situations that the helper refrain from carrying out the action until the recipient gives consent. Helpers must appreciate that they are in a relatively poor position to know just when and what kind of help is needed. As outsiders, they do not have knowledge of the actual limitations and how best to meet them. In fact, the general tendency to overestimate the extent of disability leads to the exaggerated notion that the person is more helpless than is often the case.

Who but the initiated or specifically informed would guess that Wilke, the visitor without arms, could manage very adequately at the table, at personal grooming, and at being a man around the house? The following scenes are described by Mrs. Bruckner, the mother of the boy without arms, whose home he was visiting.

At the Table

He pulled off his loafer, picked up the fork and started eating. I cannot describe how easy and graceful his motions were. He did not use his bare feet, as I had expected, but his left, black silk sock was specially made. It had been sewn like the first two fingers of a glove. He only needed the big toe, which he used like a thumb, and the first digit; an unusually large space had developed between them, like the space between a normal thumb and first finger. He did ask me to give him a cup instead of a glass, but aside from that he manipulated everything so easily and neatly that I couldn't help but compare him favorably with my own often clumsy movements. He selected a piece of bread from the bread tray and spread it with butter; everyone knows how slippery and difficult to manage hard butter is. But, unlike many of my able-bodied guests, he dropped no crumbs on my carpet and spilled no food on my tablecloth. When he had finished eating, his place at the table was orderly and clean, and I felt ungainly in comparison to his efficiency. [Bruckner, 1954, p. 177]

At Personal Grooming

. . . He bent down and wiggled out of his jacket. Then he picked it up with his toes and hung it on a hanger more neatly than my husband has ever been able to do. He wore suspenders, which he could slip off his shoulders with no trouble. His shirt had a full-length zipper, concealed in the front, instead of the usual buttons. . . . since he travels a lot on lecture tours and doesn't want to carry too much baggage, he wears only nylon or orlon shirts and underwear and washes them out each night. [Bruckner, 1954, p. 179]

At Being a Man Around the House

He told us that he danced, but didn't care much for it. He owned and operated a car and had a regular driver's license. "I do everything that any other family man attends to around the house," he said. Then he grinned and looked down at his feet. We were sitting in the living room and he had not yet put on his socks. "You can see that I painted the baby's crib last week," he said. "I love to go around barefoot, and I haven't yet been able to get all the blue paint off my feet. I do all my own painting and repairing, take care of putting up the screens and storm windows and all that sort of thing." [Bruckner, 1954, p. 181]

Can you imagine the same settings enacted differently because a helper insisted on spoon-feeding Mr. Wilke, on removing his jacket and shirt, on stirring the paint and painting the crib for him? Yet such annoying if not humiliating interference is precisely what occurred when the man escorted Viscardi across the street (see p. 312) and is repeated countless times in the lives of many persons with disabilities.

Even if the helper correctly judges that the person needs help, he or she may lack the necessary experience to know what to do to be most helpful. For instance, how could a sighted person realize without being told that a person who is blind can be accompanied more easily if he or she holds the arm of the sighted person than vice versa? Add to this the consideration that all too often the helper's own need for a pat on the back or for reassurance of being better off get in the way, and the advice *offer but don't persist* becomes obligatory.

Since the person with a disability may be too proud or otherwise restrained to ask for needed help, and since ordinary courtesy may suggest help, it is appropriate to offer help rather than waiting to be asked. However, only under special circumstances should continued efforts to help be made in the face of resistance by the recipient and generally in these instances the help should be offered again rather than administered without the person's consent. (See the case of Mary, p. 286.)

3. The third principle refers to the general manner in which help is executed. The subjects of the help study strongly opposed all fuss and emotional display in helping. Ostentatious help conveys a feeling that the helper is enhancing his or her own self-satisfaction at the cost of one less fortunate. Rather, help should be offered qui-

etly and matter-of-factly, in a way that is pointed to the demands of the situation, not to the helping relationship itself. With this precaution, such experiences as the following will be minimized:

> I went out with a teacher to a concert; we travelled by bus. I have enough vision to get on and off a bus without being told when to step and being clung to as if I would run away. Every time there was a step she would say "Step" in no quiet voice and I know everyone was looking me up and down. It made me feel like crying. [Sommers, 1944, p. 32][14]

Help offered matter-of-factly diminishes the possibility that help will be useless or hindering. It gives the person with a disability a chance to reject the help or to explain how it can best be performed. And most important of all, negative implications of subservience and devaluation will be minimized.

The authors of the help study also advance several penetrating recommendations to the person with a disability. They point out that the recipient could well take cognizance of the fact that the act of help in itself cannot be taken as a measure of how he or she is regarded, for refraining from helping may place more emphasis on the disability than casually offering assistance. They also point out that restricting help to situations of absolute necessity may foolishly eliminate much useful assistance. What is most important is a reinterpretation of the meaning of help—that is, of the reasons for which it is offered by the helper and accepted by the recipient. Just as help is offered to people in general, not because of their general state of helplessness but merely because a situation seems to call for help, so may a person with a disability realize that it can be offered *not* as to a *disabled person* but as to someone who is having difficulties in *particular situations.* This involves a reorganization of the self-concept, for as we have seen (Chapter 12) the self-concept is central to the interpretation of social relationships.

Perhaps these points sound obvious. If so, the obvious needs to be extricated from the dull and uninteresting. Consideration of help can no longer be neglected, for help *is* a problem. All too often helpers barge in and are so intent on letting the recipient or the wider group know of their solicitousness that what could have been welcomed help is resented. Likewise, the recipient all too often sees in the help relationship another indication of his or her inferiority whereas actually it may be an expression of good will toward a person having difficulties in the particular situation.

---

[14]Reprinted from *The influence of parental attitudes and social environment on the personality development of the adolescent blind,* by V. S. Sommers. New York: American Foundation for the Blind, 1944. By permission of the foundation.

Although the discussion of help referred explicitly to bodily assistance, the reasons for approving and rejecting help as a social relationship or as an expediting act apply to nonphysical help situations as well. Criddle, for example, with vision poor enough to be classed as legally blind, could not accept the services of an agency for the blind even though he was desperately in need of employment during the depression days. Sheltered employment meant to him dependency, helplessness, personal and social admission that he was inferior (Criddle, 1953, Chapter 21). Likewise, emotional help as expressed in sympathy can be welcomed or distrusted, depending on the form it takes and the meanings it conveys to the recipient. It is to the emotional relationship of sympathy and pity that we shall now give our attention.

THE PROBLEM OF SYMPATHY AND PITY

Sympathy, that basically human expression of warm concern of one person for another, does not always afford consolation. The same factors that were significant in the evaluation of curiosity and help apply to the evaluation of sympathy: self-regard, situational and personal context, wish for adjustment and desire to be understood, and the behavior of the other person. Instead of detailing these factors again, we shall analyze the problem of sympathy in a somewhat different way. Unwanted sympathy will be examined first, followed by the kind of sympathy that is potentially acceptable, referred to as empathy by some writers (Batson & Coke, 1983). The discussion, stemming from the work of Dembo and her associates (1956; 1975, Chapter 6), examines the nature of the sympathy *relationship*.

Unwanted Sympathy

Sympathy may be rejected because of the *desire for privacy*. This occurs, most commonly, when the recipient wishes to hide the disability or at least to act as if it did not make any difference. It also occurs when the person wants to be left alone with one's own personal feelings about the loss, because of a need to first get hold of oneself, or because of a wish not to burden others with one's troubles.

Sympathy may also be rejected when the recipient senses *contaminating attitudes* in the other person, such as devaluation or insincerity. Pity as we shall use it presumes a status relationship in which the other person looks down upon the recipient; it involves devaluation even though the other person may wish to help the sufferer. Sympathy contaminated with *pity* is surprisingly easy to detect. The following examples show how difficult it is for the agent to camouflage the feeling of devaluating pity. In both cases the agent probably would have acknowledged only the most honorable motives, but the undercurrent of pity makes a travesty out of the seeming benevolence:

> John, a spastic boy, related, "I went to the theater with my mother. A stranger walked up to her and said, 'I'm awfully sorry your son turned out this way.'"
>
> Nancy, a young girl, said, "I was sitting in the waiting room at a department store. A woman came up to me and offered me a quarter. She said it was because of my 'little crippled legs.'" [Foster, 1948, p. 9]

Pity, the feeling of being devaluated and not worth much, tends to cause additional suffering. It is among the most hated of all the attitudes of another person to the self.

Insincere sympathy may be expressed by the agent for the purpose of adhering to the ethical ideal of being a good person. Sometimes this implies self-aggrandizement, in which case it is rejected. However, insincere sympathy may be evaluated as proper when seen as a formal expression of politeness. Here the agent conveys only a recognition of the seriousness of the event and the intention not to intrude further into the privacy of the recipient. *Formal sympathy,* therefore, bears no great dangers, but the investigators of the sympathy study caution that it should emphasize the event and not the person. To say, "I'm sorry it happened" conveys what is needed. "I'm sorry for you" may connote devaluation. Resentment may also occur when the recipient, mistaking the sympathetic overtures for genuine feelings, assumes a concern that does not exist. Should the recipient confide in the agent, he or she is left with a feeling of having been used or beguiled into revealing private matters.

Even when the recipient may be ready to accept sympathy, the manner in which the sympathy is expressed may be disturbing. What, then, does characterize acceptable sympathy? How should sympathetic persons act? The specifications as to appropriate behavior can be seen as fitting into a human relationship that has a coherent underlying structure.

Nature of Potentially Acceptable Sympathy

The fundamental characteristics of sympathy, as delineated by the investigators of the sympathy study, are *congruence, understanding,* and *readiness to help.*

In a sympathy relationship, the feelings and perceptions of the agent and the recipient are not and cannot be identical because the content of their distress is different. The recipient is distressed over the loss itself, the agent because the recipient suffers. Their moods need not be similar. If someone is depressed, the sympathizer need not also become depressed. Instead of identity, what is required is a *congruence* of feeling and understanding of the participants. Congruence rather than identity, moreover, would seem to hold a better potential for diminishing the distress. Not only do different points of view introduce new angles, but the sympathizer can well remain free of the anxiety and fearfulness of the person in distress since these emotions act as barriers to realistic evaluation of the situation.

What makes for congruence in emotional relationships needs further study. We do know that gay attempts to divert a person suffering a loss will be felt as incongruous and "rub him or her the wrong way." The sympathy study also points out that expressions of concern that are immoderate may be very disturbing to the recipient. The reasons are several: The recipient may be so emotionally keyed up in regard to the whole disability situation that additional emotion is difficult to bear. Any strong emotional expression may also make the person feel that the situation is even more unfortunate than he or she thought it to be. It may arouse feelings of guilt in the person at having caused so much distress in others. It may lead to embarrassment because the person does not know how to act in the face of strong emotion. Furthermore, excessive emotionalism may lead the person to doubt the sincerity of the feeling and to sense self-aggrandizing motives. What is equally important, excessive emotion has the danger of making the agent imperceptive to the shifts in feelings and needs of the sufferer. Just as music may be cacophonic or harmonious, so may the emotions between two persons clash or be in tune.

The second essential characteristic, *understanding*, requires first and foremost that the agent give sufficient weight to both sides of an underlying conflict in the sufferer, the conflict between wishing to remain preoccupied with the loss on the one hand and wishing to escape the negative character of the situation on the other. Thus, the agent must have sufficient respect for the distress itself (even if he or she is unaware of its cause or ramifications) and not try immediately to dissipate it. The investigators of the sympathy study provide the following example:

> . . . a mother may be genuinely concerned over the unhappiness of her adolescent daughter, but if she tries to soothe her by saying, "It's only puppy love. You'll soon forget all about him," the daughter, even when recognizing her mother's concern, will feel that she doesn't understand and thus that she is not really sympathetic. Similarly, if someone tries to "cheer-up" an injured friend by saying, "Oh, you'll soon get a new leg," he may be felt to take lightly the feeling of loss which the

injured man experiences. It is equivalent to saying to someone bereaved, "You'll soon get a new wife!" [Dembo, Leviton, & Wright, 1956,
p. 28][15]

At the same time, because the sympathizer wishes to help bring
about emotional relief, attention to positive aspects of the situation
may be encouraged so long as it is not implied that the feelings and
concerns of the sufferer are not valid or important. In this way both
sides of the conflict are respected.

The investigators point out that the word "understanding" is not
restricted to a conscious intellectual appreciation of the diverse
meanings of the loss for the recipient. "It seems as though there is
such a thing as emotional understanding—that is, grasping the emotions of the other person directly on the emotional level without the
intermediate step of intellectual realization of these emotions" just
as one may spontaneously catch a ball suddenly thrown without intellectually deciding on a course of action (1956, p. 29). An excellent
example of such emotional sensitivity is seen in the following example of a mother comforting her son. Ohnstad knew he was going
blind as a young high-school boy. He had not been able to go to school
during the previous year, and the fear of blindness was overwhelming. His mother emotionally understood. Ohnstad recalled:

> I looked in the mirror many times daily to see if the redness in my
> eyes was going away. Sometimes they seemed clearer, and hope re-
> turned. When they looked redder than before, my heart sank. There
> was a strange tightness in my throat, a vague feeling of dread within
> me. The lids felt hot. When I awoke in the morning, matter had dried
> upon my lashes and sealed them together. I brooded over the fact that
> my classmates were going ahead in school while I sat at home doing
> nothing. I was being left behind.
> Mother called me into her room one night.
> "I thought you might like to have me read a little from the paper,"
> she said as I stood in the doorway, blinking at the light. Her intention
> was, I knew, to try and cheer me up.
> "There's a story here," she said. "I thought you might like to hear
> it." She read a few lines in her laborious broken English, then she
> stopped. "I wouldn't feel so badly about it if I were you," she said, appar-
> ently divining my thoughts. "Even if you have to stay out of school one
> year, that's nothing. You can catch up again easily."
> I said nothing, but the tears welled into my eyes and trickled down
> my cheeks. Mother's voice faltered. She dabbed her eyes with her hand-

[15]Adjustment to misfortune: A problem of social-psychological rehabilitation, by T.
Dembo, G. L. Leviton, & B. A. Wright. Reproduced from *Artificial limbs*, National
Academy Press, Washington, D.C., 1956.

kerchief. "I know it's hard," she said brokenly, "It's hard now, but some day—some day things will be better." [Ohnstad, 1942, pp. 21–22][16]

"I know it's hard, but some day things will be better" is the core of emotional understanding; it recognizes both the absorption with the difficulties and the need for eventual overcoming of the distress. Such emotional understanding can take place in young children. A child, without knowing the facts or understanding the implications, can sense distress in another and convey genuine sympathy.

The importance of emotional understanding by no means relegates intellectual understanding to second position. Intellectual understanding, by giving rise to useful suggestions that the recipient may be ready to accept, may increase the effectiveness of the help offered.

The third essential characteristic of sympathy is a *readiness to help* the recipient overcome distress. Concern that does not carry with it a willingness to put oneself out for another is felt to be insincere or at best a formal expression of sympathy, otherwise empty.

But what can the sympathizer do to help? In a particular situation, concrete suggestions may be appropriate, as when the agent informs the person of rehabilitation facilities. What we are after, however, is not a listing of the concrete ways of sympathetically "saying and doing," for this is limitless, but rather some guides that can apply to the sympathetic relationship in general. Dembo and her associates propose one important guide—namely, that the agent should be *passive* or *active,* depending upon the recipient's wishes and his or her momentary tendency to remain absorbed with, or escape from, the suffering. They point out that a deep, positive feeling on the part of the sympathizer can be conveyed without demonstrative overtures. There are times, probably not infrequent, when the sympathizer can help best by just "standing by"; there is a mutual understanding that, as the situation warrants it, the agent is ready to participate more actively. This requires that the agent be sensitive to occasions when forces in the recipient to meet and overcome the suffering can be strengthened. The authors of the sympathy study point out that the sympathizer must be ready to abandon any benevolent attempts at the first sign that he or she has proceeded beyond the willingness of the recipient to accept the offering. Because of a desire to help, the sympathizer may proceed too quickly in trying to cheer up the sufferer or may even become impatient with the recipient's slow pace at overcoming the sorrow. The sympathetic per-

[16]Reprinted from *The world at my fingertips,* by K. Ohnstad. Indianapolis, In.: Bobbs-Merrill, 1942.

son emotionally understands that "haste is made slowly." Ideally, the readiness to help is transformed into more active participation as cues are received from the recipient concerning the kind of help that will be most constructive. The actual value of the help will depend on the wisdom of both agent and recipient. It is altogether likely that sympathy, as an expression of we-group feelings, always has some positive value by giving assurance that one is of worth to another person.

Recommendations to the sympathizer as to how one may best serve the recipient have necessarily been woven into the discussion of the nature of acceptable sympathy. Management by the recipient of unwanted sympathy will not be described here, for sufficient material to understand the nature of such attempts has already been given in regard to the situations of curiosity and of help.

THE PROBLEM OF SOCIAL PARTICIPATION

"How can a blind guy be a member of the gang?" (Criddle, 1953, p. 20). Young Criddle was challenged in this way when he returned to the club where he had been a member until his accident destroyed almost all his vision. And for the first time he experienced a terrifying fear of blindness, for the consequences of blindness seemed irrevocably to include social ostracism. When a person with a disability fears the disability, what may be feared is that he or she will be left behind, out of the running, excluded from normal group activities.

"Treat Me Like Anyone Else"

To counter the threat to social acceptance and participation, the person with a disability not uncommonly appeals to the world to "treat me like anyone else!" Underlying this may be the fervent wish to hide the disability, to act like a nondisabled person, and to be treated like a nondisabled person. This was true in young Ohnstad's case during his early adjustment to his blindness. At that time he needed the conviction that he was just as he was before, that blindness in fact made no real difference. To prove this illusion he had to maintain the standards of sighted behavior as his own:

> I preferred the bruises, however, to walking around with my hands stretched out before me. It was too conspicuous. I did not want to be stared at and looked upon as helpless and *different from others*. And so I continued to bang into doors; and chairs out of their accustomed places continued to bruise and cut the flesh on the front of my legs with their sharp edges. At night my socks had grown fast to my skin, and I had to pull the scabs off with them. [Ohnstad, 1942, p. 45, italics ours]

To maintain the fiction, Karsten Ohnstad had to insist on being treated like anyone else. He even wanted people to laugh at him when he fumbled and stumbled just because this reaction would have been elicited in the case of a nondisabled person (p. 45).

But had they indeed laughed, Ohnstad would have felt just as hurt; in either case, the silence or the laughter would have been seen as stimulated by the fact of his blindness. As long as he regarded this fact as a devaluating one, identity of treatment would remain impotent to effect a comfortable acceptance in social participation. Actually, identity of treatment in many instances may point up a difference that could remain quite unobtrusive with special treatment. Serving steak to someone unable to use both hands because he or she should be treated like anyone else would more certainly call attention to the disability than had a more manageable main dish been planned. Identity of treatment may boomerang in yet another way, for unless one allows for modifications in the situation, the injunction resolves itself into an all-or-none rule: either one treats identically or one does not treat at all; that is, the person becomes excluded from the situation.

It is necessary to realize that special treatment in itself does not mean stigmatizing treatment. One does not debase a person who is deaf because one is careful to provide adequate light for lip reading. One does not debase someone with a leg prosthesis because one gears the step to a more leisurely pace. Debasement does not depend upon how similar the treatment is to the usual pattern but on underlying attitudes of prejudicial exclusion.

Minority groups in general should give heed to the important distinction between equal treatment and equal opportunity. Affirmative action plans require this distinction. That so-called equal treatment can be a snare and a delusion for both blacks and people with disabilities was eloquently expressed by a black student in the early days of the civil rights movement:

> At one time, the phrase "treat me like anyone else," could have been called the Negro national anthem. In the not too distant past, Negroes were loudly voicing the view that they were the same as whites: only this was not true. Negroes were denying their true selves by attempting to acquire characteristics which they did not have. For example, instead of saying "a little dab of Brylcream" they said "two dabs." The only thing he gained was twice the amount of "greasy kid stuff." Or take the example of schools. The Negro screamed for *integrated* schools because the Supreme Court decided he was suffering in his all black schools. So integration was tried. Except it was not integration on an equal basis—it was, "close the Negro schools and send them to the white schools." When this started happening, Afro-Americans started to awaken to the fact that they did not want integration at the cost of losing what little positive self-concept they had. No! He wanted quality education as a

Negro not as a white in "blackface." His swan song changed quickly from "treat me like anybody else" to "treat me like me." I think the same attitude would be of positive benefit for people with disabilities. They do not want to be lumped into one uncomfortable pile and treated (mistreated) by the same behavior. They want to be treated for the person they are and not what someone might think they are or should be. [Personal communication]

Inclusion Through Accommodation

Instead of identity of treatment serving as the guide to social behavior, the person with a disability and those around him or her should think rather in terms of how the person can best participate. And with this thinking new and varied possibilities emerge. A boy who is lame plays baseball:

> I played with the boys of the neighborhood, sharing in all their games and sports, even baseball. I was catcher, since that position required less getting around, and when it came my turn to bat, another boy ran the bases for me when I hit the ball. [Goldman, 1947, pp. 53–54][17]

The following account of a party that Ohnstad, who is blind, attended as a college student is reported at some length because it demonstrates how a series of accommodating modifications evolved as a natural process:

> At first those who invited me—and I myself—took it for granted that I could take no part in the fun-making. Parlor games were made for sighted persons, not for blind men. It was better for me to remain safely in one spot than to go galloping about the room crashing into furniture and knocking over the statuary. And so, while the others played games and had a good time, I sat in an easy chair like an old grandfather, smiling at the shouts and laughter of the youngsters and wistfully recalling the lost days of my youth. . . .
> The girls who selected the games, however, were on the alert.
> "You can play this one as well as the rest of us," Nan said. "All you've got to do is think about what the one who is thinking is supposed to be thinking, and—"
> To everyone's surprise, there were more games that I could take part in than we had imagined.
> "Bring your marked cards along," Chet reminded. "We're going to play five hundred or bridge or something."
> Braille cards were a novelty to the others at the party.
> "What are all these dots on here—flyspecks?" Joe asked, staring at the cards as I dealt them around.

[17]Reprinted with permission of Macmillan Publishing Co., Inc., from *Even the night* by R. L. Goldman. Copyright 1947, and renewed 1975, by Raymond Leslie Goldman.

Patty held a card out before me. "But how can you tell which is which?"

I explained the system of initials and numbers. "See these three dots? That's the letter J. And these two dots next to it? That's the letter C—the jack of clubs." . . .

Very soon I was taking almost as active a part in the fun-making as anyone else. . . . A delegation of four marched into the room.

"We are supposed to guess by their actions what book they are trying to represent," Clara said. "Two of them are sitting on the floor and another is—well, looks as if she's got a long stick and is trying to jab holes in the floor. Bob is waving his arms in a big circle as if he were turning wheels."

Bob moved slowly from one end of the room to the other uttering a dull, monotonous "hooo! hooo!" That was easy. He was a boat of some kind. Maybe a freighter. There was no book represented in all these indications of adolescence that I could make out, unless it could have been "Wynken, Blynken and Nod."

The two sailors on the floor began talking.

"Keep your head down until we get past!" The voice was piping and as boyish as a girl could make it.

"Yas sah! Dey nebbah see me whuh ah is!"

This was confusing. It might have been Robinson Crusoe and his man Friday, but where did the steamboat and the boy with the fishing pole come from!

"Ships in the Sky!" The audience was off to a catalogful of titles: *"Showboat!" "Nigger of the Narcissus!"* . . .

"Three men in a Tub," I shouted. *"Twenty Thousand Leagues Under the Sea."*

Jack leaned toward me from the other end of the davenport.

"What would a steamboat be doing twenty thousand leagues under the sea?"

"That's right," I said, turning to my informant and back to the actors again. "The Wreck of the Hesperus!"

"I don't know what they'd be doing with that pole unless they were on a—I've got it!" Clara jumped up excitedly. *"Huckleberry Finn!"*

"Right!" . . . [Ohnstad, 1942, pp. 208–211][18]

Participation was made possible at this party because Ohnstad was *not* treated like anybody else. Games were selected in which he could get along with little or no help; Clara described a little bit of the charades to him as they were being enacted; Alice helped him write down the geographic names; Ohnstad himself felt free to ask for some readily available equipment so that he could write on his own.

---

[18]Reprinted from *The world at my fingertips,* by K. Ohnstad. Indianapolis, In.: Bobbs-Merrill, 1942.

All this is special treatment, but when it is done matter-of-factly according to the requirements of the situation as they arise and change, special treatment, paradoxically, allows one *to be treated like anyone else,* for it is then that the person is not set apart from, but is made a part of, the social group. The boy who played baseball by having someone else run the bases for him felt, "I won my battle for equality among my fellows. They perceived that I wanted no special consideration and they gave me none" (Goldman, 1947, p. 54). The special treatment was not felt to be special at all. It was so natural a requirement of the situation that it led to a feeling of equality; in order to treat him *as a person* like anyone else, one had to allow special treatment and accommodation for that part of his tool equipment which was inadequate to the task.

The point is an important one and should not be glossed over with a glib acquiescence that merely gives a token nod to its substance. Participation is a preeminent requirement of group belongingness and acceptance. Without it the person all too often feels truly "different," abnormal, and not wanted. This is brought out by a young man both of whose legs were paralyzed when he was three years old. After learning to swim, he asked these questions:

> Why did I have to wait until I was 21 to learn I could be like others? Why did I always have to go to study hall when the others went out to play? [Daniels, 1948, p. 20]

What this man is decrying is his *exclusion* from activities which he could have entered. When he learned to swim, he was struck by the remarkable thought that he could do things that others did even though the performance was styled to fit his own idiosyncrasies. It was then that he began to feel like others, in spite of the fact that the details of his performance were different. *New Fountains,* a provocative play about a 16-year-old girl who recently had polio, presents a clear demonstration of how participation in the social life of her high school helped her feel a part of the community of other young people (Gilmore, 1953).

Some people are glad when others forget they have a disability. This is well and good when the disability does not have to be taken into account. However, when it is necessary or even just helpful to accommodate special needs, such forgetting is not a blessing. Marty, a woman who is deaf, addresses this point loudly and clearly:

> I once had a hearing friend who I liked very much. . . . But she was always getting carried away. Sometimes I couldn't follow her because she'd move around and I'd lose sight of her face. "Look at me," I'd have to remind her. "Oh, Marty," she finally blurted out one day, "You seem so normal, I forget that you're deaf." I was so let down and disappointed.

I'm sure *she* thought it was a compliment. "I'm not interested in being "normal," I had to tell her. "I'm deaf, and goddamn it, don't you ever forget it!" [Romano, 1980, p. 48][19]

To be sure, situations should not always be accommodated to the needs and wishes of a person with a disability. There are occasions when the necessary modifications might place undue strain on the group. For example, a person who is deaf, even though a proficient lip reader, has difficulty functioning in a large group discussion. To require that other members always face the person and watch for signs that he or she has lost the trend of the conversation could interfere with the free flow of ideas. Having an interpreter present may be one solution. However, where it is not likely or possible for special needs to be accommodated, it should be left up to the person with the disability as to whether or not he or she wishes to join the group. The person may wish to get as much out of the occasion as possible or perhaps simply to enjoy the presence of others. Alternatively, the person may wish to decline the invitation. Someone else should not make that judgment.

As part of the Dembo study, serious thought was given to the problem of participation and social acceptance (Ladieu, Adler, & Dembo, 1948). The investigators point out that exclusion from certain activities because of the *realities* of a handicap is totally different from exclusion that stems from social rejection. In the former case the person may miss the activity, but in the latter case there is hurt in the affront, which says in effect, "You are not good enough to associate with us. Keep your distance." The person with a disability may feel socially rejected when kept from activities in which participation is possible.

The Dembo study also points out that the problem of social participation is complicated by the discrepancy between what the person with a disability sees as limitations and what others see (Ladieu, Adler, & Dembo, 1948). Frequently, when others judge that certain physical characteristics preclude an activity, the person himself or herself knows that this is not so. The phenomenon of *spread* (see pp. 32–39) is one important factor responsible for this discrepancy. The recommendation is made that since the outsider cannot readily acquire information as to the variable capacities of the person with the disability, a willingness to have the person participate should be indicated, the judgment as to whether or not to do so being left up to the person himself or herself.

[19]Reprinted from the silent part, by D. L. Romano. In *Mother Jones*, 1980, 5(1), 40–49. By permission of *Mother Jones*.

THE PROBLEM OF RIDICULE AND TAUNTING

With civilized acceptance of the "Golden Rule" and the proprieties of good social form, outright ridicule and taunting of a person's physical imperfections are permitted only under special circumstances. Social sanction is given to ridiculing one's enemies; during wartime, cartoons revel in caricaturing the physical characteristics of the opponent. Where there is no evident justification for disparagement, however, ridicule may sometimes be permitted if the intention is to evoke a positive effect in the recipient. For example, an adult may belittle a child for spilling food in order, presumably, to encourage more mature eating habits.

The requirement of mourning makes possible a deeper understanding of the motives behind devaluating pity, ridicule, and taunting (see Chapter 5). In ridicule and taunting are found the most blatant expression of the self-aggrandizing requirement of mourning. Bullies are typically insecure about their own status and are impelled to prove their own worth by deriding someone else.

The kind of ridicule undertaken solely for the purpose of seeking personal advantage in the suffering of another, however, is ethically taboo. Because it is so untutored and open, it is more frequently the instrument of children who have not learned more subtle ways to express their needs. Unfortunately, it is also children who bear the brunt of ridicule, children who may be quite defenseless to cope with unrelenting jeers. An indication of how common this form of self-aggrandizement is in children is given in a study of the nicknames of children living in an orphanage (Orgel & Tuckman, 1935). Nicknames of both boys and girls referred to physical defects in about one-third of the cases. Virtually all such nicknames were derogatory and produced resentment and ill feeling.

Among adults ridicule generally occurs more covertly, though open ridicule is by no means nonexistent. A man whose face is paralyzed on the right side reports that on the job ". . . the fellows made my life miserable. They would tell jokes and make faces the way I do when I talk. Or they would say 'are you trying to be tough, talking out of the side of your face?' " (Macgregor, 1951, p. 634). Usually, however, the expression of ridicule by adults is more subtle; it may assume the character of devaluating pity cloaked with sympathetic overtones. So-called playful teasing in some instances may be a more artful expression of underlying ridicule. On the basis of interviews with 200 male college students taking corrective physical education, it was concluded that experiences with adults were far more pleasant than experiences with children of the atypical child's own age or younger (Stafford, 1947, p. 80).

Management by the Recipient

What do young children do who are the object of taunts and jeers? They may try to strike back, but when the uncertain attempts are of no avail, their desperation may be vented in crying that is full of anger and hurt. Henry Viscardi, dwarfed as a result of congenitally deformed legs, presents a heart-breaking account of just such an experience. The scene is his first day at grade school:

Mamma and Papa had wisely chosen a flat in the same block as the school. It was on 101st Street near Amsterdam Avenue. My sister Terry took me to school the first day. Clutching her hand I hoisted myself up the steps to the schoolyard. It was crowded with children, bouncing balls, playing hopscotch, and running up and down the steps. I had never seen so many children, not even at the hospital. And these were all so big. I tried to back away.

"What's the matter, Henry?" Terry patted my shoulder. "You'll be all right—soon as you get used to it."

Then I heard loud laughter. "Hey, Louie, looka the ape man."

Three big boys came toward me.

"I'll show you where your room is." Terry jerked my hand.

The laughs grew louder. "Come on, Henry," Terry urged. Her cheeks were red.

The crowd of jeering boys had grown. One of them, who had a thin face and dirty, light-colored hair, came over and shoved me. I shoved back, against his knee.

"Oh, you wanta fight, kid?"

"Cut it out, Mike," somebody yelled.

"You—you—leave my brother alone." Terry almost cried. But the circle of boys held us in.

"Hey, ape man, what you got tied to your feet, boxing gloves?"

I looked down at my mismatching boots. They weren't a bit like the shoes the other boys wore.

"I want to go home." I hung on Terry's arm, tears rolling down my cheeks.

"Sissy, sissy. . . ."

Another big boy shoved me. I lost my balance and sprawled on the cement. Terry helped me up and brushed the dirt off my clothes. I started swinging my arms. The crowd pressed in and I couldn't see my sister anywhere.

Then the bell rang, and the boys ran into the building. Terry came back. "Here," she said, "blow your nose." She gave me her handkerchief. "Your hand's bleeding." I thought I saw tears in her eyes.

"Come on," she said. "I'll take you to your teacher." [Viscardi, 1952, pp. 13–14][20]

[20]Reprinted from *A man's stature* by H. Viscardi, Jr. (1952). By permission of Paul S. Eriksson, Pubs.

Henry Viscardi's first day at school—Raymond Goldman's first day at school (see pp. 224–225). How alike they were!

As such incidents recur, the recipient tries one way of reacting and then another, hoping to find some way which will be effective. Russell Criddle reviews his attempts to cope with ridicule as a young teenager with extremely poor vision:

There had been some teasing, some mimicry which I had already learned to tolerate during my first few years as a handicapped person. I knew that I must never retaliate to the various negative reactions which children usually had toward me. The best way, I had learned, was to pretend not to be hurt, and I sensed that in this way I eliminated the feeling of remorse that both I and others would suffer if I showed resistance, or retaliated. This submission, I think, balanced the distress caused others by my handicap.

There were a few boys of the little-bully type who wouldn't let me disregard their reactions. I tried a benevolent, understanding attitude toward them, an attitude which said to the rest of the class, "They don't hurt me. I know my eyes are funny, and it doesn't bother me if they laugh."

But what was, in truth, humility struck them as aloofness, and they were further irritated. In pretending not to be hurt or not to notice them I supplied sustenance for their stupidity and their insensible concepts of blindness.

I tried to make friends with the boys, to be one of them, entering into what they wanted to consider a game of wits—laughing with them when they "pulled a good one," covering up for them if they were caught by the teacher.

Once one of the boys, pretending to be engrossed in study, let his foot stick out into the aisle so that I would trip over it. The teacher hadn't seen his foot, but I know she suspected when she asked, "What happened, Russell?"

"I slipped," I said with a laugh. The teacher understood, as did the rest of the class, and I can understand how this added to the irritation of the boy who had tripped me. He was winning the scorn of everyone. Matters soon reached the stage of a running conflict. . . .

. . . It was in study hall. The teacher was out of the room, and I was reading a history book. I had not noticed Mike [a schoolmate] as he walked down the aisle toward my desk and was not aware of him until I felt the pain of a blow against my knuckles. He had struck them with the sharp edge of a foot rule, the kind which had a thick piece of metal imbedded along one edge.

I didn't flinch, I didn't move.

He hunched his buttocks upon the top of my desk so that he was half sitting there. I raised my head until I was looking into his face. I could see that he was smiling.

"Don't you have any feeling, Criddle?" he asked in a matter-of-fact tone. I stared at him, and he struck my knuckles again.

Someone said, "Aw, Mike, cut it out!"

"I'll stop when he asks me to," Mike said. He struck again. . . .

He was saying, in effect, Look, he isn't like us. He doesn't feel pain, and loneliness, and hunger. Blindness makes him different. It makes him defenseless. There is nothing he can do but let me hurt him until I get tired of the sport. This is fun, look at me smile.

I let my eyes fall to my knuckles. They were bloody.

Afterwards I was told that I just stared at my knuckles for a moment and then screamed and lunged at Mike with a force that knocked him across one row of desks into another aisle. I sprang after him, pounding his face with my bloody knuckles until he called for help. Then I started choking him. I remember Mr. Singleton pulling me away and leading me, hysterical, to the boys' washroom. [Criddle, 1953, pp. 98–99, 101–102][21]

The strategies attempted by Criddle over the years were:

Not to retaliate. To pretend not to be hurt.

To be benevolent and understanding, an attitude that says, "I know my eyes are funny, and it doesn't bother me if they laugh."

Not to notice the jeerers; to ignore them.

To join the jeerers by ridiculing himself and covering up for them.

To return the attack; to retaliate with physical force.

Actually, none of these tactics could be effective in all or even most situations, for as long as the attacker needs someone to step on to sustain his or her own uncertain status, the abuse will continue until the desired response of suffering is elicited. Thus, ignoring the jeers, showing understanding of them, or submitting to them only provokes more vigorous attacks. The bully must get the unfortunate person to admit the superiority of the attacker.

The method of active retaliation is effective only when the person is fortunate enough to be stronger than the attacker. Then the bully does not dare provoke that person again, but will turn to an easier target. The bully seeks another scapegoat because defeat at the hands of the first has injured a vulnerable self-esteem still further, an insult that can be avenged by forcing inferiority on someone else.

In the discussion of curiosity, it was seen how the recipient may actively retaliate in nonphysical ways, for example, through biting sarcasm. However, to return the jeers of a bully is effective only when the child is more masterful at this game than is the bully. Too often a child who is ridiculed is so humiliated that the control required for

[21]Reprinted from *Love is not blind,* by R. Criddle. New York: Norton, 1953.

effective sarcastic retort is lacking. Weak submission, pretense, and angry attack seem to be easier ways to defend the self.

Recommendations

What, then, is the answer, if there is no fully adequate way for children to cope with ridicule? It is our opinion that extraordinary care should be taken to eliminate as far as possible exposure to ridicule. All too often the child "learns" to agree that he or she is indeed a pitiful object that ought to be scorned. Moreover, the power of ridicule to defeat the recipient is so great that even a single such attack in childhood can leave emotional scars.

The most general need is for the development of accepting attitudes toward disability through education at all levels of community life. In accord with democratic principles, education against religious and racial discrimination has been encouraged, and only recently has serious attention been given in the schools to the necessity for education in the overcoming of prejudice toward persons with disabilities. We need good visual aids and other methods in the elementary and high schools to inform children that physical attributes and styles of life differ widely among individuals, that within this assortment of differences lies the common core of the human being, that differences per se need not make a difference in many important areas of living together. If these views were part of the broad teaching of community and school, the problem in the case of a single child would be vastly simpler.

It is encouraging to find increasing acceptance of these views in enabling legislation and good educational materials. The development of programs to foster positive attitudes takes more wisdom and skill than one might imagine because such powerful forces as the requirement of mourning and other psychological traps can so readily undermine the effort. As we have seen, however, the effort will be on safe ground if the message is geared to the *person with a disability* rather than to the disabled person, to the coping aspects in the situation rather than to the succumbing aspects. Thinking along these lines can go far in developing constructive attitudes, not only for the benefit of someone else who is different but also for oneself as well, since no one can excel in everything. The matter of developing constructive views of life with a disability is so important that the last chapter of this volume is devoted to it.

In addition to general preparation in the schools on the matter of disability, it is sometimes helpful to pave the way specifically for a child who is markedly different and who is about to enter school or any other group. This has the possibility, at least, of abating inordinate curiosity and of furthering the realization that this child who is different is for all that a child who is the same. Sometimes the principal may be the best person to lead the discussion, sometimes the teacher, sometimes an invited speaker, and sometimes the parent. Karen's mother relates how she went to speak to the kindergarten class the day before Karen was to start school:

> "I have a little girl, just your size, named Karen," I began in a conversational tone. "She's nice and laughs a lot and has freckles and pigtails." I turned to a tot at the nearest table. "But her pigtails are not as long as yours." I had done enough public speaking to know when I had established "contact."
> "Now God didn't make Karen's legs as strong as yours," I went on, "so we have to help them get strong, so she can walk. Some children wear braces to help their teeth and Karen wears braces to help her legs. There are some things she can't do and some games she can't play. Sister will let some of you help her once in a while. But don't spoil her!" I laughed as I stood up. I went over to the doll house, admired it properly and asked the little lass in blue to show me some of the furnishings. "We have a real bureau with drawers that go in and out that will just fit in the bedroom. Karen will bring it tomorrow. Good-by, Sister, good-by, kids," I waved. [Killilea, 1952, p. 111][22]

The words were few and simple, but they struck just the right chord. They prepared the children to see a child who is really a child, so much like them, yet different in particular ways; a child who needs help, but only some of the time; a child who is managing her difficulties and can be part of the group.

Parents of children with disabilities may perhaps be heartened by the realization that with maturity their children will be better able to cope with ridicule and other difficult social situations and that among the adult population the rules have changed. Although pity is common, the public expression of ridicule tends to be more controlled. Viscardi was not taunted during his first day at college as he was upon entering first grade.

In the last analysis we need to improve society's general mental health so that the need to tear another person down in order to build oneself up will become an insignificant factor in the social relations among people. The bully, too, is a person with a disability, in this case an emotional disability, and he or she also requires help and understanding in the effort toward better adjustment.

Curiosity, discussion of the disability, help, fear of being a burden, sympathy, devaluating pity, social participation, taunting, and

---

[22]Reprinted with permission from *Karen* by Marie Killilea. © 1952 by Marie Lyons Killilea. Published by Prentice-Hall, Inc., Englewood Cliffs, New Jersey 07632.

ridicule—these interpersonal relations are especially potent in the lives of persons with disabilities. Examination of these relations not only shows that their significance is part of the broader problem of the meaning of disability to the agent and to the recipient but points the way toward more satisfying relationships. Such concepts as status value, coping, succumbing, and spread appear again and again in the analysis of everyday relationships and in the recommendations for improving them.

Yet a good deal of the burden in interpersonal relations will be borne by the person who has the disability. Although the pathology may lie with the group, the person with the disability is the one who is annoyed or hurt most directly. It is he or she who has to "take it," who has to handle the ineptitudes of others in the ordinary affairs of getting along. Because often one's own management can ameliorate or add to the difficulties, special preparation for the kinds of disturbing situations one is likely to encounter is very much in order. This topic is treated in the following chapter.

Chapter 14
Preparing the Person for Difficult Social Encounters

One way to prepare people to meet the challenge of difficult social encounters is to strengthen their sense of who they are, their sense of personal worth and human dignity. We have already discussed the powerful role of the self-concept in both the interpretation and handling of interpersonal relations (Chapter 12). There are other ways to meet the challenge, as seen in the great variety of approaches that have been developed to help a person become more skillful when interacting with others (for reviews see Bellack & Hersen, 1979; Galassi & Galassi, 1978; 1979; Rich & Schroeder, 1976; Smith, 1975; Thelen et al., 1979; Twentyman & Zimmering, 1979). The present chapter describes a few approaches that give the person an opportunity to experience alternate ways of evaluating and handling potentially disturbing social interactions. These approaches are suitable for use in support groups.

ROLE PLAYING

Role playing is a method in which problem situations are acted out by various members of the training group who have been assigned certain roles. It stems from psychodramatic methods of therapy used by Moreno (1937).

The form of the role playing can vary widely, depending on the purposes of the session. "The problem situation and the roles to be played may be defined so strictly as to constitute . . . a demonstration; or they may be set so loosely that the 'play' is highly spontaneous and the outcome all but unpredictable. The play may deal with a single incident, or it may contain a series of incidents each growing out of the preceding one. Various individuals playing parts may be instructed as to how to react if certain events take place, or they may be told to react 'naturally' " (Bavelas, 1947, p. 184).

To teach social skills, it is Bavelas' experienced judgment that effective role playing requires (1) the use of carefully planned "stereotype" situations as basic training material and (2) rather close controls of all roles being played, with the exception of the role primarily under consideration—that one being left entirely free to be played as the individual sees fit (Bavelas, 1947, p. 187).

The following is an adaptation to disability problems of an outline by Bavelas describing the succession of events in a typical role-playing session (Bavelas, 1947, pp. 187–189). Let us imagine a group of ten persons with orthopedic disabilities gathered together:

1. The session is begun with a short discussion of the general area in which the problems to be taken up lie. In our example, it is the ordinary social experiences encountered daily by a person with a disability. The group may be encouraged to describe cases or personal experiences that illustrate the various aspects of the problem.

2. If this is the first time role playing has been attempted, a few minutes should be spent preparing the group for the experience. It might be pointed out that people often think they know how they should behave, but in actuality it doesn't work out; that research has shown that living the situation by acting it out allows for direct observation and discussion of the pitfalls and positive consequences of different behaviors.

3. Two of the participants are then selected to go out of the room. Particularly if role playing is new to the group, individuals should be selected who are expected to have least trouble in entering into the spirit of the thing.

4. The problem situation to be enacted is then described to the rest of the group. This might be developed from an earlier discussion on problems of everyday relationships, but often the situation has greater teaching value if it has been carefully planned by the leader in advance of the meeting. It might be a situation in which a person with an obvious disability realizes that two strangers are staring and talking about him or her. Enough background information should be given so that not only will the problem come alive but those who

are to play the auxiliary roles (in this case the two strangers), would also have a fairly clear notion of how they are to feel and act. For example, the details might be:

(a) The two strangers, a husband and wife who are seated in a bus, watch someone with crutches and leg braces laboriously enter and find a seat. (b) The husband and wife have a child who suffered severe crippling in an accident a few years ago. (c) They watch the person intently because they are very much interested in the Canadian-type crutches being used (i.e., short crutches held by the hands). Their own son uses the long arm crutches. (d) They comment about this together in a low tone, wondering if their child could be fitted with short crutches. (e) They smile in a friendly way when the person with crutches glances in their direction.

5. Two members of the group are selected or volunteer to play the roles of husband and wife. In initial sessions, the leader may play one of these roles. If the group is very small, one person may play the husband or wife with an imaginary partner.

6. It is pointed out that the individuals out of the room who will play the person with the crutches and braces (the primary player) will not be told anything about the strangers. The primary player will simply be informed that the scene is a bus which he or she is to enter with some effort and find a seat. The primary player notices two people staring and talking about him or her.

7. Enough simple "props" are set up to bring the situation to life. In this case, chairs may be used to indicate the seats of the bus. Their arrangement is important for it should allow for different seat choices and varied behavior on the part of the main actor in interacting with the strangers.

8. The group is asked if the setting is clear. It is well for some discussion to take place that will orient the group to what to look for. Questions may be raised briefly, such as "What might the person on crutches do? Will he or she feel self-conscious? Angry? Hurt? Annoyed? Indifferent? Friendly? How will these feelings manifest themselves? Why did the person on crutches choose the seat he or she did?"

9. One of the players waiting outside is then called in. The setting is explained and the action may be started: "The problem is clear? Very well. You are entering the bus here. It takes quite a bit of effort. You notice these two people watching you. You are to find a seat and behave as any person would in such a situation." Because the primary players are asked to act the role of someone in general with their disability, they are protected from the threat of too great personal exposure. In later sessions, when the group has become more secure, personal roles labeled as such may more safely be enacted. In either case discussion of the behavior is productive.

10. This kind of situation may end by itself with the person finding a seat and, for example, gazing out the window. Sometimes the situation does not come to an end naturally if left alone. The leader must then decide when the play has gone on long enough for the purposes of the session and end it.

11. The primary player is then asked to join the group. Those aspects of the problem which the primary player is not aware of are explained (such as the fact that the strangers have a child with a disability) so that he or she can watch the second player on a par with the rest of the group. The trainer briefly sums up the action that took place in the first play without giving any interpretations. Sometimes it is helpful to outline the events briefly on a blackboard and cover it up before the second play starts. Discussion does not take place at this point. Rather the group is primed to look for differences between what they have seen and the next play.

12. The second player is called in and the procedure is repeated. The persons taking the role of husband and wife essentially repeat their previous behavior.

13. When the second play has ended, the leader sums up the action of the play and reviews what happened in the first one. The review is important because the second player must be brought up to date. If a blackboard is used, there will now be two outlines, each describing the action in one of the plays.

14. Before general discussion begins, it is usually best to ask all the actors for their reactions. This gives the players a chance to share why they acted as they did and serves to give the group additional information.

15. The meeting is then opened to general discussion. It is sometimes helpful to get a third outline on the board indicating what the group now feels would be the preferred behavior of the person with the disability. The preferred behavior should be examined in terms of principles since there is generally no one best way of doing things.

16. A member of the group who has not yet played a role is selected to act out the main role along the lines indicated by the group. The group is instructed to watch carefully for flaws in what they have set up as "preferred" behavior.

17. There is considerable value in making a tape recording of the role playing. This permits checking remembered events against the actuality and listening to nuances of verbal expression and tone.

Modifications of this type of role-playing session to fit specific conditions and purposes readily suggest themselves. A white cane and dark glasses can be substituted for crutches and braces. The group can consist of persons with diverse disabilities or similar disabilities and even of individuals with and without disabilities. The sex and age of the characters can vary. Problem situations involving help, sympathy, pity, ridicule, curiosity, or nonparticipation can be tried. The primary character need not always be a person with a disability; it may be enlightening to the person and the group to center on the role of an able-bodied person.

Bavelas (1947) points up the following advantages of role playing, illustrated here in terms of disability problems:

1. Playing a role before an "audience" makes an individual self-conscious. This self-consciousness is desirable because it makes the individual aware of his or her own actions in a new way. In general the person makes the same mistakes made unconsciously in real life; however, because of the self-reflective nature of role playing, the person is able to point out some of these errors as soon as the play is over.
2. Since the secondary roles are also played by members of the group, it is possible to get direct expression of the effects caused by the actions of the primary actor. For example, the persons playing the role of the curious strangers can report their reactions to the behavior of the person on crutches. This helps the trainees to get better insight into the effects of their actions on others.
3. Sometimes the individual who has just played the role of the person with a disability assumes the role of an able-bodied person in the very next play. This offers the stimulating experience of "feeling the difference" between the two positions.
4. The fact that sooner or later everyone takes a turn at playing a role alerts the audience to the positive and negative features of the current play.
5. Role playing has the advantage of emphasizing *showing* how one would do something rather than *telling* how one would do it. Many individuals who "talk a good game" are woefully inadequate when it comes to performing the actions.
6. Role playing is conducive to experimentation in ways of behaving. The mistakes made do not have negative consequences for real-life situations. Moreover, the atmosphere in role-playing sessions is (or ideally should be) sympathetic and constructive rather than condemning.

Assertive role playing is a special form of role playing in which two people from the group adopt antagonistic roles, one that of a person with a particular disability, and the other of a person who denies him or her access to a needed opportunity (Williams, 1979). In the following example the simulation involves a personnel manager and a person with multiple sclerosis seeking employment.

The player who is to simulate a person with multiple sclerosis is given the following profile: "You have a high school diploma and a certificate from an area vocational-technical school in clerical and business-machine skills. You are trying to return to the work force, but have recently been diagnosed as having multiple sclerosis."

The player assuming the role of personnel manager is given a series of statements that pose objections to hiring a person with multiple sclerosis. Thus, he or she begins by saying: "I'm impressed with your credentials, but our insurer insists that it screen all applications and you are not acceptable as an employee because you are a bad health insurance risk."

The person with multiple sclerosis is then asked to respond. Others in the group are encouraged to participate until an understanding of how best to deal with this problem is reached.

The personnel manager then escalates the confrontation further by stating: "I notice that you need rest periods every few hours, but we only give a 10-minute break in midmorning and midafternoon, so I'm afraid you just won't work out." Again the person with multiple sclerosis is asked to respond and others in the group join the effort to demolish the validity of this argument.

Depending on the available time, a number of prepared typical encounters with attitudinal barriers can be role played using different simulated disabilities, different problems, and different settings. The confrontation is designed to force members of the group to assert themselves in meeting the challenge of overcoming barriers to equal opportunity.

Role playing can also be used to give people practice in casually referring to their own disability as a way of putting another person at ease. An example of a humorous self-reference is given by Russell on page 274 (Scene II) and one that is matter-of-fact given by Karen on page 301. Research has shown that referring to one's visible disability in a natural way when getting acquainted has positive effects (Evans, 1976). Where the disability is not obvious, role playing may be useful in helping the person become more comfortable in self-disclosing when the situation is appropriate.

The answer to what is an appropriate situation is not always simple, however. When rehabilitation clients and professionals were asked the question "Do you advocate full disclosure to prospective employers of a handicapping condition, or hiding it when it is possible?" judgments varied, although most subjects were inclined toward disclosure (Leviton, 1973). Examples of tips offered to clients and to counselors are: *To clients* (p. 64): "Don't volunteer information, but tell the truth if directly asked." "Disclose the facts, not on an application blank, but in an interview where you can explain the irrelevancy of the handicap and emphasize your good points." "Ideally, one should be honest, but size up the employer and decide the possible effects of telling." *To counselors* (p. 65): "The client's wishes should be the determining factor when advising him." "The characteristics of the client must be taken into account: does he constitute a danger . . . ?" "The counsellor should intervene if necessary to straighten out an employer's mistaken ideas of what is involved in the handicap."

Several studies have demonstrated the positive changes that can be initiated when role playing is well planned. As part of the series of experiments already referred to on answering antiminority remarks (pp. 304–305), subjects were given training with respect to the manner and content of the most effective answers (Citron & Harding, 1950). The basic training method was role playing and discussion. In the role-playing sessions, the subjects assumed the role of the answerer to the bigot's remark. Discussion of the incident followed. Five sessions of about 2 hours each produced marked improvement in ability to answer according to principles based on general psychological knowledge, on experience with incident situations, and on the results of previous experiments. Well-prepared role playing and discussion sessions have also been used as effective methods in the training of leaders (Bavelas, 1942; French, 1944; Lippitt, 1943; Zander, 1947), management (Bavelas, 1947), foremen (French, 1945), interviewers (Barron, 1947), and, as shown in Chapter 19, the public at large.

It is Lippitt's conviction that "a training process which aims to effect changes in the behavior style of a person cannot efficiently depend upon lectures or other patterns of verbalization such as discussion. Actual experimentation in the desired 'ways of behaving' must be provided, in situations where intensive guidance and encouragement is possible, and where the pressures against making mistakes are removed" (Lippitt, 1943, pp. 291–293). Role playing is a widely accepted approach for effecting change both in behavior and attitudes.

REAL-LIFE SITUATIONS WITH A PERSON WHO "KNOWS"

Another promising teaching procedure deals directly with real-life experiences by having the person who is faced with a disability accompany someone well versed in handling disability matters on various social excursions. Russell (1949), the veteran who lost both hands in World War II, was fortunate enough to have such an experience while still in the hospital. Charley McGonegal, whose hand amputations antedated Russell's by one world war, took a drive with Russell and Tony, a hospital mate:

. . . At first we thought he was joking. How could anyone with hooks, even if he was Charley McGonegal, handle a car? We soon found out. Charley didn't have any special gadgets or gimmicks on the steering wheel or gear-shift, but he was a smooth, capable driver. After we'd driven awhile, he stopped the car and let Tony and me try it. To my surprise, I discovered it wasn't very difficult at all. I just grabbed hold of the wheel with my hooks and off we went.

But the incident that left an even deeper impression on me took place that afternoon. Charley drove us into town and we stopped off for a soda. He steered us to the most conspicuous table in the place and ordered sodas and a package of cigarets. When the waitress brought the cigarets he made quite a show of opening the package, pulling out the cigarets, passing them around and lighting them for us. Everyone in the store watched him as if it were some kind of theatrical performance which, as it turned out, it was. Charley wasn't the least bit disconcerted by their fascinated stares. He acted as cool, as unconcerned as though we were all alone.

On the way back to Reed I noticed something odd. He pulled out a silver case filled with cigarets, lit one. Then I got the point of that little performance back in the soda parlor. He purposely ordered the pack of cigarets, which he didn't really need, just to show us, in his own quiet, indirect way, how to behave with strangers gawking at you. [pp. 108–109][1]

The effectiveness of such an experience can be partly attributed to the following: McGonegal gave meaning to the situation by his behavior. Instead of indicating that the situation was threatening, he produced a totally different interpretation. Strangers gawking could gawk without ruffling the object of their curiosity. In the same way does parental teaching often proceed. The child may not be afraid to be left in the nursery school until the oversolicitous behavior and concerned look of the parent tells the child that this is and should be a dangerous situation. Situations often become fearful, embarrassing, friendly, or comfortable, depending on the meaning defined by the behavior and reaction of others.

It should not be assumed that one such experience as Russell had, however impressive it was, is enough to ensure smooth social relationships in the future. Russell had yet to suffer much bitterness in his encounters with others, for until he began to accept his disability, the experience with McGonegal could be only potentially helpful. But it was there, as part of his reservoir of meaningful recollections, to aid him when he was ready to utilize it.

Again, modifications of this procedure may be introduced. The

[1]Reprinted by permission of Farrar, Straus & Giroux, Inc. From *Victory in my hands* by H. Russell & V. Rosen. Copyright 1949 by Harold Russell & Victor Rosen. Copyright renewed © 1976 by Harold Russell.

size of the group venturing forth can be varied, as well as the situations to be experienced. Discussion of the experience may follow, or its impact may well be left for personal reflection. A second expedition to the same setting may take place so that the person can observe change in his or her own reactions. The person may be encouraged to take a lead in the ongoing social events, or may be allowed to assume a back-seat position from which to observe and experience. In any case, observing the behavior of an experienced person in a situation which is important to the learner is apt to leave him or her with an impression so potent as to produce changes in feelings and behavior.

It would be well for administrators of rehabilitation programs to reflect upon this matter. Just as provision is made for the employment of physical therapists, so ought provision be made for the employment of persons with disabilities whose adjustment and experience have taught them wisely. Opportunity could then be provided for patients to be exposed to a variety of real-life situations with a person who "knows."

REAL-LIFE SITUATIONS WITH OTHER NOVICES

Real-life situations are also experienced to advantage by groups of persons with similar disabilities, all of whom are "learners." The fact that there is likely to be a variety of reactions and interpretations of the situation tends to stimulate reappraisal of the disability and events connected with it. In an early experience, during his first pass to town from the hospital, Russell (1949) became bitterly upset when a stranger offered drinks and made reference to his hands (see pp. 273–274). He defiantly ended the episode by ordering the man away and shaking his hooks at him, threatening, "Before I give you these." The following conversation then took place among the buddies:

> "I guess maybe we better get used to have people pester us like that," one of the boys said.
> "Why the hell should we?" I said. "It's none of their damn business. Would any of us go up to somebody and ask him if he was wearing a toupee or had store teeth?"
> "Maybe they just figure we're heroes and belong to them, our great, adoring public—"
> "Nuts!"
> "Or maybe they think it's patriotic to be interested in us—"
> "Or maybe," one of the others said, "they feel kind of guilty because they're not in there pitching and so they want to make up for it by slobberin' all over us." [p. 123]

Russell learned much as a result of this experience, even though he could only gradually put it into practice. He learned that people like himself, others who had an amputation, could see some acceptable motives in the stranger. His buddies implied another way of handling the situation predicated on the proposition that they ought to get used to the behavior of strangers. Such suggestions are more apt to be taken seriously by the person when they come from someone who also has a disability; otherwise it is natural to discredit the advice because a nondisabled person "just couldn't understand."

Rehabilitation and hospital centers might well consider the feasibility of arranging excursions into the outside world by small groups of patients. There the patients will be exposed to the staring and curiosity of strangers, offers to help, and expressions of sympathy and devaluating pity, but they will experience these situations together, and together they will be able to discuss them. In so doing they may discover new meanings and more effective ways of managing. Variations, of course, may be introduced. An experienced person, with or without a disability, may be called in to join the discussion. Eventually the patient may be encouraged to venture forth alone. For this short period one is on one's own, but after returning to the temporary refuge of the hospital or rehabilitation center, the person will be able to relieve oneself of the questions and irritations encountered by sharing with others who understand.

There are other inexpensive methods by which the patient can gradually be introduced to the uncertain outside within the more protective environment of the hospital. For example, after the initial medical phases of treatment, it may be feasible to transfer the patient to a mixed convalescent ward instead of keeping him or her on a ward for people with a particular type of disability. In this way the patient comes into contact with persons with a variety of ailments who will stare, ask questions, and offer advice; the patient will be exposed to "ordinary social relations" in an atmosphere in which status differences are leveled and sympathetic understanding is more easily sensed and accepted.

SHARING LIFE EXPERIENCES THROUGH GROUP DISCUSSION

Free discussion of common problems of interaction with other people can lead to ideas never before entertained, ideas which may effect basic changes within the value system of the person and in his or her behavior. The following is a transcript of a tape recorded discussion by a group of children with cerebral palsy, ages 11 to 14 years, about their experiences in being with other people. The discussion is led by their friend and teacher (Sutter, 1954). Joe's speech is hardly intelligible, Eddy's is moderately involved, and Bobby's, Carol's, and Lily's is very clear:

EDDY: Sometimes wise guys just come along and decide to pick on you. I mean sometimes I sat just there and watched these kids the way they talk about you and the way they look at you and stare at you. I don't know. I just come to the conclusion that they just have to get used to you.

TEACHER: Good enough, Eddy.

BOBBY: Well, they kid you about your condition and some of the younger kids kid you and some of the older kids they kid you saying, "Oh, you can't run as fast, Oh, you keep falling down. Why can't you run fast and why can't you talk so good?"

TEACHER: Any of the rest of you have any experiences? Like Bobby's? Carol?

CAROL: Well, Mrs. Sutter, you know I went to Juilliard School of Music two summers ago in New York and I spent six weeks in the city and once or twice when my companion went shopping or when we were even coming out of our apartment children, I mean, children, would stop me on the street and say, "Hey, what's the matter with you" . . . because children stop me more so than adults actually and just saying "What's the matter? What's wrong with you?" And I'd say, "I have cerebral palsy." And I'd say, "I wouldn't care," and my companion would try to pull me away from it but I would just be willing to tell them."

TEACHER: It's a good thing to face these things if we have to. Yes, Joe. Joe is very anxious to say something. All right, Joe.

JOE: When you walk down the street people look at you.

TEACHER: [Repeating in order to make his remarks understandable.] People look at you.

JOE: And stare.

TEACHER: And stare. How do you feel when that happens, Joe? All right, tell us.

JOE: [Unintelligibly]

TEACHER: The best thing is to ignore them, said Joe.

ONE OF THE

CHILDREN: Yes, that's what I said.

TEACHER: Yes, it is, but how about what you're going to do about the way you're feeling inside? Yes, Bobby, what?

BOBBY: After I tell 'em I say well, take one of the kids who is about five, you know. And he said, "What's the matter with you? Can't you walk?" I said, "I've got cerebral palsy." He said, "What's that? Is it like polio?" and I said, "Something like that. If you have it, you have it and you go on."

[1 minute of discussion omitted.]

TEACHER: Eddy has wanted to say something over here. Now have you forgotten? I hope not, Eddy. You had your hand up.

EDDY: Well, I'm trying to say that many times I walk down the street and people who are a good twenty or thirty years old and they just stand there and look at you most of the time. It burns me up, the way they look at you. It doesn't even bother you if a small child looks at you but you get these grownup people. I don't know; most of the time I don't say nothing to 'em.

TEACHER: No you can't.

EDDY [continuing]: The idea is mostly ignore them but sometimes you can't. You know. As how you have to tell them something.

TEACHER: Yes, Bobby?

BOBBY: It isn't the way the grownups look at you, but I remember one time I was at the theater you know. I couldn't hold still you know. I tried to keep stiff because people were watching you know. But I just couldn't and one of them says, "Hey kid, don't you mind your manners or something."

TEACHER: Oh, yes. There could be that kind of misunderstanding.

BOBBY [Continuing]: But I couldn't keep them stiff any longer because it had been a long time.

TEACHER: Sometimes adult C.P.'s who are out in public and maybe they walk with sort of a staggering gait with which we are all sort of familiar with, aren't we?

CHILDREN: Yes, we know.

TEACHER: And other people, what do they think? [The children say something.] Yes, they think they are intoxicated. There is that sort of misunderstanding, too.

JOE [With very belabored speech]: I think sympathy people. . . .

TEACHER [Helping him out]: Oh, I'm glad you mentioned that. Sympathy people, people who are too full of sympathy.

ONE OF THE
CHILDREN: Oh you poor boy! That sort of people.

TEACHER: Tell me about it.

BOBBY: One time I met an old lady and I was sorta, I couldn't walk so good and she says, "Oh you poor little boy!" [Children laugh with amusement.]

TEACHER: And what's the answer to that? I don't know. I don't know. Do you?

BOBBY [Continuing]: She said, "You poor little boy. What's the matter with you, you drink too much soda or something?" [Children laugh.] That kind of stuff makes me sick!

TEACHER: Eddy?

EDDY: Well, last night I was in the movies and along comes someone in the town, a noseybody I should say, and he says, "Oh, leave him alone, he's a—" [Eddy then interjects] you know, I don't like to use this word "cripple," and well I just get up and I tell 'em that right off, I tell 'em, "What's it to you?" I mean, I don't know I just like to tell them so they don't bother me no more 'cause I just *hate* that word.

BOBBY: And I just hate that word. Because there's a kid up my block who's always. . . . One time I was walking down the street and this kid was with me, you know, and an old lady comes along and she almost tripped over me and she says, "Oh, he's crippled, don't touch him." [said with scorn]

TEACHER: There's that word again Eddy said he didn't like to use. Let's face that word very squarely. It's a label, isn't it, that word "crippled," it's a label and you don't like it, do you?

CHILDREN: No.

TEACHER: No. Are there any other ways of being crippled than in your legs or in your hands?

CHILDREN [Answering in unison]: Yes!

TEACHER: Yes. And in an even more important way, you know?

JOE: Inside.

TEACHER: Joe said inside and he meant?

CAROL: To be crippled in your feelings!

EDDY: About that, uh, I don't want to go back to that word, . . . about that idea of people sympathizing with you, and stuff like that. Well, there are two kinds and don't forget. There are the guys who don't look at your handicap who look at . . . uh, well, I can give you an example. A number of times when Allen a couple of years ago here would pick on me and someone would come up and say, "Lay off. He's smaller than you," or "He can't fight back as good as you" or . . . I mean they don't mention that, they don't make you understand that you are, as I said before, crippled or handicapped.

TEACHER: Yes. That is in other words, excuse me, Eddy, there may be occasions when you really do need help from somebody else but there are ways and ways of giving help. And now the other kind?

EDDY: The other kind I don't care much for.

TEACHER: I know you don't.

EDDY: I just don't like it, that's all.

TEACHER: Yes. Because one has real understanding and the other has none.

BOBBY [Excitedly]: Oh, boy! This was an experience. This was yesterday, as a matter of fact. This guy, he was walking along, you know, and he thought that I kept falling down when I was walking down the street. And he said to me, he said, "How do you feel?" and I said, "I feel fine." And he said, "What's the matter?" I said, "Well, I'm handicapped, that's all." [The rest of the children laugh.] He said, "Oh, you better see a doctor." Oh boy, that kills me.

TEACHER: Well, this is good for us to talk about. Yes, Lily.

LILY: I also find it very hard to accept the fact when people sometimes see that you can walk, let's say, all right with one cane, that you're capable. Maybe they don't see it but when you feel that you can walk perfectly well, but maybe another person doesn't see it, and they try and help you. You know they try very hard.

TEACHER: That is pretty natural. It's awfully hard not to, Lily. You know, after all these years I still have to catch myself. I want to help you. I have to remember not to. Diane, how do you feel about this?

What did the children gain from this discussion? How did it affect their reactions to the difficulties of ordinary living? We do not know. And what we can guess at is based partly on clinical observations that sharing thoughts and feelings can bring about change in outlook and partly on faith. How could it be otherwise than helpful to hear one among the group say, when affronted, "I've got cerebral palsy. . . . If you have it, you have it and you go on"? How could it be otherwise than helpful to have the children distinguish between two kinds of "sympathy," the understanding kind and the pitying kind? The fact that the children could hear each other complain about some of the annoyances on the outside, the fact that they could laugh about some of the misunderstandings, undoubtedly serves to relieve some of the burden. When this is bolstered by new understandings of one's own feelings and the feelings of others, important preparation for subsequent changes in the management of social relations has taken place.

New understanding of one's own feelings and the feelings of others can sometimes be achieved through self-examination of one's own reaction to the disability of others. A deaf woman, whose speech was quite difficult to understand, shared a discovery she made after encountering a child with cerebral palsy (Including Me, 1977). Prior to that time, she became angry toward people who constantly avoided her. She found herself having to reach out to others, having to make the first move in most situations. She couldn't understand why people wouldn't readily approach her. Why did they seem so uneasy and afraid of her when they met her? Then she met a child with cerebral palsy. Suddenly this young woman became anxious and afraid. She didn't know how to relate or communicate with this child. She wanted to pull away. Then she realized! This feeling of uncertainty and inability to communicate with the child was the same reaction other people had felt toward her. This young woman decided to help others understand her disability and herself as a person so as to ease their feelings of anxiety and make freer communication possible. One can see how sharing such a sequence of events in group discussion can help pave the way for the learning of new social skills.

Discussion of stories designed to prepare a person for experiences that might be painful has also proved useful. It has been reported (Dinkel, 1947) that a black father had considerable success in softening the shock of race prejudice upon his children through the use of stories he began telling before they had had encounters with white hostility. The fictitious black children who were the principal characters in these stories went through a series of incidents of the kind that the father anticipated his children would experience. By means of doll play he also rehearsed techniques with his children that could be used to avoid or lessen the difficulties that might befall them. When they later encountered racial antagonism, they were able to handle it more skillfully than neighboring children who had not had such careful training. Discussion of stories can also be helpful in the case of adults who find difficulty in referring to their own personal experiences and feelings. By discussing the behavior and attitudes of a character in a story, direct exposure of oneself is avoided. Favorable use of stories with adults who have an amputation has been reported (Dembo, Leviton, & Wright, 1956).

It is known that discussion is likely to be more effective in producing change when combined with actually *trying out* new ways of behaving than when it stands alone. French (1944) reports a study of retraining an autocratic leader. In spite of the fact that full discussion had taken place in the group concerning the advantages of democratic procedures in leading a discussion, one of the trainees completely regressed to his usual autocratic style when he was asked to lead. The children with cerebral palsy who shared their everyday troubling experiences could well capitalize on their discussion by some form of reality practice where the new learnings are brought to life and thus more firmly set by behavioral experience. Notice that the black father had his children *act out,* in play with dolls, the techniques demonstrated in the stories.

The learning experiences described above take place in a group whose participants share similar problems. The group may have a trained leader but need not in all cases. Much is gained when the learning experience stimulates a new look at the self and others as well as new possibilities of behavior. Insofar as the intention is to promote behavioral skills as well as cognitive restructuring and adjustive attitudes, it is advisable to use some form of reality practice in addition to observation and verbal exchange.

Chapter 15
Motivating Children in the Rehabilitation Program

The problem of learning and motivation involves incentives, rewards and punishments, goals and subgoals, success and failure, values and meanings, and much more. Whereas learning involves the acquisition of new knowledge and behavior, motivation is more strictly concerned with incentives—what propels a person to engage in an activity or to acquire knowledge.

The chapter begins with a brief review of the main notions underlying three approaches to understanding learning and motivation, namely, operant conditioning, cognitive development, and observational learning. Some basic issues are raised, followed by case demonstrations of four children and one young adult engaged in some phase of rehabilitation. Included are a home situation and institutional settings involving physical therapy, speech therapy, and a behavior problem. The chapter concludes with ten questions that ought to be checked out whenever one is examining the learning experiences of children in a rehabilitation program. Although the focus is on children, the issues raised are applicable to adults as well.

CONTINGENCIES OF REINFORCEMENT IN OPERANT CONDITIONING

The emphasis in the operant conditioning approach is on what the person does, not on what he or she feels (Skinner, 1938, 1953, 1974). Yet it should be recognized that the thoughts and feelings of the person are being increasingly solicited in both planning the program of behavior change and helping the person gain self-control (Sulzer-Azaroff & Mayer, 1977). Another important idea is that specific problem behavior is viewed as the real problem, not as a symptom of some underlying conflict. A review of the application of operant principles to rehabilitation problems appears in Fordyce (1971).

The word *operant* refers to the idea that behavior operates on the environment and thereby produces effects or consequences. It is the effects or consequences that either reinforce the behavior, maintain it, reduce it, or eliminate it. Therefore, operant methodology focuses intensely on the consequences of behavior (reinforcement contingencies) when dealing with the problem of motivation.

Briefly, there are five basic strategies that involve the provision or withholding of positive consequences on the one hand and negative consequences on the other. In the case of desirable behavior, two of these strategies are used. One involves reinforcing the occurrence of desired behavior by what is commonly referred to as a reward. Sometimes the behavior itself is intrinsically reinforcing, as when one enjoys an activity. Then an extrinsic reward is not necessary. Sometimes the behavior is accompanied with sufficient frequency by positive reinforcers that occur naturally in the environment. A specially planned positive reinforcement schedule is then unnecessary. Positive reinforcers usually take the form of approval, pleasant activities, or tangible payoffs. Should any of these not increase the frequency of the desired behavior, it is not a positive reinforcer for that individual.

The second method of reinforcing desired behavior involves the withdrawal or avoidance of an aversive stimulus when the desired behavior occurs. This method is referred to as negative reinforcement: For example, a child avoids the irritation of a neck brace by holding his or her head erect. The aversive stimulus is thereby withdrawn and the correct posture negatively reinforced.

To reduce the frequency of undesirable behavior, two kinds of punishment are used. One involves the introduction of an aversive stimulus, like scolding or spanking, as a consequence of the misbehavior. Severe punishment is not generally advocated because of its variable and complicating effects, although it is sometimes recommended when behavior is clearly self-injurious (e.g., head banging), when costs and benefits are carefully weighed, or as a last resort when other approaches have proved ineffective.

An alternative method of punishment is to withdraw something positive, such as privileges or attention, whenever the undesirable behavior occurs. Positive consequences may also be withheld by removing the individual from the enjoyable situation in which the misbehavior occurs, a procedure known as "time out."

Besides punishment, misbehavior can be extinguished when it doesn't pay off. No aversive stimulus is introduced, no "cost" is imposed. The behavior is simply no longer reinforced. Extinction can occur during the time-out period.

The five basic reinforcement strategies can be summarized as follows:

Desirable behavior

1. Positive reinforcement or reward—positive consequences are provided.
2. Negative reinforcement—aversive consequences are withdrawn.

Undesirable behavior

3. Punishment—aversive consequences are provided.
4. Punishment—positive consequences are withdrawn.
5. Extinction—nothing happens in the environment.

The use of reinforcement techniques presumes that the person knows how to perform the desired behavior; that is, that the behavior is within the individual's repertoire. If this is not the case, the problem becomes one of new learning, not only of motivation. The person then has to learn what to do and how to do it. New learning is accomplished by teaching the person to perform successive approximations to the desired goal, a process known as shaping.

There are many other features of operant methodology, the details of which may be found in a number of good sources (e.g., Honig & Staddon, 1977). For example, the timing of reinforcement is important: Reinforcement can be applied each time the specified behavior is performed, after the behavior has taken place a predetermined number of times, after a given time interval regardless of the number of times the behavior has occurred, or more irregularly. Each of these "schedules of reinforcement" is best for particular purposes.

THE PLACE OF FEELINGS, COGNITIONS, AND OBSERVATIONAL LEARNING

The procedures of operant conditioning have contributed significantly to the problem of helping people learn. Its emphases on systematic observation, explicit criteria for determining progress in learning, readiness to alter procedures on the basis of that information, and on success experiences give the technology of operant conditioning a well-deserved position of importance. Moreover, the cumulative evidence that even severely mentally limited persons can be taught to improve their self-help and social skills with the application of operant-conditioning principles has infused a vitality into the back wards of some institutions, replacing the despair and vacuousness of hopelessness with knowledge that development and learning is possible.

While underscoring these contributions of operant conditioning, we do not share the philosophical or conceptual framework of those advocates who *exclude,* or at best relegate to a position of unimportance, the cognitive and experiential life of the person. It should be pointed out, however, that those working with operant conditioning in the real world are increasingly taking cognitive and humanistic considerations into account. Thus, the authors of a manual on the use of operant techniques in the education of severely retarded children urges its readers to insure that "human emotions, insights, and intuitions are added to the procedures that we have outlined—that the all-important 'human element' be included in every interaction between adult and child. To fail to do so will insure a failure of any attempts aimed at educating the retarded child" (Larsen & Bricker, 1968, p. ii). Feelings as such are accorded a significant place in the following statement by Fordyce, known for his work on the use of operant methodology in the rehabilitation situation: "Information about and understanding of an individual's feelings can facilitate behavioral approaches by helping to identify how the person discriminates stimulus situations and by indicating what environmental events are likely to be reinforcing or nonreinforcing to him. In addition, most people identify effective or important attention from others with the other person being interested in and responsive to expressions of one's own feelings. The development of an effective treatment relationship with a client or patient . . . can be enhanced considerably by the professional's awareness of his client's (verbal or nonverbal) feelings. What is suggested here is that a more expeditious way to help the disabled person is to focus on helping him to change his behavior. It is quite possible that feelings will follow rather than lead these behavior changes" (Fordyce, 1971, pp. 77–78).

It is our position that the feelings and viewpoints of the client should always be taken seriously. Not only is the dignity of the client thereby affirmed, but the probability of successful long-term rehabilitation is furthered. The client also gains the emotional support of feeling understood when he or she is listened to and helped in sorting out alternative courses of action and ways of looking at things. Feelings, cognitions, and behavior influence each other and all are important in the rehabilitation program, although each may become a focus at different times during the rehabilitation process. *Cognitive-behavior modification* is a term expressing the interdependence of these aspects of human functioning in a growing field of research and application (Meichenbaum, 1974; Kendall & Hollon, 1979).

Operant conditioning should not be confused with the more inclusive terms "behavior modification" and "behavior therapy." The latter terms have been applied to such widely divergent approaches as desensitization, modeling, biofeedback, hypnosis, implosive therapy, psychodrama, and assertiveness training, as well as to operant conditioning. What ties behavioral approaches together is their focus on explicit behavior. Some of them are based on conditioning principles, but not all. Some of them rely on measurable behavioral criteria to ascertain change in behavior, but not all. Some of them rely heavily on events inside the person's skin, such as introspections, images, and feelings, but not all. Some of them consider feelings and cognitions to be irrelevant, but not all. A good review of many of these approaches may be found in Kanfer & Goldstein (1980).

In one sense, all intervention strategies, psychotherapy as well as behavior therapy, have as their aim the modification of behavior. The goal of psychotherapy, after all, is to help the person act more wisely as well as to feel better. What distinguishes psychotherapy from behavior therapy is its focus on the person's feelings and notions about the self and others, and the belief that the person will be enabled to conduct his or her life more adequately when feelings and cognitive misperceptions become clarified. The diversity of psychotherapeutic approaches is as great as that of behavior therapy. Transactional analysis, rational-emotive therapy, reality therapy, client-centered therapy, and the varieties of psychoanalytic therapies are all included.

It should also be made clear that although operant conditioning stresses the systematic use of principles of reinforcement, it necessarily draws upon cognitive principles. For example, the steps involved in knowledge and skill acquisition is a cognitive problem, one that is central to teaching and learning in general. The notion of shaping behavior through the mastery of small steps requires cognitive decisions as to how to proceed from the simple to the complex. For example, multiplication is based on the concept of addition and therefore addition is learned prior to multiplication. Cognitive understanding on the part of the teacher or therapist of the nature and size of sub-units or steps in learning is as vital as the application of contingencies of reinforcement.

Besides size of subunits, knowledge about the child's level of cognitive development is important in helping the child understand what is expected. Piaget, among the foremost psychologists concerned with cognitive development, holds the view that the act of perception is considerably more than a passive response to stimuli. Each individual holds a model of reality in his or her mind, a cognitive structure that includes both the specific facts and the rules of logic by which reality operates. All events are experienced in terms of this cognitive structure (Piaget, 1954; Flavell, 1963).

Piaget's theorizing is primarily concerned with how the child's model of reality changes with age. He has proposed four stages of development that represent qualitative differences in cognitive functioning. The stages overlap, although the order in which the stages are mastered is the same for all children. Knowledge of these stages decreases undue pressure on the child for behavior more mature than he or she is capable of. Thus, it would be foolhardy to expect a child to think about a concrete object in the absence of its actual presence until the child is able to represent or symbolize the object in his or her mind. This ability is not possible until Piaget's second stage of mental development has begun to emerge around age 2. Likewise, the adult will not expect a child to be respectful of the rights of others until the child has overcome "egocentric thinking" by being able to perceive the world from another's point of view. This ability is a sign of the third stage of cognitive development which begins around age 7.

The question of observational learning is also important for problems of motivation and learning. The fact is that children learn by observing others. More than that, they can be enticed to engage in an activity just because they have seen others act in a particular way. Bandura (1969), whose work has stimulated a considerable amount of research, addresses four factors involved in observational learning:

1. Factors that help the child to *attend* to the model being observed: for example, similarity of the model to the child, distinctiveness or novelty of the model's behavior, and status of the model.
2. Factors that help the child to *retain* what has been observed: for example, opportunity to rehearse what has been seen by thinking about it or imitating it.

3. Factors that affect the child's *capacity to perform* the activity: for example, the child's ability.
4. Factors that refer to *incentives to perform* the activity: for example, the apparent pleasure or displeasure of the model in what he or she is doing and rewards or punishment received by the model.

It is Bandura's view, and the one supported here, that incentives are important for eliciting behavior, but *not necessarily* for the learning of behavior. Of course, insofar as a child is motivated to perform an act, the additional practice can be expected to lead to better retention or learning.

It is noteworthy that the terms *cognitive behaviorism* and *humanistic behaviorism* are appearing in the literature, pointing the way to an amalgam between approaches that holds considerable promise. As a further expression of this trend there is a growing recognition that much is to be gained by having the person, adult, or child become an active participant in planning the strategy to be used in modifying his or her behavior, whether the approach involves psychotherapy, behavior modification, cognitive principles, or eclectic approaches.

INTRINSIC VERSUS EXTRINSIC MOTIVATION

Intrinsic motivation refers to incentives that are intrinsic to the nature of the task itself, such as the usefulness of the activity, its enjoyment, and the satisfaction derived from accomplishment. These contrast with positive incentives that are not inherent in the task itself, such as praise, tokens, and other rewards. Negative intrinsic aspects of a task such as its unpleasantness, and negative external consequences such as punishments, also are possible.

Research leads us to be cautious about the indiscriminate use of extraneous incentives and to urge maximizing intrinsic motivation wherever possible (Deci, 1975; Condry, 1977). Extraneous incentives run the risk of decreasing interest in the task itself should the outside reward be withdrawn. Consider the following experiment (Lepper, Greene, & Nisbett, 1973): Nursery school children were given drawing pens with which to play. One group had been promised a special reward (a "good player" certificate with a gold star) for engaging in that activity. The children in a second group were told about the reward only after they finished playing and a third group of children were not informed of any reward. During the following week, these children were observed during free play. The amount of time they played with the drawing pens rather than other interesting toys was taken as an indicator of intrinsic motivation. The findings were clear:

The introduction of an extrinsic reward for performing an interesting activity caused a significant decrease in intrinsic motivation. That is, children who originally had undertaken the task knowing they would be rewarded spent less time drawing in the subsequent free-play situation where no reward would be given than did those children who had unexpectedly been offered a reward or those who had not been given any reward. Moreover, the quality of the drawings made by the children was significantly poorer in the first group than in the other two groups. It is as if the first group of children attributed part of the pleasure in drawing to the anticipated reward so that the task appeared to be less enjoyable when the reward was no longer expected.

Results from the growing amount of investigation into the problem of intrinsic versus extrinsic motivation have been summarized as follows: The evidence "suggests that task-extrinsic rewards, when they are used to motivate activity, particularly learning, have widespread and possibly undesirable effects. These extend to effects on the process, as well as the products, of the task activity, and to the willingness of the subject to undertake the task at a later date. . . . In general, compared to non-rewarded subjects, subjects offered a task-extrinsic incentive choose easier tasks, are less efficient in using the information available to solve novel problems and tend to be answer oriented. . . . They seem to work harder and produce more activity, but the activity is of a lower quality. . . . Finally, . . . subjects are less likely to return to a task they at one time considered interesting after being rewarded to do it. . . ." (Condry, 1977, pp. 471–472). The advice given is that "If we wish to encourage exploration and the self-knowledge and internalization that apparently come from it, it would be wise to discover how this might be done without the offer of strong, extrinsic, task irrelevant incentives to motivate the individual to engage in the task" (p. 473). It is further urged that we rid ourselves of the illusion that people work and learn only in the face of extrinsic rewards and that we start studying intrinsically motivated behavior.

Let us clarify again the role of praise. When it is used to inform the child that his or her performance is proceeding nicely, praise can be encouraging, for it provides an important cue to the child that the activity's purpose is being fulfilled. The child also gains a sense of competence and satisfaction at being able to accomplish a valued task. In this case praise serves the same purpose as the feedback provided by a progress chart, with the added advantage that praise, *when focused on the task*, serves as a reminder of its importance. When, however, praise becomes *the* salient feature of the activity to the child, when the child "works for the praise" but not for the satisfaction of accomplishing the task, the child may become overly dependent on social approbation. The praise may reassure the child of being loved and accepted, but its role in increasing intrinsic motivation is more problematic.

It is known that both external rewards and punishment can mobilize the person's energy and attention toward the learning task. In a classical experiment (Hurlock, 1925) it was shown that school arithmetic improved most when the children were praised, next when they were reproved, and least when they were ignored. Because the praise and reproof were administered to the children in a group, no information was gained as to specific errors and correct answers. That performance was better, however, does not answer the question as to whether the children's fascination with arithmetic was better. Moreover, intrinsic motivation should not imply that the child should be ignored. Ignoring provides no reassurance that progress is being made or that arithmetic is useful.

Although punishment can motivate the child to improve behavior, psychologists are generally agreed that, unless it is carefully considered, it is easily misused. The following statement elaborates this point well: "The interpersonal aspects of the punishment situation are fraught with more hazards than those in reward. As a teacher or parent becomes emotionally upset, it is an easy matter to take out aggression on children through punishment. The children may be provocative, but the danger of injustice in punishment is great, and children are extremely sensitive to injustice. The meaning to the child of being punished by a powerful adult is complex, and regardless of the effect on immediate behavior there may arise concealed attitudes of resentment, of dislike of the work for which punishment was imposed as well as of the punishing teacher" (Hilgard & Russell, 1950, p. 49). In any case there is no evidence in support of punishment as a generally useful procedure to enhance intrinsic motivation.

Most of the studies investigating the effects of extraneous rewards on intrinsic motivation have involved tasks chosen to be intrinsically motivating. But what about dull and boring tasks? The evidence thus far leaves the question largely open. One study, for example, found that although rewards decrease interest in interesting tasks, they may enhance interest in dull tasks (Calder & Staw, 1975).

There also are circumstances where the person's intrinsic motivation to perform valued activities has been eroded by adverse life conditions, as in the case of some institutionalized persons. Extraneous incentives may then be useful in helping the person conform to particular behavior objectives in order to make management easier. Being able to eat by oneself without smearing food, for example, is a help to all concerned. The child may even find proper eating habits to be intrinsically satisfying once the skills are mastered.

The ten questions raised at the end of the chapter point to conditions that can enhance intrinsic motivation even when external rewards are also used. Let us pause with the first question: "Does the child understand the purpose of the task?" Isn't it true that all too often we make demands on children without first taking the care and time necessary to help the child understand the value, purpose, or importance of what needs to be done? The import of the second question, "Can the task be recast so that it becomes part of an enjoyable activity?" is clear, for it is easier to count on intrinsic motivation when the valence of the activity is positive. Or consider question three which stresses the importance of including the child in helping to fashion the task. Is not this principle also conducive to intrinsic motivation? So it is with the other questions. The questions guide thinking toward those conditions that support task usefulness, task enjoyment, and the satisfaction of accomplishment, the tripod upon which intrinsic motivation rests.

REHABILITATION EXHIBITS

The application of operant conditioning to rehabilitation is illustrated in the cases of John and Tom taken from Meyerson, Kerr, & Michael (1967). The three cases of Wally, Ben, and Lila that follow show minute-by-minute observations recorded by trained observers in the ecological research of Barker & H. Wright (1955) in the years 1948–1951. The cases will be drawn upon later in a series of questions that focus on important aspects of the problem under consideration.

John and His Short Attention Span

As a result of an automobile accident, John, age 18, was unable to walk. His attention span, speech, vision, memory, and muscular coordination were impaired. The occupational therapist selected learning to type by hunt and peck as a way to improve John's eye-hand coordination. However, a major problem was that John never worked for longer than 7 minutes at a time. It was observed that the therapist inadvertently had been reinforcing John's limited typing attempts by coaxing, answering a complaint, and talking with him. In their analysis, the authors (Meyerson, Kerr, & Michael, 1967) addressed themselves to four basic questions:

1. What is the "desirable" behavior? This question must be answered . . . in terms of objectively observable actions. In this case it was desired that the client engage in more typing behavior.

2. What is the criterion for success? This question must be answered in terms of frequency of specified actions, time spent at the task, speed or accuracy or adequacy of the performance, or some combination of these. . . . Since automated equipment was not available, a global set of criteria were specified . . . : (a) The client should attend to the typing task for at least 30 minutes. (b) During this period he should not demand the therapist's attention. (c) The work output in terms of lines typed should increase. (d) Accuracy of typing should improve. . . .

3. What behavior must be generated, extinguished, or altered? If desirable and undesirable behavior are incompatible, one might expect that reinforcing the desirable behavior would be sufficient to maintain it at strength. This question deserves attention, however, because the training of rehabilitation personnel to be responsive to "human needs" may lead them to reinforce undesirable behaviors concurrently with their reinforcement of desirable behaviors without being aware of what they are doing. They may not perceive that the undesirable behaviors must never be reinforced. In the present instance, for example, the occupational therapist did give moderate attention to the client for typing while he was typing, but she was also responsive to his demands for attention and was rather incredulous that paying no attention to the latter might have positive effects on the former. Extinguishing incompatible behaviors is especially important in cases of relearning, where the desired behaviors are usually present in at least minimal strength. In cases of new learning, where the desired behaviors are absent, altering behavior by means other than extinction is more important.

4. What will serve as a reinforcer? In the absence of knowledge of what has been reinforcing to the client in the past, the behavioral engineer may attempt to use an extrinsic reinforcer such as money, trading stamps, trinkets, food delicacies, or any activity of consumption that therapists may report the client engages in. . . . Social reinforcement is also possible. The latter is particularly effective with many rehabilitation clients since . . . they have been deprived, sometimes for long periods of time, of the positive social reinforcement they experienced prior to disablement. It also has the advantage of not requiring programming apparatus. In general, a good reinforcer often is that reinforcing stimulus that has been maintaining undesired behavior. In the present case, it was social reinforcement that was maintaining the client's disruptive behaviors and which could be used just as easily to reinforce behavior. [pp. 218–219][1]

[1]Reprinted from Behavior modification in rehabilitation, by L. Meyerson, N. Kerr, & J. L. Michael. In S. W. Bijou and D. M. Baer (Eds.), *Child development: Readings in experimental analysis.* Englewood Cliffs, N. J.: Prentice-Hall, Inc. 1967. Copyright © 1967 Prentice-Hall, Inc. Reprinted by permission.

The treatment in this situation consisted of two changes: (1) The typing was done in a more isolated room in order to decrease the behavior stimulated by the presence of other people. (2) Social reinforcement was made contingent upon typing behavior. The experimenter gave reinforcement for small units of work by entering the room about every 5 minutes. Without interrupting the client, the experimenter estimated the number of words typed and if the performance appeared roughly to have increased over the previous period, he or she would make some positive remark such as "You're doing very well," and then walk out. At the end of each 30-minute session in which the total output exceeded the previous session (two sessions per week), the experimenter spent 5 minutes talking with John about cars and other topics that interested him. If John had stopped for several minutes during the session, he could not exceed his previous output, and this special treat was not given.

The authors report that

> After a single 30-minute session in which such reinforcement was given but demands for attention were ignored, the client no longer attempted to engage the experimenter in conversation during the working period. . . . his typing output increased from 5 lines in the first session to 12 lines in the twelfth session, and his error rate decreased from 3 errors per line to $\frac{1}{2}$ per line.
>
> From the thirteenth through the fifteenth experimental periods, the duration of typing activity was increased to one hour with only a 5-minute reinforcement break at the half-way point. . . . He [the client] now appeared to be "well-motivated," and it was clear that further gains were possible if the regular therapist . . . gained skill in maintaining the reinforcement contingencies. [pp. 219–220]

John's case illustrates the use of extinction (ignoring bids for attention) and positive reinforcement (praise, sharing John's interests) that led to an improvement in desired typing behavior. Tom's case below demonstrates the use of shaping behavior and positive reinforcement.

Tom Learns To Fall Safely and To Walk

Seven-year old Tom is a child who has cerebral palsy. He never stood or walked unassisted in spite of coaxing, although medical opinion held that he had the physical ability to do so. The problem involved overcoming his fear of falling, learning some things that he had never done before (fall safely), and learning to perform successive approximations to the final goal of walking unassisted (shaping). It was observed that Tom seemed to enjoy being the center of attention when he refused to try to learn; that is to say, the adults were unwittingly reinforcing the no-walking behavior.

The following determinations were made:

1. Desired behavior: The child should stand and walk independently and learn how to fall safely.
2. Criteria for success: He should walk unassisted to the experimental room, and he should fall, in the approved way, on command.
3. Behavior to be generated, extinguished, or altered: He should overcome the fear of falling and experience the freedom of unassisted walking which then would allow reinforcement contingencies that occur in the natural environment to exert their continuing effects.
4. Reinforcer: Tokens (e.g., poker chips) were selected since Tom had responded favorably to these in previous work with him. They could be exchanged for a wide variety of social and material reinforcers, that is, things Tom wanted, following the treatment sessions.

A description of treatment procedures follows in some detail. Standing and walking independently: The treatment involved successive approximations to these goals. First, Tom was given two extra tokens if he scooted in his chair by himself to the experimenter's desk and pulled himself up to a standing position in order to have his coloring assignment corrected but received no extra tokens if the experimenter went to him. The authors report that after one reinforcement for coming to the desk, Tom refused to let the experimenter come to him. After a dozen reinforcements, Tom was offered extra tokens for standing at the desk without holding on. He succeeded in one 20-minute session and thereafter stood unassisted. His comments about being unable to walk changed to those about how he could stand by himself.

For the next step, two chairs were placed back to back and close enough so that Tom, while holding onto one chair, could turn and grasp the other chair. Tokens reinforced this behavior. The chairs were then gradually moved apart until it was necessary to take one or more steps without support to get from one chair to the other. At the end of the first 20-minute session, Tom was taking three unassisted steps from one chair to the other. At the next session five days later, he walked by himself into the experimental room. It is probable that during the interim, these first efforts were reinforced by praise in the nonexperimental setting and together with the reinforcing effects of walking itself, served to improve performance.

Falling safely: The ability to fall safely was important since the child's spasticity would probably result in his falling occasionally. "Falling was broken down into three phases: (1) Placing the subject's hands and knees on the mat and having him roll his body to one side. (2) Placing the subject on his knees with his body in an erect position and having him fall forward on his hands and then roll to his side. (3) Standing the subject beside the mat and having him fall to his knees, then to his hands, and then having him roll his body to one side" (Meyerson, Kerr, & Michael, 1967, p. 223). Tom was shown these successive approximations to falling, and tokens were given upon his performing the behavior on command. Tom undertook the learning task and, in four sessions of 20 minutes each, was able to fall correctly.

Lest the success of these two cases lead to exaggerated confidence, the authors included one case that showed no progress. They make clear that "behavioral experimentation is not always, or even usually, a hop, skip, and jump from isolating a problem, to devising a procedure, to successful outcome. In every case reported, there were some false starts and some difficulties of greater or lesser degree that had to be solved" (Meyerson, Kerr, & Michael, 1967, p. 235).

Wally, His Mother, and His Braces

Wally is a 4-year-old boy who is unable to walk as a result of poliomyelitis which occurred some two years earlier. The scene opens at eight o'clock in the morning with Wally sitting on a big chair in the corner of the living room, hunched over, with his face on his hands:

> 1'[2] Wally's mother went directly to stand in front of Wally's chair. She said gently, "Let's get dressed, Wally." Wally made no move to change his position. He sat with his head down on his arms. His mother picked up a T-shirt and said pleasantly, "Put your arms up, Buddy. Don't you want to get dressed?" Again Wally made no response; he just sat there, hunched up. His mother, encouraging him, said, "Hurry," as she pulled off his pajama upper quickly with no cooperation from him. His mother, with a little more urgency in her voice, said, "Put your arms up," as she held out the T-shirt. Rather reluctantly and in response not only to her words but also to her hands, because his mother put her hands on him and helped to lift up his arms, he put his arms up. At first he was languid and then he stretched, as if he rather enjoyed the stretch. His expression as he lifted his face a little was disgruntled and sleepy. His mother slipped the T-shirt over his head quickly, and gave it kind of a firm pull over his head. Wally said, "I don't like this," in rather a

---

[2]Time notation, the first minute.

whiny voice. (He seemed to refer to the tight T-shirt being pulled over his head.) His mother admonished mildly, "Wally," and obtained his cooperation. When he had his T-shirt on, his mother held him under the arms, and stood him on his feet. She suggested as she did so, "Hold onto me." He held on, but weakly, so that he wobbled. She quickly and quite efficiently pulled his pajama pants down over his seat as he was standing.

2′ She admonished him again for his general limp behavior and lack of cooperation by just saying, "Wally," in a mildly reproving voice. As soon as the pajama pants were slipped over his seat, she picked him up by the arms and put him back on the chair with his feet sticking straight out. Then she pulled off his pajamas over his feet. He already had on his shorts; they were under his pajamas. (Whether he regularly wears them under his pajamas or whether he had been partly dressed before I arrived, I don't know.) She picked up his socks and quite hastily put first one sock on and then the other. Wally braced his back as she put on his socks, but was still very limp in his head and shoulders.

3′ His mother picked up from the floor a high shoe with the brace attached and started to put it on Wally's left foot and leg. The brace extends the full length of his leg with a curved part just under the buttocks. Wally immediately responded to this by saying vehemently, "I don't want to wear that damned old brace," in a very negative voice. His mother ignored this and went on putting on the shoe and the brace. He said, "I ain't gonna wear this old brace," with more vehemence and some defiance. His mother said mildly, "You don't have to wear them long," then explained, "I have to clean your shoes first, and then I'll put your shoes on." Argumentatively Wally said, "You *did* clean my shoes the other day." His mother smiled at that, partly to me, implying that cleaning them the other day would not mean that they were clean now, but she didn't argue about it with Wally.

4′ His mother continued to lace up the shoe and fasten the brace. Wally said, whining now, more than belligerent, "I hate that brace," though still somewhat defiant. As she fastened the brace up high, he put his hand around and rubbed his hip at the place where the brace hit and said crossly, "I hate you." (This referred to his mother for insisting he wear the braces rather than to the braces, I felt.) And then he said, equally unhappy about everything, "I don't like that lady," meaning me. (I felt that I was included in his general unhappiness rather than being the cause of it.) His mother responded in quite a joking way, "You're in a bad mood, ain't ya?" trying to get him a little bit out of it.

5′ She continued, saying, "You wouldn't let your daddy see you in such a bad mood, would you?" a little bit jocular, still trying to get him out of it. Then she added, "Where did your daddy go this morning?" (I think she was trying to engage him in conversation to get him out of his negative mood.) Wally said very negatively, "I won't tell you." Then his mother said something about going where there was a big red barn. Stubbornly, Wally said, "I won't tell her where my daddy went."

(I think he sensed that his mother was trying to get him to talk partly for my benefit and he was not going to cooperate. He sounded as though he were hanging onto his bad humor and not that he was really very upset.) His mother remarked that his daddy would be home for lunch. As she was talking, she put on his right shoe and brace and fastened it. Wally whined in a very complaining voice, "These hurt me." His mother continued to fasten them without responding.

6' Wally more belligerently said, "And I ain't gonna wear them." He turned and looked at me for the first time, scowling. (The paper boy opened the door and laid the morning paper on the chair near the door.) Wally did not appear to notice him. He again whined at his mother, this time a little more as though he were pleading with her, as though he could make some progress, "Mamma, I don't want them on." His mother said conciliatorily, "I'll take them off after a while, after you've had breakfast and play a while." He responded quite argumentatively, "No, you won't." She put his feet in overall legs. His mother took his hand and pulled him to his feet. Now, with the braces on, he could stand with very little support. He held on to the chair or his mother all the time. She pulled his overalls over the braces and took out some suspenders. She sat in the chair and he stood in front of her as she fastened his overalls. She started to fasten the suspenders onto the overalls. (He was completely passive in all this dressing procedure and he didn't offer any assistance at any time.)

7' As he stood, he whined, "These braces are too heavy, I don't want them." His mother, a little reproving said, "Wally," meaning probably that he shouldn't fuss so much. Wally responded by exclaiming, "God, I don't want them." Then again more belligerently, "I'm gonna throw them in the river." Wally alternated between pleading with his mother and denouncing his braces. His mother responded, "I don't like them either. All right, when shall we do it?" meaning when shall we throw them in the river. (Her voice was joking; I don't believe he could have believed seriously that she would let him throw them in the river. It was more an effort to go along with his mood.) She added, "Next time we go across the big old river, shall we throw them in?" Wally made no response to this.

Mrs. Wolfson continued with an attempt to change the topic of conversation, "Did you see Jack bring the paper?" Wally did not answer. As he stood in front of his mother looking sleepy and disgruntled, she turned him around so that she could fasten the suspenders in the back. Then with that she was finished dressing him and said, "Okay," indicating that she was through.

She stood up and came around in front of him and took hold of one hand. He took half a dozen steps toward the kitchen as she held the one hand and walked backward toward the kitchen. She held out her other hand, possibly so that she could take both his hands and give him more help. When his mother put her hand out for his other hand, he made no response. But he stood there limply with his shoulders bowed and his head down. It seemed as though, except for the braces, he would crumple in the middle, too. Then she let go of the hand she held and held out both hands to him as one does to a baby to lure a baby that's walking, to come to you. At that he smiled for the first time, a sweet smile, at his mother. He leaned forward and fell into her arms.

8′ She picked him up with a swish and carried him halfway across the room. She put him in the chair at the east end of the dining table in the kitchen. He sat with his legs straight out, his back against the back of the chair. The chair was well pushed in to the table. The table had a cloth on it and a clear, plastic cover over the cloth.

Maud, the two-year-old sister, was in the kitchen now, waiting for her breakfast. Maud said, "That's what I want," concerning some food. Wally immediately answered in a cross, grumpy voice, "I'm going to eat them all up." Maud whined, "Buddy's going to eat them all up." His mother said, placating Maud, "Oh, no, he won't." And Wally said, "Yes, I will," teasing Maud. Maud continued to whine about how Buddy was going to eat them all up. [Barker & H. Wright, 1948–1951][3]

Wally continued to be irritable and uncooperative for several minutes more until dabbles of sugar and a hearty breakfast made him considerably more cheerful. The braces remained on for about an hour and a half, during which time Wally ate breakfast and then played actively and happily outdoors with his wagon and two cousins. At 9:20, 17 minutes before the braces were finally removed, Wally asked his mother to take them off for the first time. His mother replied warmly from the kitchen, "Well, just a minute, baby." At 9:28 Wally repeated his request, more imperiously this time, and his mother responded promptly, "Okay, just a minute." At 9:37, a final pleading from Wally brought his mother out of the house with a pair of shoes without braces.

A Physical Therapy Session with Ben

Ben is a 6-year-old child with cerebral palsy who has been a resident in a special school for 2 years. He speaks with difficulty and is not yet able to crawl or stand alone. "In the characteristic picture of Ben he is seen strapped in a chair with his arms hanging at his sides, his head tilted to one side, his mouth open, and his tongue hanging out and drooling spittle on his chin" (Barker & H. Wright, 1948–1951). It is early afternoon. Ben had just been brought into the physical therapy room: Mr. T. is the physical therapist, Miss O. the occupational therapist, and Celestia an older child with cerebral palsy:

[3]From *One of a series of records made in connection with the natural living conditions of children* by R. G. Barker and H. F. Wright. Printed by permission of R. G. Barker.

1' Mr. T. came over from working with Celestia to Ben. As he did so, he said in a very cheerful, pleasant, yet business-like way, "O.K. Brother Benrod." Ben made no response that I could see. Then Mr. T. unstrapped Ben from his chair, picked him up and laid him down on the floor. Ben seemed to accept this as just what he had expected; he displayed no particular feeling about it.

Noticing that Ben's shoelaces were unfastened, Mr. T. commented gaily and in a slightly teasing way. "How come your shoelaces are all undone?" Ben mumbled quite happily, "I didn't do it." Mr. T. replied in a gay, joking and nonchalant way, "Oh, I know, I know. You didn't do it. You *never* do it." Then Ben said happily, really enjoying himself, "Elmer did it." Mr. T. laughed restrainedly and said knowingly, "Oh, Elmer did it, huh? Yeah, Elmer always does it."

2' Mr. T. continued working with Ben's shoelaces. Benjamin talked gaily away to Mr. T. who seemed to be paying very little, if any, attention. Since he was not looking at me it was impossible for me to understand what he said. Apparently Mr. T. didn't understand either, for at one point he said questioningly, "Huh?" Ben mumbled something else still quite gaily, but I couldn't understand what he said.

3' Celestia came over and said something to Mr. T. and Mr. T. replied to her question. Benjamin made no response nor took any notice of this interaction. Mr. T. continued lacing Ben's shoes. Then Benjamin said something else to Mr. T. I didn't understand what it was but I felt sure that it was just pleasant conversation.

Mr. T. said somewhat more seriously but still in a pleasant way, "How far are you going to crawl today?" Benjamin mumbled something which I couldn't understand. I couldn't tell for sure whether he was responding to Mr. T.'s question or not.

4' Mr. T. finished with Ben's shoes and said gaily, "There you go!" Then Mr. T. picked Benjamin up from the floor. He stood him up for just a moment and then placed him on the floor on his hands and knees. Mr. T. had a little trouble getting Ben settled in this position. He moved Ben's hands close together and straight out in front of him. He moved Ben's legs so that he sat in a froglike position on the calves of his legs and his feet.

5' Miss O. walked in from the Occupational Therapy room and made a few gay, happy, cheerful remarks about the fact that Ben was going to be six very soon. Ben looked up at her but made no other response. Then Mr. T. said somewhat seriously, "Well, any little boy who's going to be six is going to have to learn to crawl." With this Miss O. and Mr. T. walked to the far end of the room. Ben did not try to say anything in response to the comments by Mr. T. and Miss O. but I'm sure he understood what they said. He sat on his hands and knees, jerking somewhat rhythmically, wiggling slightly, apparently trying to keep his balance. Ben had been placed on the floor just about in line with the doorway into the kitchen. It was a distance of nine or ten feet to the north end of the room which was established as Ben's goal in his crawling. Ben continued to sit on his hands and knees in this froglike fashion and seemed to be trying to balance himself. (Miss O. returned to the Occupational Therapy room without further comment and Mr. T. began talking with Celestia. Ben paid no attention to them.)

6′ Ben continued sitting in this froglike position. He continued balancing, wiggling slightly as though he might be trying to crawl, although it wasn't clear that this was what he was trying to do. Mr. T. looked over from where he was working with Celestia and said pleasantly, with no irritation or impatience, "Come on, Ben. Let's go." Ben made no response. He continued his rhythmical jerking and wiggling.

7′ Ben's face assumed a very serious look. He began jerking harder and wiggling more rhythmically as though he were trying earnestly to crawl. (Mr. T. continued talking with Celestia. Ben paid no attention to them at all.)

Then Mr. T. looked over at Benjamin and said with more insistence in his voice, "Come on, Ben. Crawl. Lift those knees way up. Now, your left knee, then your right." Benjamin made no verbal response but it seemed that he tried a little harder, shifting his weight so that he could slip a knee a fraction of an inch forward. So far Ben had not moved more than one or two inches from where he began.

8′ Celestia, taking up Mr. T.'s previous comment, said, "O.K. Benny. One, two," meaning that Ben should move his legs in a steady, rhythmic fashion. Her comment was very pleasant and cheerful and was not a demand of any kind. Ben, as far as I could tell, made no response to Celestia's remark. He continued his efforts to crawl. Again Celestia said quite pleasantly, "Come on. One, two." This time Ben looked over at Celestia and mocked her saying, "One, two," imitating Celestia's tone of voice. Then Ben grunted and whined just a little and tried to push himself forward along the floor.

9′ Ben wiggled and bounced quite hard again. His face screwed up into a deep frown. He whimpered as though he were almost ready to cry. Celestia chattered gaily something about Ben's sixth birthday. Ben did not respond to this but continued wiggling and trying to crawl.

At this point, Ben had moved some six or seven inches. Then Mr. T. looked over and said somewhat insistently, "Come on, Ben. Crawl." Ben did not look at Mr. T. but he half-said and half-cried, "I can't do it." But Ben continued bouncing and wiggling. As he strained very hard, he screwed up his face and his breathing was quite jerky. He shifted his weight from side to side and jerked his hands around as he endeavored to crawl along the floor.

10′ Ben made more noise of a whimpering kind, almost crying. He continued trying very hard, struggling with his movements. Ben bounced up and down on the calves of his legs, apparently using the momentum of the bouncing to inch himself forward. Ben whimpered again, and it sounded almost like crying. He kept struggling, wiggling and bouncing, trying to inch along on the floor. (Celestia walked up and down the Physical Therapy room, passing quite close to Benjamin. Ben didn't look up and made no response to her at all.)

11′ Mr. T. went over close to Benjamin. He reached down, moved

Ben's hands apart and said, "Now, get your hands apart. Keep pushing with your legs. You'll go. Pull with your hands. Come on, pull." This was said in a didactic way; it was business-like instruction given in a not very pleasant way—a type of very demanding encouragement.

12′ In response to Mr. T.'s urging, Ben intensified his efforts. He fussed louder, making a crying noise. His face was very sober. Mr. T. put his hand on Benjamin's back to be of some slight assistance although not very much. Benjamin continued to try very hard. Mr. T. said rather critically, "Ben, you're not working. You're just not working at all. Let's go. You're just getting lazier and lazier." There was no warmth or friendliness in this comment; it was straight criticism.

13′ Ben put forth even more effort. He screwed up his face, bounced and wiggled, apparently straining very hard. He managed to move forward a little. Then Mr. T. said more pleasantly, "Now, you're making headway. Just keep going." Without responding directly to Mr. T.'s comment, Benjamin continued his wiggling and bouncing. He managed to move another inch or so.

14′ Mr. T., still standing right behind Ben with his hands on Ben's back, said, "Come on, now. Quit fussing and work. Let's keep going." This was said almost bitterly. Ben continued his vigorous bouncing. He made crying noises and whimpered with the exertion. At this point Ben's noises and whimpering came very near to crying, but still Ben did not open up and bawl unrestrainedly.

15′ Perhaps in response to Ben's intensified whimpering Mr. T. stepped around behind him and lifted some of the weight from Ben's legs by pulling up the belt straps in Benjamin's jeans. This apparently helped considerably for Benjamin's fussing and crying noises diminished sharply.

16′ Ben continued his efforts to crawl, struggling along the floor. At this point he had traveled three or four feet from the initial starting place.

Marilyn [an aide] walked past and said cheerfully, "How are you doing, Benrod?" Benjamin made no response.

Then Mr. T. released his support and stepped away from Benjamin. He said insistently, "Come on, Ben. Pull 'em up. Pull 'em up." Benjamin continued bouncing although not as earnestly as he had been just before.

17′ Mr. T. said, "That's the way. Come on, now. You're moving." This was said somewhat hopefully but still demanding that Ben continue his efforts.

Ben looked up almost tearfully at Mr. T. and asked, "How far?" Mr. T. responded as though somewhat surprised that Ben should ask such a question, "How far? Just as far as you can go, that's how far." Then Ben mumbled something else which I couldn't understand. He continued to bounce and wiggle, trying to inch along the floor.

Miss O. came through from the Physical Therapy room on her way to the kitchen. She looked down at Ben and said jokingly and good-naturedly, "Aw, dry up and blow away." Ben made no response but continued wiggling and pushing. Miss O. continued on her way without saying anything further.

18′ As Benjamin wiggled and bounced, he continued making whimpering, almost crying sounds.

Celestia, who was walking back and forth under Mr. T.'s supervision, called to Ben pleasantly, "Ben, are you laughing or crying?" She repeated the same question. Ben responded, "Laughing," but it was said as though he didn't really believe it. Then Celestia replied in a pleasant, joking way, "What are you laughing at? Yourself?" Ben said, "Yes," as though he knew this weren't really true but he had to put on a good front.

Ben continued bouncing and wiggling as he struggled along. He continued making the very same sounds, however, which to me were clearly much more like crying than laughing.

19′ Mr. T., standing behind Benjamin, said, "Come on, Ben. Keep working. You're laying down. Get your knees way up." This was said insistently, with no pleasantness even attempted. Ben made no response but continued wiggling and bouncing.

Miss O., returning from the kitchen, said pleasantly, "Come on. Come on. You're not even moving." Then she walked into the Occupational Therapy room and stopped in the doorway. She turned around and looked down at Ben on the floor.

20′ She said jokingly but with sincere affection, "Oh, look at the monkey. Look at the monkey." Ben looked at Miss O. A brief smile flitted over his face at the joking comment. He quickly resumed his sober expression and continued his efforts.

At this point Ben had moved about six feet from the starting place. Mr. T., who still was standing just behind Benjamin, said pleasantly, "Can you see yourself in the mirror?" Ben replied, "No," matter-of-factly. Mr. T. said, "Well turn so that you can," in a business like way. The mirror was directly in front of Benjamin at the north end of the room. It was about five feet away from him.

21′ Benjamin continued struggling. He made whimpering sounds as he struggled along. Mr. T., still standing behind him, said insistently, "All right. Let's go. Let's go. Keep moving." Ben continued bouncing and wiggling as he struggled along. He was roughly seven feet from his starting point. Mr. T. turned away from Ben and walked toward the south end of the room where Celestia was standing.

22′ Apparently in response to Mr. T.'s leaving him, Ben began fussing a little more. He made more and more noise until he was almost crying aloud. He kept trying, however, bouncing on his haunches and pulling with his hands. The more he tried, the louder he fussed.

23′ Ben kept fussing and wiggling. His efforts were in vain, however; he had made no progress since Mr. T. went to the other end of the room. Ben continued struggling.

24′ He stopped, turned his head around and peered back at Mr. T. at the opposite end of the room. (This was the first time since he started that Ben apparently was not trying to crawl.) Mr. T., who was just standing quietly with his arms folded, tapped his foot on the floor with impatience, indicating that Ben should get busy. Then Ben promptly turned around and began trying again very hard. Again Ben whimpered very intensively, just on the verge of crying.

25′ Ben wiggled and bounced. He fussed loudly. Then he turned around again and looked at Mr. T. Since Mr. T. left, Ben had managed only to turn himself around so that instead of facing north he was almost facing east. But still he continued wiggling.

At this point Miss O. stepped into the doorway of the Occupational Therapy room and said teasingly but pleasantly, "Come on. Come over here and I'll give you a bite. Come on." She was talking about an apple which she was eating. Ben looked up at Miss O. and smiled momentarily. Then he resumed his efforts.

26′ Mr. T. said more pleasantly, "See how far you've gone Ben. Quit fussing and go up to the mirror." The mirror was three to four feet away. Benjamin made no response to Mr. T.'s insisting.

Miss O. did something with reference to the waste can which was right by the door, and she laughed very hard at whatever she had done. Ben looked up and joined momentarily in Miss O.'s hilarity. Miss O. commented gaily, "I knew that would make him laugh." Then she sat down on the edge of the trash can.

Ben resumed his wiggling and bouncing as he struggled to crawl.

27′ Miss O. stepped around behind the mirror and playfully peeped out around the other side, trying to boost Ben's spirits. Ben apparently made no response but just continued his wiggling and bouncing.

Ben intensified his efforts. As he did so his whimpers became louder and louder until they amounted to a virtual cry. From the south end of the room, Mr. T. called in a very threatening, not-to-be-questioned tone of voice, "Ben, do you want to go to the bathroom with me?" [This means a spanking.] Then Mr. T. continued, "All right then, settle down and get busy." Miss O. went into the Occupational Therapy room.

28′ Ben made no observable response to Mr. T.'s severe orders but continued with his whimpering, fussing and wiggling as he tried to crawl. Then Ben looked up into the mirror and continued with his efforts. Celestia talked glibly with Mr. T. about something that would take place on Saturday. Then she cheerfully asked Ben if he could see his face in the mirror. Ben made no response; he simply acted as though he hadn't heard Celestia's comment.

29′ Ben looked over at me briefly with no meaning in his look. Still Ben continued trying. He fussed and wiggled. Ben had moved not more than a foot or a foot and a half since Mr. T. went to the other end of the room. (Otto and Verne [children] passed through the Physical Therapy room on their way into Occupational Therapy. Ben apparently did not notice them.)

30′ Mr. T. came to the north end of the room and moved the mirror out of the way. Then Mr. T. pointed with his toe to a line on the floor and said seriously, "All right, Ben, get up to this line and then I'll put you in your chair. Let's go, now." This was said somewhat hopefully and with real promise in his voice.

31' Ben tried with renewed effort, it seemed. He bounced, wiggled vigorously and cried with a little restraint. (Ben was extremely involved in this and his efforts had been continuous from the very beginning except for the one point which I mentioned.) He continued now, wiggling, fussing, and crying as he tried to reach the point which Mr. T. designated. With all the exertion Ben began coughing a little. As he coughed he relaxed his efforts somewhat. The line to which Mr. T. had pointed was about two feet away from Ben.

32' Miss S. [school teacher] stepped into the doorway between the Physical Therapy room and the classroom and made a very bitter comment about a little boy who insisted on acting like a baby, saying that she was so tired of it she'd like to throw him in the lake. She was obviously talking about Benjamin. Ben, however, made no response. I'm not even sure that he heard her. He continued his wiggling and bouncing, trying to get to the line.

33' Miss O. and Hilda came slowly through, going from Occupational Therapy into the classroom. As Miss O. neared Benjamin, she jumped over him, put one foot on each side and came down very hard making quite a noise. This she did in a very joking, good-natured way. Benjamin made no response to this but kept trying earnestly to get to the line. (Miss O. went on into the classroom.)

Ben had managed by this time to cover about half the distance.

34' He reached his hand out as far as he could, pointed to the line and looked up questioningly at Mr. T. Mr. T., who was standing just on the other side of the line, looked down and said, "No, no. Now cut that out. That's fudging. You've got to get all the way up to the line. You've got to get your arms across and get your knees almost up there, about halfway across." This was said in a more kindly, explanatory way. Benjamin resumed his struggling, wiggling and bouncing as he tried to reach the required goal. After just a little more effort, Mr. T. said, "O.K.," with finality. Then Mr. T. went to the other end of the room and brought Ben's chair back. Ben relaxed visibly and just sat waiting quietly. Mr. T. rolled the chair up to Benjamin.

35' Mr. T. picked Benjamin up and set him down rather forcefully in his chair. Then as Mr. T. began strapping Ben in his chair, he gave Ben a lecture about what was going to happen tomorrow if Ben insisted on continuing with his fussing and crying while he was in Physical Therapy. He told Ben that he just wasn't going to have any more of this whimpering and fussing and that if he came in tomorrow and started whimpering and fussing they would go to the bathroom and Ben knew what would happen then. ("Going to the bathroom" means a spanking.) He told Ben that he was just getting lazier and lazier and he was going to have to snap out of it. Mr. T. was quite critical and very serious. There was no attempt to be good-natured or to gloss over the criticism. It was straightforward and almost bitter. Ben made no observable response to this lecture. I'm sure, however, that he understood everything Mr. T. said.

Then Mr. T., having finished strapping Ben in the chair, took hold of the back of the chair and shoved Ben out of the room with haste and dispatch. He rolled him quickly up the ramp and took him into the class-room where he left him. [Barker & Wright, 1948-1951][4]

Lila Participates in the Speech Class

Lila is an $8\frac{1}{2}$-year-old child with cerebral palsy who has lived at a special school for nine months. She has both the athetoid and spastic type of cerebral palsy. In walking, she extends her arms for balance, but falls quite frequently. Her speech is very difficult to understand. Ben, Jimmy, and Newton are three other children in the speech class, Ben being our little friend who had such a hard time in the physical therapy session. Miss B. is the speech teacher. It is the first class in the morning:

1' Lila watched with mild interest as Miss B. moved Ben's chair over so that the three were sitting in a line. Lila looked up as Jimmy, a new boy in the speech class, came in bringing a chair and set it next to Ben's.

2' Lila watched Miss B. who asked if "we should take our blow first." Miss B. was referring to the exercise of blowing toy horns. Lila smiled a little as if she liked the idea. All the children seemed to.

Miss B. gave each of the children a toy horn, telling them to blow long and hard. Lila routinely took the horn Miss B. offered her. Lila held her horn with her right hand, which she supported with her left hand. She put the horn in her mouth. She had a little difficulty getting the horn to her mouth because of the mild athetoid movements of her head.

Lila looked at Miss B. who said, "That's a good one," to Ben, who was blowing his horn rather loudly. Lila continued to blow her horn. She took the horn out of her mouth to take a breath. She put it back in the mouth to blow again. She watched Miss B. who went from one child to another, encouraging them in a friendly way.

3' Miss B. seemed to be trying to impart more enthusiasm to the children. Miss B. encouraged the children by displaying her own enthusiasm. She said to the group, "Come on, let's blow real hard." As she talked she directed her attention first to one child, then another.

Lila still held her horn with both hands. She blew it for all she was worth. She worked so hard at blowing her horn that when she took the horn out of her mouth to take a deep breath, her feet came up off the floor. The activity of trying to blow hard seemed to be such an all-over activity that when she gave out with a blast as loud as she could, her feet came up off the floor again.

Miss B. indicated this activity was over by holding out her hands and asking for the horns. Lila routinely handed her horn to Miss B.

---

[4]From *One of a series of records made in connection with the natural living conditions of children* by R. G. Barker and H. F. Wright. Printed by permission of R. G. Barker.

4′ Then Miss B. said, "Now we'll do blowing sounds." The sounds they were using were "f" sounds. Miss B. said, "Good, Newton." Lila watched as she complimented Newton on his blowing sound. Speaking with warm enthusiasm, Miss B. asked Lila, "Let's hear yours." Lila made an "f" sound vigorously. Miss B. spontaneously complimented her on it but helped her to do it more smoothly. She encouraged Lila to do it again. She said to Lila helpfully, "Let's do it again and this time do it all through your mouth." This time Miss B. held Lila's nose for her to help show her how to make the sound all through her mouth. Lila watched intently as Miss B. demonstrated and seemed to put herself wholly into this activity, trying to do it just the way Miss B. wanted it.

Lila watched intently as Miss B. asked Newton with friendly anticipation, "What do we have when we go to a picnic?"

5′ Miss B. asked Lila to give the answer to the question, "What do we have when we go on a picnic?" and Lila said, "Fun." Miss B. said, "Fine," explosively as if she were really happy with the sound Lila had made. Lila had done a good job.

The teacher went down through the rest of the children, Ben and Jimmy, with questions requiring "f" sound answers. Lila turned to watch as each of the children performed. Ben was asked a question, "What is this?" as Miss B. wrote a "4" on the blackboard. Lila watched intently and smiled at Miss B. Then Lila turned to look at the blackboard where Miss B. was writing a letter, "S". Miss B. asked Jimmy to make this sound. Jimmy made the sound.

6′ Miss B. exclaimed, "Good." Lila smiled. Lila watched with quiet interest as Miss B. indicated Ben and asked him what he had eaten his breakfast with. Ben failed to put the "s" on "spoon" and said, "poon." Miss B. in a friendly way seemed quite disappointed as she said Ben had done just what they were talking about. He had left off the "s" sound and she asked him to say "spoon." Ben did. Lila smiled as Ben got it correctly.

Lila cocked her head to the left, to watch Miss B. intently as she went back to the blackboard.

7′ Lila watched Miss B. who said, "What do we do with our eyes?" Lila said, "See," and Miss B. said, "Fine, let's clap for Lila." Then all of the children clapped and smiled. Lila smiled bashfully; apparently she enjoyed the recognition she was getting for having said the word so well. Then Lila looked over to me and smiled. I smiled back at her. It seemed that she was still happy to have done such a good job with this word.

Lila turned back to look at Miss B. She rubbed her upper lip with her hand just under her nose as if she were still a little sleepy. In rubbing her upper lip, she turned her hand over, bent it sharply at the wrist, and rubbed with the top of her wrist.

8′ Lila dropped her head to her chest. (It wasn't quite clear to me if Lila had dropped her head to her chest because she was tired or if it was just an uncontrolled athetoid movement.) She let her chin rest on her chest for just a moment. Then she raised her head and pulled it clear back; that is, she rested the back of her head on the back of her chair so that she was looking up at the ceiling.

9′ Lila pulled her head back up to look at Miss B. She watched as Miss B. said, "Now, let's make our singing sounds." Lila pursed her lips; she seemed to be doing this as thoroughly as she could, really intent upon her job. She tried to make the sounds that were indicated. She stopped and looked up as Miss B. said, "Whose name begins with an 'm' sound?" She made the sound for "m," the "m-m-m" sound rather than saying the letter "m." Lila said spontaneously, "Mattie." Lila watched Miss B. who asked next, "Whose name begins with an "l" sound?"

10′ Miss B. asked questioningly, "Does your name begin with an 'l' sound?" Lila shook her head negatively, saying, "No." Miss B. acted very surprised and indicated to her that it did. Then Lila laughed as if she recognized her mistake. Newton, who was sitting next to Lila, laughed, too, in a friendly way at Lila's mistake. [Barker & H. Wright, 1948–1951][5]

QUESTIONS TOWARD ENHANCING MOTIVATION

The five previously described cases represent a range of "techniques," of attempts on the part of the adult to motivate a child. Some of them bear promise of sound learning; others seem to impede learning and even lead to wrong learning. In discussing them we do so with the recognition that it is one thing to display wisdom under conditions of relaxed and objective appraisal and quite another thing when one is involved in the day-to-day difficult and time-demanding therapy with a child.

The problem of motivation would be vastly simpler if desirable activities were satisfying in themselves. The natural pleasure of a child when eating an ice cream cone, romping, or solving an intriguing problem is enough to ensure the positive valence of these activities. When, however, the task is at best a bother or at worst intolerably disagreeable, motivating the child becomes a challenge. There is no fun, in and of itself, in wearing braces as did Wally, in laboriously crawling as did Ben, in making "f" and "s" sounds as did Lila, and in learning to fall as did Tom. Even should the child be cooperative and motivated, the question of what else the child is learning while performing the task is of great importance. The serious and systematic consideration of the following 10 questions provides a way of highlighting important issues when reviewing one's rehabilitation practice.

[5]From *One of a series of records made in connection with the natural living conditions of children* by R. G. Barker and H. F. Wright. Printed by permission of R. G. Barker.

Does the Child Understand the Purpose of the Task?

In the authoritarian relationship between adult and child, all too often little respect is given to the rational part of the child's functioning or the child's capacity to understand and act on that understanding. There are children, to be sure, who are intellectually very limited, but in most cases some level of understanding can be achieved provided that sufficient care is taken for this purpose. In so doing, not only is understanding (reasoning, cognition) endorsed as a value, but the child's active participation is thereby encouraged. This is not to say that reasoning alone is sufficient. Nor is it to say that reasoning is always helpful. Sometimes, even, discussion and reasoning may serve to motivate the child contrariwise. In that case the child's performance provides a clue that altering one's strategy is necessary. However, exceptions to the general rule that understanding is a facilitating factor in learning is reason enough to define the exceptional conditions but not dismiss the rule.

In none of the five cases presented above was the purpose of the procedures carefully explained to the child, at least not during the period of the observational records. Ben's therapist did remark that "any little boy who's going to be six is going to have to learn to crawl" (5')[6] but did not show how wiggling was a beginning step to crawling. A film depicting a child like Ben in early stages of wiggling and in later stages of crawling is one suggested way to help bring about clarification, in this case through observational learning of an appropriate model. Parents and teachers, including those who systematically apply the principles of operant conditioning, should seriously make use of cognitive clarification as an important part of the learning process.

Can the Task Be Recast To Become Part of an Enjoyable Activity?

This principle can be exemplified in the difference between body building through calisthenics versus athletic games, or between learning to play the piano through exercises versus musical pieces. It simply takes advantage of the natural interest of the person. Its application is seen in the speech teacher's use of toy horns in developing Lila's blowing skills and her use of a question-and-answer game for drill on particular sounds. In Ben's case, some effort was made to enliven the task by playful teasing and by reminding Ben of the mirror (20'), but no real embedding of the crawling within an enjoy-

[6]Time notations in parentheses refer to corresponding portions of the records.

able activity was attempted. To Ben, crawling 10 feet was a Herculean task. To make it inviting, the journey across the floor could have been divided into different towns or stores on the way to the circus. Appropriate rewards, all in the spirit of play, could provide further incentives at each of the substations. Wally did not have to do anything with his braces except wear them; after his initial resistance the braces were forgotten for a long while in the excitement of outdoor play, and in this way they became an unobtrusive part of an activity that Wally enjoyed. John's occupational therapist had selected "hunt and peck" typing as an intrinsically interesting (and useful) task for improving eye-hand coordination. Did John concur? Tom's task, scooting in his chair and standing before the experimenter's table to have his work corrected, was part of his involvement in an enjoyable coloring activity.

Occupational therapists have devised many activities based on the principle of embedding, as when children become involved in unbuttoning exercises in anticipation of the surprise picture hidden beneath the buttoned cloth. In physical therapy there is the use of weighted doll buggies in developing the child's balance in walking. Here is an area that needs continued ingenuity by all therapists: How can skills in sitting, standing, crawling, walking, eating, dressing, talking, reading, and so on be developed by submerging the necessary drill within an intrinsically satisfying activity?

The principle of embedding need not, of course, be applied at every turn. Sometimes repetitive drill is a happy relief from fun and frolic. Sometimes an unappealing exercise may be recommended because it accomplishes far more than could be achieved through playful activity. In this case, particular care should be taken to see that the child realizes the significance of the task and is not overburdened by it. In this case also, social recognition of the child's effort and progress by some form of commendation serves both to encourage the child and to underscore the importance of persisting in accomplishing a difficult but valuable goal.

Has the Child Had a Part in Designing Some Features of the Task?

In none of the cases reported was the child asked to help decide what would take place in the learning situation. It is not proposed that the child (or adult) must always and in every detail have input into the rehabilitation program, but participating actively in setting goals, in fashioning aspects of the task, and in selecting incentives not only provides needed experience in the important area of decision making but also favors child involvement and learning. As one example, learning to spell correctly is facilitated by having children select the words they want to learn. If Ben had helped to make a game out of crawling by choosing the incentives he would find along the way to the goal line, it is likely that he would have accomplished more than he had and with less protest. Even Wally, who wanted to have nothing to do with the braces, could have been invited to decide whether he wanted to try to increase his wearing time by 1 minute or 5 minutes. Surely John could have been asked to select the task he would like to work on from among suitable possibilities contributed by both himself and the occupational therapist. Did he have a voice in deciding that he should attend to the typing task for at least 30 minutes? The underlying message is that ways should be sought to bring children into the planning and decision-making process in situations involving them. Increasingly this principle is being incorporated in many approaches to learning and motivation.

Is the Task Optimally Geared to the Child's Capabilities?

The point here is that tasks that are too difficult or too easy for the child guarantee frustration and failure on the one hand and unrealized potential on the other. A feeling of satisfaction in accomplishment is also denied because this special feeling comes when the person achieves something that is important and challenging through his or her effort—that is, near the top of the person's ability level. It is this satisfaction in accomplishment that bolsters the child's ego, that encourages the child to continue to apply effort.

The problem of gauging optimal task difficulty requires the considered judgment of all persons involved—the child as well as the adults in charge. The proof of the judgment is the child's behavior. Is the child progressing according to the rehabilitation plan? Is the child applying effort? Is the child pleased with his or her accomplishments? If the answer to any of these cues is negative, the difficulty of the task with respect to the child's particular abilities becomes a pointed question (among others) that needs reassessment. Was the distance that Ben had been asked to crawl too taxing? Was the 1 hour and 45 minutes that Wally wore his braces too long? Reviewing the evidence at regular intervals and modifying the task accordingly are marks of good rehabilitation practice.

Is the Goal Reachable Within a Time Dimension That the Child Can Deal With?

In the rehabilitation setting, it is important to establish goals that the child can reach within a relatively short period of time. Where the ultimate goal is far away, short-term goals and subgoals should be established as offering the best motivating potential. Actually, we are often unable to establish long-term goals because we do not know them. We may not be able to say with assurance, for example, that 3-year-old Suzie who has cerebral palsy and is just beginning to learn to sit tailor fashion will eventually be able to walk, with or without braces or crutches. Fortunately, immediate goals may more confidently be established in terms of recent performance, allowing small gains to be interpreted as accomplishments rather than as falling short of some future, hoped-for achievement. In the following account, a young woman in the rehabilitative phases of polio recalls:

> . . . "Come now," the therapist would lie beautifully, "you stood for twenty seconds longer yesterday," and I almost collapsed as I remembered standing for almost three hours talking to a boy who had carried my books home for me from high school. Twenty seconds! I felt as though I had been there twenty years! But in this manner my therapist increased my standing time, my confidence, and my strength. And I seriously realized that unless I tried harder, tomorrow would be no different from today, and I tried to do just a little better than I was asked to do. [Linduska, 1947, p. 116][7]

In Ben's case, even if crawling 10 feet were within his capacity, subgoals of 5 feet or even 2 feet with appropriate incentives would more readily have been felt *by the child* as attainable with reasonable expenditure of time and energy. Surely for a 6-year-old child immediate goals should be within reach in less than the 35 minutes during which Ben labored.

Is the Child's Overall Experience One of Success or Failure?

"Nothing succeeds like success" is a psychological truth of everyday life. There are important reasons for this. To begin with, success provides the person with information (not necessarily conscious) that one is on the right track. It also often enhances the attractiveness of a task whereas failure often acts contrariwise, turning an acceptable task into a disagreeable one (Cartwright, 1942; Gebhard, 1948). Comparable effects hold for anticipated success and anticipated failure. Furthermore, success normally increases the level of aspiration—that is, the goal one sets for oneself with respect to the task—whereas failure tends to decrease it (K. Lewin et al., 1944). Fi-

[7]Reprinted by permission of Farrar, Straus & Giroux, Inc. From *My Polio Past* by N. Linduska. Copyright © 1947, 1974 by Noreen Linduska.

nally, it has been shown that persons with a background of success in the particular area of concern differ significantly from those with a background of failure. The academically successful children in Sears' study (1940), for example, expected improvement well in line with their current performance, whereas those with a background of failure tended either to expect no improvement at all or to expect completely unrealizable gains.

But how will the child learn to tolerate failure if he or she experiences little of it? Fortunately, the child does not have to be taught to accept failure through repeated failure experiences. As Hilgard & Russell (1950) point out, "A better preparation for failure is to have a sufficient backlog of success experiences so that failure is not devastating" (p. 52). They remind us that it is possible to teach tolerance of failure by drawing upon success, not failure, as the regulator of conduct. In the study by Keister (1937), children were taught to accept failure by linking temporary failure with ultimate success. They were taught not to be impatient but to keep striving until success was achieved. When failure indicates that one must try a new approach it can stimulate learning, but certainly the children in the Keister study were not taught to endure lasting failure.

Whether or not success has occurred can be indicated to the child in several ways. First, there is the performance as such that may inform the child. If a child's goal is eight bull's-eye hits out of ten, for example, a score of two or nine speaks for itself. When Lila finally completed her tower, she knew she had succeeded and was obviously pleased (pp. 100–101). Charts that visually display the child's progress can also be used to good advantage. Particularly when progress is slow, it is difficult to appreciate improvement without comparing earlier performance levels. Often the judgment of others, as expressed by praise or reproof or by more tangible evidence, becomes the main indicator of success and failure. Lila, for instance, knew that she was improving her "f" sound, not as a result of the raw data presented by the sound itself but by the compliments of her teacher (4'). Positive comments also greeted John's successful efforts, and in Tom's case tokens served this purpose. That progress in learning depends on some feedback process to guide the person in the appropriate direction is clear.

Some words of caution are in order. Praise, if overdone, can make the child too heavily dependent on flattery and commendation, too sensitive to possible failure, too much concerned about status rather than the task as such. (See discussion of intrinsic motivation, pp. 357–360.) Happily, not every occasion must be designed to elicit a success experience. As the work of Barker & H. Wright has shown (1955), most of our waking hours by far are neutral with respect to success and failure (see p. 97). Likewise, in rehabilitation programs, the stimulation of success can become an overstimulation if the person is geared to it in every activity undertaken. One needs the temperance afforded by activities that are indifferent to success and failure, though it still remains true that the overall program should be marked by well-paced success experiences.

That success is a potent motivating factor leading to heightened goals and making the task at hand more pleasant, is not to be taken lightly, and yet the motivator often neglects to take this factor into account. Let us see how the principle of well-paced success fared in the experiences of Wally, Ben, Lila, John, and Tom. The analysis will concern both the relation between performance and goal as an indicator of success and the reaction of the a lults as social evaluators.

Wally may not have experienced failure, but he certainly did not feel any pride in accomplishment, the main criterion of a success experience. Moreover, he was given no indication that he was succeeding in anything worthwhile. Not once did his mother praise him during the hour and a half that he wore his braces. If anything, her acknowledgment that she did not like the braces either (7') provided social confirmation that the whole affair was disagreeable and to be avoided. As for Wally's performance as an indicator of achievement, the necessary goal structure was lacking. Moreover, the vague goal as imposed by his mother—to wear the braces until he had breakfast and played a while (6')—became vaguer still because he doubted her intentions. His mistrust evidently had some basis, for an hour and 15 minutes later he was still wearing the braces and it took three imperious reminders on Wally's part before his mother removed them. A vague and unacceptable goal, with no encouragement along the way, provided little support for striving.

To be sure, Wally was generally in an uncooperative mood (some of the reasons for which are offered in the following sections) and at the time nothing might have worked, but certain suggestions do come to mind as to what Wally's mother could have tried. She could have commented, after putting on his braces, that now he was standing nicely (6'), for without them he could do nothing but slump. At least this would have reminded him that he was accomplishing something worthwhile. She could have counted the seconds that he could stand alone or the steps that he could walk holding on with one hand or unaided, as well as kept a record of his progress. At least this would have established a concrete and realistic standard, a goal that gave meaning to his performance here and now.

In Ben's case, unmitigated failure pervaded almost the entire session, being capitalized at the end by undisguised chastisement and threats of punishment. In addition, the goal was apparently both unclear and unattainable to Ben.

Perhaps the therapeutic procedures were so similar from day to day that the therapist did not see the need to orient Ben explicitly toward the goal. If so, one of course would call this into question, since it would seem desirable to establish and make clear each day just what the objectives are and, equally important, something of the why of them. During the third minute the therapist did ask, "How far are you going to crawl today?" but the interaction was so brief that it could hardly have been a serious exploration of the task ahead. And though in the fifth minute the goal, crawling about 10 feet, was mentioned, 12 minutes later Ben whimperingly asked, "How far?" The therapist missed this excellent opportunity to clarify the situation, and instead made the goal uncertain and hopelessly out of reach by replying, "How far? Just as far as you can go, that's how far."

Early in the lesson Ben was convinced that the goal, whatever it was, was beyond his capabilities. After about 4 minutes of trying to crawl, Ben was clearly discouraged, saying "I can't do it" (9′). The therapist, busy with another child, ignored Ben until 2 minutes later, when he did instruct Ben on just how to crawl: "Now, get your hands apart. Keep pushing with your legs. You'll go. Pull with your hands. Come on, pull" (11′). But this businesslike instruction, demanding and unsympathetic, hardly served to convince Ben that he really could accomplish the task if he tried. The therapist could have pointed out that Ben already had crawled 7 inches, that yesterday he did such and such. The goal could also have been structured anew and even modified to make it more in line with what Ben could accomplish. Subgoals within a game format could have been designed. As it was, Ben strained and whimpered, almost as if he wished to prove that the task was in fact beyond him. It is noteworthy that 20 minutes after Ben started to crawl, he was not even facing the mirror, though at that time he was about 4 feet from it (25′).

Throughout the session Ben was chastised so that even if he had finally reached the goal, there would have been but small joy in its achievement. Toward the end of the session (30′) the goal was lowered but certainly not in a way that would give Ben a feeling that he had done an adequate job. Four minutes later, when Ben had virtually reached the new goal by stretching out his hand, he was in effect slapped down for "fudging." Finally, at the end of the session (35′), Ben was reprimanded and threatened in no uncertain terms. He was told that his performance was fussing, crying, whimpering, and lazy. One can hardly imagine greater defeat, for not only did he fail the goal of the therapist, but Ben's own goal of proving his effort was totally unrealized. The change in Ben's mood, which was quite cheerful at the outset, is striking. The session is an excellent example of the effects of persistent failure: the goal is lowered; the task becomes more disagreeable.

Lila's experience was very different from that of either Wally or Ben. She started out being pleased (as was Ben, but not Wally) and ended being pleased (as neither of the boys). Satisfaction with her performance, even when she was given help in bettering it, pervaded the session. The feeling of success primarily grew out of the teacher's encouragement and praise of the children's efforts and accomplishments. Satisfaction spread to the group as a whole so that success was further underscored by the smiling and hand-clapping of peers. Notice that, when Lila was corrected, it was in a positive, noncritical, certainly nondisparaging way (4', 10'). Furthermore, the goals were sufficiently immediate and clear for the children to appreciate what they were. To blow a horn, make certain sounds, and answer certain questions provided definite guides for their efforts. Though success was heavily determined by the teacher's evaluation, it was not bandied about irrespective of the child's efforts and performance.

Like that of Lila, success characterized the rehabilitation sessions of John and Tom. Praise or tokens served to indicate success, and goals were adjusted in accordance with performance so that continued progress could be made without having the individual mark time or experience repeated failure.

In summary, the following can be asked in evaluating whether well-paced success characterizes the child's experience:

Is the goal within the child's reach?
Is it flexibly gauged in terms of actual performance?
Has the child had a part in establishing it?
Are subgoals necessary to encourage striving?
Has praise been given to indicate success?
Has praise had the balance of matter-of-fact and task-oriented appraisal?
Is the child able to determine accomplishment in terms of the performance itself?
Are there sufficient interludes in the child's life where success and failure are not at stake, where the activity carries itself, either because it is accepted as a job to be done or because it is enjoyable?

What Else Is the Child Learning?

One of the most important questions we can ask in evaluating incentives is: What else is the child learning? In the case of intrinsic incentives, the verdict is positive, for to experience and value the pleasure of an activity, the satisfaction of goal achievement, the usefulness of what one is doing enhances striving. But in the case of extrinsic incentives, the end result is not as clear-cut.

If castigation predominates, the child's self-concept is in danger of being undermined. In just a single session, Ben heard (and learned?) that he was a lazy, fudging cry-baby, and in fact a total failure. More than that, he was learning that effort did not count for much (he had really worked hard for more than half an hour); it was achievement, and an unattainable one, that mattered. He also learned to dread the next session.

Even so-called playful teasing on the part of the adult may easily be misconstrued by the child. When Miss O. jokingly said to Ben, "Oh, look at the monkey. Look at the monkey" (20'), was this a delightful jest to him? When Wally's mother agreed with him in disliking his braces and that they would be tossed in the river at the first opportunity (7'), was this taken merely as sympathetic understanding? Or did this interplay also reinforce Wally's emphasis on the succumbing aspects of his disability—that the braces signified pain and trouble and his inability to walk rather than a way to help him?

As for rewards, one can well ask whether the child is learning to become overly dependent on praise or on tangible rewards for even small effort and accomplishment. The probability of this can be reduced if the required achievement becomes greater as performance improves or if the activity becomes so intrinsically satisfying that external incentives are no longer needed. When rewards are used judiciously in instances where intrinsic motivation is difficult to achieve, however, the child may become motivated. The child may learn that effort, cooperation, and progress are valued. The child may find that the newly acquired skills are themselves intrinsically satisfying.

In Chapter 8 it was pointed out that one of the value changes that promotes acceptance is subordinating physique relative to other values. At the same time, the very purpose of rehabilitation—to improve physique—serves to emphasize it. This contradiction makes it even more necessary to free the rehabilitation setting of the idea that physical achievement is all-important, that upon it one's destiny rests.

These examples are sufficient to illustrate that in the rehabilitation situation the child learns far more than the immediate task at hand. One learns about oneself and others, what is valued and what is not. One learns basic attitudes that become an influential part of orientation to life in general and to disability in particular. Questioning what else the child is learning helps to reveal the strengths and weakness of one's methods.

Are Background Factors (Time, Place, and Social Conditions) Optimal for Learning?

Especially because all of us hold preconceived notions as to the background conditions most conducive to learning, these must be consciously checked by the evidence presented in actual practice. The following is a good example of how a parent's reasonable notions turned out not to fit the facts:

> During this summer, I experimented with giving Karen her physiotherapy on the beach. It didn't work.
> I found that the cold water increased her spasticity, making already stiff muscles that much stiffer (temporarily). I found that more than twenty minutes of sun had much the same (temporary) effect.
> I then tried doing her therapy immediately after her nap and so learned something interesting, and today still inexplicable. Instead of being relaxed and "soft" immediately after sleep, as one might reasonably expect, our daughter is more spastic and it is necessary to allow one full hour to elapse from the time of waking to the start of any therapy. [Killilea, 1952, p. 149][8]

To question the background conditions of the case at hand is also necessary because individual differences in *diurnal rhythms* that influence alertness, moods, and energy are great. Wally's general mood as the scene opened at eight o'clock in the morning was resistant and fretful. Although this could be attributed to the prospect of his hated braces, it is to be observed that he became cheerful during breakfast. One wonders if Wally needed time to wake up after rising, if he is not generally disgruntled until breakfast sets him right with the world. If this is the case, one would certainly recommend postponing bracing until then.

As we well know, the factor of *social facilitation* can have a tremendous impact on the person's readiness to undertake a task. Lila's therapeutic situation made the most of this background condition. There, other children were doing the things she was asked to do. They were praised and she was praised. They were pleased with her success and she with theirs. Ben, on the other hand, had to become involved in a task very much apart from any supporting group. To be sure there were people around, but they were engaged primarily in other pursuits, their contact with Ben being more or less capricious, sometimes only adding to his misery. His therapist was also preoccupied with working with another child. In fact, he remained with Ben for only 1 minute after he placed Ben on the floor (4'). Inter-

[8]From *Karen* by Marie Killilea. © 1952 by Marie Lyons Killilea. Published by Prentice-Hall, Inc., Englewood Cliffs, New Jersey 07632.

mittently he directed Ben from afar. Several minutes later the therapist rejoined Ben and remained with him for about 10 minutes (11'–21'). It is to be observed that when the therapist left again, Ben's fussing increased as though he were crying out for someone to be "together with" him in his ordeal. During the next 8 minutes the therapist was across the room and Ben made little progress (22'–30'). In spite of the steady stream of people in and out of his orbit, Ben apparently felt very much alone.

It is not always easy to provide the social stimulation of other people. Wally was not in an institutional setting where there were other children who needed similar treatment. In such circumstances, the child may resist therapy just because playmates don't have to be bothered with it. It sets the child apart, makes the child feel different and lonely. Being aware of this, the parent may be able to draw the child's friends into certain phases of the rehabilitation program. An older child could keep score as Wally stands alone and all could rejoice in his progress. Karen's mother called the neighbors to watch Karen as she walked with her new crutches for the first time (Killilea, 1952, pp. 217–219). The important point is that care should be taken to keep the child from feeling that no other children have any interest in the rehabilitation task.

Of course, social stimulation needs to facilitate learning for it to be helpful. This is not always the case. John, for example, pursued the typing task more diligently when he became isolated from the distractions of other people. To be sure, the therapist provided social reinforcement every 5 minutes when his work merited an encouraging remark.

What Is the Attitude of the Child Toward His or Her Disability and Rehabilitation?

A child's readiness to participate in the rehabilitation program depends not only on specific conditions surrounding the task that do or do not promote enthusiasm, but also on general attitudes toward oneself and one's disability. Why did Wally hate his braces so? It may have been because the situation was poorly constructed from the point of view of specific motivating factors, but it may also have been because the braces represented for Wally "nothing but trouble." They may point to the succumbing aspects of disability to the exclusion of their significance for coping with the problems. In Ben's case, the predominant attitude was "I can't." Again, this may have been a consequence of the unfortunate way in which the task was planned but it also may reflect Ben's pervasive feeling about himself—that he is helpless, pitiful, and unable. In other words, the child comes into the situation with important needs and attitudes that will affect the child's reaction. Needless to say, what happens in the rehabilitation setting can influence for better or worse the child's attitudes toward the self and the disability.

Sometimes our best efforts to motivate a child fail just because we remain unaware of what the situation means to the child. Although such awareness often requires sensitively relating to the child, it is surprising how often we overlook even the most direct cues. Neither Wally nor Ben was asked why he felt as he did. What might Wally have said? What might Ben have said? A child's ability to contribute knowledge and understanding to the situation must always be assumed, an approach that is all too often violated just because of the devaluated status of children.

Does the Motivator Feel Friendly to the Child and the Task?

Human motivators are human beings and as such they, too, come into the situation with needs and attitudes toward the child and the disability that profoundly influence the proceedings. The enthusiasm and friendly encouragement contributed by Lila's therapist to the situation is clearly inseparable from her personality and warmth toward her pupils. On the other hand, if the adult dislikes the child, becomes easily angered and impatient, is discouraged about rehabilitation possibilities, or is basically uninterested, motivation and learning on the part of the child are likely to be undermined.

One suspects that the relationship between Ben and his therapist led to a turn-about-face in Ben's motivation, so that instead of wanting to reach the goal, however vague, he wanted not to reach it. Certainly crawling was a difficult job for Ben, but apparently he made more ado about it than was warranted. This annoyed the therapist who did not realize that by it Ben was trying to say, "See how I am trying. See how miserable I am. Give me credit for my straining and pain."

Aside from the basic issue of whether the motivator feels friendly to the child, there is the practical problem of repetitive therapy. This problem concerns motivating the motivator: How can therapy that must be carried out day in and day out continue to be of sufficient interest and challenge to the therapist so that most of the sessions are entered with enthusiasm and encouragement. This problem, of course, applies to all teachers, including parents. Part of the answer lies in the selection of personnel and part in the arrangements of the working situation.

We know that in teaching institutions, rehabilitation workers see added challenge in the daily routines because what they are doing is shared with students in training and other members of the staff. There is something new in everyday events when they are analyzed and thought about, when they have to be justified and evaluated. Other instances of the kind of social involvement that tends to keep alive one's work and interest result when visitors frequent therapy sessions and when the rehabilitation worker participates in planning and evaluating the rehabilitation program. Feeling rewarded by knowledge of the child's progress and one's own contribution to that progress further sustains continued interest. One must add, of course, that heavy case loads, long hours, and insufficient respect for the functions of the rehabilitation worker are unfavorable conditions for the kind of keen awareness we are seeking.

Parents seldom have sufficient opportunity for the kind of sharing with other adults that does so much to strengthen understanding and determination to persevere with rehabilitation procedures in spite of boredom and difficulties. Parent self-help and discussion groups, as well as more frequent contacts with visiting nurses and other therapists, are indicated. Parents, like therapists, are also motivated by knowledge of the child's progress and by being credited for their contribution to it. Of course, the genuine motivation of most parents for whom the welfare of their children is uppermost will carry them a long way.

One might wonder why theory and practice are frequently so far apart. Perhaps it is because the questions raised here are obvious only after they have been raised and because the principles that provide some of the answers are not such truisms as one might think. After all, though the motivators in the rehabilitation cases which provided our "living material" tried to be on their best behavior, being under observation as they were, not all were able to avoid even glaring errors. The ten key questions need to be raised again and again as checks against which rehabilitation procedures may be guided.

Chapter 16
The Parent as a Key Participant

Parents are an integral part of the rehabilitation process, not only because their knowledge about their child and their cooperation are needed, but also because they too need help and support in accepting their child's disability as nondevaluating and in learning to cope with the challenges that await them. For the purposes of this chapter, the terms *rehabilitation worker* and *counselor* will be used in the generic sense to refer to the professional involved—that is, the doctor, physical therapist, teacher, and so on.

QUALITATIVE ASPECTS OF A SOUND RELATIONSHIP

The following are three basic characteristics of a constructive relationship between parents and rehabilitation worker:

1. Parents must feel that the rehabilitation worker is not working against them, that together they are seeking solutions to problems.

2. They must feel that the rehabilitation worker likes their child, sees him or her as an individual, a special person.
3. They must feel that the rehabilitation worker appreciates their struggle to do the best they can for their child, that though they have shortcomings, they also have strengths and ideas.

These guideposts may appear obvious, but the complexity of attitudes on both sides of the relationship makes it important to examine those attitudes that create difficulties.

Interfering Parental Attitudes

Parents are likely to carry certain attitudes that act against the most productive use of the time spent with the rehabilitation worker. They are likely, for example, to regard the rehabilitation worker with a measure of fear and awe, emotions reminiscent of their own childhood reactions to authority figures.

Parents also often enter the relationship with a number of well-defined fears. They may expect to be blamed for any and all of the child's difficulties and fear that their guilt as a parent will be exposed. They may worry that excessive demands will be made on their financial resources, on their time, strength, and emotional involvement. They may fear that the expert will shatter their fragile hope that their child will be cured or at least appreciably helped. They may believe that the specialist will not understand their concerns and will become impatient with their desperate wish that all will be well. They may be anxious lest the child become too attached to the therapist—no small threat to those parents who are insecure about their ambivalent feelings toward their child.

Such fears can be expected to abate as the previously enumerated three points become sensed by the parent during contact with the rehabilitation worker. Achieving mutual respect and confidence, however, is not simple to accomplish, as will be further seen below.

Interfering Counselor Attitudes

The following attitudes on the part of the rehabilitation worker militate against a constructive relationship with parents:

· *"The Trouble with Children Is Their Parents."* This attitude in professional circles is more common and more resistant to change than one might suppose. There are many reasons for this. To begin with, it is a general cultural viewpoint. Then, too, the rehabilitation worker, like other adults, may harbor resentment against one's own parents. The rehabilitation worker may have added proof of the lack of wisdom of parents when parents fail to carry through the recommended plan or openly defy it. Also, there is the edict of theorists who have laid the tremendous responsibility for maladjustments in children on the parental doorstep.

Rehabilitation workers themselves, therefore, have to examine and reexamine their own feelings toward parents. Stereotypes about parents must give way to the reality of the individual parent. One is far better prepared to understand the parent if one remembers that "Parents love and hate . . . children [with disabilities] just as parents love and hate children who are not physically impaired. Parents protect, guide wisely, pamper, neglect, and even abandon children whether or not they are handicapped. Some children were unwanted, but are loved and have the security of a healthy relationship with their parents. Some children were wanted, but are unloved and insecure, whether or not they are sound of mind and body" (White, 1955, p. 470).[1]

Whether the rehabilitation worker will be positively or negatively inclined toward the parent largely depends upon how he or she perceives those parental characteristics that are found wanting. If the rehabilitation worker sees a particular parent primarily as rejecting his or her child, even hating the child and wanting to become absolved of all responsibility, then, to say the least, respect for the parent is hardly likely. If, however, the rehabilitation worker sees that parent as torn by conflict, bothered by guilt, and running away from responsibilities because of being overburdened with stresses of various sorts, then the parent's struggle becomes evident. This focus can be directed toward the growth potential of the parent in the wake of enmeshing, destructive forces. Such a focus is one of the best guarantees that the counselor will look upon the parent with an attitude of positive regard so essential in a good counseling relationship.

Of course the rehabilitation worker cannot ignore destructive parental feelings and attitudes. It must be appreciated, however, that the shortcomings of parents have their own origins, and the effort to understand and cope with them must supplant denigration of them.

• *"My Job Is to Provide the Answers."* The key to the psychological issue involved in this interfering attitude is made clear by changing the

---

[1]Reprinted from Social casework in relation to cerebral palsy, by G. White. In W. M. Cruickshank & G. M. Raus (Eds.), *Cerebral palsy: Its individual and its problems.* Syracuse University Press. By permission of Syracuse University Press.

pronoun: "*Our* job is to provide the answers." Even when many professionals are involved—physician, physical therapist, occupational therapist, speech therapist, social worker, psychologist, nurse, teacher—the knowledge, insights, and lack of insight on the part of the parent are just as essential as are the knowledge, insights, and lack of insight on the part of the professional worker. The parent must become a full and respected member of the rehabilitation team.

Since parents in most cases must assume the ultimate responsibility for their child, it is necessary that they actively participate in the rehabilitation process from the beginning. They will be less prepared for the many independent judgments they will have to make if, during their contact with the rehabilitation situation, their primary role had been that of passive listener to the wisdom of the expert. The value of having parents attend case conferences about their child, along with other members of the team, is elaborated on pages 429–431.

It is to be expected that the parents' admixture of uneasiness, fear and awe, gratitude and resentment, pride and guilt, self-dignity and self-pity will tend to keep them in a turmoil and lead them to accept their role of uninformed listener. This means that the rehabilitation worker must actively encourage questions and opinions on their part. It means that parents need time to disentangle feelings and thoughts and to absorb new information. Opportunity should be given for more than one contact with the professional worker because questions and formulatable opinions often come *after* the parent leaves the counselor's office. Parents should be asked to write out their questions for the next occasion and make certain that such questions are raised and discussed.

An important study of communication between doctors and 800 mothers (Korsch & Negrete, 1972) bears on this point. The mothers had taken their child to an emergency clinic for an acute but usually minor illness and were seen by doctors who had 1 to 3 years of pediatric experience. The visits were tape-recorded. The findings showed that the mothers were generally reticent about asking questions and opening up lines of inquiry in spite of the fact that they expressed a desire for more information when interviewed immediately after the visit. The mothers were also frequently dismayed at the doctor's disregard of their account of what chiefly worried them about their child's illness. As an example, a mother repeatedly tried to interest the doctor in the fact that her child had been vomiting, but the doctor ignored her remarks and persisted in asking her about other symptoms which, as she did not realize, related to the same basic problem of dehydration. One-fourth of the mothers in a follow-up interview said that they had not mentioned their greatest concern to the physician because they did not have an opportunity or because they were not encouraged to do so. The investigators also concluded that the session tended to have a more successful outcome when the mother had an *active* interchange with the doctor than when she remained passive and asked few questions.

Considering the professional worker as an expert who "knows best" bears upon the issue of parental rights and responsibilities. A case in point is the question of institutionalization. Is a professional person ever justified in urging that institutionalization of the child is the only reasonable course of action? Consider the following reaction of a parent:

> Mrs. Brown is completely unable to accept the recommendation of placing Susan, age five, in an institution for the feebleminded. She can admit only that Susan is retarded in physical functioning and speech. She now refuses to believe that the doctors at the center have been interested in her child and that they tried to help her the past three years. . . . [White, 1955, p. 487][2]

The right of the professional person to recommend institutionalization when the parent is opposed or has doubts about it should be seriously questioned. We must remind ourselves that at best it is difficult for an outsider to judge when the care of a child, however physically or mentally incapacitated, is too much for a family. Their love and concern may so lighten the burden that what may appear to be an unwise expenditure of family resources to others may to the parents be simply taken as self-evident. To be sure, parents need to be informed of all possibilities open to them, including institutionalization. In time they may feel that institutionalization is the only alternative, but then it is their decision and not that of someone else. Parents may then need reassurance and support for their decision.

· *"I Do Not Feel Comfortable with Disabled People."* Particularly interfering are such emotional reactions to people with disabilities as fear, aversion, and devaluating pity. Such feelings countermand one of the cardinal criteria of a constructive rehabilitation relationship—namely, that parents believe that the counselor likes and respects their child. Confidence in the specialist cannot be achieved when parents doubt that the rehabilitation worker views their child as likeable and important. Moreover, the opportunity is lost for the parent's own attitudes toward life with a disability to become more accepting.

[2]Reprinted from Social casework in relation to cerebral palsy, by G. White. In W. M. Cruickshank & G. M. Raus (Eds.), *Cerebral palsy: Its individual and community problems.* Syracuse University Press. By permission of Syracuse University Press.

In a sound relationship, the specialist conveys to the parent that a person is not a disability, that the child can partake of life's satisfactions though he or she will have a share of its sorrows. Next to eradicating the disability itself, the parents' supreme wish is that this balanced view be true. This attitude of the professional can be so comforting that parents begin to view the disability not as a tragedy but as a reality with which they can live. Also, of course, the child's own feelings and behavior will be affected by the attitudes of rehabilitation personnel.

A main antidote to emotionally negative attitudes on the part of the rehabilitation worker lies in coming to grips with one's feelings involving disability. It is hoped that a volume such as this, in exploring some important psychosocial factors, in considering attitudes involving problems of human perception and values, and in giving weight to societal practices that add to difficulties or reduce them, will provide some of the directions that such a self-analysis can take. The proposed self-analysis takes place under favorable conditions when the specialist is actually working with persons who have physical disabilities, for then emotionally he or she begins to see *people* and not simply diseased and deformed structures. As one teacher reports:

> I remember my first visit to the hospital—my feelings of revulsion at the disfiguring conditions of the children. Gradually I came to grips with myself and began to understand some of the reasons for my feelings. By the fourth clinic session, I was completely at ease. These were children who needed help. I hardly noticed the disfiguring conditions which had first repelled me. I know now, that what counts is not the handicap, but what is done with it and about it. Teaching these children is a challenge and a charge—but most of all a richly rewarding experience (*Helping the physically limited child*, 1952–1953).

In the study on doctor-patient communication described earlier (pp. 393–394), less than 5 percent of the tape-recorded sessions showed the doctor's conversation friendly or personal in nature in spite of the fact that most of the doctors believed they had been friendly (Korsch & Negrete, 1972). Recognizing what a parent is going through gives comfort. Listening to the parent's concerns shows respect as does keeping the parents from waiting too long in the waiting room. Avoiding technical language and eliciting parent questions foster understanding. Noticing something positive about the child indicates liking. Clearly, *awareness training* of what it takes to convey liking and respect for both child and parent is *urgently needed in professional schools.*

TOPICS AND UNDERSTANDINGS COMPRISING A BROAD REHABILITATION PROGRAM

In addition to the significance of the underlying emotional relationship between counselor and parent, there are many specific topics and insights that should be integrated into the total rehabilitation program. The following summary draws heavily upon a thoughtful account of parental problems in dealing with exceptional children (Laycock & Stevenson, 1950).

Parents must be helped to realize that a disability is part of the general condition of human imperfections which must be faced in themselves and in all other human beings. The problem of parents of exceptional children is therefore not unique but applies to all parents. These are not mere palliative words, for all parents must learn to accept the limitations of their children.

Parents make a tremendous step forward when they realize that any course other than acceptance of the disability as non-devaluating adds to the child's and their own difficulties.

Parents can be helped to see that it is typically not the disability as such that hinders a child's adjustment, but how the child and others regard the disability.

One of the best ways to help parents is by understanding the potentialities of their children. Instead of emphasizing the fact that the child will never walk, for example, it is better to concentrate on how the abilities of the child can be developed. In this way coping rather than succumbing aspects of the situation guide the emotional and practical life of the person (see Chapter 9). The important point is that every parent must adjust to what the child *can* do.

Parents need to understand that their exceptional child is fundamentally like all children, that "all children need an adequate and balanced diet, sufficient rest and sleep, a comfortable temperature, and activity when well rested, that all need to be loved and wanted, to have a reasonable independence in running their own lives and in making their own decisions, to feel a sense of achievement that comes from making things and doing jobs, to win the approval of others for what they are and do, and to feel that they are worthwhile individuals who reasonably come up to their own standards" (Laycock & Stevenson, 1950, p. 123).

At the same time, parents need to recognize the special problems involving the child's disability. Such recognition, however, must be coupled with precautions against the natural tendency to view all or most of the child's growing-up problems as disability-connected. (See "Spread," pp. 32–39; "Containing Disability Effects," pp. 175–178.)

Parents need to understand the different techniques that may have to be used in the education of their child.

Parents may need assistance in facing early separation from their child in hospital and school.

Parents will have questions about medical aspects—cause, course, and treatment—of the disability. There will be anxious questions about hereditary implications regarding future children and grandchildren. At this time the all too common feelings of guilt can be brought to the surface and helped to be dissipated.

Parents need to reach some understanding of the relative roles of maturation and learning in the child's development and realize that the child has to be ready for the next step before progress can be made.

The dangers of comparison with other children need to be realized, and the child's own progress needs to be accepted as the primary basis for evaluation.

Instructions as to how the parent can best help the child at home in the development of specific skills should be given. But the therapist must be careful not to make too great a demand on the parent's time and energy (or on the child's, of course), appreciating that parents have many other responsibilities in regard to maintaining the family.

Parents need to appreciate that progress in the child may require a great deal of regular practice and much encouragement, as well as untold patience on their part.

Parents should become aware of the threats to the emotional security of their children caused by continuous quarreling in the home, major disagreements between the parents in regard to child-rearing practices, inconsistent or baseless discipline, dominance or coddling of the child, the playing of favorites by the parents, and the feeling on the part of the child that he or she is a burden.

Parents need to understand important practical principles of child guidance. The usual areas of concern should be explored, such as toilet training, sleeping, eating, thumbsucking, nailbiting, bed-wetting, temper tantrums, and so forth. Parents also need understanding with respect to sibling relations, sexual development and sex education, the development of constructive social patterns of behavior, shyness and aggression, problems of discipline and, later on, the considerations involved in vocational choice.

At the same time it must be recognized that, though rules are helpful, in no case can they take the place of love for the child, of sensitivity to the child's experiences and reactions. The parent needs to grasp not only the "letter" of the rules and principles but also their spirit.

Parents also need to be prepared for the ordinary frustrations and gratifications aroused by their child's disability. Help in meeting the curiosity, rejecting attitudes, sympathy, and devaluating pity of neighbors and friends should be part of the rehabilitation effort.

Parents need to recognize the difference between problems caused by the child's disability and problems caused by social and physical barriers that prevent access to valued opportunities. Parents can be encouraged to help eliminate those barriers.

These topics cover some of the areas that should be tapped in a broad rehabilitation program involving the parents of children with disabilities. There are others. The rehabilitation team can decide which of the above topics belong to whose domain. Actually, many of them cut across specialities and, in one way or another, are related to the work of all parties involved. The importance of the rehabilitation worker as a counselor and as a person cannot be overestimated. Training and skills are essential but so are wisdom and maturity.

Fortunately, there is a wide variety of reading material to which parents can be directed for sound information concerning child development in general and matters revolving around disability in particular. Spock's classic book on baby and child care can be recommended, and its brief review dealing with the handicapped child contains basic wisdom of benefit to any parent (1976). *Your child has a future* (McCleary, 1978), sponsored by the Easter Seal Society, is an example of an excellent pamphlet for parents of children with disabilities in general. Among sources devoted to a particular type of disability, *The child with spina bifida* (Swinyard, 1964/1975), *New directions for parents of persons who are retarded* (Perske, 1973), and *Our blind children: Growing and learning with them* (Lowenfeld, 1971) are exemplary. These materials provide information concerning questions of etiology, treatment, and home management; offer lists of relevant agencies and other resources; and convey basic attitudes of realistic yet hopeful acceptance. Autobiographical accounts can also extend the horizons of parents. Of books written by parents, the one by Henderson (1954) dealing with the blindness of her child and the one by Bruckner (1954), which reveals so well the emotions in first rejecting and then meeting the challenge imposed by her son's disability, are examples. The amount of autobiographical material written by persons with disabilities is vast, and almost any of it can be helpful to parents who are reaching toward better understanding and acceptance.

The world-famous library of the National Easter Seal Society in Chicago, Ill., will provide the parent (and the professional worker) with sources of bibliographical material covering many areas of child development and disability. Other national organizations, such as the Volta Bureau in Washington, D.C., concerned with problems of deafness, and the American Foundation for the Blind, Inc., in New York City, also maintain reference and lending libraries. Guidance materials by state and national departments of education, welfare, and human services are also available.

If they are to be used to best advantage in parent-child relationships, the knowledge and insights gained must be emotionally accepted as well as intellectually understood. The readiness of the parent to face the facts can be paced with less risk if the parents are given an opportunity to "see for themselves." For example, Cruickshank (1955) has suggested that parents of mentally retarded children with cerebral palsy be given the opportunity to see their child's progress in a nursery school with other children with disabilities but who have normal mentality, when "clinical findings fail to convince parents, who cannot be expected to understand the ultimate implications of a slow rate of development; untold mental anguish and feelings of guilt of parents can be alleviated if the parents . . . convince themselves of the failure of their child to respond to educational opportunities. . . . Realistic planning should ideally allow for this phase of parent-enlightenment before further planning is undertaken" (p. 347). When parents of a child who is deaf visit a school for children who are deaf, they may be upset by the fact that the voices of the graduating seniors are far from what they had hoped could be accomplished. Their reaction, however, remains one of disappointment and not despair when learning about deafness has been taking place within a coping framework.

What needs to be stressed is that parents can deal with the present reality while maintaining hope so long as any bleak future probabilities are allowed to fall into place as the parent seeks and is ready to face such clarification (see Chapter 9 on hoping). It should be remembered that the tasks of hoping include reality surveillance, worrying, encouragement, and mourning—tasks which ultimately allow new hopes to become substituted for those that have to be given up.

It also should be appreciated that acknowledging the possibility that particular hopes for a child might be unrealistic is harder for parents than for professionals (Wright & Shontz, 1968). Evidence indicates that parents often need *both* more facts and greater support for hope than they get (Davis, 1963).

In this connection the sustaining power of religious precepts which posit in disability a divine purpose may be mentioned. Karen's mother, for example, strengthened by her religious beliefs, conveyed a comforting outlook to her child with cerebral palsy:

> . . . She [Karen] had been singing contentedly and broke off in the middle of a bar. Looking at me squarely, she asked, "Mom Pom, why did God make me a cripple?"
>
> "Here it is," I thought, "and I'm not ready after all." I breathed a swift prayer for guidance. I fully realized how much depended on my answer. I dried my hands and sat at the table beside her.
>
> "I think, Karen, because God loved you better than most people," I answered slowly. "He didn't pick Gloria or Marie or Rory [Karen's siblings] to be C.P.; He picked you. You have suffered already and you will suffer more. Not only will your body be hurt at times, but your mind and your heart. It takes a very special person to handle hurt." I moved closer to her. "Karen, whom do you think God loved more than anyone else in the world?"
>
> She pondered. "His mother, I guess."
>
> "You're right, darling, He loved His mother more than anyone else, and yet he allowed her to suffer more than anyone else. Suffering, sweetheart, is a sign of God's special love. That's why you're crippled and we are not. He just loves you more, that's all."
>
> "It's hard, but I'm really lucky. It's all right now I know." [Killilea, 1952, p. 212][3]

And Karen's mother feels that she is privileged to care for Karen:

> I had never thought that "capable" hands (the tactful way of referring to large hands) would be a source of gratitude. Nor that the years spent on tennis court and in fencing would produce anything but the problem of covering bulging biceps, summer or winter. That both would one day be a source of facility and strength in teaching my child to walk, could never have occurred to me. God works in mysterious ways. In giving me a passion for sports and an aptitude thereat, He had been equipping me since childhood for a task not entrusted to the average parent. [pp. 81–82]

Mrs. Bruckner, the mother of Billy who was born without arms, became convinced when he survived a nearly fatal illness that he was

---

[3]From *Karen* by Marie Killilea. © 1952 by Marie Lyons Killilea. Published by Prentice-Hall, Inc., Englewood Cliffs, New Jersey 07632.

born for a purpose, and as the months progressed increasingly saw the positive intent of God's work with respect to Billy (Bruckner, 1954).

Religious beliefs serve to organize one's feeling and thinking about illness and disability through value judgments of right and wrong, of purpose and ultimate meanings. But it should be clear that values also enter the scientific approach, as the discussion of acceptance of disability well testifies (Chapter 8).

The process of reevaluation can carry parents far in giving their child the love, support, and acceptance needed to face life with a disability. In the account below, a father was able to achieve an emotional and intellectual acceptance of his son's disability without specifically calling upon divine judgment. The son, Bill, had lost both arms in a car accident. The father, in service during the war, wrote his son a letter on the eve of Bill's discharge from the rehabilitation center:

> . . . He told him, in words as simple and plain as those he used in making his reconnaissance reports, about a man's rights. He said he was fighting in Korea for those rights, for his own, for Bill's, for Marty's [mother]. "For everybody's rights, Son, no matter where they live. But sometimes a guy gets mixed up. You hear so much about rights these days you begin to think you have a right to everything. Even to a body with two legs and two arms and sight and hearing and so on. But you don't. No one has a right to that kind of body. It's a gift. God gives it to you or nature gives it, or you can call it the evolutionary process, or however you want to speak of it. In big words or little words, it is a gift. And not everybody is given it. For accidents happen before birth, as well as afterward. I know a great chap who was born without arms and legs. . . .
>
> "And sometimes," he said in this letter, "even when we have a gift to begin with, it gets messed up. You know about that. And I know too, out here, because it has happened to some of the bravest men I've flown with. It's funny how a guy can get mixed up about things. He loses a leg, say; or his arms, or his sight; he begins to feel he hasn't had a fair deal; things are raw; he's been gypped; somebody's taken his right to a whole body away from him. He's all wet, Bill.
>
> "But there is a right that you do have; everybody has; and that is the right to a whole life, whether you have legs and arms, or not; no matter how different you may be. And I mean by a whole life, a life full of fun and interesting experiences (along with the hard things), and people you love, and a girl some day, and a job you like to do, and sports, and making things better for others. We are going to do our best, Bill, to help you hold on to that right. To see that nobody takes it away from you. But you have to walk to it, boy, like Guillaumet [a pilot who had suffered untold hardships and whom Bill admired]. All

your mother and I can do is stand by, and help when we can." [Smith, 1954, pp. 178–179]

THE PROBLEM OF OVERPROTECTION, DEPENDENCE, AND INDEPENDENCE

Overprotectiveness is likely to appear as one of the main problems in any study of the attitudes and behavior of parents toward children who have a disability. Research involving children with cerebral palsy (Shere, 1954), other crippling conditions (Kammerer, 1940), and adolescents who are blind (Sommers, 1944) well illustrates this concern. Moreover, the generalization can probably be made that parents tend more frequently to be overprotective toward their children who have a disability than toward those who do not. A study of thirty pairs of twins, one twin of each pair having cerebral palsy (Shere, 1954), revealed that thirteen children with cerebral palsy were judged to be overprotected, whereas none of the nondisabled twins was so judged. An enlightening account of three families differing in their degree of acceptance and overprotectiveness toward the twin with cerebral palsy and the one without is also presented in that study (pp. 129–131).

The person who has a disability often rejects overprotection. In a study of attitudes of people who are deaf toward those with normal hearing (Heider, 1941), it is reported that former pupils of schools for children who are deaf spontaneously mentioned that they are frequently overprotected by, and lose their freedom to, those with normal hearing. The following excerpt from a tape recording of a discussion between a teacher and several young adolescent children with cerebral palsy shows how strongly these adolescents feel about the need for independence (Sutter, 1954).

> BOBBY: They [my parents] don't understand that you *have* to go out and buy something.
> TEACHER: I like that, Bobby, they don't understand that you *have* to get out. Curtis, you had something to say and I want to hear it.
> CURTIS: My family babies me too much.
> TEACHER: Your family babies you too much. . . .
> BOBBY: My mother won't let me take my own bath.
> TEACHER: How old are you Bobby?
> BOBBY: Twelve.
> TEACHER: And you can walk around pretty well. All right . . . we can't leave this subject without finding out why parents feel this way. Why?
> BOBBY: They're afraid for you.
> TEACHER: They're afraid for you. Joe, does your family protect you too much, take too good care of you sometimes, do you think, or do they

let you do anything that is reasonable, going out to the store and so on?

JOE: She won't let me go to the store because a lot of my streets are dangerous and she don't trust me too much.

TEACHER: I don't think it's that your mother doesn't trust you. I think she may not trust your ability to see very clearly or well enough. Well, that's not distrusting you. Sometimes there are very good reasons for these things. Yes, Joe?

JOE: Look for a car.

TEACHER: Sometimes there are ways and means to get around these things like taking a bath or going down to the village. If we can work closely enough with your parents, the teachers and you, we all get together, maybe some of these problems can be solved. . . .

DIANE: After all, you're going to have to do it eventually. You're going to have to do it when you really are more or less on your own, when you don't have anybody to look after you you're going to have to do it and if you can't do it now while your parents are still with you, why then when something happens to them and you try to do it something terrific is liable to happen to you.

Now our problem first begins. We have to think through what overprotection signifies before we dare condemn or commend protective relationships of one person toward another.

Overprotection Negative by Definition

The term *overprotection* has a negative connotation, for too much of anything is undesirable. A certain amount of protection is good; more than that is detrimental.

Overprotective parents have been described in many ways. The following is a sample (Shere, 1954, pp. 48–49):

Overprotective parents are highly child-centered; they are eager to sacrifice themselves (and the rest of the family) for the "good" of one particular child.

They are continually helping the child, even when the child is fully capable and willing to help himself or herself; they bathe, dress, and feed the child.

They restrict the child's play—acceptant parents because they fear the child may get hurt; rejectant ones because their restriction frustrates and punishes the child.

They do not understand the child's capabilities and limitations; they set goals that are too high or are content with goals that are too low.

They monopolize the child's time; they sleep with the child, allow few friends of the child's own choosing, and persuade the child to stay at home with them.

It is not surprising to find many unfortunate effects of overprotection described in the literature. For example (Shere, 1954, pp. 51–52):

> Overprotected children are overdesirous of petting and cuddling. They like to sleep in the same room with their parents or even in the same bed with one of them. They are afraid to sleep alone.
>
> They are overconforming; they obey implicitly.
>
> They are jealous of anyone who appears to threaten their position with loved ones.
>
> They are afraid of many situations, even where there is no real danger.
>
> Their feeling of insecurity is manifested by nervous habits which may serve as emotional release or as attention-getting devices.

The behaviors described in the above lists are ominous indeed. Nonetheless, in the following sections a number of basic issues are raised that challenge the readiness with which overprotection is used as a label to indict parental behavior.

Who Is the Judge?

It might appear that with explicit criteria as to what constitutes overprotection, identification of the overprotective parent would not be difficult. The judgment as to whether the parent is overprotective, however, depends upon who is doing the evaluating. The parents themselves generally do not concur that they are being overprotective. As they see it, the help and protection they are giving the child meet the needs of the child and the realities of the situation.

Other examples illustrate the fact that the *overprotective* label depends upon point of view. The independence given children today would have been considered excessive by the Victorian parent or schoolmaster. Socioeconomic level influences standards of protectiveness. The adolescent tends to regard parental guidance and restrictions as overprotective. Difference in judgment is seen when neighbors feel that parents are underprotecting a child who is blind or deaf when that child is allowed to cross city streets, though experts and parents may believe independence is being fostered.

Glorification of Independence

The problem of overprotection is part and parcel of the cultural value placed on dependence and independence. A notion of how American middle-class society compares with other societies in this respect is provided in the important study of child-rearing practices by Whiting & Child (1953, Chapter 4).

1. Initial nurturance. Among the 38 primitive societies rated, indulgence of the infant's tendencies to be dependent is generally rather high. This is also true of American middle-class society, though 30 of the societies allowed their babies to be more dependent than ours.

2. Age at beginning of training in independence (self-reliance, responsibility). Serious efforts at independence training are begun at the median age of a little above 3.5 years for the 38 societies. American middle-class society is placed at 2.5 years. However, independence training among the American group is completed at a very late age in comparison with the societies rated.

3. Severity of independence training. American middle-class practice is placed at the median of all the societies surveyed, a high rating being given, however, for that aspect of independence concerned with the responsibility of the child for taking an adult role in the household economy (e.g., self-help in dressing, chores) and a low rating for fending for oneself without adult surveillance. The evidence further indicates that in regard to overall indulgence and severity of training as applied to a variety of behaviors (nursing and weaning, toileting, sex behavior, dependency, aggression), American middle-class society is comparatively not only extremely low in average indulgence but is also rather extreme in the severity of its socialization practices.

A major study by Sears, Maccoby, & Levin (1957, Chapter 5) contributes additional data on dependency in American children in a sample of almost 400 mothers of kindergarten children. Each was asked how much attention her child seemed to want, whether the child followed her around, whether the child objected when she left for a while, and whether the child asked for unnecessary help. On the basis of these indications of dependency, it was found that by the time the children were 5 years of age, a preponderance showed little of the dependency behavior rated; only about 20 percent showed a considerable amount (Table D:13, p. 524). There was, however, a wide variability in the attitudes of the parents toward the kind of dependent behavior investigated. About one-third showed little tolerance for such dependency; the middle third was moderately permissive, and the remaining third was lenient.

The various lines of evidence lead to the conclusion that independence is highly valued in our society. It goes along with ability, masculinity, leadership, and rugged individualism. To be independent is reassuring that one will be able to take care of oneself and not be dependent on the uncertain solicitude of others. Dependence, on the other hand, is often disvalued. It is associated with weakness, femininity, indecision, selfishness, and helplessness. No one would be startled to find a book or a chapter entitled "Growing toward Independence" but one would be rather surprised to find the heading "Growing toward Dependence." The shock might be tempered by the assumption of a typographical error, or that the chapter dealt with negative practices that lead children to grow in the wrong direction. If the author argued that children and adults need to grow toward *de*pendence, would the reader take it seriously?

This hypothetical situation indicates how deeply rooted is the conviction that independence as a goal has the weight of an axiom. Add to this the fact that disability may threaten independence and we have a combination of circumstances that makes understandable, if not completely justifiable, the tremendous emphasis placed on independence in work with persons who have a disability.

Dependence as a Value and Universal Need

As long as dependence is arbitrarily disvalued and neglected in interpersonal relations, independence becomes distorted as a goal. What happens, for example, to the warmth and friendliness between parent and child when the parent is driven to get the child to eat alone, dress alone, walk alone? These goals are important, of course, but when independence becomes virtually the dominating guide for parental behavior, the cost in emotional security is unjustifiably great. This is seen in the following example of a mother who insisted on self-reliant behavior in her 5-year-old child:

> I[NTERVIEWER]: How did you feel about it when she wanted to be with you all the time?
> M[OTHER]: Well, I had to teach her she had to be alone at times and not have me around.
> I: How do you generally react if she demands attention when you're busy?
> M: I don't pay attention to her.
> I: How about if she asks you to help her with something you think she could probably do by herself?
> M: I tell her she's supposed to do it herself, and I'm not going to help her.
> I: And then does she do it?
> M: Oh, yes, if she feels like it.
> I: Otherwise, what do you do?

M: Otherwise, I just let her alone, let her have one of her stubborn streaks, or just take things away, tell her she can't play any more if she's going to be like that. [Sears, Maccoby, & Levin, 1957, p. 164]

Several research findings are pertinent here. In the study of children with cerebral palsy mentioned earlier (Shere, 1954), the children who were *both* loved and overprotected, but not those whose overprotection stemmed from rejection, appeared to be friendly, cheerful, with a good sense of humor, and free from aggressive behavior. In the aforementioned study of patterns of child rearing (Sears, Maccoby, & Levin, *1957*) it was found that:

Punishment for dependency only made children more dependent than ever.

Withdrawal of love as a disciplinary technique and severity of punishment for aggression toward parents were significantly related to degree of child dependency.

Those mothers who had an accepting tolerant attitude toward the child's dependent behavior tended also to be affectionately warm toward the child, gentle about toilet training, low in their use of physical punishment, high in sex permissiveness, low in punishment for aggression toward parents, and high in esteem for both self and husband.

The findings of these two studies alone suggest caution in decrying dependency (or for that matter overprotection) without considering the broader parent-child relationship and the emotional needs of the child.

A great step forward was made when psychoanalytic and other theories stressed that the early period of dependency of the child on parents is important and that the need for nurturance in its broadest sense must be satisfied. Emotional support for this emphasis was given by the strong cultural and human value placed on love and acceptance and by the anxiety about social rejection, which is especially strong in our culture. Nevertheless, dependency as such is usually not posited as a desirable end in itself. Instead, it is seen as a means to emotional security or to ultimately greater independence.

We should like to extend the emphasis on dependency by submitting that the need for dependency applies throughout the life span. People have to learn how and when to become appropriately dependent on others just as they need to learn appropriate independence. To take everyday examples, a person should be able to rely on others, to ask for and accept help, to delegate responsibility. These are behaviors that require being dependent on others.

It takes learning on both the emotional and intellectual levels to value such dependency and to know when such dependency serves important needs and goals. Although the nature of dependent relationships changes over a lifetime, there is always a need for dependency, for no one can rely on the self alone. This holds true in the optimum state of health as it does when we become sick, acquire limitations, and become old.

Just as people may be excessively dependent on others, they may also be excessively independent of others. In both instances the person is denying the self and others certain values. Excessive dependence denies the obvious value of ability to do for oneself and accomplish certain goals. Excessive *in* dependence denies the less accepted value of emotional sharing. It also constricts one's range of accomplishment by negating the desirability of relying on others and delegating responsibility. Being goaded by independence, the person may insist on doing for oneself only to be depleted of energy and emotional resources that might well have been spent more usefully.

Dependence and Independence as a Partnership

The following account is a particularly telling description of the difficulty people with disabilities, as well as people without disabilities, have in recognizing that independence as a narrowly conceived overriding principle is a snare and a delusion that creates unnecessary obstacles to the wise use of one's energies. It was reported by a woman with quadreplegia who assisted at an Independent Living Center for people with disabilities (Cappaert, 1979). Someone asked her why she did not use an electric wheelchair:

> When she asked me this question I realized that I was one of the few people who spent time at the center who used a manual rather than electric wheelchair.
>
> I answered that, in my particular situation, an electric wheelchair seemed to cause more problems than provide benefits. I value the relative light weight of my manual chair when I want to be lifted up or downstairs and I value the flexibility of it when I want to fold it up and jump into a friend's car, storing it in the trunk.
>
> Besides these factors, because I use a portable respirator that must be reconnected (plugged in, turned on, etc.) each time I change locations, the ability to move myself across a room still does not really free me from the need to have another person around to help do this.
>
> I also had a feeling, I told her, that I depended upon many machines for my survival and did not welcome more time spent in worry over another machine, such as an electric chair, breaking down or needing repairs.
>
> I added that, after thinking over the alternatives, I had decided that, at least for now, I prefer to depend upon a person pushing me rather than an electric chair.
>
> But don't you want to be independent?" the woman protested to me.

For the next ten minutes our conversation went in confusing circles about just what this meant. As I felt frustrated in our talk I noticed that the question of electric vs. manual wheelchairs had almost become humorous to me. The question seemed to recur often in my life and my answers seldom seemed to satisfy the questions. It seemed that this small question was symbolic of a larger issue.

When I went through an evaluation program at the Bureau of Vocational Rehabilitation the same question seemed to creep into discussions I had with almost every member of the staff. To me it seemed that they were grasping at a mechanical device because it was a relatively simple answer to what their agency could do to help me.

When I had explained my thoughts and reasons for deciding against an electric chair the BVR staff had come back at me with the same trap, "But why don't you want to be independent?"

I refer to this attitude as a trap because it refuses to acknowledge my decision as a valid independent act. There was no way that I, as the client, could have answered that question fairly or reasonably.

Sadly, I was not surprised to get this type of response from trained social workers. However, I was surprised to hear this attitude coming from a peer. It worried me to think that disabled people are allowing the theories of "professionals" to define who they are.

To me, independence is the freedom to survey all of the available alternatives in a given situation and then use this collected information to make a conscious choice. [p. 25][4]

Some proponents of the vitally important Independent Living movement have grappled with the problem of dependence versus independence by insisting that, so long as the person "calls the shots," the person is being independant. Thus, it would be argued that the woman in the account above was no more dependent in choosing the manual wheelchair that required an attendent than would an able-bodied person be in hiring a carpenter so long as the person retains the power to make choices and to hire and fire the needed helper.

My own thinking on this matter is to retain the concept of dependence as legitimate in its own right, but to recognize that being independent, in the sense of relying on oneself, and being dependent, in the sense of relying on another person, often go hand in hand. The woman was being independent by making her own choice and by retaining the power to hire and fire. She was being dependent by requiring the services of an attendant on whom she needed to rely. Dependence as a value ought to be held in the same high regard as independence. Each alone and together can expand one's free-

[4]Reprinted from Confusing definitions of independence, by A. Cappaert. In *Rehabilitation Gazette*, 1979, 22.

dom, space of free movement, and accomplishment. This is true for all of us and the wise use of both dependence and independence requires upholding the value of both and learning through tutelage and experience.

Interdependence as a Value and Universal Need

Interdependence, a third dimension in human relationships, needs to be added to the partnership of independence and dependence so that its importance can be recognized and given due weight. Just as all of us benefit by being independent and dependent some of the time, so all of us benefit from relationships of mutual dependency. Mutual dependence occurs in families, among friends, and even among enemies. It occurs in the work place and in larger social units.

What appears to be a dependent relationship may often be better understood as one of interdependence. A worker's dependence on an employer has its counterpart in the employer's dependence on the worker, despite differences in power. A child's dependence on the parent may be matched by the parent's dependence on the child. The parent may have a deep need to keep the child dependent, or in the positive case, may enjoy ministering to the child and seeing the child grow and develop. Where a child shows too much or too little dependence or independence, it behooves us to look at the parent's needs and behavior in what more usefully should be considered a relationship of interdependence with the child.

Achieving the Independence-Dependence-Interdependence (I-D-I) Balance

Placing independence within a more balanced perspective suggests that parents, through the pressure of their own principles and those of the specialist, may be pushing children too fast and too soon toward the vague and abstract goal of independence. It suggests that the priceless quality of warmth in interpersonal relations may be usurped by the calculated zeal to teach the child independence. It suggests that ratings of overprotectiveness, which appear as central findings in research reports, may be unduly weighted by the high cultural premium placed on independence. It suggests the need for investigating the kinds of dependency and interdependency that should be fostered during the various phases of the entire life span of a person's development. It suggests that dependency and interdependency should not be seen as substitutes for independence, but as equally important values in and of themselves.

It has already been pointed out that the judgment of overprotectiveness varies not only with the person making the judgment but also with the times. Although this means that there are no universal criteria defining how much dependence, independence or interdependence is too much or not enough, there are aids that can help parents in arriving at what is for them a satisfactory course to take with their children. The following focuses on children with disabilities, although the principles apply to all children.

The opportunity for parents to *observe other children* with the same disability as that of their own child, so that they can learn what various children are able to do and what they are allowed to do, opens up new possibilities. Such observation is possible in a variety of settings, such as rehabilitation centers, special and integrated schools, and homes.

Because comparisons are often somewhat dangerous, a word of caution is in order. Although the gains from observation of other children are many, they may be offset by the ill-considered adoption for one's own child of standards based on what another can do. Even though another child of the same age has a similar disability, the principle of individual differences, of course, still holds. Since there is a strong tendency to adopt as a standard the performance of the superior child in the group, parents may need help in understanding the abilities and limitations of their own child as an individual.

Parent discussion groups provide an excellent resource for furthering awareness of what can realistically be expected of the child (Bice, 1955; Heisler, 1972). In exchanging ideas with parents and in observing other children, such reorienting notions may emerge as: "I think my child [who is blind] will be able to ride a trike too." "She [child with cerebral palsy] might be able to lace her own shoes if I gave her enough time." "I will let my child [who is deaf] go to the store. The grocer will be able to understand him." On the side of developing healthy dependency needs: "My child is too aloof from others. She needs to play more with other children." "My child is afraid to ask for help. I wonder why." And for interdependency: "We ought to depend more on my child. I think he is ready to set the table and help with the yard work if we are not too fussy." *Brainstorming,* described on pages 209–210, can be recommended as a method for generating workable ideas especially suited to parent discussion groups.

Parents also need to be informed of *special techniques* that can aid in the development of their child. Many require little in the way of mechanical equipment. As Lowenfeld (1971) points out to parents of children who are blind: "Your child, if he is totally blind, may not be familiar with the way in which legs must be moved in walking since he cannot see it done. You can help him easily in this situation. Let him stand on your shoes while you hold him by the hands. Thus he will be able to observe with his own body your movements when you walk. This should be done in such a way that your child faces the same direction as you do in walking. If you do this frequently enough while he is gaining control in standing up, he will one day step off your shoes and go through the actions of walking himself" (p. 56). The suggestions outlined by Snell (1955) are simple and beneficial: "Parents [of cerebral palsy children] complain that their children do not like to sit in a high chair or that they slide down in the chair, and after a few attempts . . . the high chair is discarded. Adjustments can be made in high chairs, such as reducing the length of the back legs slightly, so that the front of the chair is higher than the back. A piece of wood two inches wide and four inches high may be attached to the center front rim of the seat on the high chair, this padded and covered with a plastic material, so that it can be easily cleaned. The child is placed in the chair with a leg on either side of the bar so that it is not possible for him to slide out . . ." (p. 289). The importance of informing parents of "know how" would hardly require mention if it were not for the fact that simple solutions and aids are often overlooked in rehabilitation requiring such complex procedures as bracing and special education.

The idea of *creating opportunities* for specific kinds of experiences should also be raised with parents. Although this is obvious as a principle, parents need help in applying it concretely. Again an example from Lowenfeld (1971) is apt. We do not have to think very much about opportunities for moving and exploring for ordinary children, for on their own they will expand their horizons beyond their own body, from the crib to the playpen, room, house, yard, and neighborhood. But in regard to the blind child, or the child with marked physical incapacity, indifference on this score will impede growth and development. "The blind child will often remain unaware of his environment and of interesting objects in it because he cannot see them, and his other senses do not make him conscious of them. Therefore, he will often need to be taken to things, or from one place to the other before he will venture out on his own. But he is just as eager to move and explore as any other child if he is stimulated and encouraged in ways which are suitable for him" (p. 19).[5]

The creation of opportunities applies, of course, not only to locomotion. A commonsense though fallacious notion regarding deaf children, for example, is that since the child cannot hear it is futile to talk to him or her; instead, one must gesture. The parent's realization that the child must be spoken to so that speech-reading skills

[5]From B. Lowenfeld, *Our blind children* (3d ed.), 1971. Courtesy of Charles C Thomas, Publisher, Springfield, Illinois.

may be developed, even though manual language may also be used, represents a major step forward on the part of parents. Opportunity for the child to communicate with nonfamily members is also important.

However, creating opportunities is not always easy to bring about. Parents may realize how important it is for their child with cerebral palsy to have experience with a variety of adults and may look for a baby-sitter to provide this opportunity, only to have considerable trouble in finding someone willing to undertake this duty. Or, parents may be aware that their child needs the companionship of other children, but in spite of efforts to provide interesting play situations for invited children, neighbors may be reluctant to respond. The rehabilitation worker must be aware that even with the best of intentions solutions are sometimes "easier said than done." Follow-up is necessary to correct false leads and seek new solutions.

The judicious use of *reading material* (see pp. 398–399) can be invaluable in imparting to the parent constructive attitudes and factual information, the background necessary toward realizing the I-D-I balance in striving for independence, dependence, and interdependence.

Finally, the child needs the opportunity to assume *increasing responsibility* for his or her own self-help behavior as well as for activities involving other people. In an important ecological study (Barker and H. Wright, 1955) in which an institution for children with cerebral palsy was compared with a nearby rural community, one of the sharpest differences was that the institutionalized children entered far fewer positions of responsibility and status than did the rural children. Relatively rarely were they leaders, joint leaders, or responsible functionaries in a particular activity. More typically they had little power in the situation or were onlookers. Children need to become responsible actors in some of the home, school, and community settings and not serve only as auxiliary players. Parents and professionals need help in recognizing those situations where the child can take on responsibility, with or without help, and in devising other situations where they do not exist.

Barriers and Cautions

The preceding discussion may appear reasonable enough, and yet a good balance in the three areas of independence, dependence, and interdependence is typically difficult to achieve. There are many reasons for this. One set of reasons applies to environmental barriers of all sorts. Architectural barriers are legion. Appropriate play groups for children with disabilities may not be available, and so forth.

Another set of reasons applies to personal restraining forces that impede development in the three areas. I would like to mention two insidious forces that all of us, parents and professionals alike, are prey to. One is the tendency to see a child who has a severe disability as severely limited in all areas of functioning, including being able to assume responsibility. This tendency is referred to as the *negative spread effect* (see Chapter 3).

The second is the tendency to limit the child's scope of activities rather than to enlarge it because it is easier in the short run to do so. Especially during the beginning stages of learning, it may require a good deal more patience on the part of the parent to let the child do for oneself, or to include the child in decision making, or to depend on the child, than for the parent to take over. This holds for all children but is especially germane where disability is involved. Sometimes the parent is not aware that learning may be a slow and laborious process and that it is important to provide the necessary time and opportunity for that learning to occur. Sometimes the parent has a need to keep the child overly dependent; at other times, the parent is already overburdened with the time and energy demands of tending a home and making a living. This weariness may keep the parent from meeting the child's dependency needs as well as the child's need to grow in independence and interdependence. The parent may limit interaction with the child to an extent bordering on neglect and rationalize that it is good for the child to be on its own. Comparable pressures apply to professionals in their relationships with families and children.

Still another set of reasons applies to the main thrust of our concern. Until the values of independence, dependence, and interdependence are seen in relationship to each other and as equally important, human relationships must remain distorted. It behooves the parent and the professional to question explicitly whether the child is developing appropriately with respect to each of the three I-D-I value areas. Is any of these neglected? Overstressed? How can remediation take place? The I-D-I conceptualization needs to become the guiding framework. It is then that the balance needed in independent, dependent, and interdependent relations can begin to be guaged and adjusted according to our best understanding of growth-promoting opportunities.

THE BASIC VALUE OF CARING AND LOVE FOR THE CHILD

The power of caring and love for the child in sustaining both parent and child in the face of difficulties is great indeed. "Love, to be worthy of the name in any human relationship, consists of a sincere desire for the other individual's best good rather than mere self-indulgence of the one who gives the affection" (Laycock & Stevenson, 1950, p. 120). A study on adolescent blind children (Sommers, 1944) brought out that "the lack of satisfying parental love . . . produced a feeling of loss which seemed to be more injurious to the personality of the blind child than his lack of sight" (p. 103). An important review of such child-rearing practices as breast versus bottle feeding, age of weaning, and toilet training showed that these factors *as such* had little psychological significance for the child's development, whereas the attitude of the parent in carrying out the procedures was crucial (Orlansky, 1949). In a study that examined the lives of more than 250 *well-adjusted children* (Stout, 1951), it was revealed that the background information about the parents (age, religion, etc.) gives little help in accounting for the good adjustment of their children. What did stand out among the many variations in family life was the parent's belief in what is "most important of all"—namely, conveying to the children in behavior and words that they are loved, respected, and wanted.

Of course, love is not enough, as this chapter attests, but it can go far in enabling parents to deal with their behavior, feelings, and needs that impede child development. It would seem that the specific aids toward achieving a healthy dependent-interdependent-independent balance would have the best chance of being effective where love is the prevailing attitude, for then the predominant effort of the parent, consciously and subconsciously, is geared toward the child's needs, not the parent's. On the other hand, where rejection of the child, or the need to keep a child dependent, or guilt is strong, then behavior reflecting such feelings may be expected to persist. Sometimes a therapist or a parent discussion group can be of help in such instances. Hearing a disquieting attitude talked about in a permissive atmosphere makes it easier to see it in oneself. As one father while participating in a discussion group said, "If anyone had asked me before it was mentioned here if I ever felt guilty about our boy, I would have denied it; I realize now that I did" (Bice, 1950). Not to be overlooked is the fact that good feelings may also surface as a result of sympathetic discussion. Some parents may be so bothered by shame and guilt or by problems extraneous to the child that they do not realize how much affection and closeness they feel toward their child.

At the same time it must be realized that no matter how much parents love their child, they can only do so much, beyond which excessive fatigue, frustration, and other signs of psychological stress become inevitable. Also, parents need to be prepared that no matter what they do, they will be criticized by some people. There will be neighbors and friends who will view necessary care and concern as signs of oversolicitude. There will be those who will interpret parental efforts to give their child more freedom as neglect and rejection. Even well-meaning friends will not be able to understand the mature calmness of a parent toward his or her child's disability. In not understanding, they are prone to be accusing.

This chapter concludes with a deep respect for what it takes on the part of parents to rear a child to maturity. It also recognizes the enormous contribution that the broad range of rehabilitation services can make to the developing child. The best rehabilitation programs make use of the special knowledge, caring, and efforts of parents and rehabilitation personnel working as a team toward the physical, mental, and emotional development of the child.

Chapter 17
The Client as Comanager in Rehabilitation

Few professionals or clients would deny the importance of active participation on the part of the client. In an important study of professional and client viewpoints on rehabilitation issues (Leviton, 1973), subjects were asked whether there should be more client participation in decision making or more control by professionals. The professional subjects were rehabilitation hospital staff, vocational counselors, and nursing instructors; all three groups favored active client participation. This was also true of clients seeking vocational rehabilitation and members of a self-help group; however, subjects still in a rehabilitation hospital tended to support professional control. It should be stressed, however, that even when all parties concerned approve active client participation in principle, the factors that interfere with its realization are so insidious that it is necessary to examine word and deed for possible violations. A number of interfering factors were discussed in the preceding chapter.

It should also be emphasized that active participation is not, as is often assumed in practice, synonymous with "cooperative attitude." Of course professionals are pleased when clients willingly submit to all manner of test procedures, when they respond to questions fully and with enthusiasm, and above all when they follow recommendations. This is the "good" client. But it is not the active participant.

The specifications of active participation become clarified when clients are considered to be part of management. It is then that they not only contribute data to their case but also help to evaluate the data and work toward solutions; and finally that they claim veto power as well as voting privileges (except in special circumstances; see pp. 434–438). The *principle of comanagement* is an apt designation for the kind of relationship advocated. It connotes active participation by *both* client and specialist. This principle, or even philosophy, also was seen to underlie a good deal of the discussion of motivation in the rehabilitation situation and the parent as a key participant (Chapters 15 and 16).

BASIS FOR ENCOURAGING COMANAGEMENT

Reasons for participation by adults and children in the management of their rehabilitation are important. The first of these concerns the matter of self-esteem.

> . . . the worker-client relationship tends to be an asymmetrical one in which the professional person has the higher status position. Just as in the case of doctor and patient, lawyer and client, or teacher and pupil the disabled person may easily feel [himself to be] in a dependent position in which it is hoped that the wisdom of the worker will guide him through his difficulties. But it is just such an atmosphere of a wise and powerful one, on the one hand, and a dependent, suppliant one on the other hand, that so easily can nourish the feelings of inadequacy and personal inferiority that true rehabilitation seeks to avoid. The inner strength and self-respect which we wish to build in the client grows in a relationship in which the disabled person feels that he has an important role in planning his life and that what he says and what he feels is respected. . . . Even a disabled child needs to have a feeling that he knows what is happening to him and why, that he has a choice in the decisions. How much more true this is of the person who has reached adulthood with all the independence of judgment and self-determination that this implies. [Barker & B. Wright, 1952, pp. 20–21]

Inner strength and self-respect grow in a relationship when the person has a significant role in planning his or her life, when the person's suggestions and feelings are regarded as important.

Motivation to make the plan work is another important reason for stressing the participation of the client in the development as well as the execution of the rehabilitation program. One pamphlet addressed to patients emphasizes that ". . . the final result depends on you and how much you put into it. Their [staff] job is important, but yours is more important" (Rusk & Taylor, 1946, p. 85). When clients feel that they have little to do with the plan in the first place, their energies can easily be dissipated in minor complaints. They are also less apt to assume responsibility for making new decisions and adjustments as circumstances change. How often does a person, presumably vocationally rehabilitated, leave the job after 6 months as a result of relatively unimportant sources of irritation because, not having had a crucial say in the vocational alternatives, he or she has readily placed the responsibility of finding the perfect but nonexistent job in the counselor's lap! Patient responsibility forms the cornerstone of what is known as client-centered therapy (Rogers, 1951) and is certainly an essential building block of other, more directive types of psychotherapy. As Rogers (1959) has stated it, psychotherapy is the "releasing of an already existing capacity in a potentially competent individual, not the expert manipulation of a more or less passive personality" (p. 221).

A third reason for encouraging comanagement is the fact that the potential for learning is greatly increased when one is actively involved in guiding one's own behavior. That this is true for academic subjects is well known. An important volume on how to read a book (Adler & Van Doren, 1972) devotes a considerable portion to specific instructions for becoming an actively involved reader. It is suggested, for example, that the reader circle key words and phrases and raise pointed questions, such as "What does the author want to prove?"

Even where learning is nonintellectual, active participation promotes learning. A particularly illuminating example is the research on adaptation to prisms that distort vision (Held, 1965). In one experiment, prism goggles were worn under two conditions. In the active condition, the person walked for an hour along an outdoor path. In the passive condition, the person was pushed in a wheelchair along the same path for the same length of time. The degree of adaptation to the prisms achieved by the subjects who had been involved in active movement was far greater than that of the subjects who had been in the passive situation. Another example is the common experience that learning one's way around in a new city proceeds much more rapidly when one is the driver rather than a passenger in a car.

A further consideration for endorsing active client participation is the fact that our fund of knowledge is often not sufficient to enable the professional person to actually know the best course of action. Add to this the fact that scientific knowledge is neither learned nor applied as "pure knowledge" untouched by predilections of one's professional discipline, by personal prejudices, or by the biasing effects of prior information and diagnostic labels that appear in client records (Batson, 1975; Riscalla, 1973). On these grounds alone it would seem desirable to allow for the views of the client.

As a concrete illustration of this point, let us examine the controversial issue as to whether people of good intelligence should be provided higher education irrespective of the degree of physical disability. There are those who have spoken out strongly in the negative, arguing that the "overtrained" physically handicapped person will be happier in a less skilled job than when frustrated in an attempt to compete in professional fields where the possibility of real achievement is seriously limited if not impossible. Although this point of view cannot be ignored, the following issue is crucial to its evaluation: Isn't a judgment of employability at best an estimate of probability, and isn't an unwarranted wisdom assumed on the part of even the most expert vocational counselor who feels able to say with assurance that a particular individual will be unable to put his or her training to productive use? The remarks of Lowenfeld (1971) with respect to the vocational pursuits of persons who are blind have wide generality. He reminds us that any list of occupations must remain incomplete because "a singularly gifted blind man or woman can be found doing work which others—even those experienced in work with the blind—would consider impossible for a blind person. Thus we know of a highly successful blind scientist in atomic research, an equally successful blind chemist, and a physicist, and I know myself of a totally blind man who owned and ran the largest bookstore in a city with almost half a million population—and he really did run it successfully" (Lowenfeld, 1971, p. 13).[1] The fact that even those experienced in work with persons who are blind might consider these occupations impossible should have sobering implications.

It must also be remembered that employability is not related in a simple way to degree of disability, that many unforeseen social, as well as personal, forces may combine to open up opportunities for even those with the most severe disabilities. There is the enlightening fact, uncovered in a study of adults with cerebral palsy (Glick, 1953), that of those whose disabilities were categorized as mild, 7 percent were employed as compared with 22 percent and 24 percent of those with moderate and severe disabilities, respectively. The enormous potential for widening opportunities by using enabling technology, by modifying tasks to meet functional limitations, and

[1]From B. Lowenfeld, *Our blind children* (3d ed.), 1971. Courtesy of Charles C Thomas, Publisher, Springfield, Illinois.

by eliminating unjustified barriers, including architectural, legal, and attitudinal barriers, also enters vocational outcome.

Instead of giving the vocational and educational counselor the prerogative of deciding whether or not a client should be allowed to enter a particular program, it is proposed that the counselor should *assist* clients in deciding the course of their destiny by providing relevant information and by helping them consider basic issues involved in the choices. A good example of such mutual sharing in the process of vocational counseling appears on page 424. To be sure there will be instances where hindsight will prove that the client was wrong, but *there will also be instances where the counselor's misgivings will not have been borne out.*

Whether or not one agrees with the particular conclusion concerning vocational guidance, the general point should be taken seriously by all rehabilitation workers—namely, that the lack of omniscience on the part of the counselor and the special knowledge that the insider has of one's own needs, wishes, and situation, give additional support to the principle that clients in most cases should be a key planner in their rehabilitation. It is interesting that in the aforementioned study on professional and client viewpoints (Leviton, 1973), clients who supported active participation referred to the special knowledge of the insider as an important reason, whereas professionals neglected this aspect. Instead, professionals gave much weight to the idea that clients will be more likely to take responsibility for implementing mutually arrived at decisions. Although most clients did not include motivation as a reason, some members of the self-help group did. Also, both professionals and clients rarely referred to the less-than-perfect knowledge of professionals as a basis for encouraging client participation. Those who favored greater professional control, however, gave most weight to the superiority of professional knowledge.

Finally, there is the important question as to which issues belong rightfully within the inviolable domain of the adults directly involved. Some persons may regard many areas as falling within the "inalienable rights" of the individual. Choice as to having more children, even children with severe limitations, may be so regarded, as may choice concerning living arrangements, educational goals, vocational pursuits, and medical care. We have already discussed the issue of institutionalization in these terms (p. 394). The principle of self-determination may be so highly prized by some rehabilitation workers that only in the most unusual circumstances would they feel compelled to defy the wishes of the client. Other specialists see a much narrower zone for decisions that are inviolably the client's. In any case, every professional person must face the issue as to whether he or she has a right in the particular situation to make decisions or even in some cases to offer recommendations. Later we shall consider special circumstances in which the client cannot or should not be a key planner in his or her rehabilitation.

The judgment of client rights is not only made by the professional. Clients (consumers) too have views about their rights. Scott's (1960) attack against the role of agencies for the blind in creating docility and dependency in their clients was supported by broad groups of consumers who questioned whether the goals of agencies were the ones they would have chosen for themselves. Since then bills of rights for patients and for persons with disabilities have emerged on the national and international scene. Moreover, as consumers become insistent in laying claim to their rights, professional attitudes may begin to change accordingly. What initially may have been viewed as arrogant and interfering demands come to be seen as grievances that must be redressed.

IMPEDIMENTS TO COMANAGEMENT

One of the important factors that hinders comanagement on the part of the client is the helping relationship itself. The point has already been made that "help" frequently connotes an asymmetrical situation in which the one helped occupies a subservient, less powerful position. The helper is the capable one in the situation whereas the one helped is in a position of dependency. In the extreme case, the specialist occupies the position of a benevolent and authoritative parent protecting, guiding, and ordering, and the client the position of a child, naive, uninformed, and irresponsible, with negativistic and unrealistic tendencies. The helping relationship itself tends to reinforce the attitude that the expert has the answers, or at least should have the answers. The thought that the answers themselves may frequently require the judgment and decision of the client is quite alien. Instead, it becomes natural for the professional to take over and to receive the credit for successful rehabilitation. The dominance of the expert has been associated with the medical model in contrast to help as a growth promoting process in which clients comanage their rehabilitation (Anderson, 1975).

Not infrequently, of course, the client expects and wants the professional to take charge of the case completely. And there are circumstances in which such action is commendable. The acutely ill person often does not have the energy reserve, to say nothing of clarity of intellectual functioning, to become actively involved in alternatives and decisions. In such circumstances it may be important that the therapist be allowed to take over with full confidence that he or she will manage wisely.

But the client's readiness to shift responsibility to the therapist can be a significant factor interfering with the goals of rehabilitation. Especially when the outcome of the process requires unsupervised and independent action on the part of the client, it is essential that the client be brought into a directorship role as soon as feasible. It is one thing if the patient on the operating table yields to the wisdom of the surgeon, but it is quite another thing if, during the patient's convalescence, the doctor, the vocational counselor, or the physical therapist lays out the course of action without genuine consultation with the client. The specialist cannot remain at the client's elbow to see that the plan works. Aside from the question of motivation, it is important to remember that the patient who is actively engaged in steering the rehabilitation course is able to take into account needs and circumstances which, if ignored, can prevent goal realization.

The needs of the helper are also important in role determination. When professionals have a need to assert themselves, flaunt their knowledge, buttress their status, or gain power, the authoritarian role is so satisfying that it is not easily given up. There is also the specialist who does not enjoy or who becomes anxious in real give-and-take relationships. More impersonal contact with clients in an authoritarian relationship may then be preferred.

There are other factors that pose stumbling blocks in applying the principle of comanagement. They have to do with financial costs, time shortage, and the need to offer rehabilitation services to as many people as possible. The unfortunate fact is that involving the client in a comanagement role frequently takes more time than having the specialist accumulate the data and present the prescription. One can retort that time is saved in the end, but in light of severe personnel shortages and staggering numbers of clients in need, the immediate time pressures make the authoritative role of the expert expedient. One solution obviously lies in the training of more specialists. Another lies in the use of approaches which make possible more efficient use of the specialist's time without sacrificing effectiveness, and which, in their own right, promote rehabilitation. Group counseling, peer counseling, and guided reading by the client are examples. The use of special personnel able to pave the way for real participation on the part of the client and to act as a mediating link between the client and an overburdened specialist is another. The motto: "Don't get stuck with the problem; move on to the solution" is a useful reminder to prod constructive thinking.

COMANAGEMENT BY CLIENT AND PROFESSIONAL ILLUSTRATED

The following approach, used successfully by Garrett (1955) for vocational guidance with adults who have cerebral palsy, is exemplary of comanagement relationships:

> In this method a large sheet of paper is used, divided down the middle with "Assets" on the left column first and "Liabilities" on the right. Jointly counselor and counselee explore whatever both know about the client, carefully listing them in the appropriate column. Suitable items for listing are . . . ability for self-care, physical capacities, mental abilities, emotional status, vocational opportunities, hopes, ideals, aspirations, preferences, and similar data. The listings are made in terms comprehensible to the client and he may even be encouraged to do the writing. Care should be exercised lest the "Liabilities" column be greater than the "Assets" although a realistic appraisal of client strengths and weaknesses will almost always reveal more ability than disability, especially with those to whom this technique would be applicable.
>
> When the listing has been completed, occupations under consideration are then compared in detail with each asset and liability and an informal "score" of so many assets and so many liabilities is obtained. When all of the occupational groups have been completed, a rough scale of values in terms of suitability of the occupations is ready. Usually the client is ready after such a process to choose wisely, realistically, and with satisfaction to himself since he has been an active partner in the process.
>
> In this procedure, the . . . individual analyzes himself, determines those elements which have vocational significance, evaluates their specific importance to a given job, sorts and shifts the results of the process into a particular occupational pattern and determines that which suits him better than others. This process is dynamic and thus a guard against the . . . client remaining dependent, detached and avoiding reality whether of disability or of work. . . . In this process the counselor makes it clear that he does not have the answers and emphasizes this by the mutual working through of the problem. [pp. 452–453]

One could hardly accuse the counselor in the above account of having been passive. Guidance was given, but a guidance which allowed the client, even encouraged the client, to explore those aspects about the self and total situation which had vocational significance, and to determine which occupation appeared most suitable. The conclusion that "usually the client is ready after such a process to choose wisely, realistically, and with satisfaction to himself" is not to be taken lightly.

Another example of involving the client as part of management may help give meaning to the fact that the principle of comanagement has general application. A prosthetics specialist tells his patients:

> We cannot recommend a limb until we get to know you. There is no such thing as a "best" limb. The limb that is best-suited to the needs of one individual may be entirely unsatisfactory for another. The type of work you do, your personality and temperament, and the accessibility of a satisfactory limb fitter to make necessary adjustments are but a few of the factors which must be considered. *It is also important from a psychological standpoint that you yourself make the final selection. It's your limb, and you are going to wear it.* [Rusk & Taylor, 1946, p. 142, italics added][2]

The notion of full participation has been extended to the client as a coevaluator in psychological testing. In this approach, no secrets are kept from the person being tested. The purpose of the testing, its results and interpretations, are shared with the client. The client is also invited to review the psychological report itself and to contribute an addendum should there be criticisms or a need for clarification of any aspects by the client. A challenging justification for this approach, based on important philosophical, theoretical, and practical considerations is offered by Fischer (1970; 1972). In principle, number 8 of the ethical standards of psychologists, the American Psychological Association (1977) stipulates that "persons examined have the right to know the results, the interpretations made, and, where appropriate, the original data on which final judgments were based."

Even the usual administrative assignment of responsibilities in those hospitals where patients remain for a protracted period has been challenged by the idea that hospital situations should be utilized as testing grounds for the kinds of events the patient will face on the outside (Abramson et al., 1963; Kutner, 1969). Thus, it is held that the participation of patients in the decision-making process, as well as their assumption of responsibility for many everyday events in the real life of the hospital, are essential. As specific examples it is recommended that:

> If wheelchairs break down (as they seem destined to) it is the patient who must initiate spontaneous action to seek the means of repairing them. If linens, towels, soap and other shortages occur, the patient must be involved in taking the first corrective steps. If the food is poor or

---

[2]From *New hope for the handicapped,* by H. A. Rusk & E. J. Taylor. Corpright 1946, 1947, 1948, 1949 by Howard A. Rusk. By permission of Harper & Row, Publishers, Inc.

cold, the rooms too hot or too cold, the staff overzealous or indifferent, the schedules overly rigid; if there are periodic crises of personnel short-ages or absences; if recreational programs are too repetitive or pedes-trian; if life in the hospital is just too dull and dreary . . . the patient must be personally and heavily involved. These "administrative mat-ters" . . . resemble the sorts of mundane issues that the disabled individ-ual will be forced to face alone when he leaves the protection of the institution . . . To foster involvement, the staff and administration must relinquish a portion of their grip on the patient and on the program. [Kutner, 1969, pp. 17–18]

It is also recommended that there be joint problem-solving com-mittees consisting of patients and staff to deal with the overlapping concerns of living and working under the same roof.

In a study in support of this form of hospital milieu (Abramson, 1968), an experimental group of over 100 patients with severe dis-abilities underwent their rehabilitation in a hospital program similar to the one described above. One year after discharge, their status was compared with a control group of over 100 patients who had gone through a conventional rehabilitation program at the same hospital. The experimental group showed a greater degree of sustained im-provement in both self-care and ambulation and a lower mortality rate.

Regardless of the length of hospitalization, procedures can be established in all hospitals that allow the patient to function as much as possible as a responsible individual, actively participating in the rehabilitation process. Systems of progressive care are a case in point. Patients do not eat in bed if they can eat at a table; they do not live in a hospital gown if they can wear their own out-of-bed clothing; they do not enter the hospital if their self-help capability, supported by needed out-patient services, can keep them at home or at an intermediary facility. These are procedures that strength-en the functioning role and minimize the "sick" and "patient" role.

The belief that the principle of comanagement has general ap-plicability helps to reveal instances where the principle is violated. Such instances also make us appreciate how much easier it is for the professional to direct, determine, and decide rather than share mu-tually these management functions, for in spite of best intentions, one often slips into the role of "boss."

The following remarks addressed to a group of professionals rep-resent the thinking and practice in many rehabilitation facilities. They have to do specifically with vocational counseling, but the ob-jectionable principle, implied by the italicized phrases, underlies all too often the procedures in the various branches of rehabilitation:

Through a preliminary interview with the client and by studying reports from other agencies, *the counselor learns* of the disabled individual's desires, needs, and problems. This is followed by a general medical examination and any specialty examinations which may be necessary. The next step is for the *counselor to arrive* at a vocational diagnosis. This is based upon a review of medical data and the case study, and an appraisal of the client's aptitudes, abilities, interests, and background including social, economic, and psychological factors. The plan may include one or more of such services as surgery or other medical care, artificial limbs or other appliances, training for a job, occupational tools, placement, and follow-up to effect adjustment. [Italics added]

Our main point is that *both* the counselor and the client should learn of the client's desires, needs, and problems and that *both* should arrive at a vocational diagnosis. The plan evolved should be the product of the joint thinking of the rehabilitation team in which the client is a key member, not only as the object of study but also as the one who casts the deciding vote (see pp. 434–438 for exceptions).

To take another example, let us examine the following statement:

Preferably prior to an operation, or at least as soon after as possible, the surgeon, the medical social worker, and any other members of the rehabilitation team who are involved should start to build insight and understanding on the part of the patient into the problems he faces.

This advice seems to be most commendable, but how much more commendable it would be if these specialists were advised to ". . . start *to help* build insight and understanding on the part of the patient." After all, who works at the job of coming to grips with the patient's problems, of trying to understand them? Who lies awake at night thinking of the "ups and downs," the "ins and outs" and where it all will lead? The specialist may, at times, but we can be sure that the patient does so far more persistently. We must not forget that insight is built up by the person himself or herself, with the help of outsiders if they are fortunate, but only with their help. "To help build insight" reflects the emphasis that is necessary. When the specialist is said "to build insight," there is a displacement of the primary causal agent to the outsider.

The last sentence (italics added) in a quotation from a booklet addressed to hospital patients who have an amputation clearly shows how one-sided direction by the professional person often unnecessarily and perhaps unwittingly creeps in: "If you are going to turn misfortune into a valuable asset the time to start thinking about your future is while you are still in the hospital. Do not wait until you are ready to leave the hospital. *The doctor, the social worker in the hospital, the rehabilitation counselor in your district are ready to answer your question, 'where do I go from here?'* " Surely, the question of "where the patient goes from here" can be worked through only with the patient's full participation. Why not, therefore, state the matter in some such fashion? To assert that the doctor, the social worker, and the rehabilitation counselor are ready to answer this question is to place the reins in their hands, with the patient at best becoming a back-seat driver.

Based on personal experience, Kerr (1970) presents six enlightening pairs of hospital experiences to illustrate how the staff, in subtle and often nonverbal ways, prescribes a passive and devaluating role for the patient on the one hand or a role that affirms the capability and human dignity of the patient on the other. One example relates to the implicit question: "Do I [the patient] have any control over my fate, or am I just a body being run through the repair shop?"

> Perhaps the most common way of telling the patient that he is a machine in the shop for repair is the habit some staffers have of communicating with the attendant pushing the wheelchair instead of with the patient himself. The patient thus finds himself sandwiched between two white coats with one asking the other, "Now where does she go?" [p. 90][3]

How different is the following experience where the patient is encouraged to make decisions:

> I had a physical therapist who, while working within the framework of the medical prescription, let me make every decision possible concerning therapy. To be sure, the initial options were small, like which exercises we'd work on first, or which chair I'd learn to transfer into next. Later I was encouraged to make more crucial decisions such as whether it was more important to me—with my plans and obligations—to be a resident patient or a day patient. [Kerr, 1970, p. 90]

Inadvertent errors are all too easily made by all levels of staff. Thus, in-service awareness training programs, designed to sensitize staff to ways of preventing and correcting mismanagement of relationships with clients, are mandatory and should be offered regularly. Not only doctors and therapists but administrators, orderlies, and anyone else who comes in contact with clients need such continuing education. Ecological studies have revealed that in hospitals, physi-

[3]From Staff expectations for disabled persons: Helpful or harmful, by N. Kerr. In *Rehabil. Counseling Bull.*, 1970, 14, 85–94. By permission of American Personnel and Guidance Association.

cians spend relatively little time with the rehabilitation patient, as compared to other personnel (Willems & Vineberg, 1969).

There should also be training in *how to encourage clients to become comanagers in their rehabilitation.* Otherwise the insecurities and dependency needs of some or many clients, their reluctance to assume responsibility, their own misconception of the proper patient or client role, may lead them to remain passive and dependent. Audiovisual materials that demonstrate comanagement in action, such as that seen in the preceding examples of vocational guidance (p. 424) and physical therapy (p. 428) should be available to clients. A library of reels showing how clients participate in decision making on a variety of services and in various settings (agency, hospital, school) could then be drawn upon as prototypes to prepare the client for the important role of comanager.

CLIENT PARTICIPATION IN CASE CONFERENCES

Encouraging clients to become an integral part of the team at conferences in which their case is being discussed follows naturally from the comanagement principle. The word *client* will be used to refer to the adult and adolescent client, even children in many instances, to the parent and other family members—in short, anyone immediately and directly involved as deemed appropriate in the particular instance.

To be sure, more or less equal partnership sometimes occurs between a client and a single therapist—the doctor, social worker, or teacher, for example. But in the usual team approach, clients are typically excluded. Traditionally, the team approach describes case management in which several specialists (e.g., orthopedist, speech correctionist, psychologist, pediatrician, social worker, occupational therapist, physical therapist) gather together, each reporting his or her findings and arriving at conclusions as a group, but *without* the client. One of the experts then conveys certain of this information to the client. In support of this exclusionary approach, it is assumed that the presence of the client would interfere with the frank presentation of facts and would be needlessly time-consuming.

However, the decision to exclude the client should be examined in the light of the following considerations: (1) Clients get the feeling that much is being said and done behind their backs. (2) Decisions and conclusions are made, albeit in the form of recommendations, without the clients' participation. This always carries the danger that the client will be unable or unwilling to carry them out. (3) Excluding the client places the client in the position of a child who has to be told what to do without having a real voice in the telling or doing.

Even though a particular client may be too debilitated, confused, or upset to attend the conference, surely this does not hold for most clients, and full participation on the team should be the rule.

In one large rehabilitation center it is reported that after preliminary interviews and examinations by various specialists, the patient, early in his or her stay at the center, attends a staff conference at which all members of the professional visiting and consulting staffs are present: "Each person presents such of his findings as are pertinent and nonconfidential in the presence of the patient. These are discussed with the patient participating, and feasibility and length and type of rehabilitation training are estimated" (Rusk & Taylor, 1946, p. 95).[4]

There are a few reports of case conferences that include parents. One such report describes the participation of parents of institutionalized mentally retarded children (Sieffert et al., 1976): "All the team members are expected to assist the parents in participating, but it is the social worker who assumes the primary responsibility for . . . providing any needed counseling to the parents before or after the conference. The meetings are well structured but informal. Team members give reports and the parents are invited to . . . express their opinions, raise their concerns and questions, and participate in the subsequent discussion. After the meeting, a written summary of the proceedings and an agreement, specifying the institution's and the parents' respective obligations in the child's care and signed by the team leader, the social worker, and the . . . superintendent, is sent to the parents for their review and signature" (p. 238). The report concludes that "the joint meetings have worked better than any of the initiators probably anticipated" (p. 238).[5]

A second report describes case-conference participation of parents of children with cerebral palsy (Weinstein, 1968): "The procedure at the conference is to take, first, the least threatening type of information and present it in small amounts" (p. 234). The author also supports the need for a preconference meeting with staff at which parents are *not* present in order to resolve "contradictions and differences among staff members" (p. 234). Clearly, further experimentation with different case-conference formats is needed to increase understanding on such issues as whether a preconference without the parent or client is advisable or not, when it is advantageous to include a child, and so on.

[4]From *New hope for the handicapped* by H. A. Rusk & E. J. Taylor. Copyright 1946, 1947, 1948, 1949 by Howard A. Rusk. By permission of Harper & Row, Publishers, Inc.

[5]Copyright 1976, National Association of Social Workers, Inc. Reprinted with permission, from *Social Work*, Vol. 21, No. 3 (May 1976), p. 238 (quote).

The findings of systematic research may surprise us on several counts: They may show that nothing is lost if things that would unduly hurt the client are not shared at the conference. Clients may be more able than we think to withstand an honest discussion of their child's problems, *especially if matters are discussed realistically and hopefully at the same time and with full respect for the client.* Clearer criteria may be established as to which clients would find a presentation of the problems from many points of view too overwhelming. Nothing may be basically lost if even the indifferent parent or the client who is mentally quite limited is present at the conference and something valuable may be gained. The time required for explanation of technical terms may be time saved in the end, for the participation of the client at the conference makes possible the introduction of further facts and a point of view essential to a sound consideration of the total problem.

If one genuinely respects the client and is confident that most clients can win out in the striving to work through problems and go on from there, then the conviction emerges that in the long run most clients will be an asset as a full and equal member of the rehabilitation team. Parents are, after all, generally the only ones who have lived with the child for 24 hours a day over the years of the child's life. Few professional persons, in fact, can claim such intensive experience with children as part of their formal training. Does one dare to say that parents know and understand their child less than an outsider? Does one dare to say that clients in general understand themselves less than the specialist? Only in certain particulars, with some problems, in some instances. It is more correct to consider the client an expert, just as the professional worker is an expert, each bringing to the discussion an important point of view and special knowledge and understanding.

Training manuals that elaborate basic principles and offer specific and well-illustrated guidelines for conducting client-staff conferences would increase acceptance and confidence in the idea of client participation. What is needed are detailed descriptions of a variety of case conference structures and procedures so that treatment centers can be in a better position to select the most promising for particular purposes.

TERMINOLOGY AS A PROBLEM OF COMMUNICATION

If clients are to be encouraged to assume a leadership role in the management of their rehabilitation, it is important that professionals use language comprehensible to the uninitiated. Too often the specialist is unnecessarily obscure. In one study (Korsch & Negrete, 1972), almost 20 percent of the mothers who brought their children to an emergency clinic felt they had not received a clear statement as to what was wrong. In more than half the cases, the doctor resorted to medical jargon. Misunderstandings flourished; for example, one mother thought that "incubation period" meant the length of time the child was to stay in bed.

Concrete suggestions to the professional person, based on a study of tuberculosis patients (Stratton, 1957), has general applicability:

1. Words should be used that are as concrete and common as possible. In accounting for the fact that some of the most widely known words were long and technical, whereas some of the least-known words were short, the investigator concluded that direct, personal, and concrete experience with a word appears to be a more important factor for the patient's understanding than the length or technicality of a word.

2. Care must be exercised in simplifying technical terms, for although specialists know what they mean when using, for example, the figurative term "bug" for "germ," many patients take this literally and visualize a many-legged creature chewing on their lungs.

3. Anxiety may easily be created in a patient when the specialist uses terms that are misunderstood. For example, "imagine the feelings of a patient who is told that he has a *spread of disease* if he believes, like one patient, that *spread of disease* means 'cancer,' or if, like another patient, he thinks that *spread of disease* means 'the lungs are about ate up' " (p. 42).

4. Finally, the results strongly indicate that one cannot assume that the more intelligent and better-educated patient has a much better understanding of medical vocabulary or that the patient hospitalized for a protracted period is a great deal more sophisticated in terminology than the new patient. In fact, nothing should be taken for granted about the patient's knowledge of the disease and words used to describe it.

Communication and understanding are facilitated if patients are encouraged to learn some of the technical terms and concepts related to their disability. *Once the patient's role as comanager is accepted, it becomes natural that, like a new foreman, patients share in "on the job training."* Simply written and well-illustrated explanatory pamphlets can be of great value. Fortunately, there are good materials which could be used for such purposes in hospitals, clinics, and schools. Discussion of written material with the patient, if possible in groups, provides the opportunity for further clarification of misunderstandings and, what is of great importance, for the development of constructive views of life with a disability. "One can foresee the day when physicians [and other practitioners] will be schooled in ways of informing patients of conditions confronting them in terms adapted to the comprehension and emotional needs of the individual" (Barker et al., 1953, p. 316).

The issue raised here also calls into question the common practice of making a mystery of a pharmacologic prescription by using Latin abbreviations. It may be desirable in some cases to keep certain information from the patient, but the isolated case is never a justification for generalizing to the whole.

THE IMPORTANCE OF CLARIFYING THE SITUATION

Terminology is one aspect of the broader problem of clarifying the situation to the client. Barker et al. (1953, pp. 312–316) view the usual diagnostic and treatment situation as a new psychological situation for the patient, producing such behavior as conflict, caution, emotionalism, exploration, suggestibility, and vacillation. They point out that much can be done to remove the conditions causing this sort of behavior.

Among the more evident principles is "letting the patient know what will happen when." Except for considerations that may justify concealment (see pp. 434–438), this principle can do much to dispel the anxiety that thrives on the unknown. A study of patients undergoing surgery presents several lines of evidence supporting the importance of authoritative information concerning the nature and course of treatment in warding off fear (Janis, 1958).

The following memory of an incident that occurred in childhood unfortunately also has countless parallels in the experience of adults in treatment situations. How much needless anxiety could have been averted if time had been taken to inform 8-year-old Raymond of the nature of the examination:

> . . . [the doctor] replaced me on the table and measured me. So far nothing bad had happened to me, but I was still afraid. Each time he lifted me to change my position I was sure that he was going to use on me that terrible contraption that hung from the ceiling. I wanted to beg him not to, but I thought that I had better be quiet and not remind him of it. At last, while I was still unharmed, he turned to Mother and said: "Dress him, please." [Goldman, 1947, p. 27]

Certainly, adequate communication consumes time. And realistic pressures of time as well as energy limitations tend to minimize communication between practitioner and client. Nevertheless, even the harried professional must regularly pause to remember that often simple and brief explanations can relieve anxiety. Davis (1963) presents a valuable discussion of the interplay of diagnostic, professional, and institutional constraints which lead therapeutic personnel to erect barriers against the communication of relevant facts about the illness to the patient and family.

Barker et al. also call attention to office and hospital practices that serve to remove the unknown (1953, pp. 312–316). In many dental clinics, children are allowed to familiarize themselves with dental equipment and procedures before they require dental treatment. Visits by expectant mothers to labor and delivery rooms are increasingly encouraged in medical practice. Even the space arrangements for medical equipment and procedures have a psychological impact. It makes psychological sense to raise such questions as: Should control panels in the radiologist's office be exposed or concealed? Should there be a common waiting room for patients as opposed to private rooms? "These questions are not related to the patient's comfort only. The possibility of beginning treatment early, when therapy is most effective, depends upon lowering resistance to securing treatment. Likewise, the therapeutic effect of many treatments is undoubtedly influenced by the emotional reactions of the patient" (Barker et al., 1953, p. 314).

CONDITIONS FOR WITHHOLDING INFORMATION AND IMPOSING DECISIONS

The problem of communication leads ultimately to a specific and practical question: Are there not times when information ought to be withheld? So broad a question is bound to receive an affirmative answer, but in the critical consideration of its specifications insights can be found.

Certainly acute illness and trauma are states that preclude full participation on the part of the client. Physically and psychologically the client may be unable to attend to even the general circumstances of his condition, let alone the details concerning etiology, treatment, prognosis, and future planning. The best medicine for such patients may be their conviction that they are in the hands of competent specialists interested in their welfare. This reassurance frees already overtaxed adaptation resources for the main and immediate task of coping with the physiological trauma. Even in these circumstances, however, patients need to know more than is commonly assumed. They should be informed of what is happening—that they are being taken to the hospital, that they are being prepared for a blood transfusion, that doctor so-and-so will operate. This can be done in a simple and reassuring manner without the opinion of the patient being solicited. A main value of such communication is that even if the facts presented are not really comprehended by a patient in a debilitated state, the message is that the patient is a respected human being and not an object—a difference of such psychological import that it must not be passed over lightly.

The question of whether a patient with a poor prognosis, even a terminal illness, should be told remains. The common policy to disclose as little as possible in the most general terms consistent with maintaining cooperation in treatment was rarely questioned until the topic of death itself became less taboo. Kübler-Ross' work on death and dying (1969) did much to accelerate clarification of the issues involved, and an increasing majority of experts favor an affirmative answer to the question, with due consideration as to how and when to inform.

The following pro and con points, with specific reference to cancer, were made by a panel of physicians concerning whether the patient should be told (Cantor & Foxe, 1956, pp. 204–208):

Pro:

Most patients who undergo radical surgery of the face, breast, or any visible part of the body know, or what may be worse, suspect, that they have cancer anyway. The large majority live well with this knowledge. Why, then, should one embark on the surreptitious approach in the case of an internal tumor?

Besides, patients must be informed of early symptoms of possible recurrence; they will be far wiser if they have knowledge of the original process.

In the case of a fatal cancer, unless they understand the problem, patients will be more inclined to seek the services of quacks as their condition worsens.

Adult patients with a cancer of poor prognosis need to know in order to arrange their affairs wisely.

Physicians who hesitate to speak out usually act a little guilty, failing to look the patient in the eye and shifting the story. Their whole manner is conducive to the worst fears of the patient and the poorest doctor-patient relations.

Cancer, with all its publicity, is much on everyone's tongue nowadays, and with medical advances, hope can be maintained even in the worst cases.

Patients have a right to know the truth when they ask a direct question.

Con:

To most people, cancer means an inevitable and miserable end, and patients, even on their deathbed, should never be told they are dying.

The issue is not a matter of telling the truth, for even those who advocate openness will not deny the importance of glossing over certain facts and stressing the more positive.

It depends entirely on what you think the patient wants to know. Since most patients do not want the diagnosis presented to them flatly, the matter should be approached obliquely, in some such manner as "This could be a serious condition. I won't know until I have made my studies, but it needs surgery."

There are a good many patients who have lived comfortably with the knowledge that they had some serious illness, but as soon as the diagnosis of cancer was given, they did not fare well at all.

Of the six physicians on this panel, only two leaned toward the position that by and large knowledge of cancer should be shielded from the patient, and only a minority of the medical audience favored this belief. At the same time the panel members agreed that an unequivocal "always" or "never" to the original question was impossible, since special factors in the individual case may require special handling.

How the patient should be told, when and in what context, are major issues. Kübler-Ross (1969, 1970, 1974a, 1974b) feels that as soon as the diagnosis is confirmed, the patient should be informed of the seriousness of the illness but never that he or she is dying. The terminal aspect of the illness can await the time when the patient indicates an awareness of impending death and a desire to talk about it. Many other professionals, in agreement with Kübler-Ross, also feel strongly that the patient should not be given a specific number of months or years of life expectancy because it is not possible to make an accurate estimate. Moreover, should the patient survive the projected date, the patient feels that he or she is "on borrowed time." Also, the expectation of death could itself hasten death. The main idea is that not all information need be shared initially and that elaboration should proceed at the patient's pace on subsequent occasions.

There are numerous reports of patients unwilling to discuss their serious illness. In such cases the possibility that the patient's presumed need for denial may well be in direct proportion to the professional's need for denial should be considered seriously. It has been suggested that psychological defenses of the patient should be respected, but one must make sure that they exist before respecting them (Krant, 1974). How often is information withheld in the name of denial when the denial is in the physician or family?

Kübler-Ross found that patients appreciate being made aware

of the seriousness of their condition *provided that* they are also made aware (1) that there is room for hope, (2) that everything possible is being done to treat the illness and alleviate the pain, and (3) that the physician will not abandon the patient and will be there as long as needed. It will be remembered from an earlier discussion of hope (Chapter 9) that optimism for a favorable, though unlikely outcome, is sustaining and helps the person to act realistically in terms of the probable turn of events.

What do patients themselves think about divulging or concealing information? Numerous surveys have been conducted asking both healthy and terminally ill persons if they would wish to be told if they had a fatal illness. Results have consistently indicated that the great majority of both groups, typically more than 80 percent, would wish to be informed of the true nature of their illness (Hinton, 1966). In one study of 300 patients with multiple sclerosis, a frequently progressive and disabling disease that may ultimately lead to death, 90 percent believed that they should be told (Harrower & Herrmann, 1953). They spoke of wanting to plan their lives, be free from the strain of uncertainty, avoid spending money uselessly, be able to take better care of themselves physically, and remove the fear that one might be neurotic. In effect these patients said, "If I am to guide my life satisfactorily, I need to know." Of thirty-four patients with multiple sclerosis who were not told their diagnosis, only 9 percent were encouraged whereas 91 percent were discouraged. Of course, it would be helpful if there were some way to reliably identify those relatively few individuals who would fare better under the "bliss of ignorance." On the basis of the personality characteristics of patients with multiple sclerosis who wanted to be kept informed and of those who did not, it was concluded that the less differentiated, emotionally less mature persons are not concerned about medical details, whereas those persons who are more intelligent and have more mature personalities become more apprehensive when information is withheld from them.

Based on his work with surgical patients, Janis (1958) describes two types of patients requiring some form of quasi-therapeutic interview before information can be of benefit. The "overcontrolled neurotic," who tends to manifest low fear in generally threatening situations, needs help before information will activate the "work of worrying" and induce the person to deal in fantasy with potential sources of danger and discomfort so that in a moment of crisis he or she will be better prepared. The "undercontrolled neurotic," who tends to show high fear in even mildly threatening situations, will need help before information and the work of worrying can effectively serve the function of psychological preparation.

Special concern arises when it comes to informing children of their serious illness. The increasing acceptance of the idea that most people have a need to come to terms with their critical illness includes children, as well. In the light of the emotional isolation and unanswered fears that come with concealment, it is difficult to maintain the belief that children as a rule should be shielded. Even young children sense the distress of their parents and medical personnel. The danger is that the child will begin to believe that the illness is too dreadful to talk about. "In denying the child an honest relationship, we deny him the opportunity for hope" (Issner, 1973, p. 469). Although the concept of death as the cessation of biological processes is not reached until about 8 years of age, younger children associate death with such frightening ideas as separation and mutilation. Moreover, many children, fatally ill or not, have a fear of dying.

The principle of being willing to listen to the person's concerns and to respond to them within a framework of hope and caring applies to children just as to adults. But being sensitive to the child's anxieties requires being ready to hear and be aware that children (and adults) communicate their knowledge of impending death through various languages: symbolic nonverbal language, symbolic language, and plain English (Kübler-Ross, 1974b). The child who draws a picture of a grave, or of a child being run over by a truck is using symbolic nonverbal language. Children beyond the age of 10 are most likely to use symbolic verbal language. The girl in an oxygen tent who asks what will happen to her if fire breaks out and the child who asks what happened to other children who have died are using symbolic language. It is important, then, to respond to the child's need for comfort and support, and even to speak of death should the conversation drift in that direction, provided that *the message of hope and caring is the main stock into which the details of illness are blended.*

QUALITATIVE ASPECTS OF THE CO. IANAGEMENT RELATIONSHIP

Conviction that, *wherever feasible,* comanagement on the part of the client should be promoted is a belief. But it is a belief that requires more than the intellectual grasp of supporting research. It is a belief that also reflects fundamental values, a view of human potential, a statement about client rights. It is a belief that inextricably includes a deep and abiding respect for the individual. Roger's (1957) well-known phrase, "unconditional positive regard" is appropriate.

Basic respect means that the client is regarded as a person, not an object to be worked on and worked over but not worked with.

Basic respect means that clients have ideas and feelings, goals and aspirations, fears and hopes; objects don't. Further, basic respect means that the ideas and feelings of the client matter, that they must be taken into account, not ignored or lightly dismissed. It means, that in the relationship between professional and client, each must function as both a giver and receiver of information; each must have a valued role in the decision-making process.

Other qualities important in the comanagement relationship are conveyed by such terms as liking the client, being friendly, and caring and being concerned about the client's welfare. Although most professionals and clients agree with the importance of this type of involvement (Leviton, 1973), too frequently clients do not sense it in actual practice. In the study of mothers' visits to an emergency clinic described earlier (Korsch & Negrete, 1972), most of the professionals believed they had been friendly, but fewer than half the mothers had this impression, and almost 40 percent reported that the doctor had been strictly businesslike. Moreover, less than 5 percent of the tape-recorded contacts showed that the doctor's conversation was friendly or personal in nature. For the most part, the doctor paid no attention to the mother's feelings and, instead, concentrated on technical discussion of the child's condition. Civilities between the parties, such as introducing themselves or addressing each other by name, were uncommon. The findings showed that friendliness on the part of the doctor was positively related to the mother's satisfaction and compliance with the recommendations. It is to be noted that the amount of time spent with the doctor was not related to client satisfaction. In a study of forces influencing the decision to seek medical care (Shontz, 1974), it was found that, next to distrust of the physician's competence, personal dislike of the physician was the strongest restraining factor.

Whether the professional should remain emotionally neutral or be more closely involved with patients was an issue specifically addressed in the study of professional and client viewpoints (Leviton, 1973). Reasons for supporting each side of the issue were elicited in the interviews. The main findings were: "The positive meanings [of involvement] included warmth and friendliness, care and concern, understanding of and interest in the client as an individual. Involvement, in addition to being satisfying *per se* and buoying up client self-esteem was said to have positive effects upon the rehabilitation process because it improves communication and motivation. Negative meanings of involvement included excessive emotionality leading to lack of objectivity; overidentification leading to professional distress, and a 'buddy-role' leading to a loss of professional status or ability to secure compliance with prescriptions" (Leviton, 1973, p.

68).[6] For those who argue that one should be involved "but not too involved," Leviton correctly points out that it would be better not to consider this issue a quantitative matter in which there is some sort of golden mean. Rather, different qualitative aspects should be kept separate. Thus, objectivity versus nonobjectivity represents one kind of continuum, and warmth versus coldness or aloofness another. The idea is that one can be friendly, concerned and interested in the client as a person without foregoing objectivity, that is, that one optimally apply one's knowledge and professional role. The detached professional is not more likely to be objective. Instead of stressing how much involvement is too much, emphasis should be placed on the kind of emotional involvement that is helpful to the client. The disinterested party has a place in the jury box but not in professional-client relations.

We have already reviewed some of the important impediments that stand in the way of implementing useful comanagement principles in professional-client relations—impediments in the client, in the professional, and in the situation. (See also pp. 391–395, which focus on parents.) Whatever else is necessary to overcome these interfering forces, a measure that should be used by everyone is periodic examination of one's own behavior. To review one's relations with clients, to become an observer of one's own behavior, to try to see the situation from the client's point of view, can make us aware of instances that violate the principles we profess. One stops the action, so to speak, and in examining the scene, becomes cognizant of his or her own mistakes and how possibly to guard against them.

A useful self-examining technique to bring the issue of human dignity into sharp focus is that of *status substitution*. The procedure is as follows: First, the professional thinks of an actual situation involving himself or herself and a client. Then, in the mind's eye, a particular person with high status is substituted for the client, and the professional questions whether, and if so how, his or her own behavior would thereby have been altered. Finally, the judgment is made whether the difference in behavior, if any, points to behavior that needs to be corrected. For example, would you as a professional person (teacher, physician, counselor, etc.) have treated a dignitary the same way as the client (student, patient) had been treated in the situation under review? What if the client had been kept waiting without being alerted to the delay or without receiving an apology? Would a colleague have been so treated? What if a patient had been examined in front of a coterie of students in training, without explanation

[6]Reprinted from Professional and client viewpoints on rehabilitation issues, by G. Leviton. In *Rehab. Psychol.*, 1973, 20, 1–80. By permission of *Rehab. Psychol.*

and without consent? Would a very important person have been so treated? What if . . . ? What if . . . ?

Belief in the principle of comanagement in a relationship of respect and caring can go far in bringing comanagement about. But just because it is easier to subscribe to this in principle than in practice, the professional person must question at all times whether the client is at the helm helping to steer the course of rehabilitation or whether in effect the client is being paternalistically directed as a manipulable charge who is to follow through but not question why.

Chapter 18
Societal Sources of Attitudes

Factors contributing to the way people with unusual physiques are regarded have thus far focused on the perceiver. For example, misattribution and the neglect of the environment, spread and the context of disability, the insider versus outsider perspective, disability as a value loss, values and evaluation, the requirement of mourning, expectation discrepancy, and the coping versus succumbing frameworks. There is another side to attitudes, namely, the role played by society. The present chapter discusses diverse sets of factors that incline members of society toward viewing the significance of disability in particular ways.

PHYSICAL DEVIANCY AMONG LOWER ANIMALS

It is interesting that antipathy toward persons with unusual physiques is sometimes explained by pointing to comparable instances in the animal world, implying that negative reactions have an evolutionary basis. The attempt to understand human behavior in terms of animal behavior has been referred to as the "principle of genetic reductionism," and questioned in some scientific circles (Scheerer, 1954, p. 124).

In any case, the facts of animal psychology clearly debunk the myth that animals *in general* ostracize the physically deviate of their kind. Maisel (1953, Chapters 4–6) has collated many anecdotes and objective observations of research workers concerning the reaction of fish, birds, and mammals to physically exceptional members of their species. A sample will show the heterogeneity of reaction among various species:

Goldfish with amputated fins live "happily" among their fellows.

Sharks will converge on a wounded shark and eat it.

Some ants do kill their old and enfeebled. Higher ant forms do not.

Termites eat their injured, but notably where there is a shortage of nitrogenous food.

An albino penguin was observed to be loved by its family but received with hostility by strangers.

Among fish, unusual coloring is of no importance.

Baboons are ruthless toward their physical inferiors.

The wolf does not attack or avoid physically atypical wolves.

Among chimpanzees, taking the part of the underdog is not uncommon.

In the light of such variability, Yerkes, the psychobiologist who worked for half a century in the field of animal psychology, said, "I am quite unable to make with confidence any general statements" in regard to the reaction of animals to the disabled (Maisel, 1953, p. 538). Maisel, in his extensive review of this matter, has hazarded a bolder statement about icthyological ways: "If there is, indeed, a law of the deep, it might well be that anything goes, and all kinds of atypical bodies can survive" (1953, p. 479). Sometimes, of course, a weak member may not survive because of competition for food and shelter, but this is quite different from ostracism and rejection.

The fact that the fable of the ugly duckling and the metaphor of the black sheep live on as paradigms is again evidence of the proclivity of the human being to perceive the facts that fit and to fit the facts that do not. To make this point more impressive, let us look at the habits of hens, the hen being a domestic fowl under common observation. Everyone "knows" that a hen is prone to peck, even unto death, another bird who has a raw spot showing. This fact is retained and disseminated because it fits with the preconceived notion—and, in some instances, the need—that physical deviation and injury are bound to bring about rejection. The fact that fowls do not react in this way to other kinds of physical irregularities is not even noticed.

A hen that is paralyzed, for example, will maintain her pecking order and will not be relegated to the bottom of the pile (Maisel, 1953, p. 516).

Another example that shows how "naturally" our preexisting ideas and needs tend to perpetuate incorrect notions is provided by the legend of the shark. Although it is an indisputable fact that sharks do destroy wounded members of their own species, the ready anthropomorphic inference that this is motivated because of an aversion to deviation or of fear of some kind is far from the truth. But typically one does not pursue the why of the behavior, for when something is "all figured out," the disturbance produced by new facts is not welcomed. It so happens, however, that sharks distinguish what is food and not food by olfactory cues; the juices of an injured shark set up a chemical stimulus that brings on feeding behavior in other sharks (Maisel, 1953, p. 470). If the dispersion into the water could be siphoned off, shark cannibalism would not occur. The shark, evidently, is indifferent to the atypicality or injury as such.

In a word, the belief that lower life forms defile their disabled cannot be accepted as even a rough approximation.

ATYPICAL PHYSIQUE IN NONLITERATE AND NONOCCIDENTAL SOCIETIES

Just as there is a belief that "human nature" is basically "animal nature," so there is the view that the behavior of primitive societies reveals our true human nature unrepressed and uncamouflaged by the niceties and hypocrisies of civilization. Though such reasoning is questionable, anthropological horizons certainly broaden perspective, especially in replacing an ethnocentric point of view by an awareness of the otherwise unimaginable variety in the behavior of human beings.

That Spartan rule is by no means universal in primitive societies is clearly shown in Maisel's compilation of data on more than fifty tribes and societies drawn from the Human Relations Area Files at Yale University (1953, Appendix). This latter source is equivalent to an extensive survey of anthropological literature, for the material collected in the files is culled from books, articles, and records of anthropologists and other observers, abstracted, and classified so that it could be expediently used in a variety of studies. A sampling of the material is provocative:

Among the Siriono Indians, sickness not infrequently leads to abandonment and death.

In the Azande tribe, infanticide is not practiced. "Abnormal children are never killed nor do they seem to lack the love of their parents."

"A supplementary fifth finger or first toe is surprisingly common amongst these [Azande] savages who are usually proud of the addition. . . ."

Among the Navajo Indians, the ideals proscribe sadistic humor against those with physical deviations but in practice "A great deal of enjoyment is derived from commenting verbally or through pantomime on the personal afflictions, infirmities, and peculiarities" of others. Uncomplimentary nicknames are not uncommon.

Among the Masai, "misshapen and especially weakly children" are killed immediately after birth.

Among the Dieri, a tribe of Australian aborigines, "infanticide is frequent, applying to the children of unmarried girls, and to deformed children."

Among the Chagga, an East African tribe, cripples were felt to satisfy evil spirits, thereby making possible normality in others. Hence, they did not dare to kill cripples, who included children with more or less than five fingers as well as those with serious deformities.

Among the Creek Indians, where "old age is revered to excess," the aged infirm were killed only out of humanitarian reasons, such as when they might otherwise fall into enemy hands.

Among the Truk peoples of the East Central Carolines, only the healthy and strong are esteemed. The deaf and dumb are called *umes* (crazy people). Old people and the disabled are considered to be superfluous.

Among the Wogeo, a New Guinea tribe, children with obvious deformities are buried alive at birth, but children crippled in later life are looked after with loving care.

Among the Dahomeans of Western Africa, it is a singular fact that the state constables are selected from persons with deformities. Children born with anomalous physical characteristics are held to be under the guardianship of special supernatural agents. Some of these children are destined to bring good luck, and the fate of others must be determined by signs from the supernatural. They may even be "ordered" to be abandoned at the river bank.

Among the Ponape of the Eastern Carolines, "crippled and insane children" were treated like the normal children.

Among the Witoto Indians of the North West Amazons, the newborn infant is submerged in the nearest stream, for "if the child was not strong enough to survive it had better die." If the child becomes deformed later, the medicine man declares that it was caused by some evil spirit and may work ill to the tribe, making it necessary to dispose of the person.

Among the Jukun, a Sudanese Kingdom, children with deformities are not allowed to live, but are left to perish in the bush or in a cave, for it is believed that such children are begotten by an evil spirit.

Among the Semang of the Malay Peninsula, the person looked upon as a sort of chief to settle disputes and admonish if necessary was a severely crippled man who could only move with the help of a long stick.

Among the Balinese, sexual relations with "albinos, idiots, lepers, and in general the sick and the deformed," are tabooed.

Among the Palaung, an Eastern Clan, "it is lucky to have extra fingers or toes, and extremely lucky to be born with a hare-lip."

Among the Sema Nagas "the killing of idiots and similarly deficient persons, such as hunchbacks and deaf-mutes, is 'genna' (taboo)."

Among the Macri of New Zealand, people with deformities meet with little sympathy and often receive a castigating nickname.

If positive and negative attitudes toward persons with disabilities prevalent among the tribes and societies summarized by Maisel were to be tabulated, there is no doubt that negative attitudes would show a preponderance. However, sheer frequency can have such diverse significance that we can do little more than note it. For example, just because infanticide is likely to be shocking even to the most objective investigator, it is likely to be recorded as an impressive fact, whereas a benign attitude to the child with physical abnormalities is more likely to go unheeded.

Although the variety of ways in which deviant members of society are looked upon and handled in different cultures is in itself striking, it would be a mistake to conclude that "anything can happen." The role prescriptions for the aged among different societies provide an apt illustration. Though the diversity is great, a common principle emerges in the fact that all societies, as far as is known, differentiate between old age in general and the helpless state in which the individual is regarded as a sufferer and social burden (Simmons, 1952, p. 44).

Similarly, although attitudes toward physique vary among different groups, it is more than likely that all societies place a value on "body-beautiful" and "body-whole." We do know, however, that what is defined as "body-beautiful" and "body-whole" varies. Scarification among the Dahomey and Ashanti and the artificially produced protruding lips of the Ubangi are looked upon with favor in these African tribes, whereas in our society such characteristics are regarded as deformities. Circumcision in our society does not destroy the intactness of the body nor does shaving the beard. Among sections of the Orient, on the other hand, "the total absence of it [the beard], or a sparse and stinted sprinkling of hair upon the chin is as great a deformity to the features as the want of a nose would appear to us; . . ." (Hentig, 1948a, p. 78).

The question of how *economic factors* influence attitudes toward people with disabilities has barely been scrutinized in the research literature. One rare example (Hanks & Hanks, 1948) is the report that among Greenland Eskimos, where economic surplus is maintained at a very narrow margin, children born with congenital defects are often killed in infancy; those with acquired disabilities are taken care of by the family until they are deemed an economic liability, in which event they commit suicide or are abandoned. In contrast is the different treatment of individuals with disabilities by the Northern Blackfoot of the North American plains and by certain tribes in Melanesia, where the economy for the most part is adequate and the society democratic. Here, the protective obligation of the family toward the person with a disability is increased. The authors tentatively offer the following propositions: Protection of persons with physical disabilities and opportunities for social participation are increased in societies in which (1) the level of productivity is higher in proportion to the population and its distribution more nearly equal, (2) competitive factors in individual or group achievement are minimized, and (3) the criteria of achievement are less formally absolute than in hierarchical social structures and more weighted with concern for individual capacity, as in democratic social structures.

Although undoubtedly important, the role of economic factors in attitudes cannot be said to be commanding or overriding; otherwise greater consistency according to economic conditions would be expected than does in fact exist. The authors of the above study (Hanks & Hanks, 1948) note, for example, that although the Paiute of the Great Basin of North America had a margin of existence almost as precarious as that of the Greenland Eskimos, infanticide was not practiced and individuals with disabilities were not abandoned.

Religious beliefs among various societies, including our own, are referred to in various parts of the present text (pp. 66; 91; 400–401). We have noted that the stigmatization of people with disabilities can be rooted in certain religious beliefs and practices whereas other religious beliefs can serve to sustain, comfort, and give voice to the humanity of all people (Wilke, 1980).

CHILD-TRAINING PRACTICES.

There is some evidence, both interesting and challenging, that attitudes toward disability may be conditioned by child-rearing practices seemingly unconnected with disability as such. The most relevant work is that of Whiting & Child (1953) who investigated the effects of child-training methods in fifty-one cultures.

Particularly pertinent to our interest are the findings concerning the relationship between the severity of socialization practices devised to teach children to conform to adult standards of conduct and theories held in the culture to account for illness. Although these findings concern attitudes toward illness, we may presume that they are applicable to attitudes toward disability as well. The particular areas of child development that were rated for severity of socialization practices promised to be of special significance according to psychoanalytic theory. Some of the areas included were the following: oral area (e.g., weaning), anal area (toilet training), genital area (sexuality), aggression, and dependency.

One of the hypotheses borne out by the study was that those areas of child development which are severely socialized would create anxiety and therefore would be expected to be incorporated in the theories of illness in the society. For example, there were twenty-three societies with an oral theory of illness (e.g., illness is caused by eating something) and sixteen societies without such an explanation. The average severity of weaning in the first group was 12.2 on a scale from 0 to 20, and in the second only 8.9, a difference that is highly significant statistically. In our society, middle-class practices concerning oral training were rated by Whiting & Child toward the severe end, a rating consistent with the prevalence of all sorts of oral theories of illness. The results for the other areas of behavior are not as clear, but they are in the same direction.

It is worthy of note that these findings are consistent with the theory of perceived similarity in cause-effect relations discussed earlier (pp. 63–68). That is, illness is a negative state. As such its cause is sought in factors that are also negative—in the case at hand by virtue of their anxiety-laden character.

With respect to overcoming illness, Whiting & Child had expected that the therapeutic practices would show some connection with behavior that in childhood had been satisfying through a long period of indulgence on the part of adults. The findings were generally negative except for the sexual area of development. In only two cultures were sexual practices believed to have a specific thera-peutic value; in these two societies there was a very high indulgence of childhood sexuality.

Another aspect of theories of illness that was studied concerned the factor of guilt. Guilt was indicated by the belief that the patient is responsible for his or her illness, as contrasted with attribution to accident or some outside agent. The hypothesis that societies with the severest socialization practices would create the most anxiety and guilt, and therefore would tend to impute responsibility for ill-ness to the patient, was supported. The overall severity of socializa-tion practices in the middle class of our society was rated close to the top of the fifty-one cultures examined.

A second hypothesis involving guilt was also supported; namely, that societies using loss of love as a threat to induce conforming be-havior in the child should also tend to have higher ratings on imput-ing patient responsibility for illness. This hypothesis was based on the theory that guilt is due to anxiety over the loss of love of the person on whom the child is dependent.

The most general conclusion of the Whiting & Child study rele-vant to disability is that beliefs about illness are indirectly influenced by those significant early relations between child and parent that have to do with the child's conformity to adult standards of behavior. The study provides a good example of how theory—in this case a the-ory relating important phases in child development and socialization practices—can produce new knowledge and understanding.

In any discussion of early childhood experiences, *castration the-ory* has a place since it presumes to provide a primary basis for emo-tional disturbance occasioned by the sight or thought of disability. A summary of this theory follows:

> In brief, the castration complex comes about as a result of childhood experience. The child soon discovers the meaning of his genital organs and, in his earliest fantasies revolving about the love of the mother, unconsciously "posits" his penis as a rival to his father's. Fearing re-venge from the father, however, the child imagines that retribution will take the form of depriving him of his male organ. Such a drastic procedure would, in his fantasy, be the only appropriate punishment from the father for taboo Oedipal desires in which the mother be-comes an incestuous love object. Throughout his childhood, the child may extend these vague fears to encompass the notion that his father will, in one way or another, punish him for his sexual activities in gen-eral. Thus his remorse or anxieties about masturbation may be reflect-ing castratory fears.
>
> The castration complex could, according to psychoanalytic thought, be symbolically brought into play by any remotely analogous equivalent

of castration. Thus the loss of a leg, or seeing another person who has lost a leg, may stir up archaic castratory fears. Indeed, the loss of any part of the body, or the sight of such a loss, is said to be symbolically capable of recalling the Oedipal taboo and the father's potential revenge—that of cutting off or mutilating the phallus.

But could such a theoretical explanation offer a possible reason for women's reactions to disability as well? Yes, according to Freudian theory, even though women have no phallus to fear losing. For while the little boy is going through the Oedipal phase, with its taboo complications, phallus fantasies and fears, and rivalry with the father, the little girl is also experiencing incestuous desires. Indeed, she goes through two phases. Unlike her brother, who experiences only a mother fixation, and is never sexually attracted to his father, the girl child may first have a mother attachment, a survival of the oral (breast-feeding) phases of her existence. This leads her to an identification with the father, just as the boy identifies himself with his father as a rival for his mother's affections. The girl, however, discovers the difference between the sexes at an early age, and her own absence of a penis gives her a castration complex—she feels that she has been deprived of the male organ, and suffers a deep sense of loss. No longer able to rival her father, she then identifies with her mother, and makes a fantasy bid for the father's love. As opposed to the boy child's Oedipal-castratory development, the girl child passes through a phase in which the Electra complex (fixation on the father) and the castration complex are major experiences. [Maisel, 1953, pp. 551–553][1]

Clinical evidence is strong that castration anxiety does occur and can ramify to attitudes toward disability. However, this source of anxiety is not necessarily common in all societies.

HEALTH CARE MESSAGES AND FUND-RAISING CAMPAIGNS

Health care and fund-raising appeals bear a heavy responsibility in shaping societal attitudes toward illness and disability. The coping versus succumbing frameworks presented earlier (Chapter 9) provide important guidelines for evaluating such appeals. It is proposed that attitudes are adversely affected when the appeal concentrates on the suffering, sadness, dependency, and passivity of individuals who have a chronic illness or disability and minimizes the coping possibilities and active participation of the individual.

[1]From *Meet a body* by E. Maisel. New York: Institute for the Crippled and Disabled, 1953 (MS.) By permission of ICD Rehabilitation and Research Center.

Health Care Messages

Consider a cartoon selected for a Pulitzer award which portrays a small boy on crutches mournfully watching other children vigorously play football. It is captioned, "Wonder why my parents didn't give me Salk shots?" The justification for such a message is highly questionable. The cartoon arouses pity, guilt, or fear, but is clearly not compatible with constructive views of life with a disability, nor does research suggest that resulting compliance rates justify this approach. Later we shall see that there are more promising alternatives in prompting people to act sensibly with regard to their health.

Much research has been done on the problem of health care messages since Janis & Feshback's classical study (1953) on the use of *fear* in getting people to take care of their teeth. A review of years of research on the effectiveness of threat appeals (Higbee, 1969; Leventhal, 1970) demonstrates that, although fear often persuades, it *cannot* be relied upon in mass media. Its effects are too variable, sometimes prompting compliance with the recommendations, sometimes having no effect, and even sometimes leading to an increase in the objectionable practice. Research has also shown that arousing *guilt* cannot be trusted in seeking compliance (Haefner, 1956; Zemach, 1966). The many studies concerned with fear and guilt have covered a wide range of topics, such as smoking, wearing seat belts, and checking for tuberculosis or cancer. They used varying intensities of fear and different media: lectures, films, audio tapes, role playing, and printed matter. Many types of people served as subjects—from students to passersby at a fair. The studies used different criteria of effectiveness: knowledge gained, attitude change on questionnaires, expressed intention to comply with the recommendations, self-report regarding compliance, and independent verification regarding action taken.

It is common sense, but in this case not psychological sense, to believe that strong fear or guilt can be relied upon to motivate people to act sensibly concerning their own welfare. The human being is too adept at defending against such emotions by suppressing or avoiding thoughts connected with them. After all, the feeling is that one doesn't have cancer unless it is medically verified; if one feels especially afraid of cancer, why then go to the doctor for a checkup and get cancer? One wag, when faced with mounting evidence linking cancer with smoking, ruefully announced that he had finally decided to give up — — reading! A major researcher in the field concluded that when high fear messages fail to persuade, the failure frequently reflects the subject's felt incapacity to cope with the danger (Leventhal, 1970). Another factor arguing against the use of strong fear is known as *reactance* (Brehm, 1966; Wicklund, 1974; Brehm & Brehm, 1981). Reactance refers to the arousal of resistance against the threat of loss of one's freedom to choose. Instead of complying with the message, reactance, catalyzed by strong fear, can lead the person to defy the message or even to act contrary to it.

At least as important as compliance effectiveness is the basic question of whether the health care message contributes to stigmatizing or constructive attitudes regarding life with a disability. Consider the following appeal urging the public to have their eyes examined, in which a blind man is depicted with a tin cup and white cane, wearing a sign on his back captioned "My days are darker than your nights." Since blindness ought not to be made a signal for helplessness, fear, or pity, neither to the millions of people throughout the world who are blind, nor to the millions of people who will become blind, nor to the sighted majority, this succumbing approach to health care surely has no place.

If evoking fear, guilt, or pity are not to be countenanced in the effort to arouse the public to pay attention to their health, what is? Research supports the conclusion that a message, low in threat, can be presented in a believable way, and that when instructions are clear and specific and conditions are such that recommended actions are not difficult to carry out, then compliance rates increase (Higbee, 1969; Leventhal, 1970). It is not enough to be persuaded of the final goal (e.g., to stop smoking); specific steps in achieving the goal are helpful. Some conditions that make compliance easier are feasible financial costs, readily accessible health care facilities, and easily performed health care practices. The findings of a study on the personal meaning of illness (Shontz, 1974) also indicated that the way to encourage a person to seek medical help is to minimize the negative aspects of treatment, avoid implying anything that would contribute to a fear of discovery of serious illness, and emphasize the person's chances for a return to health. Notice that these factors and the factors of believability, specific instructions and ease of implementation do not require that the health care message point up the dire consequences of disease, disability, and neglect. Nor do they require that the message arouse guilt or pity.

Fund-raising

Fund-raising efforts can also be examined in terms of both attitudes conveyed and compliance, in this case monetary effectiveness. The message in fund-raising, as in health care appeals, all too frequently equates disability or illness with suffering, despair, and pity. For example, a fund-raising appeal depicts a young mother weeping over the bassinette of her newborn, brain-damaged baby. Beneath the picture is written:

700 times a day a defective child is born to bitter disappointment and a woman's tears. It is the tragic truth that one in every ten American families experiences the suffering caused by the birth of a defective child. Working together . . . we can do so much to stop this heartbreak and anguish. You can help by giving . . . to support research and treatment.

The implied supposition is that defining disability as tragedy is a valid tactic to stir the public's conscience, guilt, or fear so that people will be moved to contribute.

Such an approach ought to be challenged. If you or I were the person born with a birth defect, or the parent of such a child, would we appreciate such a message? Would it not underscore the despair aspects of our existence, a state from which we would have tried to emerge and to which we would resist being dragged back? Does it not, by default, give little weight to the possibility of meeting the challenge of living with a disability and does it not reflect, instead, pity and hopelessness as viewed by those who do not have to live with the disability? Is it not shortsighted to convey ideas in fund-raising campaigns (or in health care messages) that then have to be countered by other costly rehabilitation efforts?

Cannot the public be moved to give through appeals that reveal the abilities of the target group for whom money is being raised, that show people with disabilities actively participating in valued activities, and that indicate the constructive uses to which the funds will be put?

Research provides considerable support for these notions. In one study, for example, subjects were asked to donate money to two causes, one in which the target group was represented as "Too helpless to help themselves," and the other in which the basic message was "Help disabled people help themselves" (Harris, 1975). The subjects actually gave more money to the *less* dependent group, even though they rated the more dependent group as more needy. We can surmise that the great dependency gave rise to doubt that the solicited donation would in fact be of much help. In other studies, the more dependent person did elicit more help, but in these cases the conditions were such that the subjects could readily perceive the effectiveness of their help—that is, that it would make a significant difference to the one helped (e.g., Berkowitz & Daniels, 1963; Midlarsky, 1971).

To be sure, a condition for offering aid is to perceive the need for that aid, but when the emphasis is on great dependency, the danger is that the effectiveness of the help will be doubted, that the feeling of the futility of helping—what's the use?—will prevail. What is worse, the stress on dependency easily gives rise to the "just world phenomenon" (see p. 67); the suffering of those in need is then unconsciously felt to be deserved. Also, reactance may be aroused (see p. 452) and lead to an unwillingness to help (Berkowitz, 1973). That is, feeling "pushed into helping" doesn't favor helping. What does favor helping is fund-raising within the coping framework, where the effectiveness of the aid and the gains that will be made become the focus rather than the pitiful state of those to be helped.

Research also makes clear that helping is encouraged when those to be helped are regarded as similar to oneself. This holds for financial help (Harris, 1975) as well as other forms of helping (Krebs, 1975). Similarity, therefore, is an important factor that can be used to advantage in fund-raising campaigns and provides yet another basis for cautioning against the emphasis on desperate need and dependency: Whereas depicting great dependency implies great difference from the prospective donor, revealing common human needs, values, activities, and aspirations that are shared by the target group implies similarity.

Helping is also elicited when a model or standard of the desired behavior is provided. In one study, more money was donated for a secretary's gift when the first donation listed on the sign-up sheet was larger than in the case of a second sign-up sheet (Blake, Rosenbaum, & Duryea, 1955). In another study, more shoppers contributed to a Salvation Army Kettle in the half-minute after they saw someone donate than in the half-minute before (Bryan & Test, 1967). Where the standard of behavior is designed to provoke guilt, one might question its use, but where it serves to remind the prospective donor of worthwhile action, it can be endorsed.

Other incentives for giving can be recommended. Common sense tells us that reducing the strain of contributing will have a positive effect. Donations in one study were increased by allowing the donor to parcel out the gift through periodic paycheck deductions instead of lump sum payment (Wagner & Wheeler, 1969). We also know that benefits that accrue to a donor provide an incentive to giving. Income tax deduction for charitable causes is a case in point, as are pancake feeds, walkathons, social events, and other fund-raising efforts that provide something to the donor in return.

Thus, we have the fortunate situation that it is possible to promote successful fund-raising campaigns by approaches compatible with the coping framework. One can (1) emphasize the enabling uses of the funds raised, (2) depict the active involvement of those being helped in valued activities, (3) imply the basic similarity between target group and donor, (4) make use of modeling of appropriate actions, (5) reduce the financial strain of giving, and (6) benefit the donor in return for giving.

The following are three examples of the positive approach to fund-raising. In the first, a child with double-arm prostheses and a built-up shoe is learning to play golf. Beneath the picture are the words: "We can do a lot to help kids like Marty. But wouldn't it be great if it weren't necessary?" Information on birth defects and their prevention is given and the message concludes with a request for a donation. The second fund-raising appeal shows a blind man with dark glasses and white cane crossing a street at night while oncoming cars stop. It is captioned "STOP—HE'S ON HIS WAY." The message continues with ten points for the sighted to remember when meeting a blind person and concludes with a simple appeal for funds. The third example is headed: "Strange as it sounds, there never was a better time to have cerebral palsy." A picture depicts a person in a wheelchair viewing the statue of Lincoln at the Lincoln Memorial in Washington, D.C. Without the recent installation of an elevator, this would not have been possible. The communication lists the advances made in civil rights—accessibility to jobs, education, buildings—that were "won in the courts, on picket lines and in sit-ins . . . because they were not given" and appeals for a contribution to further the effort of people with cerebral palsy and their supporters.

As in the case of health care appeals, fund-raising campaigns must be designed to further *two goals*, not one: Besides raising money, the effect on societal attitudes toward people with disabilities must become an overriding concern. Emphasis on the catastrophic effects of disability ill prepares the public for the eventuality of coping with disability problems themselves. Because this emphasis feeds into stereotyped notions about people with disabilities that undermine their potentialities, and because it interferes with satisfactory interpersonal relations with those who have disabilities, the succumbing approach is clearly unwarranted.

Casting public appeals within the coping framework is not only desirable from the attitudinal and educational point of view, but is also very much in accord with reality. Though such feelings as fear, helplessness, and hopelessness may in some cases overwhelm the person confronted with having to live life with a disability, the will for growth and personal integrity most often shifts the balance in favor of meeting the challenge.

PUBLICATIONS, AGENCY PRACTICES, CONSUMERS

Throughout this volume we have presented instances where the contributions of researchers and other professionals have to be examined critically and regarded cautiously. After all, not only are facts in general true only until further notice, but professionals are also subject to the same psychological snares of flawed human perception as are ordinary people.

Here we shall succinctly set forth pairs of alternatives to show how the writings of professionals both reflect and influence societal attitudes. In each case, the first alternative is taken from an actual professional publication.[2] You are asked to judge which of the alternatives you would be ready to support:

Do you think that it is helpful or harmful, when writing about women who have undergone a mastectomy for breast cancer, to speak only about loss and threats to one's femininity, sexuality, and self-esteem, to refer to such women as "mastectomees," and to conclude that "Mastectomy involves a physical, emotional, and sexual assault on a woman which leaves her vulnerable and in a state of psychological ambivalence. A malignant growth has been removed from her body, yet her self-perception may be one of mutilation and sexual unattractiveness"? Or, do you think it would be more helpful to include evidence that many women do not regard a mastectomy as an affront to their femininity and that many women demonstrate an impressive ability to cope and work through their anxieties?

Do you think it is helpful or harmful when writing about craniofacial disfigurement to speak of "*victims* of craniofacial malformations," or do you think it would be more helpful to avoid emotionally loaded and extreme terms and refer, instead, to "individuals with craniofacial malformations"?

Is it helpful or harmful when describing frequently observed behavioral reactions of rehabilitation patients, to indicate only negative reactions, in fact ten of them, such as "denial" and "low frustration tolerance," and not to mention even one reaction that is positive? Or, do you think it would have been more constructive to have included such equally common reactions as "willing to apply effort," "cooperative," "reality oriented," and "hopeful"?

Do you think it is helpful or harmful to encourage hiring the handicapped by stating that "A large Chicago insurance company

---

[2]Because countless articles and books contribute to disabling myths about disability, the examples selected have not been singled out for special exposure and are, therefore, not referenced.

has found that the deaf make better-than-average file clerks and checkers because they are able to concentrate so well, unaffected by office noise and distractions"? Or, do you think it would have been better to have avoided such stereotyped thinking and referred, instead, to the fact that deaf workers are successfully employed in almost all occupations, even those where hearing is ordinarily considered to be necessary, such as in nursing and teaching?

Is it helpful or harmful to attribute the lack of employment of persons with cerebral palsy, in spite of their college degrees, to their disability; or is it more appropriate to entertain the likelihood that such environmental constraints as inadequate transportation, job scarcity, discriminatory practices, and loss of medical benefits are important contributing factors?

Is it helpful or harmful to interpret the higher self-concept ratings of congenitally blind girls in the study, as compared to the sighted girls, to mean that the blind girls distorted their answers to look good, or would it have been more helpful to have included the possibility that these girls in fact felt better about themselves?

In each of the above pairs, it is the second alternative that fits the coping framework, constructive views of life with a disability, and the facts as we interpret them.

With Scott's book, *The making of blind men* (1969), the rehabilitation community was shocked into considering the possibility that many agencies foster dependency by their paternalistic practices. Since then, the demand for greater self-determination, civil rights, and equal opportunity by consumers has gathered strength as citizens with disabilities, together with their supporters, have made their voices heard (Bowe, 1978; 1980; Bruck, 1978; Gliedman & Roth, 1980). Persistent pressure has been applied on many fronts to make a reality of two main ideas: (1) The right of people with disabilities to assume responsibility for directing their own day-to-day lives and (2) the right of people with disabilities to participate actively in the daily life of the community and to fulfill the range of social roles typical in society. The effort has contributed to significant progress in the realization of far-reaching legislation,[3] independent living centers (DeJong, 1979), and greater access to jobs and to the architectural environment. Although powerful and competing societal forces never make it easy to maintain gains and make further advances, it is clear that the action taken by people with disabilities themselves, their families, and their professional

---

[3]Noteworthy are the Rehabilitation Act of 1973 (P.L. 93–112) with its amendments, and the Education for All Handicapped Children Act of 1975 (P.L. 94–142).

and agency supporters makes a difference in the attitudes of society as expressed in what is said and done.

In a general sense, it can be said that how the culture treats *differences of all sorts* leaves its mark on the way people with disabilities are regarded. Such differences involve racial, religious, and ethnic groups; the slow learner; the two sexes; one's own shortcomings, as well as illness and disability.

At a meeting of the United Nations on "Social barriers in the integration of disabled persons into community life," the statement was correctly made that "in identifying social barriers, a distinction should be made between those arising out of social relationships and those stemming from the general social system of the country concerned, and the strategy for eliminating them should be based on a reliable analysis of the causal factors" (United Nations, 1977).

Chapter 19
Developing Constructive Views of Life with a Disability

Affirmative action in places of employment and mainstreaming in the schools can benefit from knowledge derived from theory and research on the problem of influencing attitudes.[1] The body of literature on this topic continues to grow and the findings continue to vary. Some studies show positive effects of the change attempts, some negative, and others no change. We shall be in a better position to understand these variable effects, as well as to offer recommendations for modifying attitudes, if we consider what we mean by positive attitudes. It is our position that positive attitudes must refer to *constructive views of life with a disability* and that such views are conceptualized by the coping versus succumbing frameworks. (For a review of this concept see Chapter 9.) The present chapter examines a number of attitude change procedures and recommends those that accord with the constructive orientation of the coping framework. Examples are drawn from simulating a disability, educational programs,

[1] Gordon Allport's classical book on the *Nature of prejudice,* 1954, contains a rich store of information and ideas that have relevance to overcoming prejudice in general.

and direct contact with individuals who have a disability. It will be shown that positive attitudes are fostered by exposure to constructive views of life with a disability through information and direct experience.

A LESSON FROM NEGATIVE RESULTS

Too often, attempts to change attitudes misfire, making attitudes even worse than if they were left alone. Let us take an example. In the following study, an effort was made to get people to understand what it is like to be handicapped (Wilson & Alcorn, 1969). Different groups of college students simulated blindness, deafness, and using a wheelchair for 8 consecutive hours. Results compared the experimental groups with a nonrole-playing group. On a measure of "attitudes toward disabled persons," no significant differences were found. However, the frustrations and insights described by the subjects raise serious question about the naive use of simulation approaches in awareness training. That the frustrations listed were many is not surprising, especially since the assignment directed the subjects to give "special note to specific frustrations." Rather it is the nature of the insights that alerts concern. All but one of the eighteen most frequent "new insights gained into the feelings of the disabled" revealed *negative* emotional reactions (Tables 2–4, pp. 305–6). Examples of negative and invalid insights are: blindness—loneliness, fear, helplessness; deafness—tendency to withdraw, depression, fear of others talking about you; and orthopedic disability—dependence on others, irritation at self, embarrassment. The only constructive insight listed was in the case of blindness—"greater use of other senses." Surely, most people who are blind, deaf, or who use a wheelchair in real life would regard these insights as not valid general descriptions of themselves but as capturing their feelings only some of the time and in some circumstances. They would resent having their lives typified by such pervasive negative states.

That one must become wary of role playing in awareness training is further seen in the following incident involving Paul, a child with cerebral palsy who used a wheelchair, and an assistant teacher. Eager to promote independence in her pupils, the assistant teacher persisted in her attempt to get Paul to open the restroom door by himself despite the fact that the head teacher had pointed out that the tight clearance made it impracticable for Paul to do so. The head teacher then suggested that her assistant try to do it herself using the wheelchair. In writing about this incident, the head teacher reported: "My assistant was shattered by the restriction the chair created! It was cumbersome, impossible to control. She caught her hand in the door. *Unfortunately, she did not see the need to change the door.* Rather, she pushed Paul to the room—something she had never done before! She helped him the rest of the day. I might not have noticed the unnecessary help if I hadn't been aware of the simulation downfall. My assistant and I sat down and discussed this effect. I feel better. She has not pampered Paul again" (personal communication).

The above examples should force us to think through what we wish to accomplish in trying to improve attitudes.

FACTORS UNDERLYING MISGUIDED EFFORTS

It is well for us to review briefly some of the powerful forces already discussed that press toward perceiving disability primarily in terms of negative effects. First of all, negatives dominate when the disability is seen as *the* salient fact about the person, when in effect the person is made equivalent to the disability. The perceived negative character of the disability, not having any positive context to contain the negative associations, is then spread to the person as a whole. Abilities are underrated and the person is devaluated. This factor is referred to as *negative spread.* A second factor coercing negative fixation stems from the immediate pressure to focus on problems when it is problems that one is concerned about. Unfortunately, the constructive forces that exist within individuals with a disability, their families and the wider society are often not articulated and are left instead as vaguely existing somewhere—maybe. A number of clearly motivational factors also tilt toward the negative. Thus, feeling superior may be supported by highlighting the misfortune of another (self-aggrandizing requirement of mourning). Morbid preoccupations may be satisfied. Professionals may reassure themselves of the importance of their services by stressing client difficulties and dependency. All these forces conspire to adversely affect attitudes. Instead of constructive views of life with a disability, they engender pity, fear, and at best charity.

An important reason for this boomerang effect is the "just world phenomenon." The main idea is that people have a need to bring "what ought to be" and "what exists in reality" into line with each other. Therefore, where that reality is perceived as unfortunate but difficult to change, the attempt will be to justify it. This is done by regarding the misfortune as deserved (e.g., because the person has sinned, or is lazy, or careless) just as rewards must be deserved to be acceptable. However, the alignment between what "ought to be" and "what is" can also be brought about in another way, provided that changing reality is felt to be possible. This requires that existing positives in the situation, which can be tapped and strengthened, are recognized. It is then that people can be moved to alter the current state of affairs to meet the standards of what ought to be.

The error in the approach that stresses the negative lot of people with disabilities is not that negatives and injustices are stressed, but that constructive forces that abound in people with disabilities, their families, and the wider society are neglected. After all, it is these constructive forces that must be marshalled to correct injustice.

DISABILITY SIMULATION

Using the coping versus succumbing frameworks as a base, we can select specific constructive views to be directly experienced while simulating a disability. The examples we have chosen can be used with children or adults simulating a variety of disabilities in a variety of settings. For the first example, let us suppose that we would like the public, in this case children, to appreciate that a person with a disability is not a passive recipient of trials and tribulations, but is an active agent in coping, striving, and learning how to manage. There are numerous strategies that could be adopted. Let us illustrate with the case of blindness. The child's eyes could be blindfolded and the child encouraged to navigate the classroom, becoming more and more confident as learning the layout takes place. We could direct the child to notice how much about the world is learned through other senses and to list all the new awarenesses that have thereby been gained. The child could become more adept at eating or pouring liquids without using his or her sight. The intent would *not* be to have the child discover how difficult it is to live without sight, nor how easy, but rather that it is possible to live with blindness because the person strives and learns and manages.

For the next example, let us select the constructive view that the severity of a handicap is as much a function of environmental barriers, if not more so, than of personal impairment. Let us illustrate by having participants use a wheelchair to simulate an orthopedic disability. What we need is to devise a plan whereby the participants can become aware not only of architectural barriers but of how these barriers can be reduced. To do the first and not the second is to invite pity and what is worse, justification of the lot of the disadvantaged; the reader will recall the power of the "just world phenomenon." We could have the participants cross a street, first where there is no curb cut and then where there is a curb cut. We could have them attempt to enter a restroom and stall ill-adapted for wheelchair use and then one that is architecturally accessible. We could have them discover architectural barriers in their own work, school, church, home, or recreational setting and then, in group discussion, brainstorm ways of eliminating them. The goal is to find solutions to problems, not to remain stuck with them. In fact, acting on at least one of the solutions as part and parcel of the plan would make it an attitude change effort *par excellence.* The participants could also point out ways in which society has taken the needs of the majority into account: stairs, printed matter, buses, and auditory signals are common examples. Two momentous conclusions follow: (1) Reasonable accommodations *apply to everyone.* (2) Reasonable accommodations provide a strong counterforce *against exclusion and prejudice.*

The following study was explicitly directed toward awareness of environmental conditions that contribute to difficulties experienced by elderly persons with sensory losses (Pastalan, 1974). The subjects were four architecture doctoral students specializing in environmental problems. Simultaneous sensory losses involving vision, hearing, olfaction, and touch were simulated by each subject. For example, tactile impairment was created by applying a liquid fixitive to the finger tips, visual loss by wearing lenses to simulate light scatter and glare. Each subject, while experiencing all four sensory deficits at the same time, spent at least one hour each day in one of three standardized settings: a dwelling unit, a multipurpose senior center, and a shopping center. An entire experience cycle took 3 days and this cycle was repeated for a period of 6 months. The subjects kept a daily log of their experiences and periodically held meetings to compare their observations. The discussions elicited unanimous agreement on a number of sources of environmental difficulties. For example, with respect to visual loss: "If only a single intense artificial light source is used for illumination, rather than several, the chances of inducing uncomfortable glare is increased" (p. 359). For auditory loss: "Some combination of carpeting, acoustical ceiling, and draperies absorb too much sound and make functional hearing still more problematic" (p. 359).

The daily log also recorded the trials and sense of loss experienced by the simulators. Thus, they referred to tactile difficulties with fine muscle control involved in turning pages and in adjusting pressure in gripping objects. But the point is that the experience of loss was oriented toward how to adapt and how to modify the environment. In fact, the simulation was purposefully extended over a period of half a year to allow the person to overcome the "shock-value associated with 'instant' sensory deprivation" so that, "after ceasing to be preoccupied with the deficits" the person could begin "to perceive the environment" (p. 359). This is the kind of simulation that is consistent with the coping framework. The difficulties and loss are experienced. But so are *the possibilities for personal adaptation and environmental change.*

Role reversal is a form of simulation that can be especially useful when the object is to discover how a helper can better meet the needs of a person with a particular problem in an interpersonal situation. Two examples will be described. One involves a feeding situation, the other impaired hearing.

In the feeding situation, the members of the group are first paired off. One member of the pair then feeds the other who is asked to simulate paralysis of both arms. The partners are instructed to consider how the feeding situation could be made more pleasant for both of them. After the meal is consumed, the roles are reversed, the feeder now becoming the one fed. The participants then discuss the problems encountered in each role and offer helpful suggestions. As the person fed, for example, inappropriate utensils and food portions, embarrassment, and unwanted dependency emerge as problems. As the feeder, reference is made to boredom and unsightly mastication. Suggestions for improvement pour forth. They concern size of portion, tempo of feeding, attention of the feeder, optimal distance between the two parties, the responsibility of the person being fed to inform the feeder of his or her wishes, the importance of conversation of mutual interest, and so forth.

The next example is divided into two parts. Part one prepares the group members for interacting with a person whose hearing is severely impaired. In part two the simulation takes place. First, the group directly experiences the fact that they "hear better" when they can see the speaker's face. This can be demonstrated by having the listeners indicate when they can no longer understand the fading voice of a speaker under two conditions: one where a video tape allows the person to both hear and see the speaker and one where an audio tape of the same speaker is heard but not seen. Since comprehension will persist longer under the first condition, the importance of facing a person with impaired hearing while speaking is personally experienced and becomes an obvious conclusion.

The participants then discuss other ways in which they could be reasonably helpful when interacting with a person with impaired hearing. Some of the participants may have had experience with deaf relatives and acquaintances. The leader can also contribute suggestions. Forthcoming will be recommendations regarding the importance of proper lighting, of repeating the thought in another way so the deaf person might understand more easily, of allowing the person with impaired hearing to indicate how he or she may be helped to understand, of being ready to write the thought should oral communication be unsuccessful, and so forth. Ways of trying to help that really hinder can also be explored. The tendency to shout or to interrupt the deaf person are examples.

After such a brainstorming session, the group is ready to experience simulating deafness. Ear plugs can be used for half the group who interact with their hearing partners for a specified time and then reverse roles. The instruction is for both parties to apply what they have learned. Where the lighting of the room is inadequate, appropriate changes would be made in the way of lamps and seating positions, for example.

The point already made bears repeating. What is being stressed is not how hard communication is when one's hearing is impaired, nor how easy, but that needs can be met when reasonable accommodations are made. In this case, the reasonable accommodations involve both the physical and social environment. What emerges is the recognition that both the person with impaired hearing and the normally hearing person share in the responsibility for facilitating communication. The hearing impaired person can become more skilled at speech reading and at instructing others how best to communicate; the hearing person can learn what is helpful with respect to one's own behavior and needed lighting arrangements. Would you not agree that this type of recognition, reinforced by actually practicing the new understandings, is in fact what is meant by a constructive view of life with a disability? Is not this use of disability simulation far better than having the person simulate deafness for several hours and "learn" that being withdrawn, depressed, and suspicious is what it is like to be deaf?

Notice that the method of role reversal differs from ordinary simulation procedures insofar as the person experiences the position of the insider (the person with the particular problem) and the outsider consecutively, a juxtaposition that makes more vivid the awareness that direct knowledge of both can be useful in improving the helping relationship.

Simulating a disability can also take place in the home. In the following example, a mother attempted to change her child's feelings toward a classmate who had difficulty in walking. The focus was on how the classmate manages because of her coping effort and indomitable spirit, and how Larry, the 5-year-old son, could be of help. Larry had made a remark to the effect that he and the other children thought Kate was a dope. She could not do the things they could do.

Soon after his mother suggested "that they play a game and that he should get hurt by a car and that he would go to the hospital and then get better":

> LARRY. "Here I am in the street, and a car comes whizzing along and clips the tail of my bicycle so that I am thrown off on the street. Then my friend Jim (a much older and admired boy) comes along and trips over me so that I get hurt."
>
> MOTHER. "Yes, he accidentally runs over your leg, perhaps."
>
> Larry is delighted and lies kicking on the ground in supposed pain. Mother and nurse-sister come rushing along and put him in an ambulance and take him to the hospital.
>
> MOTHER. "Now I am the doctor. Hello, little fellow. What happened to you? Oh, it is your leg. Say, it is pretty bad, and it will take a while to get well. You will have to walk stiff-legged for a few weeks."
>
> LARRY. "You mean I can't run and jump any more?"
>
> DOCTOR. "No, you must take care of it for a long while. I guess you can get up now and try to walk." He lifts Larry onto his feet. "Oh no, you cannot move like that. You must not bend your knee except by lifting it up by your hand. See, when you want to go upstairs, you must raise the leg with the hand like this."
>
> LARRY. "Oh, that is difficult. It makes my back tired before I get up the first flight of stairs." He puts forth much effort and pulls each leg onto the next step. He gets to the landing and sits down. "Say, this is not fun. Why are we playing this? I want to get well soon."
>
> The mother sits down a moment on the step too. "Well, Larry, did you ever think of what Kate has to do when she walks upstairs? She never complains but keeps right on trying. . . .
>
> LARRY. " . . . I never thought of that before."
>
> MOTHER. "Do you know how you can make it easier for Kate and have more fun yourself?"
>
> LARRY. "No. How?"
>
> MOTHER. "It makes Kate happy to have the boys and girls nice to her and not impatient with her when she is slow about getting places. Perhaps you can help the other children to be nice to her too. You know they think a lot of you, and if you showed them that you like Kate and think she is brave, they will not talk about her being a dope. That must make her feel pretty bad like it would make a soldier feel bad if you said he was a dope because he lost a leg fighting in the war." [Lippitt, 1947, p. 157]

The reader's attention is also called to the role-playing procedures outlined on pages 336–340, and to assertive role playing described on pages 340–341. So long as the focus of simulation is on ameliorating problems, participants are less likely to become mired in the succumbing aspects of disablement. In short, problems are to be experienced, but it is recommended that they be experienced within the coping framework.

THE NATURE OF INFORMATION AND EDUCATIONAL PROGRAMS

The following two studies help to reveal the importance of the nature of the information that is presented in an attitude change attempt. The first was done with sixth grade children who were told that a new child would be entering their class (Siperstein, Bak, & Gottlieb, 1977). The new child was depicted by a picture of a child with Down's syndrome and by an audio tape in which the child could not spell even simple words. A measure of attitudes toward the prospective class member was administered prior to and following discussion about the new child in small groups consisting of four children. The results indicated that the children's attitudes became more *negative* after the group discussion. This did not happen with a control group who discussed a normal looking and academically competent new class member. To understand the results of this study, it is crucial to recognize that the only information imparted to the children about the child with Down's syndrome was negative; namely, that he looked funny and was stupid. Nowhere were the interests of this child revealed, or anything positive at all, such as that he liked to play ball, enjoyed helping people, or whatever. The disability reigned supreme, devoid of any competing context.

Contrast this study with the results of another in which subjects listened to a panel discuss their physical disabilities, social lives, occupational goals, and their view of societal attitudes (Donaldson & Martinson, 1977). The attitudes of these subjects were more positive on an outcome measure than those of a control group who had not heard the panel. The point to be stressed is that the panel essentially reflected the coping framework in describing their lives. They stood out as individuals, having a range of human aspirations, achievements, failures, and concerns. Positives as well as negatives shared the stage.

These studies provide a lead into the kind of educational programs that are most promising in improving attitudes. In a word, where problems involving disability are presented within the coping framework, as part of the total lives of individuals, positive attitude change can be expected. On the other hand, where the thrust concentrates on problems and not solutions, where the disabling aspects are emphasized and the individual as a whole human being with abilities as well as disabilities is lost, then we can expect a succumbing orientation that feeds negative attitudes.

These basic ideas were put into practice in a 4-week workshop for children designed to influence acceptance of people with disabilities (Lazar, Gensley, & Orpet, 1971). The subjects of the study were

8-year-old children divided into an experimental and a control group. Both groups were administered an attitude measure prior to and following the workshop. Whereas the scores of the children in the control group actually decreased during this time period, the scores of the children who participated in the special instructional program showed a significant gain. The content of the curriculum is important in understanding its effectiveness:

1. Each day, a different creative American was studied, some of whom had disabilities (e.g., Thomas A. Edison, impaired hearing; Helen Keller, deaf and blind; Franklin D. Roosevelt, using a wheelchair). The emphasis was on the person's achievements. Personal characteristics, including disability, were treated as incidental and not of major importance.
2. Each week special guests spoke about their work. One was a teacher of educable mentally retarded children. She brought pictures of her class in various learning activities. (The children in the workshop commented that "They look just like us.").
3. Other visitors were a family of normally hearing children and deaf parents. The children in the workshop had practiced the manual alphabet before the family came so that they would have some familiarity with this method of communication. (A comment of one of the children is revelatory: "When I heard that deaf people were coming, I was scared, but I'm not any more. They are real people.")
4. A teenage girl and boy described their work as aides in a convalescent hospital. After an interesting conversation with the class, they revealed that both had epilepsy.
5. One of the counselors in the school spoke about her hidden disability. She was legally blind.

Some readers may feel that positive attitudes were fostered at the expense of reality, believing that an exaggerated picture of the accomplishments and adjustment of people with disabilities was presented. Countering this view is the fact that the range of abilities considered was wide—mentally retarded pupils on the one hand, creative people on the other—and that fulfilling the role of a parent, aide, counselor, or president is not precluded by the particular disabilities of those who functioned in these roles. Had the curriculum dealt primarily with people who had severe, multiple disabilities in institutional settings, positive gains in attitude could be assessed by measuring changes in aversion and fear, appreciation of the abilities of people with multiple disabilities, support for rehabilitation programs, and so forth.

The published report of the preceding study (Lazar et al., 1971) is unusual in that it presents the content of the educational program in sufficient detail to allow the reader to get an idea of its import. Too often publications identify the educational program by a title, or an evaluative statement such as "a pro-amputee film was shown," with little if any elaboration. Such sparseness precludes interpreting the findings in terms of the content of the material.

Studies of the effect of educational programs frequently include different types of direct contact with people who have a disability along with academic knowledge as such, so that it is not possible strictly to disentangle the effects of the former from the latter. Nonetheless, the accumulated evidence appears on balance to favor the positive impact of educational experiences involving systematic courses of study. Of all the studies reviewed, only one was found in which significant changes occurred in the *negative* direction (Cobun, 1972). All the others either showed positive change as a result of the educational intervention (e.g., Nelson, 1971; Yerxa, 1971; Rosswurm, 1980) or positive change for some of the subgroups of subjects and no change for others (Wyrick, 1964).

Knowledge about illness and disability *presented within the coping framework* belongs in the elementary school curriculum. Further, at appropriate ages, children can be taught first-aid skills such as cardiopulmonary resuscitation and protective action when a person has a seizure. These skills, just as fire drills, need to be practiced periodically. Having practiced what to do in an emergency is a constructive antidote to fear, aversion, and panic.

Television provides a particularly good educational medium for developing constructive views of life with a disability. An especially fine example is the television series *Feeling free,* which shows several children, each with a different disability, engaged in a variety of activities at school, at home, and at play (Brightman, 1977). They talk about their disability, their worries, their hopes, what is easy for them and what is hard, as well as many other things not connected with the disability. Their lives are variegated and their disability is only part of living, although an important part. They come through as children, each with a separate personality, not as disabilities.

The idea that people with disabilities are rightfully part of the broadest array of life's activities can be furthered in the public media by including them in roles totally unrelated to their disability. People with disabilities participating in TV commercials, crowd scenes, talk and variety shows, in the performing arts, and as newscasters are examples. There also are many good films, books, and pamphlets that present life with a disability constructively. Rusk & Taylor's "Living with a disability" (1953) remains a classic.

THE NATURE AND EFFECTS OF CONTACT

Ordinary experience teaches us that whether the effect of contact is on balance, positive or negative, depends upon many different possible meanings, feelings, and consequences evoked by the contact.

We shall begin by a consideration of the unit-forming factors that are implied or brought about by contact, namely, interaction, proximity, and familiarity. Generally, contact implies some form of interaction and closeness (proximity) through, for example, talking or doing things together. An increase in familiarity is also generally implied since contact means some form of direct experiencing. As was discussed earlier (pp. 68–70), such unit-forming factors tend to induce a positive sentiment or liking for the person or group (Heider, 1958) and therefore are conducive to positive attitude change.

Probing a bit further, one could say that these unit-forming factors are also vehicles for additional cognitive and affective experiences whose nature determines the final outcome with respect to attitude change. For example, although the aforementioned unit-forming factors tend to arouse a positive inclination toward the attitude object, this inclination may hardly have a chance to take hold or to prosper and may even be completely reversed should the contact evoke aversion and fear for whatever reason, or should it reinforce negative stereotypes for whatever reason, or should it otherwise be unpleasant or disturbing. On the other hand, contact can be expected to lead to positive change when it reduces aversive reactions or negative stereotypes or is enjoyable on other counts.

Yuker and his associates (1966) reviewed studies containing data on the relationship between attitudes and the *extent* of contact with persons who have a disability. Based on approximately twenty-five separate results, they concluded that "increased contact with disabled persons generally results in more positive attitudes" (p. 85). By far the great majority of the reported relationships were in the positive direction, although only about half were sufficiently reliable to reach statistical significance. Studies published since that review have not altered this picture. However, since favorable attitudes to begin with may lead to more extensive contact as well as facilitate pleasurable interactions, the causal direction between attitudes and extent of contact cannot be determined from many of these studies. According to other research (Jordan, 1971), contact *per se* seems to increase the certainty or intensity of the respondent's reaction to an attitude statement but not necessarily its positivity.

When association with a person is voluntary, a positive relationship between extent of contact and degree of enjoyment of that contact is to be expected, for ordinarily we do not seek unsatisfactory relationships. Jordan's research (1971) has led him to stress that contact brings about favorable attitudes when the contact is perceived as *voluntary* and *enjoyable.* He infers from this that where the voluntary aspects are not primary, as in integrated classrooms, or in family relationships, or in quota systems for employment, then "great attempts must be made to increase enjoyment," if we are to influence attitudes positively.

It would be strange, indeed, if enjoyable experiences were not reflected in positive scores on at least some dimensions measured by attitude tests. One study on this problem asked subjects to list the experiences they had had with a person who had a disability and to indicate in each case whether the experience was unpleasant, neutral, or pleasant (Siller & Chipman, cited in Yuker et al., 1966, p. 84). A positive correlation was obtained between the overall score, indicating how pleasant the contacts were, and four attitude measures primarily concerned with general acceptance on the personal and affective level. It should be noted, however, that a significant correlation was *not* found between the quality of contact score and the ATDP test, a scale which conceptualizes acceptance in terms of the degree to which people with disabilities are perceived as similar to nondisabled people (Yuker et al., 1966). This finding again points to the generally accepted proposition that attitudes are not unitary, that they consist of multiple components that have sufficiently different functions, origins, and consequences to merit separate evaluation (Siller, Chipman, et al., 1967; Siller, Vann, et al., 1967). In terms of the six levels of his attitude-behavior paradigm, Jordan feels that if one is interested in changing attitude-behaviors at the stereotypic or normative levels, then enjoyment as such is not especially relevant, but at the more personal and action levels, "Contact situations must be devised such that they contain aspects that are perceived as voluntary and enjoyable" (1971, p. 24).

In an attempt to reach further understanding of the relationship between contact and attitudes, Yuker and his associates reviewed about a dozen studies that provide information concerning the *type of setting* in which the contact took place (1966, Table 40). Their main conclusion is especially challenging. They felt that the differences across studies may be attributed in part to differences in the *type of information* imparted by the different types of contact. More specifically, where the setting shows the person with a disability functioning in terms of his or her capabilities, attitude measures are likely to be more favorable than in settings where the focus is primarily on the person's inadequacies and disability. Thus, contact in employment, school, or social settings is more likely to affect attitudes positively than contact in medical settings.

To be sure, studies on this problem generally are not strictly designed experiments in which the effect of initial attitudes, concomitant educational programs, or other confounding factors can be ruled out. It is therefore in the accumulation of evidence, despite methodological inadequacies, upon which confidence is gradually built. Actually, confidence is enhanced and the generalizability of results increased as additional studies, by virtue of their *variation in type of subject and setting,* are sufficiently consistent in showing positive effects of environments that highlight the person's abilities rather than deficiencies.

Let us look at a study that examined changes in attitudes toward children with disabilities as a result of an integrated school program (Rapier et al., 1972). Children in each third, fourth, and fifth grade class in the school had contact with at least one child with an orthopedic disability in their classroom for part or most of the day, as well as on the playground, in the auditorium for school events, and at a Junior Wheelchair Olympics. The attitude measure administered prior to and after a year of integration consisted of twenty items to be rated on a three-point scale: for example, Don't need help; need help; need lots of help. The results indicated a positive shift in attitude: The nondisabled children perceived the children with a disability as less weak, less in need of attention and help, and more curious than they had originally thought. Items on which the majority of children had expressed positive attitudes on the pretest continued to be supported after the year of mainstreaming.

A caveat is in order. The fact that integrating children with disabilities into regular classrooms may increase recognition of their competencies and in that sense change attitudes for the better, should not be regarded as meaning that acceptance of children with disabilities equals that of nondisabled children. The evidence on this point is conflicting. For example, in one study, grade school children more frequently expressed rejecting attitudes toward their peers who had an upper extremity amputation than toward a matched nondisabled child; the children with disabilities were more frequently liked least and less frequently liked best, for example (Centers & Centers, 1963). Yet, in another study involving two integrated camps, proportionally more of the children with disabilities than children without disabilities were listed as best friends by their normal peers (Dibner & Dibner, 1973). Nor do improved attitudes or even acceptance by the nondisabled necessarily insure that the child with a disability will sense that acceptance. The situation as experienced and judged by the child with a disability requires separate study.

Another caution is in order. Making use of a person's abilities, or even enabling the person to function adequately in socially valued activities, is one factor, but not the only factor that influences the *perception* of abilities. There is a vast difference between demonstrating someone's abilities and having someone else *appreciate* those abilities. It is expected that competitive situations are not conducive to improving attitudes toward those who suffer by comparison. We need to recognize that the social climate of the setting—its philosophical view of interpersonal valuing—is an *essential* consideration in any discussion of the type of setting affecting attitudes toward people with disabilities.

The importance of the basis for personal valuing is even more to be emphasized when it is realized that contrast effects may act to highlight a person's limitations even in the absence of competitive situations. Thus, a person who is a slow learner may appear to be more retarded when seen performing in a group of ordinary children than in a group of slow learners. What is required, then, is a social climate that will minimize such contrast effects, a social climate that is strongly infused with asset values, not comparative values (see pp. 178–183).

We must not overlook the fact that the changes in attitude evidenced in the integrated school program described earlier (Rapier, 1972) did not occur in a philosophical vacuum. The report makes explicit that not only were the children with disabilities selected with the expectation that the experience would be educationally beneficial to both them and the children without disabilities but also that the teachers took special care to provide favorable interactions between these groups. *Special care* was also taken in another study that showed the positive effects of integration. This study was of a summer camp in which individuals with disabilities were included among both the camp staff and the children (Anthony, 1969). It was found that the staff without disabilities who had not attended the camp before showed positive gains in attitude as measured by their precamp to postcamp attitude scores.

A number of investigators have proposed that direct contact in which the participants have *equal status* is conducive to the disruption of negative stereotypes and the improvement of friendly relationships (Allport, 1954; Harding et al., 1970; Ashmore, 1970). The explanation is based on the likelihood that when people occupy the same role position, as coworkers or costudents for example, their interests, competencies, and goals are more apt to be alike than when their roles are of unequal status. Negative stereotypes then become unlearned because they are incompatible with the prevailing evidence and friendships that are formed. This course of events may be interrupted, however, should competitive hostilities arise for whatever reason.

Groups of people with and without disabilities who meet over time for the express purpose of sharing feelings, problems, and possible solutions can be recommended as a promising attitude change approach. Such a group allows contact to be made on the feeling level as well as on the more intellectual and action-oriented levels. The common humanity of the group comes through when deeply felt experiences are shared. Who has not known fear and hurt, anger and resentment, hope and love, joy and reassurance?

Normalizing relationships through inclusion and accommodation is another approach to developing constructive views of life with a disability. Its main purpose is to have the learner discover for himself or herself that a person with a disability can in fact participate in a wide range of activities on a peer basis if one dispenses with assumptions about the disabling effects of disability (Wright, 1975a). The procedure is as follows:

1. The person (novice) invites someone who has a significant disability (partner) to join him or her in a variety of activities that one would ordinarily carry out with a friend. The partner may, but need not, be an acquaintance of the novice. Because it is desirable that novice and partner have something in common, a partner should be sought who belongs to the same club, school, work setting, or occupation as the novice.

2. The novice then solicits the cooperation of the potential partner by sharing the purpose of the project, explaining that the intent is to replace preconceived notions that exclude people with disabilities from many activities by knowledge provided by the partner as to how he or she can in fact participate. In effect, partner and novice join forces in bringing about attitude change. The partner is informed that he or she will be invited to do things together with the novice, that any invitation can be declined, and that the partner is free to initiate an invitation.

3. The novice then prepares a list of activities that he or she would enjoy doing with a friend. No activity is to be barred because of assumptions that the disability is too limiting or that the partner might decline. In advance of each activity, the novice lists anticipated problems.

4. Following each activity, the novice describes the occasion including any accommodations that were made, and indicates how anticipated concerns did or did not materialize.

The following account is excerpted from one project in which two young men participated (Whitacre, personal communication, 1973). The novice was a college senior and his partner a college freshman who became totally blind in grade school. They did not know each other prior to the project. The activities in chronological order were: watching television, listening to music, going to a movie, attending a lecture and slide show, drinking beer together, playing a pinball machine, attending a baseball game, double dating, shopping, fixing an automobile, playing basketball, motorcycling, and playing billiards. The excerpts describe five of these activities; the others were equally enlightening to the novice:

Drinking Beer Together

Anticipated concerns

Jim and I did not know each other very well yet and a number of questions entered my head. Should I pour his beer for him or would he prefer to do it himself? If I was doing the pouring, should I ask him if he wants more when his glass is empty or wait until he asks for some?

Events as they turned out

My anticipation proved to be greater than any real need for concern. . . . I poured the beer but then found that I didn't know whether to put the glass in his hand or on the table in front of him. I decided that I would be overreacting to Jim's blindness if I just shoved the glass into his hand, so I placed it in front of him and told him where it was. When Jim finished one I simply asked him if he was ready for another. There was no problem here. It was merely that I was wary of asking what might be a stupid question.

Playing a Pinball Machine (same evening)

Anticipated concerns

The most interesting event that topped off the evening was Jim's wanting to play the pinball machines. It seemed to me that the pleasure derived from playing pinball was watching the ball bounce around and hitting it with the replay flippers and you had to see to be able to do that. Right? Wrong!

Events as they turned out

Jim loved to see how many points he could rack up and he was quite good. He solved the problem of not knowing when to hit the flippers by hitting them constantly. It was a deviation from the standard game, but successful nonetheless. I was impressed.

Repairing an Automobile

Anticipated concerns

Since the "normal" young man usually has at least a casual interest in cars, I decided to ask Jim to help me work on mine. I don't know what I expected him to do, and I was pretty sure that asking him would seem like the dumb question of the year. The problems I anticipated were numerous. If he did accept just to humor me I didn't see how he could really be any help. He couldn't tell if a spark plug was burning improperly. He couldn't read a tach-dwell meter to set the points or adjust the carburetor. There really wasn't much that I thought he could do. Since a good deal of trouble-shooting is done with the motor running, it would be very dangerous to work close to the engine if you couldn't see the moving parts that cause injury.

Events as they turned out

When I summoned up the courage to ask Jim about it, I received the first in a long series of surprises. He said that he really enjoyed working on cars and had helped his brother at home. . . . Because of this he can offer helpful suggestions as to what the trouble might be. So that is how we started. Things progressed rapidly from then on. With a little imagination, we found all sorts of things that Jim could do to help besides offering advice. I could give him the proper wrench or socket and he could remove or tighten down any bolt on the car. He could check the tension of the fan belt. With the correct feeler gauge he could set the gap on the new spark plugs, and do a really accurate job of it, too. Although he couldn't read the tach-dwell meter he could turn the adjusting screws on the carburetor while I made the readings. He could also check the water level in the radiator by feel. This is not to say that Jim became a mechanical wizard in one afternoon but we did have a good time and Jim was able to help a good deal. It makes this project seem more worthwhile when Jim learns something new also. I sometimes feel that I'm the only one benefiting from our efforts. It's nice to know that Jim is getting more than a pestering social director out of it all.

Playing Basketball with a Group

Anticipated concerns

When I asked Jim if he would like to give basketball a try, he told me that he had played basketball before . . . at a school for the blind. He explained that the game was played by allowing those students who still had partial sight to run the ball down the court. These same players were in charge of rebounding and most of the ball movements under the basket. They were not allowed to shoot, however. All of the scoring was done by students who were totally blind. These individuals were stationed at various points on the court from which they executed their one shot. Since they remained in their fixed positions throughout the game, there was no need to see where they were in relation to the basket. It was always in the same place. Jim said that some of the players hit a good percentage of their shots. . . . Although the game could be modified for a blind team, it drastically affected how the game is played and it did not seem right to ask the sighted players on the court to give up those parts of the game that hold the greatest appeal to them. . . . The players are often strangers to each other. They either hear of a game somewhere or know one or two people who ask them to come along. Fast competition and healthy exercise are the uniting features. They enjoy making a hard drive for a layup, or tricky maneuvering around opponents to get off a good shot. The contact, speed, and mobility that had to be removed from the game to facilitate the blind are the parts that make them want to play.

Events as they turned out

It became apparent that the "blind" game did not suit the other players any more than the "normal" game suited Jim. We finally found a workable solution. Jim became the permanent freethrow shooter for our team. This way the other players had to give up making their own foul shots but got to set a normal pace for the other parts of the game. At the same time Jim could play his stationary game and take his shots from the same position each time. Jim said that his position had been almost exactly that spot when he played at the school for the blind. His shooting proved that. He made between 70 percent and 80 percent of his shots from the line. Although this experiment with basketball did not yield as easily or as completely as many of our other activities, inclusion was possible.

Billiards

Anticipated concerns

While considering the game of pool as one of our activities, I thought that perhaps this one would prove to be impracticable for Jim. Unlike basketball, there is no way to continually make the same shot. There are six "goals" instead of one. There is an infinite number of angles and combinations for possible shots. One must not only know the position of the ball one wants to shoot at but must also be aware of the fourteen other balls that may be in the way.

Events as they turned out

I was used to surprises by now. Jim accepted my invitation to play. He had played before and had developed his own system for playing. It was not a regular game but it was pool nonetheless. Jim simplified the game by shooting only at those balls that were close to a pocket. If he could hit the ball fairly directly with the cue ball it would be likely to go in. Jim would lay the cue stick down, creating a bridge between the two balls. Then he could draw the cue straight back without losing the proper angle for the shot. Jim had to rely on my eyes in order to pick out a likely shot and to show him where the balls were located in the first place, but he could then make the shot by himself, using his touch-oriented technique. There were other details that required special attention. The placement of the chalk on the same spot on the edge of the table permitted Jim to locate it with a minimum of difficulty. I assisted Jim in his selection of a cue stick. He could pick out one of the proper weight to suit his game, but he had no accurate way to tell if a stick was warped. This activity, more than any other, brought us a good deal of attention. The pool hall was crowded and it didn't take long for others to notice that Jim was blind. The looks of disbelief gradually melted away as our game progressed. Jim's shooting was not so fantastic as to produce amazement in our audience, but it did make them appreciate the fact that he was really playing the game.

As seen in these excerpts, this method of normalizing relationships emphasizes the following:

1. In deciding upon an activity, the novice is guided *solely* by those *normally* carried out with a friend. At this point the disability of the partner is to be *completely ignored* and the nondisabled state becomes the framework for thinking. The partner has the option of declining the invitation, but the novice does not have the option of determining what the partner can or cannot do.
2. However, during the activity itself, the *disability is taken*

into account as seems desirable. Where appropriate, the activity is restructured and accommodations made. The needs of other participants are also considered.

3. The partner exercises considerable leadership, although not exclusively so, in determining how best to participate. The partner's wealth of experience in learning ways to manage is respected. Sometimes workable solutions are arrived at together.

The main limitation of this approach to attitude change is that novice and partner have to be ready to associate together in a variety of settings. At the very least, it takes a fair amount of time and energy. There also is no guarantee that novice and partner, especially if strangers, would find that they like each other, a prerequisite it would seem for a successful outcome. This concern is probably lessened by the fact that at the outset both parties are willing to lend themselves to the explicit purpose of the project.

Is the project worth the effort? Can a positive outcome be expected? The report of the novice above is affirmative:

> Insofar as the purpose of this approach is to get past the stereotypes that surround the handicapped, it is effective. Perhaps the first important lesson it taught me was that in spite of my previous education about the pitfalls of "spread effects" I still held many of the old prejudices.
>
> The most telling evidence for the success of this method for overcoming stereotypes concerning the handicapped does not rely on anything so specific as the examples given so far. *What made me most aware of the change in my attitudes was the fact that it became increasingly difficult to think of reasons why Jim could not participate in a given activity. I found that I expected that he would be able to do things instead of assuming that he would not. It became almost impossible to doubt that he could take part, let alone to formulate specific questions or problems as to why he couldn't.*
>
> I cannot say whether it was specifically the nature of our normal activities that was responsible for this change or whether any enduring interaction would have produced similar results. Whatever is responsible, I appreciate more fully that Jim is a person first and a blind person second. He is different from some other people who call themselves "normal" because his handicap is more obvious than the ones some of the others carry with them. His disability does not make him less than a whole person. It is just that the parts that make up a whole man need not be and are not the same for every man.

What if Jim hadn't been so adaptable? That wouldn't matter. The point is that people are adaptable in different ways, ways that have to be allowed to reveal themselves if we are to break away from stereotypic expectations. How enduring can we expect the change of the novice's attitude to be? Can we expect it to generalize to wider groups of people with disabilities? Can we expect that in future encounters with people who have a disability he will assume abilities instead of being prey to the unbridled spread of disabilities? Can we expect that he will continue to attempt to normalize relationships by including and accommodating?

The question of the persistence and generalizability of improved attitudes must be addressed with respect to all attitude change attempts. The gains made in more than one study have been shown to be but temporary (e.g., Rosswurm, 1980). Yet we can hardly expect one experience or even a set of experiences designed to change attitudes to remain significant by themselves in the midst of repeated ongoing events that influence attitudes in the wider society. We can say with confidence that where the general ambience of the community fosters constructive attitudes toward life with a disability, favorable attitudes will more easily be sustained. Such diverse conditions and actions as fund-raising and health care messages, architectural and transportation accessibility, educational and employment opportunities, client comanagement and independent living, and human dignity and the values emphasized, are examples of general influences that weigh heavily in determining how widespread and enduring positive attitudes are likely to be.

OVERVIEW

The ideas stressed in this chapter are based on the implications of some of the concepts previously introduced. In this sense they are a capstone to the entire volume. The main points are:

1. Positive attitudes will not thrive when the predominant focus is on disabling aspects of disability.
2. Constructive views of life with a disability, conceptualized within the coping framework, provide an excellent basis for developing positive attitudes.
3. People with disabilities are not passive. They do and must actively take charge of their lives.
4. People with a disability are highly differentiated as individuals. Their disability is only one aspect, albeit an important one, of the totality of their lives. They rightfully can participate in the broadest scope of life's activities.
5. The extent of limitations is as much a function of physical and social environmental barriers, if not more so, than of personal disability.
6. Inclusion through reasonable accommodations widens opportunities for everybody and provides a strong counterforce against exclusion and prejudice.
7. Recognition of the responsibility of both parties in situations

involving interpersonal relations contributes to constructive views of life with a disability.

8. To influence attitudes positively, such constructive views must be conveyed through information and direct experience.

9. In all attitude change attempts, the negatives associated with the disability of the person and with lacks in the environment must be placed within a context where positive forces can counteract the distorting power of both negative-spread effects and the "just world phenomenon."

10. The positive context consists of two major parts. One refers to the assets and abilities of the person with a disability, the other to the hidden resources and forces in society which are there to be tapped and strengthened in the effort to bring about needed change.

11. The positives must not remain hidden and neglected when problems are being emphasized.

12. The thrust should be to seek solutions to problems, not to remain stuck with them.

13. Competitive situations are not conducive to improving attitudes toward those who suffer by comparison. What is needed is a climate that values the intrinsic worth of people and their abilities, not their comparative standing.

14. Attempts to change attitudes through simulating a disability in awareness training, through educational programs, and through direct contact with people with disabilities will benefit from the application of these principles.

15. There are many psychological snares that lead the unwary change-agent astray. In fact, all service providers, researchers, agency personnel, and others could well become cognizant of these principles. What they do and what they say impact heavily on public attitudes as well as on the lives of people with disabilities.

Bibliography

Abramson, A. S. The human community in the rehabilitation process. *Arch. Phys. Med. Rehabil.*, 1968, *49*, 60–65.

Abramson, A. S., Kutner, B., Rosenberg, P., Berger, R., & Weiner, H. A therapeutic community in a general hospital: Adaptation to a rehabilitation service. *J. Chronic Dis.*, 1963, *16*, 179–186.

Adler, A. *Study of organ inferiority and its psychical compensations.* New York: Nervous and Mental Disease Publishing Co., 1917a.

Adler, A. *The neurotic constitution.* New York: Moffat, Yard, 1917b.

Adler, M. J., & Van Doren, C. *How to read a book* (Rev. ed). New York: Simon & Schuster, 1972.

Adorno, T. W., Frenkel-Brunswik, E., Levinson, D. J., & Sanford, R. N. *The authoritarian personality.* New York: Harper & Row, 1950.

Alexander, F. Remarks about the relation of inferiority feelings to guilt feelings. *Int. J. Psychoanal.*, 1938, *19*, 41–49.

Allen, F. H., & Pearson, G. H. J. The emotional problems of the physically handicapped child. *Br. J. Med. Psychol.*, 1928, *8*, 212–236.

Allport, G. W. *Personality: A psychological interpretation.* New York: Holt, Rinehart and Winston, 1937.

Allport, G. W. The ego in contemporary psychology. *Psychol. Rev.*, 1943, *50*, 451–478.

Allport, G. W. *The nature of prejudice.* Reading, Mass.: Addison-Wesley, 1954.

Allport, G. W., & Kramer, B. M. Some roots of prejudice. *J. Psychol.*, 1946, *22*, 9–39.

Allport, G. W., & Vernon, P. E. *Studies in expressive movement.* New York: Macmillan, 1933.

American Psychiatric Association. *Diagnostic and statistical manual of mental disorders* (3d ed.). Washington, D.C.: 1980.

American Psychological Association. *Ethical standards of psychologists.* Washington, D.C.: 1977.

Anderson, T. P. An alternative frame of reference for rehabilitation: The helping process versus the medical model. *Arch. Phys. Med. Rehabil.*, 1975, *56*, 101–104.

Anthony, W. A. The effects of contact on an individual's attitude toward disabled persons. *Rehabil. Counseling Bull.*, 1969, *12*, 168–171.

Antler, L., Lee, M. H. M., Zaretsky, H. H., Pezenik, D. P., & Halberstam, J. L. Attitude of rehabilitation patients towards the wheelchair. *J. Psychol.*, 1969, *73*, 45–52.

Arluck, E. W. A study of some personality characteristics of epileptics. *Arch. Psychol.*, 1941, *37*, 263.

Asch, S. E. Forming impressions of personality. *J. Abnorm. Soc. Psychol.*, 1946, *41*, 258–290.

Asch, S. E. *Social psychology.* Englewood Cliffs N.J.: Prentice-Hall, 1952.

Asher, N. W. Manipulating attraction toward the disabled: An application of the similarity attraction model. *Rehabil. Psychol.*, 1973, *20*, 156–164.

Ashmore, R. D. Solving the problem of prejudice. In B. E. Collins, *Social psychology.* Reading, Mass.: Addison-Wesley, 1970.

Ausubel, D. P. *Ego development and the personality disorders.* New York: Grune & Stratton, 1952.

Baker, L. *Out on a limb.* New York, London: McGraw-Hill, 1946.

Baldwin, A. L. *Behavior and development in childhood.* New York: Dryden, 1955.

Balunas, L. C. A study of the relationship of acceptance of disability in self and presence of disability in others to subordination of physique in the social perceptions of men with physical disabilities. *Diss. Abstr. Int.*, 1972, *32*, 5335A.

Bandura, A. *Principles of behavior modification.* New York: Holt, Rinehart and Winston, 1969.

Bandura, A. The self system in reciprocal determinism. *Am. Psychol.*, 1978, *33*, 344–358.

Barker, R. G. The effect of frustration upon cognitive ability. *Charact. Pers.*, 1938, *7*, 145–150.

Barker, R. G. The social psychology of physical disability. *J. Soc. Issues*, 1948, *4*, (4), 28–38.

Barker, R. G., & Associates. *Habitats, environments and human behavior.* San Francisco: Jossey-Bass, 1978.

Barker, R. G. Dembo, T., & Lewin, K. Frustration and regression: An experiment with young children. *Univ. of Iowa Stud. Child Welf.*, 1941, *18* (1).

Barker, R. G., & Wright, B. A. The social psychology of adjustment to physical disability. In J. F. Garrett (Ed.), *Psychological aspects of physical disability.* Dept. of Health, Education, & Welf., Office of Vocational Rehabil., Rehabil. Service Series, 1952, (210), 18–32.

Barker, R. G., & Wright, B. A. Disablement: The somatopsychological problem. In E. D. Wittkower & R. A. Cleghorn (Eds.), *Recent developments in psychosomatic medicine.* Philadelphia: Lippincott. 1954, 419–435.

Barker, R. G., Wright, B. A., & Gonick, M. R. *Adjustment to physical handicap and illness: A survey of the social psychology of physique and disability.* New York: Soc. Sci. Res. Council, Bull. 55, 1946.

Barker, R. G., Wright, B. A., Myerson, L., & Gonick, M. R. *Adjustment to physical handicap and illness: A survey of the social psychology of physique and disability* (2d ed.). New York: Soc. Sci. Res. Council, Bull. 55, 1953.

Barker, R. G., & Wright, H. F. One of a series of records made in connection with the natural living conditions of children 1948–1951. See following reference. Spencer library, Univ. of Kansas, Lawrence, Ks.

Barker, R. G., & Wright, H. F. *Midwest and its children: The psychological ecology of an American town.* New York: Harper & Row, 1955.

Barron, M. E. Role practice in interview training. *Sociatry,* 1947, *1,* 198–208.

Barry, J. R. Behavioral classification of the physically disabled. *Psychol. Aspects of Disability,* 1971, *18,* 136–142.

Batson, C. D. Attribution as a mediator of bias in helping. *J. Pers. Soc. Psychol.,* 1975, *32,* 455–466.

Batson, C. D., & Coke, J. S. Empathic motivation of helping behavior. In J. T. Caccioppo & R. E. Petty (Eds.), *Social psychophysiology.* New York: Guilford Press, 1983.

Bavelas, A. Morale and the training of leaders. In G. Watson (Ed.), *Civilian morale.* New York: Reynal & Hitchcock 1942, 143–165.

Bavelas, A. Role playing and management training. *Sociatry,* 1947, *1,* 183–191.

Bellack, A. S., & Hersen, M. *Research and practice in social skills training.* New York: Plenum Press, 1979.

Berger, E. M. The relation between expressed acceptance of self and expressed acceptance of others. *J. Abnorm. Soc. Psychol.,* 1952, *4,* 778–783.

Berkowitz, L. Reactance and the unwillingness to help others. *Psychol. Bull.,* 1973, *79,* 310–317.

Berkowitz, L., & Daniels, L. Responsibility and dependency. *J. Ab. Soc. Psychol.,* 1963, *66,* 429–436.

Bettelheim, B. Individual and mass behavior in extreme situations. *J. Abnorm. Soc. Psychol.,* 1943, *38,* 417–452.

Bice, H. V. Fathers participate in counseling series. *Cereb. Palsy Rev.,* 1950 *11,* 1–6.

Bice, H. V. Parent counseling and parent education. In W. M. Cruickshank & G. M. Raus (Eds.), *Cerebral palsy: Its individual and community problems.* Syracuse Univ. Press, 1955, 411–428.

Blake, R. R., & Ramsey, G. V. (Eds.). *Perception—An approach to personality.* New York: Ronald Press, 1951.

Blake, R. R., Rosenbaum, M., & Duryea, R. A. Gift-giving as a function of group standards. *Hum. Relations,* 1955, *8,* 61–73.

Blakeslee, H. *Know your heart.* Public Affairs Pamphlet (137), New York, 1948.

Blank, H. R. Psychoanalysis and blindness. *Psychoanalytic Quart.,* 1957, *26,* 1–24.

Boorstein, S. W. *Orthopedics for the teachers of crippled children.* New York: Aiden, 1935.

Borman, L. D., & Lieberman, M. A. (Eds.). Self-help groups. *J. Appl. Behav. Sci.,* 1976, *12,* 261–463. (Special issue.)

Bowe, F. *Handicapping America: Barriers to disabled people.* New York: Harper & Row, 1978.

Bowe, F. *Rehabilitating America: Toward independence for disabled and elderly people.* New York: Harper & Row, 1980.

Brehm, J. W. *A theory of psychological reactance.* New York: Academic Press, 1966.

Brehm, S. S., & Brehm, J. W. *Psychological reactance: A theory of freedom and control.* New York: Academic Press, 1981.

Brickey, M. Normalization and behavior modification in the workshop. *J. Rehabil.,* 1974, *40*(6), 15–16, 41, 44–46.

Brighouse, G. *The physically handicapped worker in industry.* Pasadena: California Institute of Technology, Bull. 13, 1946.

Brightman, A. J. (Proj. Dir.). *Feeling free.* Workshop on Child Awareness, American Institutes for Research, Cambridge, Mass.: 1977. (Film)

Brown, C. *My left foot.* New York: Simon & Schuster, 1955.

Brown, M. M. Parental hopes for disabled and non-disabled siblings. Master's thesis, Univ. of Kansas, Lawrence, Ks., 1968.

Bruck, L. *Access: The guide to a better life for disabled Americans.* New York: Random House, 1978.

Bruckner, L. S. *Triumph of love.* New York: Simon & Schuster, 1954.

Bruner, J. S. Personality dynamics and the process of perceiving. In R. P. Blake & G. V. Ramsey (Eds.), *Perception—An approach to personality.* New York: Ronald Press, 1951, 121–147.

Bruner, J. S., & Postman, L. An approach to social perception. In W. Dennis (Ed.), *Current trends in social psychology.* Pittsburgh: Univ. of Pittsburgh Press, 1948, 71–118.

Bruner, J. S., & Postman, L. On the perception of incongruity: A paradigm. *J. Pers.,* 1949 *18,* 206–223.

Brunschwig, L. *A study of some personality aspects of deaf children.* New York: Teachers College, Columbia Univ., 1936.

Brunswik, E. *Systematic and representative design of psychological experiments.* Berkeley: Univ. of California Press., 1947.

Brunswik, E. *Perception and the representative design of psychological experiments* (2nd ed.) Berkeley: Univ. of California Press, 1956.

Bryan, J. H., & Test, M. A. Models and helping: Naturalistic studies in aiding behavior. *J. Personality Soc. Psychol.,* 1967, *6,* 400–407.

Buck, P. S. *The child who never grew.* Middlebury, Vt.: Paul S. Eriksson, Pub., 1950.

Buros, O. K. *The eighth mental measurements yearbook* (2 vols.). Highland Park, N.J.: The Gryphon Press, 1978.

Butts, S. V. Relationships among comparative evaluation, spread and coping effectiveness. Master's thesis, Univ. of Kansas, 1962.

Butts, S. V., & Shontz, F. C. Comparative evaluation and its relation to coping-effectiveness. *Am. Psychol.*, 1962, *17,* 326. (Abstract)

Calder, B. J., & Staw, B. M. Self-perception of intrinsic and extrinsic motivation. *J. Pers. Soc. Psychol.*, 1975, *31,* 599–605.

Cameron, P., Titus, D. G., Kostin, J., & Kostin, M. The life satisfaction of nonnormal persons. *J. Consulting Clin. Psychol.*, 1973, *41,* 207–214.

Cantor, A. J. General semantics of ambulatory proctology. In A. J. Cantor & A. N. Foxe (Eds.), *Psychosomatic aspects of surgery.* New York: Grune & Stratton, 1956, 78–88.

Cantor, A. J., & Foxe, A. N. (Eds.). *Psychosomatic aspects of surgery.* New York: Grune & Stratton, 1956.

Cappaert, A. Confusing definitions of independence. *Rehabil. Gaz.*, 1979, *22,* 25–26.

Carlson, E. R. *Born that way.* Middlebury, Vt.: Paul S. Eriksson, Pubs., 1941.

Cartwright, D. The effect of interruption, completion, and failure upon the attractiveness of activities. *J. Exp. Psychol.*, 1942, *31,* 1–16.

Cartwright, D., & Harary, F. Structural balance: A generalization of Heider's theory. *Psychol. Rev.*, 1956, *63,* 277–293.

Cattell, E., Dembo, T., Koppel, S., Tane-Baskin, E., & Weinstock, S. Social usefulness of the cosmetic glove. Unpublished, Research Division, College of Engineering, New York Univ., 1949. See Dembo & Tane-Baskin, 1955, for publication of part of the above.

Caywood, T. A quadriplegic young man looks at treatment. *J. Rehabil.*, 1940, *40*(6), 22–25.

Centers, L., & Centers, R. Peer group attitudes toward the amputee child. *J. Soc. Psychol.*, 1963, *61,* 127–132.

Chesler, M. A. Ethnocentrism and attitudes toward the physically disabled. *J. Pers. Soc. Psychol.*, 1965, *2,* 877–882.

Chevigny, H. *My eyes have a cold nose.* New Haven: Yale Univ. Press., 1946.

Chigier, E. Sexual adjustment of the handicapped. *Proc. 12th World Cong. Rehabil. Int.*, 1972, 224–227.

Cholden, L. Some psychiatric problems in the rehabilitation of the blind. *Bull. Menninger Clin.*, 1954, *18,* 107–112.

Citron, A. F., Chein, I., & Harding, J. Anti-minority remarks: A problem for action research, *J. Abnorm. Soc. Psychol.*, 1950, *45,* 99–126.

Citron, A. F., & Harding, J. An experiment in training volunteers to answer anti-minority remarks. *J. Abnorm. Soc. Psychol.*, 1950, *45,* 310–328.

Clapp, M. L. *You won't believe it.* Unpublished, circa 1976.

Cobun, J. M. Attitude changes in vocational rehabilitation counselors related to the physically disabled during induction preparation. *Diss. Abstr. Int.*, 1972, *33,* 4084A.

Cohen, J., & Struening, E. L. Factors underlying opinions about mental illness in the personnel of two large mental hospitals. *J. Abnorm. Soc. Psychol.*, 1962, *64,* 349–360.

Coleman, R. L. Organ inferiority and personality. *Diss. Abstr. Int.*, 1973, *33*, 5373B.

Collins, B. E., & Ashmore, R. D. *Social psychology.* Reading, Mass.: Addison-Wesley, 1970.

Combs, R. H., & Harper, J. L. Effects of labels on attitudes of educators toward handicapped children. *Exceptional Child.*, 1967, *33*, 399–403.

Comer, R. C., & Piliavin, J. A. As others see us: Attitudes of physically handicapped and normals toward own and other groups. *Rehabil. Literature*, 1975, *36*, 206–221, 225.

Condry, J. Enemies of exploration: Self-initiated versus other-initiated learning. *J. Pers. Soc. Psychol.*, 1977, *35*, 459–477.

Conference of Executives of Schools for the Deaf. Report of the conference committee on nomenclature. *Am. Ann. Deaf*, 1938, *83*, 1–3.

Cook, D. W. Psychological aspects of spinal cord injury. *Rehabil. Counseling Bull.*, 1976, *19*, 535–543.

Cordaro, L. L., & Shontz, F. C. Psychological situations as determinants of self-evaluations. *J. Counseling Psychol.*, 1969, *16*, 575–578.

Cowen, E. L. & Brobrove, P. H. Marginality of disability and adjustment. *Perceptual and Motor Skills*, 1966, *23*, 869–870.

Cowen, E. L., Underberg, R., & Verrillo, R. T. The development and testing of an attitudes to blindness scale. *J. Soc. Psychol.*, 1958, *48*, 297–304.

Criddle, R. *Love is not blind.* New York: Norton, 1953.

Cruickshank, W. M. The impact of physical disability on social adjustment. *J. Soc. Issues.*, 1948, *4*(4), 78–83.

Cruickshank, W. M. Educational planning for the cerebral palsied. In W. M. Cruickshank & G. M. Raus (Eds.), *Cerebral palsy: Its individual and community problems.* Syracuse: Syracuse Univ. Press, 1955, 333–369.

Cruickshank, W. M., & Bice, H. V. Personality characteristics. In W. M. Cruickshank & G. M. Raus (Eds.), *Cerebral palsy: Its individual and community problems.* Syracuse: Syracuse Univ. Press, 1955, 115–165.

Crutchfield, R. S. Conformity and character. *Am. Psychologist*, 1955, *10*, 191–198.

Cutsforth, T. D. Personality crippling through physical disability. *J. Soc. Issues.*, 1948, *4*(4), 62–67.

Daniels, A. S. I don't want to be different. *Crippled Child*, 1948, *26*(4), 20.

Davis, F. *Passage through crisis: Polio victims and their families.* New York: Bobbs-Merrill, 1963.

Deci, E. L. *Intrinsic motivation.* New York: Plenum Press, 1975.

DeJong, G. Independent living: From social movement to analytic paradigm. *Arch. Phys. Med. Rehabil.* 1979, *60*, 435–446.

Dembo, T. The dynamics of anger. In de Rivera, J., *Field theory as human science: Contributions of Lewin's Berlin group.* New York: Gardner Press, 1976. (Trans. from *Psychologishe Forschung*, 1931, *15*, 1–144.)

Dembo, T. Investigation of concrete psychological value systems. Report submitted to the U.S. Public Health Services, Inst. of Mental Health, 1953a.

Dembo, T. Devaluation of the physically handicapped person. Paper presented at Am. Psychol. Assoc., Cleveland, 1953b.

Dembo, T. Suffering and its alleviation: A theoretical analysis. Report submitted to the Assoc. for the Aid of Crippled Children, New York, 1955.

Dembo, T. Sensitivity of one person to another. *Rehabil. Literature,* 1964, *25,* 231–235.

Dembo. T. The utilization of psychological knowledge in rehabilitation. *Welfare Rev.,* 1970, *8*(4), 1–7.

Dembo. T. *Competitive and intrinsic values.* Unpublished manuscript, Clark University, 1974.

Dembo, T., Leviton, G. L., & Wright, B. A. Adjustment to misfortune: A problem of social-psychological rehabilitation. *Artificial Limbs,* 1956, *3*(2), 4–62. (Reprinted in *Rehabil. Psychol.,* 1975, *22,* 1–100.)

Dembo, T., & Tane-Baskin, E. The noticeability of the cosmetic glove. *Artificial Limbs,* 1955, *2,* 47–56.

Dibner, S. S., & Dibner, A. S. *Integration or segregation for the physically handicapped child?* Springfield, Ill.: Charles C Thomas, 1973.

Dienstbier, R. A. Positive and negative prejudice: Interactions of prejudice with race and social desirability. *J. Pers.,* 1970, *38,* 198–215.

Dinkel, R. M. The influence of nursery literature on child development. *Sociology and Soc. Res.,* 1947, *31,* 285–290.

Dollard, J., Doob, L. W., Miller, N. E., Mowrer, O. H., & Sears, R. R. *Frustration and aggression.* New Haven: Yale Univ. Press, 1939.

Donaldson, J., & Martinson, M. C. Modifying attitudes toward physically disabled persons. *Exceptional Child.,* 1977 *43,* 337–341.

Donofrio, A. F. A study of the intelligence, achievement and emotional adjustment of crippled children in an orthopedic hospital school. Doctoral dissertation, New York Univ., 1948.

Doob, A. N., & Ecker, B. P. Stigma and compliance. *J. Pers. Soc. Psychol.,* 1970, *14,* 302–304.

Dow, T. E. Social class and reaction to physical disability. *Psychol. Rep.,* 1965, *17,* 39–62.

Duncker, K. On problem solving, *Psychol. Monogr.,* 1945, *58,* 1–112.

El Ghatit, A., & Hanson, R. Marriage and divorce after spinal cord injury. *Arch. Phys. Med. Rehabil.,* 1976, *57,* 470–472.

Ellis, A. *The American sexual tragedy.* New York: Twayne Publishers, 1954.

English, W. R. Correlates of stigma towards physically disabled persons. *Rehabil. Res. Practice Rev.* 1971a, *2*(4), 1–17.

English, W. R. Assessment, modification and stability of attitudes toward blindness. *Psychol. Aspects Disability,* 1971b, *18*(2), 79–85.

English, W. R., & Oberle, J. B. Toward the development of new methodology for examining attitudes toward disabled persons. *Rehabil. Counseling Bull.,* 1971, *15,* 88–96.

Estes, S. G. Judging personality from expressive behavior. *J. Abnorm. Soc. Psychol.,* 1938 *33,* 217–236.

Evans, J. H. Changing attitudes toward disabled persons. An experimental study. *Rehabil. Counseling Bull.,* 1976, *19,* 572–579.

Faterson, H. F., as reported by Paterson, D. G. *Physique and Intellect.* New York: Appleton-Century-Crofts, 1930.

Faterson, H. F. Organic inferiority and the inferiority attitude. *J. Soc. Psychol.,* 1931, *2,* 87–101.

Feagin, J. R. Poverty: We still believe that God helps those who help themselves. *Psychol. Today*, 1972, *6*(6), 101–110.

Feldman, S. Motivational aspects of attitudinal elements and their place in cognitive interaction. In S. Feldman (Ed.) *Cognitive consistency: Motivational antecedents and behavioral consequences.* New York: Academic Press, 1966.

Fenichel, O. *The psychoanalytic theory of neurosis.* New York: Norton, 1945.

Festinger, L. Group attraction and membership. In D. Cartwright & A. Zander (Eds.), *Group dynamics: Research and theory.* New York: Harper & Row, 1953, 92–101.

Festinger, L. A theory of social comparison processes. *Hum. Relations*, 1954, *7*, 117–140.

Fey, W. F. Acceptance by others and its relation to acceptance of self and others: A revaluation. *J. Abnorm. Soc. Psychol.*, 1955, *50*, 274–276.

Fiedler, F. E., Warrington, W. G., & Blaisdell, F. J. Unconscious attitudes as correlates of sociometric choice in a social group. *J. Abnorm. Soc. Psychol.*, 1952, *47*, 790–796.

Fielding, B. B. Attitudes and aspects of adjustment of the orthopedically handicapped woman. Unpublished doctoral dissertation, Columbia Univ., 1950.

Fink, S. L. Crisis and motivation: A theoretical model. *Arch. Phys. Med. Rehabil.*, 1967, *48*, 592–597.

Finkelstein, V. *Attitudes and disabled people: Issues for discussion.* New York: World Rehabilitation Fund, 1980.

Fischer, C. T. The testee as co-evaluator. *J. Counseling Psychol.*, 1970, *70*, 70–76.

Fischer, C. T. Paradigm changes which allow sharing of results. *Prof. Psychol.*, 1972, *3*, 364–369.

Fisher, S., & Cleveland, S. E. *Body image and personality.* New York: Van Nostrand Reinhold, 1968.

Fishman, S. Self-concept and adjustment to leg prosthesis. Unpublished doctoral dissertation, Columbia Univ., 1949.

Fitzgerald, D. C. Success-failure and T.A.T. reactions of orthopedically handicapped and physically normal adolescents. *J. Pers.*, 1950, *1*, 67–83.

Flavell, J. H. The developmental psychology of Jean Piaget. New York: Van Nostrand Reinhold, 1963.

Forader, A. T. *Modification of social attitudes toward the disabled by three modes of instruction.* Unpublished doctoral dissertation, Univ. of Massachusetts, 1969.

Ford, H., in collaboration with S. Crowther *My life and work.* New York: Doubleday, 1926.

Fordyce, W. E. Behavioral methods in rehabilitation. In W. S. Neff (Ed.), *Rehabil. Psychol.* Washington, D.C.: Am. Psychol. Assoc., 1971.

Foster, I. A. How to cope with teen age problems. *Crippled Child*, 1948, *27*(4), 9.

French, J. R. P., Jr. Retraining an autocratic leader. *J. Abnorm. Soc. Psychol.*, 1944, *39*, 224–237.

French, J. R. P., Jr. Role-playing as a method of training foremen. In J. L.

Moreno (Ed.), *Group psychotherapy.* Beacon, N.Y.: Beacon House, 1945, 172–187.

Freud, S. *Complete psychological works* (Vol. 19). London: Hogarth, 1961.

Friedman, S. B., Chodoff, P., Mason, J. W., & Hamburg, D. A. Behavioral observations on parents anticipating the death of a child. *Pediatrics,* 1963, *32,* 610–625.

Fromm, E. Selfishness and self-love. *Psychiatry,* 1939, *2,* 507–523.

Galassi, M. D., & Galassi, J. P. Assertion: A critical review. *Psychotherapy: Theor. Res. Pract.,* 1978, *15*(1) 16–29.

Garrett, J. F. (Ed.). *Psychological aspects of physical disability.* Washington, D.C.: U.S. Government Printing Office, Office of Vocational Rehabilitation, Rehabilitation Service Series 210, 1952.

Garrett, J. F. Realistic vocational guidance and placement. In W. M. Cruickshank & G. M. Raus (Eds.), *Cerebral palsy: Its individual and community problems.* Syracuse: Syracuse Univ. Press, 1955, 429–461.

Garrett, J. F., & Levine, E. S. (Eds.) *Rehabilitation practices with the physically disabled.* New York: Columbia Univ. Press, 1973.

Garris, A. G. How mechanical devices and adaptive behavior can aid in the rehabilitation of severely disabled persons. In R. E. Hardy & J. G. Cull (Eds.), *Severe disabilities: Social and rehabilitation approaches.* New York: Charles C Thomas, 1974.

Gebhard, M. E. The effect of success and failure upon the attractiveness of activities as a function of experience, expectation, and need. *J. Exp. Psychol.,* 1948, *38,* 371–388.

Gergen, K. J., & Jones, E. E. Mental illness, predictability and affective consequences as stimulus factors in person perception. *J. Ab. Soc. Psychol.,* 1963, *67,* 95–104.

Gilmore, L. *New fountains* (An American Theatre Wing Community Play). New York: Nat. Foundation for Infantile Paralysis, 1953.

Glick, S. J. *Vocational, educational, and recreational needs of the cerebral palsied adult.* New York: United Cerebral Palsy, 1953.

Gliedman, J. & Roth, W. *The unexpected minority: Handicapped children in America.* New York: Harcourt Brace Jovanovich, 1980.

Goffman, E. *Stigma.* Englewood Cliffs, N. J.: Prentice-Hall, 1963.

Goldberg, L. R. Differential attribution of trait-descriptive terms to oneself as compared to well-liked, neutral, and disliked others: A psychometric analysis. *J. Pers. Soc. Psychol.,* 1978, *36,* 1012–1028.

Goldman, R. L. *Even the night.* New York: Macmillan, 1947.

Goldsmith, S. *Designing for the disabled.* New York: McGraw-Hill, 1967.

Goodwin, L. Middle-class misperceptions of the high life aspirations and strong work ethic held by the welfare poor. *Am. J. Orthopsychiatry,* 1973, *43,* 554–564.

Goodwin, R. B. *It's good to be black.* Garden City, N.Y.: Doubleday, 1953.

Grand, S. A. Reactions to unfavorable evaluations of the self as a function of acceptance of disability: A test of Dembo, Leviton, and Wright's misfortune hypothesis. *J. Counseling Psychol.,* 1972, *19,* 87–93.

Haber, L. D. Some parameters for social policy in disability: A cross-national comparison. *Health and Society,* 1973, *51,* 319–340.

Haefner, D. Some effects of guilt-arousing and fear-arousing persuasive communications on opinion change. *Technical Report No. 1, Office of Naval Research,* Contract No. Nonr 668 (12), 1956.

Haire, M., & Grunes, W. F. Perceptual defenses: Processes protecting an organized perception of another personality. *Hum. Relations,* 1950, *3,* 403–412.

Hamera, E. K., & Shontz, F. C. Perceived positive and negative effects of life-threatening illness. *J. Psychosom. Res.,* 1978, *22,* 419–424.

Hamilton, K. W. *Counseling the handicapped in the rehabilitation process.* New York: Ronald Press, 1950.

Hanks, J. R., & Hanks, L. M., Jr. The physically handicapped in certain non-occidental societies. *J. Soc. Issues,* 1948, *4*(4), 11–20.

Harding, J., Proshansky, H., Kutner, B., & Chein, I. Prejudice and ethnic relations. In G. Lindsey & E. Aronson (Eds.), *Handbook of social psychology* (Vol. V). Reading, Mass.: Addison-Wesley, 1970.

Harris, R. *Effect of perspective taking, interpersonal similarity and dependency on raising funds for persons with disabilities.* Unpublished doctoral dissertation, Univ. of Kansas, 1975.

Harrison, A. A. Mere exposure. In L. Berkowitz (Ed.), *Advances in experimental social psychology* (Vol. 10). New York: Academic Press, 1977.

Harrower, H. R., & Herrmann, R. *Psychological factors in the care of patients with multiple sclerosis for use of physicians.* New York: National Multiple Sclerosis Society, 1953.

Harvey, J. H., Ickes, W., & Kidd, R. F. (Eds.) *New directions in attribution research* (Vol. 3). Hillsdale, N. J.: Erlbaum Associates, 1981.

Hathaway, K. B. *The little locksmith.* New York: Coward-McCann, 1943.

Hebb, D. O. On the nature of fear. *Psychol. Rev.,* 1946, *53,* 259–276.

Heider, F. Ding und Medium. *Symposion,* 1926, *1,* 109–157.

Heider, F. Social perception and phenomenal causality. *Psychol. Rev.,* 1944, *51,* 358–374.

Heider, F. *The psychology of interpersonal relations.* New York: Wiley, 1958. (Republished by Erlbaum, Hillside, N.J.)

Heider, F., & Heider, G. M. Studies in the psychology of the deaf, No. 2. *Psychol. Monogr.,* 1941, *53*(5).

Heisler, V. T. Goal setting behavior of crippled and non-crippled children in situations of success and failure. Unpublished doctoral dissertation, Stanford Univ., 1951.

Heisler, V. A handicapped child in the family: A guide for parents. New York: Grune & Stratton, 1972.

Held, R. Plasticity in sensory motor systems. *Sci. Am.,* 1965, *213,* 84–90.

Helping the physically limited child. Board of Education, New York, N.Y., Curriculum Bull., Series No. 7, 1952–1953.

Henderson, L. T. *The opening doors.* Middlebury, Vt.: Paul S. Eriksson, Pubs., 1954.

Hentig, H. von. *The criminal and his victim.* New Haven: Yale Univ. Press, 1948a.

Hentig, H. von. Physical disability, mental conflict and social crisis. *J. Soc. Issues,* 1948b, *4*(4), 21–27.

Higbee, K. 15 years of fear arousal: Research on threat appeals (1953–1968). *Psychol. Bull.*, 1969, *72*, 426–444.

Hilgard, E. R., & Russell, D. H. Motivation in school learning. *Yearb. Nat. Soc. Stud. Educ.*, 1950 *49* (Part I), 36–68.

Hinton, J. Facing death. *J. Psychosom. Res.*, 1966, *10*, 22–28.

Hirsch, E. A. *Starting over: The autobiographical account of a psychologist's experience with multiple sclerosis.* North Quincy, Mass.: Christopher Publishing House, 1977.

Hobbs, N. *The futures of children.* San Francisco: Jossey-Bass, 1975.

Hohmann, G. W. Considerations in management of psycho-sexual readjustment in the cord injured male. *Rehabil. Psychol.*, 1972, *19*, 50–58.

Holst, J. C. The occurrence of blindness in Norway, *Am. J. Ophthalmology*, 1952, *35*, 1153–1166.

Honig, W. K., & Staddon, J. E. R. *Handbook of operant behavior.* Englewood, Cliffs, N. J.: Prentice-Hall, 1977.

Horney, K. *The neurotic personality of our time.* New York: Norton, 1937.

Hughes, E. C. Dilemmas and contradictions of status. *Am. J. Sociol.*, 1945, *50*, 353–359.

Hunt, J. M. How children develop intellectually. *Children*, 1964, *11*, 83–91.

Hurlock, E. B. An evaluation of certain incentives used in school work. *J. Educ. Psychol.*, 1925, *16*, 145–159.

Ichheiser, G. Misunderstandings in human relations. *Am. J. Sociol.*, 1949, *55* (supplement to No. 2), 1–70.

Including Me. (Public broadcasting television program, Lawrence, Kansas) September 15, 1977.

Institute for Physical Medicine and Rehabilitation. *Primer for paraplegics and quadriplegics.* Patient Publication No. 1, New York Univ., Bellevue Medical Center, 1957.

Interrelationships between perception and personality. (Symposium.) *J. Pers.*, 1949, *18*, 1–266.

Issner N. Can the child be distracted from his disease? *J. Sch. Health*, 1973, *43*, 468–471.

Jaffee, J. *Attitudes of adolescents toward persons with disabilities.* Unpublished doctoral dissertation, Columbia Univ., 1965.

Jaffee, J. What's in a name? Attitudes toward disabled persons. *Pers. Guidance J.*, 1967, *45*, 557–560.

Janis, I. L. *Psychological stress: Psychoanalytic and behavioral studies of surgical patients.* New York: Wiley, 1958.

Janis, I. L., & Feshbach, S. The effects of fear-arousing communications. *J. Abnorm. Soc. Psychol.*, 1953, *48*, 78–92.

Johnson, D. L. A study of rigidity in the personality of deaf children. Master's thesis, Univ. of Kansas, 1954.

Johnson, W. *People in quandaries.* New York: Harper & Row, 1946.

Johnson, W. Open letter to the parent of a stuttering child. *Crippled Child*, 1950, *28*(3), 7–9.

Jones, E. E., & Goethals, G. R. Order effects in impression formation: Attribution context and the nature of the entity. In E. E. Jones, et al. *Attribu-*

tion: Perceiving the causes of behavior. Morristown, N. J.: General Learning Press, 1971.

Jones, E. E., Kanouse, D. E., Kelley, H. H., Nisbett, R. E., Valins, S., & Weiner, B. *Attribution: Perceiving the causes of behavior.* Morristown, N. J.: General Learning Press, 1971.

Jones, E. E., & Nisbett, R. E. The actor and the observer: Divergent perceptions of the causes of behavior. In E. E. Jones et al. *Attribution: Perceiving the causes of behavior.* Morristown, N. J.: General Learning Press, 1971.

Jordan, J. E. Attitude-behavior research on physical-mental-social disability and racial-ethnic differences. *Psychol. Aspects Disability,* 1971, *18*(1), 5–26.

Jordan, J. E. Attitude-behaviors toward the disabled and disadvantaged. *Proc. 12th World Congr. Rehabil. Int.,* Sydney, Australia, 1972, 796–800.

Kahle, L. R., & Berman, J. J. Attitudes cause behaviors: A cross-lagged panel analysis, *J. Pers. Soc. Psychol.,* 1979, *37,* 315–321.

Kahn, H. A comparative investigation of the responses to frustration of normal-hearing and hypacousic children. Ann Arbor: Univ. Microfilms, Publication No. 2766. Brief summary appears in *Microfilm Abstr. 1951, 11,* 959–960.

Kammerer, R. C. An exploratory psychological study of crippled children. *Psychol. Rec.,* 1940, *4,* 47–100.

Kanfer, F. H., & Goldstein, A. P. (Eds.). *Helping people change* (2nd ed.). New York: Pergamon Press. 1980.

Kanouse, D. E., & Hanson, L. R., Jr. Negativity in evaluations. In E. E. Jones et al., *Attribution: Perceiving the causes of behavior.* Morristown, N. J.: General Learning Press, 1971.

Katz, A. H., & Bender, E. I. *The strength in us.* New York: Franklin Watts, 1976.

Katz, D., & Braly, K. Racial stereotypes of one hundred college students. *J. Abnorm. Soc. Psychol.,* 1933, *28,* 280–290.

Katz, I., Glass, D. G., & Cohen, S. Ambivalence, guilt and the scapegoating of minority group victims. *J. Exp. Soc. Psychol.,* 1973, *9,* 423–436.

Katz, I., Glass, D. C., Lucido, D. J., & Farber, J. Ambivalence, guilt, and the denigration of a physically handicapped victim. *J. Pers.,* 1977, *45,* 419–429.

Keister, H. E. The behavior of young children in failure. *Univ. of Iowa Studies in Child Welfare,* 1937, *14,* 27–82.

Kelley, H. H. The warm-cold variable in first impressions of persons. *J. Pers.,* 1950, *18,* 431–439.

Kelley, H. H. Attribution theory in social psychology, In D. Levine (Ed.), *Nebraska symposium on motivation* (Vol. 15). Lincoln: Univ. of Nebraska Press, 1967.

Kelley, H. H. Process of causal attribution. *Am. Psychologist,* 1973, *28,* 107–128.

Kendall, P. C., & Hollon, S. D. *Cognitive-behavioral interventions: Theory, research, and procedures.* New York: Academic Press, 1979.

Kerby, C. E. A report on visual handicaps of partially seeing children. *J. Exceptional Child.*, 1952, *18*, 137–142.

Kerr, N. Staff expectations for disabled persons: Helpful or harmful. *Rehabil. Counseling Bull.*, 1970, *14*, 85–94.

Killilea, M. *Karen*. Englewood Cliffs: Prentice-Hall, 1952.

Kleck, R. Emotional arousal in interaction with stigmatized persons. *Psychol. Rep.*, 1966, *19*, 1226.

Kleck, R. Physical stigma and nonverbal cues emitted in face-to-face interaction. *Hum. Relations*, 1968a, *21*, 19–28.

Kleck, R. Self-disclosure patterns of the nonobviously stigmatized. *Psychol. Rep.*, 1968b, *23*, 1239–1248.

Kleck, R. Physical stigma and task oriented interaction. *Hum. Relations*, 1969, *22*(1), 53–60.

Kleck, R., Ono, H., & Hastorf, A. H. The effects of physical deviance upon face-to-face interaction. *Hum. Relations*, 1966, *19*, 425–436.

Kogan, N. Attitudes toward old people: The development of a scale and an examination of correlates. *J. Ab. Soc. Psychol.*, 1961, *62*, 44–54.

Kogan, N., & Wallach, M. A. Risk taking as a function of the situation, the person, and the group. In G. Mandler et al. (Eds.), *New directions in psychology* (Vol. 2). New York: Holt, Rinehart and Winston, 1967.

Köhler, W. *Gestalt psychology* (2nd ed.). New York: Liveright, 1947.

Korner, I. Hope as a method of coping. *J. Consulting Clin. Psychol.*, 1970, *34*, 134–139.

Korsch, B. M., & Negrete, V. F. Doctor-patient communication. *Sci. Am.*, 1972, *227*(2), 66–74.

Korzybski, A. The role of language in the perceptual processes. In R. R. Blake & G. V. Ramsey (Eds.), *Perception—An approach to personality*. New York: Ronald Press, 1951, 170–205.

Krant, M. *Dying and dignity: The meaning and control of a personal death.* Springfield, Ill.: Charles C Thomas, 1974.

Krebs, D. L. Empathy and altruism. *J. Pers. Soc. Psychol.*, 1975, *32*, 1134–1146.

Krebs, D. L., & Whitten, P. Guilt-edged giving: The shame of it all. *Psychol. Today*, Jan. 1972, *5*(8), 50–56.

Krech, D., & Crutchfield, R. S. *Theory and problems of social psychology*. New York: McGraw-Hill, 1948.

Kübler-Ross, E. *On death and dying*. New York: Macmillan, 1969.

Kübler-Ross, E. Psychotherapy for the dying patient. *Curr. Psychiatric Ther.*, 1970, *10*, 110–117.

Kübler-Ross, E. *Questions and answers on death and dying*. New York: Macmillan, 1974a.

Kübler-Ross, E. The languages of dying. *J. Clin. Child Psychol.*, 1974b, *3*, 22–24.

Kutner, B. Professional antitherapy. *J. Rehabil.*, 1969, *35*(6), 16–18.

Ladieu, G., Adler, D. L., & Dembo, T. Studies in adjustment to visible injuries: Social acceptance of the injured. *J. Soc. Issues*, 1948, *4*(4), 55–61.

Ladieu, G., Hanfmann, E., & Dembo, T. Studies in adjustment to visible injuries: Evaluation of help by the injured. *J. Abnorm. Soc. Psychol.*, 1947, *42*, 169–192.

Landis, C., & Bolles, M. M. *Personality and sexuality of the physically handicapped woman.* New York, London: Paul B. Hoeber, 1942.

Langdon, G., & Stout, I. W. *These well-adjusted children.* Middlebury, Vt.: Paul S. Eriksson, Pub., 1951.

Langer, E. J., Fiske, S., Taylor, S. E., & Chanowitz, B. Stigma, staring, and discomfort: A novel-stimulus hypothesis. *J. Exp. Soc. Psychol.*, 1976, *12*, 451–463.

Larsen, L. A., & Bricker, W. A. A manual for parents and teachers of severely and moderately retarded children. *Institute on Mental Retardation and Intellectual Development*, 1968, *5* (whole No. 22). Nashville: George Peabody College for Teachers.

Laycock, S. R., & Stevenson, G. S. Parents' problems with exceptional children. In the Education of exceptional children. *Yearb. Nat. Soc. Stud. Educ.*, 1950, *49* (Part II), 117–134.

Lazar, A. L., Gensley, J. T., Orpet, R. E. Changing attitudes of young mentally gifted children toward handicapped persons. *Exceptional Child.*, 1971, *37*, 600–602.

Lee, D. D. A linguistic approach to a system of values. In T. M. Newcomb & E. L. Hartley (Eds.), *Readings in social psychology.* New York: Holt, Rinehart and Winston, 1947.

Leek, D. F. Formation of impressions of persons with disability. Unpublished master's thesis. Univ. of Kansas, 1966.

Lepper, M. R., Greene, D., & Nisbett, R. E. Undermining children's intrinsic interest with extrinsic rewards: A test of the overjustification hypothesis. *J. Pers. Soc. Psychol.*, 1973, *28*, 129–137.

Lerner, M. J. The desire for justice and reactions to victims. In J. Macaulay & L. Berkowitz (Eds.), *Altruism and helping behavior.* New York: Academic Press, 1970.

Leventhal, H. Findings and theory in the study of fear communications. In L. Berkowitz (Ed.), *Advances in experimental social psychology* (Vol 5). New York: Academic Press, 1970.

Leviton, G. Professional and client viewpoints on rehabilitation issues. *Rehabil. Psychol.*, 1973, *20*, 1–80.

Levy, D. M. Body interest in children and hypochondriasis. *Amer. J. Psychiatry*, 1932, *12*, 295–315.

Lewin, G. W. Some characteristics of the socio-psychological life space of the epileptic patient. *Hum. relations*, 1957, *10*, 249–256.

Lewin, K. *A dynamic theory of personality.* New York: McGraw-Hill, 1935.

Lewin, K. *Principles of topological psychology.* New York: McGraw-Hill, 1936.

Lewin, K. The conceptual representation and measurement of psychological forces. *Contr. Psychol. Theory.*, *1*(4), 1938.

Lewin, K. Field theory and experiment in social psychology: Concepts and methods. *Am. J. Sociol.*, 1939, *44*, 868–896.

Lewin, K. *Resolving social conflicts.* Lewin, G. W. (Ed.). New York: Harper & Row, 1948.

Lewin, K., Dembo, T., Festinger, L., & Sears, P. S. Level of aspiration. In

J. H. Hunt (Ed.), *Personality and the behavior disorders.* New York: Ronald Press, 1944, 333–378.

Linduska, N. *My polio past.* New York: Farrar, Straus & Giroux, 1947.

Lindzey, G., & Rogolsky, S. Prejudice and identification of minority group membership. *J. Abnorm. Soc. Psychol.,* 1950, *45,* 37–53.

Linkowski, D. C. A scale to measure acceptance of disability. *Rehabil. Counseling Bull.,* 1971, *14,* 236–244.

Linkowski, D. C., & Dunn, M. A. Self-concept and acceptance of disability, *Rehabil. Counseling Bull.,* 1974, *18,* 28–32.

Lippitt, Ronald. An experimental study of authoritarian and democratic group atmospheres. Studies in topological and vector psychology. *Univ. of Iowa Studies in Child Welfare,* 1940, *16*(3), 44–195.

Lippitt, Ronald. The psychodrama in leadership training. *Sociometry,* 1943, *6,* 286–292.

Lippitt, Ronald. To be or not to be—a Jew. *J. soc. Issues,* 1945, *1,* 18–27.

Lippitt, Rosemary. Psychodrama in the home. *Sociatry,* 1947, *1,* 148–167.

Lombroso, C. *Crime, its causes and remedies.* (Translated by H. P. Horton.) Boston: Little, Brown, 1911.

Lowenfeld, B. *Our blind children: Growing and learning with them* (3rd ed.). Springfield, Ill.: Charles C Thomas, 1971.

Macgregor, F. C. Some psycho-social problems associated with facial deformities. *Amer. Soc. Rev.,* 1951 *16,* 629–638.

Macgregor, F. C., Abel, T. M., Bryt, A., Lauer, E., & Weissmann, S. *Facial deformities and plastic surgery.* Springfield, Ill.: Charles C Thomas, 1953.

MacMillan, D. L., Jones, R., & Aloia, G. The mentally retarded label: A theoretical analysis and review of research. *Am. J. Mental Deficiency,* 1974, *79,* 241–261.

Maisel, E. *Meet a body.* New York: Institute for the Crippled and Disabled, manuscript, 1953.

Mangione, L. Personal communication, 1979.

Marinelli, R. P. State anxiety in interactions with visibly disabled persons. *Rehabil. Counseling Bull.,* 1974, *18,* 72–77.

Maslow, A. H. Dominance, personality, and social behavior in women. *J. Soc. Psychol.,* 1939, *10,* 3–39.

Maslow, A. H., & Mittlemann, B. *Principles of abnormal psychology: The dynamics of psychic illness* (rev. ed.). New York: Harper & Row, 1951.

Mason, L., & Muhlenkamp, A. Patients' self-reported affective states following loss and caregivers' expectations of patients' affective states. *Rehabil. Psychol.,* 1976, *23,* 72–76.

Matson, R. R., & Brooks, N. A. Adjusting to multiple sclerosis: An exploratory study. *Soc. Sci. Med.,* 1977, *11,* 245–250.

McAndrew, H. Rigidity and isolation: A study of the deaf and the blind. *J. Abnorm. Soc. Psychol.,* 1948, *43,* 476–494.

McCleary, E. H. *Your child has a future.* Chicago: National Easter Seal Society, 1978.

McKenna, Sr. Helen V., S.S.J., Hofstaetter, P. R., & O'Connor, J. P. The concepts of the ideal self and of the friend. *J. Pers.,* 1956, *24,* 262–271.

McLarty, C. L., & Chaney, J. A. The cerebral palsied. In R. E. Hardy & J. G. Cull (Eds.), *Severe disabilities: Social and rehabilitation approaches.* Springfield, Ill., Charles C Thomas, 1974.

Mead, M. *Male and female, a study of the sexes in a changing world.* New York: Morrow, 1949.

Meichenbaum, D. *Cognitive behavior modification.* Morristown, N. J.: General Learning Press. 1974.

Meng, H. Zur Sozialpsychologie der Körperbeschädigten: Ein Beitrag zum Problem der praktischen Psychohygiene. *Schweizer Archiv für Neurologie und Psychiatrie,* 1938, *40,* 328–344. (Reported in Barker et al., 1953.)

Meyer, A. *The common sense psychiatry of Dr. Adolf Meyer: 52 selected papers.* Lief, A. (Ed.) New York: McGraw-Hill, 1948.

Meyerson, L. Physical disability as a social psychological problem. *J. Soc. Issues,* 1948, *4*(4), 2–10.

Meyerson, L. The visually handicapped. *Rev. Ed. Res.,* 1953, *23,* 476–491.

Meyerson, L. A psychology of impaired hearing. In W. M. Cruickshank (Ed.), *Psychology of exceptional children and youth.* Englewood Cliffs, N.J.: Prentice-Hall, 1955a, 120–183.

Meyerson, L. Somatopsychology of physical disability. In W. M. Cruickshank (Ed.), *Psychology of exceptional children and youth.* Englewood Cliffs, N.J.: Prentice-Hall, 1955b, 1–60.

Meyerson, L. Hearing for speech in children: A verbal audiometric test. *Acta Oto-Laryngologica,* Supplementum 128, 1956.

Meyerson, L. Special disabilities. In P. R. Farnsworth (Ed.), *Annu. Rev. Psychol.,* Vol. 8. Palo Alto: Annual Reviews, Inc., 1957, 437–457.

Meyerson, L., Kerr, N., & Michael, J. L. Behavior modification in rehabilitation. In S. W. Bijou & D. M. Baer (Eds.), *Child development: Readings in experimental analysis.* Englewood Cliffs, N.J.: Prentice-Hall, 1967.

Midlarsky, E. Aiding under stress: The effects of competence, dependency, visibility, and fatalism. *J. Pers.,* 1971, *39,* 132–149.

Miers, E. S. Goals as we see them. Delivered in panel discussion at convention of National Society for Crippled Children and Adults, New York, N.Y. Speech printed as leaflet put out by NSCCA, 1949.

Miers, E. S. Gosh, I'm glad I'm handicapped. *The crippled child,* 1953, *31,* 4–7.

Miller, E. A. Cerebral-palsied children and their parents. *Exceptional Child.,* 1958, *24,* 298–302, 305.

Mita, T. H., Derner, M., & Knight, J. Reversed facial images and the mere exposure hypothesis. *J. Pers. Soc. Psychol.,* 1977, *35,* 597–601.

Monahan, F. *Women in crime.* New York: Ives Washburn, 1941.

Moreno, J. L. Inter-personal therapy and the psychopathology of interpersonal relations. *Sociometry,* 1937, *1,* 9–76.

Mussen, P. H., & Barker, R. G. Attitudes toward cripples. *J. Abnorm. Soc. Psychol.,* 1944 *39,* 351–355.

Morganstein, S. Disabled in action panel: The agency mentality and its crippling effects: Paternalism vs. self-determination. *The President's Committee on Employment of the Handicapped,* 1975.

National Easter Seal Society. *Portraying persons with disabilities in print.* Chicago: author, 1980.

National Health Education Committee. *Facts on the major killing and crippling diseases in the U.S. today.* New York: The National Health Education Committee, 1955.

National Sex Forum. *Sexual attitude restructuring guide for a better sex life.* San Francisco: National Sex Forum, 1975.

Nayer, D. D. They don't notice her wheelchair. *Am. J. Nurs.,* 1971, *71,* 1130–1133.

Neff, W. S. (Ed.). *Rehabilitation psychology.* Washington, D.C.: Am. Psychol. Assoc., 1971.

Nelson, O. N. Positive attitude changes toward handicapped children and special education in a beginning educational psychology class. *Diss. Abstr. Int.,* 1971, *31,* 3786A.

Newcomb, T. *Social psychology.* New York: Dryden Press, 1950.

Nirje, B. The normalization principle and its human management implications. In R. B. Kugel & W. Wolfensberger (Eds.), *Changing patterns in residential services for the mentally retarded,* Washington, D.C.: U. S. Government Printing Office, 1969, 179–195.

Nisbett, R. E., Caputo, C., Legant, P., & Maracek, J. Behavior as seen by the actor and as seen by the observer. *J. Pers. Soc. Psychol.,* 1973, *27,* 154–164.

Noonan, J. R., Barry, J. R., & Davis, H. C. Personality determinants in attitudes toward disability. *J. Pers.,* 1970, *38,* 1–15.

Ohnstad, K. *The world at my finger tips.* Indianapolis & New York: Bobbs-Merrill, 1942.

Olsen, L. S. Rehabilitation education: Knowledge, evaluation, and attitude change in families. *Diss. Abstr.,* 1968, *29,* 1790A–1791A.

Orgel, S. Z., & Tuckman, J. Nicknames of institutional children. *Am. J. Orthopsychiatry,* 1935, *5,* 276–285.

Orlansky, H. Infant care and personality. *Psychol. Bull.,* 1949, *46,* 1–48.

Osgood, C. E., Suci G. J., & Tannenbaum, P. H. *The measurement of meaning.* Urbana, Ill.: Univ. of Illinois Press, 1957.

Osuji, O. N. "Acceptance of loss"—Quantification of the concept. *Can. Rehabil. Council for the Disabled Rehabil. Dig.,* 1975, *6*(3), 3–8.

Pastalan, L. A. The simulation of age-related sensory losses: A new approach to the study of environmental barriers. *New Outlook for the Blind,* 1974, *68,* 356–362.

Perske, R. *New directions for parents of persons who are retarded.* Nashville: Abingdon, 1973.

Piaget, J. *The moral judgment of the child.* New York: Harcourt Brace Jovanovich, 1932.

Piaget, J. *The construction of reality in the child.* New York: Basic Books, 1954.

Postman, L., & Bruner, J. S. Multiplicity of set as a determinant of perceptual behavior. *J. Exp. Psychol.,* 1949, *39,* 369–377.

Randall, G. C., Ewalt, J. R., & Blair, H. Psychiatric reaction to amputation. *J. Am. Med. Assoc.* 1945, *128,* 645–652.

Rapier, J., Adelson, R., Carey, R. & Croke, K. Changes in children's attitudes toward the physically handicapped. *Exceptional Child.*, 1972, *39*(3), 219–223.

Ray, M. H. The effect of crippled appearance on personality judgment. Master's thesis, Stanford Univ., 1946.

Rich, A. R., & Schroeder, H. E. Research issues in assertiveness training. *Psychol. Bull.*, 1976, *83*, 1081–1096.

Riley, L. E., & Nagi, S. Z. (Eds.). *Disability in the United States. A compendium of data on prevalence and programs.* Columbus, O.: Ohio State Univ., Dept. of Physical Medicine, Div. of Disability Research, 1970.

Riscalla, L. M. Some uses and abuses of client records. *Am. Psychol. Assoc. Annu. Meeting,* Montreal, Canada, 1973.

Robinault, I. P. *Sex, society, and the disabled: A developmental inquiry into roles, reactions, and responsibilities.* New York: Harper & Row, 1978.

Rogers, C. R. *Client-centered therapy, its current practice, implications, and theory.* New York: Houghton Mifflin, 1951.

Rogers, C. R. The necessary and sufficient conditions of therapeutic personality change. *J. Consulting Psychol.*, 1957, *21*, 95–103.

Rogers, C. R. A theory of therapy, personality, and interpersonal relationships, as developed in the client-centered framework. In S. Koch (Ed.), *Psychology: A study of a science* (Vol. 3). New York: McGraw-Hill, 1959.

Rogers, C. R., & Dymond, R. F. (Eds.). *Psychotherapy and personality change: Co-ordinated research studies in the client-centered approach.* Chicago: Univ. of Chicago Press, 1954.

Romano, D. L. The silent part. *Mother Jones,* 1980, *5*(1), 40–49.

Rosenberg, M. *Society and the adolescent self-image.* Princeton, N.J.: Princeton Univ. Press, 1965.

Rosenberg, M. Which significant others? *Behav. Scientist,* 1973, *16*, 829–860.

Rosenberg, M., & Simmons, R. G. Black and white self-esteem: The urban school child. Washington, D.C.: *Am. Sociol. Assoc., Arnold M. and Caroline Rose Monograph Series,* 1971.

Rosenthal, R., & Jacobson, L. *Pygmalion in the classroom: Teacher expectation and pupil's intellectual development.* New York: Holt, Rinehart and Winston, 1968.

Rosenzweig, S., Fleming, E. E., & Rosenzweig, L. The children's form of the Rosenzweig picture frustration study. *J. Psychol.*, 1948, *26*, 141–191.

Rosswurm, M. A. Changing nurses' attitudes toward persons with physical disabilities. *ARN Journal,* 1980, *5*(1), 12–14.

Rotter, J. B. Level of aspiration as a method of studying personality. III. Group validity studies. *Charact. Pers.*, 1943, *11*, 255–274.

Rotter, J. Generalized expectancies for internal versus external control of reinforcement. *Psychol. Monogr.: Gen. Appl.* 1966, *80*(1), Whole No. 609.

Rubin, Z., & Peplau, L. A. Who believes in a just world? *J. Soc. Issues,* 1975, *31*(3), 65–89.

Rusk, H. A., & Taylor, E. J. *New hope for the handicapped.* New York: Harper & Row, 1946.

Rusk, H. A., & Taylor, E. J. Employment for the disabled. *J. Soc. Issues*, 1948, *4*(4), 101–106.

Rusk, H. A., & Taylor, E. J. *Living with a disability*. Garden City, N.Y.: Blakiston, 1953.

Russell, H., with Rosen, V. *Victory in my hands*. New York: Farrar, Straus, & Giroux, 1949.

Rutledge, L. Aspiration levels of deaf children as compared with those of hearing children. *J. Speech Hear. Disorders*, 1954, *19*, 375–380.

Sapir, E. Conceptual categories in primitive languages. *Science*, 1931, *74*, 578. (Abstract.)

Saul, L. J. *Emotional maturity; The development and dynamics of personality*. Philadelphia: Lippincott, 1947.

Schachter, S. Deviation, rejection and communication. *J. Abnorm. Soc. Psychol.*, 1951, *46*, 190–207.

Scheerer, M. Cognitive theory. In G. Lindzey (Ed.), *Handbook of social psychology*. Reading, Mass.: Addison-Wesley, 1954, 91–142.

Schilder, P. *The image and appearance of the human body*. London: Kegan Paul, 1935.

Schilder, P. *Medical psychology*. (Trans. & Ed., D. Rapaport.) New York: International Univ. Press, 1953.

Schiller, E. J. Creative habilitation of the cerebral-palsied child. *J. Rehabil.*, 1961, *6*, 14–15, 29–30.

Schoggen, P. Environmental forces on physically disabled children. In R. G. Barker & Associates: *Habitats, environments and human behavior* (Studies in ecological psychology and eco-behavioral science from the midwest psychological field station, 1947–1972) San Francisco: Jossey-Bass, 1978.

Scott, R. A. *The making of blind men*. New York: Russell Sage Foundation, 1969.

Sears, P. S. Levels of aspiration in academically successful and unsuccessful children. *J. Abnorm. Soc. Psychol.*, 1940, *35*, 498–536.

Sears, R. R., Maccoby, E. E., & Levin, H. In collaboration with E. L. Lowell, P. S. Sears, & J. W. M. Whiting. *Patterns of child rearing*. New York: Harper & Row, 1957.

Seidenfeld, M. A. The psychological sequelae of poliomyelitis in children. *Nerv. child*, 1948, *7*, 14–28.

Semmel, M.I., & Dickson, S. Connotive reactions of college students to disability labels. *Exceptional Child.*, 1966, *32*, 443–450.

Sharman, L. C. As I see it: Psychological aspects of acute neurological disease resulting in permanent disability. *Bull. Menninger Clin.*, 1972, *36*(3), 313–321.

Shears, L. M. & Jensema, C. J. Social acceptability of anomalous persons. *Exceptional Child.*, 1969, *36*, 91–96.

Sheerer, E. T. An analysis of the relationship between acceptance of and respect for self and acceptance of and respect for others in ten counseling cases. *J. Consult. Psychol.*, 1949, *13*, 169–175.

Shelsky, I. The effect of disability on self-concept. Unpublished doctoral dissertation, Columbia Univ., 1957.

Shere, M. O. An evaluation of the social and emotional development of the cerebral palsied twin. Unpublished doctoral dissertation, Univ. of Illinois. Ann Arbor: Univ. Microfilms, Publication No. 9140, 1954.

Sherif, M., & Cantril, H. *The psychology of ego-involvements, social attitudes and identifications.* New York: Wiley, 1947.

Shontz, F. C. Reactions to crisis. *Volta Rev.*, 1965, *67,* 364–370.

Shontz, F. C. *Perceptual and cognitive aspects of body experience.* New York: Academic Press, 1969.

Shontz, F. C. Physical disability and personality: Theory and recent research. *Psychol. Aspects Disability,* 1970, *17,* 51–69.

Shontz, F. C. Physical disability and personality. In W. S. Neff (Ed.), *Rehabilitation psychology,* Washington, D.C.: Am. Psychol. Assoc., 1971.

Shontz, F. C. The personal meanings of illness. *Adv. psychosom. Med.,* 1972, *8,* 63–85.

Shontz, F. C. Forces influencing the decision to seek medical care. *Rehabil. psychol.,* 1974, *21,* 86–94.

Shontz, F. C. *The psychological aspects of physical illness and disability.* New York: Macmillan, 1975.

Shortley, M. J. Introduction. In H. H. Kessler & D. Kerr, *Civilian amputees in action.* Washington, D.C.: U.S. Government Printing Office, 1948.

Shurka, E., Siller, J., & Dvonch, P. Coping behavior and personal responsibility as factors in the perception of disabled persons by the nondisabled. *Rehabil. Psychol.,* 1982, *27,* 225–233.

Sieffert, A., Hendricks, C. O., Marks, J., Gutierrez, P. P. Parents participate in clinical care of retarded children. *Social Work,* 1976, *21,* 238–239.

Sieka, F. L. Facial disfigurement and sex-role esteem. *Rehabil. Counseling Bull.,* 1974, *18,* 90–98.

Siller, J. Generality of attitudes toward the physically disabled. *Proc. 78th Annu. Conv. Am. Psychol. Assoc.,* 1970, *5,* 697–698. (Summary).

Siller, J., Chipman, A., Ferguson, L. T., & Vann, D. H. Attitudes of the nondisabled toward the physically disabled. *Studies in Reaction to Disability XI.* New York: School of Education, New York Univ., 1967.

Siller, J., Vann, D. H., Ferguson, L. T., & Holland, B. Structure of attitudes toward the physically disabled. *Studies in Reactions to Disability XII.* New York: School of Education, New York Univ., 1967.

Simmons, L. W. Social participation of the aged in different cultures. *Ann. Am. Acad. Pol. Soc. Sci.,* 1952, *279,* 43–51.

Simon, G. C. Construction of a univocal measure of positive attitudes toward people and its relation to change in attitudes toward amputees. *Diss. Abstr. Int.,* 1971, *32,* 2990B.

Siperstein, G. N., Bak, J. J., & Gottlieb, J. Effects of group discussion on children's attitudes toward handicapped peers. *J. Ed. Res.,* 1977, *70,* 131–134.

Skinner, B. F. *Behavior of organisms: An experimental analysis.* Englewood Cliffs, N.J., Prentice-Hall, 1938.

Skinner, B. F. *Science and human behavior.* New York: Macmillan, 1953.

Skinner, B. F. About behaviorism. New York: Knopf, 1974.

Skipper, J. K., Fink, S. L., & Hallenbeck, P. N. Physical disability among married women. *J. Rehabil.,* 1968, *34,* 16–19.

Smith, L. E. *The journey.* New York: Harcourt Brace Jovanovich, 1954.

Smith, P. B. Controlled studies of the outcome of sensitivity training. *Psychol. Bull.,* 1975, *82,* 597–622.

Snell, E. E. Physical therapy. In W. M. Cruickshank & G. M. Raus (Eds.), *Cerebral palsy: Its individual and community problems.* Syracuse: Syracuse Univ. Press, 1955, 257–293.

Snyder, C. R. The psychological implications of being color blind. *J. Spec. Ed.,* 1973, *7,* 51–54.

Snyder, C. R. *Comparisons.* Millbrae, Calif.: Celestial Arts, 1974.

Snyder, C. R., & Fromkin, H. L. *Uniqueness: The human pursuit of difference.* New York: Plenum Press, 1980.

Sommers, V. S. *The influence of parental attitudes and social environment on the personality development of the adolescent blind.* New York: Amer. Found. for the Blind, 1944.

Spiegel, L. A. The child's concept of beauty. *J. Genet. Psychol.,* 1950, *77,* 11–23.

Spock, B. *The common sense book of baby and child care.* New York: Duell, Sloan and Pearce, 1946.

Springer, N. N. A comparative study of psychoneurotic responses of deaf and hearing children. *J. Ed. Psychol.,* 1938, *29,* 459–466.

Stafford, G. T. *Sports for the handicapped* (2d ed.). Englewood Cliffs, N.J.: Prentice-Hall, 1947.

Steckle, L. C. *Problems of human adjustment.* New York: Harper & Row, 1949.

Stein, L. Reciprocal action of reward and punishment mechanisms. In R. G. Heath (Ed.), *The role of pleasure in behavior.* New York: Harper & Row, 1964.

Stern, E. M., with Castendyck, E. *The handicapped child, a guide for parents.* New York: Wyn., 1950.

Stolz, H. R., & Stolz, L. M. Adolescent problems related to somatic variations in adolescence. *Yearb. Nat. Soc. Stud. Educ.,* 1944, *43* (Part I), 80–99.

Storms, M. D. Videotape and the attribution process: Reversing actors' and observers' points of view. *J. Pers. Soc. Psychol.,* 1973, *27,* 165–175.

Stratton, A. J. Patient's concepts of tuberculosis: Observations and implications. Paper presented at the Nat. Tuberculosis Ass. Convention, Kansas City, 1957, as reported in *Newsletter for Psychologists in Tuberculosis, 4,* 38–43.

Streng, A., & Kirk, S. A. The social competence of deaf and hard-of-hearing children in a public day school. *Amer. Ann. Deaf,* 1938, *83,* 244–254.

Strong, E. K., Jr. *Change of interests with age.* Stanford: Stanford Univ. Press, 1931.

Sullivan, H. S., Perry, H. S. & Gawel, M. L. (Eds.) *The interpersonal theory of psychiatry.* New York: Norton, 1953.

Sulzer-Azaroff, B., & Mayer, G. R. *Applying behavior analysis procedures with children and youth.* New York: Holt, Rinehart and Winston, 1977.

Sutter, R. C. Acceptance and rejection. A tape recording of a discussion with cerebral palsied children presented at the International Council for Exceptional Children, Cincinnati, O., 1954.

Swinyard, C. A. *The child with spina bifida.* New York: Institute of Rehabilitation Medicine, Patient Publication Series No. 6, 1975. (Originally published, 1964.)

Thelen, M. H., & Fry, R. A. Therapeutic videotape and film modelling: A review. *Psychol. Bull.,* 1979, *86,* 701–720.

Thompson, C. With the collaboration of P. Mullahy. *Psychoanalysis: Evolution and development.* New York: Hermitage, 1950.

Thorndike, E. L. A constant error in psychological ratings. *J. Appl. Psychol.,* 1920, *4,* 25–29.

Tracht, V. A. A comparative study of personality factors among cerebral palsied and non-handicapped persons. Master's thesis, Univ. of Chicago, 1946.

Trieschmann, R. B. *Spinal cord injuries: Psychological, social, and vocational adjustment,* New York: Pergamon Press, 1980.

Twentyman, C. T., & Zimmering, R. T. Behavioral training of social skills: A review. *Prog. Behav. Modification,* 1979, *7,* 319–400.

Understanding the disabled. Prepared by the National Foundation for Infantile Paralysis and the Citizen Education Project. New York: Columbia Univ. Citizen Education Project, 1956.

United Nations. *Social barriers to the integration of disabled persons into community life.* (Report of an expert group meeting, Geneva, 1976.) United Nations, Department of Economic and Social Affairs, ST/ESA/ 62, 1977.

Vash, C. L. The psychology of disability. *Rehabil. Psychol.,* 1975, *22,* 145–162.

Viscardi, H., Jr. *A man's stature.* Middlebury, Vt.: Paul S. Eriksson, 1952.

Volkart, E. H., & Michael, S. T. Bereavement and mental health. In A. H. Leighton, J. A. Clausen, & R. N. Wilson (Eds.), *Explorations in social psychiatry.* New York: Basic Books, 1957, 281–304.

Wagner, C., & Wheeler, L. Model, need, and cost effects in helping behavior. *J. Pers. Soc. Psychol.,* 1969, *12,* 111–116.

Warfield, F. *Cotton in my ears.* New York: Viking Press, 1948.

Weinberg, N. Social stereotyping of the physically handicapped. *Rehabil. Psychol.,* 1976, *23,* 115–124.

Weinberg, N., & Williams, J. How the physically disabled perceive their disabilities. *J. Rehabil.,* 1978, *44*(3), 31–33.

Weinberg-Asher, N. The effect of physical disability on self-perception. *Rehabil. Counseling Bull.,* 1976, 15–20.

Weinstein, B. The parent counseling conference. *Rehabil. Literature,* 1968, *29,* 233–236.

Weiss, E., & English, O. S. *Psychosomatic medicine.* Philadelphia: Saunders, 1943.

Weiss, S. A., Fishman, S., & Krause, F. Severity of disability as related to personality and prosthetic adjustment of amputees. *Psychol. Aspects Disability,* 1971, *18,* 67–75.

Wenar, C. The effects of a motor handicap on personality: The effects on level of aspiration. *Child dev.,* 1953, *24,* 123–130.

Wertheimer, M. Untersuchungen zur Lehre von der gestalt. II. *Psychologishe Forschung,* 1923, *4,* 301–350.

White, G. Social casework in relation to cerebral palsy. In W. M. Cruickshank & G. M. Raus (Eds.), *Cerebral palsy: Its individual and community problems.* Syracuse: Syracuse Univ. Press, 1955, 462–500.

White, R. K., Wright, B. A., & Dembo, T. Studies in adjustment to visible injuries: Evaluation of curiosity by the injured. *J. Abnorm. Soc. Psychol.,* 1948 *43,* 13–28.

White, R. W. *The abnormal personality.* New York: Ronald Press, 1948.

Whiteman, M., & Lukoff, I. F. A factorial study of sighted people's attitudes toward blindness. *J. Soc. Psychol.,* 1964, *64,* 339–353.

Whiteman, M., & Lukoff, I. F. Attitudes toward blindness and other physical handicaps. *J. Soc. Psychol.,* 1965, *66,* 135–145.

Whiting, J. W. M., & Child, I. L. *Child training and personality.* New Haven: Yale Univ. Press, 1953.

Whorf, B. L. Science and linguistics. In T. M. Newcomb & E. L. Hartley (Eds.), *Readings in social psychology.* New York: Holt, Rinehart and Winston, 1947, 210–218.

Wicklund, R. A. *Freedom and reactance.* Hillsdale, N. J.: Erlbaum Associates, 1974.

Wilke, H. H. *Creating the caring congregation: Guidelines for ministering with the handicapped.* Nashville: Abingdon, 1980.

Willems, E. P., & Halstead, L. S. An eco-behavioral approach to health status and health care. In R. G. Barker & Associates, *Habitats, environments and human behavior.* San Francisco: Jossey-Bass, 1978.

Willems, E. P., & Vineberg, S. E. Direct observation of patients: The interface of environment and behavior. *Psychol. Aspects Disability,* 1969, *16,* 74–88.

Williams, J. M. Manifest anxiety and self concept: A comparison of blind and sighted adolescents. *Dev. Psychol.,* 1972, *6,* 349–352.

Williams, R. Demonstration of assertive role-playing for workshop on disabilities, sponsored by Personnel Services, University of Kansas, 1979.

Wilson, A. J. *The emotional life of the ill and injured; the psychology and mental hygiene of rehabilitation and guidance.* New York: Social Science Publishers, 1950.

Wilson, E. D., & Alcorn, D. Disability simulation and development of attitudes toward the exceptional. *J. Spec. Ed.,* 1969, *3,* 303–307.

Winkler, H. *Psychische Entwicklung und Krüppeltum.* Leipzig: Leopold Voss. (Reported in Barker et al., 1953, op. cit.)

Witkin, H. A., Lewis, H. B., Hertzman, M., Machover, K., Meissner, P. B., & Wapner, S. *Personality through perception: An experimental and clinical study.* New York: Harper & Row, 1954.

Wittkower, E. D. *A psychiatrist looks at tuberculosis.* London: Nat. Assoc. for the Prevention of Tuberculosis, 1949.

Wittkower, E. D., & Cleghorn, R. A. (Eds.). *Recent developments in psychosomatic medicine.* Philadelphia: Lippincott, 1954.

Wolfensberger, W. *The principle of normalization in human services.* Toronto: National Institute on Mental Retardation, 1972.

Wolff, W. *The Expression of personality: Experimental depth psychology.* New York: Harper & Row, 1943.

Woodworth, R. S., & Marquis, D. G. *Psychology* (5th ed.). New York: Holt, Rinehart and Winston, 1947.

World Health Organization. *International classification of impairments, disabilities and handicaps: A manual of classification relating to the consequences of disease.* Geneva: author, 1980.

Worthington, M. E. Personal space as a function of the stigma effect. *Environ. Behav.,* 1974, *6,* 289–294.

Wright, B. A. (Ed.). *Psychology and rehabilitation.* Washington, D.C.: Am. Psychol. Assoc., 1959.

Wright, B. A. Spread in adjustment to disability. *Bull. Menninger Clin.,* 1964, *28,* 198–209.

Wright, B. A. The question stands: Should a person be realistic? *Rehabil. Counseling Bull.,* 1968, *11,* 291–297.

Wright, B. A. Value-laden beliefs and principles for rehabilitation psychology. *Rehabil. Psychol.,* 1972a, *19,* 38–45.

Wright, B. A. Psychological snares in the investigative enterprise. In E. P. Trapp & P. Himelstein (Eds.), *Readings on the exceptional child* (2nd ed.). Englewood Cliffs, N.J.: Prentice-Hall, 1972b.

Wright, B. A. Personal perspective in mitigating suffering. *Proc. 12th World Cong. Rehabil. Int.,* Sydney, Australia, 1972c, 781–788.

Wright, B. A. Changes in attitudes toward people with handicaps. *Rehabil. Literature,* 1973, *34,* 354–357, 368.

Wright, B. A. Social-psychological leads to enhance rehabilitation effectiveness. *Rehabil. Counseling Bull.,* 1975a, *18,* 214–223.

Wright, B. A. Sensitizing outsiders to the position of the insider. *Rehabil. Psychol.,* 1975b, *22,* 129–135.

Wright, B. A. Perceived adjustment value of own troubling experiences, 1976 (unpublished).

Wright, B. A. The fortune phenomenon with quasi-insiders: Friends as compared to strangers, 1977 (unpublished).

Wright, B. A. Person and situation: Adjusting the rehabilitation focus. *Arch. Phys. Med. Rehabil.,* 1980, *61,* 59–64.

Wright, B. A., & Fletcher, B. L. Uncovering hidden resources: A challenge in assessment. *Prof. Psychol.,* 1982, *13,* 229–235.

Wright, B. A., & Howe, M. The fortune phenomenon as manifested by stigmatized and non-stigmatized groups. 1969 (unpublished).

Wright, B. A., & Muth, M. The fortune phenomenon with rehabilitation clients, 1965 (unpublished).

Wright, B. A., & Shontz, F. C. Process and tasks in hoping. *Rehabil. Literature,* 1968, *29,* 322–331.

Wright, M. E. The influence of frustration upon the social relations of young children. *Character Pers.,* 1973, *12,* 111–122.

Wright, S. R. *Social psychological effects of labor supply in the New Jersey-Pennsylvania experiment.* Paper presented at the Am. Sociol. Assoc. convention, New Orleans, August 1972.

Wylie, R. C. The self-concept: Theory and research on selected topics (Vol. 2; rev. ed.). Lincoln: Univ. of Nebraska Press, 1979.

Wyrick, J. The effect of the lecture method on attitudes toward physical disability. Unpublished master's thesis, Univ. of Kansas, 1968.

Yatsushiro, T. Political and socio-cultural issues at Poston and Manzanar relocation centers—a themal analysis. Unpublished doctoral dissertation, Cornell Univ., 1953.

Yerxa, E. Effects of dyadic, self-administered instructional programs in changing the attitudes of female college students toward the physically disabled. *Diss. Abstr. Int.*, 1971, *32*, 1931A–1932A.

Young, B. Handicapped man finds his life brighter. *Honolulu Advertizer*, July 25, 1965.

Yuker, H. E., Block, J. R., & Younng, J. H. *The measurement of attitudes toward disabled persons.* Albertson, N. Y.: Human Resources Center, 1966.

Zander, A. Role playing: A technique for training the necessarily dominating leaders. *Sociatry*, 1947, *1*, 225–235.

Zemach, M. The effect of guilt-arousing communications on acceptance of recommendations. Doctoral dissertation, Yale Univ., 1966.

Zola, I. K. The problem and prospects of mutual aid groups. *Rehabil. Psychol.*, 1972, *19*, 180–183.

Name Index

Subject Index

85 9 8 7 6 5 4 3